A Companion to the American West

BLACKWELL COMPANIONS TO HISTORY

This series provides sophisticated and authoritative overviews of the scholarship that has shaped our current understanding of the past. Defined by theme, period and/or region, each volume comprises between twenty-five and forty concise essays written by individual scholars within their area of specialization. The aim of each contribution is to synthesize the current state of scholarship from a variety of historical perspectives and to provide a statement on where the field is heading. The essays are written in a clear, provocative, and lively manner, designed for an international audience of scholars, students, and general readers.

Published

A Companion to Western Historical Thought
Edited by Lloyd Kramer and Sarah Maza

A Companion to Gender History
Edited by Teresa Meade and Merry E. Weisner-Hanks

BLACKWELL COMPANIONS TO BRITISH HISTORY

Published

A Companion to Roman Britain
Edited by Malcolm Todd

A Companion to Britain in the Later Middle Ages
Edited by S. H. Rigby

A Companion to Stuart Britain
Edited by Barry Coward

A Companion to Eighteenth-Century Britain
Edited by H. T. Dickinson

A Companion to Early Twentieth-Century Britain
Edited by Chris Wrigley

In preparation

A Companion to Britain in the Early Middle Ages
Edited by Pauline Stafford

A Companion to Tudor Britain
Edited by Robert Tittler and Norman Jones

A Companion to Nineteenth-Century Britain
Edited by Chris Williams

A Companion to Contemporary Britain
Edited by Paul Addison and Harriet Jones

BLACKWELL COMPANIONS TO EUROPEAN HISTORY

Published

A Companion to the Worlds of the Renaissance
Edited by Guido Ruggiero

A Companion to the Reformation World
Edited by R. Po-chia Hsia

In preparation

A Companion to Europe Since 1945
Edited by Klaus Larres

A Companion to Europe 1900–1945
Edited by Gordon Martel

Planned

A Companion to Europe in the Middle Ages

A Companion to Eighteenth-Century Europe

A Companion to Nineteenth-Century Europe

BLACKWELL COMPANIONS TO AMERICAN HISTORY

Published

A Companion to the American Revolution
Edited by Jack P. Greene and J. R. Pole

A Companion to 19th-Century America
Edited by William L. Barney

A Companion to the American South
Edited by John B. Boles

A Companion to American Indian History
Edited by Philip J. Deloria and Neal Salisbury

A Companion to American Women's History
Edited by Nancy A. Hewitt

A Companion to Post-1945 America
Edited by Jean-Christophe Agnew and Roy Rosenzweig

A Companion to the Vietnam War
Edited by Marilyn B. Young and Robert Buzzanco

A Companion to Colonial America
Edited by Daniel Vickers

A Companion to American Foreign Relations
Edited by Robert D. Schulzinger

A Companion to 20th-Century America
Edited by Stephen J. Whitfield

A Companion to the American West
Edited by William Deverell

BLACKWELL COMPANIONS TO WORLD HISTORY

In preparation

A Companion to the History of Africa
Edited by Joseph Miller

A Companion to the History of the Middle East
Edited by Youssef M. Choueiri

Planned

A Companion to the History of Russia

A Companion to the History of China

A Companion to the History of Japan

A Companion to the History of Latin America

A COMPANION
TO THE
AMERICAN WEST

Edited by

William Deverell

Blackwell
Publishing

© 2004 by Blackwell Publishing Ltd
except for editorial material and introduction © 2004 by William Deverell

350 Main Street, Malden, MA 02148-5020, USA
108 Cowley Road, Oxford OX4 1JF, UK
550 Swanston Street, Carlton, Victoria 3053, Australia

The right of William Deverell to be identified as the Author of the Editorial Material in this Work has been asserted in accordance with the UK Copyright, Designs, and Patents Act 1988.

First published 2004 by Blackwell Publishing Ltd

Library of Congress Cataloging-in-Publication Data

A companion to the American West / edited by William Deverell.
    p. cm. – (Blackwell companions to American history)
Includes bibliographical references and index.
  ISBN 0-631-21357-0 (hardback : alk. paper)
  1. West (U.S.) – History.   I. Deverell, William Francis.   II. Series.

  F591.C738   2004
  978 – dc22
                                            2003020378

A catalogue record for this title is available from the British Library.

Set in 10 on 12 pt Galliard
by SNP Best-set Typesetter Ltd., Hong Kong
Printed and bound in the United Kingdom
by TJ International, Padstow, Cornwall

Contents

Notes on Contributors

Stephen Aron is Associate Professor of History at the University of California, Los Angeles, and executive director of the Autry National Center Institute. He is the author of *How the West Was Lost: The Transformation of Kentucky from Daniel Boone to Henry Clay*, coauthor of *Worlds Together, Worlds Apart: A History of the Modern World from the Mongol Empire to the Present*, and coeditor of *Trading Cultures: The Worlds of Western Merchants*. He is currently completing *American Confluence: The Missouri Frontier from Borderlands to Border State*.

Michael A. Bellesiles is the author of seven books, including *Revolutionary Outlaws: Ethan Allen and the Struggle for Independence on the Early American Frontier* and *Arming America: The Origins of a National Gun Culture*. His next book is a study of the American Revolution titled *The Trial of John Burgoyne*.

William Deverell is Associate Professor of History at the California Institute of Technology. He is the author of *Railroad Crossing: Californians and the Railroad, 1850–1910* and *Whitewashed Adobe: The Rise of Los Angeles and the Remaking of Its Mexican Past*. He coauthored *Eden by Design: The 1930 Olmsted-Bartholomew Plan for the Los Angeles Region* and *The West in the History of the Nation* and coedited *California Progressivism Revisited* and *Metropolis in the Making: Los Angeles in the 1920s*.

Douglas Flamming is Associate Professor of History at the Georgia Institute of Technology. He has written several essays on the African American community in Los Angeles and is the author of the forthcoming book, *A World to Gain: African Americans in Los Angeles, 1890–1940*.

Dan Flores is A. B. Hammond Professor of Western History at the University of Montana-Missoula and specializes in western environmental history. He is the author of seven books, most recently *Horizontal Yellow*, *The Natural West*, and *Southern Counterpart to Lewis & Clark*. His work has been honored by the Western History Association, the Western Writers Association of America, Westerners International, the National Cowboy Hall of Fame/Western Heritage Center, the Denver Public Library, and the Texas Historical Association.

Chris Friday is Professor of History at Western Washington University in Bellingham, Washington, where he is currently department chair and Director of the Center for Pacific Northwest History. His publications include *Organizing Asian American Labor* and *Lelooska: The Life of a Northwest Coast Artist*. He has published articles on Asian American history, labor history, and regional history. His current work examines the multiracial nature of Pacific maritime labor markets in the nineteenth and twentieth centuries. His research interests focus generally on Asian American history, American

Indian history, racial formations, and regional history.

Philip Goff is Director of the Center for the Study of Religion and American Culture and Associate Professor of Religious Studies and American Studies at Indiana University-Purdue University Indianapolis. He is the coauthor of *Religion in America, 1945–2000* and coeditor of *Themes in Religion and American Culture*, as well as editor of *Religion and American Culture: A Journal of Interpretation*. He is currently at work on a book about Los Angeles-based religious radio at mid-century.

Sarah Barringer Gordon is Professor of Law and History at the University of Pennsylvania. Her areas of research include law, religion, and the West. She is the author of *The Mormon Question: Polygamy and Constitutional Conflict in Nineteenth-Century America*, which was awarded the Mormon History Association's Best Book Award for 2002. She is currently at work on a book about law and religion in the twentieth century.

James N. Gregory is Associate Professor of History at the University of Washington. He is the author of *American Exodus: The Dust Bowl Migration and Okie Culture in California*, which won the 1991 Ray Allen Billington Prize from the Organization of American Historians. His forthcoming book is entitled *The Southern Diaspora: How Two Great Migrations Transformed Race, Region, and American Politics*.

Ramón A. Gutiérrez is a Professor of Ethnic Studies and History at the University of California, San Diego and the Director of the Center for the Study of Race and Ethnicity. A scholar of race and ethnic relations in Latin America and the US Southwest, his publications include *When Jesus Came the Corn Mothers Went Away: Marriage, Sexuality and Power in New Mexico, 1500–1846*; *Recovering the U.S. Hispanic Literary Heritage*; *Festivals and Celebrations in American Ethnic Communities*; and *Contested Eden: California before the Gold Rush*.

Anne Hyde is Professor of History at the Colorado College. She is the author of *An American Vision* and co-author of *The West in the History of the Nation*. Her new work examines community and community formation in the nineteenth and twentieth-century Rocky Mountain West.

David Igler is Assistant Professor of History at the University of California, Irvine. He is the author of *Industrial Cowboys: Miller & Lux and the Transformation of the Far West, 1850–1920* and coeditor of *The Human Tradition in California*. His current research focuses on the American West and the Pacific Basin in the nineteenth century.

Andrew C. Isenberg is the author of *The Destruction of the Bison: An Environmental History, 1750–1920*. He has been a Fellow of the Huntington Library and a Fulbright Scholar. He has taught at Princeton University since 1997 and was awarded Princeton's Distinguished Teaching Award in 2001.

Peter Iverson is Regents' Professor of History at Arizona State University. He has written or edited 15 books, including, most recently, *Diné: A History of the Navajos* and *"For Our Navajo People"*: Diné Letters, Speeches, and Petitions, 1900–1960. In the spring of 2003 he won the outstanding mentor award from the ASU Graduate College.

Elizabeth Jameson holds the Imperial Oil & Lincoln McKay Chair in American Studies at the University of Calgary. Her scholarship focuses on the histories of women and labor in the American West. Her publications include two coedited anthologies, *The Women's West* and *Writing the Range: Race, Class, and Culture in the Women's West* (both with Susan Armitage); *All That Glitters: Class, Conflict, and Community in Cripple Creek*, and *Building Colorado: The United Brotherhood of Carpenters and Joiners in the Centennial State*.

David Rich Lewis is professor of history at Utah State University and editor of the *Western Historical Quarterly*. He is the author of *Neither Wolf Nor Dog: American Indians, Environment, and Agrarian Change* and numerous articles and essays on American Indian ethnohistory and the environment. He co-edited *Major Problems in the History of the American West*. He is currently exploring the Skull Valley Goshute and nuclear waste issues in Utah and co-editing a collection of essays titled *Refiguring the Ecological Indian*.

Karen R. Merrill is Assistant Professor of History at Williams College. She is the author of *Public Lands and Political Meaning: Ranchers, the Government, and the Property between Them* and the editor of the forthcoming book *The Oil Crisis of 1971*. She has begun work on a new book project entitled *April 1973: How a Time of Crisis Shaped American Power*.

Douglas R. Nickel is the Director of the Center for Creative Photography and Associate Professor of Art History at the University of Arizona. He is the author of essays on William Harnett and Winslow Homer, and the exhibition catalogue *Carleton Watkins: The Art of Perception*.

Jeffrey Ostler is Associate Professor of History at the University of Oregon and author of *The Plains Sioux and U.S. Colonialism from Lewis and Clark to Wounded Knee* and *Prairie Populism: The Fate of Agrarian Radicalism in Kansas, Nebraska, and Iowa, 1880–1892*.

Malcolm J. Rohrbough is Professor of History at the University of Iowa, where he teaches courses and directs graduate work in the American West. He is the author of, among others, *Aspen: The History of a Silver Mining Town* and *Days of Gold: The California Gold Rush and the American Nation*.

James P. Ronda holds the H. G. Barnard Chair in Western American History at the University of Tulsa and is a past President of the Western History Association. A specialist in the history of the exploration of North America, he is the author of many books and

essays examining the history of North American exploration. His most recent book is *Beyond Lewis and Clark: The Army Explores the West*. His current project is *The Western Writings of Washington Irving*, to be published by the Library of America.

Robert O. Self is Assistant Professor of History and Urban Studies at the University of Wisconsin, Milwaukee. He is the author of *American Babylon: Race and the Struggle for Postwar Oakland*. He is currently working on a book tentatively titled *This is a Man's World: Los Angeles and the Politics of American Manhood in the Mid Twentieth Century*.

Marguerite S. Shaffer is an Associate Professor and Director of the Program in American Studies at Miami University, Oxford, Ohio. She is the author of *See America First: Tourism and National Identity, 1880–1940*. Her current research focuses on public culture and popular environmentalism.

Elliott West, Alumni Distinguished Professor of History at the University of Arkansas, is a past President of the Western History Association and author of five books on the social and environmental history of the West. *The Contested Plains* received the Francis Parkman Prize and Caughey Prize as the year's outstanding work on American and western history, and two of his other books have received national awards. He is now writing a history of the West in the second half of the nineteenth century and a history of the Nez Perce War.

David M. Wrobel is a member of the history department at the University of Nevada Las Vegas. He is the author of *Promised Lands: Promotion, Memory, and the Creation of the American West* and *The End of American Exceptionalism: Frontier Anxiety from the Old West to the New Deal*, and coeditor of *Seeing and Being Seen: Tourism in the American West* and *Many Wests: Place, Culture, and Regional Identity*.

Introduction

WILLIAM DEVERELL

Over the past two decades, historians have rewritten the history of the American West. Inspired and challenged by deep changes within the historical discipline itself, scholars interested in the American West asked new questions of their sources, plunged into innovative subdisciplines, and took off in any number of novel directions in their teaching and their research.

That ferment, of which this volume is part, energized not only the field but the entire American historical profession. Influential essays and monographs on the West found their way into courses and reading lists addressing other regions and other historical topics altogether. Scholars who had only recently been "prominent western historians" became, simply, "prominent historians" who had stories to tell about America through western prisms. Utilizing the scholarly tools of new or newly energized subfields such as environmental history, ethnic studies, and others, western historians dug into the regional past and emerged with compelling insights about historical change in region and nation both. By reexamining conventional understandings of, for example, power and nature, or race and gender, western historians and their work often stood at the center of historical debates extending well beyond the region's geographic or political boundaries.

That excitement continues to this day and in the essays that make up this book. A number of years in the making, this collection consists of twenty-five original essays on various themes and issues in western American history. It is devoted to the nineteenth and twentieth-century history of the region. This chronological imbalance away from earlier periods has garnered thoughtful criticism, even from within the pages that follow. In "Thinking Through the West," the introductory section opening this collection, Stephen Aron contributes an essay that makes a persuasive argument that western historians encounter analytical blind spots when they inadvertently fix the West in place by concentrating only on the region's history over the past two hundred years. Such a point is well taken, and I urge readers to contemplate Professor Aron's challenges about historical period and chronology as they read and think about all of the contributions in this book. As both Aron and Elliott West, author of the introductory section's other essay, point out, the American West has not always been where it is today. How it, and we, got to be "here" is the product of historical processes every bit as much of the centuries before 1800 as after.

This book's contributors, an illustrious gathering of younger and more established scholars, have written superb essays that examine a multitude of topics. Ranging from such themes as western environmental history to the history of western tourism, and from the religious history of the modern West to the history of labor, the essays are meant to provide readers with an introduction to a particular topic, an evaluation of critical works, and an assessment of scholarly gaps in our understanding. Several essays address the same topic from the vantage point of different periods or centuries so that changes over long stretches of time might be more easily discerned.

What we hope will emerge from this volume are a cascade of fresh insights, succinct assessments, and spirited calls for additional scholarly work in western history. Our collective aim has been to produce a volume that brings together many of the insights born of twenty years' worth of scholarly reimaginings of the West's history into a book where the whole is indeed greater than the sum of the excellent parts. As the fortunate person granted the privilege of pulling these talented and patient authors and their work together, I can claim with confidence that we've succeeded.

William Deverell

Pasadena, California

Part I

Thinking Through the American West

CHAPTER ONE

The Making of the First American West and the Unmaking of Other Realms

STEPHEN ARON

This compendium, like other new collections about the history of the American West, tilts to the nineteenth and twentieth century and to that country which today makes up the western United States. That presentist and regionalist focus is in keeping with the trend in scholarship, which has emphasized the recent history of the region that is our American West (Limerick, 1987; White, 1991; Milner, O'Connor, and Sandweiss, 1994; Matsumoto and Allmendinger, 1999). But limiting western history to the more recent past and to the place that we know as the West distorts our vision. Reading present-day boundaries backwards pretends that the West is where it always was. That fixed sense of place loses sight of the contested character of the West's shifting borders. Beginning the history of the American West in the nineteenth century pushes Anglo-American conquest too much to the fore and gives it an air of inevitability. Drained of its contingencies, the westward expansion of the United States can hardly be imagined as anything but manifestly destined.

In hopes of restoring a more contingent and contested vision of western history, this essay reassesses the origins of westward expansion and the development of the "western country" during the eighteenth century. To be sure, this first western country that Americans eventually conquered, colonized, and consolidated lay east of the Mississippi River. It was not, in other words, our West. And yet, as I've argued at length elsewhere (Aron, 1994, 1996), the processes that shaped this first American West in the eighteenth century established patterns that prefigured the next century's expansion into lands further west.

It is impossible, however, to understand the making of the western country in the eighteenth century – or any century – by treating it only as a "West." Then, as now, the West was not west at all for many of the people who lived there or moved there. In the eighteenth century this western country, indeed, much of North America, was the site of population movements from various directions. It was also the focus of intensive rivalries between European empires. Through the century the whole continent, and particularly its eastern half, was very much up for grabs. The designs of French, Spanish, and British empire-builders competed with those of westward-minded Americans, and all of these expansionist schemes were entangled with the counter-colonial aspirations of diverse Indian inhabitants. Making the first American West – and subsequent ones too – required breaking the claims of these rivals (Taylor, 2001).

Above all, American control of this West involved the subjugation of Indian peoples, for whom the country was not west, or north, or south. For indigenous peoples in what was to become the eastern half of the United States, these were homelands, though some Indians were themselves relatively recent arrivals to the region (Richter, 2001). Through the eighteenth century, "eastern" Indians pursued a variety of paths to resist dispossession and dependency. These included migrations, accommodations, incorporations, confederations, and revitalizations. All proved successful for a time, especially so long as one or another European power lent support to their cause. But once those imperial rivals withdrew, Indian options narrowed and the pace of westward expansion quickened.

Frontier and Borderlands

Two terms, frontier and borderlands, loom large in this interpretation of the making of the first American West and the unmaking of other dreams. Thanks especially to Frederick Jackson Turner, western historians have long paid homage to the importance of the first. In recent years, however, the field has turned away from Turner's one hundred year old vision of the "significance of the frontier in American history." Turner's definition of frontier, his critics have maintained, is at best too vague; often, for example, Turner made frontier synonymous with West. For Turner, that West had its eastern boundary at the Appalachians, which is certainly not how the current generation of Americans imagine the region's geography. Worse still, the frontier as Turner construed it appears a sexist and ethnocentric anachronism. Thus, the western history that has been written in a Turnerian key neglected the experiences of the majority of westerners (who were not all white men) and ignored the devastating cultural and ecological casualties that accompanied the westward expansion of the United States. Given all these faults, several prominent "new western historians" have sought to excise Turner's influence and banish the word frontier from their vocabulary (White, 1991; Klein, 1997).

That would be unfortunate, for Turner's thesis, despite its age, omissions, and errors, has some lessons to impart to students of any or all of America's Wests. Indeed, Turner's recognition that the United States had many Wests explained his fascination with the nation's first West. In the lands between the Appalachians and the Mississippi, Turner discerned patterns that would shape subsequent American expansions. That insight still holds, though western historians must pay attention to the flows from other directions as well. As this essay argues, lands became Wests (and not Norths, Souths, Easts, or simply homelands), because rival claimants were vanquished.

But what to call these zones of shared and contested occupancy? Here I argue that frontier, despite its Turner-tainted past, remains a vital designation for territories where political control was undetermined and boundaries – cultural and geographic – were uncertain. Although Turner described this unsettled situation as "the meeting point between [Indian] savagery and [European] civilization," (Turner, 1994a) more recent scholarship has recast frontier in more neutral terms as the meeting point between indigenous and intrusive societies. Operating from this definition, historians have probed the intersection between Indians and Europeans and have recovered a frontier past in which cultures not only collided, but also coincided. In fact, an outpouring of new research has shown that, from the Caribbean to Canada and from the Atlantic to the Pacific, the mingling of Indian, European (and African) peoples rarely produced straightforward results. Instead, in rewriting the history of frontiers, historians have now emphasized the many unexpected twists and turns that characterized the contest for North America (Lamar and Thompson 1981; Cronon, Miles, and Gitlin 1992; Cayton and Teute 1998).

Helpful as the term frontier has been, it alone does not capture the complexity of the contest from which Wests were eventually made. Rarely, if ever, was this a two-sided competition. As this essay details, some Indian leaders struggled to build con-federations that would unite diverse Indian peoples against one or another colonial power. But these efforts were only partly successful, leaving Indians still divided against themselves. So, too, imperial powers were locked in competition with each other. Accordingly, Jeremy Adelman and I add the term borderlands to demarcate the zones in which the claims of two or more colonial empires overlapped (Adelman and Aron, 1999).

Like the word "frontier", the term "borderlands" has a problematic history. It is associated most closely with Turner's protegé, Herbert Eugene Bolton. As father of the borderlands school of history, Bolton directed attention away from the east to west orientation of Turner's frontier thesis and toward the northward expansion of Spanish-American settlements. More so than Turner's Anglo-American frontier, in which westward advance presumed Indian retreat, Bolton's work, along with that of his many students, appreciated the extended cohabitation between natives and new-comers that prevailed on the northern perimeters of New Spain. But Bolton, like Turner, paid little attention to the predicaments of Indians, and, as many several recent critics have pointed out, his preference for Catholic padres stigmatized his vision of borderlands' (Weber, 1986; Hurtado, 1995; Worcester, 1991).

As such scholarship attests, the trick is to throw out Bolton's biases without also draining the still useful borderlands bathwater. In fact, it is in combination that fron-tier and borderlands provide a vocabulary to analyze the making of American Wests. Frontier refers to territories where Indians and colonials intersected; borderlands delineate the overlay of imperial rivalries. That frontiers and borderlands went together is crucial to this interpretation, for the latter certainly shaped the nature of the former. In eighteenth-century North America, the presence of borderlands in the territory between the Appalachians and the Mississippi perpetuated frontiers in which complex cultural mixtures and accommodations often prevailed. In this telling, then, the making of the first American West (and future American Wests too) involves the demise of borderlands and the closing of one kind of frontier.

Early Encroachments: Mingling, Conflict, and Coexistence

Prior to the middle of the eighteenth century, the territory that was to become the first American West had attracted attention from Spanish, French, and English col-onizers, but it remained very much Indian countries. First among Europeans to pen-etrate the region were Spanish explorers, moving north and west from their Florida base. They soon departed, though their microbes wreaked devastation on native pop-ulations. Beginning in the late seventeenth century, French explorers, missionaries, and fur traders ventured south and west from settlements along the St Lawrence River and founded a few posts around the Great Lakes and along the Mississippi

River. In the early eighteenth century, the French added a couple of villages in what is now Illinois to their colonial presence south of the Great Lakes. Yet, impressive as the crescent of French settlements stretching from the St Lawrence to the Great Lakes and to the mouth of the Mississippi appeared on maps, they were so widely scattered and sparsely peopled that they hardly challenged the Indians' hold on the country (Eccles, 1969; Trigger, 1986; Ekberg, 1998; Usner, 1992; Thomas, 1990; Hoffman, 2001).

Indeed, the French had no interest in upsetting the area's demographic composition. After all, a diminished Indian presence would deprive French traders of the partners from whom they obtained valuable animal pelts. Marrying Indian women, these traders inserted themselves into their wives' extended families. Together, French colonists and Indians fashioned ways of living and trading that blended cultures. French colonial authorities were often displeased by the extent and uncontrolled nature of frontier mingling. Nor did they like the expense of making gifts, which native partners insisted was essential to building intersocietal understanding. But these same officials recognized that gift-giving was part of the cost of doing business with Indian fur-suppliers. Even more, French policymakers needed Indians as military allies if English colonists were to be prevented from moving west and encroaching on French (not to mention Indian) claims (White, 1991).

That threat became more menacing as the population of British North America multiplied in the early decades of the eighteenth century. In 1700, the census of the Atlantic seaboard colonies had already reached two hundred and fifty thousand. Through the seventeenth century, however, the inland spread of settlements had been limited. Almost all English colonists lived near the ocean, and no significant communities had been established above the fall lines of the major rivers that flowed into the Atlantic. Although coastal Indian peoples had been dispossessed, native groups in the Appalachian foothills and beyond retained their lands and their ability to check English expansion. But rapid population growth altered the balance of numbers and power. High birth rates and a flood of immigrants – not just from England, but from various parts of the British Isles as well as the European continent – swelled the population of the seaboard colonies to one million three hundred thousand by 1750. Included in this tally were more than two hundred thousand persons of African descent, though the transatlantic voyage and subsequent westward movements of these people were involuntary. Together, this ethnically diverse assortment of free and unfree pioneers pushed colonial settlements deeper into the interior, occupying lands above the fall lines and to the foothills of the Appalachians (Nobles, 1997; Hine and Faragher, 2000; Hinderaker and Mancall, 2003).

That advance was uneven, for some Indian groups, like the Iroquois of northwestern New York, effectively resisted colonial encroachments. A loose-knit confederacy, the Iroquois had the numbers to defend their lands. The geographic position of Iroquoia, between English and French domains, also helped by reducing the dependency of the Iroquois on one or the other European power.

Still, this borderland geography also strained Iroquois unity and security, inspiring military blows aimed not at English or French colonists, but at Indian groups to the west. Being between also exposed the Iroquois to epidemic diseases that by the seventeenth century had cut populations in half. Trading opportunities significantly depleted the stock of fur-bearing animals too, threatening the Iroquois' future access to the European goods upon which they had become more dependent. In response, the Iroquois invaded the territories of western neighbors. As in precolonial times, replenishing numbers by taking and then adopting captives remained a prime rationale for making war. But the pressures were much greater than before, and, armed with European-supplied firearms, the Iroquois had new means to wage combat. More important they had new ends: where precolonial ways of war venerated symbolic demonstrations of courage while limiting actual bloodshed, seventeenth-century Iroquois raids aimed at gaining control of fur-bearing and fur-trading territories. This they did through a series of destructive forays first against Huron towns and later against villages in the Ohio Valley. By the end of the seventeenth century, these "beaver wars" caused the disappearance of some peoples and the dislocation of many others. If not strengthened or truly unified by these invasions, the Iroquois maintained the power to hold their own ground against would be usurpers – at least through the first half of the eighteenth century (Jennings, 1984; Richter and Merrell, 1987; Richter, 1992; Dennis, 1993).

South of Iroquoia, in Pennsylvania, Indian groups already faced more immediate pressures and possessed fewer viable options. Take, for example, the situation of the Shawnees, who, like tens of thousands of European immigrants, were recent arrivals to Pennsylvania. Prior to the beaver wars, the Shawnees had inhabited villages on both sides of the Ohio River. Driven from those lands by Iroquois invaders in the late seventeenth century, Shawnees dispersed in small contingents into Alabama, Georgia, and the Carolinas, before partially regrouping in villages along Pennsylvania's Susquehanna River (Mancall, 1991). Into the second decade of the eighteenth century, peaceful relations prevailed between the Shawnees and the predominantly Quaker population of Pennsylvania. But the demographic and political character of the colony shifted decisively in the next decades. Where the colony's founder, William Penn, heeded Indian claims and preserved intercultural amity, his political successors were determined to get as much land as possible, a desire shared by the tens of thousands of non-Quaker immigrants who poured into Pennsylvania after 1710. Lacking the confederated strength of the Iroquois or the advantages of borderland positioning, Shawnees had little chance in a war against the expanded numbers of land-hungry colonists. So, instead of making a futile military stand, many Shawnees chose to migrate once again. Seeking refuge from white encroachments, several hundred Shawnees, along with other Pennsylvania Indian peoples, began trickling back into the Ohio Country after 1715 (McConnell, 1992).

The departure of Shawnees cleared lands for white pioneers, but it did not entirely erase the legacy of intercultural amity and cross-cultural exchange that had earlier characterized the Pennsylvania frontier. In Pennsylvania, and in the inland "backcountries" of other mid-Atlantic colonies, contact between Indians and Europeans brought not only conflict, but also "cultural fusion," which was, in historians Robert Hine and John Mack Faragher's estimation, "one of the most notable – and least understood – developments of early American history" (Hine and Faragher, 2000: 71). If this "composite culture" did not go as far as that jointly created by French and Indians in the Great Lakes, the results of backcountry–Indian cohabitation were sometimes startling. Mutual adaptations blurred distinctions between settler and native material lives and means of subsistence. Dwelling in similarly constructed log cabins and drawing sustenance from a comparable mix of hunting, herding, and farming, Pennsylvania Indians and settlers seemed to converge not only geographically but also culturally (Jordan and Kaups, 1989 and, for a contrasting view, Merrell, 1999).

Yet these borrowings and congruencies did not make for lasting accommodation or joint occupation. As the eighteenth century progressed, more and more of Pennsylvania's Indians headed west to the Upper Ohio Valley. But the buffer they hoped to establish between themselves and white pioneers proved fleeting. By mid-century, pioneers in Pennsylvania, as well as in the western parts of Virginia and the Carolinas, were poised to cross the Appalachian divide, to move where the rivers flowed away from the Atlantic and take control of the land of "western waters."

Britain's "Western Country" and Beyond

In the third quarter of the eighteenth century, the westward expansion of British America breached the Appalachians, but not before the Ohio Valley became the focal point of imperial competition, the starting point of a trans-Atlantic war, and the turning point in an Indian uprising that sought to restore borderland conditions.

For the British Empire, each of these episodes ended in apparent triumph. Initially unsuccessful in dislodging the French from their fort at the forks of the Ohio River, British armies ultimately wrested control of that stronghold. Likewise, early setbacks in the wider war turned into a decisive victory. In the resulting treaty of peace, France lost its North American "South," along with all its claims on the continent. Although insurgent western Indians then created havoc on the borders of British American settlement, the revolt was soon put down. Still, all these triumphs left ambiguous legacies. New France disappeared from North American maps, but Spain emerged as a rival for control of the western country, thanks to its acquisition of French claims west of the Mississippi River. Indians did not eradicate colonial rule or bring back the French, but their uprising reminded British authorities that the conquest and consolidation of the western country was incomplete. Chastened, these officials rescinded efforts to put the fur trade on a commercial basis and returned to prewar precepts of intercultural exchange. In addition, British administrators pledged to restrain the westward colonization of settlers; by the King's Proclamation of 1763, the lands from the crest of the Appalachians to the Mississippi were to stay exclusively in native hands. By 1775, however, British authorities and western Indians learned that neither royal edict nor various native strategies could keep backcountry settlers out of Indian country (Anderson, 2000; Jennings, 1988; Hinderaker, 1997; Barr, 2001; Dowd, 2002).

A quarter century earlier, the French had also tried to make the Appalachians into an impermeable boundary. To block British access to the region beyond the mountains, an army of French-Canadian colonists and Indian allies had marched to the future site of Pittsburgh, constructed a fort, and ordered English traders out of the western country. But French attempts to consolidate control over a South clashed with the ambitions of the British in the West. Unwilling to concede control of the fur trade and of so much valuable real estate to the French, the British countered by sending an armed force into the Ohio Valley.

The ensuing struggle extended to both sides of the Atlantic, but Americans now remember it as the "French and Indian War." The name is misleading, for it suggests that all Indians sided with the French and that French and Indian interests were identical. But Indians fought on both sides and for their own reasons. In the Ohio Country, where it all began, many Indians, especially those who had migrated from Pennsylvania, shared the French fear of British expansion. At the same time, they resented French attempts to monopolize trade. In addition, British leaders worked to win over Ohio Indians by promising to create a fixed boundary between colonial settlements and Indian countries. Whether aligned with the French or the British, Ohio Indians fought (or chose not to fight) for their own interests, which were best served not by total victory for one or the other colonial regime, but by a stalemate between imperial rivals and a continuing competition between their traders.

Rather than a renovated borderland, the war dealt the French out of North America. By the 1763 Treaty of Paris, Britain gained control of Canada and of French claims below the Great Lakes and east of the Mississippi River (with the exception of New Orleans, which, along with French possessions west of the Mississippi, was transferred to Spain). Flushed with victory and freed of competition with the French, British officials hatched plans to erect a much less accommodating regime across its newly won frontier. Treating Indian peoples of the Ohio Valley and Great Lakes as defeated peoples, the British commander Lord Jeffrey Amherst did not propose to negotiate; he intended to dictate the terms of intercultural relations. The practice of making presents to Indians, which Amherst viewed as mere "bribes" to "purchase good behavior," was to be eliminated (Barr, 2001: 152–3). He informed Indians that henceforth British traders would pay market prices for the pelts they obtained, and misbehaving natives would be punished by having their access to imported goods cut off.

Incensed by such unilateral impositions, Indian war parties from dozens of villages around the Great Lakes and Ohio Valley attacked British posts in the western country and raided settlements on the other side of the mountains. British authorities saw in these attacks evidence of a vast conspiracy, but the Indians' uprising was not the work of a centrally coordinated confederation. The insurgents did, however, draw inspiration from a number of prophets who offered similar visions of Indian renaissance through rituals of cultural purification. Particularly notable in awakening the spirit of cultural revival was the Delaware prophet Neolin. Traveling widely, Neolin preached a return to ancient customs and a cleansing of European influences (Dowd, 1992, 2002).

The message of Indian revitalization through de-Europeanization resonated with tremendous force throughout the Ohio Country and Great Lakes Region, but a complete detachment from colonial ways was almost unimaginable to Neolin or his adherents. Generations of cross-cultural exchange had woven items and ideas of European origin into the fabric of woodland Indian life. Even as Neolin heralded a world cleansed of European things and thinking, his home, with its "stone cellar, stairway, stone chimney and fireplace" reminded a visiting Christian missionary "of an English dwelling" (Dexter, 1899: 61, 68). Indeed, Neolin's vision bore the imprint of Christian missionization, especially in its fervent crusade against the consumption of alcohol and its threat of eternal damnation for those who resisted calls for cultural revitalization.

The Indians' incorporation of foreign elements included not only the adaptation of colonial things and colonial thinking but also the adoption of colonists. From their raids against backcountry settlements, Ohio Valley Indians brought back scores of captives, who, in keeping with long-standing practices, were sometimes adopted. These wartime additions joined the already heterogeneous population of Ohio Valley villages, which consisted of a diverse mélange of Pennsylvania Indians who had migrated west to escape Anglo-American encirclement and Illinois Indians who had drifted east to position themselves between French and British trading orbits. As part of their incorporation into multiethnic Indian communities, backcountry-born captives learned Native ways of living and thinking. Not all made the transition successfully. Enough did, however, so that when the British demanded the return of prisoners as a condition of restoring peace and trade, a significant number resisted repatriation (Axtell, 1985). Escorting the returnees back to their former homes, the British commander Henry Bouquet discovered that many considered their liberation a new captivity. Some had to be chained lest they escape back to their adopted kin, and these "continued many days in bitter lamentations, even refusing sustenance" (Smith, 1765: 27).

Although an army commanded by Bouquet won a victory against Ohio Indians and recovered the reluctant colonist-captives, the cost of putting down the uprising and the loss of fur trade revenues prompted a reversal of Amherst's vindictive policies. British officials took on the guise of French authorities and embraced a more accommodating stance. Like the French, British leaders acceded to certain Indian protocols. Gift-giving came back as the basis of trade, and British leaders renewed their promise to prevent settlers from trespassing across the Appalachians (Aron, forthcoming).

Did the King really intend to enforce this ban on westward colonization? Not according to many of his most influential subjects. As George Washington saw it, the Appalachian boundary was merely "a temporary expedient" (Abbot, 1988: 6). After all, wealthy and well-connected gentlemen on both sides of the Atlantic had schemed for decades about acquiring vast tracts of trans-Appalachian land. Anticipating an unparalleled windfall, speculators formed companies and successfully petitioned the crown for enormous grants (Bailyn, 1986). Gentlemen who missed the "present opportunity of hunting out good lands," warned Washington, "will never regain it" (Abbot, 1988: 6).

The proclamation line also displeased humbler backcountry settlers, who harbored land acquisition dreams of their own and who were contemptuous of imperial officials and their injunctions. During the mid and late 1760s, hundreds of settlers penetrated Appalachian valleys. Pushing and poaching even deeper into Indian country were scores of white hunters, who began to make regular fall and winter hunts in what are now Kentucky and Tennessee. These "long hunters" challenged the monopoly that Indian hunters had previously held as suppliers of skins and furs. Worse still from the perspective of Ohio Valley Indians, many long hunters engaged in land hunting on the side, scouting tracts for future settlements for themselves, or sometimes for wealthy speculators (Belue, 1996; Aron, 1996; Faragher, 1992).

Colonial authorities could do little in the face of the brazen defiance of long hunters; they had neither the money nor the manpower to police thousands of square miles of Appalachian frontier. The problem, it seemed to many gentry authorities, was that backcountry settlers in general, and long hunters in particular, too closely resembled the Indian peoples whose lands they invaded and whose role in the fur trade they usurped. Residents of western Pennsylvania, reported Thomas Gage, the British military commander for North America in 1772, "differ[ed] little from Indians in their manner of life" (Davies, 1972–81, vol. 1: 203). Backcountry residents, agreed Sir William Johnson, supervisor of Britain's relations with northern Indians, were "a lawless set of people as fond of independency as" Indians, "and more regardless of government, owing to ignorance, prejudice, democratical principles and their remote situation" (Davies, 1972–81, vol. 1: 225).

Admitting that backcountry people "are not to be confined by any boundaries or limits," Johnson attempted to defuse conflict by convincing Indians to withdraw from contested territory (Davies, 1972–81, vol. 1: 225). An opponent of Amherst's punitive policies, Johnson had influential friends among northern Indians, whose interests he earnestly wished to protect. But Johnson was also deeply interested in the acquisition of land to enrich himself and his friends. At Fort Stanwix in November 1768 he persuaded an assembly of more than three thousand Indians, principally members of the Iroquois confederacy, to cede their claims to lands south of the Ohio River and east of the mouth of the Great Kanawha. Almost completely absent from the council were representatives of the Shawnees and Delawares, whose villages lay closest to the lands in question. Johnson knew that these and other Ohio Indians had their own interest in the ceded lands, but he let himself believe that the Shawnees and Delawares were dependents of the Iroquois and that his negotiating partners had a right of conquest to Ohio Valley lands dating from the seventeenth-century beaver wars (Jones, 1982; Hurt, 2002).

Not surprisingly, the treaty won few friends in the Ohio Country, and militant opposition to British policies soon reemerged. Resentment ran especially high in several Shawnee villages, where enraged men denounced the pretensions of the Iroquois and the British. Adding insult to injury, the British made no allowance for gifts to Ohio Indians and failed to insist that the Iroquois share theirs. Talk of war once again dominated village councils. Even more alarming to officials of the British Indian Department was word that disenchanted Ohio Indians were putting together a confederacy. Reports that Shawnee emissaries had in 1769 traveled across Indian country disturbed colonial leaders, as did news of a well-attended conclave in which preparations for a united front against the Fort Stanwix Treaty and against further Anglo-American expansion were discussed.

To thwart the possibility of confederation, British officials worked to isolate militants. It was a time-tested strategy, and it worked again in the Ohio Country in the early 1770s. British officials detached southeastern, Great Lakes, and many Ohio Indians from the envisioned union. Great Lakes Indians decided that the lands south of the Ohio River were too distant to defend. Further south, colonial officers negotiated two treaties with the Cherokees, which kept them from joining with the Shawnees.

For their part, the Shawnees divided between peace and war camps, but the latter faction gained the upper hand after a group of backcountry ruffians murdered thirteen Shawnee and Mingo Indians in the spring of 1774. As was customary, relatives of the victims demanded revenge. Retaliation soon escalated. Matters came to a head in October 1774, when 1,100 Virginia militiamen narrowly defeated 300 Shawnee warriors at the Battle of Point Pleasant.

In the treaty conference that followed, Shawnee headmen yielded hunting rights south of the Ohio River, but were guaranteed again a firm boundary between Indian country and backcountry. Where the previous Proclamation of 1763 had set the boundary at the crest of the Appalachians, the new proposal moved the line to the Ohio River. Sensing that this divide too would not last long, hundreds of Shawnees embarked on another westward migration. This one took them across the Mississippi River into territory that France had ceded to Spain in 1763. West of what was now Britain's "western country," they sought a new and more permanent refuge.

As the third quarter of the eighteenth century drew to a close, Spain had not yet established much of a presence in the western country that lay to the east of the Mississippi River – or for that matter on its own side of the Mississippi. During the 1760s and early 1770s, Spain had dramatically expanded its holdings in North America. In addition to acquiring France's claims on the west bank of the Mississippi, Spain had planted a few missions in California. But across the Spanish "North," possessions were at best partially possessed. Older colonies in New Mexico, Florida, and Texas remained sparsely colonized, and their Indian inhabitants were incompletely conquered. That was even truer of California's isolated settlements and of those along the west bank of the Mississippi. Only a handful of Spanish officials actually inhabited the former French colonies, and these authorities made no attempt to Hispanicize the customs, manners, or language of *habitants*. For most French colonists, the change in colonial regimes made little difference. For many Indians as well, life went on as before. Just as the British in the 1760s emulated French accommodations, so, too, the Spanish in the Mississippi Valley assured Indians that trade would be encouraged and gifts would be given. Such promises attracted Shawnee migrants and inspired hope among natives who stayed east of the Mississippi that Anglo-Spanish competition might prevent a mixed Indian country from becoming a mere western country (Nasatir, 1976; Calloway, 1995).

The Revolutionary War and the Early Republic

During the final quarter of the eighteenth century, the conquest, colonization, and consolidation of the western country intensified, but the outcome of these processes remained contested and contingent. Indians resisted, as before, by migrations, accommodations, incorporations, revitalizations, and confederations. They did so, however, in a geopolitical context that was dramatically transformed by the American Revolution. The war and resulting American independence reshuffled intercultural and interimperial relations across North America, especially in the fervently disputed country between the Appalachians and the Mississippi. Into the 1790s, the fate of these lands was as yet unsettled.

The sustained colonization of trans-Appalachia coincided with the beginning of the Revolutionary War. In the same month that Massachusetts minutemen engaged British soldiers at Lexington and Concord, Daniel Boone led thirty men to the Kentucky River. There, Boone and his men commenced construction on a fort that was to be the headquarters for a new colony. Though the fort was designated Boonesborough, the proposed colony was called Transylvania, which was also the name of the company of North Carolina land speculators for whom Boone worked. Boone's employers had acquired their claim to hundreds of thousands of acres of

Kentucky lands through a purchase from the Cherokees. Accounts of the Transylvania Company's purchase and of its colony-planting disturbed rival speculators who feared being shut out of the profits from the resale of prime lands in central Kentucky. "There is something in that affair which I neither understand, nor like, and wish I may not have cause to dislike it worse as the mystery unfolds," wrote George Washington of the Transylvania Company's daring plans (Lester, 1935: 41). With their own plans for engrossing Kentucky threatened, colonial governors in Virginia and North Carolina also condemned the illegal purchase and settlement made by the Transylvania Company. The call to command the Continental Army soon diverted Washington's attentions, and the outbreak of Revolution unseated the colonial governors of Virginia and North Carolina who had voided the claims of the Transylvania Company. Still, the Transylvania enterprise had plenty of enemies among patriot elites, who looked to new state legislatures and the Continental Congress to nullify the company's presumed title. Challenges arose among trans-Appalachian pioneers as well. At least three other parties established settlements in central Kentucky in the spring of 1775. These men did not immediately recognize the ownership of the Transylvania Company, nor did most of the pioneers who moved into Kentucky that year and the next.

Through the Revolution and long after it, the questions of who owned the land and how it would be distributed were a prime concern on both sides of the Appalachians. On these questions, legislators and litigants engaged in seemingly endless wrangling. During the Revolution, though, Kentucky pioneers were more concerned with their struggle with Indians, who threatened from both north and south. That conflict, too, continued after the United States had won its independence (Perkins, 1998; Friend, 1999).

As before the Revolution, Indians divided about the best means to protect the integrity of their countries and their cultures. Among Cherokees, the decision to sell hunting lands to the Transylvania partners aggravated those divisions. In general, older headmen saw the deal as an unwelcome necessity. Younger men, however, accused these leaders of betraying their people. Two years later, after accommodation-minded leaders agreed to cede additional lands to the revolutionary governments of Georgia, South Carolina, North Carolina, and Virginia, militants moved out, establishing new towns further west in the Tennessee Valley. From this new location, which afforded better access to British supplies, the secessionists vowed to fight pioneer expansion (Perdue, 1998; Sheidley, 1999; Cumfer, 2001; Finger, 2001).

Similar generational and strategic splits afflicted Indian villages north of the Ohio River. Advocates of accommodation wished to remain neutral in the war between Britain and some of her colonists. If necessary, they were willing to concede Kentucky to settlers, but wished to see the Ohio River accepted as a permanent boundary. Again more militant factions preferred to force pioneers back to the other side of the mountains. To do so, they rallied to the British cause, or more accurately, they rallied to their own cause with British supplies. Militants also rekindled the idea of a pan-Indian confederacy. Just a few years earlier, calls for a united front against colonial encroachments won little backing in Cherokee councils. Only a handful of Cherokees joined the Shawnees at Point Pleasant in 1774. That was not surprising, for Shawnees and Cherokees had more typically fought one another for control of hunting lands south of the Ohio River. By contrast, during the Revolution, some

Cherokees and some Shawnees fought together. In the same month that the rebellious colonies declared their independence from Britain, thirteen Cherokees united with four Shawnees to kill two Kentucky men. Other joint ventures followed.

British supplies allowed loosely confederated western Indians to mount larger and longer campaigns against Kentucky settlements. In March 1777, a mixed group of two hundred Ohio Indians led by the Shawnee headman Blackfish began hit and run strikes that harassed pioneers for several months. By fall, when that year's "Indian summer" finally ended, seven stations had been abandoned; just four remained. These were in disarray, their inhabitants nearly destitute of corn and livestock. The following year, Blackfish brought another war party across the Ohio River. In February 1778, this force captured two-dozen Kentucky pioneers, including Daniel Boone. Instead of killing Boone, Blackfish adopted him, and instead of wiping out Boonesborough, the Indians determined to incorporate the pioneers at that station. Although Ohio Indians had a long and successful history of assimilating enemies, what Blackfish's band contemplated in 1778 – absorbing an entire community – was exceptionally ambitious. Too ambitious, as it turned out. Boone and several other adopted captives escaped, and Boonesborough settlers opted to defend their lands with their lives if necessary. As a counter-colonial strategy, incorporation of adversaries clearly had its limits (Aron, 1996).

By 1778, the lands around Boonesborough no longer belonged to the Transylvania Company, whose claim had been invalidated by the state of Virginia. Unfortunately for pioneers, Virginia legislators enacted new laws that only added to the disarray about ownership of land. Yet in spite of the confusion and the continuing raids of Indians, the number of trans-Appalachian colonists grew, and their range expanded into eastern and central Tennessee.

As pioneer ranks increased and as the government of Virginia allocated materiel for the defense of trans-Appalachian settlements, Americans were able to go on the offensive. A May 1779 attack against the Shawnee village of Chillicothe claimed the life of Blackfish and cost inhabitants their homes, their household items, many of their horses, and much of their food supply. A wider round of village razings the following summer left hundreds of Ohio Indians in a desperate condition. Taking the war to native villages also weakened the Indians' attachment to the British, who were faulted for failing to deliver essential supplies and promised presents. Some warriors talked of severing their ties with the British and aligning with the Americans. Yet Americans repeatedly undermined these efforts by launching indiscriminate raids that killed Indians regardless of their political allegiances. Dissatisfied with the British and hopelessly at odds with the Americans, many Ohio Indians joined the Delaware headman, Captain Pipe, in wishing openly for the return of the French. We have "never known of any other Father," Pipe told British officials, whom he downgraded as mere "brothers" (O'Donnell, 1992: 131). In fact, though, what Ohio Indians wanted was not to exchange the French for the British, but to restore a borderland in which imperial competition prevented any European empire from asserting dominance.

The end of the American Revolution bore more nightmarish tidings for western Indians. Although Indians had failed to dislodge pioneers from their trans-Appalachian settlements, they had not lost ground either. Through seven years of bloody raids and retaliations, they had inflicted heavy casualties on Kentucky settlers – seven times higher per capita than those suffered by Americans east of the

Appalachians. Nonetheless, when terms of the peace between Great Britain and the United States reached the western country, Indians discovered to their dismay that all of the lands below the Great Lakes had been ceded to the new nation. By the 1783 Treaty of Paris, some two hundred and thirty million acres of trans-Appalachian lands, all of which had supposedly been permanently guaranteed to Indians by royal decree, had now become the first West of the United States.

Of course, the remapping stipulated by the 1783 Treaty of Paris did not really alter the situation on the ground. As was the case twenty years earlier when a previous agreement in Paris had attached the western country to the British Empire, the 1783 accord could not alone make the West American. Yet, just as British officers pretended that western Indians had surrendered along with the French, so Americans prepared to dictate, not negotiate, with those whom they dismissed as defeated peoples. Indians, needless to say, did not consider themselves conquered in the 1760s or the 1780s. To be sure, in the 1780s, more than a thousand Shawnees and Delawares joined several hundred Cherokees in relocating to Spanish territory across the Mississippi. There they reunited with earlier migrants. Those who stayed behind resigned themselves to the loss of Kentucky, but a growing majority determined to contest any American occupations on the north side of the river. For ten years after the end of the Revolution their confederated resistance effectively limited the advance of American colonization north of the Ohio River and frustrated the efforts of the national government of the United States to consolidate its administration over the "Northwest Territory" (Hurt, 1996; Cayton, 1986).

Various factors contributed to the good fortunes of the Indian confederacy. First, the British betrayal was not as complete as the latest Treaty of Paris suggested. Making peace did not mean that King George III and his ministers had reconciled themselves to the loss of American colonies. Because the crown's agents viewed western Indians as crucial to recovering his majesty's possessions, they rushed to reassure their wartime partners that the alliance continued. Reneging on the treaty provision that stipulated the evacuation of British posts south of the Great Lakes, British officials promised Indians that these forts would be maintained and would dispense the gifts, trade goods, and arms that natives needed to defend their homelands. To further weaken the hold of the United States over its West, Britain returned west Florida to its Spanish enemy. This put Spain in control of the Gulf Coast and the mouth of the Mississippi. It left the western country isolated by mountains on the east and bordered by imperial rivals on the north, west, and south. For Indians, it meant that many still enjoyed the advantages of being in between (Calloway, 1987; Allen, 1992; Nelson, 1999).

The arrogance, incompetence, and divisions among American adversaries bolstered the Indian confederacy too. By treating natives as conquered peoples, by allowing murderers of Indians to go unpunished, and by failing to keep squatters from trespassing across the Ohio, Americans left Indians with little choice but to unite and fight. By contrast, the new nation lacked such common purpose or concerted power. Its own confederation of states assigned the national government too few resources to quell Indian resistance or assert control over the settlement of western lands. The ratification of a national constitution strengthened the federal government, but the army of the United States initially proved unable to break Indian defiance. First in 1790 and again in 1791, the federal government mustered its troops to attack Ohio Indians, and both times the armies were routed. In the second confrontation, an

American force, under the inept command of General Arthur St Clair, lost 630 soldiers. In terms of casualties, the battle ranked – and still ranks – as the greatest victory North American Indians ever won against the United States (Sword, 1985).

In the wake of St Clair's shattering defeat, the Indian confederacy gained confidence and followers. Word of the victory spread quickly from one village to the next, encouraging warriors from around the Ohio Country and Great Lakes to enlist in the common cause. Likewise, the fresh visions of new prophets, which foretold future victories, fired new converts and new recruits. Convinced of their military and spiritual superiority, Indian negotiators notified their humbled American counterparts that the United States must remove its citizens once and for all from lands north of the Ohio River. Indian diplomats also scorned American offers to buy additional lands. "Money to us, is of no value," an Indian diplomat lectured, "and no consideration whatever can induce us to sell the lands on which we get sustenance for our women and children" (Calloway, 1994: 181). Rather than waste so much blood and treasure trying to wrest land from its rightful inhabitants, Indian speakers proposed a cheaper alternative that would guarantee peace between peoples: the government of the United States should pay poor squatters, who would thus be compensated for "all their labor and improvements" and could then occupy land elsewhere (Calloway, 1994: 182).

Rewarding squatters with payments from the federal treasury was not what President George Washington had in mind. Washington, of course, had long despised unruly pioneers who interfered with the orderly settlement and profitable engrossment of western lands. As President, that animosity deepened. Squatters, in the view of Washington and other Federalists, deprived the national government of revenue by illegally occupying public lands, and they stirred up conflict with Indians that consumed the better part of the federal budget. Washington's displeasure, in fact, extended to more than just squatters; he was displeased with western citizens in general, who seemed to him forever ungrateful.

Certainly, the first generation of western Americans (like future generations of westerners) griped incessantly about the national government's shortcomings. Complainers, of which there were plenty, accused the Washington administration of being too conciliatory towards Indians. They blamed the government as well for its indifference to their economic prospects, which involved opening Indian lands for white settlement, guaranteeing property titles, and securing commercial opportunities (Rohrbough, 1968, 1978). This last element depended above all on bringing goods up and down the Mississippi. Yet the Spanish had closed the mouth of that waterway to American shipping, and the national government appeared too willing to accept the situation or too weak to change it.

Both the Spanish and the British attempted to exploit the gathering discontent of western Americans. In addition to inviting Indian migrants to resettle on their side of the Mississippi, the Spanish officials recognized that many Americans in the Ohio Valley were "disgusted with their Government" and surmised that weak national attachments might be easily shifted by liberal land offerings (Houck, 1909, vol. 2: 255). Taking advantage of the generous terms offered by the Spanish, several hundred Kentuckians and Tennesseans relocated in what is now Missouri. Meanwhile, the British lured American settlers to Upper Canada (Ontario) with similar inducements. Both Spanish and British officials also entered into secret talks with western leaders in hopes of detaching all or part of the trans-Appalachian territory from the United States.

Weak as its national government was and discontented as its western citizens were, the United States possessed a great and growing advantage over its imperial rivals and its Indian antagonists: numbers. In the 1790s, the American population topped four million, having doubled every twenty-five years during the eighteenth century. The trans-Appalachian segment was expanding even more quickly. By 1790, the first national census registered more than seventy thousand people in Kentucky, with another thirty thousand scattered in other western country settlements. By comparison, the population of Indians north of the Ohio River numbered only about twenty thousand, and this figure was declining as a result of wars, diseases, and migrations.

And so, in 1794, the United States sent another army to crack the power and unity of the Indian confederacy. Its commander, General Anthony Wayne, proved much abler than his predecessors. At Fallen Timbers in what is now northwestern Ohio, Wayne's troops defeated the Indian forces. It was an important triumph, though it alone was not decisive. What turned Fallen Timbers into a catastrophic defeat for confederated Indians were changes in the international scene. Locked in conflict with Revolutionary France, the monarchies of Spain and Britain decided to avoid a confrontation with the American republic. Consequently, the Spanish temporarily opened the Mississippi to American navigation, and the British betrayed their Indian allies once more. They closed their forts to retreating Indians and cut them off from resupply. Without this assistance, Indians could not stop Wayne from systematically destroying villages and burning cornfields. Surviving warriors scattered back to defend their homes. At the treaty session that followed, Wayne compelled vanquished Indians to surrender much of what was soon to become the state of Ohio (Cayton, 1998; Nelson, 1985).

Conclusion

Looking back, Fallen Timbers marked a critical turning point. Never again, would Indians in the trans-Appalachian West, or for that matter in subsequent Wests, contest American conquest from so favorable a position. In the years that followed, Indians resisted in familiar ways, but widening disparities in numbers and technology diminished their chances for all but the most ephemeral successes. That England, France, and Spain gradually withdrew from competing with the United States also tilted the balance of power further away from Indians.

As the scholar Anthony F. C. Wallace has recently reminded us, the election of Thomas Jefferson to the presidency in 1800 and the control that Jeffersonians assumed over the national government for the next generation contributed as well to the more rapid colonization of western lands and the speedier dispossession of Indian peoples (1999). In contrast to the restraints that George Washington and like-minded Federalists sought to impose on western settlement, Jefferson and his followers made territorial expansion the cornerstone of federal policy. To that end, Jefferson made lands more available by purchasing the vast Louisiana Territory and pressing Indians to cede remaining lands east of the Mississippi in exchange for tracts to the west. Jeffersonians also made lands more affordable to pioneer settlers by reducing the price and easing the terms on public land sales (McCoy, 1980).

Nonetheless, from Fallen Timbers and Jefferson's ascendance, the completion of Indian dispossession was several more decades in the making; not until British, Spanish, and French ambitions to gain or regain the region were thwarted was American possession secured. In the year of Jefferson's election, Spain's retrocession of the Louisiana Territory to France briefly reestablished a French imperial presence in North America. Jefferson feared that Napoleon aimed to reclaim all of France's former domain, in which case American expansion would be halted, and maybe even rolled back. But Napoleon's plans were altered when his army was unable to subdue rebellious slaves in Haiti. Instead of rebuilding a North American Empire, Napoleon's agents sold the Louisiana Territory to the United States in 1803. That transfer cleared imperial competitors from the western borders of the first West and deprived trans-Appalachian Indians of assistance from what had become the new West of the United States (Kukla, 2003). Within the first West, though, Britain still meddled from its posts to the north, and American officials were quick to blame the British for all troubles with Indians south of the Great Lakes. Indeed, stepped-up British aid during the War of 1812 raised Indian hopes anew. But war's end brought yet another betrayal by the British. No more would the British encourage or supply Indians south of the Great Lakes. Following the War of 1812, Spain also pulled back, ceding Florida to the American republic. By 1820, the borders of the first West had been secured, as had the hold of the United States over the region.

In retrospect, what is most striking about the making of the first American West is how long it took, particularly when compared with the more compressed chronologies of subsequent westward expansions. Through the first half of the eighteenth century, Indians and imperial rivals generally checked the inland movement of British American colonists. Judged by geographic range, French and Spanish expansion seemed far more imposing. Moreover, in contrast to the nineteenth century, when American expansion and Indian contraction went hand in hand, eighteenth-century imperialism rested, to varying degrees, on Indian acquiescence. Rather than exclusive occupations, colonial frontiers often featured more inclusive arrangements. Indeed, especially in those borderlands where colonial claims brushed up against one another, Indian peoples skillfully played imperial rivals off one another to fashion more favorable economic and diplomatic relations. Those possibilities declined as the surge of westering pioneers quickened following the Seven Years' War and accelerated even more after the American Revolution. But neither resident Indians nor imperial rivals yet conceded the trans-Appalachian realm to the United States. For a moment in the early 1790s, it appeared that a confederation of Indians, along with one or another European power, might wrest control of at least part of the region back from the United States. Although that moment soon passed, western Indians continued to resist as they could, following the well-worn paths of migrations, accommodations, incorporations, confederations, and revitalizations. Not until the 1830s did the Indians' only road left lead out of the first American West and down the "trail of tears."

REFERENCES

Abbot, W. W.: "George Washington, the West, and the Union." *Indiana Magazine of History*, 84 (March 1988), 3–14.

Adelman, Jeremy and Stephen Aron: "From Borderlands to Borders: Empires, Nation-States, and the Peoples in Between in North American History." *American Historical Review* 104 (June 1999), 814–841.

Allen, Robert S.: *His Majesty's Indian Allies: British Indian Policy in the Defence of Canada, 1774–1815* (Toronto: Dundern Press, 1992).

Anderson, Fred: *Crucible of War: The Seven Years' War and the Fate of Empire in British North America, 1754–1766* (New York: Knopf, 2000).

Aron, Stephen: "Lessons in Conquest: Towards a Greater Western History." *Pacific Historical Review*, 63 (May 1994), 125–147.

Aron, Stephen: *How the West Was Lost: The Transformation of Kentucky from Daniel Boone to Henry Clay* (Baltimore: Johns Hopkins University Press, 1996).

Aron, Stephen: *American Confluence: The Missouri Frontier from Borderlands to Border State* (Bloomington: Indiana University Press, forthcoming).

Axtell, James: *The Invasion Within: The Contest of Cultures in Colonial North America* (New York: Oxford University Press, 1985).

Bailyn, Bernard: *Voyagers to the West: A Passage in the Peopling of America on the Eve of the Revolution* (New York: Knopf, 1986).

Barr, Daniel P.: "Contested Ground: Competition and Conflict on the Upper Ohio Frontier, 1744–1784." (PhD dissertation: Kent State University, 2001).

Belue, Ted Franklin: *The Long Hunt: Death of the Buffalo East of the Mississippi* (Mechanicsburg: Stackpole Books, 1996).

Calloway, Colin G.: *Crown and Calumet: British–Indian Relations, 1783–1815* (Norman: University of Oklahoma Press, 1987).

Calloway, Colin G.: *The World Turned Upside Down: Indian Voices from Early America* (Boston: Bedford/St Martin's Press, 1994).

Calloway, Colin G.: *The American Revolution in Indian Country: Crisis and Diversity in Native American Communities* (Cambridge: Cambridge University Press, 1995).

Cayton, Andrew R. L.: *The Frontier Republic: Ideology and Politics in the Ohio Country, 1780–1825* (Kent, OH: Kent State University Press, 1986).

Cayton, Andrew R. L.: " 'Noble Actors' upon 'the Theatre of Honour': Power and Civility in the Treaty of Greeville." In Andrew R. L. Cayton and Fredrika J. Tuete (eds.), *Contact Points: American Frontiers from the Mohawk Valley to the Mississippi, 1750–1830* (Chapel Hill: University of North Carolina Press, 1998).

Cayton, Andrew R. L. and Fredrika J. Teute (eds.): *Contact Points: American Frontiers from the Mohawk Valley to the Mississippi, 1750–1830* (Chapel Hill, 1998).

Cronon, William, George Miles, and Jay Gitlin: "Becoming West: Toward a New Meaning for Western History." In William Cronon, George Miles, and Jay Gitlin (eds.) *Under an Open Sky: Rethinking America's Western Past* (New York: W. W. Norton, 1992).

Cumfer, Cynthia: " 'The Idea of Mankind is So Various': An Intellectual History of Tennessee, 1768–1810." (PhD dissertation: University of California, Los Angeles, 2001).

Davies, K. G. (ed.): *Documents of the American Revolution*, 21 vols. (Shannon, Ireland: Irish University Press, 1972–81).

Dennis, Matthew: *Cultivating a Landscape of Peace: Iroquois-European Encounters in Seventeenth-Century America* (Ithaca: Cornell University Press, 1993).

Dexter, Franklin B. (ed.): *The Diary of David McClure, Doctor of Divinity, 1748–1820* (New York: Knickerbocker Press, 1899).

Din, Gilbert C.: *Spaniards, Planters, and Slaves: The Spanish Regulation of Slavery in Louisiana, 1763–1803* (College Station: Texas A&M University Press, 1999).

Dowd, Gregory Evans: *A Spirited Resistance: The North American Indian Struggle for Unity, 1745–1815* (Baltimore: Johns Hopkins University, 1992).

Dowd, Gregory Evans: *War Under Heaven: Pontiac, the Indian Nations, and the British Empire* (Baltimore: Johns Hopkins University Press, 2002).

Eccles, W. J.: *The Canadian Frontier, 1534–1760* (New York: Holt Rinehart and Winston, 1969).

Ekberg, Carl J.: *French Roots in the Illinois Country: The Mississippi Frontier in Colonial Times* (Urbana: University of Illinois Press, 1998).

Faragher, John M.: *Daniel Boone: The Life and Legend of an American Pioneer* (New York: Henry Holt, 1992).

Finger, John R.: *Tennessee Frontiers: Three Regions in Transition* (Bloomington: Indiana University Press, 2001).

Friend, Craig Thompson (ed.): *The Buzzel about Kentuck: Settling the Promised Land* (Lexington: University of Kentucky Press, 1999).

Hatley, Thomas: *The Dividing Paths: Cherokees and South Carolinians through the Era of the American Revolution* (New York: Oxford University Press, 1993).

Hinderaker, Eric: *Elusive Empires: Constructing Colonialism in the Ohio Valley, 1673–1800* (New York: Cambridge University Press, 1997).

Hinderaker, Eric and Peter Mancall: *At the Edge of Empire: The Backcountry in British North America* (Baltimore: Johns Hopkins University Press, 2003).

Hine, Robert V. and John M. Faragher: *The American West: A New Interpretive History* (New Haven, 2000).

Hoffman, Paul E.: *Florida's Frontiers* (Bloomington: Indiana University Press, 2001).

Houck, Louis (ed.): *The Spanish Regime in Missouri*, 2 vols. (Chicago: R. R. Donnelley, 1909).

Hurt, R. Douglas: *The Ohio Frontier: Crucible of the Old Northwest, 1720–1830* (Bloomington: Indiana University Press, 1996).

Hurt, R. Douglas: *The Indian Frontier, 1763–1846* (Albuquerque: University of New Mexico Press, 2002).

Hurtado, Albert L.: "Parkmanizing the Spanish Borderlands: Bolton, Turner, and the Historians' World". *Western Historical Quarterly* 26 (Summer 1995), 149–167.

Kukla, Jon: *A Wilderness So Immense: The Louisiana Purchase and the Destiny of America* (New York: Knopf, 2003).

Jennings, Francis: *The Ambiguous Iroquois Empire: The Covenant Chain Confederation of Indian Tribes with English Colonies from Its Beginnings to the Lancaster Treaty of 1744* (New York: W. W. Norton, 1984).

Jennings, Francis: *Empire of Fortune: Crowns, Colonies, and Tribes in the Seven Years War in America* (New York: W. W. Norton, 1988).

Jones, Dorothy V.: *License for Empire: Colonialism by Treaty in Early America* (Chicago: University of Chicago Press, 1982).

Jordan, Terry G. and Matti Kaups: *The American Backwoods Frontier: An Ethnic and Ecological Interpretation* (Baltimore: Johns Hopkins University Press, 1989).

Klein, Kerwin Lee: *Frontiers of Historical Imagination: Narrating the European Conquest of Native America, 1890–1990* (Berkeley: University of California Press, 1997).

Lamar, Howard and Leonard Thompson: "Comparative Frontier History." In Howard Lamar and Leonard Thompson (eds.) *The Frontier in History: North America and Southern Africa Compared* (New Haven, 1981).

Lester, William S.: *The Transylvania Colony* (Spencer, IN: S. R. Guard & Co., 1935).

Limerick, Patricia N.: *The Legacy of Conquest: The Unbroken Past of the American West* (New York: W. W. Norton, 1987).

McConnell, Michael N.: *A Country Between: The Upper Ohio Valley and Its Peoples, 1724–1774* (Lincoln: University of Nebraska Press, 1992).

McCoy, Drew: *The Elusive Republic: Political Economy in Jeffersonian America* (Chapel Hill: University of North Carolina Press, 1980).

McDermott, John Francis (ed.): *The Spanish in the Mississippi Valley, 1762–1804* (Urbana: University of Illinois Press, 1974).

Mancall, Peter: *Valley of Opportunity: Economic Culture along the Upper Susquehanna, 1700–1800* (Ithaca: Cornell University Press, 1991).

Matsumoto, Valerie J. and Blake Allmendinger (eds.): *Over the Edge: Remapping the American West* (Berkeley: University of California Press, 1999).

Merrell, James H.: *Into the American Woods: Negotiators on the Pennsylvania Frontier* (New York: W. W. Norton, 1999).

Milner, Clyde A., Carol O'Connor, and Martha Sandweiss (eds.): *The Oxford History of the American West* (Oxford University Press: New York, 1994).

Nasatir, Abraham P.: *Borderland in Retreat: From Spanish Louisiana to the Far Southwest* (Albuquerque: University of New Mexico Press, 1976).

Nelson, Larry L.: *A Man of Distinction among Them: Alexander McKee and British–Indian Affairs along the Ohio Country Frontier, 1734–1799* (Kent: Kent State University Press, 1999).

Nelson, Paul David: *Anthony Wayne: Soldier of the Early Republic* (Bloomington: Indiana University Press, 1985).

Nelson, Paul David and Andrew R. L. Cayton: *Frontier Indiana* (Bloomington: Indiana University Press, 1996).

Nobles, Gregory: *American Frontiers: Cultural Encounters and Continental Conquest* (New York: Hill & Wang, 1997).

O'Donnell, James H., III (ed.): "Captain Pipe's Speech: A Commentary on the Delaware Experience, 1775–1781." *Northwest Ohio Quarterly*, 64 (Autumn 1992).

Onuf, Peter S.: *Statehood and Union: A History of the Northwest Ordinance* (Bloomington: Indiana University Press, 1987).

Perdue, Theda: *Cherokee Women: Gender and Culture Change, 1700–1835* (Lincoln: University of Nebraska Press, 1998).

Perkins, Elizabeth A.: *Border Life: Experience and Memory in the Revolutionary Ohio Valley* (Chapel Hill: University of North Carolina Press, 1998).

Richter, Daniel K.: *The Peoples of the Longhouse: The Iroquois League in the Era of European Colonialism* (Chapel Hill: University of North Carolina Press, 1992).

Richter Daniel K.: *Facing East from Indian Country: A Native History of Early America* (Cambridge, MA: Harvard University Press, 2001).

Richter, Daniel K. and James H. Merrell (eds.): *Beyond the Covenant Chain: The Iroquois and Their Neighbors in Indian North America, 1600–1800* (Syracuse: Syracuse University Press, 1987).

Rohrbough, Malcolm J.: *The Land Office Business: The Settlement and Administration of American Public Lands, 1789–1837* (New York: Oxford University Press, 1968).

Rohrbough, Malcolm J.: *The Trans-Appalachian Frontier: People, Societies, and Institutions, 1775–1850* (New York: Oxford University Press, 1978).

Sheidley, Nathaniel. "Unruly Men: Indians, Settlers, and the Ethos of Frontier Patriarchy in the Upper Tennessee Watershed, 1763–1815." (PhD dissertation: Princeton University, 1999).

Smith, William: *An Historical Account of the Expedition Against the Ohio Indians in the Year 1764* (Philadelphia: W. Bradford, 1765).

Sword, Wiley: *President Washington's Indian War: The Struggle for the Old Northwest, 1790–1795* (Norman: University of Oklahoma Press, 1985).

Taylor, Alan: *American Colonies* (New York: Viking, 2001).

Thomas, David Hurst (ed.): *Archeological and Historical Perspectives on the Spanish Borderlands East*, vol. 2 of *Columbian Consequences* (Washington, DC: Smithsonian Institution Press, 1990).

Trigger, Bruce G.: *Natives and Newcomers: Canada's "Heroic Age" Reconsidered* (Kingston, Ontario: McGill-Queen's University Press, 1986).

Turner, Frederick Jackson: "The Significance of the Frontier in American History." In John Mack Faragher (ed.) *Rereading Frederick Jackson Turner: "The Significance of the Frontier in American History" and Other Essays* (New York: Henry Holt and Co., 1994a).

Turner, Frederick Jackson: "Sections and Nation." In John Mack Faragher (ed.) *Rereading Frederick Jackson Turner: "The Significance of the Frontier in American History" and Other Essays* (New York: Henry Holt and Co., 1994b).

Turner, Frederick Jackson: "The Significance of Sections in American History." In John Mack Faragher (ed.) *Rereading Frederick Jackson Turner: "The Significance of the Frontier in American History" and Other Essays* (New York: Henry Holt and Co., 1994c).

Usner, Daniel H., Jr.: *Indians, Settlers, and Slaves in a Frontier Exchange Economy: The Lower Mississippi Valley before 1783* (Chapel Hill: University of North Carolina Press, 1992).

Wallace, Anthony F. C.: *Jefferson and the Indians: The Tragic Fate of the First Americans* (Cambridge, MA: Harvard University Press, 1999).

Weber, David. "Turner, the Boltonians, and the Borderlands," *American Historical Review*, 91 (January 1986), 66–81.

White, Richard: *"It's Your Misfortune and None of My Own": A History of the American West* (Norman: University of Oklahoma Press, 1991).

White, Richard: *The Middle Ground: Indians, Empires, and Republics in the Great Lakes Region, 1650–1815* (New York: Cambridge University Press, 1991).

Worcester, Donald E.: "Herbert Eugene Bolton: The Making of a Western Historian." In Richard W. Etulain (ed.) *Writing Western History: Essays on Major Western Historians* (Albuquerque: University of New Mexico Press, 1991).

CHAPTER TWO

Thinking West

ELLIOTT WEST

Bibliographical essays are not always compelling reading, so maybe it's best to start with a story.

Jean de L'Archeveque was a young man when he came to America in 1684 with the expedition of Robert Cavalier, sieur de La Salle. La Salle's goal was to establish a French presence in the lower Mississippi valley and challenge Spain's claims to the region. After missing the Mississippi's mouth (perhaps intentionally), the explorer founded a post on the Texas coast, but by 1687 his company's condition was desperate. L'Archeveque helped murder La Salle, showing what one historian has called a "precocious depravity," and managed to survive the internecine struggle that followed. Two years later a Spanish command found him, dressed and painted as an Indian, in a Native village. He vanished temporarily from the record, but by 1696 he was in Santa Fe, where he married well, insinuated his way into local society, and built a considerable business as a trader. He also developed a reputation as a leader in forays against Indians, so when authorities heard in 1720 that the French were luring plains tribes into their economic and military orbit, Jean (now called Juan) signed on with Pedro de Villasur to test the rumors. Marching to the Platte River far to the northeast, they found a village, perhaps of Pawnees, maybe Otoes, and maybe Kansas, that had in fact been courted and armed by the French. At dawn the Indians overran the Spanish camp and killed three dozen whites, including L'Archeveque and Villasur, as well as eleven Native allies.

This man's remarkable odyssey – from castaway and killer in a power play by a great imperial fantasizer, to social lion and merchant on another frontier, and to death by the indirect hand of his birth country – is a healthy reminder of the obstinate refusal of western studies to recognize boundaries, geographic, cultural, perceptual, and disciplinary. Given the prime role of the Spanish, who captured and repatriated L'Archeveque and sent him to the far rim of their empire, maybe his is a northern story, not western at all. Or is it Indian, and so to be told outward from its center in Texas, New Mexico, and Kansas? It is about international competition, multicultural blending and social climbing, politics, trade, Native diplomacy and warfare. So is this imperial history, or social, or ethnic, or economic, or military?

Here is the predicament. Tracking western historical writing and asking about its future will turn into a formless ramble unless we arrange the work into fields and broader topics. And yet whenever we explore any field or topic, we quickly find that its boundaries cannot contain what we try to put there. It is a dilemma to learn from. Arranging books and articles into historiographical categories shows us just how wide-ranging the work and insights have been; the failure of those categories at their edges teaches us that we learn most about the West when our questions ignore lines that divide what was, after all, a seamless experience.

Negotiations: Exploration and Diplomacy

Jean L'Archeveque's story rankles most with the traditional historical calendar of great western events. In *The Legacy of Conquest* (1987), arguably the most influential of the works of the "New Western History," Patricia Nelson Limerick challenges the tendency to cut off western history around 1900. Forces generated in the nineteenth century, she argues, pushed vigorously into the next. The time is ripe today to call into the question the artificial division at the other end of the nineteenth century. By the traditional view, western history generally, and certainly anything to do with imperial politics, does not really get underway until the first agents of the United States show up shortly after 1800. But as the French-Indian-Spanish L'Archeveque reminds us, the West at that point had long been hotly contested and was still very much up much up for grabs. The nineteenth century ended with one of history's greatest empires firmly in place, but when we imagine that development forward from 1800, not backward from 1900, we see this nation's westward march as one narrative being imposed on many others. Understanding the nineteenth-century West begins with recognizing that Americans stepped into a history already old. Their wresting of military and political control was inseparable from establishing mastery over how that history was told, installing themselves at its forefront, setting the country's peoples in an order of descending power, and through all this trying to impose on the West one out of many possible meanings.

Nowhere have historians been more mesmerized by eventual American success than in writing about what is traditionally treated as the inaugural episode of far western history, the Lewis and Clark expedition of 1804–6. Stephen Ambrose's fabulously successful *Undaunted Courage* (1996) is only the most recent of a long tradition largely neglectful of the broader context of the internationalized West. The Corps of Discovery seems to ascend the Missouri River into a land waiting for history to arrive. This perspective reinforces the rightness of the rise of an American empire, and, given the genuinely heroic particulars, it makes the expedition the classic expression of our national mythology – brave and questing individuals confronting the wilderness, suffering, succeeding, and being enlarged by the experience.

Lewis, Clark, and Jefferson were indeed woefully ignorant of the region explored – the President told his charges to look for mountains of pure salt and gave them a glossary for conversations with Welshmen he thought were living in North Dakota. But the reason was that the other nations that knew a lot about the West considered their geographic and ethnological knowledge precious commodities to be jealously guarded. Fifty years ago Abraham P. Nasatir (1952) compiled some of the most revealing Spanish documents on the Missouri basin before 1804, and the archaeologists W. Raymond Wood and Thomas D. Thiessen have collected and edited the journals and narratives of English and French Canadian traders from the same area and time (1985). Readers will see that America's most famous explorers visited Mandans and Hidatsas who were well supplied with awls, knives, rings, and coats, wormers, candy, and corduroy trousers. James Ronda (1998), this generation's leading interpreter of the expedition, shows that Jefferson may have known little about the West, but he was well aware that others were both interested in it and in a better position to grab it; it was the British explorer Alexander Mackenzie's call for England to colonize the Columbia River valley, not some general geographic and scientific curiosity, that sparked Jefferson's decision to send Lewis and Clark into the imagined country of Welshmen and salt mountains.

The United States, that is, entered the West in the middle of an imperial scramble that has barely begun to be explored historically. Once we pull ourselves out of the "triumphalist" perspective that assumes a momentum of events toward an American empire, the need for a far deeper investigation of the global maneuvering and domestic politics entwined in these early explorations is obvious. Donald Jackson's earlier *Thomas Jefferson and the Stony Mountains* (1981) and Ronda's more recent edited collection, *Voyages of Discovery: Essays on the Lewis and Clark Expedition* (1998), point the way, but they also make it embarrassingly clear that historians must spend more time in the extraordinarily deep archives of Spain, Mexico, England, France and (now that the Cold War has turned somewhat sunny) Russia. This multi-imperial perspective will also shift attention toward other expeditions, episodes that have been neglected to an astonishing degree. The last serious look at the Pike expedition is now more than fifty years old (Hollon, 1949), and, except for the good work by Dan Flores (1984), the forays of Freeman and Custis and Hunter and Dunbar up the Red River have been virtually ignored. Eventual control by the United States, once seen from many national angles and from a perspective across a hundred and fifty meridians, will appear more accurately as the result of long chains of circumstance, odd twists, and much luck.

This is not to say, of course, that the United States had no more going for it than other contenders. It entered the fray with comparatively superior numbers, a prodigious reproductive rate, and a growling land hunger among farmers who tended to settle where they wished. The question is, rather, how those advantages expressed themselves. Drew McCoy's *The Elusive Republic* (1980) explores how the Jeffersonian republican vision of the West mingled agrarianism with a binding trade and commerce – a measure of the nation's evolving economy and an antecedent of the mixed impulses that would drive our borders outward again at mid-century. But in the two decades since this contribution, far too little has been to done to follow McCoy's lead and examine with some exactness how American self-interest, self-perception, and self-confidence developed and were directed westward during the critical years between 1800 and 1845.

There could be no clearer evidence of pressures building up during those years than the explosive expansion during the three years following 1845. In three great gobblings – the admission of Texas as a state (1845), the acquisition of the Pacific Northwest from Great Britain (1846) and the Mexican War (1846–48) – more territory was acquired than in any other expansionist episode, including the Louisiana Purchase. In barely a blink of time the United States grew from a large republic bordered to the west by plains and mountains into a dual-oceanic, transcontinental nation of imperial proportions. Its sovereignty was extended over dozens of peoples;

into its grasp came a vast storehouse of resources including precious metals, coal, timber, rich soil, copper, and others with a value not to be realized for generations.

In contrast to the preceding period, the considerable literature on these years shows what can be gained by looking at western diplomacy from various angles. For decades the scholarly view of the war with Mexico was dominated by Justin H. Smith's jingoistic *The War With Mexico* (1919), which placed responsibility for the conflict squarely on an aggressive and obstinate Mexico and portrayed United States officials as concerned almost wholly with defending the newly acquired Texas. It is a case lesson in how a historian can examine all available documents and still be wrong. A more balanced view began to emerge with Norman Graebner's *Empire on the Pacific* (1955), which shifted our attention to the Pacific coast and to the agrarian and commercial hunger for land and ports; his book remains a challenge to scholars to look back more closely at how those desires had developed up to 1846. The next generation of historians, writing during the turbulent 1960s and 1970s, were especially attuned to questions of American power and what its exercise said about the nation's economic interests and racial presumptions. Charles Sellers's superb biography of President James K. Polk (1957) explored the impulses and maneuvering of this "continentalist," and his *The Market Revolution* (1991) offered important clues as to how America's economic transformation helped push its borders outward. Gene M. Brack's splendid slim volume, *Mexico Views Manifest Destiny* (1990), described the attempts by increasingly desperate Mexican leaders to find a way out of a political and diplomatic impasse created largely by the appallingly insensitive policies of the United States. Frederick Merk's broad-ranging studies (1967, 1972) of the annexation of Texas and the Oregon country juggle the various economic and political factors at play, as does William H. Freehling's lengthy examination of Texas annexation in *The Road to Disunion* (1990). Finally, we have a superbly researched and argued overview in David Pletcher's *The Diplomacy of Annexation* (1973), which commonsensically looks at all three episodes as interlocking, with decisions and assumptions in each affecting the others and, in the case of the war, resulting in spectacular miscalculation.

Writers also have been drawn to the cultural context of expansion. The phrase "manifest destiny," like the events of the day, takes on various meanings when turned this way and that. From Albert K. Weinberg's early study of its rhetoric (1935) through provocative shorter works by Frederick Merk (1963), William Goetzmann (1966), and Reginald Horsman (1981), the goal of historians has been to link the growth of the nation to its shifts in mood, the evolution of its collective identity, and the development of its ethnic and racial hierarchies. These, as much as economic interests and the ambitions of its leaders, help explain America's leap to the Pacific.

Plenty remains to be done on the remarkable mid-1840s, but what we have so far can suggest approaches and insights for both sides of that expansionist divide. Looking back, we need to look harder at the cultural, economic, and intellectual forces between the 1820s and 1846 as a prelude to the great gulping. Despite recent books on the expeditions of Stephen H. Long (Wood, 1966; Nichols and Halley, 1980) and John Charles Fremont (Roberts, 2000; Chaffin, 2002), for instance, there is a crying need for studies on their cultural contexts and the changes in national attitudes during the quarter century between them.

Looking ahead from 1848, it might seem that little awaits to be done. Except for the Gadsden Purchase, an after-dinner mint following the expansionist gorging, the contiguous United States was complete. But if expansion took a rest, diplomacy in its broadest meanings simply shifted its emphasis, now toward the inward tasks of exploration and self-definition.

The great surveys, for instance, can be seen as one stage of a national government and society negotiating their relationship with the newly acquired western lands and their inhabitants. Exploration is not simply an objective description of something fully established and unchanging. Rather, explorers who observed the West were simultaneously changing and even creating it. They carried their values and assumptions with them and projected them onto the lands they entered. Their mapping was a first step toward defining places, establishing their uses and arranging their peoples into an order defined by the explorers. William Goetzmann in *Exploration and Empire* (1966) first developed this theme of a West shaped by "programmed" explorers, a fresh term when Goetzmann wrote in 1966. He also showed how artistic expressions were vital documents in the creation of the West, including the illustrations accompanying government surveys. Others have followed his lead – Kevin J. Fernlund's study of the artist William Henry Holmes (2000) and James G. Cassidy's of the explorer Ferdinand Hayden (2000) – but much of the exploration after 1850 remains *terra incognita*.

The men who mapped the West also had their opinions and views of the world transfigured by the experience, of course. As they imposed their ideas onto the land, the land impressed its own realities on their thinking. Nowhere is this better demonstrated than in *A River Running West* (2001), Donald Worster's marvelous recent biography of the greatest figure of post-1850 exploration, John Wesley Powell. Powell is usually remembered as the intrepid one-armed commander of the first white expedition to ride the wild Colorado River through the Grand Canyon as well as the most vocal proponent for fundamentally revising eastern notions of the survey and proper use of the arid West. Worster plots in detail Powell's reevaluation of federal policy and shows why Powell has come to be seen as something of a prophet by contemporary environmentalists. This extraordinary figure was as well an anthropological pioneer with deep respect for Native peoples. He was profoundly changed by his work in the West. Yet, as his given names suggest, Powell never left behind all the verities of a religious upbringing, and he approached the West with the sense of confident mastery of nineteenth-century science. He never questioned the rightness of using the opening country for larger national purposes, and, sympathies aside, he assumed the inevitable and proper submergence of Indian cultures within what he considered a higher civilization.

Powell, that is, was a brilliant distillation of the exploratory process. That process was an example of a theme that runs through much of recent writing – negotiation, in this case between the outlook and notions of the early agents of a new regime of power and the western realities that bent the understanding of men like Powell into new shapes. It was a mutually influential experience. Expeditions of Ferdinand Hayden and Clarence Dutton similarly probed and tested the meanings of the West, as agrarian dream, forbidding desert, and sublime wilderness. As with George Custer's foray in his expedition into the Black Hills in 1874, prelude to the Plains Indian war and Custer's own calamity two years later, we can draw no clear distinction among exploration, defining particular places, realigning relations with indigenous peoples, and other aspects of the western story. What appears straightforward – the description of the country – bleeds always into shiftier topics of culture, mass perception, and messages found in the land.

It's Not Just the Economy, Stupid

And so it is with western economic history. Here too the story on its face seems basic enough. The nineteenth-century West experienced a series of wrenching economic transformations. Chief among them was the development of extractive industries that pulled from the land a breathtaking array of natural resources and fed them to an expanding industrial plant outside the region. An increasingly powerful and centralized national economy widened and tightened its embrace of the West. It was one of the most significant developments in the larger narrative of the Industrial Revolution.

Much of the literature has cataloged the bloom of various western industries, with a few topics – most obviously the range cattle business, mining, and agriculture – dominating the shelves. All have been refined by work that draws social and cultural distinctions within each economic development. Dean May (1994), for instance, shows how different clusters of values shaped distinctively agrarian development in a Mormon village, an Oregon settlement in the 1840s, and Idaho's Boise Valley after the Civil War. Terry Jordan's closely researched analysis (1993) explains the rise of the western cattle industry as the confluence and mingling of various outside traditions. Although their attention has been more on the humid East than the drier West, historians have begun to explore more rigorously the relation of modern capitalism to rural economies. Industries relatively neglected in the past have begun to get more attention. Timbering, for example, has begun to get something like its full due, although most writing has been on the Pacific Northwest. Lumbering elsewhere, much of it in the form of smaller enterprises crucial to local development, still offers plenty of openings for new studies.

These newer works, however, are teasers that emphasize how much is left to learn when boundaries are eroded and economic history is enlivened by other perspectives. As a case in point, consider the literature on the West's unifying industry – transportation. It was triply important to western development. As a major employer it pulled vast amounts of capital into the region; it directly encouraged many "spinoff" industries such as timber; indirectly it was arguably the ultimate stimulant of other industries requiring some connection to the world beyond.

For the most part, however, this vital topic has suffered an historical snubbing during the last generation or two. Oscar O. Winther's work of nearly thirty years, from the 1930s into the 1960s (1936, 1950, 1964), was supplemented by excellent earlier works on steamboating and roadbuilding, but all those subjects have long been ripe for a fresh look, both in their particular settings and in their impact on the West. As Patricia Limerick has pointed out (1999), the mesmerizing power of overland migration has blinded us somewhat to the extraordinary social experience of approaching the West from the sea, and to that we can add a neglect of the economic impact of maritime trade following the Mexican War and the Gold Rush. The overland experience, furthermore, has been so closely identified with the migration of families and goldseekers that historians have badly neglected one of the West's most powerful economic and social forces, freighting, which had few if any rivals as a force of local change, as an environmental abrasive, and as an introduction for many immigrants. The many thousands of young men guiding wagons across the West, after all, outnumbered, probably by at least a factor of ten or more, the number of cowboys pushing cattle along the mythic trails to Abilene or Dodge City.

One area of transportation, on the other hand, has real staying power. In sheer historiographical tonnage, railroads have overwhelmed the competition, although here too the balance is a bit out-of-whack. Much of the writing has traced the histories of individual lines. Books taking a broader perspective have traditionally focused on the construction of transcontinentals, a tradition carried on by two recent additions by David H. Bain (1999) and Stephen Ambrose (2000). Building these lines was indeed a genuine epic, but as with the fascination with family immigration on the overland trail, the mythic glare makes us squint to the point that we miss other vital parts of the railroad story. Bain at least fleshes out the extraordinary political maneuvering and the robust, often shameless promotion behind laying down the Union Pacific and Central Pacific. Historians have paid less attention to the dynamic set in motion as railroads unleashed social, cultural and political transformations in the country they entered. John Stilgoe's *Metropolitan Corridor* (1983) made the point for the nation as a whole, and Robert Athearn's *Union Pacific Country* (1971) suggested how it might be applied to the West. In *Railroad Crossing*, William Deverell (1994) narrows the geographic focus, using opposition to railroads in California to explore the part played by these vast enterprises in both the state's life and economy and its people's anxiety about where they fit in a new industrial order. James Ducker's *Men of the Steel Rails* (1983) remains an intriguing study of how a major railroad, its unions, and its workers' sense of craft shaped the structure, relations, and even the family life in communities along the tracks. Works like these should point the way toward more studies on the railroad's impact from the national to the local level. A forthcoming study by Richard White promises an even wider perspective by considering the first transcontinental as an American instance of the railroad as a force of global change.

Once we recognize the wide-ranging influence of this economic juggernaut, all sorts of new lines of investigation open up. Railroads' environmental impact, and through that their part in the assault on Indian independence, have barely begun to be studied. The same can be said about how railroads and other means of movement altered how people saw and thought about the West. The visceral responses in hundreds of overland diaries, the fear and anxiety, elation and astonishment, testify how the plains and interior West loomed large in national mental geography – as long, that is, as people had to walk across it. The railroad instantly changed that. Four months after the first transcontinental's completion, a southern diarist's single-entry dismissal of the space between Council Bluffs and the Rockies – "Passing a poor, sandy & stoney country" – suggested a region already on its way to becoming the Great Flyover. Anne Hyde (1990) has taught us how the transportation revolution was accompanied by a perceptual one, but others need to trace the connections among how people moved around the West, how transportation remade their economies, and how it rebuilt landscapes and human awareness of them.

The larger point about economic history echoes that of exploration: what seems a cleanly defined and self-contained subject will not be disentangled from its social and cultural context. As an example, consider what is arguably the most enduring theme of western economic history – colonialism. In the 1930s Walter Prescott Webb (1937) and Bernard DeVoto (1934) portrayed the West (and South) as plundered provinces. Webb and DeVoto were pulling into historical perspective complaints going back at least to territorial trans-Appalachia and reaching their most dramatic flashpoint in western Populism. These regions, the argument runs, have suffered a steady loss of wealth and have remained politically subordinate to centers of economic power elsewhere, especially the Northeast. Although the study of class and its formation, inherent to this analysis of economic inequality, remains curiously neglected, the colonial theme runs unbroken through western studies, with its finest recent representation in William G. Robbins's 1994 study *Colony and Empire*. But as Robbins shows so well, economic analysis becomes steadily more fulfilling as we refine it with an eye to western society's popular attitudes, its many ethnic components, and its mythic dimensions. Flipping through Robbins' book we find economic theorists sharing the page with the painter Frederic Remington and the novelists Owen Wister and Wright Morris. William Cronon's magnificent work on the rise of Chicago and its linkage to the West, *Nature's Metropolis* (1991), is a recent variant on colonialism, here with the great city drawing from and making over the hinterland. Cronon manages the seemingly impossible: an utterly engaging narrative about capital flow, wheat production, and regional patterns of bank deposits. He does this by writing as much a perceptual history of city and region as an economic one, and through that he tells of history of human striving and the changing meanings of the American heartland.

In a variant of colonialism, others have considered the nineteenth-century West through the lens of world systems and dependency theory. Here the West is a "periphery" manipulated by "centers" of economic power, with its settlers and indigenous peoples pushed this way and that by distant decisions and left inextricably reliant on support from the same distant sources that profit from their labor and resources. Richard White's *The Roots of Dependency* (1983) has proved a model for this approach; by considering three quite different Indian tribes he finds consistent patterns of deepening dependence as each group's economy was undermined, yet each case worked itself out in its own cultural particulars. Dependency theory has its critics. Most tellingly, they argue that the picture of a capitalist market economy reaching in to control the West, while accurate from the bird's-eye-view, misses how westerners still managed to shape events, however subtly. Here, as in the exchanges between explorers and the West, is the theme of negotiation, in this case with localities engaged in a give-and-take with outside power. This in turn means that to understand what is happening we must study the unique contours of life in each society, including how folks made their living. The harder we look, the less the usual topical boundaries make sense. The economic merges with social and cultural concerns.

The result often has unexpected insights. Sturdy traditional images of western life sometimes are suddenly shaken. Among the more important, and most emblematic, enterprises of the nineteenth-century West was the fur trade. Its chief practitioner, the mountain man, has stood tall in the popular view of the West as a misfit, social isolate, and man on the fringe. In 1963 William Goetzmann considered the personal trajectories of these characters, set the results in the context of prevailing social values and economic attitudes, and argued that this view was precisely backwards. Mountain men were amplified expressions of Jacksonian America, he wrote. The fur trade suddenly seemed less a romantic idyll of escape than an agent of economic/cultural expansion. Michael Allen has since made a similar point in a study of riverboatmen (1991). Another group typically portrayed as irredeemably outside national life – the buffalo hunters during the great slaughter of the 1870s – beg to be reconsidered in a similar way. The stark contrast between mountain men's popular image and their historical reality in turn pushes us into a new line of inquiry. What has compelled Americans to make those Jacksonian men into wild children who have run away from home? Why this cultural urge to admire them for what they supposedly rejected (but did not), to use the Jeremiah Johnsons of that time to question an economic expansion we otherwise celebrate?

The call, that is, is to bring intellectual history, broadly defined, to bear on western economic life. Half a century ago Henry Nash Smith virtually single-handedly birthed the field of American Studies with *Virgin Land: The American West as Myth and Symbol*. One could honestly say this book is about the usual episodes of economic expansion, especially the spread of an agricultural empire, governmental encouragement through railroads and the Homestead Act, and the agrarian disappointment at the century's end. But the most untutored reader quickly sees that Smith is up to something else. His interest is in the West as mass dream. His crucial documents are not legislation and the correspondence of power brokers but works of popular literature. These provide a kind of script or blueprint for what usually are treated as central events – exploration, settlement, conquest, policy making. For Smith, the economic conquest of the West was driven by the peculiar expectations and illusions of what we call, a bit condescendingly, popular culture. Looking back over the half century since his book appeared, his great accomplishment was to show us how to treat seriously the expressions of popular culture and how to explore the continuing exchanges between those expressions and their historical setting.

Richard Slotkin's trilogy on myth and the frontier – *Regeneration Through Violence* (1973), *The Fatal Environment* (1985), and *Gunfighter Nation* (1992) – is the most notable among shelves of books that have followed Smith's lead. Most can be defined as a meeting of economic, cultural, and intellectual history. This approach was made to order for the concurrent surge of interest in gendered perceptions. Feminist scholars pointed out that the title of Smith's pathbreaking book itself revealed how the rhetoric and assumptions of pioneering were dominated by male fantasies of conquest and of deflowering of virginal country, followed by planting of seeds of a masculine culture in plowed, subdued ground. Annette Kolodny first contrasted female and male visions of the frontier West in *The Lay of the Land* (1975), then delineated more fully female perceptions in *The Land Before Her* (1984). Curiously, the economic focus of most has remained that of Smith – pioneer agriculture. Particular themes have ranged from illusion and propaganda, as in David Emmons's *Garden in the Grasslands* (1971), to the aesthetic yearnings of westering farmers studied by Peter Boag in *Environment and Experience* (1992). The breadth of economic life offers so many more opportunities to apply this dynamic – perception resonating with specific settings and particular economic enterprises – to a changing nineteenth-century West, from its timbering camps and mining towns to its railroad market centers and blossoming cities. Just as wide open is the study of this same interaction among the many nationalities who arrived alongside the settlers in Smith's and Kolodny's books. What was the West, as mass dream, to its Hispanic and Asian newcomers? How did their wrestling with their expectations shape the course of change?

One area of economic history remains largely unaffected by these new trends – labor. Earlier works came close to equating labor history with the story of unionization. This focus is not so surprising, given the often hellish conditions that inspired the first organizing, especially in western mines, the dramatic rise of the Western Federation of Miners and its evolution toward the Industrial Workers of the World. The persistence of the equation of labor and union history, however, is more puzzling in light of the impact of other approaches in western scholarship. Ronald C. Brown's *Hard-Rock Miners* (1979) and Mark Wyman's *Hard Rock Epic* (1979), it is true, both bring in something of the miner's social world, yet the emphasis remains on working conditions below ground, and from that perspective the rise of unions feels proper and inevitable. And so it may have been. But by defining labor in large-scale industrial terms much of western working life is necessarily left out, and by centering it solidly in the context of unionization the temptation is to keep our attention on matters of ideology at the expense of other aspects that doubtless were more to the fore in these workers' attention. Ronald James's *The Roar and the Silence* (1998) and Sally Zanjani's *Goldfield* (1992) point one way out. By keeping the focus on one mining region, in this case the Comstock Lode and Goldfield, Nevada, James and Zanjani can tell the story of workingmen's towns, one of them the cradle of western unionism, yet still interweave the many threads of social life to achieve something close to its full texture. The results should make us hungry for something similar done in the many other laboring contexts across the transforming West.

Four recent books give us examples of the happy results when economic history is expanded and reshaped by questions rooted in intellectual, cultural, and social history. In *The Culture of Wilderness* (1996) Frieda Knobloch recasts our notions of colonization by arguing that agriculture, as defined broadly by an expanding Europe, was a conquering device that has rested on defining perceptions of land and its proper use; the details of plants and crop choices, tools and technologies, plowing techniques and aggie bulletins all become elements of an encompassing culture that overwhelms and makes over the West in its image. Hal Rothman's *Devil's Bargains* (1998) has an essentially colonialist take on the tourist industry that began in the late nineteenth century, but by grounding his argument in local examples he brings a subtlety usually missing in this old theme while also stressing how mass perception and illusion, in this case the commodification of leisure, romance, and adventure, can also be potent economic forces. Mark Fiege's *Irrigated Eden* (1999) considers southern Idaho's economic culture of ditches and potato farms as an ideological overlay on a demanding landscape – an environment that in turn subverted the colonizers' efforts to categorize and arrange natural relationships. Settlement became – here it is again! – an ongoing negotiation between human assumptions and ecological realities, with the result over time a surprising amount of common ground between the two. Gunther Peck, in *Reinventing Free Labor* (2000), crosses two sorts of boundaries. He joins labor and immigration history by studying Greek, Italian, and Mexican workers in movement around the West under the padrone system they soon began to resent and eventually to resist, and he pictures that West as a continental region in which national borders blur away in the stories of real people. Peck's concern is the neglected theme of class, but, as treated here, it teaches us just as much about the ethnic and social texture of the workingman's West.

The Tangles of Society

Social history is the craft's most loosely defined field. It has been called "leftover history," whatever remains after other topics are parceled out to other categories. It includes the history of relations among members of some larger human unit – a community, family, or political group, for instance. It might be the study of daily lives of common folk. It might focus on institutions and customs revelatory of the people who participate in them. Ultimately, however, social history is fuzzier around its edges than other fields. As we have seen, diplomatic history and economic history also refuse to stay within the lines, even if they sometimes pretend to. Social history is more honestly vague than the others, and as such it has been especially welcoming to the topics-without-borders approach.

As with other fields, social history also has yawning gaps, and as usual some of the most obvious fall outside the main events of east-to-west expansion. Simply in terms of length, the story of relations within and between social groups prior to Europeans is far more significant to western history than the few centuries after the first Spanish touch, yet this history has been abandoned almost entirely to the anthropologists. The same is largely true of the profound social changes set in motion by early European contact. There were shufflings of power and sweeping migrations; the fortunes of some peoples rose and others fell. Some tribes that whites assumed had existed from time immemorial in fact had formed only recently when related bands coalesced in response to dangers and opportunities brought by Europeans. Military and hunting societies took on new roles to meet changing circumstances. In some groups polygyny, the taking of more than one wife by a husband, was encouraged by the heightened hunting power of men on horseback (and consequently the greater work load in processing their kills), the attrition of warriors from intensified warfare, and the flaunting of higher status in more affluent times. The social, political, and spiritual position of women shifted when sedentary horticultural peoples acquired horses and adopted a seminomadic life on the plains.

Literature on westward expansion long has celebrated its theme of adaptation and change under trying and alluring circumstances. Yet nothing in the pioneer story as typically told can match the social revolutions among Indian peoples during the first several generations after European contact. Because of our tendency to place these societies outside of history, at least until whites show up in person and in substantial numbers, this turbulent, innovative chapter in the western story has been conceded almost wholly to other disciplines and to scholars not always sensitive to the dynamics and contingencies that historians favor. It is a historical area waiting to be discovered.

More has been written on interactions between Indian and Euro-American societies. Many recent historians look to Richard White's *The Middle Ground* (1991). Although set in the Great Lakes region in the previous century, his insights into the mutual evolutions of white and Indian societies, full of contingencies and cultural blending and paths not taken yet ending in white domination, offer a fruitful model for understanding the intricate patterns unfolding in the West. Before White's book

Ramón Gutiérrez also pointed the way with his *When Jesus Came the Corn Mothers Went Away* (1991), a fascinating – and to some a controversial – perspective on the evolution and adaptations of Pueblo Indian peoples from the arrival of the Spanish and of Franciscan fathers through the immediate aftermath of the Mexican War. Particularly intriguing are his insights into the Spanish penetration of the Native spiritual world and how this inner conquest left Indians subordinate in a new order of values and sexualized power. The interplay of economics, cross-cultural politics, and the role of sex in social relations has been explored also in the context of the fur trade. Sylvia Van Kirk (1983) and Jennifer S. H. Brown (1980) have both written of the Indian wives of white traders and their crucial roles in economic and cultural transactions. They were liaisons who allowed their own and their husbands' peoples access to desired goods; they were cultural interpreters to each side; they were helpmates and mothers to a rising generation that would form a connective tissue between Indians and Euro-Americans. And in their precipitous loss of standing as white society took full root, they took tragic measure of the collapse of Indian autonomy.

By neglecting the history of changing Indian societies, historians are missing crucial clues to the larger transformation of the West. The obvious themes of Native social history – the creation and sharp evolutions of communities, the key role of gender and sexuality in understanding those changes, the dramatic shuffling of power within and among societies – unfolded in dozens of different settings. In a spate of recent works on one of the most written-about episodes in western history, the California Gold Rush, we can see how much can be learned from these fresh perspectives. Malcolm Rohrbough's splendid *Days of Gold* (1997) explores the many crosscurrents of an episode that in so many ways anticipated the direction the republic was moving. In *Roaring Camp* (2000), Susan Johnson emphasizes that the creative confusion of the camps allowed a remarkable experimentation in social roles, including the bending not merely of gender and ethnic relations, but of the very meanings of those categories. *American Alchemy* by Brian Roberts (2000) sees the gold camps as testing grounds for the values and postures of men rising into the expanding middling ranks of Victorian America. He and Rohrbough both explore an equally significant route of change that Linda Peavy and Ursula Smith (1994) develop in detail in *Women in Waiting in the Westward Movement*. Wives left behind by men trudging off to find their fortunes were pressed, sometimes reluctantly, into new responsibilities and roles, thus reorienting the fundamental bearings of male and female throughout the nation.

All these fine books play on what is arguably the oldest theme in western studies – the tension between, on the one hand, the persistence of traditions and social forms brought into the West and, on the other, the innovations bred from the demands of this new setting. When pursued in these subtler contexts, this theme illuminates much more than studies of the more formal institutions that were the focus of students of Frederick Jackson Turner. As an early instance of such social history, John Mack Faragher's *Women and Men on the Overland Trail* (1979), increasingly emerges as a seminal work. It can as well be read as an early entry into the creative explosion of work in western women's history. Julie Roy Jeffrey's *Frontier Women* (1979) appeared the same year, and within a decade a cascade of new work played a vital part in rewriting and rethinking western history. Indeed, it was women's history that really began the vigorous revision of the field. Susan Armitage and Elizabeth Jameson

(1987), John Mack Faragher (1979), Sandra Myres (1982), Lillian Schlissel (1982), Glenda Riley (1981), Joan Jensen (1981), and a host of others were rattling the established telling of the tale in some cases several years before the appearance of works typically credited with birthing the "new" western history.

Nearly as influential have been studies of the ethnic West. Contrary to prevailing impressions, the most ethnically diverse region of the nation has been the West, not the Northeast, yet outside a handful of works, such as Mary Roberts Coolidge's classic *Chinese Immigration* (1909), remarkably little was written before the 1970s. Then began a flood of books and articles on the Irish, Germans (including Germans from Russia), Italians, French, Basques, Swedes, Norwegians and other Scandinavians, Greeks, Dutch, Cornish, Scots, Slavs and others. We have a book on Yugoslavs in Nevada and an article on Serbs in Arizona (there were at least two of them). Particular interest has been given to the group whose mores were farthest from the mainstream (if such a varied flood can be said to have a central channel at all): the Chinese. Their differences made them also the most victimized, although a recent work by Liping Zhu (1997) argues that, at least in the northern Rocky Mountains, Chinese fared much better and exerted more control over their fate than the usual accounts would have it.

Besides stressing the diversity of the western experience, the overall effect of this ethnic history has been twofold. The theme of the transfer and adaptation of outside traditions – yet another angle on negotiation – is exponentially more complex. And another of social history's themes, the making and remaking of communities, has been deliciously complicated as we see the process as both the creation of a patchwork of enclaves and an interaction of cultures tossed suddenly together.

Each of these variations of western social history spins off many other possibilities and together they combine into a dizzying range of topics, a few already pursued but many more waiting for attention. Merge women's and ethnic history and we have books on Chinese prostitutes and wives (Tong, 1994), Peggy Pascoe's study of middle-class missions (1990) to "save" (and to convert culturally) women outside the Protestant mainstream, and Albert L. Hurtado's 1999 examination of sexuality as a matrix of culture, gender, and class in nineteenth-century California. Follow the story of Indian communities into the reservation era and you'll find David Rich Lewis's account (1994) of three tribes' cultural negotiations to maintain some integrity during desperate economic times, Morris Foster's close tracing of the Comanches' evolving identity (1991), and Fred Hoxie's superb history of the Crow peoples' economic, religious, and social adaptations into the modern era (1995). These should be inspirations to chase after similar but unpursued topics.

There are, besides, larger areas still mostly unexamined. Considering the vigorous pursuit of African American history during the last generation, the neglect of blacks in the West during the nineteenth century has been astonishing. With a handful of exceptions, that limited attention has been on a few topics far outside the general experience – cowboys and exodusters, for instance. Quintard Taylor's *In Search of the Racial Frontier* (1998) is a magnificent breakthrough, both in terms of what it tells us and in the dozens of possibilities it opens for students in decades to come. A lot more awaits our attention. Women in the West's maturing cities, for instance, especially those of the working class, remain in the historical shadows. The evolution of rural communities – small towns and, even more, the social nets of farms and ranches in the great outback – has been barely touched. Aspects of the family, the basic social unit of any society, remain understudied. Elliott West's *Growing Up With the Country* (1989) has been followed by a few other forays, but much more could be done on what in many areas was the majority of residents – those under the age of fifteen or so. Add the ethnic component and the evolution of communities, and the questions multiply still more. Virtually no one has looked into the lives of Indian children during these transformative years, for instance.

One broad area is even more neglected than most: religion. No one can delve into the lives of ordinary westerners and not be impressed by the importance of religion as an institutional presence, as a sustaining force in individual lives, and as a means whereby people could understand the world around them. The great exception to historians' neglect has been Mormonism, one of two world religions to originate in the United States and a faith whose history is inextricably bound up with the West. In a way, however, the vast library of Mormon history emphasizes the isolation of religion from western writing. Jan Shipps, a leading authority in the field, has advanced what she calls the donut theory (2000). Western historians write literally around Utah and the Mormon experience when generalizing about their region. Scholars outside Mormon history, that is, write about the donut; Mormon historians write about the hole. Donut historians seem to work on the unstated assumption that religious history is somehow anomalous. True, there are some general treatments of particular denominations as well as works on famous missionaries like Marcus and Narcissa Whitman (Jeffrey, 1991) and Father Pierre de Smet (Carriker, 1995). Certain phases of Native American religion, notably so-called messiah movements like the Ghost Dance, have also inspired millions of words.

What is missing is an integration of religion into social experience. Because religion is treated as isolated in a distinct population like the Mormons, or as a force acting on westerners from the outside, or as something aberrant that flared up occasionally to disrupt the flow of events, we lose any sense of what religion meant to people in the dailiness of their lives. We also miss how religion, as mass spiritual expression, evolved in the changing West. An exception once again comes from an innovative study of the California Gold Rush. Laurie F. Maffly-Kipp's brilliant *Religion and Society in Frontier California* (1994) describes the "moral landscape" of the mining camps, and so doing she shows us how, once again, the mining frontier anticipated Americans' movement toward values that would dominate the next century.

Talking With Nature

There is a lovely wrinkle to recent western historiography. From the 1950s to the 1980s western history was considered peripheral and rather outdated. Then, suddenly, the study of the West was close to the center of the action. An important reason was the rise of environmental history and its invigoration of writing about America and the Atlantic world. As the influence and interest in this new field spread, a handful of exceptionally talented scholars were in position to apply its fresh approaches to western history. The attention they attracted in turn brought western studies toward the forefront of American historiography. It is not too much of a stretch to picture scholars of this new subfield, plus writers in western women's history, riding like the cavalry at full gallop over the hill, guidons fluttering and bugles a-toot, to rescue western history from obscurity. Of the four scholars most often mentioned as revitalizers – Patricia Nelson Limerick, Richard White, Donald Worster, and William Cronon – all but the first have written extensively in environmental history.

Traditionalists can argue that this is perfectly fitting, for human interaction with the environment has been central to western history since its emergence as a field. The essence of Frederick Jackson Turner's frontier thesis was the dismantling of institutions and attitudes that were thrust into settings never meant for them, then the arising of others shaped to their environmental surroundings. Turner's approach is most often counterpoised with that of Walter Prescott Webb's *The Great Plains* (1931). Webb treated the West, not as Turner's temporary engagement between an elaborated culture and the wilderness, but as a region with unique and enduring environmental traits. Western history, Webb said, consists of westerners' endless adaptation to those unchanging conditions.

Turner and Webb usually are set at either end of a historiographical spectrum, and in fact they do give us contrasting views that broaden our understanding when we play them against each other. But their writings have this in common: at heart they are accounts of people interacting with their environments over time, and in this sense what's considered the prime force in the "new" history sits squarely within the field's oldest tradition. For that matter the environment has been a central actor in the most romanticized and mythic takes on western history in potboiler paperbacks and B-movies, with square-jawed heroes showing their stuff by struggling and prevailing in a harsh world of mighty mountains, scorching deserts, blizzards, and those human figures basically equated with the wilderness, Indians and outlaws.

What, then, sets the new environmental history apart? For one thing, writers today are far more likely to describe people and their physical settings in a continuous and mutually influential exchange, rather than to recount a passing stage of interaction, as Turner did, or follow Webb's view of a plastic society molding itself to a changeless environment. Here once more is a sort of negotiation. Richard White (1992) chooses another term – a conversation. It is a useful metaphor. As they act, people in a sense are voicing their opinion, impressing on the world around them their understanding of that world and how they mean to live in it. Changed slightly or profoundly by how people act – how they speak out – the environment talks back, affecting people, who in turn are changed and respond in a somewhat new way. The conversation has no beginning or end, and it is unavoidable. Humans have no choice but to live within a nonhuman world, even if they convince themselves that it is a world of their own making, and as they affect their environment they must continually adapt to its changes and responses. This seems commonsensical on its face, but the implications are considerable. As this conversation moves along, neither side is ever the same. It follows that we can never reestablish a past environment or return to a previous social relation with the land, anymore than we can go back to being exactly who we were at the start of a discussion. This in turn throws a harsh light on the oldest, most powerful perception of the West in our cultural history – the dream of wilderness. Westering emigrants and the societies that sent them forth considered the land between them and the Pacific mostly untouched by human influence. The West was pictured, on the one hand, as pristine and virginal and, on the other, as untamed and threatening. But as soon as we recognize that all people at all times have lived in exchange with their surroundings, we see that white pioneers entered country that had been tangled in human purposes for millennia.

Ethnohistorians have followed the implications and have illuminated some of the Indians' countless environmental manipulations and their adjustments to the inevitable changes they triggered long before and after white contact. Revealing examples are Charles Bowden's *Killing the Hidden Waters* (1977) and the work of Gary Nabhan: *Enduring Seeds* (1989) and *The Desert Smells like Rain* (1982). A few have taken a step farther to consider consistent patterns among various Native and European peoples and the elaborate borrowing among these cultures. The best of these is Stephen Pyne's magnificent multi-volume study (1982, 1997, 1997) that places North America within the global use of fire, man's most enduring tool of change.

This in turn places the transformations of the nineteenth century in a far truer perspective, with changes brought by pioneers now seen on a continuum with scores of variations in an ancient process. This by no means puts all these transformations on an equal basis. To the contrary, it throws into sharp relief the astounding power of these latest conversationalists to make the world over, and by doing that to provoke from the environment responses far ruder than any before. Once that point is made another question becomes especially sharp: Why was the environmental impact of Euro-Americans so vastly greater? Sheer numbers, of course, are a large part of the answer, but equally telling were the guiding cultural impulses of these most recent arrivals. Two masterworks develop this theme. Donald Worster's *Dust Bowl* (1979), although set in the next century, stresses that the disaster of the "dirty Thirties" began with the arrival on the plains of a capitalist mindset, with its confident determination to commodify everything and the technological muscle to carry it out. In *Nature's Metropolis* (1991) William Cronon unravels the transformative strands snaking out from Chicago into a vast half-circle to the West, from the Wisconsin forests southward to the west Texas plains, that created out of previous environmental arrangements a "second nature" built to the needs and visions of a global capitalist market economy, American-style. Once encouraged to study Indian peoples' own environmental interactions, then to consider the reasons behind the staggering impact of the whites' exchanges, we are called naturally to bring the two together. The older notion of a dynamic white society entering a changeless wilderness had its equivalent version of Indian–white relations – that familiar story of whites bulling their way over Native peoples who were living in timeless balance with the natural world. The new story ends in the same way, with conquest and loss of Indian independence, but it unfolds as a far more intricate process, with all parties playing off one another within an evolving environment. Richard White's *Roots of Dependency* (1983) and its depiction of interacting economies working inexorably toward one dominating the other has already been mentioned. Some especially revealing examples concern the episode that stands in the popular mind as white America's supreme blow against the Indians' fruitful union with nature – the near-extinction of the plains bison. First a seminal article by Dan Flores (1991), then Elliott West's *The Way to the West* (1995) and Andrew J. Isenberg's *The Destruction of the Bison* (2000) tell a much messier story. Indians first responded to new opportunities of trade, making one more in a chain of countless efforts to find new advantages in a changing setting, but they soon found themselves caught in sequences of environmental, economic, and cultural change that gave an unbeatable edge to the expansive, market-oriented, white newcomers. No simple villains and noble savages here, just a normal cast of predators and visionaries, some with a lot more clout than others but all of them involved in a negotiation with their surroundings that they understood only in part.

The other side of that wilderness dream, the vision of an undefiled West as God's cathedral, has found expression in the preservationist movement, particularly the drive to create national parks as islands of natural wonder and reminders of an America before the touch of change. This vision too unravels once Indians are seen as meshed from the start in their own evolving arrangements with the land. A recent gust of books details how the creation of every national park began with the dispossession of the most recent of Indian peoples who for centuries had been using this supposedly untouched landscape: Mark Spence's *Dispossessing the Wilderness* (1999), Ted Catton's *Inhabited Wilderness* (1997), Robert H. Keller and Michael F. Turek's *American Indians and National Parks* (1998), and Philip Burnham's *Indian Country, God's Country* (2000).

By questioning the dream of wilderness, both as a savage land brought under human dominion and as sacred country rescued from development, environmental historians are redefining conquest itself. Indians lost their independence in a contest, albeit lopsided, between well-evolved and equally dynamic relationships that linked societies and their resources. And a subplot in that story was the imposition of a national fantasy on weaker peoples who had the bad luck to be living in an imagined Eden and who, like the garden's original couple, were expelled when it was decided they had no business there.

This interactive view of conquest goes well beyond such strictly human constructions as economies. The European arrival brought together two hemispheric biota that had been mostly separated for roughly ten thousand years. The result, in phrases from Alfred Crosby, the scholar who pioneered the study of this phenomenon, was a Columbian exchange and an ecological imperialism (1972, 1986). Thousands of organisms moving in each direction revolutionized human relations with their environment on both sides of the Atlantic. On the western side, Indians in some ways profited, but European invaders gained far more. The nineteenth-century West might be read as an elaborate exhibit of this process. A single animal, the horse, allowed Indian peoples a burst of power and an array of new possibilities, but the overall effect of the biological invasion, everything from cattle and sheep to weeds and worms, was a wrenching interruption of Native living patterns and the seizure of ecological space by Euro-Americans and their floral and faunal allies.

The most devastating invasion took place on the microbial level. Ironically, the West in one sense was indeed a virgin land. Indian societies had never encountered many so-called crowd diseases brought by Europeans, and, as Henry Dobyns first argued in 1966, the Natives' lack of resistance triggered devastating declines in population. Dobyns' article was followed by a remarkable outpouring of work to explain and catalog how these "virgin soil epidemics" crippled Indian societies and hastened their defeat. More recently, others have questioned the calculation of losses and have challenged the more extreme claims of population collapse (Henige, 1998), but the debate should not obscure the obvious. All now agree that Native population in 1492 was many times what was estimated twenty years ago, and even modest approximations of deaths from disease and consequent disruptions make this the worst mass catastrophe in the human record. Once again environmental insights ripple out into the cultural, in this case radically revising the long-prevailing meaning of Europe's "discovery" of America. What had been a dream of uplift, of civilization coming to the wild, becomes a nightmare, and what had seemed a mostly empty continent in 1492 looks now like a well-peopled land soon to be crowded with ghosts.

So far the discussion has focused on how environmental history has rearranged our understanding of Indian peoples, their conquest, and their elaborate relations with Euro-Americans. Something similar can be said about many other areas of nineteenth-century western history. Donald Pisani (1996), Norris Hundley (1992) and John Opie (1993) are the most widely published of several historians who have written on what Hundley calls "the great thirst," the quest for water in the nation's arid western half. Others have written histories of varied western settings as elaborate interplays between unique ecologies, cultural impulses and assumptions, and outside forces. William DeBuys' work on the upper Rio Grande (1985) and California's Imperial Valley (1999) and John Miller Morris's on the west Texas plains (1997) are among the best. Arthur McIvoy (1986) and Joseph Taylor (1999) have focused on a particular industry, fishing, as a case study of the troubling results when an abundant but vulnerable species like the salmon has its ecology manipulated by market demands and powerful technology. Paul Hirt (1994) and Nancy Langston (1995) have done something similar with the lumber industry of the Northwest, here with the story considerably complicated by our nation's romance with forests as recreational refuges. Richard West Sellars (1997) and Karl Hess (1993) turn a similar light on the innermost sancta of America's devotion to the wild; they carry the early assumptions behind national parks into the next century to trace the government's maneuvers to satisfy a public perception of a timeless natural balance.

These works, for all their variety of subject and approach, address the nineteenth-century West through common themes introduced in the new environmental history – the endless dance of human and nonhuman actors, the shaping power of cultural assumptions, capitalism's transformative force, the unpredictability of thousands of interactive variables, and the unique histories to be written as all these factors work themselves out in particular places.

Other topics beg to be investigated. The environmental consequences of some of the most familiar episodes of the nineteenth-century West are largely unexplored. Donald Worster (1992) has raised the question of "cowboy ecology" and how range science can illuminate debates about pastoral land use, and in a neglected work on environmental dynamics, *Cattle in the Cold Desert*, James A. Young and B. Abbott Sparks (1985) have traced the effects of ranching on the Great Basin. Together they emphasize how much remains unwritten on the ecology of the cattleman's West, of railroad building, and, despite a tentative start by Duane A. Smith (1987), on mining. The good work on water in the West tends toward the institutional – water law, policy and its making, political maneuvering. Water, however, carried cultural, social, and religious meanings as well, all of them reflecting and affecting how water was used and legislated. Mark Fiege's *Irrigated Eden*, mentioned above, shows how much there is to learn when we take seriously water's place in social belief, but (as usual) this integrated approach has been left almost wholly to anthropologists working in Native cultures.

If environmental historians have broken with the old duality of nature and society in most ways, in one they still cling to it. While emphatic that human influence can be found in the remotest reaches of the Wild West, they have largely ignored the nonhuman at work where people are most evident – in western cities. Since it was first designated a region by the census, the West has been the most urbanized part of the country, yet while urban environmental history is something of a hot field elsewhere in the nation, the conversation between people and nature in Denver, Phoenix, Los Angeles, San Francisco, Salt Lake City and scores of other larger and smaller urban centers has yet to be recorded and listened to. Unexamined, too, are the cultural aspects of urban environmental history. Was an urban aesthetic influenced by distinctively romanticized notions of the supposedly wild landscapes beyond the city limits? The boundary of rural and urban is still mostly to be breached.

Conclusion

Environmental history by its nature encourages the approach that has so invigorated western history. Its guiding truism, that "everything is connected to everything else," sums up nicely the impulse behind much of the best and most provocative recent work (and certainly many of the most enduring older studies). Arranging this or any discussion by area of interest is finally – and, it should be added, thankfully – misleading and self-defeating. Most of the books mentioned so far as especially revealing in one area could easily be moved to another. Annette Kolodny's *The Land Before Her* and Gunther Peck's *Reinventing Free Labor*, under economic history, could just as well have been set in environmental and social history, respectively. James Young's *Cattle in the Cold Desert*, Andrew Isenberg's *The Destruction of the Bison* and Ted Catton's *Inhabited Wilderness* all concern economic and social as much as the environmental history.

In some fields not mentioned here boundaries have been drawn and kept more rigorously – political and military history are examples – and as Sherry Smith has argued for military topics (1990), this leaves them wide open for the expansive complications we find elsewhere. In other areas noted above in passing, such as ethnic and women's history, scholars have so happily colored outside the lines that their work could easily have been given as full a treatment as economic or social history. The pattern is mottled, but the call is obvious to explore more fully the new avenues opened and to open others clearly visible but so far neglected.

There is no better illustration than an area that naturally resists boundaries, at least of the national variety: borderlands history. The field's founding spirit, Herbert Eugene Bolton, and his disciples concentrated on the northward Spanish thrust, and in the 1940s Carey McWilliams wrote of the continuing historical connection across the border from south to north, now with a concern with class and the difficulties of minorities that anticipated the new history's interests thirty years later. Recent borderlands writing has continued this tradition of northward movement, yet the questions asked and the disciplines introduced have produced a literature of exceptional range and energy. Already noted are Ramón Gutiérrez's study of the spiritual conquest of Pueblo peoples and the emergence of a hybrid system of values and belief and William DeBuys' portrait of the upper Rio Grande region as evolved cultural, environmental and economic history. Richard L. Nostrand (1992), Thomas D. Hall

(1989), and Donald W. Meinig (1971) have borrowed insights from sociology and geography to chart the structural relationships of Hispanic societies to the land's resources, to each other, and to the world beyond. Sarah Deutsch's excellent *No Separate Refuge* (1987) follows the Hispanic intrusion from the late nineteenth and into the twentieth century, out of the Southwest onto the plains, and by introducing the themes of gender and class shows us patterns of power distinctive to the borderlands, while also telling a story of exceptional persistence and adaptation. John R. Chavez (1984) considers the making of this region in yet another sense, as a mental creation of Hispanics from before the Mexican War into the next century; now we see the borderland as an overlay of cultural inventions, the triumphal east-to-west national version and, for those whose identity ran south-to-north, as a lost land.

As in all areas mentioned above, the picture changes with each of the West's parts. There were many borderlands and varied experiences. In one of the field's classics, *With a Pistol in His Hand*, Americo Paredes (1958) brings together standard sources, oral history and tradition, song, and folklore to describe the distinct culture along the Texas–Mexico border. Andres Tijerina (1998) adds another dimension by focusing on the ranching life of south Texas and David Montejano (1987) looks more broadly at ethnic relations in the making of that state. Ross Frank (2000) introduces the practical arts – pottery, furniture and blankets – as documents that tell us much about the evolution of the society and economy of early New Mexico. Douglas Monroy's focus is California (1990). With a vigorously multicultural and expansive approach, he looks at countryside and city, Mexicans and Indians and Anglos, ranchos and missions and agriculture, law and banditry and much more to trace the emergence of a distinctive Hispanic culture.

Books by Monroy, Paredes, Gutiérrez and others cheerfully resist our best efforts to stuff them into this category or that. Good history always provokes questions, and good questions will spin us off into various lines of inquiry. The results will not be easily confined, and when unconfined the creative sprawl can be considerable. The West's regional boundaries, as Richard White puts it (1991), have been a series of doors pretending to be walls. The same applies to the West as written. We look back over the long span of years. From the far side of those years Jean de L'Archeveque looks back at us. He moves through one door, then another, and another. Those doors are still open for us.

REFERENCES

Allen, Michael: *Western Rivermen, 1763–1861: Ohio and Mississippi Boatmen and the Myth of the Alligator Horse* (Baton Rouge: Louisiana State University Press, 1990).

Ambrose, Stephen E.: *Undaunted Courage: Meriwether Lewis, Thomas Jefferson, and the Opening of the American West* (New York: Simon and Schuster, 1996).

Ambrose, Stephen E.: *Nothing Like It in the World: The Men Who Built the Transcontinental Railroad, 1863–1869* (New York: Simon and Schuster, 2000).

Armitage, Susan and Elizabeth Jameson: *The Women's West* (Norman: University of Oklahoma Press, 1987).

Athearn, Robert G.: *Union Pacific Country* (Chicago: Rand McNally, 1971).

Bain, David H.: *Empire Express: Building the First Transcontinental Railroad* (New York: Viking, 1999).

Boag, Peter G.: *Environment and Experience: Settlement Culture in Nineteenth-Century Oregon* (Berkeley: University of California Press, 1992).

Bowden, Charles: *Killing the Hidden Waters* (Austin: University of Texas Press, 1977).

Brack, Gene M.: *Mexico Views Manifest Destiny, 1821–1846: An Essay on the Origins of the Mexican War* (Albuquerque: University of New Mexico Press, 1990).

Brown, Jennifer S. H.: *Strangers in Blood: Fur Trade Company Families in Indian Country* (Vancouver: University of British Columbia Press, 1980).

Brown, Ronald C.: *Hard-Rock Miners: The Intermountain West, 1860–1920* (College Station: Texas A&M University Press, 1979).

Brown, Ronald C.: *Hard Rock Epic: Western Miners and the Industrial Revolution, 1860–1910* (Berkeley: University of California Press, 1979).

Burnham, Philip: *Indian Country, God's Country: Native Americans and the National Parks* (Washington, DC: Island Press, 2000).

Carriker, Robert C.: *Father Peter John De Smet: Jesuit in the West* (Norman: University of Oklahoma Press, 1995).

Cassidy, James G.: *Ferdinand V. Hayden: Entrepreneur of Science* (Lincoln: University of Nebraska Press, 2000).

Catton, Theodore: *Inhabited Wilderness: Indians, Eskimos, and National Parks in Alaska* (Albuquerque: University of New Mexico Press, 1997).

Chaffin, Tom: *Pathfinder: John Charles Fremont and the Course of American Empire* (New York: Hill and Wang, 2002).

Chavez, John R. *The Lost Land: The Chicano Image of the Southwest* (Albuquerque: University of New Mexico Press, 1984).

Cook, Sherburn F.: *The Indian Population of the California Indians, 1769–1970* (Berkeley: University of California Press, 1976).

Coolidge, Mary Roberts: *Chinese Immigration* (New York: H. Holt and Company, 1909).

Cronon, William: *Nature's Metropolis: Chicago and the Great West* (New York: Norton, 1991).

Crosby, Alfred: *The Columbian Exchange: Biological and Cultural Consequences of 1492* (Westport, CT: Greenwood Publishing Co., 1972).

Crosby, Alfred: *Ecological Imperialism: The Biological Expansion of Europe, 900–1900* (Cambridge and New York: Cambridge University Press, 1986).

DeBuys, William E.: *Enchantment and Exploitation: The Life and Hard Times of a New Mexican Mountain Range* (Albuquerque: University of New Mexico Press, 1985).

DeBuys, William E.: *Salt Dreams: Land and Water in Low-Down California* (Albuquerque: University of New Mexico Press, 1999).

DeVoto, Bernard: "The West: A Plundered Province." *Harper's* 169 (August 1934), 355–64.

Deutsch, Sara: *No Separate Refuge: Culture, Class, and Gender on an Anglo-Hispanic Frontier, 1880–1940* (New York: Oxford University Press, 1987).

Deverell, William F.: *Railroad Crossing: Californians and the Railroad, 1850–1910* (Berkeley: University of California Press, 1994).

Dobyns, Henry F.: "Estimating Aboriginal American Population: An Appraisal of Techniques with a New Hemispheric Estimate." *Current Anthropology* 7 (1966): 395–416, 425–49.

Dobyns, Henry F.: *Their Number Become Thinned: Native American Population Dynamics in Eastern North America* (Knoxville: University of Tennessee Press, 1983).

Ducker, James H.: *Men of the Steel Rails: Workers on the Atchison, Topeka and Santa Fe Railroad, 1869–1900* (Lincoln: University of Nebraska Press, 1983).

Emmons, David M.: *Garden in the Grasslands: Boomer Literature of the Central Great Plains* (Lincoln: University of Nebraska Press, 1971).

Faragher, John Mack: *Women and Men on the Overland Trail* (New Haven: Yale University Press, 1979).

Fernlund, Kevin J.: *William Henry Holmes and the Rediscovery of the American West* (Albuquerque: University of New Mexico Press, 2000).

Fiege, Mark: *Irrigated Eden: The Making of an Agricultural Landscape in the American West* (Seattle: University of Washington Press, 1999).

Flores, Dan (ed.): *Jefferson and Southwestern Exploration: the Freeman & Custis Accounts of the Red River Expedition of 1806* (Norman: University of Oklahoma Press, 1984).

Flores, Dan: "Bison Ecology and Bison Diplomacy: The Southern Plains from 1800 to 1850." *Journal of American History* 78, 2 (September 1991), 465–85.

Foster, Morris: *Being Comanche: A Social History of an American Indian Community* (Tucson, University of Arizona Press, 1991).

Frank, Ross: *From Settler to Citizen: New Mexican Economic Development and the Creation of Vecino Society, 1750–1820* (Berkeley: University of California Press, 2000).

Freehling, William: *The Road to Disunion* (New York: Oxford University Press, 1990).

Goetzmann, William H.: "Mountain Man as Jacksonian Man". *American Quarterly* 15 (Fall 1963), 402–15.

Goetzmann, William H.: *When the Eagle Screamed: The Romantic Horizon in American Diplomacy, 1800–1860* (New York: Wiley, 1966).

Goetzmann, William H.: *Exploration and Empire: The Explorer and the Scientist in the Winning of the West* (New York: Knopf, 1966).

Graebner, Norman A.: *Empire on the Pacific: A Study in American Continental Expansion* (New York: Ronald Press Co., 1955).

Gutiérrez, Ramón A.: *When Jesus Came, the Corn Mothers Went Away: Marriage, Sexuality, and Power in New Mexico, 1500–1846* (Stanford, CA: Stanford University Press, 1991).

Hall, Thomas D.: *Social Change in the Southwest, 1350–1880* (Lawrence: University Press of Kansas, 1989).

Henige, David: *Numbers From Nowhere: The American Indian Contact Population Debate* (Norman: University of Oklahoma Press, 1998).

Hess, Karl: *Rocky Times in Rocky Mountain National Park: An Unnatural History* (Niwot, CO: University Press of Colorado, 1993).

Hirt, Paul W.: *A Conspiracy of Optimism: Management of the National Forests Since World War Two* (Lincoln: University of Nebraska Press, 1994).

Hollon, W. Eugene: *The Lost Pathfinder, Zebulon Montgomery Pike* (Norman: University of Oklahoma Press, 1949).

Hoxie, Frederick E.: *Parading Through History: The Making of the Crow Nation in America, 1805–1935* (Cambridge and New York: Cambridge University Press, 1995).

Hundley, Norris: *The Great Thirst: Californians and Water, 1790s–1990s* (Berkeley: University of California Press, 1992).

Hurtado, Albert L.: *Intimate Frontiers: Sex, Gender and Culture in Old California* (Albuquerque: University of New Mexico Press, 1999).

Hyde, Anne F.: *An American Vision: Far Western Landscape and National Culture, 1820–1920* (New York: New York University Press, 1990).

Isenberg, Andrew C.: *The Destruction of the Bison: An Environmental History, 1750–1920* (New York: Cambridge University Press, 2000).

Jackson, Donald D.: *Thomas Jefferson and the Stony Mountains: Exploring the West From Monticello* (Urbana: University of Illinois Press, 1981).

James, Ronald M.: *The Roar and the Silence: A History of Virginia City and the Comstock Lode* (Reno: University of Nevada Press, 1998).

Jeffrey, Julie Roy: *Frontier Women: The Trans-Mississippi West, 1840–1880* (New York: Hill and Wang, 1979).

Jeffrey, Julie Roy: *Converting the West: A Biography of Narcissa Whitman* (Norman: University of Oklahoma Press, 1991).

Jennings, Francis: *The Invasion of America: Indians, Colonialism and the Cant of Conquest* (Chapel Hill: University of North Carolina Press, 1975).

Jensen, Joan M.: *With These Hands: Women Working on the Land* (New York: McGraw Hill, 1981).

Johnson, Susan Lee: *Roaring Camp: The Social World of the California Gold Rush* (New York: W. W. Norton, 2000).

Jordan, Terry G.: *North American Cattle-Ranching Frontiers: Origins, Diffusion and Differentiation* (Albuquerque: University of New Mexico Press, 1993).

Keller, Robert H. and Michael F. Turek: *American Indians and National Parks* (Tucson: University of Arizona Press, 1998).

Knobloch, Frieda: *The Culture of Wilderness: Agriculture as Colonization in the American West* (Chapel Hill: University of North Carolina Press, 1996).

Kolodny, Annette: *The Lay of the Land: Metaphor as Experience and History in American Life and Letters* (Chapel Hill: University of North Carolina Press, 1975).

Kolodny, Annette: *The Land Before Her: Fantasy and Experience of the American Frontiers, 1630–1860* (Chapel Hill: University of North Carolina Press, 1984).

Langston, Nancy: *Forest Dreams, Forest Nightmares: The Paradox of Old Growth in the Inland West* (Seattle: University of Washington Press, 1995).

Lewis, David Rich: *Neither Wolf Nor Dog: American Indians, Environment and Agrarian Change* (New York: Oxford University Press, 1994).

Limerick, Patricia Nelson: *The Legacy of Conquest: The Unbroken Past of the American West* (New York: Norton, 1987).

Limerick, Patricia Nelson: "'This Perilous Situation Between Hope and Despair': Meetings Along the Great River of the West." In William L. Lang and Robert C. Carriker (eds.) *Great River of the West: Essays on the Columbia River* (Seattle: University of Washington Press, 1999).

McCoy, Drew R.: *The Elusive Republic: Political Economy in Jeffersonian America* (Chapel Hill: University of North Carolina Press, 1980).

McEvoy, Arthur F.: *The Fisherman's Problem: Ecology and Law in the California Fisheries, 1850–1980* (Cambridge and New York: Cambridge University Press, 1986).

McWilliams, Carey: *Factories in the Field: The Story of Migratory Farm Labor in California* (Boston: Little, Brown and Co., 1939).

McWilliams, Carey: *North from Mexico: The Spanish-Speaking People of the United States* ([1949], New York: Greenwood Press, 1968).

Maffly-Kipp, Laurie F.: *Religion and Society in Frontier California* (New Haven: Yale University Press, 1994).

May, Dean L.: *Three Frontiers: Family, Land and Society in the American West, 1850–1900* (Cambridge and New York: Cambridge University Press, 1994).

Meinig, Donald W.: *Southwest: Three Peoples in Geographic Change, 1600–1970* (New York: Oxford University Press, 1971).

Merk, Frederick: *Manifest Destiny and Mission in American History: A Reinterpretation* (New York: Knopf, 1963).

Merk, Frederick: *The Oregon Question: Essays in Anglo-American Diplomacy and Politics* (Cambridge MA: Harvard University Press, 1967).

Merk, Frederick: *Slavery and the Annexation of Texas* (New York: Knopf, 1972).

Monroy, Douglas: *Thrown Among Strangers: The Making of Mexican Culture in Frontier California* (Berkeley: University of California Press, 1990).

Montejano, David: *Anglos and Mexicans in the Making of Texas, 1836–1986* (Austin: University of Texas Press, 1987).

Morris, John Miller: *El Llano Estacado: Exploration and Imagination on the High Plains of Texas and New Mexico, 1536–1860* (Austin: Texas State Historical Society, 1997).

Myres, Sandra L.: *Westering Women and the Frontier Experience: 1800–1915* (Albuquerque: University of New Mexico Press, 1982).

Nabhan, Gary Paul: *Enduring Seeds: Native American Agriculture and Wild Plant Conservation* (San Francisco: North Point Press, 1989).

Nabhan, Gary Paul: *The Desert Smells Like Rain: A Naturalist in Papago Indian Country* (San Francisco: North Point Press, 1982).

Nasatir, Abraham P.: *Before Lewis and Clark: Documents Illustrating the History of the Missouri, 1785–1804* (St. Louis: St. Louis Historical Documents Foundation, 1952).

Nichols, Roger L. and Patrick L. Halley: *Stephen Long and American Frontier Exploration* (Newark: University of Delaware Press, 1980).

Nostrand, Richard L.: *The Hispano Homeland* (Norman: University of Oklahoma Press, 1992).

Opie, John: *Ogallala: Water for a Dry Land* (Lincoln: University of Nebraska Press, 1993).

Paredes, Americo: *"With His Pistol in His Hand": A Border Ballad and Its Hero* (Austin: University of Texas Press, 1958).

Pascoe, Peggy: *Relations of Rescue: The Search for Female Moral Authority in the American West, 1874–1939* (New York: Oxford University Press, 1990).

Peavy, Linda S. and Ursula Smith: *Women in Waiting in the Westward Movement: Life on the Home Frontier* (Norman: University of Oklahoma Press, 1994).

Peck, Gunther: *Reinventing Free Labor: Padrones and Immigrant Workers in the North American West, 1880–1930* (New York: Cambridge University Press, 2000).

Pisani, Donald: *Water, Land and Law in the West: The Limits of Public Policy, 1850–1920* (Lawrence: University Press of Kansas, 1996).

Pletcher, David M.: *The Diplomacy of Annexation: Texas, Oregon and the Mexican War* (Columbia: University of Missouri Press, 1973).

Pyne, Stephen J.: *Fire in America: A Cultural History of Wildland and Rural Fire* (Princeton, NJ: Princeton University Press, 1982).

Pyne, Stephen J.: *Vestal Fire: An Environmental History, Told through Fire, of Europe and Europe's Encounter with the World* (Seattle: University of Washington Press, 1997).

Pyne, Stephen J.: *World Fire: The Culture of Fire on Earth* (Seattle: University of Washington Press, 1997).

Ramonofsky, Ann F.: *Vectors of Death: The Archeology of European Contact* (Albuquerque: University of New Mexico Press, 1987).

Riley, Glenda: *Frontierswomen: The Iowa Experience* (Ames, IA: Iowa State University Press, 1981).

Robbins, William G.: *Colony and Empire: The Capitalist Transformation of the American West* (Lawrence: University Press of Kansas, 1994).

Roberts, Brian: *American Alchemy: The California Gold Rush and Middle-Class Culture* (Chapel Hill: University of North Carolina Press, 2000).

Roberts, David: *A Newer World: Kit Carson, John C. Fremont and the Claiming of the American West* (New York: Simon and Schuster, 2000).

Rohrbough, Malcolm J.: *Days of Gold: The California Gold Rush and the American Nation* (Berkeley: University of California Press, 1997).

Ronda, James, (ed.): *Voyages of discovery: Essays on the Lewis and Clark Expedition* (Helena: Montana Historical Society Press, 1998).

Rothman, Hal K.: *Devil's Bargains: Tourism in the Twentieth-Century American West* (Lawrence: University Press of Kansas, 1998).

Schlissel, Lillian: *Women's Diaries of the Westward Journey* (New York: Schocken Books, 1982).

Sellars, Richard West: *Preserving Nature in the National Parks: A History* (New Haven: Yale University Press, 1997).

Sellers, Charles Grier: *James Knox Polk, Jacksonian: 1795–1843*, 2 vols. (Princeton: Princeton University Press, 1957).

Sellers, Charles Grier: *The Market Revolution: Jacksonian America, 1815–1846* (New York: Oxford University Press, 1991).

Shipps, Jan: *Sojourner in the Promised Land: Forty Years Among the Mormons* (Urbana: University of Illinois Press, 2000).

Slotkin, Richard: *Regeneration Through Violence: The Mythology of the American Frontier, 1600–1860* (Middletown, CT: Wesleyan University Press, 1973).

Slotkin, Richard: *The Fatal Environment: The Myth of the Frontier in the Age of Industrialization, 1800–1890* (New York: Atheneum, 1985).

Slotkin, Richard: *Gunfighter Nation: The Myth of the Frontier in Twentieth-Century America* (New York: Atheneum, 1992).

Smith, Duane A.: *Mining America: The Industry and the Environment, 1800–1980* (Lawrence: University Press of Kansas, 1987).

Smith, Henry Nash: *Virgin Land: The American West as Symbol and Myth* (Cambridge: Harvard University Press, 1950).

Smith, Justin H.: *The War With Mexico* (New York: Macmillan, 1919).

Smith, Sherry L.: "Lost Soldiers: Re-Searching the Army in the American West." *Western Historical Quarterly* 29 (1998), 149–63.

Spence, Mark David: *Dispossessing the Wilderness: Indian Removal and the Making of the National Parks* (New York: Oxford University Press, 1999)

Stilgoe, John R.: *Metropolitan Corridor: Railroads and the American Scene* (New Haven: Yale University Press, 1983).

Taylor, Joseph E.: *Making Salmon: An Environmental History of the Northwest Fisheries Crisis* (Seattle: University of Washington Press, 1999).

Taylor, Quintard: *In Search of the Racial Frontier: African Americans in the American West, 1528–1990* (New York: W. W. Norton, 1998).

Thornton, Russell: *American Indian Holocaust and Survival: A Population History since 1492* (Norman: University of Oklahoma Press, 1987).

Tijerina, Andres: *Tejano Empire: Life on the South Texas Ranchos* (College Station: Texas A&M University Press, 1998).

Tong, Benson: *Unsubmissive Women: Chinese Prostitutes in Nineteenth-Century San Francisco* (Norman: University of Oklahoma Press, 1994).

Van Kirk, Sylvia: *Many Tender Ties: Women in Fur Trade Society, 1670–1870* (Norman: University of Oklahoma Press, 1983).

Webb, Walter Prescott: *The Great Plains* (New York: Grosset & Dunlap, 1931).

Webb, Walter Prescott: *Divided We Stand: The Crisis of a Frontierless Democracy* (New York: Farrar and Rinehart, 1937).

Weinberg, Albert K.: *Manifest Destiny: A Study of Nationalist Expansionism in American History* (Baltimore: The Johns Hopkins Press, 1935).

West, Elliott: *Growing Up With the Country: Childhood on the Far Western Frontier* (Albuquerque: University of New Mexico Press, 1989).

West, Elliott: *The Way to the West: Essays on the Central Plains* (Albuquerque: University of New Mexico Press, 1995).

White, Richard: *The Roots of Dependency: Subsistence, Environment, and Social Change Among the Choctaws, Pawnees, and Navajos* (Lincoln: University of Nebraska Press, 1983).

White, Richard: *The Middle Ground: Indians, Empires, and Republics in the Great Lakes Region, 1650–1815* (Cambridge: Cambridge University Press, 1991).

White, Richard: *"It's Your Misfortune and None of My Own": A History of the American West* (Norman: University of Oklahoma Press, 1991).

White, Richard: "Discovering Nature in North America." *Journal of American History* 79:3 (December 1992), 877.

Winther, Oscar O.: *Express and Stagecoach Days in California, From the Gold Rush to the Civil War* (Stanford: Stanford University Press, 1936).

Winther, Oscar O.: *The Old Oregon Country: A History of Frontier Trade, Transportation and Travel* (Stanford: Stanford University Press, 1950).

Winther, Oscar O.: *The Transportation Frontier: The Trans-Mississippi West, 1865–1890* (New York: Holt, Rinehart and Winston, 1964).

Wood, Richard G. *Stephen Harriman Long, 1784–1864: Army Engineer, Explorer, Inventor* (Glendale, CA: A. H. Clark Co., 1966).

Wood, W. Raymond and Thomas D. Thiessen (eds.): *Early Fur Trade on the Northern Plains: Canadian Traders Among the Mandan and Hidatsa Indians, 1738–1818* (Norman: University of Oklahoma Press, 1985).

Worster, Donald: *Dust Bowl: The Southern Plains in the 1930s* (New York: Oxford University Press, 1979).

Worster, Donald: "Cowboy Ecology." In Donald Worster *Under Western Skies: Nature and History in the American West* (New York: Oxford University Press, 1992).

Worster, Donald: *A River Running West: The Life of John Wesley Powell* (New York: Oxford University Press, 2001).

Wyman, Mark: *Hard Rock Epic: Western Miners and the Industrial Revolution, 1860–1910* (Berkeley, University of California Press, 1979).

Young, James A. and B. Abbott Sparks: *Cattle in the Cold Desert* (Logan: Utah State University Press, 1985).

Zanjani, Sally S.: *Goldfield: The Last Gold Rush on the Western Frontier* (Athens, OH: Swallow Press/Ohio University Press, 1992).

Zhu, Liping: *A Chinaman's Chance: The Chinese on the Rocky Mountain Mining Frontier* (Niwot, CO: University Press of Colorado, 1997).

PART II

Conquest and Its Patterns: The Nineteenth Century

CHAPTER THREE

Passion and Imagination in the Exploration of the American West

JAMES P. RONDA

Forty years ago, the distinguished western historian and documentary editor Donald Jackson wrote that it is "no longer useful to think of the Lewis and Clark Expedition as the personal story of two men." Instead, Jackson urged his readers to consider exploration in general, and the Lewis and Clark journey in particular, as "an enterprise of many aims and a product of many minds" (Jackson, 1978, vol. l: v). While this may seem common sense now, in the early 1960s it amounted to a fundamental reorientation of exploration history. With a few notable exceptions, most historians had described explorers in heroic terms, casting them as daring adventurers marching through a trackless and empty wilderness (Ronda, 1998: 299–322; Ronda, 1992: 1–2; Brebner, 1933). What Jackson offered gave voice and place to an expanded Corps of Discovery. His pathbreaking *Letters of the Lewis and Clark Expedition* exemplified that approach, opening the Lewis and Clark story to include Philadelphia scientists and artisans, St Louis merchants and rivermen, and native people throughout the continent. And Jackson's vision gave the expedition a global reach, connecting it to the Enlightenment and its many practitioners. Jackson made it plain that the exploration drama had a large cast of characters playing important parts on a grand stage.

But Jackson also understood that for much of the nineteenth century, American exploration bore the imprint of one compelling figure. Writing in 1981, he described Thomas Jefferson as "the most towering westerner of them all," clearly "the single most important figure in the early development of the American West." (Jackson, 1981: ix, 4). Jefferson was the weaver, pulling together many strands to make the whole fabric. Without diminishing the minds, experiences, and contributions of others, it seems appropriate to say that no one more completely defined American exploration of the nineteenth-century West than Thomas Jefferson. He invented a uniquely American West, one filled with his own hopes and dreams, illusions and fantasies. He launched the Lewis and Clark Expedition, the first in a long and productive series of federal probes into that invented West. He composed detailed instructions for that journey, drafting a text that both defined the American West and served as the charter for future geographic and scientific exploration. And Jefferson made exploration a national priority, an act of state and empire. Perhaps William Clark said it best when he described the president as the "Main

Spring" of the exploration enterprise (Jackson, 1978, vol. 1: 111; Ronda, 1997a: 9–10).

Jefferson himself had some sense of his own central role in western exploration. Writing to William Dunbar in 1805, he predicted that "we shall delineate with correctness the great arteries of this great country: those who come after us will extend the ramifications as they become acquainted with them, and fill up the canvas we begin." (Jackson, 1978, vol. 1: 245) Those few lines conjure up images of exploration done with the cartographer's precision, with the painter's eye for revealing detail. And the "we" in his letter suggested that the exploration enterprise would enlist the talents and energies of scientists, artists, cartographers, merchants, and travelers of all sorts and stripes. Jefferson intended to portray exploration as a rational, orderly enterprise. Explorers, statesmen, and scientists, joined in a common venture, would fill in the outline, replacing myth and empty space with fact and useful knowledge. Like his contemporaries, Jefferson believed that the twin actions of discovery and exploration would substitute fact and reality for myth and illusion. The entire Enlightenment global exploration project – one that involved Spanish, French, British as well as American explorers – was founded on those assumptions (Marshall and Williams, 1982: 7–40; Livingstone and Withers, 1999: 1–21). The Enlightenment imagined discovery and exploration as reasoned undertakings; explorers were clear-thinking agents of science and the nation-state. And of course, in this reading, any history of exploration should emphasize dispassionate Reason and the inevitable triumph of fact over fantasy.

But a closer look at the story of exploration in the American West reveals a quite different narrative, one with all the twists and turns of a mountain trail. What most often drove men and nations up that trail were the energies of passion and imagination. Passion was the fire that fueled action; imagination conjured up what passionate action hoped to find. Captain George Vancouver, surely not given to flights of fancy, confessed that explorers were caught up in the "ardor of the present age, to discover and delineate the true geography of the earth" (Vancouver, [1798], 1984, vol. 1: 275). George Forster, a naturalist with Captain James Cook's second Pacific expedition, went even farther, describing exploration as "the rage of hunting after facts" (Hoare, 1982, vol. 1: xi). Words like "ardor" and "rage" bring us face to face with the emotional history of exploration, a history that embraces myths, conjectures, illusions, and dreams. In *Arctic Dreams: Imagination and Desire in a Northern Landscape*, Barry Lopez ponders the way longing and passion shape exploration. "Desire," he writes, "causes imagination to misconstrue what it finds" (Lopez, 1986: 256). And, as Umberto Eco observes, explorers act out their parts in the theater of illusion, revealing in their every move the "force of the false" (Eco, 1998: 2–3).

At first glance the twentieth-century English writer D. H. Lawrence may appear an unlikely guide to an exploration world Jefferson thought cool and reasoned. But Lawrence spent much of his creative life traveling and exploring in remote and exotic places. In an unpublished book review written in 1926, Lawrence suggested that explorers always travel within sight of "the coasts of illusion" and yearn to land on those shores (Lawrence, 1926: vol. 1: 342–3). And, in fact, it was those very "coasts of illusion" and what they promised that prompted most journeys. Here Lawrence the artist gives shape to what Lawrence the restless traveler already knew – that behind every journey, no matter how rationally calculated, are powerful illusions and compelling dreams. Lawrence also knew what Jefferson reluctantly came to recognize. Exploring may begin with cherished dreams and glowing fantasies but often ends in uncomfortable reality and troubling disillusion.

For all his faith in Reason and Enlightenment science, Jefferson was not untouched by the fancies and visions that tempt all travelers. Some of Jefferson's illusions were geographic, reflecting current notions about the shape of the continent's rivers, mountains, and terrain. Others were anthropological, revealing his life-long scientific interest in Native American peoples and cultures. And there were deeply held expectations – often illusory – about exotic plants and animals yet to be discovered in the West.

But the most tempting illusion about the West – the one Jefferson clung to with fierce tenacity – was his faith in the West as a unique political and social environment. While other peoples and nations in the Atlantic world slid into tyranny and urban-industrial decay, the new American republic could be kept young and vibrant, renewed by the fertile lands of the West. The forces of change and decay, irresistible in the Atlantic world, could be held at bay in the West. The past would be forgotten and the future secured by the simple act of going into the West. This was Jefferson's greatest temptation, his most enduring illusion as a patron of exploration. The West promised an American Eden where republican farmers could live virtuous, self-sufficient lives beyond the reach of time and change. Explorers sent into the West were charged to map out and survey Jefferson's cherished "empire for liberty" (Onuf, 2000: 1–17).

The "empire for liberty" was founded on some of Jefferson's most passionately held illusions. Lewis and Clark, armed with Jefferson's instruction text, went in search of the empire all were sure was beyond the coast, just over the western horizon. We need to chart Jefferson's "coasts of illusion." They guided and informed the seemingly rational planning and calculated decision-making Jefferson and his successors boasted about. Throughout the century those illusions and dreams changed shape and took on new vocabularies, but their essences and lures endured. And in the twentieth century the projects and schemes of irrigation engineers, real estate developers, and highway planners advanced that same elusive western dream – the dream of paradise. Considering such dreams, we begin to appreciate the emotional, passionate history of exploration in the West.

A recent Jefferson biographer described the Virginian's presidency as "textual" (Ellis, 1997: 193). Jefferson believed that chaos could be reduced to order and human problems resolved if basic social and political texts were carefully composed and faithfully interpreted. Thoughtfully drafted constitutions and statutes were at the heart of any well-ordered civil society. Jefferson's commitment to getting the words right also extended to his exploration endeavors. As he invented an American West as a (con)text for republican virtue, so he would send explorers into that west armed with texts of inquiry. Wide reading in exploration history and travelers' accounts taught him the value of written directions for those bound on voyages of discovery. In 1793 he tried his hand at exploration planning, preparing detailed instructions for French botanist André Michaux's proposed journey across the continent to the Pacific. In retrospect that document – with its confident notions about North American geography and marvelous plants and animals in the West – was the first draft for what Jefferson wrote for Meriwether Lewis in 1803.

Throughout the spring of 1803 Jefferson wrote and circulated a preliminary instruction draft for his Pacific expedition. Advice from friends, colleagues, and fellow members of the American Philosophical Society sharpened the focus and expanded the scope of that initial document. What the President sent to Lewis on June 20, 1803 shaped not only the Lewis and Clark Expedition but also all subsequent federal exploration in the West for the remainder of the century. In a few pages Jefferson touched on nearly all the hopes, dreams, and illusions that would animate western exploration. What appears at first reading as a coolly rational, typically Enlightenment "Table of Contents" for an encyclopedia of the American West was also an expression of passion and imagination. The passion was his desire to preserve the gains of the Revolution and secure the republic; his imagination drew on a lifetime of reading about North America. Like Jefferson himself, the instructions for Lewis and Clark mix (but do not always blend) unequal measures of reliable knowledge and pure fantasy. Looking closely at this text, we begin to appreciate the complexities, confusions, and ambiguities that were at the heart of the entire exploration enterprise.

Few documents in American exploration history more fully express in their physical form and composition the spirit of rational inquiry than the instructions for Lewis and Clark. The Enlightenment exploration enterprise envisioned a well-ordered world open to thoughtful investigation by means of carefully planned journeys. Sir Joseph Banks, President of the Royal Society and Great Britain's leading exploration patron, believed that exploration ought to be organized around questions relating to the natural world – questions that had answers all reasonable investigators could agree upon. Even the most cursory look at Jefferson's instructions reveals that sense of ordered inquiry. But those same words and lines advanced a powerful set of images of the country beyond St Louis and the opportunities in a distinctly American West. Reading Jefferson's word map for Lewis and Clark we see not only the Empire of Reason in the West but an imagined place on the coasts of illusion lit by the fires of passion.

Read as expressions of both reasoned inquiry and passionate imagination, what Jefferson prepared for Lewis and Clark contains the methods of inquiry, the topics for those inquiries, and the future shape of the American West. While most discussions of the Lewis and Clark instructions begin with the expedition's core mission and the conjectural geography that informed it, we might begin by looking at the methods Jefferson intended to guide his explorers.

Like many of his contemporaries, Jefferson enjoyed the mental exercise in conjecture about remote places and exotic peoples. Pondering the character of the West in the 1790s, Jefferson wondered about the presence of llama herds and packs of mammoths. There might be Welsh Indians, volcanoes, or perhaps even a mile-long mountain of salt up the Missouri River. And conjectural geography provided the very foundation for the Lewis and Clark Expedition's core mission. Jefferson and other exploration planners were firmly convinced that exploration required making a journey. Planning could be done in the library, the conference room, or the study, but discovery and exploration demanded the physical act of moving through the landscape. Reading by itself was not enough; motion had to extend beyond turning pages or moving pen across paper. Jefferson recognized the tension between exploring from the armchair (something he spent a lifetime doing) and the importance of the journey. To undertake a journey meant work and action. Jefferson would have embraced the truth in historian Dorinda Outram's observation that "the eighteenth century believed perhaps more strongly than any other that travel makes truth" (Outram, 1999: 281). At the same time, Jefferson recognized that many of the most respected scientists were not ready to leave the quiet security of laboratories and libraries. Writing to a French correspondent in 1806, Jefferson complained that "men of science, used to the temperature and inactivity of their closet, cannot be induced to undertake" demanding western journeys. "When the route shall once be open and known," he was sure that scholars would abandon their "closets" and conjectures to become part of the exploration enterprise (Peterson, 1984: 1159).

Jefferson placed journeys at the heart of exploration. But these were not to be ordinary journeys, the kind a merchant or a casual traveler might make from one town to another. Nor did he have in mind the Grand Tour, the genteel European adventure that set young men and some young women of privilege in search of polished manners as the veneer of high culture. The making of a journey by itself was not enough. Borrowing from the experience of Sir Joseph Banks and the maritime voyages of Captain James Cook and Captain George Vancouver, Jefferson linked the journey to the act of observation. Doing that, he hoped that Americans could participate in what were already called "voyages of discovery." Drawing on one of the central ideas in the discipline of natural history, Jefferson believed that the act of observation was fundamental. As he explained to Lewis and Clark, "your observations are to be taken with great pains and accuracy, to be entered distinctly and intelligently for others as well as for your self" (Jackson, 1978, vol. 1: 62). Jefferson envisioned explorers as observant travelers making self-conscious, wide-awake journeys. What he sought was not just looking, but practiced seeing and observing. And in all of this, the recording, preservation, and dissemination of such observations were essential. Without systematic record keeping, observations would be disconnected, jumbled, and eventually lost.

Like his contemporaries, Jefferson was convinced that even the most observant travelers would make fruitless journeys unless they pursued a carefully thought-out mission. Observation without direction would become mere looking. Jefferson wanted explorers who would see with informed eyes. And it was the presence of a defined mission that could transform looking into genuine seeing and then understanding. Such a mission might have many features, aspects, and consequences but it needed to be precise enough to keep explorers from wandering from the task set before them. While textbook wisdom continues to send Lewis and Clark up the Missouri to explore the Louisiana Purchase, Jefferson had something quite different in mind. Here the power of desire and illusion came to full play in Jefferson's imagination. Persuaded that the age-old dream of a water passage through North America was geographic reality, Jefferson launched the Lewis and Clark voyage of discovery to find that water highway. Nowhere in the exploration instructions was Jefferson more explicit and more held in the thrall of imagination than when describing the expedition's central mission and the geography he believed supported it. "The object of your mission is to explore the Missouri river, & such principal stream of it, as, by it's course and communication with the waters of the Pacific ocean, whether the Columbia, Oregon, Colorado or any other river may offer the most direct and practicable water communication across this continent for the purposes of commerce" (Jackson, 1978: vol. 1: 61).

In a few sentences Jefferson managed to capture the fundamentals of a venerable geographic dream. Reaching back to the age of Columbus and the adventures of sailors like Sir Humphry Gilbert and Giovanni da Verrazzano, Jefferson found the language of the Northwest Passage both irresistible and strangely comforting. The idea of a passage from Atlantic to Pacific waters long predated the Enlightenment, but the geographic theories of the eighteenth century gave considerable aid and comfort to those who cherished the notion of a plain path to the Pacific and beyond to the riches of India and China (Allen, 1975: 1–45).

For eighteenth-century geographers and cartographers, the key words in under-standing nature were balance and symmetry. Just as the whole universe demonstrated the laws of order and balance, the earth had terrain features that mirrored that balance. Mountains at one edge of the American continent were sure to be similar to those on the other shore. The same could be said for rivers. Navigable waterways like the Hudson, the Potomac, and the Ohio were bound to have counterparts in the American West (Ronda, 1997b: 27–42). And the very soil itself – so fertile in places like Virginia, Kentucky, and the Ohio country – was sure to yield abundant crops in the lands beyond the Missouri. Little wonder that when Clark, Zebulon Montgomery Pike, and Stephen H. Long described parts of the west as an infertile desert, their observations were widely discounted.

The passage Jefferson was convinced Lewis and Clark would find was not only the key to the wealth of Asia, but the grand commercial highway into an agricultural paradise. Jefferson imagined that highway as no mere route to the markets of India and China. For him the passage was part of a much larger concern. Like many other eighteenth-century social theorists, Jefferson was convinced that all human societies passed through life stages much like the cycles of birth, maturity, and death in the plant and animal world. Those evolutionary stages were not only rooted in natural law but were inevitable and progressive. Human kind began as hunters, moved to herding semidomesticated animals, progressed to agriculture, and then descended into urban and industrial ways. Jefferson and his fellow republicans believed that virtue could thrive only in an agrarian setting. Preserving the legacy of 1776 and saving the republic meant keeping Americans rooted in the culture of agriculture. Yet Jefferson could not deny the undeniable – American farmers and planters were already deeply involved in commercial capitalism. If the children of the revolution-ary generation were to remain in a state of republican grace, they had to be provided with rich land to farm and routes to take their products to distant markets. The passage could provide just that. If Lewis and Clark could find what Jefferson was sure nature had already decreed, the republic had nothing to fear from the future.

Having once set out the mission and its geography of hope, Jefferson went about filling in the details, giving substance to his vision of what Lewis and Clark might find. Again imagination was at the heart of the enterprise. In a long section entitled "other objects worthy of notice" the president let his fancy run free. Instructing his captains to observe "the soil and face of the country," Jefferson expected Lewis and Clark to find all sorts of plants not yet known to European science. Like Banks and the expeditions he sponsored, Jefferson was convinced that such plants would have both medicinal and dietary benefit. If the West held a storehouse of plants both marvelous and useful, the country was certain to be home for animals never before seen by European eyes. Reflecting on the mastodon, the discovery of skeletal remains at Big Bone Lick, Kentucky, and the recent efforts of Charles Willson Peale to reconstruct a mastodon skeleton, Jefferson urged Lewis and Clark to keep a sharp lookout for remains or accounts of rare animals. And because Jefferson believed that extinction was not part the natural order, the West might be a Noah's Ark, a place to see plants and animals lost to the rest of the world (Jackson, 1978, vol. 1: 63; Miller, 1988).

Imagining an American West meant not only filling it with new animals but also giving it a landscape at once sublime and useful. The wonder Jefferson envisioned might come in the shape of volcanoes. For Enlightenment geographers and naturalists no terrestrial feature was more dramatic and mysterious than a volcano. Here was something that revealed the inner workings, perhaps the very nature, of the earth itself and because volcanic eruptions were both violent and unpredictable they held special significance for geographers who put so much store in order and predictability. As early as the 1780s Jefferson had speculated that there might be volcanoes in the middle of the American continent. Now here was an opportunity to make a fundamental contribution to American geology. Useful minerals, metals, limestone, saltpeter, and pit coal might add to the storehouse in this natural wonderland. But most important in this Jeffersonian image of the West was the question of climate and soil fertility. While some thought about the West in terms of the fur trade, ideological republicans like Jefferson and Secretary of the Treasury Albert Gallatin always considered the West as a farmer's paradise. In an often overlooked letter to Jefferson, Gallatin laid out his agrarian vision for the West beyond the Mississippi. "The great object [of the expedition] to ascertain is whether from its extent and fertility that country is susceptible of a large population, in the same manner as the corresponding tract on the Ohio" (Jackson, 1978, vol. 1: 33). And both Jefferson and Gallatin knew that the word "Ohio" was just another way to say a green and fertile country. If American farmers and planters were to make the West a permanent home, they needed precise information about climate, soil fertility, and seasonal change. Jefferson had no doubt that his West was a garden; Lewis and Clark were there to learn how to be good gardeners.

Imagination, illusion, and passion dominated Jefferson's thinking about mission, continental geography, and the physical character of western plants and animals. As Jefferson considered the continent west of St Louis he also filled that West with native people largely of his own making. Early in his life he had been fascinated by Indians, especially their physical presence and public oratory. For Jefferson, Indians lived in a world at once noble and debased. When some European scholars, including the distinguished French naturalist the Comte de Buffon, asserted that the American environment made animals smaller and human beings less vital and potent, Jefferson reacted swiftly to defend the New World. Prompted by cultural patriotism and his own observations, Jefferson maintained that native people showed no signs of physical decline or mental deficiency (Glacken, 1967: 681–93). As the first inhabitants of the continent, Indians were both America's oldest people and human kind at an early stage of social development. As Indians were now, Jefferson reasoned, so Anglo-Americans once were. Imagining the west as a museum – a kind of enlarged natural history "cabinet of curiosities" – Jefferson expected his explorers to find answers to questions about the course and character of human history. Lewis and Clark were ordered to gain "a knowledge of those people" and in the process learn "the names of the nations and their numbers." (Jackson, 1978, vol. 1: 62) Recognizing that the West was not an empty space, Jefferson presented his explorers with a long list of questions about native lives and cultures. He wanted to know about the territory claimed by each native group, the group's relations with its neighbors, and something of its language, cultural traditions, and economy. And Lewis and Clark were not to neglect domestic economy – matters of food, clothing, housing, and daily life. In all, Jefferson sought what anthropologists call a cultural inventory. But this was an inventory not simply for dispassionate study but one that would serve the interests of an expanding American empire. To know the names of the nations was in some way to lay claim to them.

While never acknowledging it, Jefferson implicitly recognized that the expedition's success (and perhaps its very survival) depended on friendly relations with native people. On one hand Jefferson expected his explorers to be greeted as agents of a benevolent nation, bringing the blessings of American friendship and western technology. But there was an odd ambivalence in what he told Lewis and Clark. "Treat them [Indians] in the most friendly and conciliatory manner which their own conduct will admit" (Jackson, 1978, vol. 1: 64). It was that phrase about "their own conduct" that suggests the expectation of violence. No doubt Jefferson and his captains thought they were serious about the "innocent nature of the expedition" and its hopes for the peaceful establishment of trading houses and delegations bound for Washington. But Jefferson came closer to his own fears when he urged Lewis and Clark not to put the expedition in harm's way. Harm, in the shape of native hostility, loomed large in the president's mind. In early July 1803 he wrote Lewis that it could be "expected that you will encounter considerable dangers from the Indian inhabitants" (Jackson, 1978, vol. 1: 105; Ronda, 1984). The dangers on the journey were real, but most often they came not from native people but in the changes and chances that every traveler faces in every strange country.

Read as a map to the "coasts of illusion" and the country beyond – a record of imagination and image-making – Jefferson's instructions for Lewis and Clark embody three fundamental ideas that dominated American exploration of the West throughout the nineteenth century. These ideas were not original with Jefferson but he gave them expression and the force of the federal establishment. Whether by creation or adoption, these notions became the Jeffersonian tradition for American exploration.

From the sixteenth century on it was increasingly clear that exploration beyond the bounds of Western Europe demanded the financial and organizational resources of the nation-state. Ruling elites in Spain, Portugal, France, and England all recognized that exploration served national and imperial interests. In Jefferson's time no exploration patron had a surer grasp of the relationship between exploration, science, and empire than Sir Joseph Banks. As President of the Royal Society, Banks used his considerable influence to make exploration in the Pacific a national priority (Mackay, 1979: 29). The Cook and Vancouver voyages represent Banks' skillful linking of imperial aspirations to private, commercial ambitions. And Jefferson (as president of both the nation and the American Philosophical Society) sought to do the same. What began with the Confederation Congress and the Land Ordinance of 1784 as a means to incorporate the West into the nation, now gained the power of the presidency. The West, however defined and wherever located, was bound to the federal establishment. Throughout the nineteenth century exploration continued to be sheltered under the federal umbrella. Levi Lincoln, Jefferson's Attorney General, understood this when he described the Lewis and Clark Expedition as "an enterprise of national consequence." (Jackson, 1978, vol. 1: 35) Whether the explorers were officers in the Army Corps of Topographical Engineers or civilians working in the post-Civil-War territorial surveys, it was the federal government that served as home base for the enterprises. Federal funds paid wages, bought supplies, and bore the costs of printing exploration reports. As national politics and the economy changed throughout the century, government explorers adapted their strategies to fit new circumstances.

Jefferson's letter to Lewis was filled with images of motion, passage, and encounter. The passages of the American nation were to be from east to west, or at least so it seemed from Monticello. The Lewis and Clark instructions were the first official statement of the search for east–west passages that would occupy explorers' attention for years to come. Explorers looked for water highways, military roads, and railroad routes – all tracing Jefferson's original vision of what the poet Walt Whitman would call "the passage to India." And that search for east–west thoroughfares became part of the American expansionist gospel. Here tradition and geography joined. Massive federal projects like the Pacific Railroad Surveys were inspired by ideas about passages that came directly from Jefferson and his Corps of Discovery. And perhaps it is no accident that planners of the Interstate Highway System fell under Jefferson's sway. Interstate 80, running from Atlantic to Pacific, is one more piece of that passage and its promise.

When Jefferson complained to his French correspondent C. F. de C. Volney about men of science unwilling to leave their comfortable laboratories and libraries, he touched on the third key idea that permeated American exploration in the West. Like so many of his intellectual contemporaries Jefferson measured the value of inventions and discoveries by their utility. Research in chemistry, botany, and mineralogy was of immediate service to the greatest number of citizens in the republic. Anglo-American naturalists like James Logan, John and William Bartram, and William Hamilton had already established the link between scientific study and useful applications (Greene, 1984: 253–319; Porter, 1986: 1–51). Beginning with Lewis and Clark, American geographic explorers were bent on finding information that could have practical applications. Those might be in agriculture, mining, or civil engineering, but it was useful knowledge that would sustain the republic and that deserved public support. And just beneath the surface was the belief that the West would provide the best place to apply that knowledge. In the ever-youthful West new discoveries could be tested, and if found beneficial, quickly accepted. In Jefferson's social geography the West would have no hide-bound aristocracies, wary of innovation and change.

By the time the Lewis and Clark Expedition returned to St Louis in September 1806, some of Jefferson's cherished dreams were either shattered or dented. There were no exotic animals in the West, nor did the expedition collect many plants radically different from those present east of the Mississippi. Most disappointingly, the Missouri and the Columbia did not provide an easy water passage through the western garden. What stood between Atlantic and Pacific waters was a mountain system quite unlike any Jefferson or his contemporaries imagined. The expedition sent to find an orderly West found instead a place more complex, intricate, and dis-orderly than anyone guessed. But for all its apparent failures, the Lewis and Clark

Expedition gave weight to Jefferson's key ideas. Exploration was now part of the federal agenda (Goetzmann, 1966). Passages east to west would continue to occupy expedition planners and their travelers. Perhaps most important, the connection had been fixed between useful knowledge, the expansion of the republic, and the exploration enterprise. Those ideas would come to fruition in the journeys made by two successive generations of explorers.

For all his emphasis on the role of government and the military in western exploration, the president never assumed that voyages of discovery would be the exclusive property of the federal establishment. Soon after the return of the Lewis and Clark Expedition, Jefferson told a gathering of Congressmen that he hoped some "enterprizing, mercantile young men" would venture into the West and settle there (Ronda, 1990: 44). While Jefferson had farmers in mind as his "enterprizing young men", those who took up the exploration challenge immediately after Lewis and Clark were fur traders and their corporate patrons. Such a development did not trouble Jefferson. In his mind the fur trade could play in useful role in Indian diplomacy and in preparing the West for future agricultural settlement. What did worry Jefferson and many of his contemporaries was the prospect of an unregulated trade – one that might spark violence between Indians and their new Anglo neighbors.

The quest for fur had long been one of the primary motives for North American exploration. By its very nature the trade needed to find new trapping territories. And traders had a unique opportunity to gain access to Native American geographic information. Nowhere was this fur trade exploration tradition stronger than in Canada where explorers like Peter Pond, Simon Fraser, Alexander Mackenzie, and the redoubtable David Thompson drew western Canada into the fur trade world. The intense and often murderous rivalry between the Hudson's Bay Company and the North West Company guaranteed that geographic exploration would advance at a quick pace (Allen, 1997a: 80–98).

More than one American merchant dreamed of challenging the Canadians. By the time Lewis and Clark returned to St Louis in 1806 that city was already the center for an American fur trade reaching up the Missouri to the Mandan villages. News of fur-rich streams in the Yellowstone River country and at the Three Forks of the Missouri made merchants like Manuel Lisa eager to press up the river and into the new West. No one was more ready to connect the fur business to exploration than Lisa. After hearing the Lewis and Clark stories, he hired the expedition's ablest frontiersman, George Drouillard, as his chief field lieutenant. John Colter, another Lewis and Clark veteran, also signed with Lisa. With his characteristic energy and the knowledge gained from the Lewis and Clark journey, Lisa had every reason to believe that his imagined trade empire would soon become reality (Oglesby, 1963).

Manuel Lisa might have had the necessary drive and vision required to fashion a fur trade empire in the West, but he was surely no match for John Jacob Astor. Already a prosperous New York fur merchant with close ties to the Montreal fur market, Astor was attracted by the prospect of an American fur company of international size and scope. Inspired by the imperial and geographic ideas of Peter Pond and Pond's student Alexander Mackenzie, Astor began to frame a grand design that would link the American West to fur markets in China and Europe. Jefferson imagined a West connected to the rest of the world but not infected by its social and political ills. Astor sought to integrate the West into a global economy for reasons of profit and corporate monopoly. By early 1808 Astor was ready to share the bold plan with friend and confidant De Witt Clinton, mayor of New York City and sometime lieutenant governor of New York state. As Astor explained it, he was now laying "plans on the Subject of a company for carrying on the fur trade in the United States even more extensive than it is done by the companies in Canada." (Ronda, 1990: 39). Astor's imagination was as bold as it was coldly pragmatic. In his ledger book mind, calculations of profit mixed easily with heady dreams of a rising American empire. He saw no contradiction between personal gain and the growth of the American nation. As he explained years later, his plan aimed to "extend its [the United States'] dominion over a most interesting part of the opposite coast of the North American continent, and perhaps open communications of no small moment with Japan and the East Coast of Asia" (Ronda, 1990: 260). The dream of the Passage to India was plainly far from dead.

Over the next five years Astor and his employees in the Pacific Fur Company struggled to make a daring scheme into a profitable reality. As chronicled first in Washington Irving's *Astoria; or, Anecdotes of an Enterprise beyond the Rock Mountains* (1836) Astor engaged St Louis merchant Wilson Price Hunt and a number of Canadian fur men to undertake the second American transcontinental journey (1811–1812). Astor also sent his ship the *Tonqui* on a voyage around South America to build a fur trade base at the mouth of the Columbia. Using Fort Astoria as a base of operations, the Pacific Fur Company established a series of secondary trading stations in the region. And it did appear that the company was having some initial success. Prospects brightened further when Astor struck a bargain with the Russian-American Company to carry supplies to the company's posts and transport furs to the China market in American vessels. But playing the imperial game held Astor hostage to global forces and events well beyond his control. Despite his best efforts, Astor's Western Empire was swept away by the War of 1812. Many of Astor's employees at Astoria were Canadians who feared that the war would endanger both their lives and their financial prospects. In October 1813, after hearing news that a British warship was headed toward Astoria, Astor's agents sold the post to representatives of the North West Company (Ronda, 1990: 290–1).

Despite the failure of the Pacific Fur Company and the loss of Astoria, Astor's grand scheme did leave a powerful and enduring legacy. Granting Astoria special place in his continental thinking, Jefferson insisted that "if we claim that country [the Pacific Northwest] at all, it must be on Astor's settlement near the mouth of the Columbia" (Ronda, 1997a: 63). But the impact of the Astoria idea and Astor's visionary passion went well beyond the diplomacy of empire. While Washington Irving dismissed the Astorians as "men of business little versed in science, or curious about matters not immediately bearing upon their interests," a careful reading of their memoirs and journals tells a different story (Ronda, 1990: 315). Accomplished naturalists Thomas Nuttall and John Bradbury accompanied Wilson Price Hunt's party up the Missouri and made important botanical and ethnographic observations. Hardheaded merchants and traders could no more escape the spirit of inquiry than Lewis and Clark. Astorians like Alexander Ross, Gabriel Franchere, Ross Cox, and Robert Stuart took time from their duties to make significant published contributions to ethnography, cartography, and regional history. While Jefferson's contemporaries openly acknowledged the connection between scientific exploration and national expansion, few were ready to admit that commerce, exploration, and the empire of the mind might find common ground. But the experience of the Astorians suggested otherwise. Ross put it best when he wrote that "the progress of discovery contributes not a little to the enlightenment of mankind; for mercantile interest stimulates curiosity and adventure, and combines with them to enlarge the circle of knowledge" (Ross, [1849], 1989: 3–4).

Perhaps most important for future western exploration and travel was a discovery made by Robert Stuart and his party. In 1812, eastbound from Astoria to St. Louis, Stuart and his men came upon South Pass in the Wind River Mountains. As with many such discoveries, Stuart was guided to the pass by information from Native American sources. Stuart returned to St Louis in April, 1813 and word of his "southern pass" quickly spread throughout the city. Here was the possibility of a passage over the Rockies less demanding and more commercially useful than the northern route marked out by Lewis and Clark. In a place keenly interested in the geography of the fur trade, the possibility of a route across the Rockies was important news. Joseph Charless, editor of the Missouri Gazette announced Stuart's discovery in an item entitled "American Enterprise." Charless did more than simply report exploration results. He declared that "It appears that a journey across the continent of North America might be performed with a wagon, there being no obstruction in the wheel rout that any person could dare call a mountain." This was the plain path to the Pacific – the very geography of hope that had so captivated Thomas Jefferson. While the events of the War of 1812 put a stop to such speculations, the idea of wagon trails over a southern pass did not die. Two decades later, South Pass, in present-day Wyoming, became an essential part of the Oregon Trail. While the pass was rediscovered in the 1820s by fur trader and explorer Jedediah Smith, Stuart and his Astorians deserve credit as the initial European discoverers (Ronda, 1994: 7–14).

Historians sometimes portray the War of 1812 as an Atlantic affair, an argument about neutral rights in a world at war. Caught up in the spectacle of Washington in flames and the government in flight, we miss the profound consequences of the war on the West and for the course and pace of western exploration. Government explorers and fur trade adventurers built the first American empire in the West – an empire that stretched from St Louis to Fort Astoria, from the Mandan villages to the Great Lakes and the upper Mississippi. By 1814 much of that had slipped away or appeared about to be lost. Astoria was in the hands of the North West Company, Indians on the northern plains once again looked to traders from Montreal for support and supplies, and the Great Lakes seemed once again more Canadian than American.

But dreams die hard and visions of empire can be revived by the breath of ambition, both personal and national. Even more than the events of the American Revolution, the experience of the War of 1812 gave life and intensity to a passionate nationalism – the sort of aggressive and expansionist nationalism that marked the rest of the century. No nationalist passion was more fixed in the minds of many American politicians and diplomats than the image of empire in the West. Such an empire might promise security from imperial rivals, wealth from land and fur, and perhaps even a place to relocate native people dispossessed from east of the Mississippi. National honor called for an American West; cultural survival – if Jefferson was to be believed – demanded it. Having forged the first American empire in the West, explorers were about to mark out the boundaries for the second venture into territorial expansion.

Those hard-edged imperialist expectations found fresh life in 1817 when Secretary of War John C. Calhoun undertook a systematic review of western frontier defenses. What Calhoun envisioned was the use of military force to secure the West, a goal that aimed not only at defense but an open show of strength against any potential rival. Thomas Jefferson sent heavily armed soldiers into the West in 1804. Nonetheless, his imagined West remained rooted in republican dreams of yeomen farmers in a peaceful paradise. Those hostile to his vision, so Jefferson believed, would simply vanish before American superiority. Secretary Calhoun's notions about the West were shaped by the struggles of the War of 1812. That war showed how easily an American empire in the West could be lost. To lose the West meant not only losing territory but also the promise of the American future. In 1817 the West seemed filled with powerful rivals, both Indian and European. What Calhoun and others around him envisioned was a militarized West, a place where armed force (in the shape for forts and troops) might be a permanent presence to secure the American claim. Calhoun was not the only empire-builder in President James Monroe's administration. Secretary of State John Quincy Adams openly preached a gospel of expansion and territorial acquisition. And Monroe himself plainly thought in continental terms. What emerged from these discussions was a comprehensive plan for western exploration; the first since Jefferson considered the task in 1803 (Nichols and Halley, 1995).

Linking military force to geographic exploration, Calhoun proposed what is now known as the Yellowstone Expedition, a venture that contained three interconnected journeys. The secretary intended sending large military parties up the Missouri and the Mississippi. The Mississippi Expedition, led by Colonel Henry Leavenworth, headed up the river to build Fort Snelling on the present-day site of Minneapolis and St Paul. The Missouri Expedition, commanded by Colonel Henry Atkinson, aimed at reasserting American influence on the northern Great Plains. Soldiers of the Rifle Regiment were on the plains showing the flag and displaying the force behind American claims of sovereignty. To be more precise, those troops were on the Missouri River to ensure its role as a key waterway for American expansion. And the Scientific Expedition, commanded by Major Stephen H. Long, pointed itself into the central Great Plains and the Rockies to explore the Platte, Red, and Canadian rivers. Its mission was in the tradition of useful knowledge – in this case useful military knowledge to secure the West for the republic.

While the Missouri Expedition sank in a sea of mud, disease, and petty squabbling, all hopes were increasingly pinned on the Scientific Expedition (Nichols, 1969). Stephen H. Long, an experienced civil engineer and member of the army's Topographic Bureau, shaped the Scientific Expedition to become the first American exploring enterprise to employ professional scientists. Jefferson's dream of science in the West seemed now a step closer.

For his explorer-scientists Long turned to the Philadelphia scholarly community, still the center for natural history in the new republic. There he enlisted Thomas Say, a zoologist and charter member of the Academy of Natural Sciences. Botany, by now a staple in scientific exploration, was to be the province of Dr William Baldwin. Geology, especially when applied to problems of agriculture, mining, and engineering, had also become a central feature on the exploration agenda. While not a professional geologist, Philadelphia merchant Augustus Jessup was widely read in the field and was also a member of the Academy of Natural Sciences. Long's recruits made it plain that professional science was ready to leave the laboratory and the library to brave the hazards of western travel.

Lewis and Clark recorded the West in journals and maps. The West they found was expressed in words and narratives, not by sketches and paintings. But the reading public, both in Europe and America, was hungry for visual representations and Long recognized their value. For the first time an American exploring party would take skilled artists into the field. Long hired Samuel Seymour, a talented landscape painter. Seymour provided the earliest published views of the western country. Titian Ramsay Peale, youngest son of Charles Willson Peale, was enlisted as artist-naturalist. Much like his contemporary Karl Bodmer, the young Peale could capture both the detail and the essence of a plant or animal. The presence of Peale and Seymour on the expedition is a reminder of the growing relationship between art, science, and exploration. Artists like Peale, Bodmer, and George Catlin saw themselves as combining the disciplines of art and science within the context of geographic exploration. The artists traveling with English and Spanish expeditions in the Pacific had done this first; now the idea became part of the American exploration tradition (Poesch, 1961: 20–35; Dippie, 1990).

The Scientific Expedition not only marked the first entry of American scientists and artists into the West, it was also the first time modern steam-powered transportation became part of exploration strategy. The Lewis and Clark Expedition had employed the most recent technology, whether in weapons or scientific instruments. Long now extended that tradition to include the power of steam for navigation. Colonel Henry Atkinson's Missouri Expedition had employed steamboats for their up river trip. Long also intended to use steamboats. *The Western Engineer*, Long's flagship, was an extraordinary sight as it left Pittsburgh bound for St Louis. The stern-mounted paddle wheels were dubbed "Monroe" and "Calhoun," paying tribute, as Long said, to "the two propelling powers of the expedition." But the vessel's most astounding feature was an elaborately carved dragon that served as both figurehead and steam exhaust. One bemused observer wrote, "the bow of this vessel exhibits the form of a huge serpent, black and scaly, rising out of the water from under the boat as high as the deck, darting forward, his mouth open, vomiting smoke, and apparently carrying the boat on his back" (Ronda, 1997a: 65–66).

For all Long's engineering expertise, he was not an especially skilled expedition planner. From the beginning his Corps of Discovery was dogged by a host of troubles. The *Western Engineer* proved unreliable, underpowered, and uncomfortable. Long and Major Thomas Biddle, the expedition's official record keeper, were so deeply at odds that Biddle challenged Long to a duel. More serious was Dr Baldwin's declining health and eventual resignation. Baldwin left the party in July, 1819 and died the following month. By the time Long and his fellow explorers reached their base camp "Engineer Cantonment" at Council Bluffs, twenty miles above present-day Omaha, it was plain that the enterprise was badly in need of additional personnel, fresh funds, and a clearer sense of its mission.

In early 1820 Long returned to Washington for urgent meetings with Calhoun. Persuaded that the expedition might still be of some use, Calhoun authorized new funding and additional recruits. And to make sure his message got attention, Long courted journalists eager for western news. Whether he realized it or not, Long now became the first public relations explorer, a role that John Charles Fremont would bring to perfection some years later. Most important, Long was given new exploration instructions – directions reflecting the expectation that science and empire were partners. The recent Adams–Onis Treaty (1819) between the United States and Spain attempted to establish the border between Louisiana and Spanish possessions by using the Arkansas and Red – rivers that had proved puzzling to many explorers. Long was directed to trace the Platte River to its source, then turn south to explore and map the Red and the Arkansas. The expedition was to complete its journey at Fort Smith, Arkansas. To make this an effective scientific venture, Long added Dr Edwin James and Capt. John R. Bell to the corps of explorers.

For all Long's aspirations to be a serious explorer, his expedition was poorly planned and woefully undersupplied. The party had just six extra horses, only a handful of Indian trade goods, and an inadequate number of boxes for scientific samples. With only one month's provisions, the travelers were hardly prepared for an extended western survey. Perhaps the greatest problem lay with Long himself and his own hazy conception of western geography. Conditioned by experience with navigable eastern rivers and gentle, green landscapes, Long found the West confusing and unsettling. What his eyes saw did not match what danced in his mind's eye. He mistook the Canadian River for the Red and was disconcerted by the land itself. Expedition journals were soon dotted with words like "sterile," "barren", and "arid." As Edwin James later explained, "the monotony of a vast unbroken plain, like that in which we had now traveled, nearly one hundred and fifty miles, is little less tiresome to the eye, and fatiguing to the spirit, than the dreary solitude of the ocean" (Ronda, 1997a: 67; Goodman and Lawson, 1995). For Long and James the Great Plains proved no Jeffersonian garden.

The Long Expedition is often linked to the notion of the Great American Desert. Long did place that term on his important 1823 map, prepared to accompany James's official expedition account. Convinced that much of the Great Plains was a barren land, Long told Calhoun that the region was "almost wholly unfit for cultivation, and of course uninhabitable by a people depending on agriculture for their subsistence"" (Ronda, 1997a: 68). American explorers had been using the word "desert" to describe parts of the West as early as 1805 but Long gave the idean added emphasis.

Historical geographer Martyn J. Bowden suggests that the Great American Desert image never gained wide acceptance. What endured in the American imagination was the Jeffersonian garden (Bowden, 1971: 48–79). That was the image land speculators, real estate agents, and railroad promoters used effectively in the Euro-American settling of the Great Plains after the Civil War. But, in one important way, Long and James were right. Significant parts of the West could not sustain the kinds of agriculture practiced in lands east of the Mississippi. Acknowledging the West as a land of little rain, high wind, and blazing sun, Long and James foreshadowed some of the conclusions reached in John Wesley Powell's prophetic *Report on the Lands of the Arid Region* (1878). And farmers and ranchers dusted out in the 1930s and again in the 1950s certainly would have found in Long and James some vindication for what they saw blowing in the wind.

The Long Expedition marks a major watershed in western exploration and the ideas that inspired it. While fur traders like Jedediah Smith, foreign travelers and scientists like Sir William Drummond Stewart and Prince Maximilian of Wied, and artists like George Catlin and Alfred Jacob Miller would continue to make important contributions to geographic exploration, the work of surveying the West increasingly fell to professionals within the army (Allen, 1997b: 132–189; Utley, 1997). Nothing more clearly signaled that shift than the creation of the US Army Corps of Topographical Engineers in 1838. Commanded by Colonel John J. Abert, the Topographical Engineers advanced the major government exploring endeavors before the Civil War. The Topographical Engineers represent the growing professionalization of exploration and an increased emphasis on precise measurement and cartographic technique. And no doubt the Topographical Engineers saw themselves as highly trained scientific explorers in the service of the nation.

But no explorer, whether in the era of Lewis and Clark or the age of the Topographical Engineers, was immune from the fantasies and passions of the time. The Topographical Engineers was founded and grew to maturity at a moment of intense nationalism – a time when imperialism wore the face of self-righteous Manifest Destiny. But the dreams that inspired the engineer-explorers were more than rational science and a continental United States. What William Goetzmann aptly calls the "Romantic horizon" was working its magic in art, literature, and the conception of the explorer as culture hero (Goetzmann, 1981: 11–27). Explorers in the Romantic Age thought of themselves as bold, daring travelers marching through grandly sublime landscapes, all for the greater glory of science, self, and the state. As Charlotte M. Porter explains, such travelers exemplified "the Romantic ideal of a genteel hero exploring the American wilderness with a higher vision of nature" (Porter, 1986: 41). Exploration was all about precise calculations as well as the experience of man alone in a wondrous country. Such adventurers plotted an emotional geography, one that measured both mountains and the sense of a sublime American landscape.

No Topographical Engineer more fully exemplified that tangle of dreams and illusions better than John C. Fremont did. With practical field training from experienced cartographer Joseph Nicholas Nicollet, and married to Jesse Benton, the only daughter of expansionist-minded Missouri senator Thomas Hart Benton, Fremont was uniquely placed to become the most widely known American explorer before the Civil War. He brought together a commitment to science and a Romantic temperament eager for adventure and personal glory. And few could make the eagle of Manifest Destiny scream louder than Fremont could. A popular print of the day portrayed Fremont standing atop the Rockies, a sword in one hand and an American flag with the word "Liberty" emblazoned on it in the other. Promoting himself as "The Pathfinder," Fremont became the national symbol of the explorer as hero and public man (Egan, 1977; Rolle, 1991).

Between 1842 and 1845 Fremont led three expeditions into the West. Each represented a distinct set of aspirations and expectations, both personal and national. In 1842 his first venture took him and his small party over the Oregon Trail to map South Pass and the Wind River Range. The Oregon Trail was rapidly becoming a heavily traveled and well-marked transcontinental migration route. The trail hardly needed detailed mapping. But as the American road to the Oregon country it had considerable diplomatic and imperial significance. Fremont's first expedition should be understood in the context of the Oregon Question – that diplomatic tussle between the United States and Great Britain over territorial boundaries in the Pacific North West. Fremont's show of force along the trail was one more way to demonstrate American intentions in the West. The road to Oregon was American, and so might be Oregon itself one day.

The second Fremont expedition (1843–4) was perhaps the most significant of his exploring career. Leaving St Louis in 1843, Fremont's party (now including such fur trade notables as Kit Carson, Thomas Fitzpatrick, and Alexis Godey) made a grand circuit of the West from the central plains to the Columbia River, through California, and back across the Great Basin. William Goetzmann has aptly called this Fremont's "circumnavigation of the West." (Goetzmann, 1982: 72) Graced with magnificent maps drawn by cartographer Charles Preuss, the expedition's report gained wide attention as the result of both federal and commercial press printings. And once again Jesse Benton Fremont was the invisible coauthor, giving shape and expression to her husband's notes. The 1843–4 expedition combined a symbolic statement of American expansionism – the enduring dream of empire – with genuine exploration achievement. Fremont and Preuss were the first to recognize the unique character of the Great Basin and place that name on the map. But for all this considerable scientific accomplishment, Fremont was edging closer to the role of explorer as celebrity. His third western expedition would make his destiny manifest to all.

Fremont's third western venture remains the most controversial, with debates about the explorer's instructions and intentions toward Mexican California, to say nothing of his eventual court martial after the Mexican War. In many ways his California adventure marked the effective end of his exploration career. In 1845 Fremont led a party to explore and map the sources of the Red and Arkansas rivers. What appeared a routine mission of the sort now standard for the Topographical Engineers turned into a probe into California. Once there, Fremont became embroiled in provincial politics and the Bear Flag Revolt. And when the United States declared War on Mexico in 1846, Fremont began to act as military governor of California, behavior that earned him the unending anger of General Stephen Watts Kearny.

John C. Fremont was the most widely recognized American explorer of the nineteenth century. His reports had a large reading public, and all acknowledged him as the nation's western pathfinder. But in retrospect Fremont remains an enigma, a swirl of contradictions and ambiguities. His devotion to science was genuine, if sometimes overblown. And like so many of his contemporaries he shared in the nearly mystical desire for empire in the West. All of this was wrapped in a powerful mix of self-promotion, hunger for personal glory, and the rhetoric of Romantic idealism. Fremont was a leader who held the loyalty of men like Kit Carson and Alexis Godey, no mean accomplishment. Yet he also traveled in the suspect terrain of shady business deals and shameless self-aggrandizement. If one figure points to the complexity in the history of western exploration, it is John C. Fremont (Jackson and Spence, 1970–84).

Passion and imagination defined exploration expectations and goals. Emotion and desire charted the "coasts of illusion" and gave substance to the interior country. But it was technology, whether in the shape of scientific instruments or the latest firearms that made journeys of discovery and exploration possible. At the same time, technology could act as the spark for many such journeys. New inventions captured the imagination, and there were always dreamers who saw the West as the ideal place to demonstrate the latest wonder of the age.

Perhaps no single invention of the nineteenth century more completely captured the national imagination than the steam-powered railroad. Scientists, mechanics, entrepreneurs, politicians, and visionaries were all fascinated by the promise of the iron horse. In an age of computer chips, fiber optics, and jet airplanes it is difficult for us to appreciate the sense of wonder, awe, and promise generated by the railroad idea. Animal muscle would be replaced by the tireless locomotive. Notions of time and distance might be transformed, markets would grow, and the nation could be bound by bands of steel. As Ralph Waldo Emerson said in 1844, "Railroad iron is a magician's rod, in its power to evoke the sleeping energies of land and water" (Porte, 1983: 213).

Public discussion of a transcontinental railroad began in the late 1830s, and by 1845 promoters like Asa Whitney were bombarding Congress with petitions and plans for a Pacific railway. After the Mexican War and the conquest of California there seemed even more reason for a transcontinental project. It was plain from the beginning that the federal government would sanction only one rail line west. That decision guaranteed rivalry between cities and sections. Every city – whether St Louis, Memphis, or Cincinnati – wanted to be the eastern terminal point for this iron Passage to India. The debate grew so rancorous that by the early 1850s Congress was deadlocked on the Pacific railroad question. Sectional politics and local jealousies made compromise appear unlikely.

In 1853 a solution seemed at hand. At the suggestion of several Congressmen, and with the support of Secretary of War Jefferson Davis, the gods of official government science were called upon to provide an objective answer to the route question. The Topographical Engineers were assigned the task for finding the best route across the West. Science and engineering would provide what the politicians could not. The railway dream now joined forces with the faith that science was above the political fray.

Between 1853 and 1855 six military expeditions surveyed the West. These exploring parties examined one distinctly northern route and several southern ones, giving rise to speculation that southern politics had influenced the decisions made by Secretary Davis and Colonel Abert. As fate had it, the Topographical Engineers could not reach a route consensus any more persuasive and decisive than the ones offered by the politicians. It was not until the Civil War and a northern-dominated Congress that the choice of a route from Omaha to Sacramento was made. And, in an ironic twist, the track laid by the Union Pacific and the Central Pacific did not follow any line explored by the Topographical Engineers.

It would be easy to dismiss the Pacific Railroad Surveys as an ill-starred, naive venture bound to fail. But, as William Goetzmann (1959) ably shows, we need to recognize the railroad expeditions as the first comprehensive federal survey of the West. The thirteen volumes of the *Pacific Railroad Reports* were an encyclopedia of the American West of the very kind sought by Thomas Jefferson. This was exploration systematized and organized yet with the aura of romance and empire. The *Reports* covered everything from topography and climate to geology and ethnography – all illustrated with detailed drawings and maps, many in hand-tinted color. In many ways the *Reports* were the fulfillment of what Jefferson had dreamed some fifty years before.

If Americans before the Civil War dreamed about the West in Pacific terms, after the war it was the interior West of the Great Plains and the Rockies that captured national attention. Railroad promoters, mining engineers, and ordinary dirt farmers dreamed their own dreams, giving fresh life to the Jeffersonian vision of the West as the garden of the world. Whether in Kansas or Colorado, this was to be a garden blessed with fertile foil and abundant mineral resources. The great national project now seemed to be surveying the West and then shaping it as a place safe for cows, corn, and capital. As acquisitive capitalism came to dominate post-Civil-War America, the West was imagined as the playground for ambition and wealth. If explorers only see what they are looking for, the objects of passionate desire now were gold, silver, coal, and rich topsoil. As historical geographer J. Wreford Watson suggests, "it is not what people actually see so much as what they want to see, or think they see." (Watson, 1969: 10) What was born out of those desires were the Territorial or Great Surveys – four federal explorations covering large areas of the West. No longer hunting for a Passage to India, these expeditions were in search of raw materials to feed the furnaces of industrial America.

The Territorial Surveys led by Ferdinand V. Hayden (1867–78), Clarence King (1867–72), Lt George M. Wheeler (1869–79), and John Wesley Powell (1869–79) were fundamentally different in conception and strategy from those pursued by explorers looking for routes to the Pacific. From Lewis and Clark through the 1850s, American explorers were looking for routes, particular lines to reach a single goal. While these explorers did make educated guesses about the country beyond their own line of march, they did not fan out to gain a larger view. The Territorial Surveys did just that. They often used geographic parallels like Wheeler's One Hundredth Meridian Survey or King's Fortieth Parallel Survey as ways to organize area explorations. Employing the latest cartographic and scientific methods, the Surveys sought to fill in the spaces between the lines marked out by previous explorers. And for the first time photography became an important tool in western exploration as photographers like William Henry Jackson and John K. Hillers lugged heavy cameras and glass plates to the most remote parts of the West.

The Great Surveys were often dogged by overlapping regions of study, conflicts between military and civilian control, and the clash of oversized egos. In 1879 the Surveys were terminated and the United States Geological Survey was created to continue federal exploration in the West. The men and journeys of the Great Surveys have never captured the public attention in the way that Lewis and Clark do or Fremont once did. Today only John Wesley Powell is a familiar name, one associated with his two adventures on the Colorado River. Because names like Wheeler, Hayden, and King have slipped from national memory it is easy to overlook the larger meanings in the Great Surveys. The surveys strengthened the connection between science and useful knowledge. Perhaps more important, the surveys were the final act in what many Americans believed to be the "conquest" of the West. In their reports the surveys offered a domesticated West, one where farmers and merchants could fashion prosperous lives. Wheeler, Hayden, King, and Powell found no Jeffersonian volcanoes, mastodons, or mountains of salt. What they did reveal was a West now part of the American Empire, a West that white Americans could call home.

That imperial West, the West made in so many ways by explorers' journeys, did not escape the attention of those Europeans who once had their own designs on it. George Canning, president of Great Britain's powerful Board of Trade and soon to become foreign minister, had always kept a sharp eye on the young American republic. Meeting with American ambassador Richard Rush in 1818, Canning expressed surprise at the remarkable territorial expansion of the United States. As Rush recalled it, Canning seemed "very much awake to our present and growing power." And Rush himself was astounded by what had happened in not much more than a decade. Lewis and Clark, the Louisiana Purchase, the Astorians, and a St Louis based fur trade that seemed bent on recovering what had been lost in the War of 1812 – these were events and forces that had already changed the future of the West. "Indeed," wrote the American diplomat, "we have sprung, as it were in a leap, into the rank of one of the great nations of the world" (Rush, 1818). For Rush there seemed every reason to celebrate. The passions, imaginings, and voyagings of the Jeffersonian Corps of Discovery had laid the foundation for the United States to become a continental power.

But what that larger Corps of Discovery found, described, and laid claim to did not promise equal benefit to all. Some passions destroy; some dreams turn to nightmares; some imaginings become dangerous obsessions. In his disturbing novel *Heart of Darkness*, Joseph Conrad laid bare the grimmer side of exploration. "The conquest of the earth, which mostly means the taking it away from those who have a different complexion or slightly flatter noses than ourselves, is not a pretty thing when you look at it too much" (Conrad, [1902], 1990: 4). The exploration of the American West was driven by dreams at once passionately held and coldly reasoned. Geographic exploration did not produce an unbroken line from fantasy to reality, invasion to conquest. Instead, the story was one of confusion and uncertainty, of illusions shattered and dreams unfulfilled. Journeys of empire, like those of Lewis and Clark and John Charles Fremont expanded and intensified international rivalries. Spanish officials watched nervously as waves of American explorers, travelers, and merchants swept through the Southwest. And to the north, the Astorians and later fur traders intensified friction between the United States and Canada – frictions that would not be resolved until 1846.

If exploration heightened international tensions in the West, those same journeys also troubled domestic waters. Explorers, whether private traders or army officers, carried with them claims of federal sovereignty over native people. While expediency, genuine friendship, and good judgment made relations between Lewis and Clark and Indians generally peaceful, the same cannot be said for later ventures. In the new American Empire – one forged by explorers, diplomats, and bureaucrats – Indians were expected either to vanish or meekly surrender land and power. Soon after the Louisiana Purchase, Jefferson wrote to Senator John Breckinridge making plain his continental vision. "We may lay off a range of States on the western bank [of the Mississippi] from the head to the mouth, and so, range after range, advancing compactly as we multiply." (Peterson, 1984: 1138). Such political imperialism, guided by explorers' journeys, promised just the sort of conflict Jefferson hoped to avoid. And territorial expansion also raised what was the central question in American life before the Civil War: would slavery be allowed to expand into the new western territories? Those were the very lands Jefferson hoped would secure the republic for future generations. Now the dream seemed a mean-spirited illusion. Eden bred only discord. Writing in 1820, a fearful Jefferson likened the Slave Question to holding a wolf by the ears. Whether held or set free, the wolf was bound to bite (Peterson, 1984: 1434). Jefferson's Corps of Discovery brought back many wonderful things, but they also helped put the wolf in the nation's hands.

Between 1804 and 1879 American explorers described, defined, mapped, and portrayed with paint and on glass plate the West beyond St Louis. From Lewis and Clark to Powell is but 75 years – a remarkably short span for so considerable an achievement. That achievement was built on the lives and journeys of men and women as different as William Clark, Sacagawea, John Charles Fremont, and Clarence King. Mountain men, professional cartographers, geologists, botanists, mule packers, and artists of all sorts were part of the larger Corps of Discovery. Exploration was always a matter of both imagination and reason. Henry David Thoreau, an avid reader of exploration accounts, put it best. "To travel and descry new lands is to think new thoughts and have new imaginings" (Christie, 1965: 265).

REFERENCES

Allen, John L.: *Passage through the Garden: Lewis and Clark and the Image of the American Northwest* (Urbana: University of Illinois Press, 1975).

Allen, John L.: "The Canadian Fur Trade and the Exploration of Western North America." In John L. Allen (ed.) *The Continent Comprehended* (Lincoln: University of Nebraska Press, 1997).

Allen, John L.: "The Invention of the American West: Fur Trade Exploration 1821–1839." In John L. Allen (ed.) *The Continent Comprehended* (Lincoln: University of Nebraska Press, 1997).

Bartlett, Richard A.: *Great Surveys of the American West* (Norman: University of Oklahoma Press, 1962).

Bowden, Martyn J.: "The Great American Desert and the American Frontier, 1800–1881: Popular Images of the Plains and Phases in the Westward Movement." In Tamara Hareven (ed.) *Anonymous Americans: Explorations in Nineteenth-Century Social History* (Englewood Cliffs, NJ: Prentice-Hall, 1971).

Brebner, John B.: *The Explorers of North America, 1492–1806* (New York: Macmillan, 1933).

Carter, Edward C. (ed.): *Surveying the Record: North American Scientific Exploration to 1930* (Philadelphia: American Philosophical Society, 1999).

Christie, John A.: *Thoreau as World Traveler* (New York: Columbia University Press, 1965).

Conrad, Joseph: *Heart of Darkness* ([London, 1902], New York: Dover Publications, 1990).

DeVoto, Bernard: *The Course of Empire* (Boston: Houghton Mifflin, 1952).

Dippie, Brian W.: *Catlin and his Contemporaries: The Politics of Patronage* (Lincoln: University of Nebraska Press, 1990).

Eco, Umberto: *Serendipities: Language of Lunacy* (New York: Harcourt, Brace, 1998).

Egan, Ferol: *Fremont, Explorer for a Restless Nation* (Garden City, New York: Doubleday, 1977).

Ellis, Joseph J.: *American Sphinx: The Character of Thomas Jefferson* (New York: Alfred A. Knopf, 1997).

Flores, Dan L.: *Jefferson and the Southwestern Exploration: The Freeman and Custis Accounts of the Red River Expedition of 1806* (Norman: University of Oklahoma Press, 1984).

Francis, Daniel: *Battle for the West: Fur Traders and the Birth of Western Canada* (Edmonton: Hurtig, 1982).

Furtwangler, Albert: *Acts of Discovery: Visions of America in the Lewis and Clark Journals* (Urbana: University of Illinois Press, 1993).

Glacken, Clarence J.: *Traces on the Rhodian Shore: Nature and Culture in Western Thought from Ancient Times to the End of the Eighteenth Century* (Berkeley: University of California Press, 1967).

Goetzmann, William: *Army Exploration in the American West* (New Haven: Yale University Press, 1959).

Goetzmann, William: *Exploration and Empire: The Explorer and the Scientist in the Winning of the American West* (New York: Alfred A. Knopf, 1966).

Goetzmann, William: *The West as Romantic Horizon* (Lincoln: University of Nebraska Press, 1981).

Goetzmann, William: *Exploring the American West, 1803–1879* (Washington, DC: National Park Service, 1982).

Goetzmann, William: *New Lands, New Men: America and the Second Great Age of Discovery* (New York: Viking Press, 1986).

Goetzmann, William and Glyndwr Williams: *Atlas of North American Exploration, from the Norse Voyages to the Race for the Pole* (New York: Prentice-Hall, 1992).

Goodman, George J. and Cheryl Lawson: *Retracing Stephen H. Long's 1820 Expedition: The Itinerary and the Botany* (Norman: University of Oklahoma Press, 1995).

Greene, John C.: *American Science in the Age of Jefferson* (Ames, Iowa: Iowa State University Press, 1984).

Hoare, Michael E. (ed.): *The "Resolution" Journals of Johann Reinhold Forster, 1772–1775*, 4 vols. (London: The Hakluyt Society, 1982).

Irving, Washinton: *Astoria; Or, Anecdotes of an Enterprise beyond the Rock Mountains* (Philadelphia: Carey, Lea, & Blanchard, 1836).

Jackson, Donald (ed.): *The Journals of Zebulon Montgomery Pike, with Letters and Related Documents*, 2 vols. (Norman: University of Oklahoma Press, 1966).

Jackson, Donald (ed.): *The Letters of the Lewis and Clark Expedition with Related Documents, 1783–1854*, 2nd edn., 2 vols. (Urbana: University of Illinois Press, 1978).

Jackson, Donald: *Thomas Jefferson and the Stony Mountains: Exploring the West from Monticello* (Urbana: University of Illinois Press, 1981).

Jackson, Donald and Mary L. Spence (eds.): *The Expeditions of John C. Fremont*, 3 vols. and map portfolio (Urbana: University of Illinois Press, 1970–84).

Karamanski, Theodore J.: *Fur Trade and Exploration: Opening the Far Northwest, 1821–1852* (Norman: University of Oklahoma Press, 1983).

Lawrence, D. H. *Phoenix: The Posthumous Papers of D. H. Lawrence*, ed. Edward D. McDonald (New York: Viking Press, 1936).

Livingstone, David N. and Charles W. J. Withers (eds.): *Geography and Enlightenment* (Chicago: University of Chicago Press, 1999).

Lopez, Barry: *Arctic Dreams: Imagination and Desire in a Northern Landscape* (New York: Charles Scribner's Sons, 1986).

Mackay, David: "A Presiding Genius of Exploration: Banks, Cook, and Empire, 1767–1805." In Robin Fisher and Hugh Johnston (eds.) *Captain James Cook and his Times* (Seattle: University of Washington Press, 1979).

McKelvey, Susan D.: *Botanical Exploration of the Trans-Mississippi West* (Jamaica Plain, MA: Arnold Arboretum of Harvard University, 1956).

Marshall, P. J. and Glyndwr Williams: *The Great Map of Mankind: Perceptions of New Worlds in the Age of Enlightenment* (Cambridge, MA: Harvard University Press, 1982).

Miller, Charles *Jefferson and Nature: An Interpretation* (Baltimore: John Hopkins University Press, 1988).

Morris, John M.: *El Llano Estacado: Exploration and Imagination on the High Plains of Texas and New Mexico, 1536–1860* (Austin: Texas State Historical Association, 1997).

Moulton, Gary E. (ed.): *The Journals of the Lewis and Clark Expedition*, 12 vols. (Lincoln: University of Nebraska Press, 1983–99).

Nichols, Roger L. (ed.): *The Missouri Expedition: The Journal of Surgeon John Gale, with Related Documents* (Norman, University of Oklahoma Press, 1969).

Nichols, Roger L. and Patrick Halley: *Stephen Long and American Frontier Exploration* ([1980], reprint, Norman: University of Oklahoma Press, 1995).

Oglesby, Richard E.: *Maneul Lisa and the Opening of the Missouri Fur Trade* (Norman: University of Oklahoma Press, 1963).

Onuf, Peter: *Jefferson's Empire: The Language of American Nationhood* (Charlottesville: University of Virginia Press, 2000).

Outram, Dorinda: "On Being Perseus: New Knowledge, Dislocation, and Enlightenment Exploration." In David N. Livingstone and Charles W. J. Withers (eds.) *Geography and Enlightenment* (Chicago: University of Chicago Press, 1999).

Peterson, Merrill D. (ed.): *Thomas Jefferson: Writings* (New York: Viking-Library of America, 1984).

Poesch, Jessie: *Titian Ramsay Peale and his Journals of the Wilkes Expedition* (Philadelphia: American Philosophical Society, 1961).

Porte, Joel (ed.): *Ralph Waldo Emerson: Essays and Lectures* (New York: Viking-Library of America, 1983).

Porter, Charlotte M.: *The Eagle's Nest: Natural History and American Ideas, 1812–1842* (University, AL: University of Alabama Press, 1986).

Powell, John Wesley, Grove Karl Gilbert, Clarence E. Dutton, A. H. Thompson, and Willis Drummond, Jr. *Report on the Lands of the Arid Region of the United States* (Washington, DC: Government printing Office, 1878).

Rolle, Andrew: *John Charles Fremont: Character as Destiny* (Norman: University of Oklahoma Press, 1991).

Ronda, James P.: *Lewis and Clark among the Indians* (Lincoln: University of Nebraska Press, 1984).

Ronda, James P.: *Astoria and Empire* (Lincoln: University of Nebraska Press, 1990).

Ronda, James P.: *The Exploration of North America* (Washington, DC: American Historical Association, 1992).

Ronda, James P.: "Before Covered Wagons: The Early History of the Oregon Trail." *Idaho Yesterdays*, 37 (1993), 5–15.

Ronda, James P.: "Dreaming the Pass: The Western Imagination and the Landscape of South Pass." In Leonard Engel (ed.): *The Big Empty: Essays on the Land as Narrative* (Albuquerque: University of New Mexico Press, 1994).

Ronda, James P.: *Revealing America: Image and Imagination in the Exploration of North America* (Lexington: D.C. Heath, 1996).

Ronda, James P.: "Exploring the American West in the Age of Jefferson." In John L. Allen (ed.) *The Continent Comprehended* (Lincoln: University of Nebraska Press, 1997a).

Ronda, James P.: "A Promise of Rivers: Thomas Jefferson and the Exploration of Western Waterways." In Robert C. Ritchie and Paul A. Hutton (eds.) *Frontier and Region: Essays in Honor of Martin Ridge* (Albuquerque: University of New Mexico Press, 1997b).

Ronda, James P. (ed.): *Voyages of Discovery: Essays on the Lewis and Clark Expedition* (helena, MT: Montana Historical Society Press, 1998).

Ross, Alexander: *Adventures of the First Settlers on the Oregon or Columbia River, 1810–1813* ([London: 1849], Lincoln: University of Nebraska Press, 1989).

Rush, Richard: "Richard Rush to James Monroe, London, October 1, 1818." (The Papers of James Monroe: Library of Congress, Washington, DC).

Vancouver, George: *A Voyage of Discover to the North Pacific Ocean and Round the World, 1791–1795*, 4 vols. ed. W. Kaye Lamb (Cambridge: The Hakluyt Society, 1984).

Van Orman, Richard: *The Explorers: Nineteenth Century Expeditions in Africa and North America* (Albuquerque: University of New Mexico Press, 1984).

Utley, Robert M.: *A Life Wild and Perilous: Mountain Men and the Path to the Pacific* (New York: Henry Holt and Co., 1997).

Watson, J. Wreford: "The Role of Illusion in North America Geography." *Canadian Geographer* 13 (1969), 10–27.

Wheat, Carl I. (ed.): *Mapping the Trans-Mississippi West*, 5 vols. (San Francisco: Institute of Historical Cartography, 1958–62).

CHAPTER FOUR

Environment and the Nineteenth-Century West: Or, Process Encounters Place

ANDREW C. ISENBERG

By the early 1980s, western historians had divided into two warring camps: "regionalists," who insisted that the West was a section between the Sierra Nevada and the Great Plains defined by aridity, metropolitanism, and federalism; and adherents to the "frontier" interpretation of the West, who focused on the process of change (prior to the twentieth century, for the most part) wrought by (mostly Anglo) settlers. The fratricidal debate (nicely outlined in Limerick, Milner, and Rankin, 1991, as well as Aron, 1994) dominated graduate education, conference meetings, and many major publications from its instigation until the mid-1990s. Each side grudgingly acknowledging the tenacity of the opposition, the frontierists and the regionalists have largely abandoned the contest, but they have done so without reconciliation. Rather, the armies have retreated to their trenches, and only the foolhardy, it is assumed, would venture back out into the field of the late battle.

Nonetheless, that is exactly where one must go to survey nineteenth-century western environmental history. One goes not quixotically, but of necessity. Nineteenth-century western environmental history inescapably forces one to revisit the frontier–region debate, because nearly all work in the field has hewed to one perspective or the other (and in some cases, both). Adherents to both perspectives, while disagreeing about certain fundamental tenets of western history, nonetheless have made environmental history central to their respective conceptions of the field. Because of its centrality to both interpretations, the perspective of environmental history offers western history the possibility of synthesis.

Environmental history, the study of the interactions between people and ecology over time, by its very nature calls for the integration of perspectives and methodologies. In the work of most of its practitioners, environmental history is a binary system. Human agency is one of the two parts in the system. Through a host of activities, among them hunting, agriculture, and industry, human societies transform the natural environment. The agency of the environment completes the binary model: factors such as geography, climate, and disease influence human societies. This interactive relationship between people and ecology has been described as reciprocal by Richard White (1985) and dialectical by William Cronon (1983). A few environmental historians have elaborated this definition into more complex models. Arthur F. McEvoy (1988) conceives of environmental history as the ongoing interaction among three agents of change: ecology, economy, and culture. Carolyn Merchant (1987) has added reproduction to the model as a fourth category of both ecological and social change. Fundamentally, however, environmental history remains the study of the interaction between human societies (whose constituent cultural and economic parts are complex, as McEvoy and Merchant remind us) and the natural environment (whose constituent parts are equally complex).

In the last twenty years, environmental history has been the signature field of western historians. Yet the prominence of the environment has masked the underlying division between regionalists and frontierists. In effect, frontier historians and regionalists have each focused on one side of the binary interaction that is at the heart of environmental history. Frontier historians concentrate on human agency; regionalists on the influence of the environment. In the context of western history, to study *both* the influence of people on the land and the influence of the land on its inhabitants is to be both a regionalist and a frontier historian. Indeed, despite the formal adherence of most western environmental historians to either the frontier or region interpretation, in practice most find themselves as often as not in the enemy camp.

Consideration of the environment was central to those who first established the terms of the frontier–region debate. Environment has been an integral part of frontier history since Frederick Jackson Turner's influential 1893 essay, "The Significance of the Frontier in American History." As Cronon (1987) has pointed out, the essay was environmental history in an embryonic form. The core of Turner's argument was geographic: it was the "existence of an area of free land" to the west of the Anglo-American colonies that distinguished the United States from Europe. Much of the essay centers on land use: the "continuous recession" of wilderness before settlers was, Turner argued, the dominant force in "American development." While few environmental historians would celebrate what he viewed as the transformation of "wilderness" to "civilization," they share his belief in the significance of settlers' transformation of the landscape to understanding the history of the American West (Slotkin, 1992; White, 1994; Cronon, 1987).

Turner's own conception of the possibilities of the western environment for promoting American development was largely agrarian. Even before the emergence of environmental history in the 1970s and 1980s, however, economic and western historians had elaborated on Turner's notion of the frontier to include not only agricultural land but forests and mineral deposits (Cronon, 1987). A more important innovation of post-Turner frontier historians has been the abandonment of Turner's triumphalism. Beginning in the 1970s, western environmental historians who maintained Turner's emphasis on the transforming effects of settlement often inverted his moral conclusion. Rather than celebrating the transformation of wilderness to civilization, frontier settlement became, in the words of Wilbur Jacobs, the "Great Despoliation" (1978). In more recent years, historians who work in this tradition of frontier scholarship – among them William Cronon (1983) and Alan Taylor (1998) – have wholly adopted neither the triumphalism of Turner nor the declensionism of Jacobs, but rather have viewed the frontier as a scene of complex changes in resource use by both Indians and settlers.

Regionalists, while equally dismissive of Turner's triumphalism, have assigned to the environment itself, rather than its inhabitants, the ultimate authority over the success or failure of "American development." The intellectual godfather of this brand of western environmental history was the Texas historian Walter Prescott Webb. Webb's 1957 essay, "The American West: Perpetual Mirage," defined the West not as "a shifting frontier, but as a region" between the Great Plains and the Sierra Nevada whose "overriding influence" and "shaping force" is a suffocating aridity. Like Turner – whose frontier thesis, according to Richard White, "conceptualized what was already conventional" (1994: 26), drawing on well-established nineteenth-century cultural icons of progress and peaceful settlement – Webb conceptualized notions of the arid West that had been firmly established in American culture since nineteenth-century travelers dubbed parts of it the "Great American Desert."

The writings of Webb and his contemporary, Bernard DeVoto (1934), exhibited a pugnacious, provincial pride. A residue of that provincialism rooted in personal experience persists among the regionalist historians of the West. "I know in my bones," wrote the western environmental historian Donald Worster in 1987, "that Webb was right." The West in which Worster was born and raised was a place where people tried "to wrest a living from a condition of severe natural scarcity" (1987: 146). In a series of books and essays, Worster, as Webb's chief intellectual heir, has made a case for Webb's regional history by infusing it with environmental historians' and environmentalists' concerns about the inherent limitations of nature and the unsustainability of capitalist resource exploitation (1979; 1985; 1992; 1993; 1994). Explicitly rejecting Turner's celebratory "process" in favor of Webb's western "place" of limitations and defeated expectations, Worster has argued that the arid West has dictated but two modes of production: pastoralism and irrigation. The arid environment eventually confounded even these endeavors. Drought destroyed open-range cattle ranching in southern California in the mid-1860s and in the Great Plains in the mid-1880s. Salinization of the soil and the exhaustion of underground aquifers foreshadow the end of the hydraulic West. While Webb maintained that aridity frustrated Spanish and Mexican efforts at settlement and left the region to more technologically sophisticated Anglo-Americans, Worster argued that the western climate was too severe even for Anglo-American industry; indeed, tractors and dams have only made the arid West more inhospitable.

While Worster has pushed Webb's regionalism toward an all-encompassing definition of the West, others have followed Webb's example by splitting the West into three or more subregions defined by climate and geography. In his 1931 study, *The Great Plains*, Webb divided the West into three broad regions: the tallgrass prairie, the semiarid plains, and the arid Great Basin. Similarly, in his 1957 essay on the West, he defined the states of the Mountain and Basin West – Idaho, Montana, Wyoming, Nevada, Utah, Colorado, Arizona, and New Mexico – as "The Heart of the West." On either side were the "Desert Rim States": the interior parts of California, Oregon, and Washington to the west and the western portions of North and South Dakota, Nebraska, Kansas, Oklahoma, and Texas to the east. The historian Dan Flores has extended this insight to its logical conclusion, arguing for the subdivision of the West into dozens of "bioregions," or what ecologists might call "biomes," regions characterized by a consistent floral, faunal, climatic, and geographic type (1994).

Where Worster saw a unified region, Flores sees significant variation, but like Worster, Flores has essentially elaborated on Webb's original conceptual formula. Indeed, despite the emergence of the so-called New Western History in the 1980s, at the conceptual level most western environmental historians have remained true to either Turner or Webb. In this sense, the frontier–region debate is merely the most recent manifestation of the long-standing division between those who see the environment as an *actor* (Webb and his followers) and those who see the environment as *acted upon* (Turner and his followers).

Both perspectives are inherently limited. If no longer Anglo-centric, the frontier remains decidedly anthropocentric, locating the source of environmental change in human agency. Flores's "bioregion" is more precise and sophisticated than Webb's "desert." Worster's "hydraulic West" (1985) is more intellectually engaging than Webb's 1957 characterization of western history as "brief and bizarre." Yet these elaborations on Webb's insight are ultimately no less deterministic. In short, conceptually, the terms that have shaped the study of the West for decades – frontier and region – are, when taken separately, analytically inadequate to understanding western environmental history.

In practice, to avoid both the anthropocentrism of the frontier and the environmental determinism of region, western environmental historians must remain alert to the interaction between place and process. They must be both regionalists and frontier historians, and happily, most are. Even the most combative voices in the frontier–region debate have, in their monographic work, incorporated both perspectives into their analyses. Because of the historiographical polarization of the field, however, this synthesis, while widely practiced, has remained unstated and often unrecognized.

A fully integrative understanding of the nineteenth-century western environment incorporates the perspectives of both process and place (Isenberg, 2000: 1–2). Frontier settlement was a series of ecological encounters. Newcomers (usually Euro-Americans but sometimes Indians moving into new territory) introduced exotic animals and microbes, and brought with them new land use systems and new ways of viewing the environment. While settlement was a *process* of change, *place* is also important. Newcomers encountered not only the indigenous inhabitants of the West but the non-human natural environment. The western environment was a dynamic partner in the encounter, not simply a passive subject of human contemplation and alteration. The environment imposed its constraints on both Native Americans and Euro-American settlers. Over several generations, nineteenth-century Euro-Americans reencountered western environments as explorers, hunters, farmers, ranchers, foresters, miners, and tourists. Each new encounter created its own set of relationships between people and the nonhuman natural environment. This interaction between process and place is the core of environmental history. By looking to this interaction, western history can deliver itself from its current analytical impasse.

Wildlife

According to hunters and explorers, wildlife abounded in the West in the nineteenth century. In the late eighteenth century, when Daniel Boone and his fellow long hunters traversed the Cumberland Gap into Kentucky, they found bison, elk, deer, bears, geese, and turkey in great numbers. During the course of their exploration of the Missouri and Columbia river valleys between 1804 and 1806, Meriwether Lewis and William Clark encountered dozens of different species of wildlife. Enjoined by their patron, Thomas Jefferson, to catalog the flora and fauna of the West, they carefully described the wildlife they observed. Mammals alone included antelope, bears, beaver, bison, deer, elk, mountain lions, and wolves. Not merely the diversity but the density of wildlife in North America astounded early Euro-American observers. According to some ecologists and environmental historians, the pre-Columbian West may have contained between twenty and thirty million bison, thirty-five million antelope, five million mule deer, between one and two million bighorn sheep, two million elk, and over one million wolves. The annual salmon run on the Columbia was an estimated ten to sixteen million (Reisner and Bates, 1990).

Euro-Americans interpreted North American wildlife according to their cultural lights. For some eighteenth and nineteenth-century Euro-American observers (and for some historians), the immediate temptation was to view North America as an Eden of superabundant wildlife. This view encouraged the notion that such superfluity could never be exhausted. Reflecting the late eighteenth-century rationalist notion that nature was a divinely ordered, productive machine, Jefferson believed that, despite the advance of Euro-American settlement, the extinction of any species was impossible. He contended in 1787 that "such is the economy of nature, that no instance can be produced of her having permitted any one race of animals to become extinct, of her having formed any link in her great work so weak as to be broken" (Jefferson, 1954: 53–4). When Charles Willson Peale exhibited the fossilized skeleton of a mastodon in his Philadelphia museum in 1785, Jefferson did not doubt that the species existed somewhere in the North American interior. In 1797, Jefferson conceded that while Euro-American settlement had driven large mammals from the Atlantic coast, somewhere in the West not only "elephants and lions" but "mammoths and megalonyxes" thrived. Jefferson's distinction between the settled East, where agriculture and the commercial exploitation of wildlife had eradicated many animals, and the pristine West, where a diverse variety of species remained, allowed him to believe in both Euro-Americans' progressive transformation of the land and the immutability of an abundant nature. Historians including Peter Boag (1992) and Donald Worster (1994) have seen in late eighteenth-century rationalism and its stepchild, nineteenth-century romanticism, the roots of some Americans' belief in an enduringly productive "Nature" in the West.

For others, the abundance of wildlife meant that the West was a wilderness, a term that, as the historian Roderick Nash has pointed out, means "place of wild beasts," a place of "bewilderment" (1982: 2). Working squarely in the tradition of Turnerian scholarship, Nash argued that Euro-Americans inherited long-standing cultural notions from the Old World that associated wilderness with the threats of paganism and savagery. Clearing forests and destroying wildlife, therefore, was an extension of both civilization and Christianity. Alan Taylor similarly argued that in western New York in the late eighteenth and early nineteenth century, "settlers' fears and sufferings" in the face of the "wilderness" produced "the excesses of their assault upon nature" (1998: 292). While Nash looked to Biblical references to wilderness for the sources of settlers' anxieties about the environment, Taylor looked to more proximate narratives: the stories that western New Yorkers' parents and grandparents had told them of taming the New England wilderness. Taylor maintained that these stories made settlers' wasteful destruction of such wildlife resources as passenger pigeons and fish a cultural imperative.

Whether they saw the land before them as an Eden or as a howling wilderness, settlers (and the historians who assumed their viewpoints) often saw wildlife populations as consistently large, both because they presumed the environment to be essentially static, and because they implicitly assumed that Indians' demands on wildlife populations were limited. Indian hunting was light, they argued, for one of two reasons: either Indians were too primitive to make greater demands, or they nobly sought to live in harmony with nature. In either case, both wildlife populations and Indians' harvest of game were presumed to be stable. These views tend markedly toward Turner's process-oriented history, inasmuch as they presuppose that changes in wildlife populations and in Indians' relationship to wildlife must be the results of dynamic EuroAmerican settler societies acting on a passive, stable environment and culturally static Indians. Shepard Krech, in his recent study *The Ecological Indian,* offers an excellent assessment of the changing understandings of Indian resource use (1999).

Wildlife populations in the nineteenth-century West were certainly large relative to Europe, the settled East, and to the modern United States. Consideration of western environments, however, challenges the notion of wildlife populations as either consistently superabundant or stable before the arrival of Euro-Americans. Rather than the static places that the idealistic notions of Eden and wilderness presume them to be, western environments were constantly changing. Wildlife populations were given to wide fluctuations. Unpredictable environmental factors such as predation, climatic change, fire, and competition for food depressed wildlife populations. For instance, while early twentieth-century estimates of the historic bison population ranged as high was seventy-five million, more sober analyses conducted recently by environmental historians, taking account of the environmental limitations on the population, set the upper limit of the bison population at thirty million (Flores, 1991). If wildlife populations were smaller than contemporaries' or historians' perspectives led them to believe, they were also less stable. The temporary absence of environmental factors limiting populations could produce a sharp eruption of numbers followed by a steep crash. For instance, as Arthur McEvoy (1986) has demonstrated, while early nineteenth-century salmon runs on the Pacific Coast were generally large, changes in ocean temperature, such as the intermittent warming pulse of El Niño, caused significant changes in salmon fisheries. In short, fish and wildlife populations of the West were generally smaller and much more dynamic than is often supposed (Isenberg, 2000: 11–30).

If environmental factors caused wildlife populations to fluctuate, so, too, did the influence of Indian hunters. Indians were neither too technologically primitive nor too innately noble to avoid causing significant declines in animal populations through overhunting. While most Indians sought to avoid overhunting because their subsistence depended on their restraint, caribou hunters of northern Canada, bison hunters of the Great Plains, and sea otter hunters of Alaska, among others, sometimes overexploited animal resources, according to several historians and anthropologists (Ingold, 1980: 69–75; Isenberg, 2000: 63–92; McEvoy, 1986: 19). The environment of the West prior to the first encounter with Euro-Americans was, in brief, complex and dynamic. The western environment was not a place of stability in which Indians lived in primitive harmony with nature. Environments were in constant flux, while, as scholars have shown, complex and changing Indian societies exerted their own transforming energies on the land (White, 1980, 1983; Brightman, 1993).

When Europeans encountered these complex places, they introduced dynamic new elements of change. The most important of these influences was the fur trade. Pre-Columbian Native North Americans had engaged in exchange systems that spanned the continent, but the fur trade with Euro-Americans enmeshed Indians in commercial exchanges that had far more wide-reaching influences on wildlife populations. By the first decades of the nineteenth century, Indians from the Ohio Valley, the Great Plains, the Rocky Mountains, and the Pacific Northwest were engaged in commerce with Euro-American traders that significantly depleted the populations of beaver, deer, bison, sea otters, and other animals. In the eighteenth century, French, Dutch, and English traders extended the trade in beaver pelts from New England and New York west across the Great Lakes, to the Upper Mississippi. By 1800, Indian trappers had largely exterminated beaver from these regions. Around that time, Russian traders introduced commerce in sea otter pelts in the Pacific Northwest, and Euro-American beaver trappers began operating in the Rocky Mountains. By the 1830s, the introduction of steamboats on the Missouri River had made possible the trade in bulky bison robes. Through the 1850s, Indian hunters in the plains annually supplied Euro-American traders with an estimated 100,000 bison robes.

These enterprises significantly depleted wildlife populations within decades of their onset. By the end of the 1830s, both the beaver and the sea otter had been nearly exterminated. The bison, estimated to number thirty million at the time of the Louisiana Purchase in 1803, had declined to fewer than one thousand by the end of the nineteenth century. Commercial predation drove several other North American species, including the great auk and passenger pigeon, to extinction. Seeking pelts and to rid the land of varmints, hunters and trappers reduced other species, such as the wolf, coyote, and prairie dog to near extinction. The extensive destruction of North American wildlife was not, however, merely the result of the pressure of Euro-American hunters, trappers, and traders. Rather, the combination of dynamic economic forces and a dynamic environment doomed millions of animals. The rise of the commerce in bison robes, for example, was but one factor in the near-extinction of the species; scholars also point to a prolonged drought that began in the 1840s (Flores, 1991; Isenberg, 2000; West, 1995). In the nineteenth-century plains, as elsewhere in the West, changes in the environment were a product of the interaction of process and place.

Agriculture

According to Turner (1893), the fledgling American republic of the late eighteenth century possessed a geographic advantage so unique and profound as to guarantee its prosperity. In a celebratory narrative that synthesized the dominant (if contradictory) notions of political economy of the nineteenth century, Turner argued that "free land" in the West determined the course of American economic development. Drawing on Jefferson, Turner argued that millions of acres of arable land on the western frontier meant that the nineteenth-century United States would be a nation of farmers rather than of bedraggled urban wage earners. Drawing on Henry Clay, Turner argued that the vast extent of the American agricultural empire stimulated the development of an integrated market economy. Turner, in short, equated agriculture, prosperity, and democracy.

Beginning in the 1930s, scholars have challenged Turner's facile assumptions about the relationships among free land, free labor, and a free society. Environmental historians have offered a new critique of Turner and his defenders: the process of transforming forests and grassslands into farms and ranches was not ecologically benign. Moreover, as settlers sought to tame the environment, they often found the environment taming them. Americans have idealized farming since Jefferson's time, viewing it as productive not only of crops but of moral incorruptibility and republican virtue. Ecologically, however, agriculture removes natural diversity and imposes an artificial, monocultural ecosystem usually built around the production of an exotic species. Environmental historians have catalogued consequences of agricultural production in the nineteenth-century West that Turner never imagined. The environment imposed limitations: exotic, domesticated plants and animals often proved unsuitable to semi-arid western environments. The environment was unpredictably interactive: by eliminating diverse, native species of plants and animals, agriculture facilitated the spread of weeds and pests. For these reasons, commercial farming and animal husbandry sometimes proved to be unsustainable in the nineteenth-century West.

The concept of utility dominated farmers' efforts to transform the landscape of the West. Beginning in 1785, utilitarianism was reflected in the hyperrational division of the public domain into six-mile-square townships, the subdivision of those townships into square-mile sections, and the further subdivision of those sections into quarter sections and quarter-quarter sections. As detailed by such scholars as Rohrbough and Opie, federal surveys transformed the chaos of the public lands into manageable and interchangeable commodities (Rohrbough, 1978: Opie, 1987).

Much of this land was densely forested; before it could be farmed, settlers needed to remove the trees. The geographer Michael Williams estimated that farmers cleared over 110 million acres of forests, primarily in the trans-Appalachian West, by 1850. During the decade of the 1850s, as a result of the expansion of commercial agriculture, they cleared nearly 40 million acres more. The vast majority of these forests were processed neither for fuel nor for lumber, but merely burned to remove them. In many cases, erosion and flooding followed deforestation.

According to the historian Peter Boag (1992), the ideal of the pastoral tempered the influence of utilitarianism. In the Willamette Valley of Oregon in the mid-nineteenth century, Boag argues, settlers sought to create a domesticated landscape that was simultaneously scenic and productive. This ideal of pastoralism bridged settlers' conceptions of utility and beauty. Utility eventually prevailed, however. The transformation of the landscape, once begun, did not stop at pastoralism and eventually came to include lumbering, commercial agriculture, manufacturing, and urbanization.

Utilitarianism was the guiding principle of irrigation, agriculture's most significant alteration of the land in the West. While the most extensive irrigation programs came in the twentieth century, settlers in Utah, California, and elsewhere laid the groundwork for those systems by the end of the nineteenth century. In Utah, the Latter Day Saints, relying on the church hierarchy to command labor and technological expertise, had over 16,000 irrigated acres by 1850. By 1890, 3.5 million acres were under irrigation in the West, and environmental as well as social consequences of reclamation were beginning to be seen, according to Worster (1985) and White (1995). Waterlogged soil suffered from salinization, and populations of salmon and other species of fish declined as dams blocked migration to spawning grounds.

Utilitarianism backfired in other agricultural pursuits. The ecological historian Alfred Crosby (1986) has noted that European colonists brought not only their grains but, unwittingly, their weeds and pests with them to the Americas, Australia, and New Zealand. In the late eighteenth century, according to Alan Taylor (1995), New Englanders who had settled in western New York raised record amounts of wheat until the advancing frontier of a fungus, "wheat blast," caught up to them. In the Midwest in the 1870s, farmers encountered an indigenous pest, the Rocky Mountain locust, and, by plowing up native grasses and introducing exotic crops, unintentionally transformed the landscape to facilitate its spread. The Rocky Mountain locust periodically swept through the grasslands, demonstrating a particular fondness for cereals – precisely the crops that settlers had planted. In an unmanaged environment, the locusts could find only a small number of their preferred plants among the diverse vegetation of the grasslands. Agriculture, however, eliminated that diversity in favor of cash crops. In 1877, for example, grain crops constituted 94 percent of Minnesota's cultivated acreage. The loosely cultivated soils were perfect nesting grounds for the locusts' eggs. In this altered environment, the Rocky Mountain locust spread like a biblical plague. Between 1874 and 1878, when a late April frost finally killed most of the locust eggs, the insects destroyed an estimated $200 million worth of crops, according to one study (Atkins, 1984). Locusts, like wheat blast, demonstrated that the process of settlement was in constant interaction with a dynamic environment that could impose its own terms on farmers.

Recent studies by historian Steven Hackel (1998) and geographer William Preston (1998) indicate that the interaction of Spanish colonialism with the California environment wrought similar ecological changes in the late eighteenth and early nineteenth century. European livestock populations exploded in California after the Spanish established missions, expanding from just over 200 head of cattle in 1773 to nearly 100,000 in 1805. Sheep herds grew even larger, numbering 130,000 in 1805. Many native plants were unable to withstand the grazing and trampling of domestic livestock. The introduction of exotic domesticated animals was thus followed by a proliferation of European weeds, particularly wild oats. By the twentieth century, according to the Preston, between 50 and 90 percent of California's native grasses had been replaced by European species.

If the western environment welcomed some new species, however, it rejected others. The eruption of cattle populations precipitated an equally sharp collapse shortly after mid-century. By the 1830s, Southern California's economy centered around livestock. Rancheros, who had appropriated mission lands following secularization, raised an estimated 400,000 cattle and 300,000 sheep, developing an extensive commerce in cowhide with Yankee traders from New England. After the discovery of gold in 1848, many rancheros shifted their focus from producing hides to driving cattle northward to the mines. Initially, they reaped enormous profits, but the lure of profit induced them to overstock the range. Heavy winter rains in late 1861, followed by drought in 1863–4 caused the southern California cattle ranching industry to collapse. The California historian Robert Glass Cleland (1941) estimated that 200,000 cattle in California died during the drought.

The disaster in California presaged the collapse of the free-range cattle industry in the Great Plains in the 1880s. The catastrophe figures prominently in western historiography in part because the cowboy of the plains is an enduring figure of the iconography of the American West and in part because it points to the limits that the western environment imposed on settlers' transformation of the land. Like oats and wheat in Minnesota, domesticated cattle were an exotic presence in the plains. Cattle were potentially an extraordinarily profitable investment in the 1870s and early 1880s, however. By the early 1880s, tens of millions of dollars poured into the plains, much of it from Great Britain, resulting in an estimated 7.5 million cattle grazing in the rangelands. Unlike the bison, which is an effective grazer well adapted to the cold winters on the plains, untended domesticated cattle proved to be unsuited to the western shortgrass plains. Blizzard in the southern plains in 1884–5 and in the northern plains in 1886–7, followed by a summer of drought in the north, destroyed perhaps 15 percent of the herds, according to Richard White (1994). In the aftermath of the collapse, cowboys came to resemble farm hands, raising hay to feed their herds over the winter. If nothing else, the humbling of this western icon demonstrated the power of the environment to dictate the limits of settlement and resource extraction.

Late twentieth-century readings of Turner and his frontier thesis reflected these limitations. As the historian Louis Warren (1997) has suggested, in its broad outlines, Turner's story of the disappearance of free land mirrors a twentieth-century parable of resource exhaustion: the biologist Garrett Hardin's 1968 essay, "The Tragedy of the Commons." Hardin's essay revolved around a hypothetical pasture. A number of shepherds living near the pasture have a common interest in preserving the grazing lands, but each has an individual interest in overstocking the pasture. The result – which Hardin interpreted as basic to human nature – was that the pasture was overstocked, the grass consumed, and everyone impoverished. According to Warren, in both Turner's essay and Hardin's model, free land fills up with settlers. As a result, both Turner and Hardin were ill at ease about the future. In 1893, Turner implied that, without free land, the US would become congested, impoverished, and undemocratic. In 1968, Hardin's prognosis was still grimmer: the inevitability of global resource exhaustion.

The collapse of free-range ranching in the plains in the 1880s seems, on its surface, to confirm Hardin's model: too many cattle on the Great Plains pasturage resulted in overgrazing. As both Warren (1997) and Arthur McEvoy (1986) have argued, however, the tendency that Hardin noted for societies to overexploit resources in the pursuit of private gain was not a generic human condition, but characteristic of resource use in capitalist societies. Moreover, the collapse of the free-range cattle industry in the 1880s happened not because of equal and democratic access to the grasslands. To the contrary, powerful ranchers enclosed large portions of the public domain in order to exclude homesteaders and small ranchers. Inequality, rather than equality, of access, contributed to the collapse. Such inequality was part of the extension of market capitalism to the West. The production both of grain in the Midwest and cattle in the plains was, according to William Cronon, part of a broader pattern of the commodification of nonhuman nature and the incorporation of the West into a larger capitalist economy. By "Reading Turner Backwards," as Cronon put it, borrowing the central-place theory of historical geographers, farmers and ranchers appear not as isolated settlers removed from the urban, industrial society to the east. Rather, the West was united to the East by a process of capitalist expansion. As Cronon reminds us (1991), ranchers' and farmers' very presence in the West was dictated by the economic demands of an urban society: the grain and beef they produced found its way by rail to the markets of Chicago.

Drawing, in part, on Cronon's work, Richard White (1999) has recently argued that the "spaces" that environmental historians study are not merely local. However geographically specific all places are, they are linked, through complex processes of culture and economy, to exogenous forces. While White targeted the national blinkers of most environmental historians in arguing for a transnational context for environmental history, his analysis applies equally well to the strictly regional focus of many western historians. Wheat in western New York and cattle in Southern California (and the pests and weeds that accompanied both species) were connected to English and Spanish colonialism. The locust plagues in the Mississippi Valley, salinization of the soil in California, and the collapse of the free-range cattle industry in the shortgrass plains were likewise products of the economic and political forces that had created commercial ranching and farming in the West. The consideration of place is equally important to understanding agriculture in the nineteenth-century West. The environment imposed its limits on the settlement process. The environmental context and consequences of farming and ranching were products of this interaction between the settlement process and the dynamic western environment.

Industry

In 1850, the United States was a third-rate industrial power. By 1900, it outproduced all other nations. Such remarkable economic growth depended (as it does in all capitalist economies) on three "factors of production": capital, labor, and natural resources. Perhaps more stunning than the rapidity of American economic growth was that it was accomplished by a nation chronically short of two of these three ingredients of prosperity. Capital was notoriously scarce in nineteenth-century America; until World War I, US industry depended largely on foreign investment. Likewise, labor was in short supply – a condition that largely accounts for the high levels of immigration to the US in the nineteenth and early twentieth century.

The US had an abundance of natural resources, however, particularly minerals and timber. Plentiful resources combined with a chronic shortage of capital and labor created a peculiar imbalance in American industrial development: a heavy dependence on resource exploitation. Beginning in the 1860s, American policy-makers, understanding the nature of this imbalance, enacted legislation that opened the natural resources of the West to industrial use. Land grants to railroad companies beginning with the Pacific Railway Act of 1862 donated 131 million acres – ten percent of the public domain – for logging or other exploitation to support railroad construction. The Mineral Resources Act of 1866 made available mining lands for $5 per acre. It was followed by the General Mining Law of 1872, which opened up the public domain to mining claims for nominal fees. The Timber and Stone Act of 1878 sold forests and mining lands on the public domain for $2.50 per acre. Through these industrial versions of the Homestead Act, the federal government from the early 1860s until the last decade of the nineteenth century funneled natural resources in the West into the private sector at well below the market rate.

Railroads spurred the exploitation of natural resources in the West, primarily timber and mines, as Euro-Americans reencountered the western environment as an industrial society. Logging companies built their own railroads to get access to remote forestlands. The first railroad in California was built in 1854 in Humboldt County – the center of the coastal redwood belt – to transport logs. Federal largess helped to

make lumber one of the leading industries in the US in the second half of the nineteenth century. Even before passage of the Timber and Stone Act, forests on public
lands were logged heavily. Until the last decade of the nineteenth century, according to the legal historian Charles Wilkinson, "federal timber was effectively open for
the taking, much as was the case with federal minerals and rangeland" (1992: 120).
Altogether, between 1860 and 1910, over 150 million acres of forestlands in the
United States were cleared. During this period, the timber industry was centered in
the upper Midwest, but production in the Far West was on the rise. In 1849, California produced 5,000 million board feet of lumber per year, Oregon about 17,000,
and Washington about 4,000. Fifty years later, California and Oregon each produced
over 700,000 million board feet; Washington produced as much as Oregon and California combined.

As Cronon (1991) has argued, timber resources in the upper Midwest, like grain
and beef in the grasslands, were linked to markets in Chicago. A similar spatial relationship ordered the timber economy of the Far West, where San Francisco was the
metropolitan center for the Pacific Coast lumber industry. Most companies operating in the Far West had their administrative offices and central lumberyards there.
Loggers were tied to the locality of their main resource, but like ranchers and farmers
they were also linked to an expansive capitalism.

Some forests withstood logging in the nineteenth century. On Whidbey and
Camano islands in Washington's Puget Sound, technologically unsophisticated
loggers "did little harm to the forest environment," according to White (1980). In
other places in the West, however, profligate nineteenth-century logging practices
had significant environmental consequences. In the redwood forests of Northern California, for instance, about 25 percent of each tree – the leafy top and the stump –
were left behind. Breakage from felling, moving, and decay destroyed a further ten
percent. As a result, only about 65 percent of any redwood reached the mill. When
loggers first came to the redwood forests and had not yet learned how best to harvest
the giant trees, the waste was closer to 80 percent. Trees that fell in inaccessible places
or proved to be too heavy to move were simply abandoned. Waste continued at the
mill. A circular saw made 7.5 percent of the tree into sawdust. Given the wasteful-
ness of logging, forest resources were quickly consumed (Pisani, 1985). In 1870, the
California Board of Forestry estimated that one third of the forests in the state had
already been cut.

Like lumbering, mining was an economic activity rooted in a locality but connected to far-flung economic processes. Beginning with the exploitation of gold in
California, this interaction of process and place remade parts of the West. Gold in
California was located in placer deposits, in which nuggets, dust, or flakes are exposed
among gravel. The earliest Argonauts appropriated the most easily available gold,
concentrating on panning in the gravel of riverbeds. The narrative and images of
these 49ers has dominated the popular history of the Gold Rush. It is generally
remembered as a validation of individual enterprise, as lone men panning by
streambeds were rewarded with large fortunes. For a few early and luck prospectors,
this narrative was true. Once surface gold had been removed, however, miners proceeded to placer deposits covered by greater amounts of gravel, and to a more invasive technology, hydraulic mining. Miners were no longer individual entrepreneurs,
but employees of large hydraulic mining corporations. The new method employed

water cannons to wash gold-bearing gravel through sluices designed, like a pan, to separate heavier gold from lighter soil. One or even two tons of rock had to be washed away to get one ounce of gold, resulting in millions of tons of debris washed into California's rivers. The debris caused extensive environmental damage by flooding and polluting downstream farms and clogging passages for migrating salmon.

From California, hydraulic mining technology spread to Idaho, Montana, Colorado, and the Black Hills of South Dakota between the 1860s and 1880s. Other mining technologies diffused throughout the West. Lode mining, unlike placer mining, required heavy stamp machinery to crush rock. Railroads were largely responsible for expanding lode mining throughout the interior West. Before the railroads, only the most valuable mines could be profitably exploited. It was too expensive to ship heavy mining technology overland to the mines, and then ship ore from the mines to smelters or stamp mills to process it. With the expansion of railroads, lode mining spread from the Comstock region of Nevada throughout the interior West. Likewise, the arrival of the Northern Pacific Railroad to Butte, Montana, in 1881, made possible a shift from the exploitation of the dwindling silver mines to copper.

The increasing deforestation and mining debris in the West had a curious cultural consequence: a rising interest in wilderness as a recreational space. Having encountered western environments as hunters, farmers, ranchers, loggers, and miners, Euro-Americans now came as tourists. According to William Cronon (1996), in the late nineteenth century, precisely as "wilderness" (a culturally constructed notion from the beginning) receded most rapidly, urban Euro-Americans brought their nostalgic frontier fantasies to the environment, creating the first national parks in Yosemite in 1864 and Yellowstone in 1872. In short, the commodification of nature in the nineteenth-century West created not only the industrial landscapes of hydraulic mines and cut-over forests, but the recreational spaces of the national parks.

Conclusion

If one's only tool is a hammer, goes a common aphorism, then every problem looks like a nail. In their historiographical work, many western historians have hammered upon their subject using either frontier or region as their only tool of analysis. In their historical work, however, western historians have tended to regard the perspectives of process and place as equally but differently useful devices in their analytical toolbox. In some cases, such as the drought that destroyed open-range ranching in southern California and the Great Plains, the perspective of place is apt; in others, such as the expanding frontier of deforestation, the perspective of process is appropriate. In most, such as the diminution of the bison population, environmental change was the product of the combination of human and environmental causes.

All environments create opportunities and impose constraints on their inhabitants. In the West, the process of capitalizing upon opportunities exacted significant social and environmental costs. At the same time, particularly in the arid West, the limitations of the environment often overruled its opportunities. The environmental history of the nineteenth-century West is the study of the interaction of these dynamic forces, of frontier and region, of process and place.

REFERENCES

Aron, Stephen: "Lessons in Conquest: Towards a Greater Western History." *Pacific Historical Review* 63 (1994), 125–47.

Aron, Stephen: *How the West Was Lost: The Transformation of Kentucky from Daniel Boone to Henry Clay* (Baltimore: Johns Hopkins University Press, 1996).

Atkins, Annette: *Harvest of Grief: Grasshopper Plagues and Public Assistance in Minnesota, 1873–1878* (St Paul: Minnesota Historical Society Press, 1984).

Barsh, Russel L.: "The Substitution of Cattle for Bison on the Great Plains." In Paul A. Olson (ed.) *A Struggle for the Land: Indigenous Insight and Industrial Empire in the Semiarid World* (Lincoln: University of Nebraska Press, 1990).

Boag, Peter G.: *Environment and Experience: Settlement Culture in Nineteenth-Century Oregon* (Berkeley: University of California Press, 1992).

Brightman, Robert: *Grateful Prey: Rock Cree Human–Animal Relationships* (Berkeley: University of California Press, 1993).

Bunting, Robert: *The Pacific Raincoast: Environment and Culture in an American Eden, 1778–1900* (Lawrence: University Press of Kansas, 1997).

Cleland, Robert Glass: *The Cattle on a Thousand Hills: Southern California, 1850–80* (San Marino, CA: Huntington Library, 1941).

Cronon, William: *Changes in the Land: Indians, Colonists, and the Ecology of New England* (New York: Hill and Wang, 1983).

Cronon William: "Revisiting the Vanishing Frontier: The Legacy of Frederick Jackson Turner." *Western Historical Quarterly* 18 (1987), 157–76.

Cronon, William: *Nature's Metropolis: Chicago and the Great West* (New York: Norton, 1991).

Cronon, William: "The Trouble with Wilderness; or, Getting Back to the Wrong Nature." *Environmental History* 1 (1996), 7–28.

Crosby, Alfred W., Jr.: *Ecological Imperialism: The Biological Expansion of Europe, 900–1900* (New York: Cambridge University Press, 1986).

DeVoto, Bernard: "The West: A Plundered Province." *Harper's Magazine* 149 (1934), 355–64.

Flores, Dan: "Bison Ecology and Bison Diplomacy: The Southern Plains from 1800 to 1850." *Journal of American History* 78 (1991), 471–82.

Flores, Dan: "Place: An Argument for Bioregional History." *Environmental History Review* 18 (1994), 1–18.

Hackel, Steven W.: "Land, Labor, and Production: The Colonial Economy of Spanish and Mexican California." In Ramón Gutiérrez and Richard J. Orsi (eds.) *Contested Eden: California Before the Gold Rush* (Berkeley: University of California Press, 1998).

Hardin, Garrett: "The Tragedy of the Commons." *Science* 162 (December 13, 1968), 1243–8.

Hughes, J. Donald: *American Indian Ecology* (El Paso: Texas Western Press, 1983).

Hutchinson, W.H.: "The Remaking of the Amerind: A Dissenting Voice Raised Against the Resurrection of the Myth of the Noble Savage." *Westways* (October 1972), 94.

Ingold, Tim: *Hunters, Pastoralists, and Ranchers: Reindeer Economies and their Transformations* (Cambridge: Cambridge University Press, 1980).

Isenberg, Andrew C.: *The Destruction of the Bison: An Environmental History, 1750–1920* (New York: Cambridge University Press, 2000).

Jacobs, Wilbur: "The Great Despoliation: Environmental Themes in American Frontier History." *Pacific Historical Review*, 47 (1978), 1–26.

Jefferson, Thomas: *Notes on the State of Virginia*, ed. William Peden (New York: Norton, 1954).

Jefferson, Thomas: "A Memoir on the Discovery of Certain Bones of a Quadruped of the

Clawed Kind in the Western Parts of Virginia." (10 March 1797). In Keir B. Sterling (ed.) *Selected Works in Nineteenth-Century North American Paleontology* (New York: Arno, 1974), reprinted from *Transactions of the American Philosophical Society* 4 (1799).

Jordan, Terry: *North American Cattle-Ranching Frontiers: Origins, Diffusion, and Differentiation* (Albuquerque: University of New Mexico Press, 1993).

Kelley, Robert L.: *Gold vs. Grain: The Hydraulic Mining Controversy in California's Sacramento Valley* (Glendale, CA: Arthur H. Clark, 1959).

Krech, Shepard, III: *The Ecological Indian: Myth and History* (New York: Norton, 1999).

Leibhardt, Barbara: "Interpretation and Causal Analysis: Theories in Environmental History." *Environmental Review* 12 (1988), 23–36.

Lewis, Meriwether and William Clark: *History of the Expedition Under the Command of Lewis and Clark*, 3 vols. ed. Elliott Coues (New York: Dover, 1965).

Limerick, Patricia Nelson, Clyde A. Milner II, and Charles E. Rankin (eds.): *Trails: Toward a New Western History* (Lawrence: University Press of Kansas, 1991).

McEvoy, Arthur F.: *The Fisherman's Problem: Ecology and Law in the California Fisheries, 1850–1980* (New York: Cambridge University Press, 1986).

McEvoy, Arthur F.: "Toward an Interactive Theory of Nature and Culture: Ecology, Production, and Cognition in the California Fishing Industry." In Donald Worster (ed.) *The Ends of the Earth: Perspectives on Modern Environmental History* (New York: Cambridge University Press, 1988).

McPhee, John: *Assembling California* (New York: Farrar, Straus, and Giroux, 1993).

Matthiessen, Peter: *Wildlife in America*, rev. ed. (New York: Penguin, 1987).

Merchant, Carolyn: "The Theoretical Structure of Ecological Revolutions." *Environmental Review* 11 (1987), 265–74.

Nash, Roderick: *Wilderness in the American Mind*, 3rd ed. (New Haven: Yale University Press, 1982).

Opie, John: *The Law of the Land: Two Hundred Years of American Farmland Policy* (Lincoln: University of Nebraska Press, 1987).

Pisani, Donald: "Forests and Conservation, 1865–1890." *Journal of American History* 72 (1985), 340–59.

Preston, William: "Serpent in the Garden: Environmental Change in Colonial California." In Ramón Gutiérrez and Richard J. Orsi (eds.) *Contested Eden: California Before the Gold Rush* (Berkeley: University of California Press, 1998).

Reisner, Marc and Sarah Bates: *Overtapped Oasis: Reform or Revolution for Western Water* (Washington, DC: Island Press, 1990).

Rohe, Randall E.: "Hydraulicking in the American West: The Development and Diffusion of a Mining Technique." *Montana: The Magazine of Western History* (1985), 18–35.

Rohrbough, Malcolm J.: *The Land Office Business: The Settlement and Administration of American Public Lands, 1789–1837* (New York: Oxford University Press, 1968).

Rohrbough, Malcolm J.: *The Trans-Appalachian Frontier: People, Societies, and Institutions, 1775–1850* (New York: Oxford University Press, 1978).

Schmitt, Peter J.: *Back to Nature: The Arcadian Myth in Urban America* (Baltimore: Johns Hopkins University Press, 1990).

Sherow, James Earl: *Watering the Valley: Development along the High Plains Arkansas River, 1870–1950* (Lawrence: University Press of Kansas, 1990).

Slotkin, Richard: *Gunfighter Nation: The Myth of the Frontier in Twentieth-Century America* (New York: Harper Collins, 1992).

Taylor, Alan: *William Cooper's Town: Power and Persuasion on the Frontier of the Early American Republic* (New York: Vintage, 1995).

Taylor, Alan: "'Wasty Ways': Stories of American Settlement." *Environmental History* 3 (1998), 291–310.

Turner, Frederick Jackson: "The Significance of the Frontier in American History." American Historical Association *Annual Report* (1893), 199–227.

Warren, Louis: *The Hunter's Game: Poachers and Conservationists in Twentieth-Century America* (New Haven: Yale University Press, 1997).

Webb, Walter Prescott: *The Great Plains* (Boston: Ginn & Co., 1931).

Webb, Walter Prescott: "The American West: Perpetual Mirage." *Harper's Magazine* 214 (1957), 25–31.

West, Elliott: *The Way to the West: Essays on the Central Plains* (Albuquerque: University of New Mexico Press, 1995)

White, Richard: *Land Use, Environment, and Social Change: The Shaping of Island County, Washington* (Seattle: University of Washington Press, 1980).

White, Richard: *The Roots of Dependency: Subsistence, Environment, and Social Change among the Choctaws, Pawnees, and Navajos* (Lincoln: University of Nebraska Press, 1983).

White, Richard: "American Environmental History: The Development of a New Historical Field." *Pacific Historical Review* 54 (1985), 297–335.

White, Richard: "Animals and Enterprise." In Clyde A. Milner, Carol A. O'Connor, and Martha A. Sandweiss (eds.) *The Oxford History of the American West* (New York: Oxford University Press, 1994).

White, Richard: *The Organic Machine: The Remaking of the Columbia River* (New York: Hill and Wang, 1995).

White, Richard: "The Nationalization of Nature." *Journal of American History* 86 (1999), 976–86.

White, Richard and Patricia Nelson Limerick: "Frederick Jackson Turner and Buffalo Bill." In James R. Grossman (ed.) *The Frontier in American Culture* (Berkeley: University of California Press, 1994).

Wilkinson, Charles F.: *Crossing the Next Meridian: Land, Water, and the Future of the West* (Washington, DC: Island Press, 1992).

Williams, Michael: *Americans and Their Forests: A Historical Geography* (Cambridge: Cambridge University Press, 1989).

Wishart, David J.: *The Fur Trade of the American West, 1807–1840* (Lincoln: University of Nebraska Press, 1979).

Wood, W. Raymond: "Plains Trade in Prehistoric and Protohistoric Intertribal Relations." In W. Raymond Wood and Margot Liberty (eds.) *Anthropology on the Great Plains* (Lincoln: University of Nebraska Press, 1980).

Worster, Donald: *Dust Bowl: The Southern Plains in the 1930s* (New York: Oxford University Press, 1979).

Worster, Donald: *Rivers of Empire: Water, Aridity, and the Growth of the American West* (New York: Pantheon, 1985).

Worster, Donald: "New West, True West: Interpreting the Region's History." *Western Historical Quarterly* (1987), 141–56.

Worster, Donald: *Under Western Skies: Nature and History in the American West* (New York: Oxford University Press, 1992).

Worster, Donald: *The Wealth of Nature: Environmental History and the Ecological Imagination* (New York: Oxford, 1993).

Worster, Donald: *An Unsettled Country: Changing Landscapes of the American West* (Albuquerque: University of New Mexico Press, 1994).

Worster, Donald: *Nature's Economy: A History of Ecological Ideas*, 2nd ed. (New York: Cambridge University Press, 1994).

Wyman, Mark: *Hard Rock Epic: Western Miners and the Industrial Revolution* (Berkeley: University of California Press, 1979).

CHAPTER FIVE

Engineering the Elephant: Industrialism and the Environment in the Greater West

DAVID IGLER

The American West perches on the cutting edge of the world's post-industrial economy. Recessionary times notwithstanding, new computer-based technologies appear from places like Palo Alto and Seattle faster than it takes to reboot a five-year-old laptop. The West's biotech industries evolve at a dizzying rate, offering new curatives to our immune systems and synthetic additives to our diets. Travel to Aspen, Las Vegas, or Monterey, and we participate in the multibillion-dollar tourist industry that draws visitors from around the globe, a "devil's bargain," in historian Hal Rothman's words (1998), between local prosperity and environmental despoliation condemned by Edward Abbey as "industrial tourism" (1968). Some western cities comprise industries in and of themselves – Los Angeles, for instance, which transmits images of California's wealth and beauty to the world via satellite and celluloid. Old and new industries alike profit from the advantages of the region's location, including Pacific Rim markets to the west and a constant inflow of Latin American laborers from the south. The region also continues to exploit the world's fascination with an imagined western past: rugged individualism and sublime landscapes translate into marvelous advertising scenarios best personified by the Marlboro Man. The rub, of course, is that large-scale industries have guided developments in the American West for a very long time, and yet rarely do we imagine a western past with industrialism at its core. The Marlboro Man *works* precisely because Philip Morris situates him in a landscape free from the big cattle companies and daily wages that structured the lives of real cowboys.

Americans benefit from the high-tech, entertainment, and tourist industries driving today's western economy while celebrating an Old West in which industry plays little part. To unravel this paradox we should consider *when* industry gained its foothold in the West. Specifically, during what time period can we mark the region's industrial transformation? World War II, according to Gerald Nash, provided the watershed event for the region's growth and integration with a transnational economy (1985, 1999). Aircraft, shipbuilding, steel manufacturing, and infrastructure developed rapidly and made victory possible in the Pacific theater. Wartime production brought hundreds of thousands of laborers to the West Coast, spurring urban and suburban expansion from San Diego to Seattle. In just a few short years, the "Nash Thesis" contends, federal spending and wartime necessity transformed the West from a "backward colonial region" to "an economic pacesetter for the nation." Furthermore, the postwar military-industrial complex sustained the region's burgeoning economy with accelerated growth in manufacturing, electronics, aerospace, and the service sector. Simply put, World War II industrialized the American West.

While few historians question the war's tremendous impact on the West, many others see it as *one* rather than *the* watershed event. Roger Lotchin (1994, 2000), Paul Rhode (1994), and other historians find important continuities in the region's twentieth-century industrial economy. Ample evidence supports this case. Irrigated agribusiness, with its novel production and marketing techniques, boomed between 1900 and 1920. Public and private utilities, banking, and the oil industry thrived in the twenties. Western manufacturing experienced appreciable gains during the thirties, and the Depression decade also witnessed the construction of the West's mammoth dams and water projects that promoted agribusiness and urban expansion alike. From this perspective, industrial expansion predated wartime preparedness and set the stage for the war's powerful impact on the region and nation.

Yet viewing the twentieth century as *the* proving ground of western industrial growth presents a curious question. Why would economic developments in the late nineteenth-century West have lagged so far behind the industrializing East? A growing body of scholarship on late nineteenth-century western industries rejects this assumption. Look back from the vantage point of 1900 and we find industrial activity and large-scale corporations across the western landscape. Look back from 1900 and we discover numerous watersheds signaling the region's industrial transformation – the birth of the Western Federation of Miners, the vast investment capital generated in the Comstock Lode, the completion of the transcontinental railroad, the rise of big cities, and the California Gold Rush, to name only a few. These events, moreover, only highlight the more subtle industrial trends, such as the worldwide migration of wage laborers, the integration of large western companies, or the steady consumption of natural resources throughout the region by various extractive industries. Seen in this light, the late-nineteenth-century West's incorporation paralleled and reflected those eastern trends commonly associated with US industrialism.

It's time to bring the West into historical discussions of industrial America, and, in the process, to reconsider industrialization's temporal, spatial, and functional components. Indeed, the American West provides a perfect setting to explore a topic ignored by most scholars of industrial America: the dynamic interplay between economic modernization and the natural environment. US industrialism both shaped and was shaped by the environment, and nowhere did this tension play out more prominently than in the American West. Western mining, timber, ranching, land reclamation, and many other activities held immediate and long-term repercussions for social and natural communities. These industrial sectors spearheaded a broad-based crusade to engineer natural landscapes and overcome environmental obstacles (like aridity) that conditioned western economic development. Across the West – from San Francisco to Denver, Butte to Coos Bay – industrial activity transformed not only the economy and society, but also nature.

Can we identify a uniform industrial process in the West prior to 1900? Some typical industrial characteristics stand out, such as the integration of production and marketing, economies of scale, and, as James Gregory describes in chapter thirteen of this volume, the expansion of the wage labor system. Other factors seem more particular to western industries, like the dominance of large landowning and resource-extractive firms. These characteristics notwithstanding, did different locales in this remarkably diverse region share the same path toward industrial development? This question lands us in the conceptual thicket of defining "the West" as a unified region. Perhaps, as historian Edward Ayers argued in a recent forum on American regionalism, "we have been thinking of regions in unnecessarily brittle ways. Maybe we should think of regions less as sheer geographic areas and more as systems of widely varying reach, power, and density. . . . Rather than trying to aggregate American life into as few regions as possible we might instead multiply boundaries to embrace more of the complexity, even allowing boundaries to overlap and cross" (1999: 43). Ayers's suggestion – to think of region in terms of flexible systems and overlapping boundaries – seems particularly fruitful when we consider transregional and global forces like industrialism and the environment.

Late nineteenth-century western industrialism certainly exemplified a complex process structured by "systems of widely varying reach." Economic growth and market relations unified that process, and yet distinct areas in the West embarked on different developmental paths that reveal the complicated nature of western incorporation. To understand this transitional period in regional and national history, we should embrace both the parts and the whole: the individual enterprises and locales that propelled incorporation as well as the larger contours of industrial change. An inclusive framework is necessary, one that incorporates economic and social factors as well as natural systems and ecological impacts.

Where Is the West in Industrial America?

Indebted to the pioneering work of Alfred Chandler (1977), most scholars depict the late nineteenth century as a period of rapid and stunning change in which corporate capitalism and new types of production and consumption transformed the very basis of American society. Corporate enterprises grew larger and they served as both symbol and primary agent of industrial change. The manufacturing system, in particular, led to new relationships between workers and employers, producers and consumers, urban and rural areas. Big factories – billowing smoke and employing continuous shifts of immigrant workers – represented the most common image of US industrialization. But the massive factory in and of itself fails to capture the many layers of social change as well as industry's impact on natural communities. By spotlighting the eastern factory system, leading scholars like Walter Licht and Alfred Chandler have also failed to account for industrialism's geographic spread and variations.

Simply put, the literature on late nineteenth-century US industry maintains a large blind spot for the American West. Walter Licht's recent synthesis, *Industrializing America*, surveys the growth of "a wide belt of industry that covered New England, the Middle Atlantic States, and the Midwest" as well as "new marketing centers in the West, and mineral discoveries in the mountain states" (1995: 117). If Licht now had the chance to address the complexities of western industrialism, he quickly dismissed that opportunity because western developments "occurred as extensions of the industrial core of the country that stretched from Lynn, Massachusetts, to Philadelphia and west to Chicago." The West is clearly peripheral to the *real* story of American industrialization, and, according to Licht, corporate formation in the Pacific Coast states "would not occur until the twentieth century and would pale in comparison to the industrial heartland fashioned a century earlier" (ibid.: 117). Like many historians, Licht contends that one "industrial core" transformed the nation during the late nineteenth century, rather than viewing industrialism as a sweeping force that impacted communities throughout the nation.

Chandler's *The Visible Hand* similarly ignores the business and industrial transformation of the West. Chandler's concept of the "modern business enterprise" – which emerged from the integration of mass production and marketing and gave rise to a new class of middle managers – was manufacturing-based and "grew and spread with surprising swiftness." Yet his representative firms only "spread" so far. Despite Chandler's attempt to chart the rise of this "most powerful institution . . . in the entire American economy," the westernmost portion of that economy and *its* industrial activities received no attention (1977: 285–6). In these and many other histories of American industrialization, close attention to regional variation is trumped by a preoccupation with big manufacturers ("by whatever route they took to size") as the most important form of modern capitalist enterprise (ibid.: 347). This focus has obscured two significant industrial trends. First, the manufacturing-based economy expanded across *all* regions, from the postbellum textile mills of Dalton, Georgia, to the factory-built plows that broke the Great Plains, to the thriving industrial neighborhoods south of San Francisco's Market Street. Second, modern business systems developed in sectors other than manufacturing, and it is in these other sectors that we can also find industrialism's effect on social communities and the natural landscape.

In the American West, the natural landscape and a seemingly inexhaustible resource bounty functioned as driving forces behind industrial development. The 1849 California Gold Rush established the pattern. During the five years following James Marshall's discovery at Sutter's Mill, miners extracted over $400 million in gold from the Sierra placers. By 1875, mining corporations has sifted and blasted free over $1 billion in gold deposits and $300 million in silver from the West's landscape. This resource wealth created unprecedented capital for regional and national markets, while the inflow of merchants and laborers turned the West into a microcosm of the world's business community. The simultaneous rush on western lands received less attention than the region's ongoing mineral discoveries; even though the land rushes arguably held greater implications for the region's economic growth. Settlers of modest means grabbed small plots by hook and crook, while capitalized investors utilized land laws and public networks to carve out large expanses of the western terrain. Rather than regulating access to the public domain, federal land policy produced an institutional vacuum quickly exploited by Gold Rush profiteers to accumulate western acres en masse. Industrial enterprise in the West secured its footing on this basis, quite literally from the ground up.

Land, resources, and natural communities provided the means for capitalized firms to expand across the west. West Coast timber companies (including the Union Lumber Company, the Pacific Lumber Company, and the St Paul and Tacoma Lumber Company) clear-cut large stretches of old-growth redwood, Ponderosa pine, and Douglas fir based on private rights to millions of acres. Highly capitalized mining corporations (utilizing both hydraulic and hard rock technologies) extracted the West's deposits of gold and silver through contiguous mineral claims, and quickly reinvested their profits in other land-based operations. The Southern Pacific and Northern Pacific Railroads, firms financed by government gifts of the public domain, remained the region's largest landowning corporations throughout the nineteenth century. By striking private deals with western industrialists, these railroads passed their bounty into the hands of other rising business enterprises. If the nation as a whole witnessed a dramatic rise in resource acquisition and extraction during the late nineteenth century, it was in the West that land and resource consolidation provided the largest stimulus to industrial development. These interlocking patterns of land rights, resource acquisitions, and extractive enterprises are critical for understanding the region's diverse industrial activities during the late nineteenth century. For a closer look at these activities and the firms that initiated them, we may start not at the west's industrial urban cores but instead on the margins and borderlands.

All Over the Landscape: The Pacific Basin

Geopolitical boundaries have always played an instrumental role in defining the American West. The Louisiana Purchase (1803), Mexican–American War (1846–8), Gadsden Purchase (1853), the purchase of Alaska (1867), and the annexation of Hawaii (1898) each extended westward US territorial boundaries. Though fixed and definite on one level, boundaries also reveal the fluid and dynamic nature of actual circumstances in borderland regions. At times, the West's borders could become hardened and politicized – for instance, to close the Mexican-American War, curtail Chinese immigration, or allocate the region's water resources among individual states. Yet geopolitical borders were also something of an artifice; Mexicans *and* Americans easily moved north and south, some Chinese migrants (with much greater effort) circumvented the Exclusion Acts, and state water agreements often fell victim to nature's own allocations. Industrial activities, too, transcended geopolitical borders in the West. Investment capital, wage laborers, technologies, and natural resources circulated freely within and beyond the region – indeed, the movement across national borders (or transnationalism) represented one of western industry's strongest impulses throughout the late nineteenth century.

The business networks that developed between the Pacific Coast and Hawaii are a case in point. Strong commercial ties transected the Pacific Basin decades before the California Gold Rush brought industrial enterprise to the west. Nearly a thousand vessels traded on the California coast between 1786 and 1848, for example, and their itineraries spanned the globe from ports in London, Canton, Callao, Hawaii, and Tahiti. American, Russian, French, and British merchants established a highly profitable trade in furs, hides, and trade goods alongside the Pacific whaling industry during the 1830s and 1840s. Hawaii emerged during these years as the hub for the Pacific's growing commercial network, due in large part to the hundreds of international ships that annually stopped over for supplies, laborers, and more often than not, sexual encounters. The California Gold Rush suddenly shifted international attention away from Hawaii to the mainland, but the islands' natural resources would continue to entice western capitalists once gold fever waned.

Enter the San Francisco merchant Claus Spreckels, who built one of the nation's largest sugar corporations between 1875 and 1890 by consolidating the California Sugar Refinery Company, the Oceanic Steamship Company, and the 40,000-acre

Spreckelsville sugar plantation in Hawaii. Like his contemporaries James J. Hill of the Great Northern Railway and mining magnate George Hearst, Spreckels was an unabashed empire-builder who viewed Hawaii as more than just a resource outpost. To his firm's Maui sugar cane fields Spreckels brought the labor and technological expertise that turned crop production into a massive enterprise. Hawaiian sugar exports to California surged from 25 million pounds in 1875 to ten times that amount in 1890. Between the islands and the mainland, Spreckels' corporation had successfully integrated shipping lines, sugar refining, marketing, and an international labor force (Hawaiian, Japanese, American, and Chinese) to rationalize economies of scale and scope. Spreckels typified the American industrialist who sought control over all factors of production, even if Hawaii seemed like the last place in the world to find his type.

We can draw a number of conclusions from this brief example. First and foremost, Spreckels' operation shows how transnational factors influenced western industrialism. It drew upon pan-Pacific labor flows, resource extraction in Hawaii, processing in California, and in the process, the firm created a business system unhindered by geopolitical boundaries. In these ways, the Spreckels case demonstrates a continuing feature of western enterprise as a whole – the drive to migrate across borders for opportunities and wealth. Second, the geographic region important to Spreckels' endeavor was not the "American West" per se, but rather, the different locales that allowed him to fashion, as Ayers writes of region, a business system "of widely varying reach, power, and density" (1999: 43). Spreckels' corporation forged new regional connections in the process. Finally, if we look behind Spreckels' San Francisco sugar processing factory as the end point of the enterprise, we can see that environmental factors conditioned each stage of the industry's development. Sugar cane and sugar beet production required large stretches of land in Hawaii and California – land cleared of native species for exogenous ones. This newly formed cropland necessitated terracing and irrigation to create a new hydrologic system. Spreckels' successful land grabs in Hawaii, furthermore, only followed an epidemiological onslaught that thinned the native population by 90% during the previous 100 years. The final outcome was one of sweeping replacements. Sugar cane production filled biological, ecological, and economic niches with pan-Pacific laborers, introduced species, and the basis of a transnational economy. The ecological changes in Hawaii, though easy to overlook, actually played a primary role in the sugar industry that now tied the islands to the Pacific Coast.

Mining the US–Mexico Border

Hawaii provides one example of these transnational and ecological characteristics; the US–Mexico border offers another case. "Are we afraid of an imaginary border line?" asked *Overland Monthly* writer John Aldrich in 1909, as he looked across the border and proposed a "New Country for Americans" (Brechin, 1999: 346). Even then, Mexico was hardly a new country for US investors. By 1902, eastern capitalists like the Guggenheims and William Cornell Greene and westerners like George Hearst, James Haggin, and D. O. Mills controlled 70 percent (over $500 million) of total foreign investments in Mexico, the culmination of decades of cross-border investments in Mexican land and natural resources. The border region between Arizona and Sonora comprised a fluid meeting point where industrial workers and natural resources flowed back and forth between the two nations.

Western historians have long recognized the Phelps Dodge mining firm as the industrial powerhouse north of the border. The company's copper mines around Bisbee, Arizona began to pay off shortly after the Southern Pacific Railroad completed its second transcontinental link at Deming, New Mexico in 1882. Between 1890 and 1913, copper extraction and processing soared from 14 million pounds to over 157 million pounds, due in some measure to the technological innovations in the electrolytic refining of copper by Phelps Dodge engineer James Douglas and geologist Thomas Sterry Hunt. In many ways, Phelps Dodge fashioned the typical American industrial operation in southern Arizona – company towns, company-friendly public officials, and a landscape dotted by towering smokestacks that discharged toxic emissions across the segregated neighborhoods of native-born Americans, northern and southern Europeans, Mexican and Chinese laborers.

Yet Bisbee's industry inhabited only one side of the border, as historians Samuel Truett (1997) and John Wirth (2000) have recently shown. Immediately south of the border in Cananea, Sonora, American investor William Greene began building "an empire of his own" based on almost four million acres of rangeland, timber, and mining claims (Truett, 1997: 168). The Greene-Cananea Copper Company (later acquired by the Amalgamated Copper Company) integrated both vertically and horizontally to include copper extraction and processing, railroad transportation, timber, water, and food production for the city's 20,000 residents. By World War I, Truett writes, "a vast territory on both sides of the international border had been overlaid by an interlocking mosaic of mines, smelters, sawmills, ranches, farms, and working communities, all linked to the economic fortunes of copper mining" (Truett, 1997: 163). Industrial production alone did not unite this border region. The natural environment must also be added to the equation – the common desert landscape, the flow of natural resources north and south, and the deleterious ecological impacts of copper production.

Copper production and urban growth radically altered the environment on both sides of the border. The Phelps Dodge operation in Bisbee created all the atmospheric and water pollution problems associated with smelting copper ore. The company also clear-cut timber from the surrounding Mule Mountains while its cattle herds overgrazed the hillside range; both activities increased the frequency of, and the destruction caused by, floods that periodically swept through town. Cananea, meanwhile, sent hazardous fumes north across the border and soon had to take out "smoke permits" for the right to pollute Arizona farm and rangeland with toxic emissions. The Cananea mines dumped tailings into nearby gulches, only for them to be carried by floods into the streams and town water supply. Environmental health risks abounded, particularly for those workers who inhaled poisonous gases emitted from the reduction works. By the early twentieth century, therefore, Cananea and Bisbee shared a common experience of stunning industrial growth, international market connections, and serious (though localized) environmental pollution. The two company towns were "neighbors by nature," Truett writes (1997), and neighbors engaged in the joint mission of transforming nature.

Engineering California's Farmland

Unlike Pennsylvania steel towns or Detroit auto assembly plants, the Hawaiian sug-arcane fields and the Sonoran desert seem like odd locations to chart the growth and transformation of US industrial enterprise. This is precisely the point, and historians would benefit by observing the machinations of similar peripheral places. Frontiers – both geographic and business ones – often demanded the technological, organiza-tional, and intellectual adaptations that produced successful industrial operations. The American West's distance from the nation's "industrial heartland" may have actually accelerated rather than delayed economic innovations. Yet a quick survey of indus-trializing centers like Bisbee and Butte (copper), Nevada's Comstock region (silver), Coos Bay (lumber), and Los Banos (ranching) may reveal few characteristics that were intrinsically "western." They shared some traits common to extractive industry and they often utilized San Francisco as a banking and marketing center, yet they evolved in a more local setting than the "Great American West." Industrialism was a national and regional phenomenon, but industrial impacts were felt first and fore-most on the local level.

Industrial agriculture shows the importance of the local setting. California agri-culture, for instance, took root in a radically different natural environment from the eastern or midwestern farming regions. The Golden State's Mediterranean climate (uneven winter precipitation and long dry summers) forced ranchers and growers to experiment with everything from crops and farm machinery to new labor systems, a pattern recently analyzed by historians Steven Stoll (1998) and David Vaught (1999). By 1890, Californians had fashioned a remarkably dynamic and diverse agricultural landscape. While some growers moved haltingly toward business innovation, the largest landholders leapt headlong into industrial agriculture and distinguished their operations with million-dollar capitalization, factory-sized labor forces, managerial organization (including lobbyists, engineers, and lawyers), new technologies, and ver-tically integrated production units. This latter trend typified the southern San Joaquin Valley, where the nation's largest corporate farmers and ranchers subjected the land-scape to industrial power.

If one had the financial resources and desire, the southern San Joaquin Valley *could* become an agriculturist's paradise. Yet its physical deficiencies seemed all too appar-ent in the late nineteenth century. Part desert and part boggy lowland, traversed by shifting watercourses that sometimes filled a series of expansive lakes, and beset by malaria-infested swamps, this landscape by its very nature troubled many interested parties. "Is it necessary or right," asked California's US Senator Aaron A. Sargent in 1886, "to keep forever these polluting areas, or can engineering science and public necessity obviate them?" (Sargent, 1886: 19) Most Californians wholeheartedly shared Sargent's vision of improving nature's handiwork. But private industry rather than "public necessity" would drive these changes, and two giant corporations, the Kern County Land Company and Miller & Lux, would reap the rewards.

Like many of the West's largest corporations, these two firms held business part-nerships, properties, and subsidiary operations throughout the region. The Kern County Land Company, headed by James Ben Ali Haggin, drew its capital from a variety of San Francisco business ventures and joint mining projects with George Hearst in Nevada's Comstock Lode, South Dakota's Black Hills, and, finally,

Montana's Anaconda Copper Mining Company. By the 1870s, this mining syndicate had also amassed a ranching empire that stretched across Mexico and the American Southwest. In the southern San Joaquin Valley Haggin secured close to 60,000 acres of railroad claims and purchased the surrounding water rights from small irrigation companies with the promise of cheap water for farmers. He next orchestrated the passage of the 1877 Desert Land Act and enlisted an army of "dummy entrymen" to help him grab more irrigable land under the Act's provisions. Within the next decade, the Kern County Land Company operated an integrated cattle and crop business atop a vast irrigation system. The Kern County Land Company was a massive firm even by California standards; by 1900 it had grown even richer upon the discovery of oil fields underfoot. These and neighboring oil reserves would greatly contribute to the state's industrial potential in the twentieth century.

Haggin's operation was impressive, Miller & Lux's was even more so. Henry Miller and Charles Lux arrived in Gold Rush San Francisco in 1850 and soon formed a meat wholesaling partnership. Cultivating strong ties with the city's leading bankers, the two partners began integrating the business backwards by purchasing herds of cattle, acquiring extensive rangeland, and developing irrigation systems to grow fodder. At one end of the business sat the firm's large slaughterhouse that fed San Francisco's burgeoning population. The other end of Miller & Lux's business fanned out horizontally from San Francisco into the Santa Clara and San Joaquin valleys, northern Nevada, and eastern Oregon. Through the artful use of public land laws and government agents, the firm soon owned over 1.25 million acres, though Miller suspected his company's strategically located riparian water rights allowed it to "control ten times the land we actually own" (Igler 2000: 169). With annual meat sales exceeding $2 million and a 1,200-person labor force to rival most eastern factories, Miller & Lux ranked among the *nation's* top 200 industrial enterprises at the turn of the century. Texas's celebrated ranchers may have produced more cattle than Miller & Lux, yet the Texans paled by comparison in terms of business modernization.

These two firms illustrate a primary characteristic of late nineteenth-century California agribusiness: Big is good, and bigger is even better when it comes to property holdings and the ability to transform the landscape with capital and labor. But place two large enterprises with competing developmental agendas in a valley with limited resources, add the basic fact of aridity, and the perfect scenario arises for cutthroat corporate competition. This situation played out between 1879 and 1886, when the Kern County Land Company and Miller & Lux battled over the Kern River's meager flow in three hearings of the West's most notorious water rights case, *Lux v. Haggin*. Like industrial enterprises throughout the West, these firms quickly turned to litigation when conflicts arose over who had the right to engineer nature.

Perhaps more interesting than these firms' legal maneuverings was their shared vision for engineering the landscape, an endeavor that San Joaquin Valley agribusiness firms continued throughout the twentieth and into the twenty-first century. The surrounding desert required irrigation and the swampy lowlands required reclamation. The meandering streams needed to fulfill their destiny as efficient water-delivery aqueducts while the shallow lakes wasted tillable land. There were holding reservoirs to construct, canals to dig, and extensive acreage to scrape and level. These tasks demanded capital, labor, and technical support, all of which the two companies possessed in spades. Through a confidential agreement to share the local water supply and divide the basin in half (the Kern County Land Company to the east, Miller & Lux to the west), the two companies proceeded with their engineering plans and the Valley's unregulated landscape gave way to industry's demands.

Corporate competition *and* cooperation therefore played a role in transforming this landscape, and it remained one of the most profitable (and ecologically damaged) agribusiness centers throughout the twentieth century. The Kern County Land Company and Miller & Lux did not represent the norm for western agriculture as a whole. Instead, a remarkably diverse agricultural economy developed from one locale to another, with growers in some regions (like Oregon's Willamette Valley) welcoming industrial adaptations and others (Utah, for instance) resisting technology and capitalist trends. However, the Kern County Land Company and Miller & Lux do symbolize the increasing power and presence of industrialized agriculture in the late nineteenth-century West, as well as the fact that agribusiness thrived on its ability to engineer the natural environment. Today's mobile irrigation systems, computer-controlled river flows, and multinational firms are not so much unique agribusiness adaptations as they are the most recent incarnations of late nineteenth-century industrial practices.

Trunks to Stumps: The Pacific Northwest's Linchpin

Few industries better characterized the West's resource-extractive economy than logging, and no place matched the timber resources of the Pacific Northwest. Forests make up less than half the total land base of Oregon, Washington, and Idaho, but, according to Dale Goble and Paul Hirt, those forests "largely define the region in the popular imagination" (1999: 411). This regional identity has a long lineage, at least since Lewis and Clark reported on their 1805 winter camp at Fort Clatsop by the Columbia River. By the late nineteenth century, William Robbins argues, these same Pacific Northwest's forests had become "the last frontier for a migrating logging and lumbering industry" (1988: 3). Transnational relationships predated this "last frontier." Most notably, Hudson's Bay Company built a water-powered sawmill near Fort Vancouver in 1828 that utilized a Hawaiian labor force and exported the cut to Hawaii. While this commerce hardly comprised a burgeoning transnationalism, it did anticipate the external capital, immigrant labor, and export markets that arrived two decades later with the California Gold Rush. Dozens of sawmills appeared almost overnight on the Willamette and Columbia rivers, Puget Sound, and Coos Bay, matching San Francisco's "voracious appetite" for timber and other resources. "In short order," Robert Bunting writes, "the lumber industry became the Northwest's commercial linchpin" (1997: 125).

San Francisco capitalists financed the sawmills, ports, and transportation systems that linked California markets to the forests of Oregon and Washington. By 1875 San Francisco financiers "dominated" Coos Bay's export economy and by 1884 the Portland *Oregonian* could refer to that port town as "a part of California" (Robbins, 1988: 13, 17). Colonial relationships with California, and later with St Paul and Chicago, drove the timber economy through boom and bust cycles. The big transition from regional to national corporations began in 1900, when the Minnesota-based Weyerhaeuser Timber Company purchased 900,000 acres of timberland in Washington and initiated a new phase of industrial logging.

Weyerhaeuser's move into Washington also sheds light on internal differences transecting the Pacific Northwest. "The term *Pacific Northwest*," Thomas Cox suggests, "seems more an appellation of geographic convenience than a label for an area with a genuine regional character and identity" (1999: 465). Oregon had smaller mills scattered amongst the less accessible forests west of the Cascades, and Oregonians remained wary of outsider financiers intent on exporting their natural wealth. Washington, by contrast, developed larger sawmills and ports to match its "development- and growth-oriented" business environment.

What we should recognize here is important to industrial activity elsewhere: industrialism unleashed complex layers of economic dependence and power even within a seemingly cohesive region. Bernard DeVoto's characterization of the American West as a "plundered province" therefore simplifies a far more complicated situation (1934). Rural areas paid tribute to urban centers, most of which remained dependent on San Francisco markets and finance institutions. San Francisco, in turn, sent capital east while retaining enough to finance its own developmental projects. Some projects empowered San Francisco, but others (such as investing in Los Angeles's growth) ultimately undercut San Francisco's regional power. Thus, industrialization initiated dynamic relationships on the local, regional, and national levels, making the question of who did the plundering and by what means less apparent than other factors, like the industry's environmental impact.

The timber industry's impact may seem glaringly obvious. The timber industry removed the landscape's most defining feature – its trees. And yet recent studies have developed a deeper understanding of this process on two levels: the connection to broader industrial activities throughout the West, and the more localized impact on specific ecosystems. On the first level, the timber industry harvested a resource vital to the development of almost every other western industry. Railroads required endless rail ties and timber for bridges. The mining industry consumed entire forests for mineshaft supports and flumes. Agriculture and irrigation demanded fencing and canal construction material. The towns and cities of the heavily urbanized West utilized timber even more than the hinterland industries, especially a city like San Francisco, given its recurring experiences with urban fires between 1850 and 1906. Therefore, timber extraction in the Pacific Northwest and elsewhere supported resource exploitation and industrial enterprise throughout the entire West. Timber proved vital to the region's economic infrastructure because it quite literally comprised that physical infrastructure.

The local setting is equally significant for understanding the timber industry's ecological impact. Due to technological and transportation limitations, lumbermen stayed close to rivers and bay ports during the late nineteenth century. The impact on riparian areas was tremendous, including clear-cut riverbanks and streams filled with debris, heavy erosion on land and heavier sediment levels in the waterways, and hundreds of splash dams that restricted salmon runs on Pacific Northwest rivers. Sawdust from mills, Joseph Taylor has argued, "literally suffocated" the incubating salmon eggs (1999: 56–7). The invention and widespread use of the steam donkey in the 1880s expanded these local environmental effects. The steam donkey allowed access to previously isolated timber in the hilly terrain, according to one contemporary account, by drawing logs "up through the forest, threshing and beating and groaning, tearing up small trees and plowing great furrows in the earth" (Bunting,

1997: 148). Clear-cutting became far more efficient with such technology, culmi-
nating in a landscape of butchered forests and fire-prone debris. Forest fires, once a
vital and regenerative component of the forest ecosystem, increased in frequency and
size. As Thomas Cox contends, forest fires now "burned hotter and more destruc-
tively than before, consuming organic matter in the topsoil and crowning to destroy
stands as the old ground fires seldom had" (1999: 466). The new destructive role
of fire in the Pacific Northwest's forests increased in the early twentieth century, and
perhaps ironically, the US Forest Service's fire suppression policy intensified this
situation (Langston, 1995; Bramwell, 2000).

Industrial activity in the Pacific Northwest therefore sprung from its own economic, geographic, and ecological setting. Timber extraction also reinforced industrial activities throughout the West. Washington and Oregon's timber industry, like
extractive activities across the American West in the late nineteenth century, did not
initiate environmental changes to the landscape. The region's forest and riparian
ecosystems had a long history of transformations caused by human actions and nonhuman forces. But industrial activities did bring new and revolutionary changes that
profoundly altered the relationship between human economies and nature's economy,
between exploitable resources and dynamic ecosystems.

"Supreme Possibilities" and Hula Dancers:
Excavating the Industrial Past

After 1900 the West experienced growth in almost every existing industrial sector
as well as the birth of many new industries that would have seemed unimaginable
during the previous fifty years. California led this economic trend, as Samuel N. Goldy
predicted in his 1903 publication, *The Era of California's Supreme Industrial Possibilities.* "There is no section of the world," Goldy wrote, "when weighed in the
balance with California that equals her advantages of location, resources, raw materials, fertility of soil, and climate. Political economists, statisticians, and historians
agree that California is an 'empire within herself'" (1903: 31). Goldy saw a bright
industrial future for the state, led by firms like his own, the Goldy Machine Company.
All that California required, he observed, was to "develop the industrial force of the
people . . . and California will then win a position as a world-power, commensurate
with her vast resources, formidable, indeed, but with kindliness to all who come
within her borders" (ibid.: 32–3). If the coming decades proved Goldy overly
optimistic about Californians' "kindliness" toward some immigrant workers, much
of his other prophesizing came true. California assumed the lead in the West's
twentieth-century transformation (due in no small measure to federal spending),
and by the century's end, the Golden State would rank sixth in *national* economies
worldwide. What Goldy failed to recognize was the level of industrial activity prior
to 1900, as well as how that activity developed differently in various parts of the
American West. Historians should not be so shortsighted, and western historians in
particular should capitalize on the opportunity to make industrialization a central
theme of study.

The critical intersection and interplay between the parts and the whole – between
the many sub-regions and the entire West – stands out as a profitable direction for
future research. Numerous issues could serve to bridge these spatial and historical

scales. Transnational dynamics, for instance, strongly influenced social, cultural, and industrial-political developments across the American West, including labor migrations, technology and capital flows, or the movement of foreign firms into the West. Some companies, such as Greene-Cananea Copper, migrated south across the US border in search of resources and industrial opportunities. Other industrialists, like Claus Spreckels, established the initial corporate ties in what would later become the Pacific Basin's vast transnational marketplace. These two enterprises represent just the tip of an iceberg, and future work in this direction may be less focused upon specific corporate enterprises and more concerned with the broader issues encompassed by globalism. The point is a simple one: western industries acquired their social, intellectual, economic, and ecological resources from around the world, long before globalism became a debated public issue in the late twentieth century.

Greater attention to distinct developmental patterns can also shed light on the relationship between local, regional, and national industrialism. The Far West's industrial economy, for example, sprang initially from the phenomenal Sierra gold strikes and the vast terrain seized during the Mexican American War. The subsequent rush on land and resources constituted a pivotal phase of US expansion and corporate development. The large-scale capitalist enterprises that soon appeared in the Far West developed clear emphases: innovative and multilayered approaches to resource extraction and processing, vast land acquisition to consolidate assets and overcome environmental risks, and large itinerant labor forces to engineer natural landscapes. Miller & Lux and the Kern County Land Company clearly illustrate these patterns. However, the Far West's developmental trends did not necessarily dominate elsewhere. Western industrialism assumed different characteristics as a result of many factors, including international borders (the Southwest and the Pacific Northwest), religion (Utah and the Great Basin), strong labor activism (the Rocky Mountain states), and so on. A greater appreciation for these patterns can enrich our understanding of the West's parts and its whole.

Given the predominance and continuing impact of extractive industries in the West, the intersection between industry and the natural environment will remain almost unavoidable in the coming years. From one industrial sector to another throughout different locales, the overarching task of engineering the natural landscape was remarkably consistent. Reducing this process to the simple "exploitation" of natural resources fails to credit western industries with much ingenuity, nor does it recognize industry's goal of creating an orderly and efficient landscape. The Pacific Northwest timber industry certainly harvested trees with the greatest possible speed. But those same companies also employed workers to construct roads and rails, build dams on rivers to hold logs, cut firebreaks, and construct mills to finish the product. Each stage of this process sought to replace complex interdependent landscapes with efficient systems of production, and each stage clearly involved human labor. Here we may find one of the most important topics for future inquiry. In some ways, those workers who labored for the West's extractive industries represented the most direct link between the natural environment and industrial America. Richard White has argued this point most succinctly: "Labor rather than 'conquering' nature involves human beings with the world so thoroughly that they can never be disentangled" (1995: 7). Making the desert "blossom as a rose" for industrial agriculture or razing the hills of Seattle to make a more efficient city placed workers in direct contact with the environment, and these endeavors were part and parcel of western large-scale enterprise.

Our present high-tech, information age economy takes great pains to downplay the interdependencies between new industries and the natural environment. Silicon Valley industries seem so clean and healthy – just observe the Lycra-bound executives joyfully peddling their way up Palo Alto's Sand Hill Road on any given morning – until one considers the concentrated chemical byproducts of microchip production or Silicon Valley firms' assault on open space during the past two decades. The West's leading industries, including biotechnology, tourism, agribusiness, and entertainment appear equally ecofriendly because they attempt to engineer nature in aesthetically pleasing ways. The same cannot be said about the extractive industries that dominated the western past or the manufacturers that epitomized the nation's industrial transformation. But, then as now, by isolating the environmental impacts from industry's advance we have created what William Cronon has called in a slightly different context, a "landscape of obscured connection" (1991: 340). The new industries dodge much criticism because they appear to transcend the environmental constraints and repercussions of the past.

Efforts to reconcile this disconnect have increased in recent years. From Rachel Carson's call to arms against the chemical pesticide industry (1962) to grassroots movements for environmental justice, people inside and outside institutions of power are illuminating the many ways industrial production impacts the environment in which we live. The American West has a lot to come to terms with in this regard, and people like Kristi Hager of Missoula, Montana see no time to waste. On the bright Sunday morning of July 9, 2000, Hager and over 100 like-minded individuals strapped on their hula skirts and began swaying back and forth to the tune "Cool Water." It was a short five-minute dance with just a brief encore, performed far from any theater or stage. The performance, strangely enough, had a great deal to do with industrial and environmental legacies, and the setting could have hardly been more appropriate. Hager's hula dancers swayed at the edge of Butte, Montana's Berkeley Pit, also known as the epicenter of the nation's largest Super Fund cleanup site.

The rim of the Berkeley Pit is the place to stand if one desires a stunning perspective on the West's industrial past. Though abandoned by its owner-operator Atlantic Richfield (ARCO) in 1979, the Pit currently contains 30 billion gallons of maroon-colored water laced with sulfuric acid and a gritty brew of heavy metals (including zinc, nickel, cadmium, and arsenic). Run-off into the Pit from the adjacent, long defunct copper mine shafts contributes an additional half million gallons each day. The Pit itself dates back to 1955, when copper mining in Butte transitioned from core extraction through mine shafts to the open pit method. The environmental (and health) costs of copper extraction go back to the creation of the Anaconda Copper Mining Company in the 1870s. Between then and now, copper mining around Butte has exacted a deadly toll on every feature of the landscape – streams and soils, fish and fowl, workers and their families. The cleanup cost today is almost unimaginable. Few people even chance a guess at what "cleanup" would entail. Those details were likely far from Kristi Hager's mind as she danced to "Cool Water" above the Pit. Instead, she simply hoped "to create a lot of good will for a place that needs all the positive feelings it can get" (MacCartney, 2000). Connie Poten, another dancer, remarked that "maybe we'll take (the dance) on the road to all the copper mines" (MacCartney, 2000). What this would accomplish is anyone's guess. But it just may bring some attention to the environmental legacies that are a product of the West's industrial production over the past 150 years.

As cleanup proceeds in the following decades, we have the opportunity to influence the meaning of sites like the Berkeley Pit. How should we remember such places as part of our history? A strong argument can be made for preserving many features of the Butte landscape as one massive historical landmark. As a landmark, the Berkeley Pit, mine shafts, and abandoned buildings could commemorate the countless individuals who labored and died around Butte, a place once known as the "Richest Hill on Earth." As a landmark, this area would also testify to the ways copper mining and other western industries contributed to the nation's industrial revolution. The Butte landmark, warts and all, would stand as a tribute to western industrialism – heroic to some viewers, shocking to others, but important to all. In the meanwhile, hula dancers and Marlboro Men alike will continue to perform their homage to the West's industrial past. It is our duty as teachers, writers, readers, and citizens to assess the multiple meanings embedded in sites like the Berkeley Pit, and to keep these sites a visible part of the West's – and nation's – historical legacy.

REFERENCES

Abbey, Edward: *Desert Solitaire: A Season in the Wilderness* (New York: McGraw-Hill, 1968).

Adelman, Jeremy and Stephen Aron: "From Borderlands to Borders: Empires, Nation-States, and the Peoples in Between in North American History." *American Historical Review* 104 (June 1999), 814–41.

Adler, Jacob: "The Oceanic Steamship Company: A Link in Claus Spreckels' Hawaiian Sugar Empire." *Pacific Historical Review* 29 (1960), 257–69.

Adler, Jacob: *Claus Spreckels: The Sugar King in Hawaii* (Honolulu: University of Hawaii Press, 1966).

Aldrich, John. "A New Country for Americans: The West Coast of Mexico." *Overland Monthly* 54 (August 1909), 216–24.

Aron, Stephen: *How the West Was Lost: The Transformation of Kentucky from Daniel Boone to Henry Clay* (Baltimore: Johns Hopkins University Press, 1996).

Ayers, Edward: "A Valley Divided." *Humanities* 20 (July/August 1999), 43.

Barron, Hal S.: *Mixed Harvest: The Second Great Transformation in the Rural North, 1870–1930* (Chapel Hill: University of North Carolina Press, 1997).

Bramwell, Lincoln: "Aggressive Fire Suppression: The US Forest Service's 10 AM Policy and Interagency Hotshot Fire Crews." (MA thesis: University of Utah, 2000).

Brechin, Gray: *Imperial San Francisco: Urban Power, Earthly Ruin* (Berkeley: University of California Press, 1999).

Bunting, Robert: *The Pacific Raincoast: Environment and Culture in an American Eden, 1778–1900* (Lawrence: University Press of Kansas, 1997).

Carson, Rachel: *Silent Spring* (Boston: Houghton Mifflin, 1962).

Chandler, Alfred D.: *The Visible Hand: The Managerial Revolution in American Business* (Cambridge, MA: Harvard University Press, 1977).

Cleland, Robert Glass: *A History of Phelps Dodge, 1834–1950* (New York: Alfred A. Knopf, 1952).

Cobb, James C.: *Industrialization and Southern Society, 1877–1984* (Lexington: University of Kentucky Press, 1984).

Cochran, Thomas: *Two Hundred Years of American Business* (New York: Oxford University Press, 1977).

Cochran, Thomas: *Frontiers of Change: Early Industrialism in America* (New York: Oxford University Press, 1981).

Cornford, Daniel " 'We all live more like brutes than humans': Labor and Capital in the Gold Rush." In James J. Rawls and Richard J. Orsi (eds.) *A Golden State: Mining and Economic Development in Gold Rush California in California History* (Berkeley: University of California Press, 1998/99).

Cox, Thomas R.: *Mills and Markets: A History of the Pacific Coast Lumber Industry to 1900* (Seattle: University of Washington Press, 1974).

Cox, Thomas R.: "Changing Forests, Changing Needs: Using the Pacific Northwest's Westside Forests, Past and Present." In Dale D. Goble and Paul W. Hirt (eds.) *Northwest Lands, Northwest Peoples* (Seattle: University of Washington Press, 1999).

Cronon, William: *Nature's Metropolis: Chicago and the Great West* (New York: W. W. Norton and Company, 1991).

DeVoto, Bernard: "The West: A Plundered Province." *Harper's* 169 (1934), 355–64.

Freyfogle, Eric: "*Lux v. Haggin* and the Common Law Burden of Modern Water Law." *University of Colorado Law Review* 57 (Spring 1986), 485–525.

Flamming, Douglas: *Creating the Modern South: Millhands and Managers in Dalton, Georgia, 1884–1984* (Chapel Hill: University of North Carolina Press, 1992).

Gates, Paul Wallace: *Landlords and Tenants on the Prairie Frontier: Studies in American Land Policy* (Ithaca: Cornell University Press, 1973).

Gates, Paul Wallace: *Land and Law in California: Essays on Land Policies* (Ames: Iowa State University Press, 1991).

Goble, Dale D. and Paul W. Hirt (eds.): *Northwest Lands, Northwest Peoples: Readings in Environmental History* (Seattle: University of Washington Press, 1999).

Goldy, Samuel N.: *The Era of California's Supreme Industrial Possibilities* (San Jose: Press of Muirson and Wright, 1903).

Hampton, Edgar L.: "A Day in Camp." *Seattle Mail and Herald*, September 6, 1902.

Igler, David: "When is a River not a River? Reclaiming Nature's Disorder in *Lux v. Haggin*." *Environmental History* 1 (April 1996), 52–69.

Igler, David: "The Industrial West: Region and Nation in the Late Nineteenth Century." *Pacific Historical Review* 69 (2000), 159–92.

Igler, David: *Industrial Cowboys: Miller & Lux and the Transformation of the Far West, 1850–1920* (Berkeley: University of California Press, 2001).

John, Richard R.: "Elaborations, Revisions, Dissents: Alfred D. Chandler, Jr.'s, *The Visible Hand* after Twenty Years." *Business History Review* 71 (Summer 1997), 151–200.

Jung, Maureen A.: "Capitalism Comes to the Diggings: From Gold-Rush Adventure to Corporate Enterprise." In James J. Rawls and Richard J. Orsi (eds.) *A Golden State: Mining and Economic Development in Gold Rush California in California History* (Berkeley: University of California Press, 1998/99).

King, Joseph E.: *A Mine to Make a Mine: Financing the Colorado Mining Industry, 1859–1902* (College Station: Texas A&M University Press, 1977).

Lamoreaux, Naomi R. and Daniel M. G. Raff (eds.): *Coordination and Information: Historical Perspectives on the Organization of Enterprise* (Chicago: University of Chicago Press, 1994).

Langston, Nancy: *Forest Dreams, Forest Nightmares: The Paradox of Old Growth in the Inland West* (Seattle: University of Washington Press, 1995).

Lawrence, William D.: "Henry Miller and the San Joaquin Valley." (MA thesis: University of California, Berkeley, 1933).

Licht, Walter: *Industrializing America: The Nineteenth Century* (Baltimore: Johns Hopkins University Press, 1995).

Liebman, Ellen: *California Farmland: A History of Large Agricultural Landholdings* (Totowa: Rowman and Allanheld, 1983).

Lotchin, Roger W.: "California Cities and the Hurricane of Change: World War II in the San Francisco, Los Angeles, and San Diego Metropolitan Areas." *Pacific Historical Review* 63 (August 1994): 393–420.

Lotchin, Roger W.: *The Way We Really Were: The Golden State in the Second Great War* (Urbana: University of Illinois Press, 2000).

MacCartney, Leslie: "Hula Dancers Perform at Lip of Berkeley Pit." *The Montana Standard* (July 11, 2000).

McGerr, Michael: "The Price of the 'New Transnational History.'" *American Historical Review* 96 (1991), 1031–72.

McNeill, J. R.: *Something New Under the Sun: An Environmental History of the Twentieth-Century World* (New York: W. W. Norton, 2000).

McWilliams, Carey: *Factories in the Field: The Story of Migratory Farm Labor in California* (Boston: Little, Brown and Company, 1939).

Malone, Michael P.: *The Battle for Butte: Mining and Politics on the Northern Frontier, 1864–1906* (Helena: Montana Historical Society Press, 1995).

May, Dean L.: *Three Frontiers: Family, Land, and Society in the American West, 1850–1900* (Cambridge: Cambridge University Press, 1994).

Miller, M. Catherine: *Flooding the Courtrooms: Law and Water in the Far West* (Lincoln: University of Nebraska Press, 1993).

Miller, Henry: "Autobiographical Statement." (Hubert Howe Bancroft Collection: Bancroft Library, University of California, Berkeley).

Nash, Gerald: *The American West Transformed: The Impact of the Second World War* (Bloomington: Indiana University Press, 1985).

Nash, Gerald: "A Veritable Revolution: The Global Economic Significance of the California Gold Rush." In James J. Rawls and Richard J. Orsi (eds.) *A Golden State: Mining and Economic Development in Gold Rush California in California History* (Berkeley: University of California Press, 1998/99).

Nash, Gerald: *The Federal Landscape: An Economic History of the Twentieth-Century West* (Tucson: University of Arizona Press, 1999).

Navin, Thomas R.: "The 500 Largest American Industrials in 1917." *Business History Review* 44 (1970), 360–86.

Niemi, Albert, Jr.: *State and Regional Patterns in American Manufacturing* (Westport: Greenwood Press, 1974).

Ogden, Adele: "Trading Vessels on the California Coast, 1786 to 1848." (Ogden Collection: Bancroft Library, University of California, Berkeley).

Opie, John: *The Law of the Land: Two Hundred Years of American Farmland Policy* (Lincoln: University of Nebraska Press, 1987).

Osborn, John: *Railroads and Clearcuts* (Spokane: Keokee Publishers, 1995).

Paul, Rodman: *California Gold: The Beginning of Mining in the Far West* (Cambridge, MA: Harvard University Press, 1947).

Paul, Rodman: *The Far West and the Great Plains in Transition, 1859–1900* (New York, Harper & Row, 1988).

Peterson, Richard: *The Bonanza Kings: The Social Origins and Business Behavior of Western Mining Entrepreneurs, 1870–1900* (Lincoln: University of Nebraska Press, 1977).

Pisani, Donald: *From the Family Farm to Agribusiness: The Irrigation Crusade in California and the West, 1850–1931* (Berkeley: University of California Press, 1983).

Preston, William: *Vanishing Landscapes: Land and Life in the Tulare Lake Basin* (Berkeley: University of California Press, 1981).

Rawls, James J. and Richard J. Orsi (eds.): *A Golden State: Mining and Economic Development in Gold Rush California in California History* (Berkeley: University of California Press, 1998/99).

Rhode, Paul: "The Nash Thesis Revisited: An Economic Historian's View." *Pacific Historical Review* 63 (August 1994) 363–92.

Robbins, Jim: "Butte Breaks New Ground to Mop Up a World-Class Mess." *The New York Times* (July 21, 1998).

Robbins, William G.: *Hard Times in Paradise: Coos Bay, Oregon, 1850–1986* (Seattle: University of Washington Press, 1988).

Robbins, William G.: *Colony and Empire: The Capitalist Transformation of the American West* (Lawrence, Kansas: University Press of Kansas, 1994).

Rothman, Hal: *Devil's Bargains: Tourism in the Twentieth-Century American West* (Lawrence, Kansas: University Press of Kansas, 1998).

Sargent, Aaron A.: "Irrigation and Drainage," *Overland Monthly* 8 (July 1886), 19.

Sklar, Martin J.: *The Corporate Reconstruction of American Capitalism, 1890–1916* (Cambridge: Cambridge University Press, 1988).

Stannard, David E.: *Before the Horror: The Population of Hawai'i on the Eve of Western Contact* (Honolulu: University of Hawaii Press, 1989).

St Clair, David J.: "The Gold Rush and the Beginnings of California Industry." In James J. Rawls and Richard J. Orsi (eds.) *A Golden State: Mining and Economic Development in Gold Rush California in California History* (Berkeley: University of California Press, 1998/99).

Stoll, Steven: *The Fruits of Natural Advantage: Making the Industrial Countryside in California* (Berkeley: University of California Press, 1998).

Storper, Michael and Richard Walker: *The Capitalist Imperative: Territory, Technology, and Industrial Growth* (New York: Oxford University Press, 1989).

Taylor, Alan: *William Cooper's Town: Power and Persuasion on the Frontier of the Early American Republic* (New York: Alfred A. Knopf, 1995).

Taylor, Joseph E., III: *Making Salmon: An Environmental History of the Northwest Fisheries Crisis* (Seattle: University of Washington Press, 1999).

Trachtenberg, Alan: *The Incorporation of America: Culture and Society in the Gilded Age* (New York: Hill and Wang, 1982).

Treadwell, Edward F.: *The Cattle King: A Dramatized Biography* (New York, Macmillan, 1931).

Truett, Samuel: "Neighbors by Nature: Rethinking Region, Nation, and Environmental History in the U.S.–Mexico Borderlands." *Environmental History* 2 (1997), 160–78.

Tyrrell, Ian: "American Exceptionalism in an Age of International History." *American Historical Review* 96 (1991), 1031–72.

Vaughan, Tom: "Bisbee's Transition Years, 1899–1918." *Cochise Quarterly* 14 (1984), 4–7.

Vaught, David: *Cultivating California: Growers, Specialty Crops, and Labor, 1875–1920* (Baltimore: Johns Hopkins University Press, 1999).

Walker, Richard: "California's Debt to Nature: Nature Resources and the Golden Road to Capitalist Growth, 1848–1940." *Annals of the American Association of Geographers* (forthcoming).

White, Richard: *The Organic Machine: The Remaking of the Columbia River* (New York: Hill and Wang, 1995).

White, Richard: "The Gold Rush: Consequences and Contingencies." *California History* 77 (Spring 1998), 43–54.

White, Richard: "The Nationalization of Nature." *Journal of American History* 86 (Dec. 1999), 976–84.

Whitehead, John S.: "Noncontiguous Wests: Alaska and Hawai'i." In David M. Wrobel and Michael C. Steiner (eds.) *Many Wests: Culture and Regional Identity* (Lawrence: University Press of Kansas, 1997).

Wirth, John: *Smelter Smoke in North America: The Politics of Transborder Pollution* (Lawrence, Kansas: University Press of Kansas, 2000).

Wiebe, Robert H.: *The Search for Order, 1877–1920* (New York: Hill and Wang, 1967).

Worster, Donald: "World Without Borders: The Internationalizing of Environmental History." In Kendall E. Bailes (ed.) *Environmental History: Critical Issues in Comparative Perspective* (Lanham, MD: University Press of America, 1985).

Zunz, Olivier: *Making America Corporate, 1870–1920* (Chicago: University of Chicago Press, 1990).

CHAPTER SIX

Mining and the Nineteenth-Century American West

MALCOLM J. ROHRBOUGH

Early Mining in North America

Indian peoples as miners

Indian peoples were the first miners. From very early times, native peoples in the Southwest mined turquoise. The sources of most of the turquoise in both early and recent times was probably the Los Cerrillos mountains in present-day northern New Mexico. Here archeologists have found extensive pre-Spanish excavations, including tens of thousands of tons of turquoise mining debris. There are also other deposits in the Hachita mountains and in the Jarilla hills, but the best evidence points to the Zuni mining in the Los Cerrillos as the chief source of supply in earliest times. Although Cerrillos was "the mother lode of turquoise in the New World," to quote researchers, there were probably other sources, tapped through trade links with Rio Grande Pueblos, notably the Tano, and later the Queres of San Felipe and Santo Domingo. With the emergence of large-scale mining at Cerrillos, a turquoise-trading center developed in the Pueblo communities in Chaco Canyon. As the Chaco Canyon Pueblos created a monopoly of the turquoise trade, they also began to cut and finish turquoise as well as to trade it. By about 900 AD, skilled craftsmen traded finished stones and art objects as well as raw turquoise. These finished artistic objects came to have religious as well as economic significance. As the demand for turquoise in all its forms grew, so did the number of mines in production, and by the twelfth century, perhaps as many as 120 mines were active producers. Only the rise of the tourist industry after World War II would create a demand for turquoise equal to this first great mining enterprise within what is now the United States (Harbottle and Weigand, 1992).

Early Indian peoples also mined copper in the upper reaches of present-day Minnesota and the Upper Peninsula of Michigan. Copper was an important trade item, making its way in several forms down the Mississippi and its tributaries and across the Great Lakes Region. As trade expanded among Indian peoples, copper items were surely among the most valuable, and the more so since, because of their small size, they could be easily transported long distances. It seems likely that the Ojibwe had mined every significant Lake Superior site known there prior to contact with Europeans. The evidence of widespread trade networks is the presence of Ojibwe copper in many Mississippian, Cahokian, and southwestern sites.

Spanish peoples as miners

Among European peoples who made attempts to exploit the mineral riches of the western hemisphere, the Spanish were the preeminent miners. They came to Mexico in the early sixteenth century to mine gold and silver – it turned out to be largely silver – with a long mining tradition and skills developed and nurtured over centuries of mining in Europe. They rapidly prospected Mexico, to which they brought the three basic methods of gravity separation: nuggets found on the ground; separation by water; and separation by air. All three methods would later be used by Mexican and American miners throughout the nineteenth, and well into the twentieth century. The first great mining strikes within present-day Mexico occurred in the middle of the sixteenth century, and these discoveries led to the establishment of great silver mines at Zacatecas and San Luis Potosi. These mines were owned by entrepreneurs, worked by slave labor (generally Indian), and paid a tribute to the Spanish Crown. Over two centuries, Spanish mining developed a high degree of skill (by the standards of the day) in dealing with local mineral deposits, although production from the mines in Mexico began to decline after 1750. Attempts at recovery seemed on the verge of success when they were overtaken by political events.

The beginning of the French Revolution in 1789 opened a quarter century of warfare in Europe that led to demands for independence on the part of Spain's colonies in the western hemisphere. The movement for Mexican independence was part of this revolutionary upsurge, and, after several years of conflict, the independent Republic of Mexico was proclaimed in 1821. This prolonged period of political and economic instability associated with wars and revolutions kept mining enterprise local and reduced in scale (Young and Lenon, 1970).

Mexican peoples as miners

Among the skills inherited from its colonial antecedents, the new, independent Republic of Mexico counted mining. The Spanish had been the most effective national group in exploiting the new mineral wealth of the western hemisphere. The Mexican peoples were heirs to mining deposits (generally silver) that were vast but in decline. At the same time as they worked to revive the silver empire of the Spanish, individuals and other miners in small groups continued to prospect for mineral wealth, especially gold, throughout the wide range of mountainous areas of Mexico, including Sonora and Baja California. The discoveries within the present area of the United States included gold placers in what is today New Mexico, copper in Arizona and New Mexico, silver in Arizona, and quicksilver in California. Although their mining success was modest, the skills the Mexican miners inherited and developed would become significant with the discovery of gold in Upper California in 1848. It is important to remember that the Spanish (and later the Mexicans) bequeathed to miners the techniques and technical terms that became the basis of much of the early mining in the North. At the earliest stages of mining in California, in the summer and fall of 1848, the arriving American prospectors consulted with the Mexicans (and to a lesser extent, the Chileans) about the most likely sites and the best techniques (Young and Lenon, 1970).

Early American mining

The first English settlers in Virginia, acting on the Spanish model of mineral wealth, spent time searching for precious metals. Soon, by necessity, they and subsequent generations there and throughout the English colonies in North America would focus on land and agriculture.

The most significant mining enterprise in the independent American nation before the middle of the nineteenth century was associated with lead. There were two separate areas of lead mining during the late eighteenth and early nineteenth centuries. The first was located in what would become the state of Missouri, some seventy miles south of St Louis. This area in St Francis County produced nine million tons of pig lead, most of this after 1800. The second, located at the intersection of what would become the states of Illinois, Wisconsin, and Iowa was bigger in area but less rich. Significant towns emerged to mark the sites of the mining enterprises in this second area: Galena, Illinois, Mineral Point, Wisconsin, and Dubuque, Iowa. Both of these lead deposits were known and exploited by native people before the arrival of the Europeans. The lead mining enterprises of the Mississippi Valley served as an important training ground for miners and entrepreneurs concerned with the exploitation of mineral resources. This lead mining experience produced technical skill, a body of mining law, and a series of failed policies on the part of the United States government. All these qualities would become significant in the large-scale mining enterprise associated with gold and silver in the American West (Wright, 1996).

In the 1840s, miners on the Keneenaw Peninsula in Michigan began to find and exploit significant copper deposits. Copper production rose steadily, and the leading mining conglomerate, the Calumet and Hecla mining company, became enormously productive and profitable. Between 1871 and 1921 this company would become one of the most profitable enterprises in the history of mining, and one of the few to reward its shareholders on a consistent basis (Joralemon, 1936).

The first significant gold mining within the continental United States took place in the states of North Carolina and Georgia in the 1820s and 1830s. Camped on the rushing streams of the Appalachian Mountains, this first generation of American miners panned and washed for gold. Placer gold discoveries in Georgia produced a crowd of prospective miners between 1828 and 1830. Gold production there reached $110,000 in 1828, a dramatic figure for the period that would within a generation be dwarfed by events in California.

The California Gold Rush and the Expansion of Mining Across the American West, 1848–98

The California Gold Rush thrust mining into the center of the expansion of the American nation and began a series of new chapters in the development of the American West. On January 24, 1848, at about ten o'clock in the morning, James W. Marshall, employed by the entrepreneur John Sutter to construct a saw mill on the American River, picked some flakes of mineral out of the tail race. By this act, Marshall set on foot a series of events that would change the history of California, the history of mining, and the lives of hundreds of thousands of 49ers and their families (Paul, 1947; Rohrbough, 1997; Holliday, 1999).

Table 6.1 Gold Production in California, 1848–60

Fiscal Year	Gold Produced in California (in $)
1848	245,301
1849	10,151,360
1850	41,273,106
1851	75,938,232
1852	81,294,700
1853	67,613,487
1854	69,433,931
1855	55,485,395
1856	57,509,411
1857	43,628,172
1858	46,591,140
1859	45,846,599
1860	44,095,163
1861	41,884,995
1862	38,854,668
1863	23,501,736
1864	24,071,423
1865	17,930,858
1866	17,123,867
1867	18,265,452
1868	17,555,867
1869	18,229,044

Paul, Rodman W. *California Gold. The Beginning of Mining in the Far West*

From the welter of newsprint and stories passed from one astonished citizen to another, there quickly emerged two acknowledged truths. First, the gold in California was real and abundant: in the six years from 1849 to 1855, the Argonauts harvested some $300 million in gold from California. Second, the gold was available to everyone, regardless of education, family name, and technical skill: it was a game with an infinite number of winners that anyone with a pick, pan, and shovel could play. That tens of thousands would engage in this game within the year testified to its great appeal.

The discovery of gold in California triggered the greatest mass migration in the history of the young Republic up to that time, some 80,000 in 1849 alone and probably 300,000 by 1854, an immigration largely male and generally young but not exclusively either, by land across half a continent and by sea over thousands of miles of ocean to new and heretofore unimagined adventure and wealth. The first 49ers came from up and down the West Coast, from Sonora and Oregon, and then from the Hawaiian Islands. By the middle of autumn1848, the news of the gold in California had reached the eastern states, where it rapidly spread from Maine to Mississippi, from Wisconsin to Florida, and eventually around the world. In response, the overland schooners embarked from county seat towns and villages across the breadth of the nation, from subsistence farms in the Ohio valley and from the great plantations of the lower Mississippi River valley. Its appeal was universal, for those who joined the procession in 1849 and over the next dozen years embraced every class, from the wealthy to those in straitened circumstances, from every state and territory, including slaves brought by their owners to the gold fields. And the rush to California soon became an international event with immigration from all over the world, including contract laborers from China and lawyers from Paris, professional miners from Wales and merchants from Chile. California would become in a few short years the most cosmopolitan place in the world, and San Francisco the most cosmopolitan city.

A wide range of motives drove future 49ers (or Argonauts) who proposed to go to California. Wealth was the first and most obvious, but the array of others included escape from the limited horizons of the village, the farm, or the shop, and the daily demand of labor associated with these places; and for others, the urge to participate in the pioneering adventure of American at mid-century. Men of all ages and conditions made plans to go to California, and a surprising number of women wished to join them.

Those who determined to go often did so in a "company" with their friends and neighbors. The company was a replica of the local community from which they had come. Companies traveled to the gold fields by sea and overland. The journey by sea could begin at any season, anywhere along the coast, and could make the long voyage around Cape Horn or could opt for the shorter route across Panama. The cost was substantial, on the order of $1,000 for individual members of the company. But the sea-going Argonauts (as they became known) could carry with them to California quantities of goods for resale at high prices. The overland 49ers faced a formidable journey across half the continent. The obstacles included great distances and the monotonous character of much of the landscape, the towering mountain ranges and deserts to be crossed, and the fears of attack by hostile Indians.

The newly arrived Argonauts settled in varied places in California, including the growing cities of San Francisco, Sacramento, and Stockton. The 49ers also established themselves in the many small towns and villages on the routes to the gold fields or near to the diggings, and they went in large numbers into the many gold camps established beside the gold-bearing streams of the sierra. There were hundreds of mining camps in the California gold country. Some were as large as substantial villages; others were simply crossroads with a single street carved out of the forest to accommodate a few stores. These small urban places prospered in proportion to the mines they served. Their commercial establishments included stores for supplies, a boarding house, a restaurant or two, perhaps a doctor and a lawyer, a small entertainment place with a bowling alley, and one or more saloons.

The mining "company" had its origins in a work unit. As early as the summer and fall of 1848, observers had commented on the advantages of working in groups of at least three or four. Most companies settled on six to eight. By the mining season of 1849, mining in groups was universal. Most companies operated one or more "cradles." However, the basic unit of work in the California Gold Rush – at least for the first half-a-dozen years – was the human body. The hard, repetitive labor of digging, carrying, and washing was often done in swift, ice-cold, moving water. Contrasting with the icy water of the snowmelt watercourses was the heat of the summer California sun, beating down on the bars and into the still canyons. The work was exhausting. During the long work days that stretched into a long mining season, 49ers drove themselves forward on a daily basis through a combination of restless energy, hope, self-interest, and group loyalty. The mining companies carried over to living arrangements. For the 49ers, it was cheaper and more efficient to live and work in groups. From five to eight men would occupy a large tent or cabin as close to the work site as possible, where they would take turns cooking, cleaning, and making trips to the larger camps for food and mail.

The act of mining in California in the middle of the nineteenth century is easily described. Gold was found in the nooks and crannies of old stream beds and in the bottoms of existing water courses, where it had been left by thousands of years of the movement of water carrying the mineral downstream to the point when the strength of flow was insufficient to support the weight. Thus, water was a crucial agent in early gold mining, as an instrument in transporting and dropping the mineral, and as a force for its separation from the dirt around it. The first miners – often tutored by early arriving Mexicans – quickly mastered the primitive techniques by which moving water flowing through a tin pan would separate the gravel which would be carried off by the force of the flow of water from the heavier gold particles, which would sink to the bottom of the pan, where they could be easily retrieved and stored in a small sack. The widespread presence of gold in the streams draining the western slope of the Sierras and in gold stream beds – where it might be uncovered by removing a layer of top soil – meant an accessibility that made the early Gold Rush an open exercise for everyone. All that was necessary to participate were the most elementary and easily available tools.

Furthermore, the search for gold was uninhibited by institutional influences. Access to the rivers, streams, and valleys was unrestricted; no licenses were issued by any kind of central authority (although the State of California levied a tax on alien miners in 1850). The issue of land ownership was in abeyance for the land was sparsely settled and largely unclaimed in a European sense (except for the tracts of John Sutter). The California Indians were sufficiently weakened by two generations of the mission experience and the trauma associated with its destruction to offer little or no resistance, although this would not prevent American miners and politicians from an undeclared war against California's Indian peoples.

As mining sites became more crowded – the number of miners in the gold fields grew from 50,000 in 1849 to 100,000 in 1850 to 125,000 in 1851 – the American miners increasingly exhibited hostility toward other national groups. The issue began as a struggle over attractive mining claims supported by the xenophobic argument that the mines were for Americans alone. The initial targets were the Mexicans, soon followed by the Chileans and the French. This animosity toward foreigners reached a climax with attacks on the Chinese – who came in numbers after 1851 – the group most different by appearance and culture. Anti-Chinese agitation became a focus of politics in San Francisco over the last half of the nineteenth century. Hostility toward the Chinese was not confined to California but spread across the breadth of the mining West.

Advances in technology quickly changed the nature of mining. The first new machine was the "rocker" or "cradle" earlier in use in the gold mines of Georgia and North Carolina. The cradle was a rectangular box six or eight feet long, open at the foot, and with a coarse grate and sieve at its head; the bottom was rounded, with small cleats nailed across. The principle was the same as panning for gold: namely, to let the water do the work of separating the gold from the gravel. The difference was the economy and efficiency provided by a machine that would allow men to pool their labor into larger units. The pan and the cradle, both relying on the washing action of the water, both simple to purchase or easy to make from a few boards of lumber, provided the technology for the first two years of the California Gold Rush. The universality of both instruments – in spite of prices rising in accordance with supply and demand – insured that every prospective Argonaut could have access to the latest technology in the gold fields (Young and Lenon, 1970).

Mining was changing in other ways, too. By the close of 1849, some miners had banded together to construct dams to divert stream beds for washing. Mercury to separate the gold particles from gravels was rapidly introduced, and, by the beginning of 1851, miners had begun what they called quartz mining, that is to say, the retrieval of gold-bearing rock from deep shafts, the crushing of these gravels, and their processing to capture the gold. River damming, hydraulic mining, and quartz mining gradually restricted, the opportunities of individuals in favor of large-scale companies with substantial capital that soon sold shares to the public. Simple placer mining – individuals or small groups digging and washing gravels – had been replaced by larger units of production with new techniques. Individuals had become parts of larger companies, with increased investment in season-long mining enterprises. The expanded opportunities for gold recovery were associated with concentrations of capital and, increasingly, the sale of shares to the public. Capitalists (or even individuals of modest means) could invest in distant gold mining enterprises or water companies (almost as profitable as gold) without leaving the comfort of their homes in San Francisco.

It is impossible to overestimate the significance of the California Gold Rush for mining in the American West. The dozen years of the Gold Rush would produce an explosive immigration to the gold fields; transform California into an American state; establish the basic institutional forms for mining (that would later be codified in the Mining Law of 1872), especially the principle that mining was to proceed without interference from the federal government; serve as a laboratory for the development of mining technology for the next half century, especially as an introduction to the Comstock Lode, where so many of these technical skills were perfected; and introduce the large-scale forms that would transform mining from an individual into a corporate enterprise, with a large labor force, sophisticated technology, large capital investment, and with absentee ownership and financing. California also proved that, in the face of mining strikes, neither well-meaning individuals nor governments at any level could protect the rights of Native Americans from rapacious prospectors, and the California experience would introduce a future in which foreign miners (especially non-English speakers) would be subject to discrimination and harassment. California would also be the site of the first struggles over mining and the environment.

The discovery of gold in California and the rush of people west in response to it helped to define the nature of westward expansion for a decade. The western vanguards of the young nation had, heretofore, been headed north to Oregon. Marshall's discoveries changed the direction of that advance from Oregon to California, and gave new and dramatic meaning to the term Manifest Destiny.

The Comstock Lode

The successor to California in mining techniques and the enlarged forms of technology, capital, and enterprise was the Comstock Lode. The discovery of rich veins of silver ore in the Comstock Lode near Virginia City, Nevada in 1859 shifted the focus in mining away from gold to silver. Mining operations on the Comstock Lode rapidly grew to enormous proportions, including deep shafts down to 2,000 feet, mammoth processing plants with stamp mills to process the raised ore, and the first great mining town, Virginia City, that grew to an estimated 30,000 people within a decade. Along with new technical aspects associated with processing silver ore, the Comstock also pioneered the finances of mining. For the first time, stock in mining companies was sold to the public on a large scale. Mine owners and others quickly came to grasp that greater profits could be made manipulating stock than in raising and processing ore. The reason for the success of the stock scheme was that it offered the opportunity for anyone to enjoy the financial bonanzas associated with the Comstock Lode. The Comstock produced $300 million in precious metal from 1859 to 1880. A fortunate few, the so-called "Silver Kings," built extravagant mansions on San Francisco's Nob Hill. The mining experience of the Comstock Lode also brought into stark relief for the first time a quality that could later come to characterize mining throughout the nineteenth and well into the twentieth century; namely, the dramatic contrast between the leisured lives and lifestyles of the score who made great fortunes and the living and working conditions of tens of thousands of miners who labored underground in the harshest work world for $3 a day (Paul, 1963; Peterson, 1977).

The profits from the Comstock Lode generated large sums that soon sought investment in mining enterprise elsewhere. George Hearst was the best known of the future investors. The Comstock also refined mining skills at all levels, from engineers to superintendents to miners. It was the laboratory that created a core of expert knowledge that would be carried, with its practitioners, to the new mining strikes across the West. As a mining enterprise, the Comstock was extraordinarily long lived, producing for almost a generation into the 1880s, with cycles of downturn as the leads played out followed by extensive searches for new rich veins. Virginia City became the first permanent mining town that grew into a city, the model for Leadville, Colorado, Lead, South Dakota, and Butte, Montana (Paul, 1963).

Colorado to Alaska

The discovery of gold at the edge of the Front Range of the Rocky Mountains in Colorado in 1858 began a surge of immigration that rivaled the passage to California a decade earlier. In the summer of 1859, perhaps 75,000 so-called "59ers" crossed the plains to the mining region in the eastern foothills of the Rockies. This large number of miners established several mining camps, of which Central City and Blackhawk were most significant, with Denver as the supply and financial center. The surge in immigration led to the organization of Colorado as a territory in 1861 (Paul, 1963).

Like Nevada before it, Colorado's future lay in silver mining. Twenty years after the first gold strikes in Colorado came the dramatic bonanzas in silver. First at Leadville (1877) and then Aspen (1879), these silver strikes seemed to presage the successors to the Comstock Lode. The development of large silver mining operations needed capital, mining skills, and railroads. These were all in place by the middle 1880s (Leadville's first railroad dated from 1880; Aspen's, from 1887), and the silver ore flowed out of the mines in astonishing quantities.

In addition to other necessary mining skills and resources, silver generated political influence across the American West, and the Silver Block in the Senate enacted the Sherman Silver Purchase Act (1890) that provided for the Treasury Department to purchase large quantities of the domestic production of silver, enough to keep the price of American silver well above the world price. This artificial support left silver vulnerable to changes in the economic and political landscape. With the onset of the economic crisis of 1893, President Grover Cleveland called a special session of Congress to repeal the 1890 Silver Act. With the price of silver cut in half, almost every silver mine in the West immediately shut down. The perceived destruction of the silver industry became a long-lasting grievance of the West against the "gold bugs" of Wall Street. The western demand for the unlimited coinage of silver at the ratio of sixteen to one became the centerpiece of the emerging Populist Party and later the Democratic Party (Rohrbough, 1986).

In the early 1860s, prospectors in search of placer gold had made notable strikes in Idaho (1860–2) and Montana (1862–4), where the claims were rich, remote, and small-scale. Idaho and Montana seemed to offer the reincarnation of early Gold Rush California, in which individual prospectors and small companies reaped substantial profits. Because of the inaccessibility of these locales and the severity of the winter climate, mining in Idaho and Montana began as a seasonal enterprise, with miners and support groups retreating to Colorado and Utah during the prolonged winter months (Paul, 1963).

Montana's mining future was significant indeed, but it lay in copper mining. The spread of electricity into home and industry beginning in the 1870s led to a dramatic rise in demand for copper. The most important deposits in the West were in Montana and Arizona. The first would be the great producer of copper in the last part of the nineteenth century, the latter, the producer of the twentieth century. In Montana, copper was discovered in the vicinity of Butte, and copper-mining operations quickly eclipsed gold or silver. The great mining operations around Butte made the town "the richest hill on earth," made fortunes for a few ruthless entrepreneurs, and became the site of endless litigation and violence. In 1887, the mines around Butte replaced Michigan's Keewenah peninsula as the leading copper producer in the world (Paul, 1963; Malone, 1981).

Gold remained the object of widespread prospecting throughout the American West, even as the changes in technology and financing reduced most mining to another dimension of industrial America. The best example of gold mining as rational industrial enterprise on a grand scale was the Homestake Mine in Lead, South Dakota. In response to George Armstrong Custer's announcement of gold in the Black Hills of Dakota Territory, a large mining rush took place there beginning in 1875. Undeterred by conflicts with Indian peoples (the great Sioux War of 1876 would culminate in Custer's defeat at Little Big Horn), prospectors laid off hundreds of mining claims in the Black Hills. Agents of George Hearst bought some of the most promising and established a large mining operation that took the name of one of the original claims, the Homestake. Over the next half century, the Homestake would become one of the most profitable gold mines in the world, adding immeasurably to the Hearst fortune (providing the financial foundation for William Randolph Hearst's newspaper empire), and becoming the prototype for a large multiethnic workforce in a company town. The workforce involved miners from most of the Eastern European countries, plus the Welsh. The town was Lead. The recently formed union of miners affiliated with the Western Federation of Miners struck for higher wages in 1909. The company broke the union within six months. Mining resumed and production and profits remained high for the next half century. Most of the $500 million in gold produced in the Black Hills has come from the Homestake (Cash, 1973). The closing of the Homestake mine in 1995 was a landmark in the mining experience in the West.

The last great gold mining rush on this continent began in Alaska in 1898. Rumors of rich gold strikes in the Yukon valley, near Fairbanks, and along the coast sent tens of thousands north from the continental United States. In the midst of corporate mining in the American West as another vast industrial enterprise, here in Alaska was the prospect of a rebirth of the dream of California's early years: rich claims to be worked by individuals and small groups. The claims were indeed rich, but the gold deposits were distant and the landscape and climate hostile. Probably fewer than half those who began the journey actually reached the gold fields, but the strikes in Alaska and the 98ers provided a vivid final chapter – notably assisted by reporters and photographers – to a half century of searching for gold across the breadth of the American West (Marks 1994; Morgan, 1967).

Nineteenth-century mining: developments and consequences

By the close of the nineteenth century, the economic dimensions of mining enterprise had spread across the American West. The product of the mines caught the eye of the public, but to mining entrepreneurs at several levels, processed ores were only the most obvious of many opportunities for profit. Buying and selling claims was the first of these opportunities. Promising sites were soon crisscrossed with claims (under the Mining Law of 1872, a claim covered an area of about ten and one half acres), and these claims were freely sold or traded, as the first mine owners attempted to profit from their holdings without making further investment. Later, as the mines matured as mining operations and as speculative vehicles, the owners sold stock to the public. Rumors, innuendo, stories spread to local newspapers could drive stock prices up or down. Stock manipulation was an important ingredient of mining enterprise, beginning with the Comstock Lode and extending across the American West to the gold mines in Alaska at the turn of the century. The silver mining town of Aspen, Colorado provides a useful case study of this evolution of mining claims: eager prospectors laid off more than 7,000 mining claims around Aspen , and of these fewer than 25 became producing mines, and of the producers, only six paid dividends to the shareholders. Yet speculators and the public alike, driven by the occasional spectacular returns from mines, invested heavily in such mining companies (Paul, 1963; Rohrbough, 1986).

Mining had other influences that spread out in endless concentric circles beyond the mining claim. It was a collective enterprise, and the concentrated nature of the economic venture that brought together so many people meant the appearance of towns. Boomtowns, producing towns, towns in decline, and ghost towns all became part of the mining experience of the West. Every major mining city had surrounding satellite towns, where energetic town builders hoped to profit. There were many avenues to profit: speculation in town sites, hotels and boarding houses, an entertainment industry (almost always gambling and prostitution), and eventually schools and churches. The latter were always greeted with a sigh of relief, reflecting, as they did, signs of permanence. And the final steps were the connections with the outside world, through which people and supplies would arrive and the products of the mines would be shipped. These began with tracks, which led to trails, roads for stagecoaches and wagons, and finally the railroad. The arrival of the railroad was a sign that the town might very well become a city, that the richness of its mines had been authenticated and its prospects recognized as bright by eastern investors (Smith 1967, 1974; Rohrbough, 1986).

The development of mines and towns, the buying and selling of stock, and the plans for a railroad reflected a continuing symbiotic relationship between East and West. Mines in the West needed eastern capital to develop and, beginning with the Comstock Lode, western mine owners looked to eastern investors for support. The geographic designation was a figure of speech, of course, for the capital necessary to develop mines or towns or railroads might come from San Francisco or, later, from Denver. But the implication was the same: mining was an enterprise that demanded a high degree of capitalization. It was a variety of late-nineteenth-century industrial enterprise, and it needed capital for investment in technology, transportation, and professional management.

The last was a new dimension that became increasingly important as mining assumed ever larger dimensions. As the technology of mining evolved rapidly in the last half of the nineteenth century – the Comstock Lode represented a dramatic technological advance over the placers of California's streams – so too did the demand for trained professionals to manage mining exploration, mining development, and the mining workforce. The practical information that emerged in western mines made its way to the professional mining schools, and they, in turn, graduated mining engineers who made their way around the West and eventually around the world (Spence, 1970; Young and Lenon, 1970).

Mining in the West gave rise to a large body of law. The Mining Law of 1872 was simple enough on paper, but on the ground it admitted of endless variations. And in a world where a fortune might be found in a tract as small at ten feet by ten feet, the stakes were high. The latitude allowed in staking claims inevitably assured that claims would be overlapping. As some of the claims turned out to be valuable, so the legal disputes rose in proportion. Furthermore, as claims changed hands rapidly, each separate transaction offered opportunities for fraud, misunderstanding, and legal action. Mining lawyers often became as wealthy as mine owners – not surprisingly, for they were the arbiters of who owned what, when, and where.

Over two generations, what started out as individual prospectors on a lone quest in California had evolved into a world of huge capital investment, advanced technology, and mining by professionals in shafts two thousand and five hundred feet under the surface across the American West. In a sense, these changes reflected the transformation in the national workplace generally. Mining in the American West – that began as the most individual of enterprises set against the backdrop of a magnificent and often hostile landscape – had been transformed by technology and capital into another industrial enterprise.

But amidst these triumphs of technology, human ingenuity, and endless human labor, several unhappy by-products emerged. Mining stocks became synonymous with fraud and dishonesty, the more so as the market turned out to be increasingly a European one, where investors were viewed as endlessly gullible. Mining itself turned out to be infinitely unstable, with rich strikes this year followed by dry holes the next year. And the recruitment, training, and continuing (often growing) use of a large-scale professional labor force injected the issue of labor wages and conditions into an already complex equation. Beyond these important issues, stood three that deserve special attention.

Mining turned to be a dangerous experience for Indian peoples in the American West. Mixed with the traditional hostility toward Indians was the attraction of great wealth in remote often mountainous regions. So the search for mineral wealth carried miners into the highest mountains and most inhospitable landscapes, heretofore the last refuge of Indian peoples. And these invasions sometimes took place on lands guaranteed to Indian people by treaty. Nor did the government of the United States move to defend these treaty rights, but, instead, generally permitted the mining rushes to proceed while attempting to make additional treaties as a screen of legality.

The California Gold Rush was a particularly horrific example of the impact of mining on Indians. Driven by a general hostility toward Indians, the intrusion of mining parties into the highest reaches of the Sierra, and the inaction associated with the closure of mining in the winter, American miners began seasonal winter campaigns against California Indians. These semiofficial military expeditions, undertaken with the support of the state government, evolved into campaigns of annihilation. The lethal encounters between miners and Indians spread across the West, wherever precious minerals were found or might be found. The spontaneous rush into the Black Hills led directly to the destruction of Custer's 7th cavalry command. Skirmishes between wandering mining parties and Indian peoples continued into the 1890s (Hurtado, 1988).

The second unhappy by-product of the spread of mining was the growing violence associated with it. This violence assumed two forms. The first was the hostility of American miners toward foreign miners. This began in California, and in 1850 the California state legislature passed a tax on foreign miners. Mexican, Chilean, and French miners were the targets, all non-English-speaking and resented because of their mining success. This hostility spread with the spread of mining across the West, and the most persistent target became the Chinese.

Attacks on the Chinese lasted for a half century and had their origins in the universality of the Chinese presence throughout the West, their hard work for low wages, clannish behavior, and perceived hostility to Christianity and assimilation. That low-wage jobs and self-contained communities had been forced on the Chinese did not seem to occur to their persecutors. Chinese had been brought in to construct the transcontinental railroads. With the railroads completed, they were turned loose and gradually gravitated to the mining communities of the West, where they inherited the worst mining claims. That their claims were presumed played out did not lessen the hostility against them. Violent anti-Chinese riots in Denver, Colorado in 1880 and Rock Springs, Wyoming in 1885 were directed against Chinese miners and laborers who had refused to support strikes. Chinese miners in the American West remained vulnerable to vigilante actions well into the 20th century (Zhu, 1997).

Another dimension of violence pitted mine owners against their workforces. In the California Gold Rush, men initially worked for others as a means of accumulating a stake to strike out on their own. Beginning in the Comstock Lode, underground mining became a permanent condition. The work was hard, repetitive, and dangerous. As underground mining spread from gold to silver, from silver to copper, and from copper to lead and coal, working miners expanded in numbers and across the West for the rest of the century. Parallel to the labor unrest that appeared in the East and Middle West, so labor–owner conflicts spread across the West. Miners sought better wages (or at least stable wages) and the eight-hour day. Pursuant to these ends, they organized. Some of the unions that emerged were traditional in their demands (wages and hours); others were more radical in calling for basic changes in the distribution of power and wealth.

The appearance of union organizers, from the Knights of Labor to the Western Federation of Miners and the Industrial Workers of the World, aroused hope in miners and implacable hostility in mine owners and superintendents. Some of these confrontations ended tragically, such as at Ludlow, Colorado, where a strike of miners in the coal industry turned violent. An example of the intense control exercised by owners was the "lock-out" of miners at the Homestake Mine in Lead, South Dakota, in 1909, and the subsequent breaking of the union by the owners. Throughout, in many cases, the mine owners had the support of the state government in their battles against the unions. The use of state militia against the miner's camp at Ludlow was only one example. In this pattern, the mining West reflected the labor struggles across the nation (Byrkit, 1982; McGovern, 1972).

The creation of a large professional mining force in the industrial setting in the West led to the hiring of large numbers of recent immigrants. Mining became a symbol of the opportunities associated with new immigrant workers, who would start on the bottom of the economic ladder, at work in the most dangerous and difficult of all occupations. This pattern created isolated ethnic communities in mining cities and that, in turn, sometimes led to conflict as a result of hostility toward the supposedly clannish nature of new immigrant groups and their perceived economic threat. That immigrants sometimes were brought in as strike-breakers gave foreigner miners a reputation as "scabs." The isolation of the immigrant communities within a large mining workforce also worked against union organization for a common goal. This hostility toward immigrants increased as hard rock mining came on hard times in the 1890s (Wyman, 1979).

At least one immigrant group, the Irish mining community in Butte, Montana, found a degree of prosperity nevertheless. Over a generation, from 1885 through the close of World War I, Irish miners created a life of stability and full employment in the copper mines of Butte. Supported by a management that succeeded in making the town its own and the mines a form of economic opportunity for all, this immigrant group maintained a remarkable degree of cohesion and expansion. At the turn of the century, Butte was (proportionately) the most Irish town in America. Marcus Daly, the creator and chief executive of the Anaconda Copper Mining Company, raised on a poor family farm in rural Ireland, had determined to assist his fellow countrymen. He was also noteworthy in his attempts to keep the Anaconda Company in western hands and prevent its control from falling to eastern financiers (Emmons, 1989).

Finallly, in the rush to exploit the natural wealth of the West – in this case mineral wealth – individuals and groups paid scant attention to the landscape. The competition for wealth and the inhospitable conditions, the seemingly infinite western landscape as it stretched forth around them meant that the issue of despoiling the land was not a matter of concern. The results of mining were especially severe in this respect. California's interior valleys were dug out over two generations, many streams changed course, the detritus of a generation of hundreds of thousands of miners – whether tailings or old camp sites – littered the landscape (Smith, 1987).

As mining assumed a larger scale, the damage became more severe. The most injurious was hydraulic mining, in which powerful streams of water washed away hillsides. Persistent mining by hydraulic methods polluted many California steams and river, carrying the by-product downstream into agricultural areas. By the late 1860s, debris from hydraulic mining had clogged rivers and raised their water level to flood the valleys. In the 1870s and 1880s, conflict between farmers in the Sacramento River valley and miners in the Sierra Nevada reached the courts and the state legislature. In an 1884 decision, the California courts ruled mines a public nuisance. The victory of agriculture began a lengthy process of restricting the heavy pollution of mining (Kelley, 1959).

Several different kinds of threats to the landscape continued throughout the mining West. The Comstock Lode produced a different set of natural liabilities. As the mines burrowed underground to a level of 2,000 feet, they demanded ever greater quantities of timber to shore up the working areas. One writer described the Comstock mines as the "tomb of the forests of the Sierras." The silver mines cut and used 600 million feet of timber for the mines, denuding the hillsides for miles around Virginia City (Paul, 1963).

The industrial dimension of mining had other public by-products. Great mining enterprises such as the Anaconda had smelters that produced poisonous smoke that lay like a blanket over the city of Butte. The scores of stamp mills in Lead, South Dakota operated twenty-four hours a day with a deafening racket. And in the twentieth century, the Climax molybdenum mine at Climax, Colorado would produce a vast lake of chemical by-products. These developments and others like them threatened the natural environment and the health of the people who lived and worked in these mining operations (Smith, 1987).

Mining in the Twentieth Century

The history of mining in the twentieth century is the story of the gradual decline of traditional mineral products in the face of foreign competition mixed with the discovery and exploitation of new mineral resources. Among the most important of the new minerals were molybdenum and uranium. The first was a mineral used in hardening steel, and it became a vital ingredient for the steel industry. The Climax Moly mines, at 11,500 feet in Climax, operated at full employment through the 1930s in some of the worst economic years of the Great Depression and in the midst of the worst and most taxing physical conditions in the history of mining. Climax molybdenum was a symbol of 20th mining: it was a vital new product produced by an industrial process, involving a highly capitalized company and a professional workforce that worked at the face in deep mines. It also polluted the landscape with reckless abandon, reflecting the context of the time and the lack of oversight associated with that generation (Voynick, 1978).

The second of the new minerals that caught the attention of mining entrepreneurs in the twentieth century was uranium. First extracted in the early years of the century for radioactive research in America and Europe, the coming of atomic energy during World War II and the arms race with the Soviet Union after 1945 generated an immediate demand for high-grade uranium ore. These high prices led to a nineteenth-century mining rush in the second half of the twentieth century: prospectors with Geiger counters (now in four wheel drive vehicles), instant new towns, vigorous speculation in uranium claims. Salt Lake City became the financial center of a burgeoning trade in uranium stocks. The more than 300,000 claims filed in four Utah counties attest to the boundless enthusiasm for the new bonanza. Within a few years, the search for uranium had spread across the western landscape. The important new uranium discoveries were on the Colorado Plateau, at the confluence of the states of Colorado, New Mexico, Utah, and Arizona. In response to the new deposits, by 1955, eight hundred mines were producing high-grade uranium in this area of the American West, a modern mining enterprise that generated $100,000,000 a year (Amundson, 2002).

Responding to the shortage of oil and its skyrocketing price in the early 1980s, scientists and representatives from oil companies fanned out across the Western Slope in Colorado in search of shale that could produce an alternative oil product. Once again, the potential for a rich mining bonanza produced a surge of prospectors, town site speculation, and the spread of rumors about small fortunes already made and big fortunes on the horizon. As it turned out, shale was not an economically viable alternative as a source of petroleum. As the prospect of an economic bonanza faded, many citizens on the Western Slope thought themselves ill used by large corporations who had held out of the prospect of large economic benefits and, just as quickly, disappeared. Mining enterprise and industry has struck hard times in the last half of the twentieth century. Copper mining in Arizona has been challenged by large producing mines in South America, and as the company has tried to cut wages and benefits, a series of depleting strikes has dotted the western mining landscape. The longest-lasting of these was a strike against the Phelps-Dodge mines at Bisbee, Arizona between 1980 and 1990. The failure of the strike was a final reminder of the changes in western mining as the end of the twentieth century approached.

With the passage of a law to allow gold to reflect the world market, the price immediately rose from $35 an ounce to several hundred dollars, peaking at almost $700. The surge produced the opening of several closed mines, once again profitable at such prices. But the bulk of the production has remained in the Soviet Union and South Africa, and the decision of those two governments to sell substantial quantities of bullion on the world market reduced the price in dramatic fashion. The price has hovered at around $250 an ounce for some years now, and only the most productive mines in still in operation. The decision of the Homestake Mine in Lead to cease its mining operations was a powerful indicator of the changing fortunes of gold mining (Smith, 1998).

In the wake of these mining changes and adaptations, gold mining has become the business of giant companies, most of them based in Canada, that process hundreds of tons of ore every day for a return as low as a quarter ounce per ton. The search for mining sites in the American West has produced an intense controversy between those who favor economic development and those who decry the environmental damage to the landscape generated by huge open-pit mining operations. Consider the recent example of a Canadian-based gold mining company mining near Summitville, Colorado. Between 1985 and 1992, the company developed an open-pit, cyanide-heap leech mine at 11,500 feet. In these eight years, the company mined some 10 million tons of ore, crushed the product, and ran the gravels through a solution of sodium-cyanide that picked up the gold. In 1992 the company declared bankruptcy, leaving in its wake one of the most massive cleanup sites in the history of the Superfund. Endless litigation is now underway over the results of this mining operation, made the more complicated by two nations involved (Shagun, 1998).

Most recently, the attempts of the large Canadian mining company to begin mining operations almost within sight of Yellowstone National Park provoked a loud outcry that led the federal government to intervene to stop the opening of the mine. But the final adjudication of the issue was a compromise, under which the company received other lands that it might mine at a greater distance from national parks. The environmental impact on the landscape would, presumably, be the same, but the damage would be far less visible (Glidden, Ralph: conversations with the author 1997, 1998, 1999).

The close of the twentieth century finds mining enterprise in the American West notably enlarged in scale, but far removed from the highly competitive game without rules that characterized it after 1848. Although demands for minerals in industry have not diminished and, indeed, have increased, prices for minerals reflect a world supply and demand. Mineral deposits are just as rich in distant settings, labor is cheaper, and concerns about the environment are muted.

A final new dimension of mining in the twentieth century is the rising concern over the environment. As the West has become the nation's playground, hikers, bikers, canoers, white water rafters, climbers, and campers have visited this striking landscape in unheard of numbers. National Parks, such as Yellowstone, have been overwhelmed. But a wider public has taken up the cause of the West as never before, whether through organizations such as the Sierra Club or simply in individual expressions of opinion. Large numbers have rallied to protect the rest from large-scale mining that does obvious damage to the landscape. Politicians have responded. The on-going conflicts between environmental purity and beauty on the one hand and economic development on the other remain unresolved.

REFERENCES

Amundson, Michael A.: *Yellowcake Towns: Uranium Mining Communities in the American West* (Boulder: University Press of Colorado, 2002).

Byrkit, James W.: *Forging the Copper Collar: Arizona's Labor Management War of 1901–21* (Tucson: University of Arizona Press, 1982).

Cash, Joseph H.: *Working the Homestake* (Ames, Iowa State University Press, 1973).

Emmons, David M.: *The Butte Irish: Class and Ethnicity in an American mining Town, 1873–1925* (Urbana: University of Illinois Press, 1989).

Goldman, Marion S.: *Gold Diggers and Silver Miners: Prostitution and Social Life on the Comstock Lode* (Ann Arbor: University of Michigan Press, 1979).

Greever, William: *Bonanza West: The Story of Western Mining Rushes* (Norman: University of Oklahoma Press, 1963).

Harbottle, Garman and Philip Weigand: "Turquoise in Pre-Columbian America." *Scientific American* 266, 2 (February 1992), 78–85.

Holliday, James: *The World Rushed In: The California Gold Rush Eperience* (New York: Simon and Schuster, 1981).

Holliday, James: *Rush for Riches: Gold Fever and the Making of California* (Berkeley: Oakland Museum of California and University of California Press, 2000).

Hurtado, Albert L.: *Indian Survival on the California Frontier* (New Haven, CT: Yale University Press, 1988).

Jameson, Elizabeth: *All That Glitters: Class, Conflict, and Community in Cripple Creek* (Urbana, University of Illinois Press, 1998).

Joralemon, Ira B.: *Romantic Copper* (New York: D. Appleton-Century Co., 1936)

Kelley, Robert L.: *Gold vs. Grain: The Hydraulic Mine Controversy in California's Sacramento, Valley* (Glendale, CA: A. H. Clark Co., 1959).

King, Joseph E.: *A Mine to Make a Mine: Financing the Colorado Mining Industry, 1859–1902* (College Station: Texas A & M University Press, 1977).

Lingenfelter, Richard E.: *The Hardrock Miners: A History of the Mining Labor Movement in the American West, 1863–93* (Berkeley: University of California Press, 1974).

Malone, Michael: *The Battle for Butte: Mining and Politics on the Northern Frontier, 1864–1906* (Seattle: University of Washington Press, 1981).

Mann, Ralph: *After the Gold Rush: Society in Grass Valley and Nevada City, California, 1849–1870* (Stanford: Stanford University Press, 1982).

Marks, Paula Mitchell: *Precious Dust: The American Gold Rush Era, 1848–1900* (New York: W. Morrow, 1994).

McGovern, George and Leonard F. Guttridge: *The Great Coalfield War* (Boston: Houghton Mifflin, 1972).

Morgan, Murray C.: *One Man's Gold Rush: A Klondike Album* (Seattle: University of Washington Press, 1967).

Paul, Rodman W.: *California Gold. The Beginning of Mining in the Far West* (Cambridge, MA: Harvard University Press, 1947).

Paul, Rodman W.: *Mining Frontiers of the Far West, 1848–1880* (New York: Holt, Rinehart and Winston, 1963).

Perry, Tony: "Rights and Rites Clash in Mine Plan." *Los Angeles Times* (February 9, 1998).

Peterson, Richard: *The Bonanza Kings: The Social Origins and Business Behavior of Western Mining Entrepreneurs, 1870–1900* (Lincoln, University of Nebraska Press, 1977).

Petrik, Paula: *No Step Backward: Women and Family on the Rocky Mountain Mining Frontier* (Helena: Montana Historical Society Press, 1987).

Rohrbough, Malcolm: *Aspen: The History of a Silver Mining Town, 1879–1893* (New York: Oxford University Press, 1986).

Rohrbough, Malcolm: *Days of Gold. The California Gold Rush and the American Nation* (Berkeley: University of California Press, 1997)

Shagun, Louis: "As U.S., Canadian Lawyers Wrangle, a Colorado Mine Emits Its Poisons." *Los Angeles Times* (March 3, 1998).

Smith, Duane A.: *Mining America: The Industry and the Environment, 1800–1980* (Lawrence: University Press of Kansas, 1987).

Smith, Duane A.: *Rockv Mountain Mining Camps: The Urban Frontier* (Bloomington: University of Indiana Press, 1967).

Smith, Duane A.: *Silver Sage: The Story of Caribou, Colorado* (Boulder, CO: Pruett Publishing Co., 1974).

Smith, Gordon: "Dreams of Gold: Mining's Massive Scale." *San Diego Union-Tribune* (January 20, 1998).

Spence, Clark C.: *British Investments and the American Mining Frontier, 1860–1901* (Ithaca: Cornell University Press, 1958).

Spence, Clark C.: *Mining Engineers and the American West: The Lace-Boot Brigade* (New Haven: Yale University Press, 1970).

Thompson, Sharon Elaine: "Roots of the Turquoise Trade." *Lapidary Journal* (1966).

Voynick, Stephen: *The Making of a Hardrock Miner: An Account of the Experiences of a Worker in Copper, Molybdenum, and Uranium Mines in the West* (Berkeley, CA: Howell-North Books, 1978).

West, Elliott: *Contested Plains: Indians, Goldseekers & The Rush to Colorado* (Lawrence KS: University Press of Kansas, 1998).

Wyman, Mark: *Hard Rock Epic: Western Miners and the Industrial Revolution, 1860–1910* (Berkeley: University of California Press, 1979).

Young, Otis E. and Robert Lenon: *Western Mining: An Informal Account of Precious Metals Prospecting, Placering, Lode Mining, and Milling, on the American Frontier from Spanish Times to 1893* (Norman: University of Oklahoma Press, 1970).

CHAPTER SEVEN

Law and the Contact of Cultures

SARAH BARRINGER GORDON

For the purposes of this essay, which introduces the reader to current work in the field of western legal history and major trends in the scholarship over the past half century as well as to the bibliography that follows, legal history is concerned with the role of laws, legal institutions, and legal cultures in the nineteenth-century West. The topic is an enormous one, especially when one considers that, for much of the time, different and diverging legal worlds competed for dominance – or even for survival – in unstable and unpredictable environments. The legal landscape of the west, one might say, changed as much in the nineteenth century as the physical landscape, making almost every major event and trend a possible object of study. What follows, therefore, is a summary of the major insights of work in the field, as well as suggestions for further research, rather than an exhaustive treatment. The legal history of the West, although it has at times been mired in stagnant or celebratory wallows, has seen innovative new work over the past generation, which has invigorated and challenged the field.

Like the rest of western history, the historiography of law has suffered a prolonged identity crisis. For decades, historians debated whether the nineteenth-century West was fundamentally a violent, vengeful, even "lawless" place. See, for example, Eugene Hollon's *Frontier Violence, Another Look* (1974), which summarizes the literature to date on violence and concludes that "the general public expected the frontier to be violent and would not have it any other way." The rueful pride that many white Americans have taken in their legacy of violence should not obscure the fact that much of the debate about law and order in the West was itself constructed as a coming-of-age myth. In this myth, winners (usually) shed the blood of losers, yet still earned the admiration of their peers and historians. The eventual, reluctant acceptance of the rule of law, in this view, was not an unmitigated gain. Instead, it represented both maturation and loss of innocence.

A second, more romantic strain of this debate envisioned a "rugged" or "rustic" yet effective justice imposed by mountain men and then settlers who had moved beyond regular law courts and officers. In this vision, honest and simple settlers imposed a rough order that suited their pioneering spirit. Warlike Indian tribes and violent outlaws who violated the norms of rustic justice were subdued eventually by the army or Indian agents, or frontier marshals such "Wild Bill" Hickok and Wyatt

Earp. Another branch of this strain conceives of the western wilderness as a "state of nature," in which pioneers touched roots of justice and humanity that were buried in more corrupt, "civilized" regions. In this second vision, the vast territories of the nineteenth-century West provided a refuge for people whose physical courage in migration was rewarded by the simplicity and honesty of frontier society and its basic legal rules.

The stale historiographical debate over law and order, which in part traced its roots back to Frederick Jackson Turner's frontier thesis, was reconfigured for legal historians in the mid-twentieth century by another scholar from Wisconsin, James Willard Hurst. According to Hurst, law acted as a "release of energy," paving the way for settlement and development. Hurst's ground-breaking study of the lumber industry in Wisconsin, *Law and Economic Growth* (1964), invigorated the field of legal history, as well as leading many historians to reconsider the place of law in economic history. Hurst's analysis of law and development, which traces the impetus for economic growth to the proper legal climate, created a third and starkly different way to look at law and legal development in western history. Hurst's work places legal rules at the center of western history, rather than at the periphery. There is not much room for alternative legal cultures in such a vision, however, and Hurst has been criticized for his failure to include the legal histories of Native Americans, just to give one example.

The debate over the relationship of law, and lawfulness, to western history has been further enriched over the past two decades by a fourth, arguably more inclusive approach, which focuses on the transmission of law with the migration of people. Instead of leaving the legal system behind, settlers brought their law with them, using legal concepts and rules to govern their relations in wagon trains, just to take one example, as well as to structure new settlements and enterprises. John Philip Reid's influential *Law for the Elephant* (1980), studied the legal habits and patterns of behavior that migrants brought with them as they traveled the overland trail in the mid-nineteenth century. Attention to the migration of laws along with the people who obey or defy them allows for a richer and more layered sense of legal development.

The insight into the "law-mindedness" of European-American settlers, however rich in attention to the legal world of white migrants, must be supplemented by attention to the myriad native legal cultures that existed on the ground before widespread migration, or that were imposed under Spanish or French rule in territories that were acquired through the 1803 Louisiana Purchase or the Mexican American War (1846–48). The study of the law of expansion through treaty, for example, is a field that deserves more attention from contemporary scholars. Outside the rich scholarship on treaties with Native American tribes discussed later in this essay, the classic work in the field remains Everett Somerville Brown's *The Constitutional History of the Louisiana Purchase* (1920).

The violent conflict and presumed lawlessness that has been the subject of many fictional as well as historical treatments of the West was often based in dramatic conflicts between two different legal cultures, each of which rewarded or punished behavior differently the other. Because it makes sense to think of law and legal order as both a system of meaning and the institutional structures that enforce the political power of the state, it is possible to conceive of a given geographic location as containing more than one legal culture, even if there was a single, dominant political system. Native American, Chinese, and Mexican legal traditions, just to name a few, varied widely in their approaches to questions of property rights, marriage, murder, and so on. The "contact of cultures" that historians refer to when they talk about Native and European peoples encountering each other in early colonial North America, could readily be extended to the far more cosmopolitan trans-Mississippi West of the nineteenth century. Much of this essay, therefore, will be devoted to works that have probed the contacts and conflicts that are unique to western legal history, and that have shaped important and vital aspects of local and national law, including immigration, federalism, marriage, citizenship, and religious liberty.

Studies that document the imposition of Anglo-American law and legal traditions in colonial Hawaii, the territorial Rocky Mountain West, and early California all treat this contact of cultures. Sally Engle Merry's recent *Colonizing Hawai'i* (2000) is a superb account of the transformation of a society through law and legal rules, as well as of the resistance to that transformation. As Merry shows, religious conviction and sectarian legal principles were vital early aspects of the discourse of colonization, as were the assertion of control over sexuality and marital relationships. David Langum's *Law and Community on the Mexican California Frontier* (1987) shows the profound uneasiness that Anglo-Americans experienced when living outside a common law system. The collision between a less formal, yet more hierarchical, system for dispute resolution under Mexican law and the litigious, yet arguably also more predictable, adjudication of suits under the common law system, meant that neither side could rest easy in the legal world of the other.

Equally important, legal traditions and conflict over legal regimes developed not only between Anglo-Americans and those with whom they came in contact, but also within the dominant culture. The most important example of this internecine conflict is the case of territorial Utah, settled in the late 1840s and then controlled by the Church of Jesus Christ of Latter-day Saints, commonly called "Mormons." Despite the separation of church and state elsewhere in the country, in Utah religious faith demanded a theocratic government. Mormons also rejected the common law, and provided that the decisions of the church "could not be legally questioned." Most important, from the perspective of outsiders, was the practice of polygamy, and the fundamental alteration of the law and practice of marriage that the union of one man with more than one woman entailed. We now have extensive research into the conflict that polygamy created with the rest of the country, including this author's *The Mormon Question* (2002), which focuses on the constitutional struggle between the Saints and their opponents, as well as the relationship of marriage to broader understandings of law, citizenship, and democracy. Kathryn Daynes' *More Wives Than One* (2001) examines the myriad ways in which change of marital structure affected the broader Mormon society and economy. Among the most interesting developments within Utah was the creation of a well-documented, functioning alternative legal system operated by the church, which is explored in Edwin Firmage and Richard Collin Mangrum's *Zion in the Courts* (1988). Because much vital archival material is owned by the LDS Church, however, and access to these materials is restricted, it is not likely that the internal functioning of church courts will be subjected to rigorous analysis in the foreseeable future.

Woman suffrage, too, found its first major successes in the West. Wyoming and Utah, both territories rather than states, enacted woman suffrage bills in 1869 and 1870. Although Wyoming's statute was described as a ploy designed to lure women settlers, and Utah's was primarily crafted with an eye to increasing the Mormon majority in territorial elections, there can be no doubt that the cause of women's rights in the West drew considerable attention to both territories, and to subsequent action by western states. The debate over suffrage for women in the rest of the country, and the re-visioning of political community that the extension of the power of the franchise beyond white men entailed, was also tinged with regional interests and biases. As this author points out in her article "The Liberty of Self-Degradation," (1996), eastern critics of western woman suffrage freighted western experiments with the burden of proving the worth of suffrage for all women. Equally important, the relationship between woman suffrage and questions of race, expansionism and empire converged in debates over citizenship for women, as Allison Sneider demonstrates in "Reconstruction, Expansion and Empire" (1999).

Other areas of interest to legal historians include the development of law in relative legal vacuums. Although it is a mistake to assume that the West itself was devoid of legal cultures prior to Anglo-American settlement, it is also the case that some isolated communities experienced legal vacuums for short periods of time. For example, California after 1848 no longer belonged to Mexico, yet Mexican law still governed the territory. However, no written copies of the Mexican code were available in northern California, nor had Mexican settlement occurred so far north. Thus after the discovery of gold at Sutter's Mill, the gold fields in the late 1840s were, from a formal perspective, "ungoverned." Miners in these early days participated in the drafting of legal codes that protected property rights of small stakeholders, and provided for equitable access for newcomers. Modern scholarship has repudiated older work that assumed the gold fields were ruled only by violence. Andrea McDowell's "From Commons to Claims" (2002) analyzes the codes of 175 mining communities drafted before 1860, demonstrating instead the remarkable care that stakeholders took to create property regimes that respected the rights of outsiders. Similar informal regulations governed behavior in the early Nevada silver mines, as well.

Although the topic remains largely unexplored, it seems likely that cowboys also developed alternative legal traditions, especially in rules and behavioral codes governing cattle drives, which conflicted with the broader culture. The custom of the open range, for example, which was based on the federal government's tacit approval of free and unregulated grazing on federally owned lands, was initially recognized in many western states and territories by statute or judicial decision. By the end of the century, however, abuse and overgrazing transformed a practice that had lured ranchers and cowboys to develop vast herds of free roaming cattle. As Andrew Morriss shows in his "Miners, Vigilantes & Cattlemen" (1998), violence and conflict marked the collapse of customary practice that had sustained the spread of cattle ranching and the creation of cowboy culture.

Additional research in both these fields could help us determine how and when distinctive legal cultures emerged from the creation of communities defined primarily in terms of their labor, rather than faith or ethnicity. Equally important, such research may lead us to further qualify (or confirm) the claims of John Phillip Reid who argues in his essay "The Layers of Western Legal History," that "the adjective 'western' in western legal history is geographic, not normative" (1992). The role of vigilantism or even "lawlessness" in such communities, which preoccupied historians until recent scholarship demonstrated that communities previously assumed to be ruled by brute force were in fact not wholly anarchic, should not be confused with the endeavor to discern and describe a distinctive legal culture. Robert Dykstra and Jo Ann Manfra's recent article "The Circle Dot Cowboys at Dodge City," (2002) on the novel *The Log of a Cowboy*, for example, concludes that the fictional treatment of events in Dodge City in 1882 actually provide new evidence for law reform movements in the fabled town. Martha Umphrey's examination of legal history through the lens of Owen Wister's *The Virginian*, "The Dialogics of Meaning" (1999), although it does not tell us about a separate legal culture for cowboys, tells us that it was popular to claim that there was such a culture, and that it was especially admirable. The relationship between beliefs about law, fictional treatments, and western legal history, deserves further exploration.

The law of the western territories – especially in comparative perspective, which might also provide some indications as to the reaction of the federal government to local difference – also remains an understudied field. We have excellent work on the drafting of new state constitutions for territories seeking entrance into the Union, including Christian Fritz's "The American Constitutional Tradition Revisited" (1994), and Gordon Bakken's *Rocky Mountain Constitution Making, 1850–1912* (1987), which confirms that drafters at constitutional conventions viewed themselves primarily as participating in a larger American constitutional order, rather than inventors of a new tradition. Research into state and territorial judges tends to support the thesis that for the most part, legal professionals strove to be included among their peers in the rest of the country, rather than to make a mark as iconoclasts or radical revisionists. John Guice's *The Rocky Mountain Bench: The Territorial Supreme Courts of Colorado, Montana, and Wyoming* (1972), and John Wunder's *Inferior Courts, Superior Justice* (1979), as well as the work of Christian Fritz on California Supreme Court Justice Ogden Hoffman (1991), demonstrate that at every level most judicial officials identified themselves with the broader American legal system of the eastern States, and strove to impose legal uniformity, rather than to differentiate themselves from the East.

However, recent scholarship has not generally focused on the way territorial governments actually functioned, and whether distinctive legal regimes emerged in the interstices of federal oversight. Older studies remain central to this branch of the field. Much of the work is political and legislative rather than explicitly legal in conception, however useful it is to legal historians eager to know more about the territories. Earl Pomeroy's *The Pacific Slope* (1965) and Howard Lamar's *The Far Southwest* (1966), remain the foundational works in the field, although neither was written from an explicitly legal perspective. The example of Utah, especially, presents a distinct conflict between the legal concepts and ideals employed by federal officials sent from Washington, and the territorial legislature and even the governor, until the forced removal of Brigham Young from office in the late 1850s.

Much innovative and probing work has been in studying legal developments growing out of the West's peculiar geographic attributes, including both mineral wealth and aridity, and environmental issues generally. The law of mines and mining, which combines both the customary rules and administration of justice at placer diggings in the gold fields with Spanish and Mexican mining laws, state and federal legislation, and judicial decisions that explicated both formal and customary law, has long been of interest to legal historians. In addition to the work on gold and silver fields mentioned above, Charles Shinn's fascinating but undocumented *Mining Camps: A Study of Frontier Government* (1965) and Rodman Paul's *Mining Frontiers of the Far West* (1963) remain the most complete studies of mining customs. In general, modern research has shown that the law assumed that miners would use resources productively, and that development was to be encouraged and nurtured, primarily by giving local tradition the force of law. The impetus behind the codification of mining law at the state and federal level was generally toward privatization of mineral rights, which led to far greater concentration of wealth in the mining industry than early drafters planned or hoped.

Water law has also been central to western development, especially in the ascendancy of the doctrine of "prior appropriation," which holds that the first to put water to a "beneficial use" establishes a right to future use of the water. Donald Pisani's *Water, Land, and Law in the West* (1996) collects his essays on the law of water rights, as well as federal irrigation policy and water reclamation, forest policy, conservation, and public land. As Pisani shows, the doctrine of prior appropriation was not unheard of elsewhere. Yet its triumph in the West commodified water, and sustained the development of dams, irrigation ditches, and canals that diverted water primarily to private users. Although the doctrine was by no means universally welcomed, attempts throughout the nineteenth century at broad reform were unsuccessful. Established users, which included not only agricultural interests but hydraulic miners in California, supported private control of water throughout the West. Their interests were undergirded by widespread acceptance of the theory that, in general, government intervention in the market would force inequity and lack of productivity on most citizens, while benefiting a few favorites.

Environmental law, specifically the law of fishing, in both rivers and sea, also has attracted the attention of legal historians, first among them Arthur McEvoy, whose *The Fisherman's Problem* (1986) studies the depletion of California's fisheries. McEvoy's book documents the devastation wrought by a policy that privatized a common resource, subjecting it to a private industry's search for profit and the social pressures of race and racism that characterized the political and legal climate of nineteenth-century California. The relationship of law and public policy to the preservation of natural resources is so vital and enduring that many legal histories not traditionally considered works in environmental history should be added to the list. This includes not only the work of Donald Pisani but also Willard Hurst's treatise on the lumber industry in Wisconsin, *Law and Economic Growth* (1964), mentioned at the outset of this essay.

The control of formerly public resources, including water law and fishing rights, also profoundly affected the rights of Indians, especially when definitions of "beneficial use" and the leasing of reservation land were at issue. Irrigation, for example, expanded greatly in the late nineteenth century, transforming formerly arid land into valuable farmland. Yet the policy known as "allotment" introduced by the Dawes Act of 1886, which provided for distribution of reservation land to tribal members as private owners, undermined the value that would have flowed to tribes through the increased agricultural productivity of reservation lands. In many cases, non-native farmers acquired the allotted lands within a generation of the introduction of the policy, as Donald Pisani showed in his "Irrigation, Water Rights, and the Betrayal of

Indian Allotment" (1986). Forced "assimilation" of native peoples into the private property rules of the American legal system characterized the last decade of the nineteenth century, and continued throughout much of the twentieth.

The broader relationship of Native Americans to western legal history has produced some of the most insightful and innovative work in the field, beginning in the 1940s with the classic work of Karl Llewellyn and Adamson Hoebel, *The Cheyenne Way* (1941), which focused on the sophisticated legal culture of the Cheyenne before the end of the buffalo, and including John Philip Reid's recent work *Patterns of Vengeance* (1999), which studies a concept as fundamental as the law of "vengeance" across a spectrum of tribes. Much work remains to be done, however, on the many and varied legal structures of tribal cultures, and their change over the course of the nineteenth century. In many cases, tribal laws that existed before sustained contact and white settlement were challenged, and often ignored, by state and federal officials. In addition, native cultures from the East were transplanted to new, western locations through the forced removals in the 1820s and 1830s and beyond.

Work on federal law relating to Indians is extensive, and includes explorations of the nature and limits of the sovereignty of tribes in American constitutional and statutory law, the status of treaties, and the recognition of tribal judgments in federal courts. Sidney Harring's *Crow Dog's Case* (1994), an examination of Sioux law and territorial sovereignty in the late nineteenth century, as well as of the federal law of native peoples and their rights, argues that Indian law and history should be more fully integrated into basic legal concepts, such as land policy, expansionism, and economic development. Despite federal courts' description of native tribes as "domestic, dependent nations" with limited yet valid claims to their lands, Indian peoples endured repeated, uncompensated violation of treaty and other property and personal rights in the nineteenth century that have been the subject of litigation and controversy in the twentieth and twenty-first centuries. Blue Clark's *Lone Wolf v. Hitchcock* (1994) examines the law of Indian treaties, and the relationship of treaty obligations to the legal experience of Native Americans in the nineteenth century. As a result of the unique and imperiled position of Indians and their legal cultures throughout the century, the recovery of native law and society through careful historical work cries out for additional scholarly attention.

Asian-Americans' migration to North America in the nineteenth century also created multiple layers of contact and often conflict. Recent scholarship in the field has emphasized not only that laws such as the Chinese Exclusion Act of 1882, which prohibited the immigration of Chinese laborers for ten years, were discriminatory and oppressive. As Erika Lee put it recently in her article "Enforcing the Borders: Chinese Exclusion along the U.S. Borders with Canada and Mexico, 1882–1924" (2002), Chinese were, literally, the first to be described as "illegal immigrants," as the national policy prior to 1882 had been the recruitment rather than the restriction of immigrants. Over the past two decades, scholars have also studied immigrants' resistance to legal restrictions, and their attempts to use the legal system to mitigate the effects of new legislation that violated legal principles that had traditionally governed state and national immigration policy. Scholars working on Asian-American communities have begun to document the legal strategies of Chinese immigrants, concentrating especially on federal courts and administrative agencies, and their dealings with those who sought to enter or remain in the United States. Lucy Salyer's *Laws Harsh as*

Tigers (1995), for example, argues that modern immigration law and administrative agencies were created, literally, to deal with the "Chinese Question," transferring legal questions for the first time away from courts and the rule of law, and into political and bureaucratic venues. Todd Stevens' "Tender Ties" (2002) documents the tensions between the right of husbands recognized in American law, and the racial restrictions of exclusions policy. When Chinese husbands sought to admit their wives, he demonstrates, husbands' rights often won out against racial discrimination.

As Richard Cole and Gabriel Chin argue in a recent historiographical overview of the scholarship, "Emerging from the Margins of Historical Consciousness" (1999), Chinese and Chinese Americans are the most heavily studied Asian communities for the nineteenth century, and California and federal law remain the focus of most research. The study of other Asian communities in the nineteenth century, as well as work on the internal legal culture of Chinese communities, has yet to be undertaken in depth. Equally vital, historians have only begun the extensive work needed on state and local laws, especially those outside California, which throughout most of the nineteenth century were every bit as important as federal law.

For both Native and Asian Americans, the connections and comparisons between legal paradigms for other immigrant groups and races remains largely unexplored. Citizenship, federalism, and equal protection, just to name a few important themes in nineteenth-century legal history, arguably cannot be thoroughly explored without understanding the multiple and contested roles of native peoples, immigrants, and non-Europeans. In many senses, it was in the West that the racial dichotomy of black and white never made sense. The study of the legal experiences of those whose very presence challenged white Americans to remake their laws and legal standards is vital to an appreciation for the development of American law in the broadest sense.

The recent growth and innovation of western legal history are remarkable and praiseworthy, sustaining even the publication of a journal devoted to the topic. *Western Legal History: The Journal of the Ninth Judicial Circuit Historical Society* began publication in 1988. Yet, like the rest of western history, there is no consensus on precisely what the West means in legal terms, if it means anything at all. Nor does it seem likely that such a consensus will emerge in the near future. This is both the strength and the bane of the field – a guest who must constantly explain her presence at the dinner table not only is prone to acquire an inferiority complex. She is also likely to develop an acute sense of why she is there, and how her presence makes a difference to those around her.

REFERENCES

Allen, James B.: " 'Good Guys' vs. 'Good Guys': Rudger Clawson, John Sharp, and Civil Disobedience in Nineteenth-Century Utah." *Utah Historical Quarterly* 48, no. 2. (Spring, 1980), 148–74.

Arnold, Morris S.: *Unequal Law Unto a Savage Race: European Legal Traditions in Arkansas, 1686–1836* (Fayetteville, University of Arkansas Press, 1985).

Asher, Brad: "Their Own Domestic Difficulties: Intra-Indian Crime and White Law in Western Washington Territory, 1873–1889." *Western Historical Quarterly* 27 (Summer, 1996), 189–209.

Asher, Brad: *Beyond the Reservation: Indians, Settlers, and the Law in Washington Territory, 1853–1889.* (Norman, OK: University of Oklahoma Press, 1999).

August, Ray: "Gringos v. Mineros: The Hispanic Origins of Western American Mining Law." *Western Legal History* 9 (Summer/Fall, 1996), 147–75.

August, Ray: "Cowboys v. Rancheros: The Origins of Western American Livestock Law." *Southwestern Historical Quarterly* 96, 4 (April, 1993), 475–88.

Baade, Hans W.: "The Historical Background of Texas Water Law." *St Mary's Law Review* 18 (1986), 1–98.

Bakken, Gordon Morris: "Admiralty Law in Nineteenth-Century California." *Southern California Quarterly* 58 (1976), 499–514.

Bakken, Gordon Morris: *The Development of Law on the Rocky Mountain Frontier* (Westport, CT: Greenwood Press, 1983).

Bakken, Gordon Morris: *Rocky Mountain Constitution Making, 1850–1912*, (Westport, CT: Greenwood Press, 1987).

Bakken, Gordon Morris (ed.): *Law in the Western United States*, (Norman, OK: University of Oklahoma Press, 2000).

Baxter, John O.: *Dividing New Mexico's Waters, 1700–1912* (Albuquerque, N.M., University of New Mexico Press, 1997).

Beeton, Beverly: *Women Vote in the West: The Woman Suffrage Movement, 1869–1896*, (New York: Garland Publishing, 1986).

Bigler, David L.: *Forgotten Kingdom: The Mormon Theocracy in the American West, 1847–1896*, (Spokane, WA: Arthur Clark Co., 1998).

Boessenecker, John: *Gold Dust and Gunsmoke: Tales of Gold Rush Outlaws, Gunfighters, Lawmen, and Vigilantes* (New York, John Wiley, 1999).

Brosnan, Kathleen A.: *Uniting Mountain and Plain: Cities, Law, and Environmental Change along the Front Range* (Albuquerque: University of New Mexico Press, 2002).

Brown, Everett Somerville: *The Constitutional History of the Louisiana Purchase* (Berkeley: University of California Press, 1920).

Butler, Ann M.: "Still in Chains: Black Women in Western Prisons, 1865–1910." *Western Historical Quarterly* 22. (November, 1991), 18–35.

Cannon, Kenneth L., II: "Mountain Common Law: The Extralegal Punishment of Seducers in Early Utah." *Utah Historical Quarterly* 51, 4 (Fall, 1983), 308–27.

Carlson, Leonard A.: *Indians, Bureaucrats, and Land: The Dawes Act and the Decline of Indian Farming*, (Westport, CT: Greenwood Press, 1981).

Carrico, Richard L.: "Spanish Crime and Punishment: The Native American Experience in Colonial San Diego." *Western Legal History* 3 (Winter 1990–Spring 1991), 21–33.

Case, Suzann Espenett: "Almeda Eliza Hitchcock." In Mari J. Matsuda (ed.) *Called From Within: Early Women Lawyers of Hawai'i* (Honolulu: University of Hawaii Press, 1992).

Chuman, Frank F.: *The Bamboo People: The Law and Japanese Americans*, (Del Mar, CA: Publisher's Inc., 1976).

Clark, Blue: *Lone Wolf v. Hitchcock: Treaty Rights and Indian Law at the End of the Nineteenth Century*, (Lincoln, NE: University of Nebraska Press, 1994).

Cole, Richard P. and Gabriel J. Chin: "Emerging from the Margins of Historical Consciousness: Chinese Immigrants and the History of American Law." *Law and History Review* 17, 2 (Summer, 1999), 325–64.

Cresswell, Stephen E.: *Mormons & Cowboys, Mooshiners & Klansmen: Federal Law Enforcement in the South and West, 1870–1893* (Tuscaloosa, AL: University of Alabama Press, 1991).

Cutter, Charles R.: *The Legal Culture of Northern New Spain, 1700–1810* (Albuquerque, NM: University of New Mexico Press, 1995).

Cutter, Charles R.: "Judicial Punishment in Colonial New Mexico." *Western Legal History* 8 (Winter 1995–Spring 1996), 114–29.

Daynes, Kathryn: *More Wives Than One: Transformation of the Mormon marriage system, 1840–1910* (Urbana: University of Illinois Press, 2001).

Dykstra, Robert R. and Jo Ann Manfra: "The Circle Dot Cowboys at Dodge City: History and Imagination in Andy Adams's *The Log of a Cowboy.*" *Western Legal History* 13, 1 (Spring, 2002), 19–40.

Ebright, Malcolm: "Frontier Land Litigation in Colonial New Mexico: A Determinant of Spanish Custom and Law." *Western Legal History* 8 (Summer–Fall, 1995), 198–226.

Firmage, Edwin Brown and Richard Collin Mangrum: *Zion in the Courts: A Legal History of the Church of Jesus Christ of Latter-day Saints, 1830–1900* (Urbana, IL: University of Illinois Press, 1988).

Friedman, Lawrence M. and Robert V. Percival: *The Roots of Justice: Crime and Punishment in Alameda County, California, 1870–1910* (Chapel Hill, NC: University of North Carolina Press, 1981).

Fritz, Christian G.: *Federal Justice: The California Court of Ogden Hoffman, 1851–1891* (Lincoln, NE: University of Nebraska Press, 1991).

Fritz, Christian G.: "Popular Sovereignty, Vigilantism, and the Constitutional Right of Revolution." *Pacific Historical Review* 63 (February, 1994), 39–66.

Fritz, Christian G.: "The American Constitutional Tradition Revisited: Preliminary Observations on State Constitution-Making in the Nineteenth-Century West." *Rutgers Law Journal* 25 (Summer, 1994), 945–98.

Garrison, Tim Alan: *The Legal Ideology of Removal: The Judiciary and the Sovereignty of Native American Nations* (Athens, GA: University of Georgia Press, 2002).

Gates, Paul W.: *History of Public Land Law Development* (Washington, DC: Public Land Law Review Commission, 1968).

Gates, Paul W.: *Land and Law in California: Essays on Land Policies*, (Ames: Iowa State University Press, 1991).

Gordon, Sarah Barringer: "'The Liberty of Self-Degradation': Polygamy, Woman Suffrage, and Consent in Nineteenth-Century America." *Journal of American History* 83, 4 (December, 1996), 815–47.

Gordon, Sarah Barringer: *The Mormon Question: Polygamy and Constitutional Conflict in Nineteenth-Century America* (Chapel Hill, NC: University of North Carolina Press, 2002).

Grossman, Lewis: "John C. Fremont, Mariposa, and the Collision of Mexican and American Law." *Western Legal History* 6 (Winter/Spring, 1993), 16–50.

Guice, John D.: *The Rocky Mountain Bench: The Territorial Supreme Courts of Colorado, Montana, and Wyoming, 1861–1890* (New Haven, CT: Yale University Press, 1972).

Hall, Kermit L.: "Hacks and Derelicts Revisited: American Territorial Judiciary, 1789–1959." *Western Historical Quarterly* 12, 3 (1981), 273–89.

Harbison, J. S.: "Hohfeld and Herefords: The Concept of Property and the Law of the Range." *New Mexico Law Review* 22 (1992), 459–99.

Harring, Sidney L.: *Crow Dog's Case: American Indian Sovereignty, Tribal Law and United States Law in the Nineteenth Century* (Cambridge, Cambridge University Press, 1994).

Hart, Richard E. (ed.): *Zuni and the Courts: A Struggle for Sovereign Land Rights* (Lawrence, KA: University of Kansas Press, 1995).

Hastings, David W.: "Frontier Justice: The Court Records of Washington Territory, 1853–1889." *Western Legal History* 2 (Winter 1989–Spring 1990), 79–87.

Haywood, C. Robert: *Cowtown Lawyers: Dodge City and its Attorneys, 1876–1886* (Norman: OK: University of Oklahoma Press, 1988).

Hietter, Paul T.: "How Wild Was Arizona? An Examination of Pima County's Criminal Court, 1882–1909." *Western Legal History* 12 (Summer–Fall, 1999), 183–209.

Hoebbel, E. Adamson: "The Political Organization and Law Ways of the Comanche Indians." *Memoirs of the American Anthropological Association* 5 (1940).

Hollon, W. Eugene: *Frontier Violence, Another Look* (New York, Oxford University Press, 1974).

Hollon, W. Eugene: "Law and Order." In Howard R. Lamar (ed.) *The New Encyclopedia of the American West* (New Haven, CT: Yale University Press, 1998).

Hurst, James Willard: *Law and the Conditions of Freedom in the Nineteenth-Century United States* (Madison: University of Wisconsin Press, 1956).

Hurst, James Willard: *Law and Economic Growth: The Legal History of the Lumber Industry in Wisconsin, 1836–1915* (Cambridge, MA: Harvard University Press, 1964).

Janisch, Hudson: "The Chinese, the Courts, and the Constitution: A Study of the Legal Issues Raised by Chinese Immigrants in the United States, 1850–1902." (JSD dissertation: University of Chicago, 1971).

Katz, Ellen D.: "The Six Companies and the Geary Act: A Case Study in Nineteenth-Century Civil Disobedience and Civil Rights Litigation." *Western Legal History* 8, 2 (Summer–Fall, 1995), 227–71.

Kim, Hyung-Chan: *A Legal History of Asian Americans, 1790–1990*, (Westport, CT: Greenwood Press, 1994).

Lamar, Howard R.: *The Far Southwest, 1846–1912: A Territorial History* (New Haven CT: Yale University Press, 1966).

Langum, David J.: *Law and Community on the Mexican California Frontier: Anglo-American Expatriates and the Clash of Legal Traditions, 1821–1846* (Norman, OK: University of Oklahoma Press, 1987).

Langum, David J.: "The Legal System of Spanish California: A Preliminary Study." *Western Legal History* 7 (Winter 1994–Spring 1995), 6–23.

Lee, Erika: "Enforcing the Borders: Chinese Exclusion along the U.S. Borders with Canada and Mexico, 1882–1924." *Journal of American History* 89, 1 (June, 2002), 54–86.

Libecap, Gary D.: *The Evolution of Private Mineral Rights: Nevada's Comstock Lode* (New York: Arno Press, 1978).

Limerick, Patricia N.: "Judging Western History: From the Battlefield to the Courtroom." *Western Legal History* 14 (Winter–Spring, 2001), 11–18.

Linford, Orma: "The Mormons and the Law: the Polygamy Cases, Parts I & II." *Utah Law Review* 9 (1965, 1966), 308–70, 543–91.

Llewellyn, Karl and E. Adamson Hoebbel: *The Cheyenne Way: Conflict and Case Law in Primitive Jurisprudence* (Norman, OK: University of Oklahoma Press, 1941).

McClain, Charles J., Jr.: "In re Lee Sing: The First Residential-Segregation Case." *Western Legal History* 3 (1990), 179–96.

McClain, Charles J. and Laurene Wu McClain: "The Chinese Contribution to the Development of American Law." In Sucheng Chan (ed.) *Entry Denied: Exclusion and the Chinese Community in America, 1882–1943* (Philadelphia, Temple University Press, 1991).

McClain, Charles J.: *In Search of Equality: The Chinese Struggle Against Discrimination in Nineteenth-Century America* (Berkeley, CA: University of California Press, 1994).

McCurdy, Charles W.: "Stephen J. Field and Public Land Law Development in California, 1850–1866: A Case Study of Judicial Resource Allocation in Nineteenth-Century America." *Law and Society Review.* 10 (Fall/Winter, 1976), 235–66.

McDowell, Andrea G.: "From Commons to Claims: Property Rights in the California Gold Rush." *Yale Journal of Law and the Humanities* 12. (Winter, 2002), 1–72.

McEvoy, Arthur F.: *The Fisherman's Problem: Ecology and Law in the California Fisheries, 1850–1980* (New York, Cambridge University Press, 1986).

McKanna, Clare V.: "Chinese Tongs, Homicide, and Justice in Nineteenth-Century California." *Western Legal History* 13 (Summer–Fall, 2000), 205–38.

McKanna, Clare V.: *Homicide, Race, and Justice in the American West, 1880–1920* (Tucson, University of Arizona Press, 1997).

Merry, Sally Engle: *Colonizing Hawai'i: The Cultural Power of Law* (Princeton: Princeton University Press, 2000).

Miller, Charles W.: *Stake Your Claim! The Tale of America's Enduring Mining Laws* (Tucson, AZ: Westernlore Press, 1991).

Mooney, Ralph James: "Matthew Deady and the Federal Judicial Response to Racism in the Early West." In Charles McClain (ed.) *Asian Americans and the Law: Historical and Contemporary Perspectives* (New York: Garland Publishing, 1994).

Morris, Andrew: "Miners, Vigilantes & Cattlemen: Overcoming Free Rider Problems in the Private Provision of Law." *Land & Water Law Review* 33 (1998), 581–696.

Nunis, Doyce B., Jr.: "The 1811 San Diego Trial of the Mission Indian Nazario." *Western Legal History* 4 (Winter 1991–Spring 1992), 47–58.

Paul, Rodman W.: "Mining Law." In Howard R. Lamar (ed.) *The New Encyclopedia of the American West.* (New Haven, CT: Yale University Press, 1998).

Paul, Rodman W.: *Mining Frontiers of the Far West, 1848–1880* (New York: Holt, Rinehart and Winston, 1963).

Petrik, Paula: "'Send the Bird and Cage': The Development of Divorce Law in Wyoming, 1868–1900." *Western Legal History* 6 (Summer–Fall, 1993), 153–81.

Petrik, Paula and John R. Wunder: "Women, Legal History, and the American West." *Western Legal History* 7 (Summer–Fall, 1994), 193–9.

Pfeffer, George Anthony: "Forbidden Families: Emigration Experiences of Chinese Women Under the Page Law, 1875–1882." *Journal of American Ethnic History* 6 (1986), 28–46.

Pisani, Donald J.: "Irrigation, Water Rights, and the Betrayal of Indian Allotment." *Environmental History Review* (Fall, 1986), 157–76.

Pisani, Donald J.: *To Reclaim a Divided West: Water, Law, and Public Policy, 1848–1902* (Albuquerque: University of New Mexico Press, 1992).

Pisani, Donald J.: *Water, Land and Law in the West: The Limits of Public Policy, 1850–1920,* (Lawrence, KA: University of Kansas Press, 1996).

Pomeroy, Earl S.: *The Pacific Slope: A History of California, Oregon, Washington, Idaho, Utah, and Nevada* (New York: Knopf, 1965).

Prucha, Francis Paul: *American Indian Treaties: The History of a Political Anomaly* (Berkeley: University of California Press, 1994).

Przybyszewski, Linda C. A.: "Judge Lorenzo Sawyer and the Chinese: Civil Rights Decisions in the Ninth Circuit." *Western Legal History* 1 (1988), 23–56.

Reich, Peter L.: "Western Courts and the Privatization of Hispanic Mineral Rights since 1850: An Alchemy of Title." *Columbia Journal of Environmental Law* 23 (1998), 57–87.

Reichard, David A.: "The Politics of Village Water Disputes in Northern New Mexico, 1882–1905" *Western Legal History* 9 (Winter 1996–Spring 1997), 8–33.

Reid, John Philip: *A Law of Blood: The Primitive Law of the Cherokee Nation* (New York: New York University Press, 1970).

Reid, John Philip: *Law for the Elephant: Property and Social Behavior on the Overland Trail,* (San Marino, CA: The Huntington Library, 1980).

Reid, John Philip: "The Layers of Western Legal History." In John McLaren, Hamar Foster and Chet Orloff (eds.) *Law for the Elephant, Law for the Beaver: Essays in the Legal History of the North American West* (Pasadena, CA: Ninth Judicial Circuit Historical Society, 1992).

Reid, John Philip: *Patterns of Vengeance: Cross-cultural Homicide in the North American Fur Trade,* (Pasadena, CA: Ninth Judicial Circuit Historical Society, 1999).

Reid, John Philip (2002). *Contested Empire: Peter Skene Ogden and the Snake River Expeditions* (Norman, OK: University of Oklahoma Press, 2002).

Ridge, Martin: "Disorder, Crime, and Punishment in the California Gold Rush." *Montana, the Magazine of Western History* 49, 3 (Autumn, 1999), 12–27.

Salyer, Lucy E.: *Laws Harsh as Tigers: Chinese Immigrants and the Shaping of Modern Immigration Law* (Chapel Hill, NC: University of North Carolina Press, 1995).

Scheiber, Harry N. and Charles W. McCurdy: "Eminent Domain Law and Western Agriculture, 1849–1900." *Agricultural History* 49 (1975), 112–30.

Schuele, Donna C.: "Community Property Law and the Politics of Married Women's Rights in Nineteenth-Century California." *Western Legal History* 7 (Summer–Fall, 1994), 244–81.

Shinn, Charles H.: *Mining Camps: A Study in American Frontier Government* ed. Rodman W. Paul ([1885]; New York: Harper & Row, 1965).

Skogen, Larry C.: *Indian Depredation Claims, 1796–1920* (Norman, OK: University of Oklahoma Press, 1996).

Sneider, Allison Lee: "Reconstruction, Expansion, and Empire: The United States Woman Suffrage Movement and the Re-Making of National Political Community." (PhD dissertation: University of California at Los Angeles, 1999).

Stevens, Todd: "Tender Ties: Husbands' Rights and Racial Exclusion in Chinese Marriage Cases, 1882–1924." *Law and Social Inquiry* 27, 2 (Spring, 2002), 271–305.

Strickland, Rennard: *Fire and the Spirits: Cherokee Law from Clan to Court* (Norman, OK: University of Oklahoma Press, 1975).

Traub, Stuart H.: "Rewards, Bounty Hunting, and Criminal Justice in the West: 1856–1900." *Western Historical Quarterly* 19 (August, 1988), 287–301.

Umbeck, John R.: *A Theory of Property Rights: With Application to the California Gold Rush* (Ames, IA: Iowa State University Press, 1981).

Umphrey, Martha Merrill: "The Dialogics of Legal Meaning: Spectacular Trials, the Unwritten Law, and Narratives of Criminal Responsibility." *Law and Society Review* 33 (1999), 393–423.

Van Wagenen, Lola: "In Their Own Behalf: The Politicization of Mormon Women and the 1870 Franchise." *Dialogue: A Journal of Mormon Thought* 24, 4 (Winter, 1991), 31–43.

Vaughan, Benjamin F., IV: "Property-rights problems and Institutional Solutions: Water Rights and Water Allocation in the Nineteenth-Century American West." (PhD dissertation: University of California, Berkeley, 1997).

Wunder, John R.: *Inferior Courts, Superior Justice: A History of the Justices of the Peace on the Northwest Frontier, 1853–1889* (Westport, CT: Greenwood Press, 1979).

Wunder, John R.: "The Chinese and the Courts in the Pacific Northwest: Justice Denied?" *Pacific Historical Review* 52, 2 (May, 1983), 191–211.

Wunder, John R.: "Territory of New Mexico v Yee Shun: A Turning Point in Chinese Legal Relations in the Trans-Mississippi West." *New Mexico Historical Review* 65 (July, 1990), 305–18.

Wunder, John R.: *Native Americans and the Law: Contemporary and Historical Perspectives on American Indian Rights, Freedoms and Sovereignty* (New York: Garland Publishing, 1996).

Wunder, John R.: "Law. (What's Old about the New Western History?)." *Western Legal History*. 10 (Spring–Fall, 1997), 85–116.

Zerbe, Richard O. and C. Leigh Anderson: "Culture and Fairness in the Development of Institutions in the California Gold Fields." *Journal of Economic History* 61 (2001), 114–43.

Zhu, Lipzing: *A Chinaman's Chance: The Chinese on the Rocky Mountain Mining Frontier* (Niwot, CO: University Press of Colorado, 1997).

CHAPTER EIGHT

Native Americans in the Nineteenth-Century American West

DAVID RICH LEWIS

On a hot August afternoon, sitting quietly on a hillside overlooking the Bear River just north of where it crosses from Idaho into Utah, it is hard to imagine the chill of a January morning at minus twenty degrees Fahrenheit. Shimmering heat waves rising above the summer fields in the distance obscure the memory of ice crystals hanging in the winter air and steam rising from pockets of open water along the frozen river. The muffled drone of a tractor somewhere over the horizon drowns out the sounds of people screaming, horses crying, the pop of pistols and the dull thump and crash of wagon guns turning the frozen earth like no plow ever could. I sit in a place forty minutes from my home, but one hundred and forty years distant from a past that has marked generations of Northwestern Shoshones, as well as the Mormon settlers and volunteer soldiers who contested that space.

On that bitter January morning in 1863, Colonel Patrick E. Connor and his California Volunteers slaughtered nearly 300 people and left them in the snow. On the scene of carnage a stone monument was erected in the 1930s to control the history of the event. On its side, two plaques by the Daughters of the Utah Pioneers celebrate the "battle" against "hostile" Indians and the heroism of Mormon families who nursed wounded soldiers. The only challenge to the ownership of that history appears on the south side of the monument – an inlaid stone metate, silent witness to the *Neme* experience, to the Shoshone women and children killed that morning.

That is how the story stood until the 1980s when Brigham Madsen researched and retold this nineteenth-century event (Madsen, 1985). While his documentary sources and focus on conflict and victimization reflected some of the biases of an older style of Indian history, his sensitivity to oral testimony and the Shoshone side of that story mirrored changes taking place in the western history profession. In the wake of his investigation, the National Park Service added a third plaque and the Idaho Historical Society and Idaho Department of Transportation erected a large road sign that dominates the nearby stone monument. In them, locals saw the power of the history they had controlled slipping away. Before Madsen, it was the Battle of Bear River with tributes to heroic soldiers and Mormons settlers who withstood Shoshone depredations. After Madsen, it could only be the bloody Bear River Massacre for dominion over the fertile Cache Valley and overland trail, and the recognition of Northwestern Shoshone families, then and now, who bear the burden of that contest to control land and history.

Conflict, warfare, and death have dominated the American popular imagination and histories about Native Americans in the nineteenth-century American West. Indians and that story of conflict have been portrayed in film and print as western in space and time. Every kid in my generation (and the generation before and after) knew that Indian meant nineteenth-century Plains Indian – mounted warriors in feathers and leathers, sweeping down through the red rock and sand of Monument Valley to attack the cowboy and his drove, the frontier homesteader, the stagecoach, the cavalry. Monument Valley was the quintessential western environment and all Indians became Plains Indians in our imaginations. The schools served up Squanto and Massasoit every November, and maybe a last Mohican for the bookish, but non-Plains Indians and events like Bear River did not register in the same way, or they did not register at all. Eastern Indians seemed, if anything, prologue to the *real* Indian story that was nineteenth-century Plains, western, and "frontier." Even authentic western Indians who did not openly engage the US Army or who lived in settled villages were out of the picture – hence no Southern Paiutes or Hopis, even though they actually were in the area of Monument Valley. On top of that, we told ourselves that it all ended in 1890 anyway, at Wounded Knee, at Frederick Jackson Turner's demarcation of the end of the frontier. The wars ceased and Indians disappeared into Wild West shows, into drink at the end of the trail, into isolated reservations where they became the poor farmers and the very cowboys they once fought.

Reality is always more messy than popular imagination. American Indians did not disappear in 1890 and they were never just western. That makes it difficult to discuss the historiography of nineteenth-century Indian history without stretching the definition of the West in both time and space. Although it may have begun that way, Indian history is not a subset of nineteenth-century western history. Over the years it has moved well beyond the bounds and debates of western history. Scholars have come to realize that there is more to the story than warfare and victimization, more than Native peoples acting as foils for triumphant nationalism, more than Euro-American perceptions of who Indians were and are. With the emergence of interdisciplinary ethnohistorical research in the 1950s and 1960s, the focus began to shift from dramatic moments of conflict and death, from strictly policy and contact studies, to integrative sociocultural studies and a new Indian-centered history. Researchers began to ask larger theoretical questions that bridged East–West regional peculiarities and strict eighteenth, nineteenth, and twentieth-century chronologies, uncovering continuities once hidden by master narratives of frontier victimization and assimilation or disappearance. The histories became more complex in their questions and in their telling, just as Indian experiences were more complicated than the images we grew up with. Nineteenth-century Indian history is no longer simply about the Plains, about the West, about conflict and assimilation. It is also about the metate on the fourth side of the Bear River Massacre monument, about the present of the Indian peoples who placed it there, about trying to own and trying to share the past.

This essay offers a starting place for exploration of the past topics and present trends in writing nineteenth-century American Indian history. No single essay can cover this voluminous literature adequately. For those seeking additional information, I begin by offering some bibliographic works and then move on to textbooks and studies of nineteenth-century Indian policy. After that I will discuss prominent themes that have emerged in the field within the framework of a limited number of overlapping topical categories: military history, tribal and regional histories, economics and environment, family and gender, biography, social and cultural issues, and finally who controls the Indian past and how and by whom that history should be written. Out of necessity I will try to limit examples to works on the nineteenth century and Indian groups residing in the American West. But befitting the dynamism of the field and the reality that many of the best histories do not fit neatly within those parameters, my choices will be flexible in time and in space.

Bibliographies and Historiographies

American Indian history has a venerable past and boasts a tremendous volume of scholarship judging by the published bibliographies. However, in 1982 Reginald Horsman assessed the field as a "well-trodden path," with lots of promise but very little innovation in method or topical originality. While ethnohistorical perspectives were slowly percolating through the discipline of history, studies of white perceptions of Indians, policy histories, and the persistence of "traditional blood-and-thunder accounts" kept it a parochial subfield of a parochial frontier history (Horsman, 1982: 242). Horsman's was a rather pessimistic, glass half-empty assessment, but one need only consult the major bibliographies and historiographic essays of the 1970s and early 1980s to understand his reasoning (Prucha, 1977, 1982; Malone, 1983). Historians were not pushing the envelope in focus, theory, or interpretation as far as one might have expected three decades after the founding of the American Society for Ethnohistory and a decade after Robert F. Berkhofer's call for a "new Indian history" (Berkhofer, 1971).

But Horsman captured the field on the cusp of enormous change, just as the methodological promise of ethnohistory was beginning to bear fruit in history graduate programs. The interdisciplinary conversations that emerged between historians and anthropologists during Indian Court of Claims cases of the 1950s and 1960s were being embraced by an activist generation of Indian and non-Indian scholars. Anthropologists had been quicker to integrate ethnohistorical methods of archival research and document analysis, but by the 1980s historians had begun utilizing ethnographic materials and fieldwork methods. Native American Studies programs emerged as disciplinary mixing grounds, as an alternative to traditional academic and intellectual divisions. Eclectic essay collections like Calvin Martin's *The American Indian and the Problem of History* (1987) demonstrated both the intellectual promise and unevenness of this methodological dialogue.

In many ways, the D'Arcy McNickle Center for the History of the American Indian at the Newberry Library in Chicago was at the center of this historiographic revolution. Founded in 1972, the Center brought together anthropologists and archaeologists, historians, linguists, tribal historians and teachers, writers and novelists, PhD candidates, post-doc fellows, and senior scholars, Indians and non-Indians to explore the Newberry's holding and to share their work. Under the direction of historians Francis Jennings and Frederick Hoxie, the Center produced an extensive bibliography series published in conjunction with Indiana University Press, two collections of historiographic essays that demonstrated the interdisciplinary vibrancy of the field (Swagerty, 1984; Calloway, 1988), and a bibliography that expanded the scope of sources noted in Francis Paul Prucha's bibliographies of Indian–white relations (Miller, Calloway, and Sattler, 1995). In addition, the Center held annual symposiums and workshops out of which grew a series of Occasional Papers. The Center nurtured and encouraged the "new Indian history" and interdisciplinary ethnohistorical analysis at every turn, most importantly through the people it brought together – McNickle Center fellows who raised the level of inquiry by setting off in new directions and returning to tell old stories in new ways.

By 1995 when R. David Edmunds surveyed the field, he was able to boast about the explosion in the quality of American Indian history in general. More recently, Donald Fixico (1997) and Russell Thornton (1998) have each edited volumes on the health, wealth, and methodological promise of Indian history and Native American Studies. For western historians, simply perusing the "Recent Articles" section of the *Western Historical Quarterly*, or looking at paper submissions to the Western History Association annual conferences, indicates the growing interest in and sophistication of the field of American Indian history.

Policy and Textbooks

The name that dominates nineteenth-century Indian policy studies is Francis Paul Prucha. More than any other individual, Prucha defined the field and covered it thoroughly in a series of books and articles examining Indian policy from the Trade and Intercourse Acts, to Jackson and removal, to religious reform and the Grant Peace Policy, to the allotment of reservations. His two-volume opus, *The Great Father* (1984), is a solid, carefully researched reference narrative explaining Indian–white relations and policy up to 1980. A more recent companion volume, *American Indian Treaties* (1994), explores the nuances and political meanings of treaty-making between Indians and whites. Both books are straightforward and unapologetic in their accounts of policy approaches and outcomes, and of the brutality of Indian–white relations. Yet both tend to tease out the positives of federal paternalism over Indian peoples. Politicians and reformers are well intentioned, outcomes approach the inevitable, and treaties that promise sovereignty, however limited, are political anomalies. As policy histories – and excellent ones at that – both books tell us more about Euro-Americans than about Indians, but then that is the nature of most policy studies.

Others have pursued studies of Indian policy from different angles. Robert F. Berkhofer, Jr. (1978) offers one of the most interesting approaches, tracing Euro-American intellectual traditions and the resulting images of Indians in order to explain American Indian policy. The result is an enormously readable intellectual history that ranges widely across religious, scientific, and popular conceptions of the Indian, at each stage relating those images to an evolving federal Indian policy and the American imperative of remaking Indians in their own image.

Where Berkhofer painted with a broad brush over time and space, others focused on more specific policy periods, particularly the period following the Civil War where church joined state to reform and assimilate. Among the best of the numerous policy studies is Robert H. Keller, Jr.'s (1983) work on Protestantism and Indian reform. Keller outlines the efforts of religious societies to deal with the structural problems of reservations in the West, to reform entrenched federal bureaucracies, and to supply and support missionary agents. Clyde Milner's (1982) excellent case study of Quakers among the Pawnee, Oto, and Omaha, and Milner and Floyd O'Neil's *Churchmen and the Western Indians* (1985) detail the good intentions and failed promise of religious reform. In the end the Protestant churchmen and women proved little better – and in some cases, worse – than the federal government in caring for Indians, body or soul.

Perhaps the most significant of the nineteenth-century policy studies with a more decidedly western focus is Frederick E. Hoxie's *A Final Promise* (1984). Hoxie offers a counterbalance to the prevailing "good intention" policy arguments by tracing the abandonment of Indians and the breakup of reservation lands in the wake of the 1887 Dawes General Allotment, or Severalty Act. Placing Indian policy in the context of a rapidly changing white society where racial distrust and exploitation marked white Americans' relationships with immigrants and "others," Hoxie marks the shift from the rhetoric of assimilation to the practice of marginal incorporation that was the nineteenth century's legacy to the twentieth. In the end, the irony is that marginalization held out more hope for Indians (and other racial groups) to survive and explore cultural renewals than the alternative of forced homogenization. Since then, and because of that, Hoxie concludes, "the Indians are winning" (Hoxie, 1984: 244).

Textbooks that treat nineteenth-century Indian history are largely policy and chronology driven. Few take time to incorporate discussions of native cultures and perspectives, and fewer focus on anything but a westward-moving frontier. Arrell Morgan Gibson (1980) wrote one of the more culturally sensitive textbooks for its time, followed more recently by James Wilson's excellent narrative *The Earth Shall Weep* (1998). Anthropologist Edward Spicer redirected attention to the Spanish and Mexican borders in his *Cycles of Conquest* (1962), and Roger Nichols (1998) compared US and Canadian Indian relations. Text readers by Albert Hurtado and Peter Iverson (2001), Roger Nichols (1999), and Frederick Hoxie, Peter Mancall, and James Merrell (2001) are excellent updated snapshots of the field combining previously published essays and primary documents. But in covering prehistory to the present all of these textbooks are, out of necessity, quite general about the nineteenth-century West. Robert M. Utley's *The Indian Frontier of the American West* (1984) addresses the topic most specifically, but conflict and warfare dominates the narrative, leaving little room for cultural analysis from the "other" side of the frontier.

Indians and the Military

It has been difficult to distract academics or the public from the drama of Indian wars. Most of the older histories of Indians and the American West emphasized this warfare and the victimization of Indian peoples. Most were more properly histories of military leaders, campaigns, and engagements in which Indians just happened to be the engaged. They explored the tactical movements, worldviews, perceptions, and experiences of white soldiers with Indians in a foreign western landscape. The better ones like Robert Utley's *Frontier Regulars* (1973) might include discussions of Indian war leaders and some of the reasons compelling their "uprisings" and "outbreaks," but the focus was clearly elsewhere. Even the immensely popular *Bury My Heart at*

Wounded Knee (Brown, 1970), which purported to tell the Indian side of the story, in essence told the same tale but with a different tone. Indians were still victims with little agency and less hope.

While the historiography of Indian victimization seemed an improvement in terms of the symbolic politics in the 1960s and 1970s, it obscured the reality of Indian agency and power. Indeed, the outcome of the Indian wars is undeniably known. Few would argue that Indians won much in the end, but few would also argue that Indians were simply helpless children. Indeed, both active and passive resistance afforded some choices and outcomes that pure victimization cannot explain. Clearly we need to understand the Indian side of the story and include them as military participants rather than hostiles or passive victims, to include their voices and conflicting perspectives in the creation of that narrative of warfare. Books like Anthony McGinnis' *Counting Coup and Cutting Horses* (1990) detail intertribal warfare on the Northern Plains – Indians as actors in their own military dramas with their own agendas. Thomas W. Dunlay (1982) complicates the story with his study of Indian scouts. Jerome Greene (1994) and Colin Calloway (1996) have each edited collections of Plains Indian's testimonies about battles that we know so well from the US Army's perspective. And while biographies of white military officers privilege their perceptions, there is room for more complex stories that include Indians, like Joseph C. Porter's biography of John Bourke (1986).

Tribal Histories

It is generally acknowledged that what we call "tribes" today were, in many instances, creations of nineteenth-century treaties, policies, and cultural circumstances. Even band level organization is difficult to ascertain in some instances. This point has been driven home most recently by Alexandra Harmon's elegant study of evolving Indian identities in the Pacific Northwest, *Indians in the Making* (1998). Harmon demonstrates that there is no simple or straightforward story of tribal continuity, but rather an ongoing evolution of Indian communities and identities from pre-contact to the present. Tribes and native peoples organized and reorganized their lives and cultures in both a positive ongoing internal dialogue and as adaptive strategy in dealing with others, Indian or non-Indian. Rather than viewing such change as negative, Harmon argues that this story of transforming identities over generations demonstrates the real "creativity, ingenuity, and resilience" of Indians in Washington specifically and American Indians generally (Harmon, 1998: xi). That same kind of "ethnogenesis" is evident in the earliest contact periods on the southern Plains (Anderson, 1999) and over the long term among groups like the Prairie Potawatomi who made practical decisions over time about their cultural identity (Clifton, 1977).

Despite this recognition, tribal or reservation-based histories remain at the heart of American Indian historiography. The fundamental organizing principle of the multi-volume *Handbook of North American Indians* (Sturtevant, 1978–present) is by culture area and tribe. The University of Oklahoma Press's "Civilization of the American Indian" series (begun in 1932), helped establish the pattern. These studies generally tell the story of a tribe from prehistory or contact to the late nineteenth or early twentieth century, committing the most space to discussions of nineteenth-century Indian–white relations: treaties, reservations, wars, allotment, and the breakdown of reservations. Although fairly traditional in approach and uneven in quality, some, like Edmund Danziger's, *The Chippewas of Lake Superior* (1978), John Ewers', *The Blackfeet* (1958), and Donald Worcester's, *The Apaches* (1979) stand out as enduring studies of Indian communities. Other historians pursued tribal histories more narrowly as test cases for native peoples struggling with reservation life and federal assimilation policies. William Hagan (1976) explored United States–Comanche relations and their struggles with reservation life while Donald Berthrong (1976) recounted the ordeal of Cheyennes and Arapahoes removed to Indian Territory.

Because of the growing recognition of the problems in defining tribes as static entities, tribal histories have had to become more sophisticated or become irrelevant. Individuals who are part of those communities or who have spent considerable time there have written some of the most significant tribal histories in the last two decades. They recognize that the present informs the past – that the nineteenth-century communities they wish to uncover have not disappeared, nor have they remained static. They also recognize that the history they write has tremendous legal and sociocultural consequences. Therefore, most include extended discussions of the twentieth century as more than mere post-frontier epilogues. These studies explore not only the outward resistance of native peoples to the crush of nineteenth-century westward expansion, but also their internal cultural rationales, their inventiveness and resilience, their strategies for controlling their own destinies even when their options were so narrowed by colonial powers.

Native scholars like Veronica Tiller (1983) and Steve Crum (1994) have explored the experiences of their own tribes. In the process they have braved both tribal politics and the politics of the academy. Father Peter J. Powell, adopted Northern Cheyenne, dedicated his scholarly career to explaining the complex worldview of the Northern Cheyenne in two multi-volume histories, particularly *People of the Sacred Mountain* (1981) which explores nineteenth-century Cheyenne politics and society. Martha Knack's masterful *Boundaries Between* (2001) embraces a complex multi-band, multi-state Southern Paiute ethnohistory from 1775 to 1995, the culmination of years of study. Others, including Peter Iverson (1981, 2002), Loretta Fowler (1987), and Frederick Hoxie (1995), have produced sensitive and complex nineteenth-century tribal histories that incorporate fieldwork and oral history, that stress the agency and inventiveness of Indian peoples, and that connect the people to their place, region, and present.

Tribes themselves have teamed with academic research centers to produce tribal histories and oral history collections for use in court cases or in their own educational systems. The best example of this collaboration is the University of Utah's American West Center, under the direction of Floyd A. O'Neil. A non-Indian who grew up on the Uintah-Ouray Ute Reservation, O'Neil cut his teeth supervising the Doris Duke American Indian Oral History Project for the Intermountain West – arguably one of the largest and strongest of the regional collections. O'Neil turned those tribal contacts into long-term educational partnerships. He worked with tribes to obtain outside grants, and then teamed Native scholars with center personnel in the research, writing, and publication of dozens of books, including histories of the Western Shoshone (Inter-Tribal Council of Nevada, 1976), Hupa (Nelson, 1978), Northern Ute (Conetah, 1982), Tohono O'odham (Erickson, 1994), and Santa Ana Pueblo (Bayer et al., 1994). For four decades, O'Neil helped tribes put history to work for them, on their own terms, creating resources for Indian school children and tribal leaders alike.

Studying regions as opposed to specific tribes offers an alternative to the problems inherent in narrower tribal histories. Regional perspectives allow for broader considerations of intertribal politics, trade, and social interactions, for looking at Indians in relation to regional environments, and for teasing out the variability in contact experiences, which in turn demonstrates the variety of responses and agency of different groups at the same time. This regionalist tradition appears strong in the Pacific Northwest where, as Harmon (1998) points out, identities were so complex and fluid prior to and through contact. Robert Ruby and John Brown utilized this approach in a number of works, specifically their classic *Indians of the Pacific Northwest* (1981). The Southwest has also been the focus of such integrated regional studies, most recently sophisticated explorations of intercultural exchange like James Brooks' *Captives and Cousins* (2002). For scholars, the problem of regionalism comes down to the size and complexity of the research involved, and of constructing coherent narratives that still do justice to the individual stories. State-level studies are another option, such as Rennard Strickland's (1980) compact history of a complex Oklahoma Indian experience. One of the most interesting efforts occurred in Utah. Forrest Cuch (2000), Northern Ute and director of the Utah State Division of Indian Affairs, edited a collection of Utah tribal histories, each prepared by collaborating Indian and non-Indian scholars – the ultimate combination of tribal histories by tribal members framed on a regional level.

Economics and Environment

For years, the fur trade and buffalo economy of the Plains dominated discussions of nineteenth-century Indian economic activities and environmental consequences in the West. Fur trade scholars introduced the issue of expanding market capitalism and its impact on native economies and environments. Arguments ranged over issues of Indian needs, wants, and cultural or religious proscriptions, the emergence of hunting territories, the competing understandings of trade and gift exchange, and the relative economic values Indians and Euro-Americans placed on each other's goods. World systems theory emerged to explain economic contact and dependency, only to be redefined in light of the extent of Indian agency by what has come to be called "Middle Ground" analysis – that intermediate period of political and economic contact in which neither Indian nor Euro-American actors held total sway (White, 1991). The outcome has been a more complex and nuanced picture. On the environmental side of the equation, early studies downplayed Indian impacts on the environment and stressed a kind of ecological nobility and stasis that robbed Indians of their agency as humans and ignored profound environmental changes, or else chalked those up to European contact. Cultural ecologists studied native actions and adaptations to their environments. Functionalist arguments hid the diversity of human imaginations in any single environment, while structuralist insistence on the dominance of cultural imperatives might push the imagination too far. Defining the reciprocal influences between culture and nature was as hard academically as it must have been in real life.

A number of fur trade studies focused on the nexus between native economies and the environment. Arthur Ray's *Indians in the Fur Trade* (1974) explored culture, ecology, and exchange through Hudson's Bay Company records, and traced the shifting patterns of Indian participation in that trade. Calvin Martin (1978) turned the field upside down with his provocative, if ill-supported, thesis that the fur trade was less economic than cultural as Indians assailed beavers who, they believed, had broken their reciprocal relationship and caused the epidemics ravaging native peoples. Martin's thesis precipitated an essay series (Krech, 1981) assailing his scholarship with more functionalist explanations for Indian participation in the fur trade.

The need to define more precisely not only how the environment shaped human societies, but also how humans shaped the environment and the social consequences of that ongoing and exponential process has generated important recent studies. Shepard Krech's book *The Ecological Indian* (1999) provides a balanced assessment of Indians as human actors within their environments. In dismantling myths that obscure both the material and ideational complexity of Indian motivations and human–land relationships, Krech has provoked the wrath of those satisfied with simplistic and romantic images of an "ecological Indian." Likewise, Andrew Isenberg's more complex analysis of the destruction of the North American bison (2000) eschews the simple story of racism, capitalism, and the hide trade. Isenberg identifies the multivariate factors (human and biological) in the buffalo's demise stretching back hundreds of years, including active Indian participation independent of the conditions of trade alone, and the ongoing social and environmental ramifications of their actions. Elliott West's magnificent *The Contested Plains* (1998) explores the power humans exert on their perceived and effective environments through their different "imaginings" of the same land. Conflicting visions of how to utilize existing resources (grass, bison, horses, gold, and livestock) resulted in shifts in power, environmental change, and social reorganization. New cultural and environmental imaginings of resources emerged and things changed again as one group undercut another to capture and control the energy of the Plains. West's sophisticated interdisciplinary analysis demonstrates the reciprocal interplay of culture and environment better than most.

Finally, studies by Richard White (1983), David Rich Lewis (1994), and Brian Hosmer (1999) are connected by virtue of their common focus on Indians, land, markets, and sociocultural change. They also share the strength of being comparative case studies – a difficult research task, but one that expands the power of analysis far beyond the specifics of any single group or time period. White explores the variable interplay of culture, environment, and the market in the processes whereby Indian peoples became dependent. Lewis picks up the story from the point of dependence and explores native agency and strategies for dealing with assimilationist reservation agriculture programs in light of the reciprocal impacts of environmental, subsistence, and social change. Hosmer examines the processes of market incorporation and Indian efforts to direct that social and economic process, and shape their political future. Each stresses the agency of Indian peoples in negotiating social and economic change, even when those choices were limited; each traces persistence, adaptation, and change; and each weighs the cultural, ecological, and materialist explanations of a process that stretches over three centuries.

Family and Gender

Just as the study of women in western society has exploded in the last three decades, so has the effort to create a more inclusive three-dimensional portrait of Indian women and families. Anthropologists and fur trade scholars did most of the pioneering analysis of Indian women's roles and the ethnogenesis of mixed blood families and communities. Sylvia Van Kirk (1980), Jennifer S. H. Brown (1980) and Jacqueline Peterson and Jennifer Brown (1985) address the experiences of Indian women and fur trade families. Perhaps more importantly they explore the meanings of an emerging *métis* ethnic group. The role of these new peoples cannot be ignored or underestimated. As Melissa Meyer (1994) and others have demonstrated, Indians of mixed descent emerge as a distinct ethnic group and frequently play pivotal roles in the social and political evolution of their tribes – sometimes as cultural brokers, or cultural conservators, or as agents for more radical change. Understanding inter-marriage and the nature of mixed blood social and cultural development will help us create a more complex picture of Indian ethnic/racial identity and agency, both in the past and present. The same is true for studies of gender diversity or homosexuality in a native context (Lang, 1998).

From images of Indian women as subservient drudges, the historiographic trend has been to highlight the types and methods of female power and status in both traditional and transitional society. Works like Albert Hurtado's *Indian Survival on the California Frontier* (1988) remind us of the victimization of women under the mission system, but elsewhere women emerge as important mediators of directed change, particularly in the context of reservation life with its biological and cultural assault on the family. Two recent essay collections – Nancy Shoemaker's *Negotiators of Change* (1995) and Laura Klein and Lillian Ackerman's *Women and Power in Native North America* (1995) – provide excellent overviews of the field. More specific case studies by Carol Devens (1992) and Katherine Osburn (1998) explore the responses of women to the colonization or assimilation efforts of Euro-American missionaries and federal Indian agents, from the Great Lakes to the Colorado Plateau. These studies demonstrate that while Indian women generally had more authority and respect in tribal societies than did their European counterparts, and while their status generally declined after contact, they remained active and creative in preserving the family and resisting their own sociopolitical marginalization. Generational studies of Indian women (Boyer and Gayton, 1992) and families (Starita, 1995) help us see this process over time.

Biography

Compared to the recent explosion of biographies and autobiographies of ordinary twentieth-century Indians, biographies of nineteenth-century Indians are largely limited to prominent male warriors or religious leaders, or to Sacajawea and Sarah Winnemucca, seemingly the only females in the West worthy of extended discussion. Among others, Tecumseh and Tenskwatawa, Black Hawk, Kenekuk, John Ross and Major Ridge, Ouray, Joseph, Red Cloud, Crazy Horse, Sitting Bull, Cochise, Geron-imo, Wovoka, and Quanah Parker have garnered much attention. Two particularly interesting biographies of a lesser-known individuals are E. Richard Hart's *Pedro Pino*

(2003) and Scott Christensen's *Sagwitch* (1999). Sagwitch survived the 1863 Bear River Massacre, went on to embrace Mormonism, yet remained thoroughly Shoshone. Christensen's biography is even more significant as a marker of the changing nature of biographical research. Christensen learned the Shoshone language, balanced his archival work with extensive oral testimonies, and was deeply involved with Sagwitch's descendents in producing the biography – recognizing and respecting the present of the past he was trying to narrate.

Another group of biographies and autobiographies exist of nineteenth-century, boarding-school-educated individuals who emerged as leaders of pan-Indian organizations, but these works speak more to their twentieth-century experience. Many more biographies of more ordinary nineteenth-century American Indians appear as journal articles or in collections of biographical essays on leadership (Edmunds, 1980). Two of the more insightful collections are by James Clifton (1989) and Margaret Connell Szasz (1994). Each of these explore the lives of lesser-known individuals who acted as cultural brokers or mediators, highlighting the multiple paths individuals (as opposed to groups) take in responding to contact and culture change and in defining and redefining what it means to be an Indian.

A number of nineteenth-century "as-told-to" autobiographies of more ordinary men and women exist, collected in the early twentieth century by ethnographers conducting what they saw as the "salvage anthropology" of a disappearing race. Two Crow autobiographies are particularly interesting cultural snapshots. Frank Linderman's *Pretty-shield* (1932) and Peter Nabokov's *Two Leggings* (1967) describe what life was like for the last generation of pre-reservation Crow Indians. Read together, these books provide a gendered analysis of Crow subsistence, warfare, medicine, and society. Two Leggings and Pretty-shield's voices are strong and compelling, and the personal stories they tell make larger points so much more human and immediate than the same points made in synthetic historical narratives.

Social and Cultural

This section presents a variety of studies that speak to broadly defined social and cultural issues in nineteenth-century American Indian history, from education to the law, from leadership to religious expression. To begin, let me suggest three works in particular that demonstrate the possibilities of broad social and cultural analysis. James Ronda's *Lewis and Clark Among the Indians* (1984) is, at first glance, a book about American exploration and images of Indians. But within that narrative, Ronda uncovers the multiple sides of the contact equation, offering Indian interpretations – group by group – of contact based on extensive analysis of tribal beliefs and customs. Ronda helps us glimpse native religious beliefs, trade and intertribal relations, subsistence practices and gendered divisions of labor, the power and role of sexual contact, and the cultural divides between Indians and between Indians and whites. Albert Hurtado's *Indian Survival on the California Frontier* (1988), the most extended work of Indian family and community social history, uses quantification to round out his analysis of California mission Indian experiences up to the mid-nineteenth century. On the other end of the century, Peter Iverson's *When Indians Became Cowboys* (1994) offers much more than an economic analysis of Indians and the cattle industry in the West. Iverson looks at the cultural processes whereby Indians adopted and adapted the appearance, image, attitudes, and lifestyles of rural Americans, particularly ranchers, to the point where cowboys and Indians came to share more in common with each other than they did with urban members of their own racial groups. All three authors explore the social relations of native groups to explain contact and its consequences, taking Indian social and cultural manifestations seriously in order to give Indians primacy in new constructions of older narratives.

Historians and anthropologists have spent a great deal of time examining issues of Indian political organization and leadership, and recently have deepened their social analysis of those institutions in flux. Catherine Price (1996) and Rebecca Kugel (1998) demonstrate the importance of recognizing the culturally fluid nature of Lakota and Ojibwe leadership in the mid-nineteenth century. Both historians privilege Indian worldviews and eschew simplistic progressive–traditional dichotomies in their analysis of internal social dynamics. They also recognize group factionalism, not as a negative as portrayed by earlier scholars, but – as Loretta Fowler (1982) suggests – as a rational and functional social response to assimilative pressures and culture change. Likewise, Brad Asher (1999) has explored the relationship between Indians and the Washington territorial courts and found that individuals used the law to interact and negotiate with non-Indian neighbors. This innovative social strategy "beyond the reservation" complicates the more common story of Indian dispossession in the federal courts.

The history of Indian education has seen explosive growth in the last decade, evolving from studies of policy to studies of the social world of boarding schools. Early works described the paternalistic good intentions of these schools, followed by studies that emphasized the coercive nature of power and the cultural genocide that marked boarding schools. Recently, a more nuanced interpretation has emerged that explores both the power and powerlessness of Indian students, the positives, possibilities, and pitfalls of boarding schools as experienced by a range of individuals. Most western case studies explore the twentieth-century experience using Indian letters and oral histories, but a handful extend that analysis back into the nineteenth century. David Adam's *Education for Extinction* (1995) introduces the subject and debates, while case studies like Devon Mihesuah's *Cultivating the Rosebuds* (1993), Michael Coleman's *American Indian Children at School* (1993), and Clyde Ellis's *To Change Them Forever* (1996) indicate both the good and bad elements of educational institutions and stress the complex cultural motivations and responses of students. These works reinforce studies of twentieth-century boarding schools, which suggest there is no hegemonic story of passive Indian victimization, but that Indian responses varied greatly as they adapted elements of white institutions to their own needs. In the end, nineteenth-century boarding schools decimated Indian populations and languages, but they also produced the very individuals who worked to preserve and revitalize Indianness in the twentieth century.

Studies of Indian religions in the nineteenth-century American West tend to be either broadly generalized surveys, ethnographic accounts of group-specific myths and worldviews, histories of Christian contact and an emergent religious syncretism, or discussions of specific revitalization movements like the Ghost Dance, Sun Dance, or peyotism. In the past, emphasis on the breakdown of "traditional" religions has obscured the reality of persistent Indian inventiveness and receptivity to change, but likewise an over emphasis on native incorporation and "indigenization" of

Christianity hides real instances of ritual loss. Revitalization – depicted as a universal cultural response to contact, suffering, and change – needs to be assessed as a variable response given the sociocultural differences within and between groups. And finally, we need to recognize that, as Bonnie Sue Lewis (2003) points out, Indian conversions to Christianity were (and are) real and at times complete, but that the individuals or groups did not necessarily abandon their cultural or racial identities. A number of studies navigate these issues in order to get at the nature and meaning of Indian religious practice in the context of the immense physical and social changes associated with reservation life. Joel Martin (2001) provides an excellent general survey of religious practices and issues. Joseph Jorgensen's *The Sun Dance Religion* (1972) is an early example of the power of combining comparative ethnographic data and historical events contributing to the adoption of the Sun Dance religion. Russell Thornton's (1989) analysis of the Ghost Dance in terms of native demographics and Christopher Miller's (1985) and Larry Cebula's (2003) works on plateau prophetic movements and Christianity offer new (if contested) ways of looking at revitalization movements. While changing nineteenth-century religious practices are sensitive and at times difficult subjects to research, they remain essential components for understanding Indian societies, past and present.

Finally, a number of studies consider nineteenth-century Native American oratory, arts, and material culture, items that can tell us more about the individual people, societies, and cultures that produced them than histories with loftier foci. A number of authors have collected the fragments of Indian voice preserved in official documents and private accounts. While mere bullet points of what undoubtedly were longer, more eloquent and sophisticated discussions and speeches, these snippets offer us Indian voices that are now beyond the reach of fieldwork and oral history methods. Peter Nabokov's *Native American Testimony* (1999) provides broad temporal and geographic coverage, while a host of others, like Theda Perdue's *Nations Remembered* (1993) and William Coleman's *Voices of Wounded Knee* (2000) provide oral collections of more focused groups and events. Indian art and material culture has received more attention and sophisticated analysis in books like Joyce Szabo's *Howling Wolf and the History of Ledger Art* (1994), William Wroth's *Ute Indian Arts & Culture* (2001), or Nabokov and Easton's *Native American Architecture* (1988). Even modern fiction such as James Welch's *Fools Crow* (1986) or family "memoirs" like N. Scott Momaday's *Way to Rainy Mountain* (1969) provides important insights into nineteenth-century Indian societies in motion.

Writing Indian History

The most prominent issue facing the field of Native American history currently is one that other fields have grappled with and worked through: Who should write Indian history? Whose voice should be privileged, or at least granted more weight, in the sources used, the writing of, and the audience for Indian history? It is both a healthy discussion marking the maturity of the field, and an unfortunate one, indicating the anger and mistrust that lies under the surface. It has emerged in part from the controversies over the repatriation of Indian artifacts and remains, the commercial usurpation of Indian arts, crafts, and ceremonies, and in part from a desire to control educational sources, methods, content, and perhaps history itself.

While the debate has existed and appeared in many places over time, the most focused critique was offered by nine Indian authors in the winter 1996 *American Indian Quarterly*, later expanded to twelve contributors and edited by Devon Mihesuah as *Natives and Academics* (1998). The authors argue that Indian history should have an Indian voice. The problem as they saw it is that academic histories do not reflect a Native American perspective, that Indians have no editorial control over what is written about them, and that the studies profit academics without benefiting Indian peoples. Non-Indian scholars are charged with taking and using privileged information from informants on the one hand, and with ignoring living Indians and oral testimony on the other. Some go so far as to indicate that only Indians should write Indian history, and one ventures into the identity wars by dismissing mixed-blood commentators as people living beyond tribal cultures and therefore beyond "Indianness."

Several senior scholars and the editor of the collection try to balance the more extreme critiques while buttressing the essential message: oral traditions are important resources; more Indians need to be mentored into a reformed academic system; history has an impact on the present; and scholars should respect the people they work with. They stress the benefits not only of an Indian voice, but of a more inclusive perspective, collaboration, and understanding.

The essentialist argument that only X, Y, or Z can understand and write the histories of X, Y, or Z is not new, nor will it withstand rigorous thought. Neither will the idea that any group has exclusive rights to interpret or control the past. The absolutist straw-man depiction of all scholars working in the field as intellectually corrupt and ethically bankrupt is disingenuous at best and counterproductive at worst. Yet, at heart, this collection distills some of the fundamental methodological questions and critiques of authorship and higher education that deserve serious discussion by those working in Native American ethnohistory, and recognition by those thinking of entering the field. It should not be lightly dismissed or ignored, but embraced in dialogue and the spirit of understanding.

Conclusion

At the beginning of the twenty-first century, I sit on an academic hillside overlooking a historiographic past that is difficult to see clearly or inclusively. Nineteenth-century American Indian history is a vibrant field with many important topics and books eluding coverage. But several broader trends do emerge: the methodological resonance of ethnohistory that inserted culture into contact and historic chronologies; the incorporation of Indian voice and perspective; the recognition of Indian agency – power and choice – as well as victimization; the complexity of individual actions, motivations, and beliefs, in addition to the complex workings of larger sociocultural systems; and the struggle to listen, ask, and communicate new and meaningful questions and discoveries, for everyone.

Like the stone monument marking events that took place along the Bear River in January of 1863, we need to recognize the danger in claiming exclusive ownership of the past or rights to the creation of history. The dynamic power of history comes in the interpretive dialogue between peoples, in the recognition of the emic and etic, internal and external perspectives, in the connections between past and present. We need to respect that dialogue, and remember that the future will always have the last interpretive word, like the metate on the fourth side of that stone monument.

REFERENCES

Adams, David Wallace: *Education for Extinction: American Indians and the Boarding School Experience, 1875–1928* (Lawrence: University Press of Kansas, 1995).

Anderson, Gary Clayton: *The Indian Southwest, 1580–1830: Ethnogenesis and Reinvention* (Norman: University of Oklahoma Press, 1999).

Asher, Brad: *Beyond the Reservation: Indians, Settlers, and the Law in Washington Territory, 1853–1889* (Norman: University of Oklahoma Press, 1999).

Bayer, Laura, with Floyd Montoya and the Pueblo of Santa Ana: *Santa Ana: The People, the Pueblo, and the History of Tamaya* (Albuquerque: University of New Mexico Press, 1994).

Berkhofer, Robert F., Jr.: "The Political Context of a New Indian History." *Pacific Historical Review* 40, 3 (August 1971), 357–82.

Berkhofer, Robert F., Jr.: *The White Man's Indian: Images of the American Indian from Columbus to the Present* (New York: Alfred A. Knopf, 1978).

Berthrong, Donald J.: *The Cheyenne and Arapahoe Ordeal: Reservation and Agency Life in the Indian Territory, 1875–1907* (Norman: University of Oklahoma Press, 1976).

Boyer, Ruth McDonald and Narcissus Duffy Gayton: *Apache Mothers and Daughters: Four Generations of a Family* (Norman: University of Oklahoma Press, 1992).

Brooks, James: *Captives and Cousins: Slavery, Kinship, and Community in the Southwest Borderlands* (Chapel Hill: University of North Carolina Press, 2002).

Brown, Dee: *Bury My Heart at Wounded Knee: An Indian History of the American West* (New York: Holt, Rinehart and Winston, 1970).

Brown, Jennifer S. H.: *Strangers in the Blood: Fur Trade Company Families in Indian Country* (Vancouver: University of British Columbia Press, 1980).

Calloway, Colin G. (ed.): *New Directions in American Indian History* (Norman: University of Oklahoma Press, 1988).

Calloway, Colin G. (ed.): *Our Hearts Fell to the Ground: Plains Indian Views of How the West was Lost* (Boston: Bedford/St. Martin's, 1996).

Cebula, Larry: *Plateau Indians and the Quest for Spiritual Power, 1700–1850* (Lincoln: University of Nebraska Press, 2003).

Christensen, Scott R.: *Sagwitch: Shoshone Chieftain, Mormon Elder, 1822–1887* (Logan: Utah State University Press, 1999).

Clifton, James E.: *The Prairie People: Continuity and Change in Potawatomi Indian Culture* (Lawrence: The Regents Press of Kansas, 1977).

Clifton, James E. (ed.): *Being and Becoming Indian: Biographical Studies of North American Frontiers* (Chicago: Dorsey Press, 1989).

Coleman, Michael C.: *American Indian Children at School, 1850–1930* (Jackson: University of Mississippi Press, 1993).

Coleman, William S. E.: *Voices of Wounded Knee* (Lincoln: University of Nebraska Press, 2000).

Conetah, Fred A.: *A History of the Northern Ute People* (Salt Lake City: University of Utah Printing Service for the Uintah-Ouray Ute Tribe, 1982).

Crum, Steven J.: *The Road on Which We Came, Po'i pentun tammen kimmappeh: A History of the Western Shoshone* (Salt Lake City: University of Utah Press, 1994).

Cuch, Forrest S. (ed.): *A History of Utah's American Indians* (Salt Lake City: Utah State Division of Indian Affairs and Utah State Division of History, 2000).

Danziger, Edmund J., Jr.: *The Chippewas of Lake Superior* (Norman: University of Oklahoma Press, 1978).

Devens, Carol: *Countering Colonization: Native American Women and Great Lakes Missions, 1630–1900* (Berkeley: University of California Press, 1992).

Dunlay, Thomas W.: *Wolves for the Blue Soldiers: Indian Scouts and Auxiliaries with the United States Army, 1860–90* (Lincoln: University of Nebraska Press, 1982).

Edmunds, R. David (ed.): *American Indian Leaders: Studies in Diversity* (Lincoln: University of Nebraska Press, 1980).

Edmunds, R. David: "Native Americans, New Voices: American Indian History, 1895–1995," *American Historical Review* 100, 3 (June 1995), 717–40.

Ellis, Clyde: *To Change Them Forever: Indian Education at the Rainy Mountain Boarding School, 1893–1920* (Norman: University of Oklahoma Press, 1996).

Erickson, Winston: *Sharing the Desert: The Tohono O'odham in History* (Tucson: University of Arizona Press, 1994).

Ewers, John C.: *The Blackfeet: Raiders of the Northwestern Plains* (Norman: University of Oklahoma Press, 1958).

Fixico, Donald L. (ed.): *Rethinking American Indian History* (Albuquerque: University of New Mexico Press, 1997).

Fowler, Loretta: *Arapahoe Politics, 1851–1978: Symbols in Crises of Authority* (Lincoln: University of Nebraska Press, 1982).

Fowler, Loretta: *Shared Symbols, Contested Meanings: Gros Ventre Culture and History, 1778–1984* (Ithaca: Cornell University Press, 1987).

Gibson, Arrell Morgan: *The American Indian: Prehistory to the Present* (New York: D. C. Heath, 1980).

Greene, Jerome: *Lakota and Cheyenne: Indian Views of the Great Sioux Wars, 1876–1877* (Norman: University of Oklahoma Press, 1994).

Hagan, William T.: *United States–Comanche Relations: The Reservation Years* (New Haven: Yale University Press, 1976).

Harmon, Alexandra: *Indians in the Making: Ethnic Relations and Indian Identities Around Puget Sound* (Berkeley: University of California Press, 1998).

Hart, E. Richard: *Pedro Pino: Governor of Zuni Pueble, 1830–1878* (Logan: Utah State University Press, 2003).

Horsman, Reginald: "Well-Trodden Paths and Fresh Byways: Recent Writings on Native American History." In Stanley I. Kutler and Stanley N. Katz (eds.) *The Promise of American History: Progress and Prospects* (Baltimore: Johns Hopkins University Press, 1982).

Hosmer, Brian. *American Indians in the Marketplace: Persistence and Innovation Among the Menominees and Metlakatlans, 1870–1920* (Lawrence: University Press of Kansas, 1999).

Hoxie, Frederick E.: *A Final Promise: The Campaign to Assimilate the Indians, 1880–1920* (Lincoln: University of Nebraska Press, 1984).

Hoxie, Frederick E.: *Parading Through History: The Making of the Crow Nation in America, 1805–1935* (New York: Cambridge University Press, 1995).

Hoxie, Frederick E., Peter C. Mancall, and James H. Merrell (eds.): *American Nations: Encounters in Indian Country, 1850 to the Present* (New York: Routledge, 2001).

Hurtado, Albert L.: *Indian Survival on the California Frontier* (New Haven: Yale University Press, 1988).

Hurtado, Albert L. and Peter Iverson (eds.): *Major Problems in American Indian History* 2nd edn. (Boston: Houghton Mifflin, 2001).

Inter-Tribal Council of Nevada: *Newe: A Western Shoshone History* (Reno: Inter-Tribal Council of Nevada, 1976).

Isenberg, Andrew C.: *The Destruction of the Buffalo: An Environmental History, 1750–1920* (New York: Cambridge University Press, 2000).

Iverson, Peter: *The Navajo Nation* (Westport, CT: Greenwood Press, 1981).

Iverson, Peter: *Diné: A History of the Navajos* (Albuquerque: University of New Mexico Press, 2002).

Iverson, Peter: *When Indians Became Cowboys: Native Peoples and Cattle Ranching in the American West* (Norman: University of Oklahoma Press, 1994).

Jorgensen, Joseph G.: *The Sun Dance Religion: Power for the Powerless* (Chicago: University of Chicago Press, 1972).

Keller, Robert H., Jr.: *American Protestantism and United States Indian Policy, 1869–82* (Lincoln: University of Nebraska Press, 1983).

Klein, Laura F. and Lillian A. Ackerman (eds.): *Women and Power in Native North America* (Norman: University of Oklahoma Press, 1995).

Knack, Martha C.: *Boundaries Between: The Southern Paiutes, 1775–1995* (Lincoln: University of Nebraska Press, 2001).

Krech, Shepard, III (ed.): *Indians, Animals, and the Fur Trade: A Critique of Keepers of the Game* (Athens: University of Georgia Press, 1981).

Krech, Shepard, III: *The Ecological Indian: Myth and History* (New York: W. W. Norton and Company, 1999).

Kugel, Rebecca: *To Be the Main Leaders of Our People: A History of Minnesota Ojibwe Politics, 1825–1898* (East Lansing: Michigan State University Press, 1998).

Lang, Sabine: *Men as Women, Women as Men: Changing Gender in Native American Cultures* (Austin: University of Texas Press, 1998).

Lewis, Bonnie Sue: *Creating Christian Indians: Native Clergy in the Presbyterian Church* (Norman: University of Oklahoma Press, 2003).

Linderman, Frank B.: *Red Mother* (New York, 1932); reprinted as *Pretty-shield: Medicine Woman of the Crows* (Lincoln: University of Nebraska Press, 1972).

Lewis, David Rich: *Neither Wolf Nor Dog: American Indians, Environment, and Agrarian Change* (New York: Oxford University Press, 1994).

Madsen, Brigham D: *The Shoshoni Frontier and the Bear River Massacre* (Salt Lake City: University of Utah Press, 1985).

Malone, Michael P. (ed.): *Historians and the American West* (Lincoln: University of Nebraska Press, 1983).

Martin, Calvin: *Keepers of the Game: Indian–Animal Relationships and the Fur Trade* (Berkeley: University of California Press, 1978).

Martin, Calvin (ed.): *The American Indian and the Problem of History* (New York: Oxford University Press, 1987).

Martin, Joel W.: *The Land Looks After Us: A History of Native American Religion* (New York: Oxford University Press, 2001).

McGinnis, Anthony: *Counting Coup and Cutting Horses: Intertribal Warfare on the Northern Plains, 1738–1889* (Evergreen, CO: Cordillera Press, 1990).

Meyer, Melissa L.: *The White Earth Tragedy: Ethnicity and Dispossession at a Minnesota Anishinaabe Reservation, 1889–1920* (Lincoln: University of Nebraska Press, 1994).

Mihesuah, Devon A.: *Cultivating the Rosebuds: The Education of Women at the Cherokee Female Seminary* (Urbana: University of Illinois Press, 1993).

Mihesuah, Devon A. (ed.): *Natives and Academics: Researching and Writing about American Indians* (Lincoln: University of Nebraska Press, 1998).

Miller, Christopher L.: *Prophetic Worlds: Indians and Whites on the Columbia Plateau* (New Brunswick: Rutgers University Press, 1985).

Miller, Jay, Collin G. Calloway, and Richard A. Sattler (comps.): *Writings in Indian History, 1985–1990* (Norman: University of Oklahoma Press, 1995).

Milner, Clyde A., II: *With Good Intentions: Quaker Work Among the Pawnees, Otos, and Omahas in the 1870s* (Lincoln: University of Nebraska Press, 1982).

Milner, Clyde A., II, and Floyd A. O'Neil (eds.): *Churchmen and the Western Indians, 1820–1920* (Norman: University of Oklahoma Press, 1985).

Momaday, N. Scott: *The Way to Rainy Mountain* (Albuquerque: University of New Mexico Press, 1969).

Nabokov, Peter (ed.): *Two Leggings: The Making of a Crow Warrior* (Lincoln: University of Nebraska Press, 1967).

Nabokov, Peter (ed.): *Native American Testimony: A Chronicle of Indian–White Relations from Prophesy to the Present, 1492–2000*, rev. edn (New York: Penguin Putnam, 1999).

Nabokov, Peter and Robert Easton: *Native American Architecture* (New York: Oxford University Press, 1988).

Nelson, Byron, Jr.: *Our Home Forever: A Hupa Tribal History* (Salt Lake City: University of Utah Printing Service for the Hupa Tribe, 1978).

Nichols, Roger L.: *Indians in the United States and Canada: A Comparative History* (Lincoln: University of Nebraska Press, 1998).

Nichols, Roger L. (ed.): *The American Indian: Past and Present*, 5th ed. (New York: McGraw-Hill, 1999).

Osburn, Katherine M. B.: *Southern Ute Women: Autonomy and Assimilation on the Reservation, 1887–1934* (Albuquerque: University of New Mexico Press, 1998).

Perdue, Theda: *Nations Remembered: An Oral History of the Cherokees, Chickasaws, Choctaws, Creeks, and Seminoles, 1865–1907* (Norman: University of Oklahoma Press, 1993).

Peterson, Jacqueline, and Jennifer S. H. Brown (eds.): *The New Peoples: Being and Becoming Métis in North America* (Lincoln: University of Nebraska Press, 1985).

Porter, Joseph C.: *Paper Medicine Man: John Gregory Bourke and His American West* (Norman: University of Oklahoma Press, 1986).

Powell, Peter J.: *People of the Sacred Mountain: A History of the Northern Cheyenne Chiefs and Warrior Societies, 1830–1879, with an Epilog, 1969–1974*, 2 vols. (New York: Harper and Row, 1981).

Price, Catherine: *The Oglala People, 1841–1879: A Political History* (Lincoln: University of Nebraska Press, 1996).

Prucha, Francis Paul: *A Bibliographical Guide to the History of Indian–White Relations in the United States* (Chicago: University of Chicago Press, 1977).

Prucha, Francis Paul: *Indian–White Relations in the United States: A Bibliography of Works Published 1975–1980* (Lincoln: University of Nebraska Press, 1982).

Prucha, Francis Paul. *The Great Father: The United States Government and the American Indians*, 2 vols. (Lincoln: University of Nebraska Press, 1984).

Prucha, Francis Paul: *American Indian Treaties: The Political History of a Political Anomaly* (Berkeley: University of California Press, 1994).

Ray, Arthur J.: *Indians in the Fur Trade: Their Role as Hunters, Trappers, and Middlemen in the Lands Southwest of Hudson Bay, 1660–1870* (Toronto: University of Toronto Press, 1974).

Ronda, James P.: *Lewis and Clark among the Indians* (Lincoln: University of Nebraska Press, 1984).

Ruby, Robert H. and John A. Brown: *Indians of the Pacific Northwest: A History* (Norman: University of Oklahoma Press, 1981).

Shoemaker, Nancy (ed.) *Negotiators of Change: Historical Perspectives on Native American Women* (New York: Routledge, 1995).

Spicer, Edward H.: *Cycles of Conquest: The Impact of Spain, Mexico, and the United States on the Indians of the Southwest, 1533–1960* (Tucson: University of Arizona Press, 1962).

Starita, Joe: *The Dull Knifes of Pine Ridge: A Lakota Odyssey* (New York: G. P. Putnam's Sons, 1995).

Strickland, Rennard: *The Indians in Oklahoma* (Norman: University of Oklahoma Press, 1980).

Sturtevant, William C. (gen. ed.): *Handbook of North American Indians*, 20 vols. (Washington DC: Smithsonian Institution, 1978–present)

Swagerty, W. R. (ed.): *Scholars and the Indian Experience: Critical Reviews of Recent Writing in the Social Sciences* (Bloomington: Indiana University Press, 1984).

Szabo, Joyce: *Howling Wolf and the History of Ledger Art* (Albuquerque: University of New Mexico Press, 1994).

Szasz, Margaret Connell: *Between Indian and White Worlds: The Cultural Broker* (Norman: University of Oklahoma Press, 1994).

Thornton, Russell: *We Shall Live Again: The 1870 and 1890 Ghost Dance Movements as Demographic Revitalization* (New York: Cambridge University Press, 1986).

Thornton, Russell (ed.): *Studying Native America: Problems and Prospects* (Madison: University of Wisconsin Press, 1998).

Tiller, Veronica Velarde: *The Jicarilla Apache Tribe: A History, 1846–1970* (Lincoln: University of Nebraska Press, 1983).

Utley, Robert M.: *Frontier Regulars: The United States Army and the Indian, 1866–1891* (New York: Macmillan, 1973).

Utley, Robert M.: *The Indian Frontier of the American West, 1846–1890* (Albuquerque: University of New Mexico Press, 1984).

Van Kirk, Sylvia: *"Many Tender Ties": Women in Fur Trade Society in Western Canada, 1670–1870* (Norman: University of Oklahoma Press, 1980).

Welch, James: *Fools Crow* (New York: Viking Penguin, 1986).

West, Elliott: *The Contested Plains: Indians, Goldseekers, and the Rush to Colorado* (Lawrence: University Press of Kansas, 1998).

White, Richard: *The Middle Ground: Indians, Empires, and Republics in the Great Lakes Region, 1650–1815* (New York: Cambridge University Press, 1991).

White, Richard: *The Roots of Dependency: Subsistence, Environment, and Social Change among the Choctaws, Pawnees, and Navajos* (Lincoln: University of Nebraska Press, 1983).

Wilson, James: *The Earth Shall Weep: A History of Native America* (New York: Grove Press, 1998).

Worcester, Donald E.: *The Apaches: Eagles of the Southwest* (Norman: University of Oklahoma Press, 1979).

Wroth, William (ed.): *Ute Indian Arts & Crafts: From Prehistory to the New Millennium* (Albuquerque: University of New Mexico Press, 2001).

CHAPTER NINE

Western Violence

MICHAEL A. BELLESILES

American violence has never been geographically determined. Certainly the violence of the Civil War, based largely in the eastern half of the country, exceeded anything that ever occurred in the West. Nonetheless, there are those who believe that the West as a region is somehow directly responsible for the violent nature of American society. The causality remains vague, but seems to have something to do with an imagined "Wild West" in the latter half of the nineteenth century. Historians have subjected this perception to a withering critique over the last thirty years, convincingly demonstrating that the Wild West was more about farming, mining, and building communities than about gunplay. Scholars differ on the actual number of homicides in the West, but generally agree that the rate was no higher on average than in the contemporary urban East or the South.

It is important to distinguish three kinds of violence: state-sanctioned, personal, and impersonal (or structural). The second is most notorious, with the image of the gunfight, the walk-down on the town's main street, permanently embedded in the public consciousness from its origin with Owen Wister's *The Virginian* (1902) through recent western films. Yet the first violence, committed under the authority of the state, proved most significant to the conquest of the West by the United States. Impersonal violence, the killing and maiming resulting from unregulated industrialization, claimed the most casualties. In each category, little difference can be found between the nature of violence in the West and in the rest of the country.

There is a continuing debate over the relative levels of personal violence in the West. Police and court records certainly contain a great deal of violence; the core question is: How do those levels compare with the rest of the country? The major political issues rarely concerned acts of violence, but more often focused on moral, ethnic, and economic matters, with all three closely linked. The search for scapegoats often focused on the Chinese. Generally that anger was expressed politically, often violently. Most often it was what historian Ralph Mann (1982) called "perceptions of disorder." For much of American history, whites tended to assume that violence was a cultural characteristic of nonwhite groups. The West was no different in this regard either. "According to the American-born," Mann writes, "vice as well as violence was the near-exclusive province of the 'Spanish'" (1982: 50).

The West may have long been a less brutal place than the East. There is evidence indicating that conflicts among the pre-Columbian Plains Indians were less lethal than those among the Indians on the eastern seaboard (Smith, 1937; Secoy, 1992; Ambrose, 1975). Much of this distinction could be the result of the far lower population density of the West, but the general attitude toward warfare appears distinctive on the Plains. Western Indians preferred to count coup, to register their success by hitting their opponent with a war club and then retreating, rather than by capturing and killing entire villages. With violence more a ritual than an end in itself, it was possible for both sides to claim victory after a battle resulting in few deaths.

The pattern was different among the Pueblo Indians of New Mexico. Battles were much more brutal, and losers were often exterminated and, perhaps, eaten (Gumerman, 1988; Adler, 1996). Certainly Puebloan battles with the Spanish showed less contentment with symbolic victories. But Natives were by then responding to high levels of savagery. When Francisco Coronado attacked Tiguex pueblo in retaliation for their killing some Spanish horses, he burned the town and its inhabitants. When the Spanish completed their conquest of the region at the end of the sixteenth century, they regularly turned to terror as a means of maintaining control. In 1599 Don Juan de Onate responded to the killing of thirteen Spaniards at Acoma by attacking the pueblo, killing most of its inhabitants, and condemning the survivors to slavery, after ordering a foot cut off of all the men.

Such tactics seemed to work, as the pueblos remained pacified until 1680. In that year the New Mexico Indians rose in revolt, killed more than 15 percent of the 2,350 Spanish settlers, and drove the rest from the region. Twelve years later the Spanish returned under Diego de Vargas, though it was necessary to repress another uprising among the pueblos in 1696.

It must be noted that most Spanish battles with western Indians were nowhere near as devastating as those that occurred on the east coast in the early seventeenth century. However, the clash of European powers accelerated violence in the West. Slave raids encouraged by the Spanish and French led to constant wars among the western Indians. Each war fed the demand for revenge, producing ever more violence. Most notable were the Comanche attacks on the New Mexico pueblos in the 1760s, which destroyed Pecos and Galisteo, and the Apache raids on the Spanish provinces in the 1770s, which killed more than 1,500 people in five years.

As Patricia Limerick (1987) has pointed out, the very concept of the "West" is the product of conquest, and thus of violence. Indians conquered the lands of other tribes, as when the Sioux seized the territory of the Crow and Kiowas along the Platte in the early nineteenth century. The European-American western frontier resulted from armies moving against native peoples. This violence was unmistakable, and marked the periods of contact, conquest, and conversion.

Violence associated with the Spanish conversion of Indians to Catholicism is too often overlooked. Spanish missionaries hoped to "reduce" the Indians to a well-disciplined Christianity. Doing so almost exterminated some tribes. In California, the Franciscans brought 54,000 Indians to Christ, most of whom were made into veritable slaves of the missions in the process. Those unwilling to convert were often whipped into faith; soldiers pursued those who fled their Christian fathers, often bringing back the survivors in chains for public whippings. When Fray Junipero Serra established his first mission in 1769, an estimated 72,000 Indians lived in California from the San Francisco Bay south; by 1820 that population had fallen to an estimated 18,000.

As on the east coast, the western part of North America witnessed rebellions by the white settlers against their European masters. Starting in 1811, a series of uprisings in Texas contested Spanish control. The Spanish authorities reacted to each of these insurrections harshly. When General Jose Arredondo crushed the rebellion led by Bernardo Gutierrez de Lara in 1813, he killed hundreds of Texans. Conflict continued through 1821, with Texas losing more than half of its Spanish-Mexican population in these years before becoming part of the new Republic of Mexico.

Mexico never succeeded in establishing large, self-sufficient settlements on its northern frontier, and erred in its liberal immigration policy. As a consequence, the United States' conquest and subsequent annexation of the West through the 1846–8 Mexican War was remarkably rapid and required little military action. The Texas rebellion of 1836 included an exchange of slaughters: Santa Ana ordered the execution of the 370 prisoners taken at the Alamo in San Antonio, and of another three hundred after the Battle of Goliad; American Sam Houston allowed his troops to kill hundreds of Mexicans after the Battle of San Jacinto. California fell in the ensuing war between the United States and Mexico with much less loss of life. Forty poorly armed men surprised the small Mexican garrison at Sonoma, taking the garrison and its guns without firing a shot. Monterey, the provincial capital of California, surrendered to this force, now under the leadership of John C. Frémont, without offering any resistance. The Battle of Los Angeles ended with four deaths among the pro-US forces and none for the Mexican garrison. New Mexico fell to General Stephen Kearny's forces without a battle. When Kearny marched on to California, he met serious resistance from Andres Pico's Mexican lancers at the Battle of San Pascual. But Kearny made it through to San Diego, claimed victory, and the province fell to the United States.

Immediately after the Mexican War, the discovery of gold in the foothills of the Sierra Nevadas drew thousands of men to the West. If ever there was a formula for personal violence born of chaos, the Gold Rush was it. And yet somehow the Gold Rush regions remained remarkably nonviolent. Miners displayed an astounding respect for American legal customs. Visitors to the Gold Rush region repeatedly expressed their surprise that even towns lacking a single permanent building already had elected mayors and sheriffs. Travelers commented on the way in which goods were left lying around busy streets undisturbed, doors bore no locks (and tents could not be locked), and miners would mark mining claims with personal possessions, confident that these goods, and their claims, would be respected by others.

When a crime was committed, Gold Rush communities preferred the sheriff and judge to handle the matter. In the absence of established authority, the community acted collectively to try and sentence the miscreant, with the most common punishment being a whipping followed by exile from the area. Disputes were rarely settled individually, and miners generally did their best to follow what they thought of as correct legal procedures.

Historians of the Overland Trail have found this same respect for the legal norms of American society. John Philip Reid's important books (1980, 1997) on the subject provide compelling evidence that the overland migrants hoped to bring customs of both personal and social behavior with them to the West. Reinforcing recent research on California miners, Reid found little evidence of social chaos during the great migration west. Travelers on the Overland Trail complained when a companion used profanity; they had little tolerance for theft or violence. Despite the monotony and stress of the westward migration, personal violence rarely disrupted the journey. Homicides occurred on the Overland Trail, and were treated with shock and horror; the migrants sought the capture of the perpetrator, turning him over to either the Army or other local authority if at all possible. There is little evidence of callousness toward violence or a quick willingness to take the law into private hands. And, most telling, Reid discovered that most murders occurred at the beginning of the Overland Trail, well before the stress of the journey and the supposed collapse of social order. If anything, the contemporary narratives, journalism, and diaries of the nineteenth-century West can be a bit dull for their adherence to normality.

Fictional accounts emphasize attacks on Overland Trail migrants by Indians. There were two such major assaults: the 1854 Snake Indian attack on the Ward party that cost the lives of nineteen migrants, and the 1860 assault on the Otter–Van Orman train by the Shoshone which cost thirty-two migrants their lives. But the largest massacre of white civilians in western history was the Mountain Meadows Massacre of 1857 in which a Mormon gang and their Indian allies killed one hundred migrants.

Far more common were white massacres of Indians. Most of these slaughters occurred in the Civil War and Reconstruction period. The US Army was far from uniformly successful though, suffering a number of humiliating defeats at the hands of the Plains Indians. In the 1850s the Sioux fought the Army to a standstill, slaughtering Lieutenant John L. Grattan and his thirty men in 1854 and forcing the United States to abandon the Overland Trail for several years during the Civil War.

The Civil War transformed the response of the government to western Indians. No longer was Washington content to negotiate agreements with Indians as sovereign peoples. This was the beginning of the government's reservation policy, a more passive form of violence. The nature of warfare in the West shifted as well, as small scale encounters gave way to wars of extermination. The first of these was launched against the Navajo in 1862, in what the Navajo called *nahondzod*, the time of fear. The US Army swept in and forced the Navajo out of their traditional homes in the area of Canyon de Chelly, marching them hundreds of miles east to the desert bordering Texas. In 1863 General James Carlton warned that any Indians found off the reservation would be considered hostiles and subject to attack. Kit Carson was placed in charge of the forced removal of the Navajo, a task he conducted in the old way. Aided by Ute allies, Carson carefully maneuvered the Navajo into a hopeless situation, seizing or destroying their food stores and engaging in small encounters that left a few dead and the Navajo demoralized. By the time Carson swept into Canyon de Chelly in January 1864, he had killed one hundred Navajo and reduced the survivors to a state of starvation from which they saw no escape but surrender. Far more Navajo died from the hardship of their "long walk" to the reservation at Bosque Redondo than in Carson's campaign. Ironically, the US Army led the Navajo back to their ancestral homes in 1868, the real point of the campaign not being to move but to control the Navajo.

The US war on the Plains Indians was brutal but sporadic. Combatants on each side killed civilians indiscriminately; among the Indians, the old, women, and children probably suffered more deaths than the warriors did. During the years between

1865 and 1898, the Plains Indians killed 919 US soldiers. More than a third of this total fell at the Fetterman Massacre in 1866 and Little Bighorn in 1876. But, as in the East, the Indians continued to undermine their own success by fighting one another. Many tribes supplied valuable assistance to the US Army, while others continued traditional conflicts with modern weaponry. The Sioux, for example, killed over one hundred Pawnee at Massacre Canyon in 1873, forcing the Pawnee out of Nebraska.

On a few occasions, civilians slaughtered groups of Indians. The latter were almost always peaceful people, for it was easier to attack the nearest passive Indians rather than the more aggressive tribes that might actually fight back. In 1860 California ranchers in the Humboldt Bay area killed an estimated 185 peaceful Wiyots in response to some cattle thefts by a different Indian tribe. Such attacks did not go unchallenged in the white community. After the slaughter of the Wiyots, Edwin C. Waite, editor of the Nevada City *Journal* wrote that wars against the Indians were "schemes to plunder" generally instigated by whites (Mann, 1982: 116–17).

Though groups of civilians occasionally played a role in slaughtering Indians, that task fell mostly to state militia or the Army. In 1864, the Colorado militia under Colonel John Chivington attacked the Cheyenne village at Sand Creek, which was officially under the protection of the US Army. With outrageous savagery, Chivington's men fired on the sleeping village with howitzers, spending the rest of the day raping, sexually mutilating, and murdering the survivors, mostly women and children. The militia, which had killed some two hundred Indians and launched a war with the Cheyenne, claimed a great victory and displayed body parts to cheering Denver crowds. The US Army condemned this massacre, but four years later committed another at the Washita in Oklahoma. Colonel George A. Custer's 7th Cavalry attacked a reservation village that was, again, theoretically under government protection. Custer's troops killed Black Kettle, an ally of the whites, and one hundred other Indians. When nearby Indian warriors rushed to aid the village, Custer retreated, leaving behind Major Joel Elliott and his patrol of eighteen men, all of whom were killed. The Tucson Committee of Public Safety launched its own massacre in 1871. A mixed militia force of Anglos, Mexicans, and Papago Indians, under the command of Jesus M. Elias, attacked the Apache village at Camp Grant, Arizona, killing one hundred Apaches, only two of whom were adult males. Elias's men suffered no casualties and sold twenty-seven Apache children into slavery, in violation of the Thirteenth Amendment of the Constitution.

The most famous white massacre of Indians came at the "battle" of Wounded Knee in 1890. While attempting to disarm a group of Sioux camped at Wounded Knee Creek, South Dakota, members of the 7th Cavalry under the command of Colonel James Forsyth opened fire on the Indians. Using Hotchkiss guns, troops fired on fleeing Sioux, regardless of age or gender. The Indians fought back, killing twenty-five soldiers but suffering 150 dead and fifty wounded (forty-four of the dead were women, eighteen children).

There were a number of other massacres in the West in the nineteenth century. Most often the victims were Chinese, but many Mexicans also fell victim to angry white mobs. Nearly two dozen Chinese were killed in Los Angeles in 1871, supposedly in retaliation for the murder of a white man. In 1885 a mob of white workers in Rock Springs, Wyoming, outraged that the Chinese would not join their strike against the Union Pacific Railroad, attacked the Chinese section of town, killing twenty-eight men and driving hundreds of Chinese into the surrounding hills. That same year, a group of whites in Pierce, Idaho, lynched five Chinese men suspected of involvement in the murder of a white man, while another group of whites killed two Chinese workers in Squak Valley, Washington, for no apparent reason. Two years later, in 1887, another white mob killed ten Chinese at Log Cabin Bar, Oregon. During these years, mobs also drove the Chinese out of Seattle, Tacoma, and Eureka.

The emphasis in most books on the West on individual acts of violence is particularly interesting because of its great distance from reality. Violence in the West has tended to be collective, as was true elsewhere in the nation prior to the twentieth century. Yet it is very hard to shake the perception that there is something especially individualistic about the West. As Richard White has written, the irony of that perception is that "the American West, more than any other section of the United States, is a creation not so much of individual or local efforts, but of federal efforts. More than any other region, the West has been historically a dependency of the federal government" (1991: 57). Certainly, the government has maintained a near monopoly on the use of violent force. It was the Army that conquered the West and stationed troops along the Overland Trail. The Army oversaw the removal of the Cherokee and other eastern Indians to Oklahoma on the Trail of Tears, a journey that claimed thousands of lives. Sanctioned by the state, police and soldiers fired on striking workers throughout the West. More positively, federal marshals helped to establish legal order in the West and secured the conquered territory for its new settlers. A leading historian of western law enforcement, Frank Prassel, has observed that the western settler "probably enjoyed greater security in both person and property than did his contemporary in the urban centers of the East" (Prassel, 1972: 22).

Nonetheless, writers search for the distinctiveness of the West. Most conclude that it is found in gun use. Westerners went about "brandishing revolvers and rifles in the ordinary course of daily affairs," making the West "one of the most heavily armed populations in the world" (Brown, 1994: 394). But surely such daily use of firearms would be reflected in the contemporary court records and newspapers. Certainly farming and mining must have been difficult with the need to brandish rifles and pistols all day. Most writers fail to think through precisely the full meaning of their imagery, or to consider exactly how the West might be contrary. For instance, the mythical "Code of the West" that required rapid and violent response to any insult, is really no different from the code of male honor that existed elsewhere in the United States at that time. The "imperative of personal self-redress" insisted upon by so many authors flies in the face of the court records. Those living in the western US made use of the legal system with the same regularity as other Americans, and in the same way: primarily civil actions. Far too many writers give primacy to fictional evidence over the normative conduct found in contemporary records. That insults often resulted in violence is a cultural value attached to males in societies as diverse as the American South, Italy, and Japan. But there is usually more talk than action to such cults of masculinity, more chest-thumping aggression than actual bloodshed. That such displays of masculine honor happened on an almost daily basis in the American West is pure fantasy.

The romantic vision of the West spills over into the one truly violent social force of the West: vigilantism. Generally just another name for a lynch mob, vigilante action is often portrayed in the western context as upholding law and order in the absence of established legal systems. Yet the specifics almost always speak to motivations basically no different from those of southern lynch mobs, and yet western lynch mobs rarely earn the condemnation directed at southern mobs. Yet mobs in both the South and the West operated with similar terrorism and often for the same racist reasons. Many scholars of the West identify "belief systems" to explain western violence, yet rarely mention racism, which was probably the single most prominent cause of violence in the West.

Many writers repeat the formula that, as Harry S. Drago wrote, "in a world where all men – or nearly all – went armed, gun law became the only law, at least the only effective law" in the West (1975: vi). Such scholars offer a Hobbesian vision of the West, with the law completely ineffective or nonexistent, and social chaos necessitating violence in order to just survive. The vigilantes thus appear, oddly enough, as agents of order. The ideology of western vigilantism is usually identified as having three components: self-preservation, the right of revolution, and popular sovereignty. These elements have almost nothing to do with actual lynchings, though everything to do with justifications put forth by lynchers. The vigilante image is part of a larger mythology of a lawless West in which average people had to assert the supremacy of justice by illegal actions. Close analysis reveals a different story.

Those who romanticize vigilantism perceive it as an expression of democratic populism. Their victims would have a different view. Lynching, at its core, represents an effort to make a violent end run around the law. Given the chance, the victims, overwhelmingly Hispanic and Asian, would have preferred a judge to a mob. Much recent scholarship indicates that the law often operated as it is supposed to; though often racially changed, the courts respected the technical rules of evidence and justice. In fact, what many vigilantes objected to was precisely this respect for the rule of law, which they saw as dangerously liberal and excessively respectful of the rights of the accused. Vigilance committees were more about enforcing conformity than punishing criminals (see Mann, 1982; McGrath, 1984; McKanna, 1997, 2002).

Vigilante movements often served as a cover for economic or political feuds. Texans excelled at feuds and lynchings. The most lethal of these long-term battles was the San Sabra County War of 1893 to 1898, which claimed twenty-five lives. Twenty-four more lost their lives in the Sutton–Taylor feud, which grew out of Civil War politics and lasted thirty years. The highest yearly average came in the Lee–Peacock feud of 1867 to 1871, in which twenty people were killed. With the exception of the vigilante actions in the town of McDade between 1877 and 1886, which produced a death toll of twenty-three, the victims of the vigilantes were usually black or Hispanic. Though members of the lynch mobs often claimed to be upholding the law, they operated in the presence of fully functional legal systems. Their objection was to the failure of these legal systems to share their prejudices or the court's failure to act with sufficient speed and brutality. Several recent studies of western vigilante groups reveal that they acted after courts had found unpopular defendants innocent or had passed sentences considered too lenient. Close study generally makes it difficult to grant these lynch mobs legitimacy (see, e.g., Prassel, 1993; Barr, 1996; Carrigan, 1999).

When not racist in orientation, lynch mobs tended to be expressions of class conflict. In the last quarter of the nineteenth century the West experienced a concentration of land-ownership similar to the enclosure movement in eighteenth-century Scotland. Members of the western elite sought to create empires of land at the expense of their less prosperous neighbors. Wealthy ranchers used every means at their disposal, including hired gunmen, to dispossess those living on Congressional land grants. This battle over land marks the one real distinction between western violence and that in the rest of the country, while indicating the force of class conflict in the West. The only violence elsewhere in the US similar to these western wars of enclosure came in the South, where whites used the courts and the Ku Klux Klan to dispossess black landowners, driving thousands of freedmen into tenancy. All other components of the western class wars could be discovered elsewhere in the country as elites employed vigilante groups, marshals, Pinkertons, and the US Army to win control of the West.

Sometimes these conflicts captured sufficient attention to be labeled a "war," that very word choice helping to determine public perception. The first and most complicated of these economic battles came in New Mexico with the Lincoln County War of 1878–81. The violence began as a contest between two factions competing for economic and political advantage, adherents of James Dolan or Alexander McSween. With local law enforcement entirely on the side of Dolan, the McSween faction turned for support to hired gunmen, including Billy the Kid. When the US Army intervened, it acted in the interest of the Dolan faction, and played a role in McSween's murder. But the conflict did not end there, as several criminals took advantage of this lawlessness created in part by the government, and the "war" only ended with Pat Garrett's shooting of Billy the Kid (Utley, 1989; Nolan, 1992).

In 1884 Granville Stuart, the most powerful cattleman in Montana, created a private lynch mob to operate as vigilantes, seeking out and killing those he identified as criminals. Most of the thirty-five victims of "Stuart's Stranglers" were in fact horse-thieves operating out of the Missouri Breaks. The vigilantes, claiming to act in the name of law and order, did not arrest these criminals for trial; they simply killed them. Judging by the murals in the capitol building, the state of Montana approved of these murders.

Eight years later, neighboring Wyoming was home to the Johnson County War. But the Wyoming cattlemen proved less effective than Stuart's gang as they targeted not just rustlers, but also innocent citizens. Calling themselves "Regulators" in an effort to forge a link to an American tradition of extralegal action, these Wyoming vigilantes killed two rustlers before being confronted by a posse of local citizens who resented this violation of legal procedures. The Regulators were saved only by the intervention of the US Army, and there were no further deaths. But the ensuing response demonstrated that vigilantism enjoyed little popular support in Wyoming, as the 1892 election resulted in the defeat of the pro-vigilante Republicans.

The most unusual of these class-based conflicts came in the Mussel Slough area of California, thirty miles south of Fresno. Farmers and the railroads held competing land claims and turned to the courts for resolution. In 1879 federal judge Lorenzo Sawyer found in favor of his friend Leland Stanford of Southern Pacific. On May 11, 1880, a confrontation between the two sides produced the bloodiest civilian gunfight in western history, leaving seven men dead – five farmers and two supporters of the railroads. Walter J. Crow, who died in the encounter while fighting for the railroads, took more lives in this single shootout, three, than did any other known gunfighter on a single day (Brown, 1991: 87–127).

Other forms of industrial action were far more common than such wild shoot-outs, and were no different from elsewhere in the post-Civil War United States. The earliest labor actions, including the bitter California miners' strike of 1869, did not produce violence. Labor violence started in the east with the Great Strike of 1877 in Pittsburgh, and spread west as mine and business owners indicated a willingness to employ hired thugs against workers. Strikes led to violence at Couer d'Alene in 1892, Leadville in 1894, Telluride in 1901, Cripple Creek in 1903–4, Wheatland in 1913, Ludlow in 1914, Everett in 1916, Butte in 1917, Centralia in 1919, and Los Angeles in 1920. Just as they did against the Molly Maguires in Pennsylvania's coal fields, the industrialists employed spies to infiltrate, disrupt, and destroy the unions, and could always draw upon the militia and US Army to enforce their will. Some businesses, such as Wells Fargo and Southern Pacific, even had their own police force dedicated to keeping the unions under control. Both rich and poor used violence in the West as they did in the East. But, as elsewhere, the rich could always bring more force to bear for a longer time. This ability to sustain violence matched the elite's skill at manipulating the political and legal systems for their own benefit, guarantee-ing success in their effort to gain control of western resources.

There is an aspect to class-based violence that is rarely explored: industrial acci-dents. The word "accident" gives the impression that the tens of thousands of annual workplace deaths in the late nineteenth century were unavoidable. But that is far from the case. All major industries, mines, and railroads vigorously acted to prevent the imposition of state safety regulation while refusing to implement any safety stan-dards themselves. The result was an astoundingly high level of violence far exceed-ing the numbers killed in personal encounters. According to the Interstate Commerce Commission, the single act of coupling railway cars led to the death of 433 workers plus an additional 11,277 injurious accidents in 1893 alone. Here was violence on a grand scale that dwarfs personal violence in the West, and yet has found its way into few films.

The image of the Wild West, as Robert Dykstra (1968) has convincingly demon-strated, is grotesquely exaggerated. For instance, Butch Cassidy came from a respectable and supportive Mormon family, did not suffer privation or denial, and did not learn to use a gun until he was eighteen. Gunplay was not the norm in his robberies, the threat of violence usually proved sufficient to open bank vaults and scare off a posse. Visions of heroism come back to earth when we read of the sheriff in Montpelier, Idaho, who did not own a gun, pursuing the Wild Bunch on a bicycle. Cassidy benefited from a liberal legal system in which judges and juries released defendants for lack of evidence and technical violations of the law, with light sen-tences and paroles for those found guilty, and in which sheriffs generally adhered to strict legal procedures. The governor of Utah even met with Cassidy in an effort to cut a deal with the crook. The easy accessibility of guns transformed "a big dumb kid," as a girlfriend described Cassidy, into a celebrity criminal.

But such a reality, in which Butch Cassidy did not shoot anyone during his career as a criminal in the United States, does not generally generate much interest. Even reputable historians fall for the gunslinger image of the West. Daniel Boorstin (1965) described the events in Lincoln County in 1878 as "open warfare," in which "more than sixty men had been killed." The actual figure is twenty (perhaps twenty-one). The Johnson County "War" is often portrayed as a bloodbath; two people were murdered. From sources unknown, several scholars have followed Richard M. Brown in claiming that "By the 1860s, man-to-man gunfighting was an established practice in the West," and that there "were thousands of Western gunfighters" (Brown, 1991: 60). The standard vision of the West is one in which nearly every settler resorted to violence. Clifford Trafzer (1990) saw little difference between Kit Carson and Billy the Kid, who, he held, "had something in common – they were killers."

There were gunslingers and killers in the West, though most came nowhere near their public image. Boorstin (1965) credits Wild Bill Hickok with between thirty and eight-five killings; the actual number is either seven or eight (see Rosa, 1996). There were psychopaths like Billy the Kid and John Wesley Hardin. Hardin, who sided with the racist Taylor faction in the Sutton–Taylor feud, killed twenty men between 1868 and 1878, a record for western gunmen. But such serial killers exist in any society. It is the aggregate that matters. No one knows how many professional gunmen there were in the West in the nineteenth century, but the rarity may be suggested by the origins of the words "gunfight" and "gunslinger." Both are fictional products: Stephen Crane coined the word "gunfight" in a story in *McClure's Magazine* in 1898, while "gunslinger" first appeared in 1928.

Historians of the western frontier disagree over the number of homicides in the late nineteenth century. Some hold that there were fewer murders than in contemporary eastern and European cities, while others find comparable rates. For instance, Robert Dykstra's 1968 analysis of five cattle towns found a homicide rate of 1.5 murders per year. Richard A. Bartlett (1974) summarized the nature of the cattle towns well: they were not "sleepy little religious communities. When the herds arrived, there was plenty of noise, fights, gambling, whoring, and general carousing – but it was under control." Four people, including Wild Bill Hickock, were murdered in Deadwood, South Dakota, in 1876, its first year as a town. The community responded by establishing a police force and did not experience an equal level of homicide in the nineteenth century. There were differences between towns; Bodie, California, suffered twenty-nine homicides in the years from 1877 to 1883. But then Bodie, unlike many other western towns, made no effort to control firearms. As Richard White (1991: 332) wrote, "Those towns such as Bodie and Aurora that did not disarm men tended to bury significantly more of them. Society as a whole was able to control personal violence when the community desired to do so," though it flies in the face of the popular image of streets blocked by corpses. In his pathbreaking book on frontier violence (1974), W. Eugene Hollon argued that the frontier generally "was a far more civilized, more peaceful and safer place than American society is today." One should probably qualify that statement by stating that it was so for white settlers. But it is very difficult to generalize, as the circumstances and statistics of acts of violence differ in each county studied.

The pattern evident in most of close studies of western communities is of extreme violence in the first year or two of settlement, followed by long periods of relative peace until the end of the nineteenth century when homicide rates again rose. Two constants that did not seem to differ notably from other parts of the country or from more recent times are the gendered nature of physical violence and its relation to alcohol. As is the case today, men tend to be both the perpetrators and chief victims of homicide; most studies finding men committing more than 90% of the murders. Additionally, most acts of individual violence in the West in the last half of the nineteenth century seem to have involved alcohol, a great many occurring in or near bars (McKanna, 1997, 2002; Mocho, 1997; Taylor, 1979; Slatta, 1987).

The easy availability of firearms, especially handguns, in the aftermath of the Civil War made killing easier. One study of California in these years found guns used in 60 percent of the homicides (McKanna, 2002: 11). No less an expert than Bat Masterson described the single purpose of the revolver: "Always remember that a six-shooter is made to kill the other fellow with and for no other reason on earth" (O'Neal, 1979: vii). Those shootings that did occur tended, as today, to be quick affairs in which the victim never had a chance to defend himself, shootings from ambush being particularly common. In an age when doctors knew next to nothing about treating a gunshot wound, most shootings ended as fatalities.

Communities acted to control such violence in a number of ways. Stricter law enforcement including forbidding the carrying of firearms within town limits was one approach, as were laws against "exhibiting dangerous weapons." Many towns turned to temperance and prohibition in hopes of lowering the number of drunken brawls. A California newspaper editorialized "The habit of going armed in a farming region anywhere in California seems an insult to law and order. . . . The presence of arms engenders strife." (McKanna, 2002: 86) Wild Bill Hickok, quoted in the *Abilene Chronicle* June 8, 1871, agreed, proclaiming "There's no bravery in carrying revolvers in a civilized community. Such a practice is well enough and perhaps necessary among Indians or other barbarians, but among white people it ought to be discontinued" (Rosa, 1969: 63). Frank R. Prassel (1993) has argued that contemporary newspaper reporting on crime was closer to reality than current perceptions. Crime features in the *New York Times* were primarily about domestic violence on the east coast; reports of violence "relate to the West in only about one instance in ten, a ratio almost exactly the same as population distribution in the period." (Prassel, 1993) Meanwhile, western papers were far more interested in politics and agriculture than in crime.

And yet the image of the Wild West has proven durable, resistant to historical research. More people are shot in the opening scene of the Wild Bunch than in the entire nineteenth century in Dodge City. Louis L'Amour killed more fictional characters in shoot-outs in the pages of his books than were killed in gunfights during the entire history of the period usually known as the Wild West. Most of what the public receives about America's western heritage is filtered through the media. Historians have expended a great deal of energy over the last thirty years attempting to convince the public that the Wild West of the movies and television never existed. Their efforts have had little seeming impact; the westerns keep on coming and public officials continue to make references to our frontier heritage as the best explanation for current levels of violence. But then the images are so much more satisfying than the reality. That historians are hard put to find examples of the classic walk-down does not for a moment diminish the dramatic power of such a scene in films made at the end of the twentieth century.

The power of this fictional imagery can lead to directly contradictory information. Thus one historian (Brown, 1994: 393), in discussing Frederic Remington's painting, "What an Unbranded Cow has Cost," which shows eleven men dead or wounded, wrote, "No western gun battle over unbranded cattle or range rights claimed as many lives as Frederic Remington's painting suggests. But the picture . . . captures the spirit of the no-duty-to-retreat gunplay that characterized violence in the 19th-century West." At one and the same time, this scholar tells the reader that the myth is both false and true.

The twentieth century brought the West into line with the rest of industrial America, which meant a higher homicide rate. As western cities grew, the number of murders increased. This development is rather ironic, especially given that most accounts of western violence end in 1900. But then there is nothing unusual about violence in the West in the last century, except for the occasional dramatic event in Los Angeles (see, e.g., Woolsey, 1979). In 1943, US servicemen swept through the city's streets beating up a wide variety of non-Anglos in the Zoot Suit Riot. The Watts Riot of August 1965 marked the beginning of a wave of inner-city disturbances that shattered the complacency of white Americans. Many whites were shocked that, in the aftermath of the passage of the Civil Rights Act, race riots broke out, not in the South, but in the West. What had been largely ignored was the long simmering anger of urban African Americans over their poverty, mistreatment by largely white police forces, and confinement to ghettos. After six days of burning, looting, and shooting, thirty-four people were killed and more than a thousand injured. Few of the causes of black anger had died down by May 1992, when the truly bizarre "Rodney King Riot" claimed fifty-three lives. Furious that an all-white jury had freed the police officers charged with beating a black driver named Rodney King – a beating caught on videotape – thousands of African Americans in the poorest neighborhoods of Los Angeles took to the streets, beating whites and Koreans, and destroying an estimated billion dollars worth of property. There is evidence that other ethnic groups, including whites and Latinos, joined in the violence. For a few days near the end of the twentieth century, the popular perception of an exceedingly violent West existed in reality on the streets of Los Angeles.

Over the years, many writers on the western United States have made vague calls about what are perceived of as high levels of violence. Yet such calls are rarely accompanied by any indication of what that level of violence may have been, let alone any statistical evidence. It is only in recent years that scholars have made a concerted effort to discover the actual number of violent acts in the West, with most of their attention focusing on the traditional post-Civil-War Wild West period. The entire country suffered in these years from a dramatic increase in violent crimes, much of it racially determined, the continuation of the war under a different guise. Except for the mythological images, the western experience of violence was no different from most of the United States. In this particular at least, the West was a part of the United States from its first absorption to the present day.

REFERENCES

Adler, Michael A. (ed.): *The Prehistoric Pueblo World, A.D. 1150–1350* (Tucson, AZ: University of Arizona Press, 1996).

Ambrose, Stephen E.: *Crazy Horse and Custer: The Parallel Lives of Two American Warriors* (New York: Doubleday, 1975).

Argersinger, Peter H.: *The Limits of Agrarian Radicalism: Western Populism and American Politics* (Lawrence, KS: University Press of Kansas, 1995).

Atherton, Lewis: *The Cattle Kings* (Bloomington, IN: Indiana University Press, 1961).

Ayers, Edward L.: *Vengeance and Justice: Crime and Punishment in the Nineteenth-Century American South* (New York: Oxford University Press, 1984).

Bancroft, Hubert Howe: *Popular Tribunals*, 2 vols. (San Francisco: A. L. Bancroft & Co., 1887).

Barr, Alwyn: *Black Texans: A History of African Americans in Texas, 1528–1995* (Norman, OK: University of Oklahoma Press, 1996).

Bartlett, Richard A.: *The New Country: A Social History of the American Frontier, 1776–1890* (New York: Oxford University Press, 1974).

Beeton, Beverly: *Women Vote in the West: The Woman Suffrage Movement, 1869–1896* (New York: Garland Publishing, 1986).

Bolton, Herbert Eugene (ed.): *Spanish Exploration In The Southwest 1542–1706* (New York: Scribner's 1916).

Boorstin, Daniel J.: *The Americans: The National Experience* (New York: Random House, 1965).

Brooks, Juanita: *The Mountain Meadow Massacre* (Norman, OK: University of Oklahoma Press, 1991).

Brown, Dee: *Bury My Heart at Wounded Knee: An Indian History of the American West* (New York: Holt Rinehart & Winston, 1970).

Brown, Dee: *The Fetterman Massacre: An American Saga* (London: Barrie and Jenkins, 1972).

Brown, Richard Maxwell: "Historiography of Violence in the American West." In Michael P. Malone (ed.) *Historians and the American West* (Lincoln, NE: University of Nebraska Press, 1983).

Brown, Richard Maxwell: *No Duty to Retreat: Violence and Values in American History and Society* (New York: Oxford University Press, 1991).

Brown, Richard Maxwell: "Violence." In Clyde A. Milner, II, Carol A. O'Connor and Martha Sandweiss (eds.) *The Oxford History of the American West* (New York: Oxford University Press, 1994).

Brundage, W. Fitzhugh (ed.): *Under Sentence of Death: Lynching in the South* (Chapel Hill, NC: University of North Carolina Press, 1997).

Byrkit, James: *Forging the Copper Collar: Arizona's Labor-Management War of 1901–1912* (Tucson, AZ: University of Arizona Press, 1982).

Calloway, Colin G. (ed.): *Our Hearts Fell to the Ground: Plains Indian Views of How the West was Lost* (Boston: Bedford Books of St Martin's Press, 1996).

Cameron, Ian and Douglas Pye (eds.): *The Book of Westerns* (New York: Continuum, 1996).

Cannon, Lou: *Official Negligence: How Rodney King and the Riots Changed Los Angeles and the LAPD* (New York: Times Books, 1997).

Carrigan, William D.: "Between South and West: Race, Violence, and Power in Central Texas, 1836–1916." (PhD dissertation: Emory University, 1999).

Conot, Robert: *Rivers of Blood, Years of Darkness* (New York: Morrow, 1968).

Costo, Rupert and Jeannette Henry Costo (eds.): *The Missions of California: A Legacy of Genocide* (San Francisco: The Indian Historian Press for the American Indian Historical Society, 1987).

Couve de Murville, M. N. L.: *The Man Who Founded California: The Life of Blessed Junípero Serra* (San Francisco: Ignatius Press, 2000).

Deverell, William F.: *Railroad Crossing: Californians and the Railroad, 1850–1910* (Berkeley, CA: University of California Press, 1994).

Deverell, William and Tom Sitton (eds.): *California Progressivism Revisited* (Berkeley, CA: University of California Press, 1994).

Drago, Harry S.: *The Great Range Wars: Violence on the Grasslands* (Lincoln, NE: University of Nebraska Press, 1970).

Drago, Harry S.: *The Legend Makers: Tales of the Old-Time Peace Officers and Desperadoes of the Frontier* (New York: Putnam, 1975).

Dubofsky, Melvyn: *We Shall Be All: A History of the Industrial Workers of the World* (Chicago: Quadrangle Books, AHM Publishing Co., 1969).

Dubofsky, Melvyn: *Industrialism and the American Worker, 1865–1920*. 3rd ed. (Arlington Heights, IL: Harlan Davidson, 1996).

Dunlay, Tom: *Kit Carson and the Indians* (Lincoln, NE: University of Nebraska Press, 2000).

Dykstra, Robert R.: *The Cattle Towns* (New York: Knopf, 1968).

Dykstra, Robert R.: "To Live and Die in Dodge City: Body Counts, Law and Order, and the Case of Kansas v. Gill." In Michael A. Bellesiles (ed.) *Lethal Imagination: Violence and Brutality in American History* (New York: New York University Press, 1999).

Ehle, John: *Trail of Tears: The Rise and Fall of the Cherokee Nation* (New York: Doubleday, 1988).

Einstadter, Walter J.: "Crime News in the Old West." *Urban Life* 8 (1979), 323–30.

Eisenhower, John S. D.: *So Far From God: The U.S. War with Mexico, 1846–1848* (New York: Random House, 1990).

Escobar, Edward J.: *Race, Police, and the Making of a Political Identity: Mexican Americans and the Los Angeles Police Department, 1900–1945* (Berkeley, CA: University of California Press, 1999).

Faragher, John Mack: *Women and Men on the Overland Trail*. New Haven, CT: Yale University Press, 1979.

Fehrenbach, T. R.: *Lone Star: A History of Texas and the Texans* (New York: Macmillan, 1968).

Fritz, Christian G.: "Popular Sovereignty, Vigilantism, and the Constitutional Right of Revolution." *Pacific Historical Review* 63 (1994).

Gordon-McCutchan, R. C. (ed.): *Kit Carson: Indian Fighter or Indian Killer?* (Niwot, CO: University Press of Colorado, 1996).

Gumerman, George J. (ed.): *The Anasazi in a Changing Environment* (New York: Cambridge University Press, 1988).

Gutiérrez, Ramón A.: *When Jesus Came, the Corn Mothers Went Away: Marriage, Sexuality, and Power in New Mexico, 1500–1846* (Stanford, CA: Stanford University Press, 1991).

Halaas, David F.: *Boom Town Newspapers: Journalism on the Rocky Mountain Mining Frontier, 1859–1881* (Albuquerque, NM: University of New Mexico Press, 1981).

Hammond, George P. and Agapito Rey (eds.): *Narratives of the Coronado expedition, 1540–1542* (Albuquerque, NM: University of New Mexico Press, 1966).

Hammond, George P. and Agapito Rey (eds.): *The Rediscovery of New Mexico, 1580–1594: The explorations of Chamuscado, Espejo, Castaño de Sosa, Morlete, and Leyva de Bonilla and Humaña* (Albuquerque, NM: University of New Mexico Press, 1966).

Hammond, George P. and Agapito Rey: *Don Juan de Oñate: Colonizer of New Mexico, 1595–1628* (Albuquerque, NM: University of New Mexico Press, 1953).

Henige, David: *Numbers from Nowhere: The American Indian Contact Population Debate* (Norman, OK: University of Oklahoma Press, 1998).

Hoig, Stan: *The Sand Creek Massacre* (Norman, OK: University of Oklahoma Press, 1961).

Holliday, James S.: *The World Rushed In: The California Gold Rush Experience* (New York: Simon and Schuster, 1981).

Hollon, W. Eugene: *Frontier Violence: Another Look* (New York: Oxford University Press, 1974).

Horsman, Reginald: *Race and Manifest Destiny: The Origins of American Anglo-Saxonism* (Cambridge, MA: Harvard University Press, 1981).

Hurtado, Albert L.: *Indian Survival on the California Frontier* (New Haven, CT: Yale University Press, 1988).

Hyde, George E.: *Red Cloud's Folk: A History of the Oglala Sioux Indians* (Norman, OK: University of Oklahoma Press, 1937).

Ireland, Robert M.: "Homicide in Nineteenth-Century Kentucky." *Register of the Kentucky Historical Society* 81 (1983), 134–53.

Johnson, Susan Lee: *Roaring Camp: The Social World of the California Gold Rush* (New York: W. W. Norton, 2000).

Josephy, Alvin M.: *The Civil War in the American West* (New York: A. A. Knopf, 1991).

Kavanagh, Thomas W.: *Comanche Political History: An Ethnohistorical Perspective, 1706–1875* (Lincoln, NE: University of Nebraska Press, 1996).

Kessell, John L., Rick Hendricks, and Meredith D. Dodge (eds.): *Blood on the Boulders: The Journals of Don Diego de Vargas, New Mexico, 1694–97* (Albuquerque, NM: University of New Mexico Press, 1998).

Kessell, John L., Rick Hendricks, and Meredith D. Dodge (eds.): *That Disturbances Cease: The Journals of Don Diego de Vargas, New Mexico, 1697–1700* (Albuquerque, NM: University of New Mexico Press, 2000).

King, Cameron H. (ed.): *Revised Statutes of Arizona* (Prescott, AZ: State of Arizona, 1887).

Knaut, Andrew L.: *The Pueblo Revolt of 1680: Conquest and Resistance in Seventeenth-Century New Mexico* (Norman, OK: University of Oklahoma Press, 1995).

Lamar, Howard R. (ed.): *The New Encyclopedia of the American West* (New Haven, CT: Yale University Press, 1998).

Lane, Roger: *Violent Death in the City: Suicide, Accident, and Murder in Nineteenth-Century Philadelphia* (Cambridge, MA: Harvard University Press, 1979).

Lapp, Rudolph: *Blacks in Gold Rush California* (New Haven, CT: Yale University Press, 1997).

Lepore, Jill: *The Name of War: King Philip's War and the Origins of American Identity* (New York: Knopf, 1998).

Limerick, Patricia Nelson: *The Legacy of Conquest: The Unbroken Past of the American West* (New York: W. W. Norton, 1987).

McGrath, Roger D.: *Gunfighters, Highwaymen, and Vigilantes: Violence on the Frontier* (Berkeley, CA: University of California Press, 1984).

McKanna, Clare V.: *Homicide, Race, and Justice in the American West, 1880–1920* (Tucson, AZ: University of Arizona Press, 1997).

McKanna, Clare V.: *Race and Homicide in Nineteenth-Century California* (Reno, NV: University of Nevada Press, 2002).

Mann, Ralph: *After the Gold Rush: Society in Grass Valley and Nevada City, California, 1849–1870* (Stanford, CA: University of California Press, 1982).

Mocho, Jill: *Murder and Justice in Frontier New Mexico, 1821–1846* (Albuquerque, NM: University of New Mexico Press, 1997).

Montell, William: *Killings: Folk Justice in the Upper South* (Lexington, KY: University Press of Kentucky, 1986).

Morgan, Edmund S.: *American Freedom, American Slavery: The Ordeal of Colonial Virginia* (New York: W. W. Norton, 1975).

Nolan, Frederick W.: *The Lincoln County War: A Documentary History* (Norman, OK: University of Oklahoma Press, 1992).

O'Neal, Bill: *Encyclopedia of Western Gunfighters* (Norman, OK: University of Oklahoma Press, 1979).

Patterson, Richard M.: *Butch Cassidy: A Biography* (Lincoln, NE: University of Nebraska Press, 1988).

Paul, Rodman W.: *Mining Frontiers in the Far West, 1848–1880* (New York: Holt, Rinehart and Winston, 1963).

Perdue, Theda and Michael D. Green (eds.): *The Cherokee Removal: A Brief History with Documents* (Boston: St Martin's Press, 1995).

Phillips, Charles and Alan Axelrod (eds.): *Encyclopedia of the American West*, 4 vols. (New York: Simon and Schuster Macmillan, 1996).

Pinkerton, Allan: *Strikers, Communists, Tramps and Detectives* (New York: G. W. Carleton & Co., 1878).

Pitt, Leonard: *The Decline of the Californios: A Social History of the Spanish-Speaking Californians, 1846–1890* (Berkeley, CA: University of California Press, 1966).

Prassel, Frank R.: *The Western Peace Officer: A Legacy of Law and Order* (Norman, OK: University of Oklahoma Press, 1972).

Prassel, Frank R.: *The Great American Outlaw: A Legacy of Fact and Fiction* (Norman, OK: University of Oklahoma Press, 1993).

Price, L. Bradford (ed.): *General Laws of New Mexico* (Albany, NY: W. C. Little & Co., 1880).

Reddy, Marlita A. (ed.): *Statistical Record of Native North Americans* (Detroit: Gale, 1993).

Redfield, H. V.: *Homicide North and South* (Philadelphia: J. B. Lippincott & Co., 1880).

Reid, John Philip: *Law for the Elephant: Property and Social Behavior on the Overland Trail* (San Marino, CA: Huntington Library, 1980).

Reid, John Phillip: *Policing the Elephant: Crime Punishment, and Social Behavior on the Overland Trail* (San Marino, CA: Huntington Library, 1997).

Reid, John Phillip: *Patterns of Vengeance: Crosscultural Homicide in the North American Fur Trade* (Pasadena, CA: Ninth Judicial Circuit Historical Society, 1999).

Revised Codes of North Dakota (Bismarck, N.D.: State of North Dakota, 1896).

Robbins, William: *Colony and Empire: The Capitalist Transformation of the American West* (Lawrence, KS: University Press of Kansas, 1994).

Roberts, David: *Once They Moved Like the Wind: Cochise, Geronimo, and the Apache Wars* (New York: Simon and Schuster, 1993).

Rosa, Joseph G.: *The Gunfighter: Man or Myth?* (Norman, OK: University of Oklahoma Press, 1969).

Rosa, Joseph G.: *Wild Bill Hickok: The Man and his Myth* (Lawrence, KS: University Press of Kansas, 1996).

Ruby, Robert H. and John A. Brown: *Indian Slavery in the Pacific Northwest* (Spokane, WA: A. H. Clark & Co., 1993).

Sankewicz, Robert M.: *Vigilantes in Gold Rush San Francisco* (Stanford, CA: Stanford University Press, 1985).

Savage, W. Sherman: *Blacks in the West* (Westport, CT: Greenwood Press, 1976).

Saxton, Alexander: *The Indispensable Enemy: Labor and the Anti-Chinese Movement in California* (Berkeley, CA: University of California Press, 1971).

Schultz, Duane P.: *Month of the Freezing Moon: The Sand Creek Massacre* (New York: St Martin's Press, 1991).

Secoy, Frank Raymond: *Changing Military Patterns of the Great Plains Indians* (Lincoln, NE: University of Nebraska Press, 1992).

Slatta, Richard W: "Comparative Frontier Social Life: Western Saloons and Argentine Pulperias." *Great Plains Quarterly* 7 (1987).

Slotkin, Richard: *The Fatal Environment: The Myth of the Frontier in the Age of Industrialization, 1800–1890* (New York: Atheneum, 1985).

Slotkin, Richard: *Gunfighter Nation: The Myth of the Frontier in Twentieth-Century America* (New York: Atheneum, 1992).

Smith, Helena Huntington: *The War on Powder River* (New York: McGraw-Hill, 1966).

Smith, Marian W.: "The War Complex of the Plains Indians." *Proceedings of the American Philosophical Society* 78 (1937), 425–61.

Sonnichsen, C. L.: *I'll Die Before I'll Run: The Story of the Great Feuds of Texas* (New York: Harper, 1951).

Stewart, George R.: *Committee of Vigilance: Revolution in San Francisco, 1851* (Boston: Houghton Mifflin, 1964).

Taylor, Quintard: *In Search of the Racial Frontier: African-Americans in the American West, 1528–1990* (New York: W. W. Norton, 1998).

Taylor, William B.: *Drinking, Homicide, and Rebellion in Colonial Mexican Villages* (Stanford, CA: Stanford University Press, 1979).

Trafzer, Clifford: *The Kit Carson Campaign: The Last Great Navajo War* (Norman, OK: University of Oklahoma Press, 1990).

Unruh, John D. Jr.: *The Plains Across: The Overland Emigrants and the Trans-Mississippi West, 1840–1860* (Urbana, IL: University of Illinois Press, 1979).

Utley, Robert M.: *The Last Days of the Sioux Nation* (New Haven, CT: Yale University Press, 1963).

Utley, Robert M.: *Frontiersmen in Blue: The United States Army and the Indian, 1848–1865* (New York: Macmillan, 1967).

Utley, Robert M.: *Frontier Regulars: The United States Army and the Indian, 1866–1891* (New York: Macmillan, 1973).

Utley, Robert M.: *A Clash of Cultures: Fort Bowie and the Chiricahua Apaches* (Washington, DC: Department of the Interior, National Park Service, Division of Publications, 1977).

Utley, Robert M.: *The Indian Frontier of the American West* (Albuquerque, NM: University of New Mexico Press, 1984).

Utley, Robert M.: *Billy the Kid: A Short and Violent Life* (Lincoln, NE: University of Nebraska Press, 1989).

Vandal, Gilles: *Rethinking Southern Violence: Homicides in Post-Civil War Louisiana, 1866–1884* (Columbus, OH: Ohio State University Press, 2000).

Vestal, Stanley: *Warpath and Council Fire: The Plains Indians' Struggle for Survival in War and in Diplomacy, 1851–1891* (New York: Random House, 1948).

Weber, David J.: *The Mexican Frontier, 1821–1846: The American Southwest under Mexico* (Albuquerque, NM: University of New Mexico Press, 1982).

Weber, David J.: *The Spanish Frontier in North America* (New Haven, CT: Yale University Press, 1992).

White, Richard: "The Winning of the West: The Expansion of the Western Sioux in the Eighteenth and Nineteenth Centuries." *Journal of American History* 65 (1978).

White, Richard: *"It's Your Misfortune and None of My Own": A History of the American West* (Norman, OK: University of Oklahoma Press: 1991).

Wise, Winifred E.: *Fray Junípero Serra and the California Conquest* (New York: Scribner, 1967).

Wister, Owen: *The Virginian* (New York: Macmillan, 1902).

Woolsey, Ronald C.: "Crime and Punishment: Los Angeles County, 1850–1865." *Southern California Quarterly* 61 (1979).

Wyman, Mark: *Hard Rock Epic: Western Miners and the Industrial Revolution, 1860–1910* (Berkeley, CA: University of California Press, 1979).

Zhu, Liping: *A Chinaman's Chance: The Chinese on the Rocky Mountain Mining Frontier* (Niwot, CO: University Press of Colorado, 1997).

CHAPTER TEN

Bringing It All Back Home: Rethinking the History of Women and the Nineteenth-Century West

Elizabeth Jameson

Creation Stories

This essay began with a deceptively simple invitation: Write 7000 words about women in the nineteenth-century West. This seemingly straightforward task raises a series of dilemmas. They start with where to begin.

A history of nineteenth-century westward expansion might start with the Louisiana Purchase. Or perhaps with Lewis and Clark. A Spanish Borderlands historian might begin with Mexican independence from Spain, or with the Mexican–American War. The excruciating Texas history classes of my childhood began with Moses and Stephen F. Austin, and jumped to the war for Texas independence. Histories of states have discernible if arbitrary starting points, and it is possible to add a few women here and there to long-familiar plots. To Lewis and Clark, add Sacajawea; to frontier opportunity, add the first woman suffrage victories, in Wyoming Territory in 1869 and Utah in 1870. But adding women to the frontiers of national expansion bypasses most women and evades the question of which women a history of the nineteenth-century West should include.

A history focused not on the West itself, but on the people who sojourned or settled there, raises essential questions about women, the West, and the nineteenth century. *Which* women? The *hispanas, indias, mestizas* of Northern New Spain? The Lakota, Cree, and Blackfoot women of the northern Plains, whose territory crossed what became the Canadian border? African American Exodusters who migrated West after the Civil War? The Presentation Sisters and Sisters of Loretto who founded schools and hospitals in the West? Mormon women who pushed their handcarts to Utah in the 1850s? Each group could cite different events – epidemics, wars, famines, legislation, religious persecution or vocation – that dated their particular women's Wests, particular periods of changing gender options. From the perspectives of all the women whose lives intersected in what is now the American West, when does the nineteenth century begin and end?

Which woman, whose story, should open this history?

Perhaps Maxiwidiwiac, a Hidatsa woman who dated her birth from a smallpox epidemic, brought by traders, which killed over half her tribe in 1837. "I was born," she said, "in an earth lodge by the mouth of the Knife river, in what is now North

Dakota, three years after the smallpox winter" (Wilson, 1981: 7). Her birth coincided with the end of one period in Hidatsa history, 1787–1845, when three independent Hidatsa villages stood at the mouth of the Knife River, before the horse and hide trade brought enormous changes in the gender roles of northern Plains tribes. Horses from New Spain arrived on the northern Plains during the eighteenth century. Horses and guns made it easier for men to kill many buffalo quickly, transforming the economies of tribes that had previously hunted on foot for collective subsistence. Demand for buffalo hides depleted the herds, intensified women's labor tanning hides to prepare them for market, and altered the relationships between women and men (Hanson, 1987; Klein, 1983).

The Hidatsa economy combined hunting and agriculture. European trade goods like iron hoes also altered women's collective labor in their gardens. Agricultural change wove throughout the history Maxiwidiwiac learned from her grandmother, who taught her that the Hidatsa emerged from Miniwakan, or Devils Lake, in present-day North Dakota, bringing ground beans and potatoes from their home under the water. Maxiwidiwiac measured change in gardens. The Hidatsa, she said, learned of corn and squashes from the Mandan, and ultimately joined them near the mouth of the Heart River (Wilson, 1987).

After the disastrous smallpox epidemic, the survivors moved up the Missouri and built a joint village at Like-a-fishhook bend. She continued: "We lived in Like-a-fishhook village about forty years, or until 1885, when the government began to place families on allotments," or private plots of land (Wilson, 1987: 8). Whites also, she said, brought weeds, like thistle and mustard, new seeds for oats, wheat, watermelons, and onions, and for vegetables she considered inferior, like turnips, and big squashes.

Like-a-fishhook village became part of the Fort Berthold Indian Reservation, where, after 1885, missionaries and government agents worked to teach Indians the virtues of Christianity, private property, and patriarchal nuclear families. Maxiwidiwiac moved from an earth lodge in a village, where she was surrounded by other women and kin, to an isolated square log cabin. Her son learned English, converted to Christianity, and entered a history that charted progress in human development "from savagery to civilization" (Turner, 1993b: 60). Maxiwidiwiac became increasingly separated from other women, her story increasingly marginal to a history of the American West.

A history of the women in the nineteenth-century West could start with Maxiwidiwiac. Or it could follow the trajectory of Albert Hurtado's *Intimate Frontiers* (1999), beginning at the California Spanish missions where, in 1775, Father Junipero Serra reported the marriages of three Spanish soldiers to Native women neophytes. The same year some 800 Kumeyaay Indians revolted against rapes and missionary rule by burning Mission San Diego and killing three Spaniards. A history of women in the American West might start on the northern frontiers of New Spain, with missionary efforts to eradicate native marriage and kinship practices, and with the new peoples born of such intimate encounters.

Or it could open in Guangdong, in the Pearl River delta, where some women of the nineteenth-century West traced their ties to the place they called Gold Mountain. By the mid-nineteenth century, loss of land, high taxes, unemployment, a rapidly growing population, scarce food, the Opium Wars, the Taiping Rebellion, the Red

Turban uprisings, and interethnic warfare led many men to emigrate to the US West to work on railroads, mines, and farms. They left behind "grass widows" whose labor maintained their families and underwrote the men's journeys. Chinese women's long separations resembled the experiences of Euro-American "Gold Rush widows" who maintained homes and families "back east" while men grubbed for elusive fortunes in the western diggings. The key difference was that US Chinese exclusion laws prevented Chinese women from joining their husbands (Chan, 1986; Tsai, 1994; Yung, 1995; Peavy and Smith, 1990, 1994). One impoverished Chinese miner wrote his "Beloved Wife" during their long separation: "Because I can get no gold, I am detained in this secluded corner of a strange land" (Applegate and O'Donnell, 1994: 215). Women left behind in men's international migrations gave long years of separate toil to forge the material and emotional infrastructure of the western workforce and western capital.

The same could be said of the women who came west with their husbands. Consider Catharine Doran, born in Ireland in the early 1830s, who married Edward Doran during the disastrous famine years of 1845–49. She bore twelve children and buried three, as the Dorans moved to Wales, to the lead mines of Shullsburg, Wisconsin, and then to Colorado, where her husband and sons mined gold and silver for a daily wage. Her daughters married miners, their options limited, in mining towns where the only industry hired only men, to providing domestic services at home or for pay. An 1899 fire consumed the boarding house that Catharine ran to support herself in her widowhood; after that she had to rely on her children (Jameson: 1998).

We could start with another mother, with Polly Holmes and her husband Robin, who came as slaves from Missouri to the Willamette Valley in 1844, brought by Nathaniel Ford, who belatedly, five years later, honored his promise to free them. In a landmark legal battle for their children in 1853, recently described by the historian Quintard Taylor (1997), Robin and Polly Holmes won a victory against slavery when the judge in *Holmes v. Ford* refused to sanction slaveholding in the free state of Oregon (Taylor, 1997; Taylor and Moore, 2003).

The women of the nineteenth-century West traced their roots along a web of worldwide routes: from China, Mexico, Canada, and Europe, from the American South, Midwest, and East, from beneath the waters of Devils Lake. The fact that they were women distinguished their lives and options from men's. Maxiwidiwiac gardened rather than hunted buffalo. Kumeyaay women were raped. Catharine Doran bore twelve children, fed and clothed her family and boarders; she did not mine. Robin Holmes filed the suit against Nathaniel Ford that freed his children. We can only assume that Polly participated, that the court case emanated from shared parental longing. But just as gender distinguished women's lives from men's, so also race, class, and cultures distinguished what it meant to be a woman in the shifting gender systems of a nineteenth-century social world in enormous flux. The tangled trajectories of western women's histories were forged within inextricably linked systems of gender, race and ethnicity, labor and kinship, sexuality and life cycle, as well as the more public histories of politics and empire that charted how, throughout the nineteenth century, the US claimed the West.

Maxiwidiwiac, Polly Holmes, and Catharine Doran, the women of northern New Spain, the grass widows and Gold Rush widows left behind – these diverse women shared at least one bond. Their lives challenged triumphal histories of westward expansion, not just because they were poor, or immigrants, or on the losing sides of imperial conquests, but also *because they were women*. The history of America moving west subordinated the intimate details of reproduction, kin, adaptation, and survival that anchored their lives. First authored by Frederick Jackson Turner in 1893, a familiar history followed Americans' movements west through a series of frontiers that separated America from Europe and forged national progress and identity. Turner's frontiers – the dividing lines between "savagery and civilization" – belonged sequentially to Indian traders, hunters, soldiers, ranchers, miners, and farmers (Turner, 1993b). Men's jobs defined these frontiers and charted increasingly advanced stages of human development (Cronon et al, 1986).

Progress, in this history, moved from east to west. It moved upward from savagery to civilization, as white Americans conquered the wilderness, and as "primitive peoples" became "new nations." And a third line of progress assumed that public life was more important, historically, than private life. History progressed, Turner said, as people moved "from families into states" (Turner, 1993a: 49). In a famous passage in which he outlined how frontiers promoted democracy and individualism, Turner made a fleeting and indirect reference to women. "Complex society," he wrote, "is precipitated by the wilderness into a kind of primitive organization based on the family" (1993b: 82). History then progressed as men formed territories and governments, as they established states – the real subjects of history. The "primitive" social units of private life buried women in a history of the nation in which they were largely invisible. They remain marginal, if not entirely buried, in many recent New Western Histories as well (Limerick, 1987; White, 1991). It is very hard to bring into common focus the histories of a place, the American West, usually written from the vantage of public politics, economics, and conquest, and the lives of all the people who have called it home.

Conceptual Journeys

A generation of new histories complicated and disrupted Turner's narrative with the stories of people whose journeys did not always move from east to west, whose lives did not always improve, who did not always share a common standard for calculating progress. The social movements of the 1960s raised new questions about the historic roots of grass-roots activism, questions that generated new histories, including histories of western women. In 1980 Joan Jensen and Darlis Miller's important essay, "The Gentle Tamers Revisited," surveyed the existing literature. From that point western women's histories multiplied, their sheer variety challenging the imaginative capacity to write diverse stories at the center of a common past. That challenge charts the messy process of reconceiving history. Feminist historian Gerda Lerner eloquently outlined the steps, which begin, she suggested, when we "add a woman and stir" (1981). Next we see how women stretch the limits of inherited histories. And only then can we begin to try to imagine new plots, new stories, from the perspectives of an expanded cast.

From the perspectives of western women, we are somewhere in the middle of this historiographic journey. Putting women into the history of the American West changes more than the cast of historical actors. It challenges the subjects of a history that privileges the state over people, plots that privilege national expansion over more ambiguous stories of loss and gain, the assumption that history is always made by public figures, not through mundane private acts.

The first step in an ongoing journey of historical reconception was to assert that western women *had* histories, and that no accurate history could omit them. The issue was posed as early as 1941, by an unnamed "dean" of the historical profession, who observed "that Turner's theory is overwhelmingly a masculine one, with the role of women in western settlement almost entirely neglected" (Pierson, 1961: 149). The field of western women's history is commonly dated from Jensen and Miller's 1980 summary of the scholarship from which western women's histories could be built, and their call for a multicultural research agenda that would write women of all races and classes into western history. Western women's history as a distinct field of historical research may be dated from two conferences, the 1983 Women's West Conference, and Western Women: Their Land, Their Lives, in 1984, which built new professional networks and collaborations, sparked new questions, produced two path-breaking anthologies (Armitage and Jameson, 1987; Schlissel, Ruiz, and Monk, 1988), and ultimately generated new interpretative frameworks.

Historians began the add-and-stir process from the perspectives of western history, women's history, or racial ethnic history. Each field added women to frameworks that could not hold them. Susan Armitage pushed that point home as she opened the Women's West conference, evoking a mythic territory called "Hisland," a place where:

> . . . under perpetually cloudless western skies, a cast of heroic characters engages in dramatic conflict, sometimes with nature, sometimes with each other. Occupationally, these heroes are diverse; they are mountain men, cowboys, Indians, soldiers, farmers, miners, and desperadoes, but they share one distinguishing characteristic – they are all men. . . . This mythical land is America's most enduring contribution to folklore: the legendary Wild West.

"The problem with Hisland," Armitage continued, "is that many people believe it is history, and some of those people are historians" (Armitage, 1987: 9). To replace myth with history, she suggested, historians should add the missing women and see the West through their eyes.

Doing that was not so easy. Whatever their training, historians added women to a past they already saw through histories that raised limited questions for a limited female cast. The constricted plots and timelines of nineteenth-century Turnerian frontiers reduced the potential cast of new female characters and the arenas in which they acted. Scholars trained in western history began with concepts of frontier democracy, opportunity, and individualism that could accommodate women by focusing on the democratic opportunity of woman suffrage, first achieved in western states and territories. Women's historians began with the gender roles prescribed for an eastern white elite, and with concepts of race grounded in the black/white categories of the US South. They questioned whether suffrage was an adequate index of liberation, asking instead whether women could stretch their prescribed gender roles in the West. Julie Roy Jeffrey concluded in *Frontier Women*: "I hoped to find that pioneer women used the frontier as a means of liberating themselves from stereotypes and behaviors I found constricting and sexist. I found that they did not" (1979: xv–xvi).

For women of color, however, the limited frameworks of suffrage and elite gender roles did little to illuminate multiple inequalities of race, gender, class, and colonialism, or multiple strategies of resistance. Were the frontiers of American expansion liberating for Native American women? Did the Mexican American War free Mexican women from oppressive gender roles? Beginning with the inherited plots and characters of a history of (mostly white) westward migration, the first corrective steps reinscribed some of the racial and class biases of older western histories. Historians of racial ethnic women critiqued western women's histories that projected white women's experiences as the norm, and added inequalities of gender and sexuality to histories of race and colonialism (R. González, 1987; Castañeda, 1992, 1990; Jameson, 1988; Perales, 1997). Seeing women of color as historical actors stretched the conceptual limits of histories focused on liberation and opportunity, and expanded the timeline of a history that began only when white Americans arrived from the East. New frameworks were needed to connect race, class, and gender and to reconceive historical periods from multicultural perspectives (Jameson and Armitage, 1997b). In practice, it has often been as hard to decenter white women as to decenter the story of westward expansion.

The limits of older frameworks became evident as historians identified common stereotypes of western women, the female counterparts of mythic western men. Across all racial and ethnic groups, the stock stereotypes divided women into good women and bad, all of them judged wanting by the histories that generated them. "Good" white women were either suffocating civilizers who ended the frontier good times as they battled saloons and insisted on schools and churches, or they were oppressed drudges, reluctant pioneers dragged West and done in by overwork and a land that was too much for them. The stereotypical good women were asexual, the "bad" ones hypersexual hellraisers or whores (Stoeltje, 1975). For women of color, degrees of "goodness" and "badness" also reflected the racist assumptions of colonialism. The better the woman, the more acculturated to European values, the lighter her skin, the more likely she was to be Christian, and to emulate the Virgin. Bad women were darker, non-Christian, and immoral. The stereotypical "good" Indian woman, based on Pocahontas, was a princess who could be a hero of western history only by helping white men conquer her people (Green, 1976). The "bad" Mexican woman was a Pocahontas figure viewed from the other side: Malintzin Tenépal, called "la Malinche," Cortés's guide and interpreter, who bore his son, and was vilified by her own people as a sell-out who slept with the enemy (Candelaria, 1980; Del Castillo, 1977).

The stereotypes inhabited a public masculine territory that offered no way for women to win. The good women were not man enough for the West. The best stayed hidden in domestic seclusion, far from the public arenas where history was made. Those who, like good men, were sexual, competent, self-reliant, active, and adventurous became, by definition, bad women.

Such one-dimensional stereotypes highlighted the assumptions and the plots that reduced women to distorted caricatures. Getting past the stereotypes required multi-dimensional actors whose lives raised more complex issues than either/or questions about liberation and oppression. That challenging process can be traced through two staples of western history: free land and the frontier.

Frontiers to Crossroads

The conceptual frameworks of Turner's frontiers necessarily excluded women. The sequence of economies from hunting to farming through which nineteenth-century intellectuals charted the progress of civilization erased women's labor. The historical gaze that saw the frontier from the East assumed that a feminized wilderness and savagery lay on the other side, waiting for the penetrating advance of frontiersmen. Those assumptions multiply erased indigenous women, as savages and as women inseparable from the wilderness.

If women were scarce on Turnerian frontiers, that fantasy reflected a shred of reality. For women, frontiers meant an excess of men. In California, a year after the Gold Rush began, the US census counted twelve men for each woman. In Colorado, a year after the Pike's Peak boom, there were 16.5. Western states and territories remained disproportionately male well into the twentieth century. As late as 1920, there were 175 men in Alaska for each hundred women; 122 in Arizona; 120 in Montana; 148 in Nevada. The odds evened somewhat in agricultural areas, where family migration was more common. By 1920 Kansas had only 104 men per hundred women; Oregon and South Dakota, 113; California, 112.[1]

These dry numbers held the key to women's options in much of the nineteenth-century West. An excess of men intensified demands on women's labor and sexuality, both indirectly, as for the American Indian women of the Northern Plains coping with increasing numbers of buffalo hides, and directly, as in the marriages and rapes at the Spanish missions. In the fur trade, as on other cross-cultural frontiers, native women acted as cultural intermediaries, both voluntary and coerced, and as economic and intimate partners who literally birthed new peoples throughout the Americas (Van Kirk, 1980). An estimated 80 percent of nineteenth-century fur trappers married during their years in the trade; over half married Indian women, a fourth married Hispanic women of the northern Spanish Mexican borderlands (Swagerty, 1980). What that meant for the women is harder to discern through limited and filtered sources, but the personal meanings appear to have covered a spectrum from emotional intimacy to violent abuse.

The fact that men outnumbered women meant different things to historians, depending on the interpretative frameworks through which they considered women's options. From the assumptions of the mythic West, it meant that western men "gave" women the vote to lure them westward, that opportunity lay in a land with so few women that even an ugly woman could marry. James Barnes, who left New York in late 1849 for the California gold fields, drew a different conclusion. He complained that "females are too scarce," so that "[W]hat are here think themselves better than the Angels in heaven."[2]

From women's own perspectives, the significance of their scarcity varied. An excess of men could offer the opportunity to earn money providing food, shelter, and sex for men. It could also mean isolation from other women, and vulnerability to violence and abuse. For Euro-American women, the journey West and the first years establishing farms and homes could be far from liberating, bounded by childbearing, hard work, and hunger for other women's company. The first feminist histories of female frontiers made it clear that for women the good times came later, after homes and farms were established, after constant childbearing stopped and the children could help, after neighbors arrived (Rasmussen et al, 1976; Jameson, 1987; Petrik, 1987).

Indeed, the narrow focus on frontiers defined by the scarcity of white Americans obliterated a post-frontier history of women's efforts to build community institutions, like schools, libraries, hospitals, and churches. It erased, too, a history of women's organizing to achieve suffrage. Frontier explanations of suffrage fit only Wyoming, which wrote woman suffrage into its new territorial constitution in 1869, and Utah, which followed in 1870. If we accept the crude measure by which the Superintendent of the Census declared the frontier closed in 1890, the definition that drew the frontier along an unbroken line of settlement with two or fewer people per square mile, then woman suffrage was not won on the frontier. It came later, after there were more women, with lighter workloads and childbearing responsibilities, and more time to organize. The demography of gender suggests a post-frontier "fault line," the significance of which remains to be examined. All the western states, except Wyoming, Alaska, and, perhaps, Nevada, adopted woman suffrage after the ratio of men to women dropped below three to two. Suffrage contests throughout the West challenge rosy scenarios of democratic western guys generously giving the little ladies the vote. Studies of suffrage campaigns in Colorado, Montana, California, Oregon, and elsewhere draw more realistic pictures of women activists who lobbied and organized for decades to try to win the franchise (Stefanco, 1987; Wright, 1974; Petrik, 1987; Jensen, 1986; Moynihan, 1983, Gullet, 2000).

What frontier opportunity meant for different women appeared in starkly separate relief when viewed through the lens of another staple topic of westward expansion, access to free land. Without belaboring the obvious – that the land was neither unoccupied nor free for the taking – US land policy held very different promises for women of different races, and for married and unmarried women. The Homestead Act of 1862 allowed women, for the first time, to claim an independent stake in the land, if they were single or heads of households, at least twenty-one years of age, and citizens or immigrants who had filed for citizenship. Previous land allocation measures included women only through their relationships to men. The Oregon Donation Act of 1850, for instance, gave 320 acres to American men who had settled in Oregon before 1850, and granted them another 320 acres for their wives.

When Congress passed the Homestead Act, it still envisioned a nation of family farmers, where husbands and wives would work as partners. The details evolved by which the federal government ultimately distributed almost 250 acres, but the Homestead Act established the basics: the government offered a homesteader 160 acres, more, eventually, in arid areas, in exchange for a small filing fee, living on the land, and improving it for a specified time – usually five years.

Homesteading offered an unprecedented opportunity for women, and thousands took it. By all available calculations, single women ranged from around 5 percent of all homesteaders in early settlements to one in five after 1900; they were slightly more successful than men in achieving final title to their claims (Patterson-Black, 1975; Nelson, 1978). Women's successes, however, could not be measured by how long they lasted on their land. The most complete examination of a sample of single women homesteaders showed that only 40 percent stayed on their land much longer than the time required to claim it. Homesteads were investments that financed a number of dreams: millinery shops, boarding houses, and university degrees, or the chance to expand joint marital landholdings. Women homesteaders married later than their contemporaries, and brought their own financial stakes to their marriages. The promise of the land drew women whose options elsewhere were more limited. A third of the women who homesteaded in North Dakota came from other countries, including 5 percent from Canada, where women could not file for land in their own names (Lindgren, 1996).

But the same land policies that spelled new promise for single white women held very different meanings for American Indians. The principles of private property and family farms laid the foundations of US Indian policy as well as the Homestead Act. The Dawes Act of 1887 severed tribal lands and assigned land allotments to individual nuclear families; it governed US Indian policy until 1934. Private family farms, it was assumed, would help "raise" and "civilize" Indians, a civilizing mission that included efforts to teach women "appropriate" gender roles, based on models of female domesticity and submissiveness to male authority. These policies operated in North Dakota on the Fort Berthold Reservation, where government agents moved Maxiwidiwiac to a family land allotment, and at the Devils Lake Sioux Reservation near the site where Hidatsa history began. Government employees and missionaries worked to reverse a traditional division of labor in which women planted and harvested, by giving agricultural equipment, stock, seeds, and legal title to family lands to Native American men. Hidatsa women like Maxiwidiwiac continued to garden. So did white women on neighboring homesteads. But the gardens that offered new access to private property for white settlers signified great losses for Hidatsa women, who no longer owned their gardens or enjoyed the company of women in collective family agriculture (Hanson, 1981; Wilson, 1987; Albers, 1974, 1983).

Federal policies that supported family farms and nuclear families generated very different options for women who homesteaded independently or as wives, and for their Hidatsa and Dakota neighbors for whom the "opportunity" to homestead private family farms forged new dependencies on men who controlled family land and wages (Albers, 1974, 1983; Patterson-Black, 1976; Kohl, 1986; Harris, 1993; McKeown, 1961; Stewart, 1961; Corey and Gerber, 1990). Indian women's efforts to escape the "promises" of American civilization redefined resistance from the warfare that reverberated across the Plains through 1890 to a spectrum of more mundane acts like burning down BIA schools, exercising tribal divorce practices, continuing religious practices and ceremonies, and ignoring the Field Matrons who came to teach proper domestic values (Wall, 1997; Jacobs, 1997; Emmerich, 1997; Osburn, 1997).

Single women homesteaders stretched the promise of free land to meet their own goals, and stretched the temporal boundaries of a farmers' frontier well into the 20th century, filing in significant numbers into the 1920s. Homesteading acquired more contested significance as the same land policies that wrote opportunity into the Homestead Act wrote losses of land, status, and culture into the assumptions of the Dawes Act.

As the women slotted into frontier histories stretched these histories' timeframes, plots, and assumptions, it became increasingly apparent that the frontier could be stretched only so far. Historians sought new frameworks that would center women, and particularly women of color, as leading actors in their own lives. The focus shifted from staking out women's territory within western history, to the expanded focus of a multicultural history of women in the West.

By the late 1980s, new histories, with women of color in the center, reconceived frontiers themselves. Instead of lines that marked the western boundaries of advancing Americans, frontiers became meeting grounds that illuminated inequalities of race, class, and conquest. The multicultural cast of new western histories redefined frontiers as crossroads and borderlands where conquest, accommodation, and resistance inscribed contested legacies. Sarah Deutsch's *No Separate Refuge* (1987) redefined frontiers as zones of cultural interaction. Placing Hispanic women at the center of an Anglo-Hispanic frontier that moved north from New Mexico to Colorado, Deutsch charted how cultural interaction redefined relationships of race and class as well as gender. This frontier extended from 1880 to 1940, and progressively eroded Hispanic women's control and status as Hispano/as became dependent on wage work in the mines, railroads, and beet fields of an Anglo-controlled capitalist marketplace.

While Deutsch redefined frontiers as cultural interactions, Peggy Pascoe offered a new metaphor to shift the paradigm, suggesting "that historians of women in the West replace the current emphasis on frontierswomen – mythic or real – with a new definition of our field and that we learn to see our task as the study of women at the cultural crossroads" (1991a; 43–4). Placing women of color at the centers of cross-cultural relationships would illuminate the intertwined axes of race, class, and gender that forged inequalities throughout the West.

The conceptual power of multicultural and cross-cultural frameworks to recast historical subjects and questions hinged on the concept of historical agency, and particularly the historical agency of women and people of color. Putting women of color at the historical center redefined historical arenas and historical acts. Pascoe focused on the interactions between white women reformers and the women of color they sought to help, and on interracial marriage (Pascoe, 1990, 1991b, 1991c). Deena González approached the Mexican–American War from the perspectives of the Spanish-Mexican women of Santa Fe, for whom the story began long before US conquest, as they developed the cultural reservoir of practices from which women resisted colonial power. Women's relationships with traders, merchants, soldiers and spouses demonstrated that acculturation was not a one-way street to Americanization. González, for instance, reinterpreted Doña Gertrudis Barceló, who owned a gambling house and a saloon, as a woman who took Americans' money as they learned Spanish and local customs (D. González, 1993, 1999). Such histories broadened the concept of resistance to include daily negotiations among people with unequal power. Women at the cultural crossroads generated neither tales of heroic triumph nor of tragic victimization, but rather a more contested and murky set of exchanges and strategies that fostered survival and cultural persistence in the face of massive social dislocations.

The legacies of unequal power in cross-cultural exchanges, though, raised cautions about how much historical weight historians might ask women of color to carry. Antonia Castañeda (1992) critiqued racist assumptions embedded in the multicultural agenda as she surveyed the decade of scholarship after the "The Gentle Tamers Revisited" (Jenson and Miller, 1980). In particular, she criticized multicultural histories that did not examine the ideologies and politics of race, sex, class, and empire.

While a focus on multiculturalism and cross-cultural relations wrote multiracial histories, it did so most often on white terms, leaving unexamined assumptions that white women's histories defined the norm. Histories that focused on conquest and intercultural exchange included women of color only in relationship to whites, and not on their own terms, or in separate, often segregated communities where survival strategies and support systems were forged (Castañeda, 1992; Jameson, 1988). A pioneer anthology by radical women of color named this historical burden: women at the cultural crossroads became *This Bridge Called My Back* (Anzaldua and Moraga, 1981).

Cultural crossroads thus led some historians away from the centers of cultural exchange, which so usefully uncovered power relationships, to the distinct histories of women of many races and cultures recorded by historians of African American women, Chinese and Japanese women, the women of many American Indian cultures, European ethnic women, and Mexican American women – each racial ethnic term itself a difficult choice, constructed and adopted in unequal social relationships, carrying its own burden of history (Glenn, 1985). The 1997 Jameson and Armitage anthology *Writing the Range: Race, Class, and Culture in the Women's West* attempted to address the dilemma of telling a multicultural history without narrowing the focus to intercultural relationships or to a single racial ethnic group (Jameson and Armitage, 1997). It organized articles chronologically around successive waves of settlement and conceptually around the issues of identity, adaptation, and empowerment that particular groups of women encountered in their respective Wests. That framework reflected a growing awareness of the enormous challenges of western women's history: the methodological, conceptual, and ethical challenges of recovering and bringing into common focus *on their own terms* the lives of all the women who had ever lived in the American West.

Sin Fronteras

The conceptual difficulty lay in connecting women whose lives often revolved around private spaces that isolated them from women of other races, classes, and regions of the West. Intercultural frontiers connected the unequal exchanges of the marketplace, court, and political systems to the intimate arenas of sexuality and marriage. As the definitions of historical acts widened, so did the concept of historical agency, which included daily acts of survival as well the exercise of public and political power. Women's power to control their own bodies established one test of agency. Access to memory, to the historical legacies of intimate and private frontiers, defined another.

As women and men of different classes and cultures met throughout the nineteenth-century West, their intimate personal encounters illuminated shifts in local power. In San Antonio, for example, Anglo newcomers, who were mostly men, enhanced their power by marrying daughters of the Tejano elite. But as Anglo power increased, the children of these unions moved from Catholicism to Protestantism and adopted English names (Dysart, 1976). Where economic and social control was more shared, children's acculturation patterns – as reflected in names, religion, and their own marriage partners – remained more mixed as well. In Santa Fe, from US conquest until the railroad brought increased Anglo settlement after 1880, intermarriages most often united working-class Spanish Mexican women and Irish

Catholic men who acculturated to their wives' communities. The larger historical reality, however, is that most women did not intermarry (Miller, 1962; D. González, 1999; Johnson, 1987).

Multicultural histories that focused on cross-cultural exchanges erased women whose lives centered around people of their own heritages. Traditional ethnic histories often denigrated immigrant women and women of color as backward because they did not assimilate to American culture. While their husbands and children learned English in schools and in the marketplace, homebound women maintained the languages and the domestic and religious practices of their homelands. Private domestic practices might be valued, however, as acts that preserved heritages subsumed in histories that measured progress by assimilation.

The intimate impacts of colonialism and the personal meanings of cross-cultural frontiers extended far beyond intermarriages, to grimmer legacies of rape and venereal disease, and to acts that disrupted practices of marriage, divorce, and inheritance. As the Spanish missions and the Dawes Act demonstrated, conquest disrupted indigenous systems of marriage, kinship, and gender. Spanish missionaries and civil authorities tried to obliterate Native American religions, and sexual and marriage practices. American missionaries and government personnel continued the effort to establish patriarchal nuclear families in the nineteenth-century West.

Rapes, prostitution, venereal disease, and the epidemics that ravaged native populations all further disrupted cultural practices. By the mid-nineteenth century, the surviving minority of California Indian women experienced dramatically lowered fertility, which further endangered their peoples' survival (Hurtado, 1988). Changing economies, like the horse and hide trade, eroded women's power relative to men. That power shift reverberated from loss of productive and economic control to the virtual disappearance by the late-nineteenth century of cross-gender roles that had provided a range of options for Native women in at least thirty-three tribes (Blackwood, 1984; Medicine, 1983).

Public power was never separate from such private arenas. Laws throughout the West defined, both directly and indirectly, who could marry, inherit, and divorce. A series of laws to limit Asian immigration, most notably the Chinese Exclusion Act of 1882, slowed the migrations of Chinese and Japanese women to a trickle, mostly wives of merchants. The exclusion of women forged largely male communities, led to extreme age differences between wives and husbands, and largely restricted the ability to reproduce to the middle class (Yung, 1995; Chan, 1991).

People of all races resisted the regulation of intimacy more extensively than the public record can reveal, since the most fundamental resistance was to continue forbidden intimate practices beyond public scrutiny and control. The variety of ways that people sought to control their own intimacy and reproduction redefined agency, and established its limits. Legal practices shifted in part through women's active uses of the courts. Women in California and Montana used local courts to extend the grounds for divorce to mental cruelty (Griswold, 1982; Petrik, 1987). In Montana, local practices inscribed class distinctions as well. The courts in middle-class Helena reduced the severity of physical and emotional abuse a woman had to suffer before gaining a divorce, while in the working-class mining town of Butte, judges were more sensitive to charges of nonsupport that might make a woman dependent on government assistance. Better, the court decisions suggested, to let women leave such marriages and find men who were better providers. As women left abusive marriages, they began to change the legal limits of the abuse and neglect a woman must endure before filing for divorce. Other legal restrictions prompted extralegal resistance, as historian Judy Yung (1995, 1999) demonstrated through the coaching book her mother memorized to meet the immigration criteria to join her husband in California. Yung estimated that a majority of Chinese women entered the country through such fabrications, providing a clear example in which private sources and oral traditions were more accurate than official sources, which reflected only the stories that successful immigrants memorized (Yung, 1995, 1999).

Efforts to control intimate practices of marriage, sexuality, reproduction, and inheritance illuminate social power throughout the West, the stakes for all the players, and the limits of women's historical agency. Intimate frontiers, as Albert Hurtado eloquently demonstrated, could be brutally unequal. The violent bounds of intimacy could define a rapists' frontier, established in practice against conquered and subordinate women. That violent frontier was vividly etched in the story of Amelia Kuschinsky, an adolescent servant in Shasta County, California (Hurtado, 1999). Probably impregnated by her master, Amelia died an excruciating death in 1860, the result of a forced abortion. Her mute body defined the limits of women's agency in systems of unequal power. Sometimes, simple survival was the ultimate act of resistance. Amelia Kuschinsky could stand for many women who did not survive to exercise historical agency, to control their own lives, or to inscribe their own memories in recorded history.

Such wrenching histories force a return to the categories of liberation or oppression that described the stereotyped women of Hisland, and to the concept of historical agency that includes daily ordinary acts as historical practices that maintain and transform cultures. Historical inclusiveness expanded the cast of western women. That cast redefined agency and activism to transcend the divisions of public/private and liberation/oppression that characterized the western frontiers and Victorian gender prescriptions with which western women's histories began, recasting agency and empowerment to encompass an enormous range of possible acts and goals. What the West held for nineteenth-century women depended on what they sought and what they left to find it, on a complex calculus of gain and loss. For women of all races and classes, the arenas of agency included access to public power, but they also included private control of households, property, reproduction, and sexuality.

Efforts to control intimate relationships illustrate the varying degrees of power that women exercised in arenas both private and public. If Amelia Kuschinsky bore mute testimony to private powerlessness, some women were able, with support, to resist. Activist responses to domestic violence began long before battered women's shelters. Prostitutes protected one another from pimps and customers while other women campaigned more publicly to expand the definitions of cruelty that justified divorce. Activism might include the private strategy of a battered wife in Victor, Colorado, who left her abusive husband with the help of neighboring miners who boarded with her so she could support her children. The daily labor required to support four children by taking in laundry and running a boarding house was not liberating, but it represented a degree of agency and control over domestic abuse.[3]

If we do not force women into models of activism defined by public organizational leadership, but instead ask what issues engaged women, we can gain new insights into historical agency. If women's activism is defined not in terms of public leadership, but as any act to empower women, or improve their lives, or to benefit the lives of others, then activism defines a spectrum from private acts of resistance to organizations fully mobilized to achieve clearly articulated agendas for change. Activism could include Maxiwidiwiac's speaking her native language rather than English, other Native American women's getting pregnant to get sent home from a government boarding school, or burning down the BIA school at the Round Rock Reservation in California, or adapting to new systems of land tenure, religion, and family. Activism could include private acts like teaching other women about birth control, public personal acts like filing for divorce, public community acts like establishing libraries and sewing machine cooperatives, and mobilizing politically for woman suffrage, community property rights, and reproductive choice (Wall, 1997; Emmerich, 1997; Jameson, 1987; Rasmussen, et al, 1976; Hampsten, 1982; Jensen, 1981). And activism could include telling the stories silenced in state-centered histories.

The historical legacies of unequal power also bequeathed unequal access to memories. One example will suffice. The children of the borderlands, descendants of the intermarriages on the northern frontiers of New Spain, traced their lineages to Spaniards, Africans, and many indigenous Indian peoples. The Spanish Mexican frontiers privileged the Spanish identity; after American conquest, "whiteness," on American terms, privileged northern and western Europeans. The legacy of these multicultural frontiers included children who literally embodied their parents' private intimacy, and who embodied the ensuing power relations that privileged or punished particular strands of that heritage, who grew up learning that they were Spanish or Mexican, not Indian, *mulato*, or *mestizo*. A similar history endures in blood quantum requirements for tribal enrollment. It endures, too, in efforts to recover and reconceive histories far from the intimate roots of intercultural frontiers.

These searing histories inform a final metaphor of the cross-cultural legacy, inscribed by Gloria Anzaldua in *Borderlands-La Frontera* (1987), a place where the mixed heritages of unequal power relationships hold the power to silence. The effort to reclaim those silenced voices and memories guided Cordelia Candelaria (1980) and Adelaida Del Castillo (1977) who reinterpreted La Malinche as an adapter and survivor, the symbolic *india* mother of *mestizo/as* long alienated from their maternal roots. Anzaldua recorded the personal costs of survival, moving from the metaphor of crossroads as sites of exchange, to cultural crossroads embodied in individual lives:

> To survive the Borderlands
> you must live *sin fronteras*
> be a crossroads.

Bringing It All Back Home

This essay, like the women of the nineteenth-century West, violates the conventions of western history, evading the bounds of both time and place. Its timelines have slopped over the edges of the nineteenth century, to the eighteenth-century frontiers of New Spain; it has followed single women homesteaders, Chinese immigrants, and the Hispanic women of northern New Mexico all well into the 20th century.

I have, with deliberate cowardice, evaded defining the precise boundaries of the West. From a state-centered perspective, it might be argued that the American West was not established until 1846–8 when the US took the Southwest in the Mexican–American War and established the 49th parallel as the boundary with Canada. If we include Hawaii and Alaska, timelines and boundaries become further confused.

Mapping the West from women's perspectives may present challenges as intricate and challenging as fitting them into the timelines and conceptual frameworks of national histories. Women themselves might map their Wests in terms of the distance to water or from neighbors and kin, the abundance of wood or buffalo chips for cooking, or, in the telling metaphors of some white pioneers' memoirs, as a territory centered ninety miles from nowhere, seventy miles from a lemon (Nelson, 1989; Howell, 1987; Yates, 1949).

Adding women uncovers the messy issues lurking in editor William Deverell's deceptively simple invitation. For different women the century begins and ends at different dates, or has no meaning as a historical period. The West shifts its boundaries and its promises. "Western women" as a collectivity shatter into distinct individuals and groups whose histories do not always touch. This essay began with individual women, because individual lives illuminate larger processes of work, conquest, intimacy, kinship, resistance, and agency more vividly than strained efforts to write a single narrative of all women in the American West. They challenge histories that move from the top down, from east to west, from nation to hinterland, histories that happen *to* people, from the outside in. The ultimate act of living *sin fronteras* may be to reconceive history while reclaiming memory.

A generation of new histories has greatly expanded the potential cast of an inclusive western history, one that could include ordinary women and men of all races and classes, the social ancestors of the contemporary West. But that expanded cast has not yet claimed the center of a New Western History. So long as history remains the story of the region, or the state, it cannot hold the multiplicity of people who have lived in the West, or moved through it, who built its communities, its economies, its social institutions. No single linear story can hold so many voices. But collectively they invert or shred all the assumptions of Turnerian frontiers: that westward movement brought progress, that civilization lay on the Euro-American side of the frontier line and savagery and feminized nature on the other, that progress lay in ascending an economic hierarchy from hunting and gathering to farming, and, most of all, that progress moved from the primitive world of family and household to the more advanced arenas of the nation state.

Reversing that final trajectory leads to a history of gender in the nineteenth-century West that includes men whose daily lives were not written in public histories of national expansion. New histories have begun to explore how men as diverse as George Custer, miners, cowboys, cross-dressers, and cabin-mates defined masculinity in the West (Murphy, 1999; Johnson, 1993, 2000; Jameson, 1998; Basso, McCall, and Garceau, 2001). The discovery that gender roles shape men's options paralleled the recognition that whites are privileged by race, and rich people by class. New histories of masculinity have the power to scrutinize the mythic stereotypes of western men that remain powerfully etched in popular culture. And they direct attention to the intimate arenas of the nineteenth-century West where many men, at least temporarily, shared domestic and social spaces with other men. Historians of western manhood are challenged to avoid the early mistakes of western women's history that ignored inequalities of race and class, and to examine the systems of power in which men of all races operated, including men's power over women.

Adding women to the nineteenth-century West fundamentally changes the story. First, the focus on nineteenth-century Anglo pioneers suggested that we needed to recast the idea of western "opportunity" to include the competing pulls of what women left and what they found in the West. Because for many women the first period of settlement was hardest, they took us past a romantic emphasis on the frontier period, to the more complex processes of adaptation and community building.

Once we began to add women, we confronted the diversity of people whose stories we need to hear and to tell to be historically accurate. With a longer time frame and more inclusive cast the story became one of encounters among successive waves of settlers. Those encounters were recast by many historians as the histories of conquest and colonization. From women's perspectives they also became intimate encounters that, at one end of a spectrum, added rape and sexual exploitation to the violence of conquest, and, at the other, resulted in intimate cultural exchanges and new *mestizo* and *métis* peoples. Those relationships, involving people of different races, cultures, and classes, as well as different genders, can only be understood if we seem them from the perspectives of all the actors.

There is considerable tension between the story of the nation and the stories of the many peoples who have lived in what is now the American West. That tension can take us far beyond the question of how to add women to existing western histories, to the far more interesting question of what stories it is important to tell, and how to tell a history of social relationships from the perspectives of all the participants.

Bringing the story of a place and its people into common focus is part of the unresolved challenge of western women's histories. If the Hidatsa creation story began beneath the waters of Miniwakan, and the national creation story began on the East Coast of North America and moved west through successive frontiers, a history that fully integrates the women of the American West remains in the process of creation. As we think about what women actually did – from keeping house in sod shanties, to tanning buffalo hides, to working for temperance and resisting slavery – history becomes not a linear journey from east to west but a chronicle of myriad activities that link home and community, daily survival and public policy. Inverting the final trajectory of Turner's frontiers, western women took us from frontiers to crossroads to human relationships forged inside brothels and kitchens, within sod and adobe houses and earth lodges. We are challenged to imagine a multivocal history of relationships and complex identities forged in private arenas that were, for most people, the daily sites of history.

NOTES

1 These statistics, and others in this article, were calculated from *Bicentennial Edition, Historical Statistics of the United States, Colonial Times to 1970* (Washington, DC: US Department of Commerce, 1970), Series A, 195–209.

2 Barnes, James to Sister Mary from Sac[ramento], 30 July 1854: James S. Barnes Collection, Bancroft Library, University of California, Berkeley, quoted with permission.
3 Oral history interview, Beulah Pryor, Colorado Springs, Colorado, May 6, 1979.

REFERENCES

Albers, Patricia C.: "The Regional System of the Devil's Lake Sioux." (PhD dissertation: University of Wisconsin, Madison, 1974).
Albers, Patricia C.: "Sioux Women in Transition: A Study of Their Changing Status in Domestic and Capitalist Sectors of Production." In Patricia C. Albers and Beatrice Medicine (eds.) *The Hidden Half: Studies of Plains Indian Women* (Latham, MD: University Press of America, 1983).
Albers, Patricia C. and Beatrice Medicine (eds.) *The Hidden Half: Studies of Plains Indian Women* (Latham, MD: University Press of America, 1983).
Anzaldua, Gloria: *Borderlands-La Frontera: The New Mestiza* (San Francisco: Spinster/Aunt Lute Book Company, 1987).
Anzaldua, Gloria and Cherrie Moraga (eds.): *This Bridge Called My Back: Writings by Radical Women of Color* (New York: Kitchen Table/Women of Color Press, 1981).
Applegate, Shannon and Terence O'Donnell: *Talking on Paper: An Anthology of Oregon Letters and Diaries* (Corvallis: Oregon State University Press, 1994).
Armitage, Susan: "Through Women's Eyes: A New View of the West." In Susan Armitage and Elizabeth Jameson (eds.) *The Women's West* (Norman: University of Oklahoma Press, 1987).
Armitage, Susan and Elizabeth Jameson (eds.): *The Women's West* (Norman: University of Oklahoma Press, 1987).
Basso, Matthew, Laurel McCall, and Dee Garceau (eds.): *Across the Great Divide: Cultures of Manhood in the American West* (New York: Routledge, 2001).
Beeton, Beverly: "Woman Suffrage in Territorial Utah." *Utah Historical Quarterly* 46, 2 (1978), 100–20.
Blackwood, Evelyn: "Sexuality and Gender in Certain Native American Tribes." *Signs* 10, 1 (1984): 27–42.
Candelaria, Cordelia: "La Malinche, Feminist Prototype." *Frontiers* 5, 2 (Summer 1980), 1–6.
Castañeda, Antonia I: "Gender, Race, and Culture: Spanish-Mexican Women in the Historiography of Frontier California." *Frontiers* 11, 1 (1990), 8–20.
Castañeda, Antonia I: "Women of Color and the Rewriting of Western History: The Discourse, Politics, and Decolonization of History." *Pacific Historical Review* 61 (November 1992), 501–33.
Chan, Sucheng: *This Bittersweet Soil: The Chinese in California Agriculture, 1860–1910* (Berkeley: University of California Press, 1986).
Chan, Sucheng: *Entry Denied: Exclusion and the Chinese Community in America, 1882–1943* (Philadelphia: Temple University Press, 1991).
Corey, Elizabeth and Philip L. Gerber: *Bachelor Bess: The Homesteading Letters of Elizabeth Corey, 1989–1919* (Iowa City: University of Iowa Press, 1990).
Cronon, William, Howard R. Lamar, Katherine G. Morrissey, and Jay Gitlin: "Women and the West: Rethinking the Western History Survey Course." *Western Historical Quarterly* XVII, 3 (July 1986), 269–90.
Del Castillo, Adelaida R.: "Malíntzin Tenépal: A Preliminary Look into a New Perspective." In Rosaura Sánchez and Rosa Martínez Cruz (eds.) *Essays on La Mujer* (Los Angeles: UCLA Chicano Studies Center Publications, 1977).
Deutsch, Sarah: *No Separate Refuge: Culture, Class, and Gender on an Anglo-Hispanic Frontier in the American Southwest, 1880–1940* (New York: Oxford University Press, 1987).

di Leonardo, Micaela: "The Female World of Cards and Holidays" *Signs* 12, 3 (Spring 1987), 440–53.

Dysart, Jane. "Mexican Women in San Antonio, 1830–1860: The Assimilation Process." *Western Historical Quarterly* 7, 4 (October 1976), 365–75.

Emmerich, Lisa E: "'Save the Babies': American Indian Women, Assimilation Policy, and Scientific Motherhood, 1912—1918." In Elizabeth Jameson and Susan Armitage (eds.) *Writing the Range: Race, Class, and Culture in the Women's West* (Norman: University of Oklahoma Press, 1997).

Glenn, Evelyn Nakano: "Racial Ethnic Women's Labor: The Intersection of Race, Gender, and Class Oppression." *Review of Radical Political Economics* 17, 3 (Fall 1985), 86–108.

González, Deena J.: "La Tules of Image and Reality: Euro-American Attitudes and Legend Formation on a Spanish–Mexican Frontier." In Adela de la Torre and Beatríz M. Pesquera (eds.) *Building with Our Hands: Directions in Chicana Scholarship* (Berkeley: University of California Press, 1993), reprinted in Vicki L. Ruiz and Ellen Carol DuBois *Unequal Sisters: A Multicultural Reader in US Women's History*, 2nd edn. (New York: Routledge, 1994).

González, Deena J.: *Refusing the Favor: The Spanish-Mexican Women of Santa Fe, 1820–1880* (New York: Oxford University Press, 1999).

González, Rosalinda Méndez: "Distinctions in Western Women's Experience: Ethnicity, Class, and Social Change." In Susan Armitage and Elizabeth Jameson (eds.) *The Women's West* (Norman: University of Oklahoma Press, 1987).

Green, Rayna: "The Pocahantas Perplex: The Image of Indian Women in American Culture." *Massachusetts Review* 16, 4 (1976), 698–714.

Griswold, Robert; *Family and Divorce in California, 1850–1880* (Albany: State University of New York Press, 1982).

Gullett, Gayle: *Becoming Citizens: The Emergence and Development of the California Women's Movement, 1880–1911.* (Urbana: University of Illinois Press, 2000).

Hampsten, Elizabeth: *Read This Only to Yourself: The Private Writings of Midwestern Women, 1880–1910* (Bloomington: Indiana University Press, 1982).

Hanson, Jeffrey R.: "Introduction." In Gilbert L. Wilson *Buffalo Bird Woman's Garden* (St. Paul: Minnesota Historical Society Press, 1987).

Harris, Katherine: *Long Vistas: Women and Families on Colorado Homesteads* (Niwot, CO: University Press of Colorado, 1993).

Howell, Anabel: *Ninety Miles from Nowhere* (Peralta, NM: Pine Tree Press, 1987).

Hurtado, Albert L.: *Indian Survival on the California Frontier* (New Haven: Yale University Press, 1988).

Hurtado, Albert L.: *Intimate Frontiers: Sex, Gender, and Culture in Old California* (Albuquerque: University of New Mexico Press, 1999).

Jacobs, Margaret D.: "Resistance to Rescue: The Indians of Bahapki and Mrs. Annie E. K. Bidwell." In Elizabeth Jameson and Susan Armitage (eds.) *Writing the Range: Race, Class, and Culture in the Women's West* (Norman: University of Oklahoma Press, 1997).

Jameson, Elizabeth: "Women as Workers, Women as Civilizers: True Womanhood in the American West." In Susan Armitage and Elizabeth Jameson (eds.) *The Women's West* (Norman: University of Oklahoma Press, 1987).

Jameson, Elizabeth: "Toward a Multicultural History of Women in the Western United States." *Signs* 13, 4 (1988), 761–91.

Jameson, Elizabeth: *All That Glitters: Class, Conflict, and Community in Cripple Creek* (Urbana: University of Illinois Press, 1998).

Jameson, Elizabeth and Susan Armitage: *Writing the Range: Race, Class, and Culture in the Women's West* (Norman: University of Oklahoma Press, 1997a).

Jameson, Elizabeth and Susan Armitage: "Editors' Introduction." In Elizabeth Jameson and Susna Armitage (eds.) *Writing the Range: Race, Class, and Culture in the Women's West* (Norman: University of Oklahoma Press, 1997b).

Jeffrey, Julie Roy: *Frontier Women: The Trans-Mississippi West, 1840–1880* (New York: Hill and Wang, 1979).

Jensen, Joan M.: *With These Hands: Women Working on the Land* (Old Westbury, NY: The Feminist Press; New York: The McGraw-Hill Book Company, 1981).

Jensen, Joan M.: "'Disenfranchisement Is a Disgrace': Women and Politics in New Mexico, 1900–1940." In Joan M. Jensen and Darlis A. Miller (eds.) *New Mexico Women: Intercultural Perspectives* (Albuquerque: University of New Mexico Press, 1986).

Jensen, Joan M. and Darlis A. Miller: "The Gentle Tamers Revisited: New Approaches to the History of Women in the American West." *Pacific Historical Review* 49, 2 (May 1980), 173–213.

Johnson, Susan L.: "Sharing Bed and Board: Cohabitation and Cultural Difference in Central Arizona Mining Towns, 1863–1873." In Susan Armitage and Elizabeth Jameson (eds.) *The Women's West* (Norman: University of Oklahoma Press, 1987).

Johnson, Susan L.: "A Memory Sweet to Soldiers: The Significance of Gender in the History of the American West." *Western Historical Quarterly* XXIV, 4 (November 1993), 495–518.

Johnson, Susan L.: *Roaring Camp: The Social World of the California Gold Rush* (New York: W. W. Norton, 2000).

Klein, Alan M.: "The Political Economy of Gender: A Nineteenth-Century Plains Indian Case Study." In Patricia Albers and Beatrice Medicine (eds.) *The Hidden Half: Studies of Plains Indian Women* (Latham, MD: University Press of America, 1983).

Kohl, Edith Eudora: *Land of the Burnt Thigh* ([1938], rpt. St. Paul: Minnesota Historical Society Press, 1986).

Larson, T. A.: "Petticoats at the Polls: Woman Suffrage in Territorial Wyoming." *Pacific Northwest Quarterly* 44 (April 1953), 74–79.

Larson, T. A.: "Woman Suffrage in Wyoming." *Pacific Northwest Quarterly* 56 (April 1965), 57–66.

Larson, T. A.: "Montana Women and the Battle for the Ballot." *Montana: The Magazine of Western History* 21 (1973), 24–41.

Larson, T. A.: "Idaho's Role in America's Woman Suffrage Crusade." *Idaho Yesterdays* 18 (Spring 1974), 2–15.

Larson, T. A.: "The Woman Suffrage Movement in Washington." *Pacific Northwest Quarterly* 67 (April 1976), 49–62.

Lerner, Gerda: "Placing Women in History." In Gerda Lerner *The Majority Finds Its Past* (New York: Oxford University Press, 1979).

Lerner, Gerda: *Teaching Women's History* (Washington, DC: American Historical Association, 1981).

Limerick, Patricia Nelson: *The Legacy of Conquest: The Unbroken past of the American West* (New York: W. W. Norton & Company, 1987).

Lindgren, H. Elaine: *Land in Her Own Name: Single Women as Homesteaders in North Dakota* ([1991], rpt. Norman: University of Oklahoma Press, 1996).

Loeb, Catherine: "La Chicana: A Bibliographic Survey." *Frontiers* 5, 2 (1980), 59–74.

McKeown, Martha Ferguson: *Them Was the Days: An American Saga of the 70s* (Lincoln: University of Nebraska Press, 1961).

Medicine, Beatrice: "Warrior Women – Sex Role Alternatives for Plains Indian Women." In Patricia Albers and Beatrice Medicine (eds.) *The Hidden Half: Studies of Plains Indian Women* (Latham, MD: University Press of America, 1983).

Miller, Darlis A.: "Cross-Cultural Marriages in the Southwest: The New Mexico Experience, 1846–1900." *New Mexico Historical Review* 57, 4 (October 1962), 355–59.

Moynihan, Ruth Barnes: *Rebel for Rights: Abigail Scott Duniway* (New Haven: Yale University Press, 1983).

Murphy, Mary: "Making Men in the West: The Coming of Age of Miles Cavanaugh and Martin Frank Dunham." In Valerie J. Matsumoto and Blake Allmendinger (eds.) *Over the Edge: Remapping the American West* (Berkeley: University of California Press, 1999).

Myres, Sandra L.: *Westering Women and the Frontier Experience, 1800–1915* (Albuquerque: University of New Mexico Press, 1982).

Nelson, Paula M.: "No Place for Clinging Vines: Women Homesteaders on the South Dakota Frontier." (MA thesis: University of South Dakota, 1978).

Nelson, Paula M.: *After the West Was Won: Homesteaders and Town-Builders in Western South Dakota, 1900–1917* (Iowa City: University of Iowa Press, 1989).

Osburn, Katherine: "'To Build Up the Morals of the Tribe': Southern Ute Women's Sexual Behavior and the Office of Indian Affairs, 1895–1932." *Journal of Western History* 9, 3 (Autumn 1997), 10–28.

Pascoe, Peggy: *Relations of Rescue: The Search for Female Moral Authority in the American West, 1874–1939* (New York: Oxford University Press, 1990).

Pascoe, Peggy: "Western Women at the Cultural Crossroads." In Patricia Nelson Limerick, Clyde A. Milner II, and Charles E. Rankin (eds.) *Trails: Toward a New Western History* (Lawrence; University Press of Kansas, 1991a).

Pascoe, Peggy: "Introduction: The Challenge of Writing Multicultural Women's History." *Frontiers* XII: 1 (1991b), 1–4.

Pascoe, Peggy: "Race, Gender, and Intercultural Relations: The Case of Interracial Marriage." *Frontiers* XII, 1 (1991c), 5–18.

Patterson-Black, Sheryll: "Women Homesteaders on the Great Plains Frontier." *Frontiers* 1, 2 (Spring 1976), 67–88.

Peavy, Linda and Ursula Smith: *The Gold Rush Widows of Little Falls* (St. Paul: Minnesota Historical Society Press, 1990).

Peavy, Linda and Ursula Smith: *Women in Waiting in the Westward Movement: Life on the Home Frontier* (Norman: University of Oklahoma Press, 1994).

Perales, Marian: "Empowering 'The Welder': A Historical Survey of Women of Color in the West." In Elizabeth Jameson and Susan Armitage (eds.) *Writing the Range: Race, Class, and Culture in the Women's West* (Norman: University of Oklahoma Press, 1997).

Petrik, Paula: *No Step Backward: Women and Family on the Rocky Mountain Mining Frontier, Helena, Montana 1865–1900* (Helena: Montana Historical Society Press, 1987).

Pierson, George Wilson: "American Historians and the Frontier Hypothesis in 1941." In Lawrence O. Burnette, Jr. (comp.) *Wisconsin Witness to Frederick Jackson Turner: A Collection of Essays on the Historian and the Thesis* (Madison: The State Historical Society of Wisconsin, 1961).

Rasmussen, Linda, Lorna Rasmussen, Candace Savage, and Anne Wheeler: *A Harvest Yet to Reap: A History of Prairie Women* (Toronto: Women's Press, 1976).

Scharff, Virginia: "The Case for Domestic Feminism: Woman Suffrage in Wyoming." *Annals of Wyoming* 56, 2 (Fall 1984), 29–37.

Schlissel, Lillian, Vicki Ruiz, and Janice Monk (eds.) *Western Women: Their Land, Their Lives* (Albuquerque: University of New Mexico Press, 1988).

Smith, Henry Nash: *Virgin Land: The American West as Symbol and Myth* (Cambridge: Harvard University Press, 1950).

Stefanco, Carolyn: "Networking on the Frontier: The Colorado Women's Suffrage Movement, 1876–1893." In Susan Armitage and Elizabeth Jameson (eds.) *The Women's West* (Norman: University of Oklahoma Press, 1987).

Stewart, Elinore Pruitt: *Letters of a Woman Homesteader* (Lincoln: University of Nebraska Press, 1961).

Stoeltje, Beverly: "A Helpmate for Man Indeed: The Image of the Frontier Woman." *Journal of American Folklore* 88, 347 (January-March 1975), 27–31.

Swagerty, William R.: "Marriage and Settlement Patterns of Rocky Mountain Trappers and Traders." *Western Historical Quarterly* 11, 2 (April 1980), 150–80.

Taylor, Quintard: *In Search of the Racial Frontier: African Americans in the American West* (New York: W. W. Norton & Company, 1997).

Taylor, Quintard and Shirley Anne Wilson Moore: *African American Women Confront the West, 1600–2000* (Norman: University of Oklahoma Press, 2003).

Tsai, Shih-shan Henry: *China and the Overseas Chinese in the United States 1868–1911* (Fayetteville: University of Arkansas Press, 1983).

Tsai, Shih-shan Henry: "Chinese Immigration, 1848–1882." In Sucheng Chan, Douglas Henry Daniels, Mario T. Garcia, and Terry P. Wilson (eds.) *People of Color in the American West* (Lexington, MA: D. C. Heath and Company, 1994).

Turner, Frederick Jackson: "The Significance of History." First presented as a talk to the Southwestern Wisconsin Teachers' Association and published in the 1891 *Wisconsin Journal of Education*, here referenced from Martin Ridge (ed.) *History, Frontier, and Section: Three Essays by Frederick Jackson Turner* (Albuquerque: University of New Mexico Press, 1993a).

Turner, Frederick Jackson: "The Significance of the Frontier in American History," first presented at the Historical Congress in Chicago at the World's Columbian Exhibition of 1893, originally printed in *Annual Report of the American Historical Association for the Year 1893* (Washington, DC: Government Printing Office, 1894), here referenced from Martin Ridge (ed.) *History, Frontier, and Section: Three Essays by Frederick Jackson Turner*. (Albuquerque: University of New Mexico Press, 1993b).

Van Kirk, Sylvia. *Many Tender Ties: Women in Fur Trade Society, 1670–1870* (Norman: University of Oklahoma Press, 1980; Winnipeg: Watson and Dwyer, 1980).

Wall, Wendy L.: "Gender and the 'Citizen Indian'." In Elizabeth Jameson and Susan Armitage (eds.) *Writing the Range: Race, Class, and Culture in the Women's West* (Norman: University of Oklahoma Press, 1997).

White, Richard: *"It's Your Misfortune and None of My Own": A History of the American West* (Norman: University of Oklahoma Press, 1991).

Wilson, Gilbert L.: *Goodbird the Indian: His Story* ([1914], rpt. St. Paul: Minnesota Historical Society Press, 1965).

Wilson, Gilbert L.: *Waheenee: An Indian Girl's Story* ([1921], rpt. Lincoln: University of Nebraska Press, 1981).

Wilson, Gilbert L.: *Buffalo Bird Woman's Garden* ([1917], rpt. St. Paul: Minnesota Historical Society Press, 1987).

Wright, James Edward: *The Politics of Populism: Dissent in Colorado* (New Haven: Yale University Press, 1974).

Yates, Emma Hayden Eames: *Seventy Miles from a Lemon* (London: Hammond, Hammond Co., 1949).

Yung, Judy: *Unbound Feet: A Social History of Chinese Women in San Francisco* (Berkeley: University of California Press, 1995).

Yung, Judy: *Unbound Voices: A Documentary History of Chinese Women in San Francisco* (Berkeley: University of California Press, 1999).

CHAPTER ELEVEN

Empire and Liberty: Contradictions and Conflicts in Nineteenth-Century Western Political History

JEFFREY OSTLER[1]

The West has always occupied a crucial position in American political thought. In the late eighteenth century, political theorists found in the West the solution for the ancient problem of the fragility of republican government. In the past, republican liberties had always given way to despotism. Poised on the edge of a vast continent and with seemingly limitless potential for expansion, however, the US would be able to overcome the fate of past republics. Some theorists looked to the West to solve the plague of factionalism. In *The Federalist* number 10, James Madison argued that dangerous factions advocating a "rage for paper money" or "an equal division of property" might inflame a single state, but were less likely to cause a "general conflagration" in a large multistate republic. Therefore, Madison declared, it was necessary for the new nation to "extend [its] sphere."[2] For others, an expanding republic was desirable because it would enable the reproduction of the essential condition for liberty: widespread land ownership for white men. A citizenry of property holders would possess the independence necessary to exercise vigilance against tyranny. In this way, western expansion would become, in Thomas Jefferson's phrase, "an empire for liberty" (Stephanson, 1995: 22).

In his 1801 inaugural address, at a time when the United States claimed no territory west of the Mississippi River, Jefferson expressed confidence that the nation's present extent would be sufficient for the "1,000th & 1,000th generation" (Ford, 1905: 196). Much sooner than Jefferson imagined – a mere five generations – the United States had completed its continental expansion. By the close of the nineteenth century, it seemed to many Americans (although by no means all) that Jefferson's vision had been realized, that the United States had indeed become a successful empire of liberty. It was in this triumphant moment that western US history was founded. Frederick Jackson Turner did not use republican language, but his thesis that the existence of "free land" allowed for the creation and reproduction of American democracy in a frontier environment proclaimed the fulfillment of Jefferson's dream. Nineteenth-century American democracy, however, was hardly universal. Not only were many groups excluded, expansion had a deleterious impact on conquered peoples. This was especially true for Native Americans. Their struggles to preserve freedom reveal American democracy's limitations in particularly striking fashion. Even for white men, Jefferson's vision of democracy may have been realized mostly in myth, with Madison's forecast that western expansion would contain radical egalitarianism nearer the mark.

Although Madison, Jefferson, and Turner all accepted the limitations of democracy within the American polity and were unconcerned with the impact of America's continental imperialism on conquered peoples, their terms – liberty, democracy, and empire – offer a framework for a political history of the West in the nineteenth century. This essay sees freedom and democracy as contested and problematic ideas whose implications were worked out through political struggles. Following recent calls for greater attention to nineteenth-century US expansion as a form of imperialism (Kaplan and Pease, 1993), this essay treats US empire-building as a process that was political in the broadest sense of the term, a process involving a wide range of conflicts and accommodations between and among groups on both sides of "the frontier." This approach broadens the scope of western political history and returns to a question, foundational to US political philosophy and western US historiography: What were the political implications of western expansion?

For a generation and more after Turner's thesis, Turner's answer to this question strongly influenced American historiography. Key moments in progressive historiography's story of the struggle between the people and the interests such as Jacksonian democracy and Populism had the frontier as the central protagonist. But after Turner's thesis was discredited in the 1930s and 1940s, American political historians turned away from the West. Historians of the frontier and the western United States continued to write political history, but they seldom made the West vital to American political development.

From 1945 through the 1980s, western political historians produced studies of distinctive western institutions such as territories and western-oriented federal agencies, biographies of western politicians, political histories of western states, and studies of social movements (nicely summarized in Owens, 1983). Some of this work revealed or sought to explain distinctive western political patterns. For example, one study found that the struggle for political supremacy in the mining town of Butte, Montana, was shaped by economic conditions more often found in the West than elsewhere in the country. Other scholars attempted, with only partial success, to explain the puzzling question of why woman suffrage was adopted earlier in many western territories and states than elsewhere (Malone, 1981; Larson, 1970).

Not surprisingly, scholars also turned their attention toward the People's Party of the 1890s, a movement that powerfully articulated farmers' and workers' grievances against the inequality and political corruption of an industrializing economy. Before 1945, scholars of Populism had followed Turner in treating Populism as a quintessentially "frontier" movement (Hicks, 1931). In contrast, post-1945 scholarship focused on the distinctiveness of western subregions. Scholars of Rocky Mountain Populism, for example, found that in contrast to other parts of the country farmers did not constitute the majority of Populist support but that the movement also relied on stock grazers and, especially, workers (Larson, 1986).

During these years, most American political historians were uninterested in regionalism or western politics. Yet, one subregion, the Midwest, became a crucial site for the influential "new political history." This school, which emerged as part of the "new social history" of the 1970s, used social science concepts and quantitative analysis of voting behavior to show that the late nineteenth-century party system was structured by blocks of "ethnocultural" voters responding to religious and cultural concerns (mandatory public education and prohibition) rather than economic issues. Although some of the new political history's key studies were situated in western states, they were less concerned with regional difference than national patterns (Luebke, 1969). When new political historians considered western distinctiveness, they argued that, in contrast to other parts of the country, there were no strong ethnocultural divisions in western states. Consequently, voters lacked strong partisan ties and political parties were comparatively weak (Kleppner, 1983).

Meanwhile, outside the conventionally defined boundaries of political history, scholars produced several works that dealt with politics in a broader sense. Some historians revealed the political processes by which Anglos dispossessed Hispanics of their land following the United States' conquest of Mexico (Pitt, 1966). Others examined the politics of race and labor and showed how labor leaders used Sinophobia to unify white workers against an external "threat" (Saxton, 1971). This and other political work on race and labor, as well as scholarship in western women's history (Armitage and Jameson, 1987), formed a critical foundation for the rise of the "new western history" in the late 1980s and early 1990s.

New western historians do not necessarily think of themselves as specialists in political history. Certainly, however, their project of critically examining western history to find a demythologized and therefore more "usable past" has political implications. Moreover, many of their works have engaged important themes in political history. New western historians have written eloquently on the decline of democracy in the West's "hydraulic empire" (Worster, 1985). They have named the brutal history of conquest and traced its present-day legacy of racial and ethnic diversity (Limerick, 1987). They have drawn renewed attention to patterns of electoral politics, the politics of social movements and race relations, and the development of the state (White, 1991).

While the new western history has problematized democracy and shown that empire-building advanced some people's liberty while destroying others', critics have suggested that its vision of politics remains limited. In the view of some, by retaining "the frontier" and "West" as categories, the new western history retains a colonial orientation that elides the perspectives and agency of many enclaved and historically subordinated people living under US domination (Klein, 1996). In a similar vein, others (Chan, 1994; Gonzáles, 1999; Castañeda, 1992) have argued that the new western history's "multiculturalism" overstates intercultural harmony and gives insufficient attention both to the oppression and agency of subordinate groups, especially women of color. Still others maintain that in contesting Turner's celebratory narrative of democracy, new western historians have produced a revalued, but similarly monolithic, account of the dominant American political culture as one uniformly characterized by the liberal values of individualism and acquisitiveness (Johnston, 1998).

My call for a broader political history of the nineteenth-century American West requires drawing not only on the "new western history" but also its critics. In addition, work by historians in distinct but sometimes overlapping fields (e.g., Chicano history, Native American history, women's history), along with scholarship in other disciplines, offers important perspectives on the politics of empire building. Taken together, a diverse literature enables us to examine key political issues connected with the expansion of the United States between 1800 and 1900. How would markets be structured? What would be the role of the federal government in managing expansion? What would be the relationship between newly developed regions of the United States and older centers of power? What labor systems would develop? What would be the position of conquered peoples in the American political economy? How would peoples facing conquest and incorporation respond to wrenching change? How would race, ethnicity, and class affect social hierarchies? How much cultural autonomy would be possible? Who would have civil and political rights, and what would these mean in practice? What would liberty mean, and for whom, in a continental empire?

In the early 1800s, even as Thomas Jefferson was declaring land enough for thousands of generations, Ohio Territory was preparing for admission as a state and northwest speculators were eyeing, and squatters were encroaching on, tribal lands. In the South, slaveholders and small farmers looked west to the new states of Kentucky and Tennessee and to Indian country beyond. The speed and energy of US expansion in the early nineteenth century reflected the partial settlement of previous political conflicts within the new polity. One conflict concerned the fears of some segments of the national elite that overly rapidly expansion would encourage social disorder and even pull apart the fragile republic that had been so carefully stitched together. The Northwest Ordinance (1787) spoke to these worries by giving the federal government strong controls over territories. At the same time, by allowing new states to gain admission to the union quickly and on an equal footing with older states, it encouraged the republic's rapid extension.

The federal government had also played an important role in abating unrest of the frontier's poor. In 1794, President George Washington led a military expedition against farmers of western Pennsylvania, who refused to pay a federal excise tax on whiskey. The "Whiskey Rebellion," like the earlier Regulator movement and Shays's Rebellion, defended the "homestead ethic," the belief in "an enduring body of values centered on the belief in the right of rural Americans to have and hold a family-size farm" (Brown, 1991: 90). In criticizing monopolists, land speculators, and wealthy parasites, the whiskey rebels exemplified the dangerous spirit of faction that Madison feared. The threat of force, rather than its actual use, was sufficient to extinguish the flames in western Pennsylvania.

Despite the appearance of an orderly process of expansion and the absence of poor people's revolts on the early nineteenth-century frontier, significant tensions remained between rich and poor, speculators and homesteaders, the respectable classes and the rabble, and whites who owned slaves and those who did not. Although most farmers accepted some forms of commercial activity, they also believed that economic activities should be regulated by moral considerations. Along with artisans and laborers in the early republic, small farmers generally held a "producer ideology" that saw labor as the source of wealth. Non-producers (speculators, bankers, and lawyers) engaged in illegitimate activities that threatened the well-being of family and community. Moral economy provided the basis for a powerful critique of social inequality and could lead to radical political challenges to economic privilege.

Although agrarian radicalism produced frequent sparks, these seldom burst into flame after 1800. Several factors modulated potential conflicts. In Kentucky, many squatters (epitomized by none other than Daniel Boone) became speculators.

Eventually, a general consensus in "private ownership of land[,] . . . in the liberty to distill and drink whiskey without interference from federal tax collectors, and in the promise of some form of commercial development" bridged social cleavages among whites (Aron, 1996: 123).

Political structures also regulated conflict. Universal suffrage for white men undergirded the development of a political system in which political parties competed for votes by employing patronage and symbols. Despite his wealth in land and slaves, Andrew Jackson and his supporters presented him to the public as a "common man." Jackson's crusade against the Second Bank of the United States at once tapped into and channeled deep strains of antimonopoly feeling among western farmers as well as eastern artisans and workers. Henry Clay's "American system," attacked by Jacksonians as a scheme of monopoly, also attracted ordinary men of the West who looked to the orderly development of railroads, markets, and small manufactures to ensure economic security for patriarchal, sober families and communities. At first, Whigs were very vulnerable to Democrats' attempts to associate them with aristocracy. However, when their 1840 presidential nominee, William Henry Harrison, proudly embraced a log cabin as his place of birth, the symbolism of frontier democracy became the currency of both parties.

Harrison's campaign also made clear the dependency of democracy upon conquest. Like Andrew Jackson, whose defeat of Muskogee (Creek) militants at the Battle of Horseshoe Bend (1814) was vital to his reputation as a war hero, Harrison capitalized on his attack on a multitribal alliance of Indian militants in what became known as the Battle of Tippecanoe (1811). A Whig broadside for the 1840 campaign (see Figure 1) depicts a series of vignettes from the candidate's life. Of course, there is the log cabin itself and the candidate plowing the family homestead. Along side these bucolic images, "Tippecanoe" is also shown defeating savage resistance.

Historians have usually failed to consider the United States' colonization of Indian people and their responses to be part of American political history. The links to conquest in Jacksonian/Harrisonian democracy suggest the shortsightedness of this omission as do the connections between empire and liberty in American political theory. In more concrete ways as well, America's history of conquest and colonization is very much a political history. The ideology of manifest destiny, which decreed an inevitable process by which a superior "Caucasian race" would simply exterminate or absorb an inferior "red race," denied this reality. Indians were supposed to simply vanish. In fact, however, various forms of Native resistance ensured that US expansion was political.

US policymakers in the early republic hoped they could have "expansion with honor," that Indians would readily accept US offers to purchase their land and eagerly embark upon the road to "civilization." In fact, however, treaty-making involved bribery, intimidation, deal-making, resistance, and capitulation – in short, the stuff of politics. As they were being negotiated, and after they had been signed, treaties frequently provoked political conflict within Indian communities.

In the first decade of the 1800s, as US citizens encroached on native lands, Indian leaders divided over how to respond. Some favored selling land and selective adoption of American ways. Others, however, like the Shawnee prophet Tenkswatawa ("The Prophet") and his brother Tecumseh, called upon Indians from Georgia to Michigan to resist American expansion. These militant leaders forecast a cataclysmic

GEN. WILLIAM HENRY HARRISON

Figure 1 *General William Henry Harrison*. Library of Congress, Prints & Photographs Division, LC–USZ62–31.

event in which Euro-Americans would either be destroyed or their oppressive presence removed (Dowd, 1992).

Tecumseh and The Prophet are well-known figures in American history. Both are symbols of the courageous, if ultimately futile, struggle of a doomed race. Unlike the Whiskey Rebellion or slave revolts, however, which presented real challenges to elite authority and had significant ramifications even in "defeat," the movement led by these and countless other Indian leaders has usually not been considered part of US political history. Unlike other forms of resistance, Indian resistance, is often seen as atavistic, misguided (although perhaps heroic), and ultimately inconsequential. This denial of resistance is a legacy of the nineteenth-century imperial ideology of the "vanishing American," which proclaimed the inevitability of Indian disappearance to justify specific actions (and nonactions) that led to extermination and dispossession (Dippie, 1982).

Of course, on its own terms native militancy in the early nineteenth century failed. Militants were unable to prevent the conquest of Indian lands in trans-Appalachia. However, prophesies of Euro-American removal continued to inspire resistance under Black Hawk in Illinois in the early 1830s and among the Seminoles in Florida into the 1840s. Furthermore, although scholars have never pinned down a link from the early nineteenth-century militants to the so-called Prophet Dance movements of the Pacific Northwest and the Ghost Dance movements of 1870 and 1890, it is not far-fetched to think that early-century militants inspired leaders of these later anticolonial movements.

After the defeats of the militants during the War of 1812, Indians used other tactics to resist US expansion. Armed with treaties previously and newly negotiated, they struggled to prevent the government from implementing its new policy of removing all tribes west of the Mississippi. The Cherokee case illustrates the complexities of the politics of removal, while at the same time showing that defeat was not absolute.

Although a minority of Cherokees were sympathetic to militancy, in the early 1810s accommodationist leaders allied with the US against the Muskogees to gain US support to preserve Cherokee lands. Despite this alliance, however, Americans identified Cherokees as a target for removal in the late 1810s. Although they faced potentially crippling factionalism, Cherokees were able to prevent removal for the moment. Their success was due in part to the majority's adoption in 1817 of a series of reforms, sometimes referred to as the first Cherokee Constitution, that central-ized authority and created greater administrative accountability. This was another step in what scholar Theda Perdue has termed the "centralization of power in response to white pressure," a major theme in Cherokee political history (1979: 32).

Cherokees also gained support from allies within the American polity. Missionar-ies, who believed that the special moral status of the United States required it to uphold Indian treaties and that removal would hinder the Cherokees' further advance toward Christian civilization, were especially important. Advocates of removal even-tually judged that Cherokees were strong enough to make removal too costly.

During the 1820s most Cherokees continued to pursue a policy of selective adop-tion of Christian civilization and the development of stronger structures of national sovereignty to preserve their land and communities. They skillfully appealed to the American judicial system and in *Worcester v. State of Georgia* (1832) won a partial endorsement of tribal sovereignty against the claims of Georgia. Nonetheless, Presi-dent Jackson, the Indians' "Great Father," found himself powerless to protect "his children" (Rogin, 1975). The doctrine of states' rights tied his hands, and Georgians continued to pressure Cherokees into accepting removal. As in the past, Cherokees remained divided. In 1835, a minority of Cherokees, mostly those from the accul-turated class of wealthy slaveholders, signed the Treaty of New Echota and agreed to removal. Despite protests by the majority of Cherokees and many sympathetic Americans, the US army forced most of the Cherokees to move to Indian Territory in 1839 at the cost of great suffering and loss of life.

Yet Cherokee resistance had not been futile. In his decision in *Worcester* and his earlier opinion in *Cherokee Nation v. State of Georgia* (1831), Chief Justice John Marshall established a doctrine of Native American sovereignty that would later provide the basis for many Indian people to assert important rights. Marshall's "domestic dependent nations" formulation certainly fell short of placing Indian nations on an equal footing with European nations, but it nonetheless recognized that Indian nations possessed significant elements of sovereignty. One might think of Marshall's decisions as occurring solely within the realm of US constitutional law, yet his reasoning depended upon the Cherokees' and other tribes' prior exercise of military and diplomatic efforts. Marshall recognized that Europeans had first nego-tiated treaties to achieve peace with formidable foes and that thereafter Indians had exercised sovereignty in their dealings with European nations and the US. The fact that the cases came before him at all was predicated upon the project of Cherokee nation-building that had been underway for decades. Had the Cherokees been unable to press their claims at this time, it is likely that the development of US Indian law would have been substantially different, with important ramifications not only for political relations between Indian communities and the American state but for inter-tribal relations as well.

The Cherokee story exposes the limitations of liberty in an expanding empire by revealing how the United States trampled on Cherokee self-determination. It also calls attention to complex connections between expansion and slavery. In accom-modating to the US, Cherokees had become a "mirror of the republic" (Young, 1981) not only by adopting a written constitution but also by holding African American slaves. White southern slaveholders, however, were not flattered by this form of imitation; they were an influential source of pressure for removal.

If a majority of Euro-Americans north and south eventually achieved a consensus around Indian removal, it was much more difficult for them to agree on the place of slavery in an empire of liberty. Jefferson himself advanced two possible resolutions of this dilemma. At times, he hoped that slavery would eventually die out; this, however, became increasingly untenable with the westward extension of King Cotton's rule. Jefferson also sought release from the obligations of Enlightenment egalitarianism by exploring the theory that Negroes were not fully human.

With the exception of an abolitionist minority, what concerned most white Americans about slavery was not the contradiction between ideals of liberty and democracy and the actual condition of enslaved millions. Rather, they feared slavery's threats to the liberties of white men. Pro- and anti-slavery forces articulated their positions in the idiom of republicanism. For white southerners, Michael Morrison writes, slavery "promoted equality by meliorating class conflict and ensured liberty by making exploitation of white workers and independent agriculturists unnecessary" (1997: 6). Slavery, for white northerners, "retarded the progress of the nation, degraded white workers, and contravened the fundamental republican principles of liberty and equality" (ibid.: 7).

Both of these arguments, in different ways, smoothed over class divisions among whites. The first did so by a paternalistic ethic that bound together the class of slaveholders to which Jefferson belonged and the yeomen he celebrated. The second did so through an individualistic ethic that united capital and labor through a shared hostility not only to slavery, but to African Americans in general. The muscular expressions of Manifest Destiny that culminated in the US conquest of much of northern Mexico in the late 1840s intensified nationalist white supremacy on both sides of the slavery debate while at the same time the territorial question strengthened sectional loyalties. It was perhaps in these ways, rather than through Madison's geographic diffusion of faction, that the extension of empire discouraged antimonopoly radicalism. After the decline of a mostly urban movement of discontented artisans in the late 1830s, there were few radical flames for Madison's extensive empire to contain until after the Civil War. Workers and farmers remained committed to a moral economy, but nationalism and intraracial solidarity, along with relative economic prosperity and the strength of party loyalties, dampened discontent in the 1840s and 1850s.

From 1846 to 1861 the central issue in American politics was the question of slavery's place in the territories. The fact that the status of slavery was unresolved in most of the trans-Mississippi West fed the fears and fantasies of northerners and southerners alike. Both sections saw the soon-to-be created territories and states of the West as the means by which the opposing section could realize its grand scheme to seize control of the government and destroy liberty throughout the nation. Thus, upon the question of whether chattel slavery would be allowed in California, or Texas, or Kansas, hinged the fate of the republic. By throwing into question the balance of power between the North and South, the extension of empire made Lincoln's divided house unable to stand.

By 1865, the North's idea of liberty had triumphed. Never again in a nation that recognized the equal creation of all men would there be chattel slavery. "Free" white labor would not have to compete with the labor of enslaved African Americans. But if this particular form of slavery had been destroyed, white men continued to perceive other threats to their liberty.

The post-Civil-War American West was a very different place from the one Jefferson had envisioned in 1800. Although there were numerous small farmers in places like Nebraska, Oregon, and even California, the scale of commercial activity in Gold Rush San Francisco or the extent of land concentration in the Central Valley suggested that the republic might be unable to reproduce the conditions necessary for Jeffersonian democracy. It was not just that there was an increase in commerce and larger holdings of land. The Industrial Revolution had brought qualitative changes: the transcontinental railroad with its annihilation of space and time, the use of new technologies in mining, and the existence of a class of permanent wage laborers.

In Turner's famous essay he asked his readers to stand at Cumberland Gap and "watch the procession of civilization" and then to go to South Pass to see "the same procession" again (Turner: 1920: 12). For Turner the "process" of western expansion had repeated itself. In fact, however, although there were many similarities in empire-building on both sides of the Mississippi, there were marked differences. In part, these were due to geography (the Far West was more arid and mountainous and had much more gold and silver), but the post-Civil-War development of the American West involved more than the extension or modification of already existing eastern institutions in a new environment. Two things were different about empire-building in the trans-Mississippi West in the century's second half. First, it occurred in conjunction with the national development of industrial capitalism. Second, it involved the conquest and incorporation of different peoples.

The political conflicts of this period can be described without much exaggeration as a "Western Civil War of Incorporation" (Brown, 1991: 43–4). The metaphor of incorporation is especially apt to describe the project of western empire-building in an era of industrialization. Not only did empire-builders engage in acts of conquest, they sought to "incorporate" all the West's peoples into an industrial order ruled, like the new corporations, by principles of ordered hierarchy. Yet this process met substantial opposition across a wide spectrum of overlapping groups. In various ways and at different times, Mexicans, Native Americans, workers, and small ranchers and farmers all resisted the consolidation of the new order.

As they had earlier, Indian people evaluated the threat from US expansion in different ways. Sometime in the early 1860s, a Crow boy named Plenty Coups had a vision in which he saw buffalo coming from a hole in the earth and spreading over the plains. Suddenly the herd disappeared, and out of the hole came animals that at first looked like buffalo, but they were spotted and had odd tails and behaved strangely. Then, Plenty Coups saw a fierce storm descend upon a dark forest. When the storm passed, only one tree was left standing, the home of the chickadee. Later, tribal elders interpreted Plenty Coups' vision to mean that "white men will take and hold this country and that their Spotted-buffalo will cover the plains." The storm was the "white man and those who help him in his wars," and the tree that remained standing represented the Crows. Like the chickadee who was small but wise, the Crows must survive through "peaceful relations with the white men, whom we could not stop even though we would" (Linderman, 1930: 73–4).

Plenty Coups' vision reflected a growing Crow consensus around a plan of alliance with the United States. This strategy was designed to avoid being destroyed by the massive invasion of Americans; it also sought to enlist US aid against another expansionary threat, the Teton Sioux (Lakotas). The Crows' accommodationist approach might be seen as simple capitulation to US domination. Yet Crows used their alliance to make important claims. In the 1880s, as the government tried to take more of their land and force them to become "civilized," ordinary Crow people used techniques of passive and active resistance. Although Crow leaders disagreed among themselves about diplomatic tactics – when to dig in their heels, when and what to concede – they were often able to "calibrate their accommodation to American power, appearing friendly while resisting [Americans'] demands" (Hoxie, 1995: 119). For the most part, Crow political victories were partial and defensive, but they survived the storm.

Factionalism often plagued Indian communities as they struggled to cope with US colonialism. The removal of the Cherokees aggravated political tensions while at the same time it destroyed the constitutional government, schools, and missions that had earlier enabled Cherokees to resolve their differences (Perdue, 1979). The result was chaos and political violence. The coming of the Civil War reawakened tensions as Cherokee slave holders argued for an alliance with the Confederacy, while others favored neutrality or joining the Union. After the war, the Cherokees signed a treaty with the United States but they continued to suffer from social and economic class distinctions and conflicting values. In the 1890s, when the government decided to allot Cherokee land, familiar divisions were played out once more. Wealthier

Cherokees got most of the best land, while poorer, conservative Cherokees refused to accept allotments and so lost what little they had.

The consequences of factionalism in Native American communities has generally been seen as negative. Yet internal divisions did not necessarily signify weakness. During the 1862 Minnesota Uprising, Ojibwe warriors joined in militant Dakotas' attacks on Euro-American settlements, whereas civil leaders remained neutral. In this situation, civil leaders "were able to capitalize on their image as 'friendly Indians' and extract concessions from the Americans" (Kugel, 1998: 84). The "contradictory yet symbiotic relationship" between the warriors and civil leaders endured throughout the nineteenth century. Although the balance of power shifted against the Ojibwes over time, they achieved meaningful victories. As late as 1898, warriors at the Leech Lake reservation (Minnesota) declared war on the US and then repulsed US troops sent to subdue this unexpected and little-known uprising. Civil leaders exploited the situation by arguing to US authorities that they alone could mediate the confrontation. In agreement for their help, authorities agreed to provide long overdue treaty annuities, investigate timber fraud, and drop plans to remove the Leech Lake Ojibwes to the White Earth reservation.

While the cases of the Crows and Ojibwes highlight the political skills of Native leaders who resisted through controlled accommodation, other leaders, in the spirit of the early nineteenth-century militants, proposed a wholesale rejection of the American empire. Plenty Coups' vision offered one way to preserve native liberty. The Wanapam prophet Smohalla, the Paiute Wovoka, and many others, who foresaw the end of the present world, the removal of Europeans, and the coming of a new world in which game would be restored and deceased ancestors return to life, charted another.

Scholars of the 1889–90 Ghost Dance generally have not treated it as a political movement. In his classic study of the Ghost Dance, ethnologist James Mooney portrayed it as akin to the great religions of the world. Like Jesus or Buddha, the Ghost Dance prophet Wovoka preached a doctrine of peace and the brotherhood of all mankind. Tribes that adopted the Ghost Dance endorsed Wovoka's pacific doctrine with the exception of the Lakotas, among whom the prophet's teachings "assumed a hostile meaning" (Mooney, 1896: 787). Mooney's thesis of Lakota exceptionalism assigned to the Lakotas responsibility for the massacre at Wounded Knee (December 29, 1890) while at the same time obscuring the ways in which the Ghost Dance contested colonialism. After the slaughter at Wounded Knee Wovoka downplayed his teaching of a world-renewing, European-removing apocalypse. However, his prophesies and the dance itself constituted an ideological and practical challenge to US domination. The ghost shirts Lakotas wore to make themselves invulnerable to bullets did not signify an impending uprising, but instead revealed their knowledge that their defiance of colonialism might provoke a government crackdown. The carnage at Wounded Knee has been seen as proof of the futility of these shirts and the Ghost Dance itself. Yet in the twentieth century Indians have continued to work for freedom from imperial domination. The Ghost Dancers' visions and their will to resist have provided one source of inspiration.

If the post-Civil-War subjugation of Indian peoples revealed continuities with earlier phases of empire-building, the conquest and incorporation of Mexicans marked a significant contrast. The Treaty of Guadalupe Hidalgo (1848) extended

American liberties to Mexicans by protecting corporate and individual land title and guaranteeing Mexican men legal and political rights. However, the treaty contained nothing to prevent Anglos from classifying Mexicans according to the racialized ideology of Manifest Destiny. The rapid expansion of industrial capitalism into Texas, California, and New Mexico, resulted in significant losses of Mexicans' land and their incorporation (for the most part) into the lower classes of a new industrial order. Like Indians, Mexicans employed an array of strategies to counter, deflect, channel, and adjust to new conditions.

Mexicans sometimes revolted. In July 1859 Juan Cortina and others rode into Brownsville, Texas, and released Mexican prisoners, raided Anglo-owned stores, and killed four Anglos who had escaped punishment for murdering Mexicans. Cortina then retreated to the countryside, where he recruited a force five to six hundred strong and kept Brownsville under siege. Not until December, with the arrival of US troops, did the "Cortina War" begin to wind down. Although Anglos alleged that Cortina was nothing more than a "bandit," his uprising was political. Cortina issued two proclamations that emphasized "loss of land either through legal manipulation or through intimidation; the impunity with which Anglos killed Mexicans, and the arrogance of Anglo American racism, 'so ostentatious of its own qualities'" (Rosenbaum, 1981: 44). Although the US defeated the Cortina rebellion, it left a significant legacy. This and other uprisings (the "Skinning Wars" of the early 1870s and the El Paso "Salt War" of 1877) demonstrated to Anglos that "overt land dispossession, expulsions, and other repressive measures were not safe options" (Montejano, 1987: 33). Given Anglos' relatively small numbers along the border, these uprisings encouraged them to practice what Montejano nicely phrases as "benevolent *patronismo.*"

A more endemic form of protest was social banditry. In California, Texas, and New Mexico the acts of quasi-mythic figures like Joaquín Murieta and Mexican communities' celebration of them through ballads and stories had important consequences. Folklore, according to Rosenbaum, "kept pride alive and provided examples for other forms of violent resistance when provocation was great enough" (1981: 60–1).

More commonly, Mexicans countered incorporation through nonviolent means and various strategies of negotiation with Anglo elites. The strength of Mexican political power depended upon demographics and the degree of Anglo economic penetration. In places like central Texas and northern California, where Mexicans were quickly outnumbered, Anglos fairly easily dispossessed and disenfranchised them. In southern Texas, New Mexico, and parts of southern California, however, Mexican elites often made alliances with Anglo merchants and lawyers and helped broker the establishment of the new order. In so doing, they preserved a measure of autonomy for themselves and sometimes for Mexican communities. Even in these places, however, Anglos eventually captured political power. In Santa Barbara, Californios controlled politics until the early 1870s when a tourist and real estate boom enabled Anglos to seize control of the city government. Anglos passed laws against bullfights and bearfights and reorganized the city's wards to reduce Mexican representation. By 1880, Mexicans had become in Camarillo's terms "foreigners in their own city" (1979: 76).

Mexicans exercised political power the longest in New Mexico Territory, where an impressive number held political office and effectively used alliances with Anglos to enhance personal economic interests. In some instances *patróns* protected poorer Mexicans, but overall in the late 1800s small Mexican farmers and ranchers lost communal and private land and faced escalating racial violence. At the same time, Mexican women became increasingly impoverished. While a few resisted encroachments, their resistance occurred mostly within the private spaces of family and church (González, 1999). Still, outward resistance surfaced, especially in rural areas where Mexicans participated in long-running skirmishes such as the Lincoln County War that involved complex and shifting alliances against Anglo land monopolization. In 1889, a full-scale uprising emerged when the Gorras Blancas (White Caps) started cutting the fences of large Anglo ranchers and destroying railroad property and other sites of Anglo economic power. In 1890, El Partido del Pueblo Unido (the United People's Party) tried to capitalize on the Gorras Blancas movement and took the issues of land monopolization and political corruption into the arena of electoral politics. Led by a coalition of middle-class Hispaños, Anglo labor leaders, and a few *patróns*, with the support of small-propertied and working-class Anglos and Mexicans, the People's Party swept the election of 1890. Under Populist pressure, the next territorial legislature established a court to resolve land claims, but this process bogged down in litigation. By 1894, the People's Party was weakened by internal class and ethnic divisions. Furthermore, the antimonopoly position of the party's Hispanic leaders was grounded more in support of laissez-faire economic development than communal land claims. To most of the party's followers, rooted in the moral economy of the Gorras Blancas, it seemed that these leaders were simply a new class of *políticos*.

By 1900 Mexicans throughout the Southwest had lost much of their land and autonomy. In urban areas, Mexicans formed *barrios*, a strategy that allowed them to regulate the pace of social change and thus ensured ethnic and community continuities. For Mexicans in New Mexico and Colorado, seasonal wage labor allowed them to survive in the new economy while at the same time maintaining "control over their own enclaves" (Deutsch, 1987: 39).

The proletarianization of Mexicans, related to the consolidation of industrial capitalism in the West, revealed the emergence of a dual labor system in the West. The top tier, which consisted of managerial and skilled workers, was the domain of white workers; the "bottom tier" of unskilled, low-paying jobs was occupied by nonwhite workers (White, 1991: 283–4). Native- and foreign-born workers (the latter including immigrant groups whose claims to "whiteness" were contingent) often occupied the bottom tier. This system was created and maintained through political struggles, and it had political consequences.

In the Far West, the process of racialization involved the reproduction of free white labor's antebellum antislavery/antiblack ideology and its extension to other nonwhite groups. Many African Americans looked to the West as a "place of economic opportunity and refuge from racial restrictions" (Almaguer, 1994: 3). African Americans who came to California's gold fields, for example, experienced a brief period of relative toleration, but, as Taylor points out (1998: 85), "traditional racial parameters were soon established." In the 1850s, white supremacists in the California legislature introduced several bills to restrict free Black immigration. The near passage of one of these in 1858 resulted in an exodus of ten percent of California's African American population to Canada. In the meantime, African Americans faced local, state, and federal laws that restricted their civil and political liberties. African

Americans organized to make known their grievances and to demand equal rights. Despite significant gains during Reconstruction, when black men throughout the West won the right to vote and an impressive number occupied elective office, by the 1890s ongoing economic, social, and political discrimination seriously limited freedom for African Americans in the West.

White workers also discriminated against Chinese immigrants. Almaguer argues that, anti-Chinese sentiment "served as a major force for the organization of white skilled labor" and "diverted the attention of unskilled workers and the unemployed from the privileged position that unionized, skilled occupations were developing at the time" (1994: 179). The rise of the Workingmen's Party in 1877 under the demagogic leadership of Denis Kearney was the major vehicle through which Chinese became western labor's "indispensable enemy" (Saxton, 1971). Racialization led to the 1882 Chinese Exclusion Act and numerous instances of violent attacks on Chinese throughout the West, the most notorious of which was the Rock Springs, Wyoming, massacre, in which white workers killed fifty-one Chinese strikebreakers. Yet Chinese were not simply passive victims of oppression. Recent scholarship has emphasized that Chinese immigrants employed a range of strategies to defend themselves against the anti-Chinese movement (Wong and Chan, 1998). They, too, were political actors.

While there is certainly a need for more study of Chinese immigrants' responses to the anti-Chinese movement, scholarship on the anti-Chinese movement itself might also profit from a more political approach. Although theorists of racialization have emphasized that race is socially and politically constructed, they often portray racializing practices as though they simply involved the unmediated outworking of the dominant culture's racial ideology. Theories of social construction might profitably be extended to analyze the actual politics of racial exclusion, including the politics of Sinophobia within the western labor movement. Before the emergence of the Workingmen's Party there was extensive cooperation between trade unions and "anticoolie" clubs; moreover, labor leaders like Henry George argued that Chinese immigration threatened to replace "a population of intelligent freemen" with one of "serfs and their masters" (Saxton, 1971: 101). Still, in July 1877, California's organized labor movement focused primarily on the dangers of capital's growing concentration and its undue political power. Socialists in the movement, especially, were far more concerned to win the eight-hour day and nationalization of the railroads than to restrict Chinese immigration. The story of how Sinophobia quickly overwhelmed these more progressive tendencies is well known, but the politics that defeated the non-racialized alternative remain obscure.

The last two decades of the century saw few signs that white labor's vision of democracy might be expanded to include nonwhite workers. Even industrial unionists, whose structural position made them the most likely group to move toward interracial unions, remained exclusionary. The Knights of Labor and Western Federation of Miners were anti-Chinese and almost always adopted an exclusionary position toward African Americans, Mexican Americans, and southern and eastern European immigrants. In 1903, William "Big Bill" Haywood announced that the WFM would organize Japanese and Chinese workers, but, as Jameson (1998: 158) points out, "[i]t was easier to endorse inclusion than to practice it." Not until the 1930s would the West see significant class solidarity across racial and ethnic divisions.

If the logic of white workers' exclusionary tendencies smoothed over their internal differences and softened their antagonism toward employers, the West's dual labor system scarcely prevented class conflict among Euro-Americans. Even labor leaders who focused primarily on racial exclusion linked this demand to a broader critique of capitalist exploitation. Furthermore, whether informed by a producer ethic with roots in Jacksonian democracy or by a more class-conscious socialism, many white workers and farmers saw the growing concentration of economic power rather than nonwhites as the main threat to liberty. In sharp contrast to the 1840s and 1850s, when dangerous factions of the sort Madison feared produced few flames, after 1865 it often seemed that a vast multistate republic would fail to contain movements advocating paper money and an equal distribution of property. Whether with hope or fear, many saw in the Granger uprising (1870s), the Populist revolt (1890s), or the miners' strikes at Coeur d'Alene (1892 and 1899) and Cripple Creek (1894) the beginnings of great upheavals.

Whether drawing on Turner or repudiating him, western historians have often treated western radicalism as nothing more than disappointed individualism. Farmers and workers came together only when their personal dreams of upward social mobility and property acquisition were dashed (Schwantes, 1987; Limerick, 1987). Yet, western radicalism was not simply a pathological species of liberalism. Radical political movements in the West were informed by alternative visions of society as a cooperative commonwealth and were deeply rooted in earlier movements with a strong sense of moral economy, as well as being nourished by new strains of radicalism brought to America by European immigrants (Johnston, 1998). Students of American political development need to take seriously these and what Berk (1994) has called other "repressed alternatives" and seek political explanations for their outcomes rather than simply assuming that they were never viable or erasing them altogether.

In a general sense, James Madison was at least partly right when he predicted that a large republic would inhibit a "general conflagration." The sheer size of the late-nineteenth-century United States was among the many factors that worked against the emergence of a stronger labor organization, not only because it contributed to uneven economic development but because it multiplied conditions of localism and isolation and hindered large-scale coordination. Furthermore, although the West did not actually draw millions of discontented workers from eastern cities, the myth of a western "safety valve" itself reinforced ideas of upward social mobility that many wage laborers found persuasive and thereby lessened radicalism's appeal. A Madisonian logic was especially salient when labor and agrarian radicals sought power through electoral politics. The 1892 People's Party, a movement that had the potential to realign the party system's axis along class lines, was unable to build on early gains in the Great Plains and Mountain West states and was forced into a watered-down coalition with free-silver Democrats. Populism needed to make a quick breakthrough in a near majority of states in 1892, but this was an almost impossible task under a decentralized party system in a large republic (Ostler, 1993).

The defeat of Populism marked a significant victory for the forces behind industrial capitalism nationally and in the West. Nonetheless, Populism left an impressive legacy that would nourish a variety of urban and rural reform movements in the early twentieth century. Agrarian radicalism reemerged in new forms in the twentieth century, and labor unrest continued to challenge capitalist hegemony well into the 1940s and beyond.

Populism also played an important role in furthering woman suffrage. Not all Populists supported woman suffrage, but by opening up public space for women, the movement's political culture encouraged women to assert their right to the ballot (Goldberg, 1997). In states like Colorado and Idaho, where women won the vote in the 1890s, their achievements were closely related to Populist success. Populism provided momentum for victories in other states in the early twentieth century. Why, then, did women achieve the vote earlier in the West than elsewhere? Once again, the extension of liberty in one sector of society was related to its denial elsewhere. One of the reasons why woman suffrage was easier to accept in the West was "because it could not alter the racial balance of power in the region, where white racial hegemony was firmly established by the turn of the century" (Mead, 1999: 283).

At the beginning of the nineteenth century, few Americans would have predicted that the US empire would reach the shores of the Pacific so quickly. For Jeffersonians, Turner surely among them, the closing of the frontier produced profound anxiety about the future of democracy. Yet there remained ways to imagine how further extension of empire could perpetuate liberty. One possibility was to bring new land into yeoman ownership through irrigating the West's arid spaces. Another looked to empire overseas. The annexation of Hawaii and the Philippines in 1898 marked a new phase in American imperialism. Part of the ideological justification for imperialism was the bringing of freedom to oppressed peoples of the world; advocates of imperialism also used Jeffersonian arguments to explain that empire would ensure democracy at home. Economic growth, essential to the mitigation of class conflict, required new markets to absorb America's excessive agricultural and industrial production (Williams, 1969). Such markets would ensure the continued well-being and independence of small farmers; for urban labor, abundance meant upward social mobility. Early-twentieth-century imperialism required an adjustment of Jeffersonian terms to the realities of an increasingly urban, industrial economy, but it also revealed the continued dependence of democracy on expansion and domination. Nonetheless, the meanings of liberty and even the legitimacy of empire itself remained open questions. Only through politics would their answers become known.

NOTES

1   For their many excellent suggestions, I would like to thank Gerry Berk, Richard Maxwell Brown, Shari Huhndorf, Robert Johnston, Jim Mohr, Peggy Pascoe, Barbara Welke, and the graduate students in my fall 1999 seminar on western US historiography.
2   Alexander Hamilton, James Madison, and John Jay, *The Federalist Papers* ([1788], New York: The New American Library, Inc., 1961), 83–84.

REFERENCES

Almaguer, Tomás: *Racial Fault Lines: The Historical Origins of White Supremacy in California* (Berkeley, University of California Press, 1994).

Armitage, Susan and Elizabeth Jameson (eds.): *The Womens' West* (Norman: University of Oklahoma Press, 1987).

Aron, Stephen: *How The West Was Lost: The Transformation of Kentucky from Daniel Boone to Henry Clay* (Baltimore: Johns Hopkins University Press, 1996).

Berk, Gerald: *Alternative Tracks: The Constitution of American Industrial Order, 1865–1917* (Baltimore: Johns Hopkins University Press, 1994).

Brown, Richard Maxwell: *No Duty To Retreat: Violence and Values in American History and Society* (New York: Oxford University Press, 1991).

Camarillo, Albert: *Chicanos in a Changing Society: From Mexican Pueblos to American Barrios in Santa Barbara and Southern California, 1848–1930* (Cambridge, MA: Harvard University Press, 1979).

Castañeda, Antonia I.: "Women of Color and the Rewriting of Western History: The Discourse, Politics, and Decolonization of History." *Pacific Historical Review* 61 (November 1992), 501–34.

Chan, Sucheng: "Western American Historiography and Peoples of Color." In Sucheng Chan, Douglas Henry Daniels, Mario T. García, and Terry P. Wilson (eds.) *Peoples of Color in the American West* (Lexington, MA: D. C. Heath, 1994).

Deutsch, Sarah: *No Separate Refuge: Culture, Class, and Gender on an Anglo-Hispanic Frontier in the American Southwest, 1880–1940* (New York: Oxford University Press, 1987).

Dippie, Brian W.: *The Vanishing American: White Attitudes and US Indian Policy* (Middletown, CT: Wesleyan University Press, 1982).

Dowd, Gregory: *A Spirited Resistance: The North American Indian Struggle For Unity, 1745–1815* (Baltimore: Johns Hopkins University Press, 1992).

Ford, Paul Leicester (ed.): *The Works of Thomas Jefferson*, vol. 9 (New York and London: G. P. Putnam's Sons, 1905).

Goldberg, Michael Lewis: *An Army of Women: Gender and Politics in Gilded Age Kansas* (Baltimore: Johns Hopkins University Press, 1997).

Gómez-Quiñones, Juan: *Roots of Chicano Politics, 1600–1940* (Albuquerque: University of New Mexico Press, 1994).

González, Deena J.: *Refusing the Favor: The Spanish-Mexican Women of Santa Fe, 1820–1880* (New York: Oxford University Press, 1999).

Gyory, Andrew: *Closing the Gate: Race, Politics, and the Chinese Exclusion Act* (Chapel Hill: University of North Carolina Press, 1998).

Hicks, John D.: *The Populist Revolt: A History of the Farmers' Alliance and the People's Party* (Minneapolis: University of Minnesota Press, 1931).

Hoxie, Frederick E.: *Parading Through History: The Making of the Crow Nation in America, 1805–1935* (New York: Cambridge University Press, 1995).

Jameson, Elizabeth: *All That Glitters: Class, Conflict, and Community in Cripple Creek* (Urbana: University of Illinois Press, 1998).

Johnston, Robert Douglas: "Beyond 'The West': Regionalism, Liberalism, and the Evasion of Politics in the New Western History." *Rethinking History* 2 (Summer 1998), 239–77.

Kaplan, Amy and Donald E. Pease (eds.): *Cultures of United States Imperialism* (Durham: Duke University Press, 1993).

Klein, Kerwin Lee: "Reclaiming the 'F' Word, Or Being and Becoming Postwestern." *Pacific Historical Review* 65 (May 1996), 179–215.

Kleppner, Paul: "Voters and Parties in Western States, 1876–1900." *Western Historical Quarterly* 14 (January 1983), 49–68.

Kugel, Rebecca: *To Be the Main Leaders of Our People: A History of Minnesota Ojibwe Politics, 1825–1898* (East Lansing: Michigan State University Press, 1998).

Larson, Robert W.: *Populism in the Mountain West* (Albuquerque: University of New Mexico Press, 1986).

Larson, T. A.: "Woman Suffrage in Western America." *Utah Historical Quarterly* 38 (Winter 1970), 7–19.

Limerick, Patricia Nelson: *Legacy of Conquest: The Unbroken Past of the American West* (New York: W. W. Norton, 1987).

Linderman, Frank B.: *American: The Life Story of A Great Indian, Plenty-Coups, Chief of the Crows* (New York: The John Day Company, 1930).

Luebke, Frederick C.: *Immigrants and Politics: The Germans of Nebraska, 1880–1900* (Lincoln: University of Nebraska Press, 1969).

Malone, Michael P.: *The Battle for Butte: Mining and Politics on the Northern Frontier, 1864–1906* (Seattle: University of Washington Press, 1981).

Mead, Rebecca J.: "How the Vote Was Won: Woman Suffrage in the Western United States, 1868–1914." (PhD dissertation: University of California Los Angeles, 1999).

Montejano, David: *Anglos and Mexicans in the Making of Texas, 1836–1986* (Austin: University of Texas Press, 1987).

Mooney, James: *The Ghost-Dance Religion and the Sioux Outbreak of 1890*, Fourteenth Annual Report of the Bureau of Ethnology, 1892–93, pt. 2 (Washington, DC: GPO, 1896).

Morrison, Michael A.: *Slavery and the American West: The Eclipse of Manifest Destiny and the Coming of the Civil War* (Chapel Hill: University of North Carolina Press, 1997).

Ostler, Jeffrey: *Prairie Populism: The Fate of Agrarian Radicalism in Kansas, Nebraska, and Iowa, 1880–1892* (Lawrence: University Press of Kansas, 1993).

Owens, Kenneth N.: "Government and Politics in the Nineteenth-Century West." In Michael P. Malone (ed.) *Historians and the American West* (Lincoln: University of Nebraska Press, 1983).

Perdue, Theda: *Slavery and the Evolution of Cherokee Society, 1540–1866* (Knoxville: University of Tennessee Press, 1979).

Pitt, Leonard: *The Decline of the Californios: A Social History of the Spanish-Speaking Californians, 1846–1890* (Berkeley: University of California Press, 1966).

Rogin, Michael Paul: *Fathers and Children: Andrew Jackson and the Subjugation of the American Indian* (New York: Alfred A. Knopf, 1975).

Rosenbaum, Robert J.: *Mexicano Resistance in the Southwest: "The Sacred Right of Self-Preservation?"* (Austin: University of Texas Press, 1981).

Saxton, Alexander: *The Indispensable Enemy: Labor and the Anti-Chinese Movement* (Berkeley: University of California Press, 1971).

Schwantes, Carlos A.: "The Concept of the Wageworkers' Frontier: A Framework for Future Research." *Western Historical Quarterly* 18 (January 1987), 39–55.

Stephanson, Anders: *Manifest Destiny: American Expansionism and the Empire of Right* (New York: Hill and Wang, 1995).

Storti, Craig: *Incident at Bitter Creek: The Story of the Rock Springs Chinese Massacre* (Ames: Iowa State University Press, 1991).

Taylor, Quintard: *In Search of the Racial Frontier: African Americans in the American West, 1528–1990* (New York: W. W. Norton, 1998).

Turner, Frederick Jackson: "The Significance of the Frontier in American History." In *The Frontier in American History* (New York: Henry Holt and Company, 1920).

Watkins, Marilyn P.: *Rural Democracy: Family Farmers and Politics in Western Washington, 1890–1925* (Ithaca: Cornell University Press, 1995).

White, Richard: *"It's Your Misfortune and None of My Own": A History of the American West* (Norman: University of Oklahoma Press, 1991).

Williams, William Appleman: *The Roots of Modern American Empire: A Study of the Growth and Shaping of Social Consciousness in a Marketplace Society* (New York: Random House, 1969).

Wong, K. Scott and Sucheng Chan (eds.): *Claiming America: Constructing Chinese American Identities During the Exclusion Era* (Philadelphia: Temple University Press, 1998).

Worster, Donald: *Rivers of Empire: Water, Aridity, and the Growth of the American West* (New York: Pantheon, 1985).

Young, Mary: "The Cherokee Nation: Mirror of the Republic." *American Quarterly* 33 (1981): 3–25.

PART III

Exceptionalism or Regionalism? The Twentieth-Century American West

CHAPTER TWELVE

African Americans in the Twentieth-Century West

DOUGLAS FLAMMING

There are two fundamental themes in black western history. One is the tension between the ostensible equality of the West and the obvious racial discrimination that blacks experienced there. The other, related to the first, is the question of regional distinctiveness. Did the West offer African Americans a better life than was available to them in the Jim Crow South or the Ghetto North?

With these themes in mind, this essay will explore Afro-western history from roughly the 1890s to the 1990s, dividing the century into three distinct periods: 1) the half century between 1890 and 1940, during which African American westerners were relatively few and lived on the periphery of black America; 2) the quarter century between 1940 and 1965, during which World War II and postwar trends transformed the black West into a place largely indistinguishable from the black North; and (3) the final third of the century, during which the black West became, for better or worse, the trendsetter for American race relations. My aim is to trace the principle themes of black western history – the tension between ideal and reality, and the question of regional distinctiveness – through each of these phases by focusing on black migration, living conditions, community leadership, and cultural production.

Until the past two decades, most historians of the black West (and they were few) focused on the nineteenth century and positioned their studies in the framework of Turnerian debates. These works dealt with settlers and soldiers, as shown in the regional surveys published in the 1970s – Michael Lauren Katz, *The Black West* (1971; revised 1987) and Sherman W. Savage, *Blacks in the West* (1976) – which placed African American pioneers, cowboys, and buffalo soldiers on the historiographical map. Historians of the black West continue to explore the nineteenth century (without the bows to Turner), in works ranging in style and scope from Dolores Hayden's gendered analysis of the Biddy Mason story (1989) to Monroe Billington's *New Mexico's Buffalo Soldiers, 1866–1900* (1991).

Most new scholarship on blacks in the West has focused on the twentieth century, with an appropriate emphasis on urban history. Several historians pioneered this field, especially Lawrence B. de Graaf, whose dissertation, "Negro Migration to Los Angeles, 1930–1950," was far ahead of its time (1962). In 1970, de Graaf published his seminal article, "The City of Black Angels: The Emergence of the Los Angeles

Ghetto, 1900–1930," and since then he has continued to publish on the African American experience in California (1975; 1980; 1996). In his 1975 essay, "Recognition, Racism, and Reflections on the Writing of Western Black History," de Graaf argued that the black urban experience was the most glaring gap in western historiography. Several studies, which varied widely in quality, answered this challenge: Douglas Henry Daniels' social history of black San Franciscans in the late nineteenth and early twentieth century (1980); Emory Tolbert's study of the Universal Negro Improvement Association (UNIA) in Los Angeles (1980); Keith Collins' work on black Los Angeles in the 1940s (1980); and Quintard Taylor's early work on African Americans in the Pacific Northwest (1977, 1979, 1991, 1995).

Black western history broke through after 1990, with the publication of numerous high-quality studies. Albert Broussard offered *Black San Francisco* (1993) along with pathbreaking work on African American life in the more distant landscapes of Hawaii and Alaska (1998; 2002). Quintard Taylor's monograph on Seattle's Central District (1994); and Shirley Moore's analysis of Richmond, California (2000), provided community studies on seldom studied urban centers. Marilynn Johnson's *The Second Gold Rush* (1993) and Gretchen Lemke-Santangelo's *Abiding Courage* (1996) examined California's East Bay communities during the critically important 1940s.

Los Angeles, easily the largest black community in the West during most of the twentieth century, has rightly garnered considerable attention. Recent work includes: overviews by Lonnie G. Bunch, III (1988, 1990); Douglas Flamming's work on the evolution of the city's black community prior to World War II (1994, 1999, 2001b, 2004); Kevin Leonard's examination of LA's multiracial environment during the World War and early Cold War periods (1992); Josh Sides' study of the community from the late 1930s to the Watts rebellion of 1965 (1996, 1998, 2004); and Gerald Horne's left-leaning reinterpretation of that uprising (1995). In all of these studies, the central issues are migration, community development, discrimination, political mobilization, and civil rights activism – themes similar to community studies of eastern cities, but with an eye toward regional twists.

Specialty studies have enriched our understanding of region and race. Works on black music in the West have been a welcome addition, especially those focusing on Los Angeles, which include an oral history of jazz on Central Avenue (Bryant, et al., 1998), Bette Yarbrough Cox's documentation of the city's musical traditions (1996), and articles on the rise of gospel and Gangster Rap (Djedje, 1989; Djedje and Meadows, 1998; Kelly, 1994). Works on high-profile Afro-westerners, such as the famed architect Paul R. Williams and classical composer William Grant Still, have deepened our appreciation of both the opportunities and restrictions facing blacks in the region (e.g., Hudson, 1993). Black art and literature have also received attention from historians (Flamming, 2001a). Articles on the black West have appeared in history journals large and small. Master's theses and PhD dissertations have been plentiful, and more are in progress. State-level surveys, such as B. Gordon Wheeler's *Black California: A History of African Americans in the Golden State* (1993) have reached a broader reading public, as have a number of locally published booklets on communities or black leaders. Museums throughout the region have brought the subject to a larger public.

The historiographical surge of the 1990s reached its zenith with the publication of Quintard Taylor's monumental survey, *In Search of the Racial Frontier: African*

Americans in the American West, 1528–1990 (1998). This book should be required reading. Based on an exhaustive review of the literature as well as his own primary research, Taylor's survey is especially useful for its emphasis on the twentieth-century urban experience. Rich in detail, it addresses "the central paradigm in the history of African Americans in the American West. Did the West represent the last best hope for nineteenth- and twentieth-century African Americans? Was it a racial frontier beyond which lay the potential for an egalitarian society?" (Taylor 1998: 17).

Equally important in helping to answer these difficult questions is Walter Nugent's rich demographic history, *Into the West: The Story of Its People* (1999). Nugent's study includes virtually every ethnic and racial group, and his regional scope is breathtaking. The title of the book has the ring of a study focusing on the nineteenth century, but in fact Nugent's chapters are heavily weighted toward the twentieth. *Into the West* explains the population patterns of the region with a clarity and comprehensiveness that no book ever has.

A third new book deserves special notice – *Seeking El Dorado: African Americans in California*, edited by Lawrence B. de Graaf, Kevin Mulroy, and Quintard Taylor (2001). This anthology, brilliant in its conception, begins with an extended introduction (by de Graaf and Taylor), "African Americans in California History, California in African American History," which offers everything its title promises – a state-level overview of Afro-Californian history that also serves to frame the 13 original essays that follow. Written by specialists in the field but intended to reach a wider audience, these pieces range chronologically from the Spanish colonial period to the 1990s, touching on every major regional theme along the way. *Seeking El Dorado* is the model state-level anthology. These three books place the black western experience in a broader context and, taken together, offer a powerful education on the black West.

Black Westerners on the Periphery, 1890–1940

The urban West was a distinctive place for black Americans during the half century from 1890 to 1940. Compared to the hostility that blacks confronted in the Jim Crow South and the Ghetto North, blacks westerners faced less overt racial prejudice. But at the same time, they crashed into the nationally universal barriers against people of color, especially barriers to well-paying employment. What Quintard Taylor has written of Seattle's blacks – that they "faced the paradox of racial toleration and limited opportunity" – held true in varying degree for Afro-westerners everywhere (Taylor, 1998: 39).

The rise of the black urban West began in the South during the 1890s. This was a particularly brutal decade for Afro-southerners, as the tenuous gains they had made during Reconstruction were stripped away in a violent plague of lynching, disfranchisement, and segregation. Jim Crow took over with a vengeance, and the South became a place to be *from*. From 1890 to 1940, millions of blacks left the South. Most moved North, to industrial cities such as Chicago, Cleveland, and Pittsburgh. World War I, and the labor shortage it created in northern cities, sparked the Great Migration, a massive demographic shift that took half a million black Americans from rural South to industrial North, or, to borrow the title of a classic study, from plantation to ghetto (Meier and Rudwick, 1966). The Great Migration fostered a steady South-to-North trend that continued steadily, if less explosively, through the 1920s and 1930s.

But some blacks moved west instead of north. They migrated westward in much smaller numbers, and, in so doing, they encountered conditions and created communities unlike those found in either the South or the North. In 1900 not a single city in the trans-Missouri West had a black population exceeding four thousand; the black populations of Denver, Los Angeles, Oakland, Omaha, Portland, San Francisco, Seattle, and Spokane *combined* barely topped ten thousand. By 1940 that had changed, especially in Los Angeles, which, with nearly 64,000 black residents, was *the* Black Metropolis of the West. But other black communities in the West remained relatively small, even on the verge of World War II. Among major western cities in 1940, Denver had a black population of 7,836; Oakland, 8,462; Portland, 1,931; San Francisco, 4,846; and Seattle, 3,789. Despite these relatively small populations, or perhaps because of them, most western blacks viewed their own region as the true "promised land."

But not all migrants saw their promised land in the city. Between the 1870s and World War I, the classic era of western homesteading, many Afro-southerners saw in western lands their best hope for a family farm. Individual families took their chances, of course, but black settlers often tried a group approach – safety and success in numbers. Black towns (or "colored colonies," as black promoters called them) flourished in the West as they did in no other region. Oklahoma had the most black towns, because of its land-rush availability and its easy access from the South, but most western states had one or more black towns (Hamilton, 1991). Most colored colonies struggled, as did white agricultural colonies, because small family farms proved almost impossible in the arid West. Homesteading peaked in the 1910s and was basically a dead letter by the 1920s (Nugent, 1999: 131–58), even though some black Okies, like their poor-white counterparts, sought deliverance in western agriculture as late as the 1930s (LeSeur, 2000).

Then there were the soldiers. Black military aspirations hinged partly on the notion that service for one's country ought to result in greater respect and liberties for blacks (especially those in uniform). Such aspirations clashed with white fears about black men with guns, a deeply rooted paranoia which itself helps explain why the US Army placed its black units in isolated, segregated western forts. The result, in some explosive instances, was conflict and tragedy.

But it was the city people – Douglas Daniels' "pioneer urbanites" (1980) – who became the heart and soul of the black West, not the soldiers and homesteaders, who largely faded from view. For black migrants to western cities, the region promised full and equal incorporation into American society and politics. In the West of 1890 to 1940, that was very much a *dream*, not a reality, but for black migrants to Los Angeles, Seattle, San Francisco, Oakland, Denver, and countless other towns and cities, a powerful part of their lives was the ongoing struggle to make their Western Dream an urban reality.

These black migrants may be broadly categorized as "middle class." The best evidence suggests that they were largely from the urban, not rural, South, and that they were people of some means, at least from a black standpoint. At the turn of the century, a one-way train ticket from the South to the West Coast cost about $40, meaning that a family of four had to have about $150 in savings to even get on the train, and that was no small amount of money in the turn-of-the-century South. Because successful blacks in the South were often the targets of white violence, increasing numbers felt the need to leave Dixie. Letters sent home from out West, and stories passed around by Pullman porters, set up a selective chain migration. Poorer Afro-southerners looking for factory work moved North; more affluent Afro-southerners had wider options, and some saw the West, with its extended distance from the South and its heralded egalitarianism, as their best chance.

The West's black newcomers were optimistic about their newly adopted region, and they said so unabashedly. We no longer think of cities like Los Angeles and San Francisco as "western" places, but in the first half of the century those cities promoted themselves as such, and black leaders promoted "the West" as eagerly as white leaders. They believed in what might be called the Western Ideal – the notion that the American West was the most egalitarian of all places, a region in which racial prejudice would give way to equal opportunity, in which anyone, regardless of ancestry, could succeed through hard work, intelligence, and a little pluck. Black boosters in the urban West extolled the virtues of their region and, with typical western élan (or western defensiveness) they sometimes mocked those who remained back East.

This was not a naive embrace of white booster rhetoric. Instead, blacks used the Western Ideal to promote civil rights in their newly adopted home. When white boosters talked about western freedom and egalitarianism, they were not talking about race. They assumed there would be a racial hierarchy and that whites, especially whites of northwestern European ancestry, would be on top. But in the West, the rhetoric of equality was on the table for all to use, and black leaders wielded it to their advantage. They did so by trumpeting the Western Ideal and, simultaneously, condemning the racism of white western society that prevented the realization of that ideal. As William Deverell and Douglas Flamming have suggested elsewhere, this evolved into a regionally specific language of civil rights agitation (Deverell and Flamming, 1999).

To what extent did actual black living conditions in the West support the notion of a distinctly better life for African Americans? Only to a limited extent, but there were bright spots, most notably the real estate situation. The black West's residential opportunities compared favorably with those in the South and North. At any time during the period 1910 to 1940, blacks in major western cities enjoyed the highest home ownership rates in the nation, usually 30 percent or higher (Taylor, 1998: 233).

By the 1920s, identifiable "black" sections had emerged in most western cities – Los Angeles' Central Avenue district, for example, or Seattle's Jackson Street. This occurred in part because black residents often clustered together, as ethnic groups will. But Afro-westerners increasingly found themselves hemmed in by racially restrictive real estate covenants, which allowed all-white residential areas to keep out the colored people, including Asians, Mexicans, and sometimes Jews. Restrictive covenants were a national trend that gained steam in the 1920s and continued through the 1940s, but they were especially insidious to black westerners because real estate and home ownership were such an important aspect of their well-being and regional outlook, which helps explain why western blacks led the legal charge against restrictive covenants.

But despite the black "districts" and the restrictive covenants, Afro-westerners were less concentrated than their black peers back East. Prior to World War II, the West did not really have any black ghettos or slums. Even in Los Angeles in the

1920s, it would have been nearly impossible to find a single block of housing which was completely black. What's more, western "black" districts were strikingly hetero-geneous – filled as they were with a diverse assortment of working-class whites (native born and immigrant), Jews, Chinese, Japanese, Filipinos, and ethnic Mexicans. The particular mix was different from city to city, but there was always a mix, and there was little overcrowding prior to the 1940s.

If black residential opportunities gave the West a distinctive flavor, employment opportunities (or rather the lack thereof) gave it national feel. In every region, African Americans held most of the low-status, low-wage jobs, and almost none of the higher-status, high-paying ones. There was no law anywhere against job discrimination. It may have been a sin to hire "whites only," but it was perfectly legal. Black job seekers in the West who sought employment in fields not traditionally open to blacks were simply told, "we don't hire colored." Labor unions did not help either. The American Federation of Labor (AFL) was committed to white supremacy and its unions excluded *all* nonwhites – African American, Asian, or Mexican. In strong labor-union cities, such as San Francisco and Seattle, blacks were therefore shut out of skill trades and most industrial jobs, except for when employers called on them to break strikes. That is one reason why Los Angeles – which pro-labor advocates hated for its pow-erful anti-union establishment – was a favored destination for blacks moving West.

Black westerners found niches in the region's service economy, especially in the areas of transportation, domestic work, and the restaurant and hotel trades. Every major western city was a Pullman porter enclave, and the black men who rode the rails as porters, waiters, and cooks held what were then good, if arduous, jobs. For a brief time during World War I, blacks in Seattle held jobs in the shipyards. After-ward, though, they were kicked out. Seattle's black men then found jobs as stew-ards, waiters, and later musicians on the steamship passenger lines that ran up and down the West Coast. They could make over forty dollars a month – good money. Seattle's black women, also kicked out of the shipyards after the war, were forced back into domestic work; but as maids in Seattle in the 1920s, they could also earn about forty dollars a month (by comparison, black domestics in the South earned from four to eight dollars a month).

White western bigotry was obvious, but blatant hostility against Afro-westerners was relatively uncommon. There were glaring exceptions, especially where South met West, in Oklahoma and Texas, which witnessed bloody racial conflicts during and after World War I. On the West Coast things were calmer, except in Los Angeles, where the black population was growing fastest and, right along with it, a white back-lash, which included a rise in police brutality against blacks and the (brief) rise of the 1920s Ku Klux Klan. But overall, black westerners were less likely to confront viru-lent bigotry than the kind of "polite racism" that Broussard illuminates in his work on San Francisco (1993). What do we make of the "polite racism" of the West? Although racial conditions were better than in the South or North, Broussard's ulti-mate point is that even a city's "progressive" reputation could mask the more insid-ious structural obstacles to full equality of opportunity (1993). Still, for those who lived daily without the threat of southern-style racial violence, without the pain inflicted by the northern "Hawk," polite racism was something like progress.

Racism in the West was never black and white. As a growing number of western historians have emphasized, we must understand the significance of nonblack racial minorities in shaping the urban West and the ways in which blacks interacted with Asian and Mexican groups. This is easier said than done, as the work on this topic so far demonstrates. Fortunately, the "New Western History" has given us a broad historical literature on nonblack racial minorities: the successive waves of Asian immigrants – Chinese, Japanese, and Filipinos – as well as the ethnic Mexican communities. Somehow, though, studies of Asians, blacks, and Mexicans have not connected with each other. It is as if the West's racial minority groups existed side by side but seldom interacted. This may, in fact, have been the case. Recent studies seeking to explore the interactions among multiple racial groups have been hard pressed to find the information they need to draw firm conclusions about the multiracial West (Taylor, 1991; Flamming, 2004).

The relationship among blacks and these other racial minorities remains unclear. In some instances, they competed for jobs, decent housing, and business clientele. At times, each seemed to be struggling to top the others in a complex hierarchy of race. In other circumstances, however, they found common ground as disadvantaged minorities scorned by most whites, restricted to poorer neighborhoods, and harassed by the police. Black contemporaries found it as difficult to interpret the situation as historians do today. Did white racial prejudice against Japanese and Mexicans work to the advantage of blacks? Did it created a buffer against white–black confrontation? Did it place blacks on a higher rung of the western racial hierarchy? Or did the presence of multiple racial minorities only stir up tensions against all people of color? For historians of the black West, this topic represents their most important task word – and their most difficult.

Black leaders in the pre-World War II West were a well-educated, underemployed group, who, in many respects, were not unlike black leaders elsewhere in the nation. African American leaders formed local and state branches of national organizations: the Afro-American Council (ACC); the National Association for the Advancement of Colored People (NAACP); the UNIA; the Federation of Colored Women's Clubs; and the Urban League. But the nationalization of black civic action can be overstated. As Emory Tolbert's work on the UNIA in Los Angeles shows, and as other community studies indicate, the western branches of national organizations often operated differently. Most national organizations were headquartered in New York, and the western branches, being so far away, had considerable autonomy to do as they pleased. In New York, the UNIA and NAACP were virtually at war in the 1920s. In Los Angeles and other West Coast cities, the leaders and activities of the two organizations were basically identical.

Above all, black western activists were pragmatic. They formed political alliances with sympathetic whites, even as they heralded the importance of racial solidarity among blacks. They worked simultaneously to break down job discrimination and to build up black-owned businesses. They embraced the integrationist NAACP and (while it lasted) the nationalist UNIA. They tried whatever might work to make their lives better. Black ideological disputes that divided blacks back East – first between W. E. B. Du Bois and Booker T. Washington, and later between Du Bois and Garvey – never seemed to carry much weight out West.

Through the early twentieth century, black leaders back East grew increasingly interested in their western brethren. Beginning in the 1910s and thereafter through the 1920s and 1930s, they would tour the black West as celebrities, after which they would fill their national black publications with praise of the West and its people. But the strongest praise for the black West was the NAACP's decision to hold its 1928 national convention in Los Angeles. The convention was held at the newly built, black-owned Somerville Hotel on Central Avenue; the hotel, Central Avenue, and Los Angeles were all a smash. The 1928 Convention marked an interesting moment in western black history: the region was coming of age, but it was coming of age differently than black communities back East, as W. E. B. DuBois pointed out in his glowing *Crisis* account of the Los Angeles convention. Western blacks seemed to him more confident, more prosperous (Flamming, 2001a).

In the arts, though, some black westerners were restless, especially when the Harlem Renaissance took New York by storm in the 1920s. Manhattan received a small but influential group of young western-born writers and artists, who were in search of what Los Angeles writer Arna Bontemps called "Negro-ness," a soul-full quality they found lacking out West (and assumed would be abundant in the South and North). Joining Bontemps in Harlem were writers Langston Hughes (Kansas) and Wallace Thurman (Salt Lake City and Los Angeles), and the artist Aaron Douglas (Nebraska). This group formed the vital core of the "New Negro" phase of the Renaissance. All had been raised in largely white neighborhoods and schools, which was not that unusual for the West at that time, and all felt that they had somehow been deprived of their racial birthright, "Negro-ness." (Not all artists pined for Harlem. The sculptor Sergeant Johnson left the East for San Francisco, where he developed by the 1920s a unique style that blended black American themes with the international and cosmopolitan trends of the Bay area.) After some successes and failures in Harlem, most of these westerners filtered back to the West during the 1930s, where their careers took new and different turns. But had they not been drawn to black New York in the mid-to-late 1920s, the Harlem Renaissance would have been a different, less interesting phenomenon. Attempts to create a Harlem-style literary Renaissance on the West Coast faltered, but the region saw more success in music.

By the 1920s, diverse musicians – jazz, classical, and gospel – were increasingly drawn to the West. From Kansas City to Phoenix, from Seattle to San Diego, black jazz musicians such as Jelly Roll Morton and Kid Ory explored new terrain. But classical music was also much loved out West, especially in larger cities such as Los Angeles, which had a middle class that supported classical work. The composer William Grant Still, whose *Symphony No. 1, Afro-American* won acclaim even then, moved permanently from New York to Los Angeles in the early 1930s and won for himself a steady career as a composer in Hollywood. Although the rise of gospel as a major commercial force would come later, the West Coast was already emerging as a center for gospel singers and composers.

Hollywood, located just miles from the heart of black Los Angeles, brought its own dilemmas. The industry's breakthrough moment in 1915 – the box office smash *Birth of a Nation* – was an unabashedly racist film which portrayed southern blacks as dangerous beasts and the Ku Klux Klan as knights in shining armor. Black entertainers sought work in Hollywood anyway, but the studio system excluded blacks, unless they were needed to play demeaning, stereotypical roles. Black writers found no opportunities in the studio system. In the 1930s, Wallace Thurman tried to break in, without success, and when Langston Hughes finally got to write a filmscript, the studio turned his story into a humiliating portrayal of happy-go-lucky slaves, prompting a distraught Hughes to leave town. Black actor Clarence Muse, on the other hand, accepted the "darkey" role and became an affluent celebrity. Hattie McDaniel's 1939 Oscar for her role in *Gone With the Wind* was a first for African Americans, but one that did little to break down racial barriers in motion pictures (Cripps, 1993).

In the arena of electoral politics, black westerners were active and vocal but generally too few in numbers to have much influence. In the South, blacks were still disfranchised. In the North, the Great Migration created large black Republican districts, as reenfranchised migrants cast ballots for the Party of Lincoln. By comparison, blacks in the West lacked political clout. Outside of the states bordering on the Midwest, they simply did not have the numbers to make a difference at the state or local level. One exception was Los Angeles, which elected California's first black legislator in 1918, when voters from the 74th Assembly District sent Frederick Madison Roberts to Sacramento (Flamming, 1994). But even in the 74th, already termed the "Black Belt" of Los Angeles, African Americans were a relatively small minority of the population. Many residents in the 74th could not vote – Asians, Mexican immigrants, and new European immigrants – which boosted black political clout. But in the end Roberts won because he received large numbers of white votes, a phenomenon that might have happened only in the West. Roberts did not have much clout, but he was able to win some minor improvements in California's civil rights statutes and provide other helpful services for education and business in his district. Roberts would hold his seat in Sacramento until the New Deal realignment (Flamming, 2001b).

The 1930s were something of a transition decade for western blacks. In cities throughout the region there were signs that regional distinctiveness was receding. Cities in the southwest became more black and less brown, due to the government's Mexican and Filipino repatriation campaigns. The New Deal, meanwhile, wrought a fundamental change in American politics. Western blacks, like their counterparts throughout the nation, made their historic shift from the Part of Lincoln to the Party of Roosevelt. In Los Angeles, this meant the political demise of Frederick Roberts. In 1934 he was defeated by Augustus F. Hawkins, a black UCLA graduate who created a new biracial coalition in the Central Avenue district (now the 62nd Assembly District), bringing together blacks and working-class whites under a New Deal, pro-labor banner, thus setting the stage for World War II-era politics (Flamming, 2001b).

In the half century before World War II, black westerners experienced a tension between regional distinctiveness and nationalization, but for this period, the striking thing was how distinctive the black West was. Afro-western communities were smaller, more dispersed, and more middle-class than their counterparts back East. They were self-consciously "western" in outlook and in their civil rights campaigns. Their lives were far better than they had been in the American South, and they were arguably better than black life in the North. Black westerners were a long way from the well springs of black politics and culture back East, and they knew it. Some were proud of that distance, others distraught. But regional distinctiveness did not last, because the rapid changes following Pearl Harbor fundamentally transformed the West, including the black West.

World War II and the Northernization of the Black West, 1941–1965

World War II, to borrow a phrase from Albert Broussard's work, was "the great divide" in Afro-western history (1993). As several powerful studies demonstrate (Johnson, 1993; Sides, 2004), the "Second" Great Migration, sparked by wartime labor shortages in West Coast military plants, did for the black West what the "First" Great Migration had done for the North. It brought massive gains in black population, opened high-paying factory jobs to black workers, sparked a white backlash, and created vastly overcrowded and underserviced black neighborhoods. The surge in black population enhanced black political and economic power in the West, but it also fostered racial tensions and created black neighborhoods that earned the designation "ghetto." In the process, the black West became very much like the black North. For a generation, 1940 to 1965, the black West was effectively absorbed into the national (read: northern) mainstream.

With the war heating up, West Coast aircraft and shipbuilding plants needed labor badly. Eventually they got it, by employing vast numbers of white women and, finally, black men and women. African Americans were last to get the jobs, which was no surprise, but as they did, the region's coastal cities were transformed by massive black in-migration. The numbers were staggering. In 1940, California, Oregon, and Washington had a combined black population of 134,295. Ten years later, they boasted 504,392 black residents, an increase of 276 percent. A half century of gradual black population growth in the West – growth resulting mostly from urban-born, middle-class blacks – suddenly gave way to a population explosion. Older black residents in West Coast cities were uneasy about the newcomers. They contributed to overcrowding and, to hear the old-timers tell it, they had bad manners in public. Older, middle-class blacks were embarrassed by and cold toward the newcomers, and the newcomers resented it. Northern black communities, such as Chicago, had experienced similar tensions during the First Great Migration a generation earlier, but these tensions were new to the West.

Several studies have recovered the perspective of the migrants themselves (Johnson, 1993; Chamberlain, 2003; Spickard, 1993; Sides, 2004; Lemke-Santangelo, 1996), most of whom were southern-born females. The wartime migrants were not the uneducated, rural Afro-Southerners that many West Coast whites and old-timer blacks complained about at the time. They were instead a family-oriented, God-fearing, hard-working, community-minded lot – and admirably flexible in their new and bewildering metropolitan environment. Maya Angelou's version, in her famous autobiography *I Know Why the Caged Bird Sings*, would agree in large part with this assessment; but Angelou offers a grittier – perhaps more ironic – view of what could happen to family, religion, work, and community in the press of wartime California.

Had every migrant been a college-educated angel, there still would have been a white backlash. The number of blacks was just too huge, and the fears of American whites too deep. Many white workers protested against black employment in the defense plants and black membership in unions. Many more fought against the black "invasion" of white residential areas. Eventually, blacks were able to get good industrial jobs, but they were seldom able to expand their residential possibilities. The result was massive overcrowding and stress in the West Coast's increasingly black neighborhoods.

The multiracial environment seemed to give way to a black–white environment. The Japanese were shipped to internment camps in the interior. In most West Coast cities, African American newcomers moved quickly into what had been, only yesterday, Little Tokyos. Japanese exile, coupled with the monumental black influx, meant that West Coast whites now saw blacks as the primary embodiment of the race problem. The one exception, perhaps, was Los Angeles, which experienced the so-call Zoot Suit Riot against Mexicans in 1943. This incident, in which white Navy men stationed in the city stormed the streets seeking and stripping down Zoot-suited Mexican youth was more an exercise in mass public subordination than a "riot," but it demonstrated ominous possibilities. Not all of the servicemen who got out of hand were white. Outside Seattle, black servicemen at Fort Lawton rioted against discriminatory treatment and even lynched an Italian prisoner of war. In general, race relations in the West became increasingly tense and shifted toward black–white dynamics similar to those back East.

But if there were whites who sought to curb opportunities of newly arrived blacks, there were also whites who saw in them the potential for new political alliances. With the rise of the CIO in the 1930s, some white unionists sought to bring African Americans into the labor movement and committed themselves to black civil rights. During and after the war, these left-leaning white liberals joined with pro-union blacks to form a biracial political alliance organized around industrial unionism. Postwar McCarthyism dashed the possibilities of these popular-front alliances. Mainstream liberals – black and white – were thrown on the defensive, desperately trying to distance themselves from any taint of Communism. The Left's stated concern for black civil rights put mainstream black leaders in a bind, because in the 1950s African American leaders could not afford the political fallout of such associations. The national NAACP therefore banned Communists from its membership in 1951, and West Coast NAACP leaders dissociated themselves from Left-leaning newspapers and organizations. This was a national, not regional, trend, but it had a profound impact on the West Coast's suddenly large black communities, as works by Marilynn Johnson and others so ably demonstrate.

The 1950s saw two other significant trends in black western life, one positive, one ominous. On the positive side, better housing opened up for blacks who could afford it. In the late 1940s and early 1950s, the US Supreme Court handed down two decisions, in cases sponsored by the NAACP and argued by LA's leading black attorney, Loren Miller, which ruled first that restrictive covenants were unenforceable and ultimately that they were unconstitutional. Miller wrote a valuable book on civil rights and the US Supreme Court (1966), but both legal battles in the West and Miller himself deserve more historical analysis. Problems continued for blacks wanting to buy homes in all-white neighborhoods, but in virtually every city middle-class and professional blacks found their way to better housing and higher ground – the Sugar Hill phenomenon. In Los Angeles, for example, blacks with sufficient funds were able to buy into the formerly white neighborhoods west of Central Avenue in the hills along Western Avenue. Ultimately they bought into prestigious Baldwin Hills, which was and remains one of the premier African American neighborhoods in the nation. That was the good news.

The bad news was what happened to the older black districts. In the words of one jazz musician, LA's Central Avenue "just went to pot" in the 1950s (Bryant et al., 1998). In the 1940s, Be-Bop jazz had swept the West Coast by storm and headed east. Los Angeles, Central Avenue in particular, was where things were happening in black American music. But somehow it did not last. The better black-owned stores and classy nightclubs moved to Western Avenue or shut down. Residents along Central were now mostly poor and too often unemployed. Housing deteriorated, services lagged, black crime and white police brutality became locked in a vicious cycle. Similar trends occurred on Seattle's Jackson Street, San Francisco's Fillmore District, just about everywhere.

Within the black community, a class divide became obvious and seemed somehow related to the alienation of the working-class African American neighborhoods. Beyond the obvious explanations historians always trot out, it is difficult to know exactly what happened to the West Coast's established black thoroughfares. No study adequately details their decline. Poverty, neglect, police brutality, and intraracial class divisions had been around for a long time, and overcrowding had been an established fact since the early 1940s. Something bad happened to the black West's older neighborhoods in the 1950s, and we need to know more about it.

Part of the problem was clearly overcrowding, for black migration to the West in the 1950s was overwhelming (a topic that has been understudied and needs a close examination). Defense jobs were no longer driving black migration, but black migrants flooded into West Coast because there was a new "push" in Dixie. After the war, southern cotton planters adopted the mechanical cotton picker with startling rapidity and that old southern scourge, sharecropping, suddenly disappeared. All to the good – except that hundreds of thousands of Afro-southerners were unceremoniously displaced, and neither the new agricultural economy nor the southern urban economy offered them any alternatives. Hundreds of thousands moved west, not because they had high hopes or because it was a promised land, but because they had nowhere else to go.

The migration figures from 1950–70 convey the magnitude of what might be called the Mechanization Migration. From 1950 to 1970, the black population of Oakland jumped from 47,526 to 124,710, while black San Francisco rose from 43,502 to 96,078. In LA, the black population skyrocketed from 171,209 to 503,606, an absolute increase of 332,397! This momentous demographic shift was bound to create problems, combined as it was with rising black unemployment and already distressed neighborhoods.

On the surface, though, racial progress seemed evident in the urban West through the mid-1960s. Whites and blacks in every major western city established interracial organizations and committees, private and public, to improve race relations. An increasing number of white Democrats now supported civil rights and racial liberalism, as a recent biography of California Congressman Philip Burton demonstrates. In Los Angeles, Kenneth Hahn, a white liberal elected by an overwhelmingly black district, became an unwavering champion of black civil rights on the Los Angeles County Board of Supervisors, one of the most powerful political bodies in the West. No book-length study of Hahn exists, and one is badly needed. An increasing number of blacks were elected to western state legislatures, and these political leaders deserve careful study.

By the early 1960s, Democratic Party liberalism meant racial liberalism, and liberals in many western state houses gained clout, especially in California. Western states passed legislation to deal with equal employment and housing, two of the most difficult and racially charged issues in modern America. In Los Angeles, as the political scientist Raphael Sonnenshine demonstrates in his book, *Politics in Black and White* (1993), an effective liberal coalition emerged between southside blacks and westside Jews. The result was three blacks on the LA City Council in 1963, including future mayor Tom Bradley. A scholarly biography of Bradley is sorely needed; it could shed light on the paradox of black success amidst black decline in the West of the 1950s and 1960s.

To compliment these favorable political trends in the West, racially liberal politics were on the upswing back East. After bloody and heroic struggles, the Civil Rights Movement in the South achieved two astonishing victories. When Congress passed the Civil Rights Act of 1964, it dismantled Jim Crow segregation and, more important for blacks outside the South, it outlawed job discrimination on account of race, the first national law to do so. A year later, responding to the Civil Rights Movement's last great campaign in Selma, Alabama, Congress passed the Voting Rights Act, which crushed the disfranchisement laws that had kept southern blacks down for so long, and which promised to dramatically enlarge the number of blacks within the dominant Democratic Party. When President Lyndon Johnson signed the Voting Rights Act into law in early August 1965, racial liberalism reached its peak in American politics. At that moment, when Americans back East thought about race relations and the African American experience, almost no one thought about the black West. That was about to change.

The Black West as Trendsetter, 1965–2000

In 1965, two events occurred – one loud, one quiet – which forever transformed both the perception and reality of black life in the American West. The loud event was the Watts uprising. The quiet event was the passage, in Washington, DC, of the Immigration Act of 1965. It would be decades before anyone noticed that the law had transformed the West. By that time, everyone would know about the black West.

On August 11, 1965, only five days after Johnson signed the Voting Rights Act into law, the nearly all-black section of Watts (within the Los Angeles city limits) burst into flames in the most costly race riot America had ever seen. As a stunned nation watched the "Watts riot" on television, black westerners burned and looted their own neighborhoods with impunity, destroying symbols of white control, such as retail stores and police cars. Historically, the term "race riot" originated back East; it meant white mobs assaulting black neighborhoods. Overnight, the West redefined the term to mean black mob violence in ghetto areas. Blacks and sympathetic academics dismissed the idea, put forth by some politicians, that Watts was a spontaneous, unfocused "riot" of hoodlums; instead they called Watts a necessary "political uprising," prompting an almost surreal linguistic debate over the meaning of urban uprisings. But the term was unimportant compared to the event's impact on American politics and life.

Watts had far-reaching, largely unintended effects, one of which was to make the West Coast the touchstone of America's racial politics. In the "long hot summers" that followed, black communities throughout the nation staged their own uprisings in what became something of a political ritual patterned after the Los Angeles model. In the West, most major cities had uprisings of varying ferocity and scope, including, on the West Coast, Seattle, Portland, San Francisco, and the East Bay cities; in the interior, Las Vegas (whose small community grew very rapidly during and after World War II), Phoenix, Tucson, and Denver, as well as some plains cities, such as Omaha and Wichita.

Since 1965, the Watts uprising has been well known but not well understood. The riot prompted a spate of journalistic books seeking to explain it, and a few social science dissertations seeking to place it in context. None of these accounts paid much concern to the long history of the black West or even that of black Los Angeles. And none has adequately explained the timing of the thing, or its regional dynamics. The historian Gerald Horne offers the most recent and most thorough account in *Fire This Time: The Watts Uprising and the 1960s* (1995). One of Horne's key arguments – that a successful Afro-Communist movement in 1950s Los Angeles would have prevented the uprising – will win few converts, but his contention that the riots laid the foundation of California's Black Power movements seems undisputable.

Black Power and black nationalism, which took African American communities by storm in the late 1960s and which had a profound impact on America's racial politics, were both centered in California. Oakland's radical trio – Huey Newton, Bobby Seale, Eldridge Cleaver – and their Black Panther Party still fascinate Americans. The Panthers themselves were given to autobiographies, but academic histories have been oddly lacking. Less dramatic than the Panthers, but influential in the long run, was Los Angeles's Manulana Ron Karenga, who vigorously promoted Afro-cultural nationalism, including Kwanza, his own invention, which is now celebrated along with Christmas and Hanukkah in public schools throughout in the nation. Karenga and his organization – United Slaves – deserve more attention from historians, and a history of Kwanza itself would be especially fruitful. A full-blown *western* history of black Power and black nationalism is needed, one that explains why the Panthers and Kwanza came out of the urban West, instead of, say, New York, Chicago, Houston, or Atlanta.

How did we get from the Black Panthers in the 1960s to the gang warfare of the 1980s? The Panthers foremost purpose was the protection of blacks from assaults by white police; but by the mid-1980s, black-on-black gun battles among street gangs, most notably the Bloods and Crips, were taking a terrible toll on what was now called "the underclass" in what was now called "the inner city." Some Los Angeles writers, such as Lynell George (1992) and Mike Davis (1992), pointed a finger at the LAPD and the Reagan-era budget cuts for inner-city programs. The appearance of crack cocaine on the West Coast about 1980 had something to do with it, but we do not know how or why. Several works have explored the lives of the gang members themselves with journalistic flare (e.g., Bing, 1992); but the links between structural explanations and interpersonal accounts are difficult to make. Whatever the explanation, the rise of gang-related murders began on the West Coast, especially in Los Angeles, and spread throughout the West, becoming part of African American life in virtually all big cities eastward to the Mississippi.

One wonders whether there was any relationship between poor-black alienation and the new immigration. The Immigration Act of 1965, intended by eastern

Congressmen to increase immigration from southern and Eastern Europe, unintentionally flooded the West with millions of immigrants from all over Latin America and East Asia. Some Asians, especially the Chinese and Indians, were highly educated or very wealthy upon arrival; but others – Vietnamese and the Hmong from Cambodia – were desperately poor. Millions of Central Americans were poor and desperate, and they crammed into poorer neighborhoods throughout the West. We need to know much more about this process, particularly how it affected the African American communities who were, in many cases, simply overrun.

Another quiet trend in black western life – suburbanization – was probably also related to the new immigration. Lawrence B. de Graaf, ever the historiographical pioneer, has been working on this topic (de Graaf, 2001). His recent work has focused on Orange County (south of Los Angeles County), which was for many years a staunchly Republican and high-income area (which earned from some academics the designation "post-suburban," because it never had any urban to start with). De Graaf discovered a trend toward black suburbanization in the 1980s. He initially speculated that black suburbanites were clustering together in quasi-ghetto neighborhoods, but, more recently, he has commented on the more widespread trend of black suburban scattering, which has led many suburban blacks to feel cut off from their black roots and alienated from the nonblacks living around them.

But if suburbanization and decentralization of black communities is a new and important trend, it is clear that the West Coast's inner cities have become powerful engines of popular culture, exporters of what is hip. From Gangster Rap to the new Gospel, from Wesley Snipes to Kobe Bryant, the West Coast, especially Los Angeles, sets many a national standard. Even the leading black intellectuals back East – who are truly *national* intellectuals, in a way W. E. B. Du Bois could only dream of – have their roots in the West, including Cornell West (out of Oakland) and Robin D. G. Kelly (Los Angeles County). We might usefully ask how we got from Hattie McDaniel to Halle Berry; from Lena Horne to Whitney Houston; from Jackie Robinson to Shaq. What have those transitions meant, regionally and nationally?

In the past two decades, black leaders in the West have become an increasingly eclectic, increasingly wealthy, group. Prior to World War II, an aspiring middle class, many of them holding blue-collar occupations, led the region's black communities. During and after the war, this leadership class was augmented by new aggressive leaders, some with a decidedly pro-labor outlook, who arrived with the wartime migration (Sides, 2004). But today black leaders are truly professionals, operating at the top of American society, not just black-American society. They are also, increasingly, entertainers and professional sports stars. How, for example, would one classify the occupation of Magic Johnson? Yet there is no denying his influence on and importance to African American development in Los Angeles and many other American cities. Beyond the stars, there are politicians, such as Maxine Waters, whose faces are equally prominent in national circles. Another set of black leaders are low-profile, inner-city crusaders, who have been struggling to save their neighborhoods and their people from violence, drugs, economic neglect, the police, and the flood of new immigrants. Then there are black elected officials who govern mostly non-black, immigrant communities, most notably Compton, California, which became virtually all black after the Watts uprising. Compton then elected a full slate of black officials, and blacks continue to run the town, but Compton is now overwhelmingly

Latino in population – an immigrant, non-voting population that is often vocal in its opposition Compton's African American leadership.

Historians of the late twentieth-century West will, of course, have to grapple with the Rodney King events – videotaped beating, first trial and acquittal, riot, second trial and conviction. All of these, like Watts in 1965, focused national attention on Los Angeles, although this time no one was surprised. Once the police officers were acquitted in April 1992, everyone expected a black uprising, which erupted within minutes. What followed was a new phenomenon in American race relations: the non-stop, live-on-national-television riot, with the added novelty of skycam shots rolling in from a swarm of newscast helicopters. Also new was the nature of the uprising itself, for what began as black-against-white rage, rapidly turned into a confusing multiethnic, multiracial (including Asian and white) uprising. Most people arrested by the LAPD were undocumented Latino immigrants, the very people who were squeezing poor blacks out of low-wage employment. The cover of *Newsweek* magazine showed a young black man, fist raised, fire raging in the background – Watts revisited. But 1992 was not Watts, as everyone soon realized. What exactly it *was* deserves historical analysis. One thing that is clear: unlike Watts, it was not copied in black communities around the country. It seems also to have engendered black population shifts in the region.

Since 1970, black population trends within the West have been chaotic and surprising. Between 1970 and 1990, the black population of Los Angeles actually decreased; so did that of San Francisco. During the same twenty years, San Diego's black population soared from 53,000 to 104,000, an astonishing peacetime surge, especially given Los Angeles' decline. San Diego's gains may have to do with the military presence there. The rise of African Americans in the post-Vietnam voluntary military has been remarkable, and, because of the West's huge investment in military bases, this has undoubtedly had an effect on the western experience. The widely scattered and relatively few Buffalo Soldiers of old have long commanded the attention of historians; all the more should the numerous and highly concentrated African American soldiers and sailors of the late twentieth century. Blacks, the military, and the West since Vietnam would be an eye-opening book. So, too, would a book on black wealth in the West since Watts. LA's traumatic events – Watts, Rodney King, and the O. J. Simpson Trial – have obscured the less dramatic but equally significant rise of a black elite and professional class in the region. It is time, for example, for a careful historical study of Baldwin Hills. But this is an essay on region, and the relative wealth of upper-class African Americans is no longer a regional matter.

Long before the end of the twentieth century, "the West" ceased to be a beacon of hope for African Americans. So did the North. Since 1980, and for the first time ever in American history, blacks have been voluntarily moving *to* the South instead of away from it. West Coast African Americans have been in the procession. This is a demographic shift of major importance, and one that deserves careful analysis. If black in-migration is an important topic in western history, then black out-migration should be, too. Like all other racial and ethnic groups in American society, blacks now move from region to region, city to city, without attaching any millennial notions of deliverance to the move. There are no more promised lands. For the first half of the twentieth century, the West stood as a place of deliverance from the everyday brutalities of the Jim Crow South and the ghetto North. In the 1940s, that hopefulness survived the Second Great Migration, and in many respects regional political gains in the 1950s and early 1960s gave credence to the view. Then came Watts. Since 1965, the West has been a national trendsetter, but its message has not been one of hope.

As an ideological construct and as a political-economic structure, "region" has all but died out in urban America. If this loss of regional distinctiveness causes us to bemoan the debilitating homogenization of a frantic consumer culture, it might also be seen as a positive good, at least from the perspective of race relations. For middle-class, professional, and elite blacks, and for working-class blacks with an eye toward upward mobility, regional convergence means that one's life chances are about equal in any major city in the country – be it Boston, Los Angeles, or Atlanta; Indianapolis, Phoenix, or Montgomery. For better and for worse, trends in modern race relations still begin on the West Coast, as they have for the past thirty-five years. But regionalism is vanishing, slowly but surely. Virtually all American cities and towns are becoming complicated multiracial, multiethnic places, as western cities long have been. And "polite racism," long the standard out West, is becoming the national norm. Let us hope that polite racism is not the best we can do. Can black western history help? Perhaps. For by telling us where we have been it informs our actions in the present and our dreams for the future. Or, as Langston Hughes wrote in his poem, *History*: "The past is a mint / of blood and sorrow / that must not be true / of tomorrow."

REFERENCES

Angelou, Maya: *I Know Why the Caged Bird Sings* (New York: Random House, 1970; Bantam reissue, 1993).

Billington, Monroe: *New Mexico's Buffalo Soldiers, 1866–1900* (Niwot: University Press of Colorado, 1991).

Bing, Leon. *Do or Die* (New York: HarperPerennial, 1992).

Broussard, Albert S.: *Black San Francisco: The Struggle for Racial Equality in the West, 1900–1954* (Lawrence, KS: University Press of Kansas, 1993).

Bryant, Clora: *Central Avenue Sounds: Jazz in Los Angeles* (Berkeley: University of California Press, 1998).

Bunch, Lonnie: *Black Angelenos: The Afro-American in Los Angeles, 1850–1950* (Los Angeles: California Afro-American Museum, 1988).

Bunch, Lonnie: "A Past Not Necessarily Prologue: The African American in Los Angeles." In Norman M. Klein and Martin J, Scliesl (eds.) *20th Century Los Angeles: Power, Promotion, and Social Conflict* (Claremont, CA: Regina Books, 1990).

California History (fall 1996) – a special issue devoted to "African Americans in California."

Chamberlain, Charles D.: *Victory at Home: Manpower and Race in the American South during World War II* (Athens, GA: University of Georgia Press, 2003).

Collins, Keith: *Black Los Angeles: The Maturing of the Ghetto, 1940–1950* (Saratoga, CA: Century Twenty One Publishing, 1980).

Cox, Bette Yarborough. *Central Avenue – It's Rise and Fall (1890–c. 1955): Including the Musical Renaissance of Black Los Angeles* (Los Angeles: BEEM Publications, 1996).

Daniels, Douglas Henry: *Pioneer Urbanites: A Social and Cultural History of Black San Francisco* (Philadelphia: Temple University Press, 1980; reprinted, Berkeley: University of California Press, 1990).

Davis, Mike: *City of Quartz: Excavating the Future in Los Angeles* (New York: Verso, 1990).

de Graaf, Lawrence B.: "Negro Migration to Los Angeles, 1930–50" (PhD dissertation: University of California, Los Angeles, 1962).

de Graaf, Lawrence B.: "The City of Black Angeles: The Emergence of the Los Angeles Ghetto, 1890–1930." *Pacific Historical Review* 39, 3 (August 1970), 323–52.

de Graaf, Lawrence B.: "Recognition, Racism, and Reflections on the Writing of Black Western History." *Pacific Historical Review* 44:1 (February 1975), 22–51.

de Graaf, Lawrence B.: "Race, Sex, and Region: Black Women in the American West, 1850–1920." *Pacific Historical Review* 49:1 (February 1980), 285–314.

de Graaf, Lawrence B.: "Significant Steps on an Arduous Path: The Impact of World War II on Discrimination against African Americans in the West." *Journal of the West* 35, 1 (January 1996), 24–33.

de Graaf, Lawrence B., Kevin Mulroy and Quintar Taylor (eds.): *Seeking El Dorado: African American California* (Seattle: University of Washington Press, 2001).

Deverell, William and Douglas Flamming: "Race, Rhetoric, and Regional Identity: Boosting Los Angeles, 1880–1930." In R. White, R. and J. M. Findlay (eds.) *Power and Place in the North American West* (Seattle: University of Washington Press, 1999).

Djedje, Jacqueline Cogdell: "Gospel Music in the Los Angeles Black Community: A Historical Overview." *Black Music Research Journal* 9, 1 (Spring 1989), 35–77.

Djedje, Jacqueline Cogdell and Eddie S. Meadows: *California Soul: Music of African Americans in the West* (Berkeley: University of California Press, 1998).

Flamming, Douglas: "African Americans and the Politics of Race in Progressive-Era Los Angeles." In William Deverell and T. Sitton (eds.) *California Progressivism Reconsidered* (Berkeley: University of California Press, 1994).

Flamming, Douglas: "A Westerner in Search of 'Negro-ness': Region and Race in the Writing of Arna Bontemps." In V. Matsumoto and B.Allmendinger (eds.) *Over the Edge: Remapping the American West* (Berkeley: University of California Press, 1999).

Flamming, Douglas: "The *Star of Ethiopia* and the NAACP: Pageantry, Politics, and the Los Angeles African American Community." In William Deverell and T. Sitton (eds.) *Metropolis in the Making: Los Angeles in the 1920s* (Berkeley: University of California Press, 2001a).

Flamming, Douglas: "Becoming Democrats: Liberal Politics and the African American Community in Los Angeles." In Lawrence B. de Graaf, Kevin Mulroy, and Quintard Taylor (eds.) *Seeking El Dorado: African American California* (Seattle: University of Washington Press, 2001b).

Flamming, Douglas: *A World to Gain: African Americans in Los Angeles, 1890–1940* (Berkeley: University of California Press, 2004).

George, Lynell: *No Crystal Stair: African Americans in the City of Angels* (New York: Anchor Books, 1992).

Hamilton, Kenneth Marvin: *Black Towns and Profit: Promotion and Development in the Trans-Appalachian West, 1877–1915* (Urbana: University of Illinois Press, 1991).

Hayden, Dolores: "Biddy Mason's Los Angeles, 1856–1891." *California History* 68, 3 (Fall 1989), 86–99.

Horne, Gerald: *Fire This Time: The Watts Uprising and the 1960s* (Charlottesville: University Press of Virginia, 1995).

Hudson, Karen E.: *Paul R. Williams, Architect: A Legacy of Style* (New York: Rizzoli, 1993).

Hughes, Langston: *The Panther and the Lash: Poems of Our Times* (New York, Knopf, 1967).

Johnson, Marilynn S.: *The Second Gold Rush: Oakland and the East Bay in World War II* (Berkeley: University of California Press, 1993).

Katz, William Loren: *The Black West* (Garden City, NY: Doubleday, 1971; rev. edn., Seattle: Open Hand Publishing, 1987).

Kelly, Robin D. G.: *Race Rebels: Culture, Politics, and the Black Working Class* (1994; New York: The Free Press, 1996).

Lemke-Santangelo, Gretchen: *Abiding Courage: African American Migrant Women and the East Bay Community* (Chapel Hill: University of North Carolina Press, 1996).

Leonard, Kevin Allen: "The Impact of World War II on Race Relations in Los Angeles." (PhD dissertation: University of California, Davis, 1992).

Leonard, Kevin Allen: "Migrants, Immigrants, and Refugees: The Cold War and Population Growth in the American West." In Kevin J. Fernlund (ed.) *The Cold War American West, 1945–1989* (Albuquerque: University of New Mexico Press, 1998).

Leonard, Kevin Allen: " 'In the Interest of All Races': African Americans and Interracial Cooperation in Los Angeles during and after World War II." In Lawrence B. de Graaf, Kevin Mulroy, and Quintard Taylor (eds.) *Seeking El Dorado: African Americans in California* (Los Angeles: Autry Museum of Western Heritage, in association with the University of Washington Press, 2001).

LeSeur, Geta: *Not All Okies are White: The Lives of Black Cotton Pickers in Arizona* (Columbia, MO: University of Missouri Press, 2000).

Matsumoto, Valerie J. and Blake Allmendinger (eds.): *Over the Edge: Remapping the American West* (Berkeley: University of California Press, 1999).

Meier, August and Elliott M. Rudwick *From Plantation to Ghetto: An Interpretive History of American Negroes* (New York: Hill and Wang, 1966).

Miller, Loren: *The Petitioners: The Story of the Supreme Court of the United States and the Negro* (New York: Pantheon Books, 1966).

Moore, Shirley Ann Wilson: *To Place Our Deeds: The African American Community in Richmond, California, 1910–1963* (Berkeley: University of California Press, 2000).

Nugent, Walter: *Into the West: The Story of Its People* (New York: Alfred A. Knopf, 1999).

Savage, Sherman W.: *Blacks in the West* (Westport, CT: Greenwood Press, 1976).

Sides, Josh: "Battle on the Home Front: African American Shipyard Workers in World War II Los Angeles." *California History* (Fall 1996), 250–63.

Sides, Josh: " 'You understand my condition': The Civil Rights Congress in the Los Angeles African American Community, 1946–1952." *Pacific Historical Review* 67 (May 1998), 233–57.

Sides, Josh: *L.A. City Limits: African American Los Angeles from the Great Depression to the Present* (Berkeley: University of California Press, 2004).

Taylor, Quintard: "The Emergence of Black Communities in the Pacific Northwest, 1865–1910." *Journal of Negro History* 64, 4 (Fal, 1979), 342–51.

Taylor, Quintard: "the Great Migration: The Afro-American Communities of Seattle and Portland during the 1940s." *Arizona and the West* 23, 2 (Summer 1981), 109–26.

Taylor, Quintard: "Reflections on Two Decades in Pursuit of African American History in the Pacific Northwest." In Linda Harris, Joseph Franklin, and Stephen McPherson (eds.) *Voices of Kuumba III: An Anthology of the Northwest African American Writers Workshop* (Portland OR: Portland Public Schools, 1991).

Taylor, Quintard: *The Forging of a Black Community: Seattle's Central District, 1870 through the Civil Rights Era* (Seattle: University of Washington Press, 1994).

Taylor, Quintard: "The Civil Rights Movement in the American West: Black Protest in Seattle, 1960–1970." *The Journal of Negro History* 80, 1 (1995), 1–14.

Taylor, Quintard: *In Search of the Racial Frontier: African Americans in the American West, 1528–1990* (New York: W.W. Norton, 1998).

Tolbert, Emory J.: *The U.N.I.A. and Black Los Angeles: Ideology and Community in the American Garvey Movement* (Los Angeles: UCLA Center for Afro-American Studies, 1980).

Wheeler, B. Gordon: Black California: The History of African Americans in the Golden State (New York: Hippocrene Books, 1993).

CHAPTER THIRTEEN

The West and Workers, 1870–1930

JAMES N. GREGORY

"Is there something unique about Seattle's labor history that helps explain what is going on?" a reporter asks me on the phone during the World Trade Organization protests that filled Seattle streets with 50,000 unionists, environmentalists, students, and other activists in the closing days of the last millennium. "Well, yes and no," I answer before launching into a much too complicated explanation of how history might inform the present without explaining it, and how the West does have some particular traditions that have made it the site of bold departures in the long history of American class and industrial relations. But, I caution, we probably should not push the exceptionalism argument too far. "Thanks," he said rather vaguely as we hung up 20 minutes later. His story the next day included a twelve-word quotation.

The conversation, I realize much later, revealed some interesting tensions. Not long ago the information flow might have been reversed, the historian might have been calling the journalist to learn about western labor history, a body of research that until the 1960s had not much to do with professional historians, particularly those who wrote about the West. And his disappointment at my long-winded equivocations had something to do with those disciplinary vectors. He had been hoping to tap into an argument that journalists know well but that academics have struggled with. Call it western labor exceptionalism. It holds that work and class have meant something different in the West than in other regions and that labor relations have been, as a consequence, more turbulent and more radical than elsewhere.

It is an argument that circulates widely in celebratory popular histories of the West. But it gains strength as well in many of the textbooks used to teach state and regional history. These typically include a chapter or two which narrate an exciting story of militant uprisings and violent strikes beginning in the mines and railroad camps of the Gilded Age, moving through early twentieth-century incidents like the Ludlow massacre and the Seattle General Strike, continuing with the maritime struggles that closed port cities in 1934, and usually ending with the farmworker struggles of the 1960s and 1970s. Articulated or not, the message is that the West's labor history is as special as its settlement history, filled with riveting episodes of high drama and danger. The Wobblies (Industrial Workers of the World [IWW]) become in these accounts the West's favorite labor movement, beloved for the same reasons as cowboys: for their recklessness, their violence, and their failure.

That popular narrative stands in some tension to academic understandings of work, class, and labor in the West. In the last few decades historians have opened wide the field of labor history, pushing into issues and terrains that had previously been segregated or ignored. The result has been an impressive cross-fertilization of subfields and an important crop of new arguments and insights. Today's labor history no longer fits neatly into a couple of distinct chapters and no longer focuses so tightly on strikes and radicals. Arguments about western labor exceptionalism have not disappeared, but they have become more complicated as labor historians have argued that issues of work, class development, and industrial relations lie near the heart of western historical change and regional identity.

Separate Strands

Western history and labor history had a curious and awkward relationship through most of the twentieth century. Professional historians paid little attention to workers, unions, or class until the 1960s. But outside of the history departments, a rich literature of labor history began to develop early in the century, actually two literatures: one produced by left-wing novelists and journalists, the other by economists.

Academic labor history was largely a project associated with labor economists. The study of industrial relations had emerged in the progressive era under the guidance of the University of Wisconsin economists John R. Commons and Selig Perlman. Moving, they claimed, away from the morality-based or revolutionary arguments about unions and class, the labor economists tried to understand what they thought to be the natural progress of an industrializing democracy towards a collective bargaining system of labor relations. History became important to their discipline because it enabled them to show the evolutionary trajectory and pick out the conditions that advanced or retarded the construction of what they regarded as a rational and efficient set of relations between workers, unions, and employers.

Their students took an early interest in the West, particularly in San Francisco, which by the early twentieth century had established a reputation as the most tightly unionized major city in America. The labor economists set out to understand why, tracing in careful detail the history of unions, strikes, and labor radicalism from the Gold Rush on, focusing much attention on the way that labor shortages gave unions early advantages in the West. Some of those early studies remain impressive today, especially Ira Cross's *A History of the Labor Movement in California* (1935) which displays the labor economists' trade mark methodology: deep historical empiricism. There is nothing shoddy about the research nor abstract about the conceptualization. The labor economists treated history with a reverence that even the most archive-bound historian would admire.

Another subject also drew interest. The Industrial Workers of the World, with their commitment to revolutionary industrial unionism and disdain for bargaining and negotiation over wages and working conditions challenged the labor economists' model of industrial relations almost as much as they challenged the craft unions of the American Federation of Labor. Carlton Parker set out to explain this aberrant movement, producing a classic study, *The Casual Laborer and Other Essays* (1920), that relied on psychological concepts to argue that the movement was a response to social conditions: dangerous social environments produced dangerous men.

In the decades that followed, labor economists would branch out to study all of the basic industries of the West and most of the cities where labor movements had flourished. These books were notable for their focus on institutional dynamics, on how unions were built and how they functioned. Some remain classics: Paul Taylor's *The Sailor's Union of the Pacific* (1923); Vernon Jensen's *Lumber and Labor* (1945); Grace Stimson's *Rise of the Labor Movement in Los Angeles* (1955).

But the legacy of the labor economists is much bigger than any specific list of books. Hundreds of dissertations and master's theses that poured out of the economics departments and industrial relations institutes laid down a carpet of descriptive studies of industries, unions, strikes, bargaining, and the politics of labor. The labor economists also built the archives that today preserve invaluable collections of union and business records. At a time when western history libraries like the Huntington and Bancroft were rejecting such materials, much of the region's industrial and labor history was being preserved as well as written by members of another discipline.

Besides the strong institutional focus, some other features of this labor-economics literature are notable. One is that it paid little attention to concepts of regionalism or the frontier development issues that occupied western historians, relying more on the specificity of industry than a specificity of place. As a result, much of this labor history was not explicitly western. It was set in the West, but the regional effect was not much explored. Another characteristic that particularly catches the eye of today's historians was the economists' inattention to solidarities and fragmentations based on race, ethnicity, gender, or even class. The tight institutional focus on unions left little room for social analysis. A third characteristic might also be mentioned: these works tended to underplay conflict and violence. It was partly a matter of tone – the clinical style of expression – and partly because the economists theorized violent industrial relations as a passing historical phase and often moved their studies through such episodes to reach the stable systems of negotiation and controlled conflict that they saw as modern and inevitable.

Labor Noir

This last tendency stands in sharp contrast with the other labor history project that shadowed the work of the economists through the first two thirds of the twentieth century. Its modes of expression were novels and journalistic histories, and its tone was strident and sensationalist. Out of this stream of literature would come some of the most enduring understandings of western work and labor, especially the understanding that the West claimed a uniquely violent and uniquely radical heritage.

The founders of this tradition were socialist writers who at the turn of the century tried to publicize the struggles underway in the mining camps, wheat fields, and seaports of the West. Images of industrial violence had figured in the fiction of late-nineteenth-century regional colorists like Mary Hallock Foote, whose 1894 novel *Coeur d'Alene* had told the story of the Idaho mining wars from the viewpoint of the owners and managers, making dynamite-throwing strikers into one of the dangers that heroic westerners faced on the road to civilization. The radical writers flipped the perspective, while building up the image of the West as zone of class violence. The early classics include Frank Norris's *The Octopus* (1901), a haunting portrait of farmers taking up arms against the Southern Pacific Railroad; Jack London's *Martin Eden* (1908) and *Valley of the Moon* (1913), semi-autobiographical tales of young people wandering through a western workscape filled with brutality and terror; Upton Sinclair's *King Coal* (1917), the nightmarish story of the Colorado Ludlow massacre, and *Oil!* (1927), his saga of wealth and class conflict in southern California.

In these works the West was gaining a labor noir literary tradition that would blossom further in the 1930s both in fiction and journalism. The novels of John Steinbeck, especially *The Grapes of Wrath* (1939), Chester Himes' *If He Hollers Let Him Go* (1945), Carlos Bulosan's *America is in the Heart* (1946), and Alexander Saxton's *Bright Web of Darkness* (1958) are examples of the rich vein of popular-front fiction that deepened the images of the West as a land of repression for those who sought merely to work and live. Violence by the privileged against the poor was key to this regional counternarrative. Using and turning the West's mythic associations with opportunity and violence, the labor noirists preached that the region's dreams had become nightmares.

The labor noir historians worked with similar themes. Louis Adamic was first. In 1931 the Slovenian-born writer published what quickly became one of the best selling histories of American labor, *Dynamite: The Story of Class Violence in America*. Notable for its provocative primary thesis that class violence caused by ruthless industrial conditions was endemic to American history, it also seemed to argue a secondary theme that the West was the location for the worst expressions of that violence. Moreover the book resurrected and romanticized the IWW, lavishing a good portion of its energy on stories of violence by, and especially against, Wobblies, many of whom in 1931 were still languishing in prison. Adamic had spent a number of years associating with Wobblies when he lived in Los Angeles. They become the forlorn heroes of his book and, in a move that other journalists would follow; he regionalized them, turning them into westerners. He celebrates the basic principles of the organization, especially its plan for One Big Union as "a typically Western idea – big: the sky was the limit" (157).

Events in the 1930s added to the growing interest in labor's past and the market for such books. The explosion of strikes and organizing that attended the early New Deal found some of its most dramatic expression on the West Coast, where the 1934 longshoreman's walkout led to a four-day-long general strike in San Francisco and sympathy strikes in ports up and down the coast. The passage of the National Industrial Relations Act in 1935 set off the greatest era of labor activism in American history as two union federations (the older American Federation of Labor and the new Congress of Industrial Organizations) competed to organize millions of workers into unions. For the next twenty years labor would be big news and labor history enjoyed its greatest era of public interest. Professional historians still paid little attention, but journalists and publishers now realized that there was a market for books on the subject.

Many of the popular histories of western places and other regional-color journalism of the middle decades of the century emphasized labor issues and labor history, their authors typically following Adamic's lead and focusing on episodes of conflict and violence. Among the volumes still worth reading are Richard Neuberger's engaging portrait of the Pacific Northwest, *Our Promised Land* (1938); Anna Louis

Strong's West Coast observations in *I Change Worlds* (1940); and Murray Morgan's *Skid Road: An Informal Portrait of Seattle* (1951).

More important still are Carey McWilliams' books: *Factories in the Field* (1939) and *Ill Fares the Land* (1942) about farm workers; *Brothers Under the Skin* (1943), *Prejudice: Japanese-Americans* (1944), *A Mask for Privilege* (1948), and *North From Mexico* (1948) about immigration, racial prejudice, and the western industrial order; *Southern California: An Island on the Land* (1946) and *California: The Great Exception* (1949), in which he develops his regional interpretation. In those eight books written over the course of ten years, the Los Angeles attorney/journalist/editor/historian brought the labor noir tradition to its pinnacle of sophistication and influence, creating ideas and agendas that would reshape much more than labor historiography.

An implicit thesis of western labor exceptionalism had been running through the noirist literature all along, but apart from casually reasoned assertions about western traditions of individualism and violence, there was no theory to support it. McWilliams produced one. Spelled out in his 1949 book, *California: The Great Exception*, it formally argues the uniqueness of California's labor history but easily extends to most of the rest of the West. Describing what he calls the "total engagement" of labor and capital in a no-holds-barred cycle of industrial conflict, McWilliams' explanation starts with Ira Cross's insight that tight labor markets gave an early and fairly continual advantage to western workers. But the heart of his thesis is a blend of Frederick Jackson Turner's history and Robert Park's sociology. McWilliams argues that class tensions in the West were continually exacerbated by the pace of population growth and the "absence of well-established forms of social organization" (133). The lightning-quick development process caused labor movements to organize early and demand much. It made capitalists just as aggressive and ready to use "strong arm tactics" (172). Absent what he took to be the usual institutions of order and tradition, labor relations in the West developed, said McWilliams, a pattern of violence and militancy on both sides.

The New Labor History

It was not until the historical profession started into its social historical turn that labor history became part of academic history. The journal *Labor History* was founded in 1960 and soon began to publish the work of a group of historians who had veered from the institutional focus established by the labor economists. E. P. Thompson's magisterial *The Making of the English Working Class* (1963) became the touchstone for the "New Labor Historians" who followed its lead in using social history to probe beyond unions into work and social life, class formation, and the traditions of radical politics. The Northeast, with its early industrialization and its well-preserved sources, was the favorite site for most of the new labor historians, but a few western studies appeared in the late 1960s and early 1970s with many more to follow in the next decades. Two regional labor history organizations were founded in the late 1960s and early 1970s: the Southwest Labor Studies Association based in California and the Pacific Northwest Labor History Association which holds its annual meetings in Oregon, Washington, and British Columbia. Bringing together academic historians, trade unionists, and nonprofessionals interested in the subject, the two organizations have provided the principle institutional support for western labor history over the past thirty years.

The labor historians' biggest accomplishment has been to explore in expanding detail the world of work, while overturning the singular image of "the worker" and replacing it with "working people" of great diversity and multiple contexts. From rural school teachers to hard-rock miners, from oil workers in southern California to cannery workers in Alaska, from Native American hop pickers to African American ship stewards, up and down the social structure and across the broad geography of the West the labor historians of recent decades have mapped, counted, and richly described its working people.

Several challenging new understandings of the late-nineteenth- and early-twentieth-century western working class have emerged from all of this social history. One focuses on its industrial composition; the other on its ethnic configurations. Carlos Schwantes is responsible for the most ambitious argument about the complexity of the western workscape. He argues that the western economy was distinct from other regions because of the high proportion of wageworkers of a particular kind. The Northeast and Midwest had cities and large urban working classes. Much of the wage work in the West took place outside the cities, in the region's mining towns, lumber camps, cattle ranches, canneries, fishing villages, and in the mobile encampments of railroad workers who laid and repaired the tracks, farm workers who followed the crops, and on board the thousands of steam ships, lumber schooners, and fishing boats which plied the coastal and inland waters of the West Coast. Seasonal and economically unstable, these western industries depended upon a highly mobile work force composed largely of young men who often moved from one kind of work to another and who also moved seasonally through the western cities, working on the docks, filling up the skidrows, getting through the winters. Schwantes develops the concept of the "Wageworkers' Frontier" arguing not only the distinctive features of the western working class but also urging western historians to put aside covered wagons and recognize the centrality of wage work in the development of the region (1987, 1994).

Not everyone agrees with all aspects of this description. Richard White, whose synthesis of western history, "It's Your Misfortune and None of My Own" (1991) incorporates many of the key insights and contributions of the new labor history, stresses the continuing importance of family-scale farming and household labor through the early-twentieth-century West. Obscured too in the wageworkers' frontier argument are the working lives of most women, whose labors were typically home centered. And it may be that wage work in other regions shared some of the circulatory and unstable characteristics that Schwantes assigns rather exclusively to the West. Still, it is clear that the scholarship of the past generation has given us a new picture of not only the places and ways of work but of the West itself in the formative late nineteenth and early twentieth centuries.

Equally dramatic are the new understandings of who worked. The economists and noirists imagined the worker as male, white, and of no particular ethnic background. The new labor history has dug deeply into the complexities of race, ethnicity, and gender and discovered in these categories new reasons to contemplate the distinctive nature of western labor. This region had different patterns of ethnicity than any other: more Native Americans, Latin Americans, and Asian Americans, fewer African

Americans than the South, and fewer southern and eastern Europeans than the Northeast. And those ethnicities overlaid the patterns of work and class in particular ways.

Scholars have mapped a kaleidoscope of ethnic occupational niches: Norwegians,
Native Americans, Italians, Portuguese, Chinese, Japanese, and Filipinos in the fishing
industries; lumber camps filled with other Scandinavians, Germans, and old stock
Yankees; cattle ranches attracting Mexican Americans, African Americans, Native
Americans, and various whites; Chinese, Irish, Italian, eastern European, and Mexican
men building the railroads; Portuguese, Italian, and Mexican women canning the
fruits and vegetables; crews of almost every description harvesting the crops. The
mining camps were especially complicated, changing ethnic compositions over time
and place, with strong showings of Irish, Cornish, Welsh, Mexicans, Italians, Slavs,
Hungarians, Finns, and Chinese in some settings, and very different mixes in the next
mining region or the next generation. Two recent books have given us new ways to
think about the connections and interactions between these different western
workers. In *Reinventing Free Labor: Padrones and Immigrant Workers in the North
American West 1880–1930* (2000) Gunther Peck explores the labor-contracting
system, exposing one of the key institutions that supported and mediated these ethnic
solidarities. In *American Workers, Colonial Power: Philippine Seattle and the Transpacific West, 1919–1941* (2003) Dorothy Fujita-Rony shows a community not in isolation but in circulation, with Filipina/o workers crossing every sort of boundary,
interacting with every sort of western American, pushing their way into the labor
movement, and creatively contesting marginalization.

Deciphering the lines of power and hierarchy within the western ethnic kaleidoscope has been a challenge. Most historians see a two-tiered, racialized labor market
in which whites controlled jobs in any sector that offered reasonable wages while
racial minorities were pressed into marginal occupations, principally service and
unskilled laboring jobs (Takaki, 1989; Almaguer, 1994). But others have struggled
to reconcile that binary logic with a social system of such diversity. The South had a
two-tiered labor market. Does the same term apply to the West? Quintard Taylor has
argued that African American opportunities in some parts of the West were situated
in a three-sided competition that involved Asian Americans as well as whites (1998).
In *The White Scourge: Mexicans, Blacks, and Poor Whites in Texas Cotton Culture*
(1997) Neil Foley situates Latinos within another triangulation and within an evolving discourse of whiteness.

The field has been slower to develop the issue of gender, despite early and eloquent pleas by Joan Jenson and Darlis Miller (1980), among others. It was not until
the late 1980s that books about female workers appeared in any number and the coverage is still thin. There are now books on waitresses (Cobble, 1991), school teachers (Weiler, 1998), , cannery and field workers (Ruiz, 1987), and a few studies of
unions and organizations like the Women's Wage Earner Suffrage League of San
Francisco (Englander, 1992). That some of the best studies focus on women of color
can be counted as one of the triumphs of recent western history. Evelyn Nakano
Glenn's *Issei, Nisei, War Bride* (1986), Vicki Ruiz's *Cannery Women, Cannery Lives*
(1987) Sarah Deutsch's *No Separate Refuge* (1987), and Judy Yung's *Unbound Feet*
(1995) have been breakthrough books on several fronts. But much more needs to
be done. Something new has occurred in the last few years as scholars have figured
out how to bring homeworking wives into labor history. In Dana Frank's *Purchasing*

Power: Consumer Organizing, Gender, and the Seattle Labor Movement, 1919–1929 (1994) the labor movement is understood to consist of families, and the family is understood to have consuming powers as well as producing powers, all of which makes gender issues and women's actions not peripheral but central to the fate of any labor movement. Mary Murphy follows a similar strategy in *Mining Cultures: Men, Women, and Leisure in Butte, 1914–41* (1997).

Western Labor Radicalism

While the labor history of the past generation has fractured our images of work and workers, it has also reorganized understandings of the West's labor movements and their relationship to the region's politics. Forgotten organizations like the Workingmen's Party of California (WPC) have been rediscovered. Others, like the Knights of Labor and the Union Labor Party, that had been disparaged by labor economists have gained new glory. And the old standards, the IWW and the American Federation of Labor (AFL), have received full makeovers. As with the project of demographic recentering, the scholarship on labor movements has created an appreciation for the diversity of labor-related institutions, politics, and ideologies while raising their collective profile. Thanks to these efforts, workers' movements figure more prominently than ever in the newer interpretations of western political history.

Rethinking radicalism was one of the earliest and most consistent projects of the new labor history, which has in general sought to place radical movements within American political traditions and establish their continuing importance. Not surprisingly, it began with the Industrial Workers of the World. In the mid sixties a number of books heralded the resurrection of interest in an organization that seemed to speak to some of the concerns and styles of a new protest generation. Joyce Kornbluh (1964), Robert Tyler (1967), Joseph Conlin (1969), and Melvyn Dubofsky (1969) turned the once feared Wobblies into forerunners of the Congress of Industrial Organizations (CIO) and the civil rights, and free speech movements. They also, and more carefully than before, distinguished between the peculiarities of its eastern operations and constituents and its western wing.

The Wobblies became the jumping-off point for a much wider investigation of western radicalism. Dubofsky set this up in a widely read article, "The Origins of Western Working Class Radicalism" (1966), in which he drew attention to the Western Federation of Miners (WFM), the militant, socialist-linked union that helped launch the IWW. Dubofsky turned the WFM into the prototype for western radicalism. He argued that the mining region had seen industrialization in its most advanced, most rapid, and most brutal form. Taking on the noirist Turnerians, who saw labor militance as an expression of western individualism and frontier conditions, he argued it was instead a response to the West's mature corporate structures. This was a West, he said, that Karl Marx understood better than Frederick Jackson Turner.

These ideas helped inspire a long stream of follow-up studies focused on the region's resource-extraction workers, especially miners. Easily a dozen important books and many more articles and dissertations have looked at hard-rock mining and coal mining in various western settings. Many endorse the descriptions of class struggle and miner radicalism, most recently Elizabeth Jameson's fine-grained social history of Colorado's mining district *All That Glitters: Class, Conflict, and Community in Cripple Creek* (1998); J.Anthony Lukas' *Big Trouble* (1997), a 750-page narrative centered on the trial of three WFM leaders charged in the 1905 bombing murder of Idaho's retired governor ; and Laurie Mercier's *Anaconda: Labor, Community, and Culture in Montana's Smelter City* (2001), which explores the lasting pattern of community unionism in the copper capital. But others complicate the image of mining as the motherlode of western radicalism. In *The Butte Irish: Class and Ethnicity in an American Mining Town, 1875–1925* (1989) David Emmons focused on the largest and most powerful local in the Western Federation of Miners, finding not radicalism and class war but a relatively conservative, ethnically based union that went thirty years without a strike while dominating the city proudly called the "Gibraltar of Unionism."

Meanwhile another group of scholars has followed the trail of WFM and IWW radicalism into different industries and spaces: into the woods where a succession of radical unions of timberworkers and shingle weavers culminated in the formation of the CIO-affiliated International Woodworkers of America in the 1930s; into maritime transportation where, according to Bruce Nelson (1988) and Howard Kimeldorf (1988), the radicalism of sailors and longshoreman in the 1930s owed much to the traditions of syndicalist organizing that Wobblies and before them WFM activists had developed; and into the fields where it meets up with Mexican traditions of radicalism in studies by Cletus Daniel (1981), W. Dirk Raat (1981), James Sandos (1992), Devra Weber (1994), and Camille Guerin-Gonzales (1994).

The explorations of the WFM-IWW tradition of western radicalism have parallelled, and to some extent been in competition with, another stream of scholarship that has focused on western cities and their labor movements. The cities saw the rise of craft unions of the American Federation of Labor in the late 1880s and before that the rise and fall of various Workingmen's parties and the Knights of Labor. These movements have taxed the interpretative powers of the new labor history much more than the recognizable radicalism of the WFM and IWW. The unglamorous AFL had long been described as conservative, exclusive, and apolitical, and along with the Workingmen's Parties and Knights' Assemblies had been implicated in the West's worst episodes of xenophobia.

The scholarship has gone in two directions, one emphasizing the role and legacy of white supremacy, the other finding idealism and a legacy of labor power. Alexander Saxton pioneered the first in *Indispensable Enemy: Labor and the Anti-Chinese Movement in California* (1971), a book that laid the groundwork for what was later called "whiteness studies". Its subject was the Workingmen's Party of California, which had come to power in San Francisco in 1879 and had played a large role in rewriting the state's constitution that same year. The WPC had been largely ignored by earlier labor scholars, who found the party's combination of class-conscious and anti-Chinese politics embarrassing and also confusing. Confusing, because it was axiomatic that ethnic hatreds undermined labor movements. Saxton turned that axiom around, showing that racism helped the Irish, German, and native protestant white workers of San Francisco overcome their differences and the resulting white-working-class solidarity laid the groundwork for one of the most effective urban labor movements of the Gilded Age. Subsequent studies by Gwendolyn Mink (1986), Sucheng Chan (1986), Roger Daniels (1977), Chris Friday (1994), and Tomás Almaguer (1994), have followed the scheme of xenophobia through the anti-Chinese campaigns led by Knights of Labor activists in various parts of the West in the late 1880s and the anti-Japanese and anti-Filipino politics of the AFL unions after the turn of the century.

But other historians found more than xenophobia in these movements and, while acknowledging their racism, have been equally intrigued by their power to mobilize large numbers of white workers behind labor-centered and transformative political visions. Dan Cornford (1987), Neil Shumsky (1991), Jules Tygiel (1992), and David Brundage (1994) are among those who have explored the Gilded Age radicalism that animated WPC and Knights activism. The American Federation of Labor has also been historiographically refurbished, emerging in recent studies as more idealistic, class-conscious, and politically involved than earlier scholars believed. Michael Kazin's *Barons of Labor: The San Francisco Building Trades and Union Power in the Progressive Era* (1987) explores the sources of labor power in the decades when San Francisco was known as "Labor's City," contending that the AFL practiced a form of pragmatic syndicalism that, while not revolutionary, looked to "workers to transform society in their own image" (150). Dana Frank (1994) joins Robert Friedheim (1964) and Jonathan Dembo (1983) in assigning a still more radical countenance to the Seattle AFL that waged the General Strike of 1919 and in the aftermath tried to build an infrastructure of labor-owned banks, stores, a laundry, a daily newspaper, a union theater, even a film company in the early 1920s. Samuel Gompers liked none of it and he warred often with these western city federations.

These studies of urban labor movements expose the uneven geography of the most recent phase of labor history: the work has concentrated on a few spaces (Rocky Mountain mining districts, Northwest forests, California's valleys) and a few cities, especially San Francisco where the volume of labor-related studies has had a noticeable effect on other aspects of the city's historiography. The political and social history of San Francisco has been extensively revised in the past two decades by urban historians sensitive to issues of class formation and labor politics (see Lotchin, 1974; Decker, 1978; Ethington, 1994; Issel and Cherney, 1986). Seattle's history has also been extensively rewritten. Richard Berner's three-volume city history may well be the most comprehensive labor-centered study of a city's institutional development found anywhere (1991, 1992, 1999).

But other cities await similar efforts, especially Los Angeles. The City of Angels was the West's fastest-growing metropolis in the early twentieth century and different in so many respects from the spaces that labor historians have come to know best. Because of its unique economy (oranges, oil, and entertainment) and demography (large numbers of Latinos and Jews instead of the Irish–Chinese axis), many of the equations labor historians have used to understand other parts of the West do not apply. That may be why no one has yet figured out how to put labor into the LA story. Calling it the "Open Shop city" and treating it as the flip side of San Francisco makes for dramatic reading but bad history. The city was complicated. It was the site of an aggressive open shop campaign, but also home to an impressive pattern of electoral radicalism (first by socialists, later by Upton Sinclair's EPIC movement). It had a promising AFL union movement early in the century which lost strength after World War I, but unionism remained alive and often highly innovative in the oil suburbs, the Mexican-American community, the Jewish eastside, among municipal water and power employees, and in the entertainment sector. As yet we know more about Chicano working-class life and activism through the studies by George Sanchez (1993), Ricardo Romo (1983), Gilbert Gonzalez (1994), Francisco Balderama (1982), Douglas Monroy (1999), and Matt Garcia (2001) than we do about most other parts of this metropolitan working class. But that is changing. New books about a working class suburb (Nicolaides, 2001) and white-collar corporate culture (Davis, 2000) are finally opening up the field of Los Angeles labor history.

The western labor history of recent years shows other weaknesses in addition to its incomplete geography. The field's strength has been social history and community- or industry-based studies, and it is only now beginning to appreciate cultural and political history. A handful of recent works explore the relationship between labor and the cultural institutions of the region. Mike Davis (1990), Kevin Starr (1990, 1996), Anne Loftis (1998), and Stephen Schwartz (1998) have called attention to the literary radicalism that flourished in Los Angeles and San Francisco and that helped remake images of the West and its workers. Steven Ross's *Working-Class Hollywood: Silent Film and the Shaping of Class in America* (1998) opens another window on the laborist cultural crusades of the early twentieth century, as unions and radicals struggled to control not just print media but some of the dream machines of the young century. For years folklorist Archie Green has been urging a different strategy for exploring the cultural influences of workers and their movements. He introduced the concept of "laborlore" almost three decades ago in *Only a Miner: Studies in Recorded Coalmining Songs* (1972) and demonstrated it recently in *Wobblies, Pile Butts, and Other Heroes: Laborlore Explorations* (1993). Maybe it is time for someone to follow his lead.

It is also time for labor historians to pay more attention to political institutions. Much of the new labor history has examined political ideas and actions without attending closely to the governmental and party systems in which they are embedded. What did it mean for labor that so many western cities lacked the entrenched two-party or single-machine political systems common in the Northeast? How much did that contribute to the effectiveness of Workingmen's parties, Union Labor parties, and labor's interest in other political initiatives? Patterns of political development helped make the West a distinctive region in both the Gilded Age, when many state constitutions were written or rewritten, and in the Progressive era, when many western states reorganized governmental capacity and party systems. Labor historians have been paying attention to courts, parties, and governmental agencies in studies that focus on other parts of America. We need to bring that focus to bear on the West.

Attention to politics may also encourage western labor historians to think more about the West itself. Some already do, Schwantes certainly, but others have been casually inattentive to the issue of regionalism, using western cities and other spaces without worrying about their westernness. This has its advantages: it has kept labor historians from falling into the parochial habits that plague some other western historical endeavors. But it robs both the western field and the labor field of potential insights. New efforts at synthesis are overdue; indeed it would be healthy if western labor historians would just argue about some of the field-defining theses that have been advanced. Schwantes "wageworkers' frontier" argument needs a full airing. Nearly twenty years ago, Michael Kazin advanced a tentative but smart revision of Carey McWilliams' "great exception" thesis for California's urban labor movements

(1986). It was ignored. We need to change that. It is time to figure out how the rich social history that has been compiled over the last few decades adds up. What does it mean? It is fine to be cautious and empirical and tell the journalists when they call that the West's labor history is "complicated." But that can be risky in a sense too. Non-academicians have proved their ability in the past to take over the subject and make it respond to felt needs.

REFERENCES

Adamic, Louis: *Dynamite: The Story of Class Violence in America* (New York: Viking, 1931).

Allen, Ruth: *Chapters in the History of Organized Labor in Texas* (Austen: University of Texas Press, 1941).

Almaguer, Tomás: *Racial Fault Lines: The Historical Origins of White Supremacy in California* (Berkeley: University of California Press, 1994).

Anderson, Karen: "Work, Gender, and Power in the American West." *Pacific Historical Review* (November 1992), 481–99.

Balderama, Francisco E.: *In Defense of La Raza: The Los Angeles Mexican Consulate and the Mexican Community, 1929 to 1936* (Tucson: University of Arizona Press, 1982).

Berner, Richard C.: *Seattle 1900–1920: From Boomtown, Urban Turbulence, to Restoration* (Seattle: Charles Press, 1991).

Berner, Richard C.: *Seattle, 1921–1940: From Boom to Bust* (Seattle: Charles Press, 1992).

Berner, Richard C.: *Seattle Transformed: World War II to Cold War* (Seattle: Charles Press, 1999).

Brown, Ronald C.: *Hard-Rock Miners: The Intermountain West, 1860–1920* (College Station, TX: Texas A & M University Press, 1979).

Brundage, David: *The Making of Western Labor Radicalism: Denver's Organized Workers, 1878–1905* (Urbana: University of Illinois Press, 1994).

Bulosan, Carlos: *America is in the Heart* (New York: Harcourt Brace, 1946).

Butler, Anne M.: *Daughters of Joy, Sisters of Misery: Prostitutes in the American West, 1865–1890* (Urbana, University of Illinois Press, 1985).

Chan, Sucheng: *This Bittersweet Soil: The Chinese in California Agriculture, 1860–1910* (Berkeley, University of California Press, 1986).

Clark, Norman: *Milltown: A Social History of Everett, Washington* (Seattle: University of Washington Press, 1970).

Cobble, Dorothy Sue: *Dishing It Out: Waitresses and Their Unions in the Twentieth Century* (Urbana: University of Illinois Press, 1991).

Conlin, Joseph: *Bread and Roses Too: Studies of the Wobblies* (Westport, CT: Greenwood, 1969).

Cordier, Mary: *Schoolwomen of the Prairies and Plains* (Albuquerque: University of New Mexico Press, 1992).

Cornford, Daniel: *Workers and Dissent in the Redwood Empire* (Philadelphia: Temple University Press, 1987).

Cornford, Daniel (ed.): *Working People of California* (Berkeley: University of California Press, 1995).

Cross, Ira: *A History of the Labor Movement in California* (Berkeley: University of California Press, 1935).

Daniel, Cletus E.: *Bitter Harvest: A History of California Farmworkers 1870–1941* (Ithaca: Cornell University Press, 1981).

Daniels, Roger: *The Politics of Prejudice: The Anti-Japanese Movement in California and the Struggle for Exclusion* (Berkeley: University of California Press, 1977).

Davis, Clark: *Company Men: White Collar Life and Corporate Culture in Los Angeles 1892–1940* (Baltimore, Johns Hopkins University Press, 2000).

Davis, Mike: *City of Quartz: Excavating the Future in Los Angeles* (New York and London: Verso, 1990).

Decker, Peter: *Fortunes and Failures: White-Collar Mobility in Nineteenth Century San Francisco* (Cambridge, MA: Harvard University Press, 1978).

Dembo, Jonathan: *Unions and Politics in Washington State 1885–1935* (New York: Garland, 1983).

Derickson, Alan: *Worker's Health, Workers' Democracy: The Western Miner's Struggle, 1891–1925* (Ithaca: Cornell University Press, 1988).

Deutsch, Sarah: *No Separate Refuge: Culture, Class, and Gender on an Anglo-Hispanic Frontier in the American Southwest, 1880–1940* (New York: Oxford University Press, 1987).

Dubofsky, Melvyn: "The Origins of Western Working-Class Radicalism, 1890–1905." *Labor History* 7, 2 (1966), 131–54.

Dubofsky, Melvyn: *We Shall Be All: A History of the Industrial Workers of the World* (Chicago: Quadrangle Books, 1969).

Dubofsky, Melvyn: *The State and Labor in Modern America* (Chapel Hill: University of North Carolina Press, 1994).

Emmons, David: *The Butte Irish: Class and Ethnicity in an American Mining Town, 1875–1925* (Urbana: University of Illinois Press, 1989).

Emmons, David: "Constructed Province: History and the Making of the Last American West." *Western Historical Quarterly* (Winter 1994), 437–60.

Englander, Susan: *Class Coalition and Class Conflict in the California Woman Suffrage Movement, 1907–1912: The San Francisco Wage Earner's Suffrage League* (San Francisco: Mellen Research University Press, 1992).

Ethington, Philip J.: *The Public City: The Political Construction of Urban Life in San Francisco, 1850–1900* (New York: Cambridge University Press, 1994).

Foley, Neil: *The White Scourge: Mexicans, Blacks, and Poor Whites in Texas Cotton Culture* (Berkeley: University of California Press, 1997).

Foote, Mary Hallock: *Coeur d'Alene* (Boston: Houghton Miflin, 1894).

Frank, Dana: *Purchasing Power: Consumer Organizing, Gender, and the Seattle Labor Movement, 1919–1929* (New York: Cambridge University Press, 1994).

Friday, Chris: *Organizing Asian American Workers: The Pacific Coast Canned Salmon Industry, 1870–1942* (Philadelphia: Temple University Press, 1994).

Friedheim, Robert L.: *The Seattle General Strike* (Seattle: University of Washington Press, 1964).

Fujita-Rony, Dorothy B.: *American Workers, Colonial Power: Philippine Seattle and the Transpacific West, 1919–1941* (Berkeley, University of California Press, 2003).

Garcia, Matt: *A World of Its Own: Race, Labor, and Citrus in the Making of Greater Los Angeles, 1900–1970* (Chapel Hill: University of North Carolina Press, 2001).

Glenn, Evelyn Nakano: *Issei, Nisei, War Bride* (Philadelphia: Temple University Press, 1986).

Gonzalez, Gilbert G.: *Labor and Community: Mexican Citrus Worker Villages in a Southern California County, 1900–1950* (Urbana: University of Illinois Press, 1994).

Green, Archie: *Only a Miner: Studies in Recorded Coalmining Songs* (Urbana: University of Illinois Press, 1972).

Green, Archie: *Wobblies, Pile Butts, and Other Heroes: Laborlore Explorations* (Urbana: University of Illinois Press, 1993).

Guerin-Gonzales, Camille: *Mexican Workers and American Dreams: Immigration, Repatriation, and California Farm Labor, 1900–1939* (New Brunswick: Rutgers University Press, 1994).

Himes, Chester: *If He Hollers Let Him Go* (Garden City, NY: Doubleday, Doran & Co., 1945).

Ichioka, Yuji: *The Issei: The World of the First Generation Japanese Immigrations, 1885–1924* (New York: Free Press, 1988).

Isern, Thomas D.: *Bull Threshers and Bindlestiffs: Harvesting and Threshing on the North American Plains* (Lawrence: University Press of Kansas, 1990).

Issel, William and Robert W. Cherny: *San Francisco, 1865–1932: Politics, Power, and Urban Development* (Berkeley: University of California Press, 1986).

Jameson, Elizabeth: *All That Glitters: Class, Conflict, and Community in Cripple Creek* (Urbana: University of Illinois Press, 1998).

Jameson, Elizabeth and Susan Armitage (eds.): *Writing the Range: Race, Class, and Culture in the Women's West* (Norman: University of Oklahoma Press, 1997).

Jenson, Joan and Darlis A. Miller: "The Gentle Tamers Revisited: New Approaches to the History of Women in the American West." *Pacific Historical Review* (1980), 173–213.

Jensen, Vernon: *Lumber and Labor* (New York: Farrer & Rinehart, 1945).

Jensen, Vernon: *Heritage of Conflict: Labor Relations in the Nonferrous Metals Industry up to 1930* (Ithaca: Cornell University Press, 1950).

Kazin, Michael: "The Great Exception Revisited: Organized Labor and Politics in San Francisco and Los Angeles, 1870–1940." *Pacific Historical Review* (August 1986), 371–402.

Kazin, Michael: *Barons of Labor: The San Francisco Building Trades and Union Power in the Progressive Era* (Urbana: University of Illinois Press, 1987).

Kimeldorf, Howard: *Reds or Rackets? The Making of Radical and Conservative Unions on the Waterfront* (Berkeley: University of California Press, 1988).

Kornbluh, Joyce: *Rebel Voices: An I.W.W. Anthology* (Ann Arbor: University of Michigan Press, 1964).

Laslett, John H. and Mary Tyler: *The ILGWU in Los Angeles, 1907–1988* (Inglewood, CA: Ten Star Press, 1989).

Lembcke, Jerry and William M. Tattam: *One Union in Wood: A Political History of the International Woodworkers of America* (New York: International Publishers, 1984).

Lemke-Santangelo, Gretchen: *Abiding Courage: African American Migrant Women in the East Bay Community* (Chapel Hill: University of North Carolina Press, 1996).

Lingenfelter, Richard E.: *The Hardrock Miners: A History of the Mining Labor Movement in the American West, 1863–1893* (Berkeley: University of California Press, 1974).

Loftis, Anne: *Witnesses to the Struggle: Imaging the 1930s California Labor Movement* (Reno: University of Nevada Press, 1998).

London, Jack: *Martin Eden* (New York: Macmillan, 1908).

London, Jack: *Valley of the Moon* (New York: Macmillan, 1913).

Lotchin, Roger: *San Francisco 1846–1956: From Hamlet to City* (New York: Oxford University Press, 1974).

Lovin, Hugh T. (ed.): *Labor in the West* (Manhattan, KS: Sunflower University Press, 1989).

Lukas, J. Anthony: *Big Trouble* (New York: Simon and Schuster, 1997).

McWilliams, Carey: *Factories in the Field* (Boston: Little, Brown, 1939).

McWilliams, Carey: *Ill Fares the Land* (Boston: Little, Brown, 1942).

McWilliams, Carey: *Brothers Under the Skin* (Boston: Little, Brown, 1943).

McWilliams, Carey: *Prejudice: Japanese-Americans* (Boston: Little, Brown, 1944).

McWilliams, Carey: *Southern California: An Island on the Land* (New York: Duell, Sloan, & Pearce, 1946).

McWilliams, Carey: *A Mask for Privilege* (Boston: Little, Brown, 1948).

McWilliams, Carey: *North From Mexico* (New York: Monthly Review Press, 1948).

McWilliams, Carey: *California: The Great Exception* (New York: Current Books, 1949).

Malone, Michael: *The Battle for Butte: Mining and Politics on the Northern Frontier* (Seattle: University of Washington Press, 1981).

Mellinger, Philip J.: *Race and Labor in Western Copper: The Fight for Equality, 1896–1918* (Tucson: University of Arizona Press, 1995).

Mercier, Laurie: *Anaconda: Labor, Community, and Culture in Montana's Smelter City* (Urbana: University of Illinois Press, 2001).

Mink, Gwendolyn: *Old Labor and New Immigrants in American Political Development: Union, Party, and State, 1875–1920* (Ithaca: Cornell University Press, 1986).

Monroy, Douglas: *Rebirth: Mexican Los Angles from the Great Migration to the Great Depression* (Berkeley: University of California Press, 1999).

Morgan, Murray: *Skid Road: An Informal Portrait of Seattle* (New York: Viking, 1951).

Murphy, Mary: *Mining Cultures: Men, Women, and Leisure in Butte, 1914–1941* (Urbana: University of Illinois Press, 1997).

Nelson, Bruce: *Workers on the Waterfront: Seamen, Longshoremen, and Unionism in the 1930s* (Urbana: University of Illinois Press, 1988).

Neuberger, Richard: *Our Promised Land* (New York: Macmillan, 1938).

Nicolaides, Becky: *My Blue Heaven: Life and Politics in the Working-class Suburbs of Los Angeles, 1920–1965* (Chicago: University of Chicago Press, 2002).

Norris, Frank: *The Octopus* (New York: Doubleday, 1901).

Parker, Carlton: *The Casual Laborer and Other Essays* (New York: Harper, Brace, and Howe, 1920).

Peck, Gunther: *Reinventing Free Labor: Padrones and Immigrant Workers in the North American West, 1880–1930* (Cambridge and New York: Cambridge University Press, 2000).

Petrik, Paula: *No Step Backward: Women and Family on the Rocky Mountain Mining Frontier, 1865–1900* (Helena: Montana Historical Society Press, 1987).

Quam-Wickham, Nancy: "Petroleocrats and Proletarians: Work Class and Politics in the California Oil Industry, 1917–1925." (PhD dissertation: University of California, 1994).

Raat, W. Dirk: *Revoltosos: Mexico's Rebels in the United States, 1903–1923* (College Station, TX: Texas A & M University Press, 1981).

Robbins, William G.: *Hard Times in Paradise: Coos Bay, Oregon* (Seattle: University of Washington Press, 1988).

Romo, Ricardo: *East Los Angeles: History of a Barrio* (Austin: University of Texas Press, 1983).

Ross, Steven: *Working-Class Hollywood: Silent Film and the Shaping of Class in America* (Princeton: Princeton University Press, 1998).

Ruiz, Vicki: *Cannery Women, Cannery Lives* (Albuquerque: University of New Mexico Press, 1987).

Sanchez, George J.: *Becoming Mexican American: Ethnicity, Culture, and Identity in Chicano Los Angeles, 1900–1945* (New York: Oxford University Press, 1993).

Sandos, James: *Rebellion in the Borderlands* (Norman: University of Oklahoma Press, 1992).

Saxton, Alexander: *Bright Web of Darkness* (New York: St Martins, 1958; rpt. Berkeley: University of California Press, 1997).

Saxton, Alexander: *Indispensable Enemy: Labor and the Anti-Chinese Movement in California* (Berkeley: University of California Press, 1971).

Schwartz, Stephen: *From West to East: California and the Making of the American Mind* (New York: Free Press, 1998).

Schwantes, Carlos: "The Concept of the Wageworker's Frontier: A Framework for Future Research." *Western Historical Quarterly* (January 1987), 39–55.

Schwantes, Carlos: *Hard Traveling: A Portrait of Work Life in the New Northwest* (Lincoln: University of Nebraska Press, 1994).

Sellars, Nigel Anthony: *Oil, Wheat, & Wobblies: The Industrial Workers of the World in Oklahoma, 1905–1930* (Norman: University of Oklahoma Press, 1998).

Shunsky, Neil Larry: *The Evolution of Political Protest and the Workingmen's Party of California* (Columbus: Ohio State University Press, 1991).

Sinclair, Upton: *King Coal* (New York: Macmillan, 1917).

Sinclair, Upton: *Oil!* (New York: A & C Boni, 1927).

Starr, Kevin: *Material Dreams: Southern California through the 1920s* (New York: Oxford University Press, 1990).

Starr, Kevin: *Endangered Dreams: The Great Depression in California* (New York: Oxford University Press, 1996).

Steinbeck, John: *The Grapes of Wrath* (New York: Viking, 1939).

Stimson, Grace: *Rise of the Labor Movement in Los Angeles* (Berkeley: University of California Press, 1955).

Strong, Anna Louis: *I Change Worlds* (New York, Henry Holt, 1940).

Taft, Philip: *Labor Politics American Style: The California State Federation of Labor* (Cambridge, MA: Harvard University Press, 1968).

Takaki, Ronald: *Strangers from a Different Shore: A History of Asian Americans* (Boston: Little, Brown, 1989).

Taylor, Paul: *The Sailor's Union of the Pacific* (New York: Ronald Press, 1923).

Taylor, Quintard: *In Search of the Racial Frontier: African Americans in the American West, 1528–1990* (New York: W. W. Norton, 1998).

Tygiel, Jules: *Workingmen in San Franciso, 1880–1901* (New York, Garland, 1992).

Tyler, Robert: *Rebels in the Woods: The I.W.W. in the Pacific Northwest* (Eugene: University of Oregon Press, 1967).

Weber, Devra: *Dark Sweat, White Gold: California Farm Workers, Cotton, and the New Deal* (1994).

Weiler, Kathleen: *Country Schoolwomen: Teaching in Rural California 1850–1950* (Berkeley: University of California Press, 1998).

White, Richard: *"It's Your Misfortune and None of My Own": A New History of the American West* (Norman: University of Oklahoma Press, 1991).

Wyman, Mark: *Hard-Rock Epic: Western Miners and the Industrial Revolution, 1860–1910* (Berkeley: University of California Press, 1979).

Yung, Judy: *Unbound Feet* (Berkeley: University of California Press, 1995).

Zavella, Patricia: *Women's Work and Chicano Families, Cannery Workers of the Santa Clara Valley* (Ithaca: Cornell University Press, 1987).

CHAPTER FOURTEEN

Societies to Match the Scenery: Twentieth-Century Environmental History in the American West

DAN FLORES

In 1893, on the banks of the North Fork of the Red River in the peach-colored prairies of Oklahoma Territory, a group of Southern Plains Indians gathered around a Kiowa shaman named Buffalo-Coming-Out in hopes of seeing something magical. Only two decades before, the Kiowas, Comanches, and Southern Cheyennes had been buffalo people. But somehow, mysteriously, the animals had disappeared, and many Southern Plains people believed they had returned to earth, specifically to Hiding Mountain (which the whites called Mount Scott) in the Wichita Range. So Buffalo-Coming-Out performed his ceremony and his followers watched the mountains expectantly (Powell, 1969, vol. 1: 281–2). But unless it took the form of the Wichita Mountains National Wildlife Refuge, established 14 years later as one of the first of the new century's scattered (and rather small) national bison ranges in the West, Buffalo-Coming-Out's magic must have struck his people at the time as insufficient to slow the spinning world, let alone reverse it.

Buffalo-Coming-Out's people were inheritors of traditions in western America that stretched back 12,000 years or more, to the very arrival of human beings in North America. Although this ancient West had been dynamic, what the Kiowas and other native peoples were confronting in the 1890s was a truism of modern history: as a result of cultural and continental linkages, the rate of change had somehow switched into fast-forward, throwing history into a kind of Doppler Shift. *Everything* in the American West seemed to be changing at the beginning of the twentieth century, and no shamanic magic – not in Oklahoma on the Great Plains, or in the Rockies or on the Pacific Coast, or in the far-flung western territories in the Southwest, Alaska, and Hawai'i – appeared capable of reversing the trend. And in no area of human endeavor was this accelerating change more evident, and gravid, than in the most basic realm of all, the relationship between human beings and "nature," or the environment that makes up our habitat as a species.

The West of this new twentieth century had been a long time assuming its modern form. But in 1900 the environmental condition of the American West was fundamentally different – and by orders of magnitude – than had been the case when the previous century commenced. With the passage of the land from native Indian and Eskimo, Polynesian, and Spanish hands to American ones, an ecological revolution as profound as any since the Pleistocene extinctions ten centuries before visited the

West of the contiguous United States, as well as (and out of many of the same causes) Hawai'i and Alaska. As catastrophe theorists would have it, a natural world that had been in a wobbly homeostasis had shifted. While built on the old world, this was a new one. As the twentieth century dawned, the West was seeking a new equilibrium. To many of those who remembered the way life had been, as the Crow leader Plenty Coups famously observed in Montana, history seemed to have ended. But of course it had not.

The Old West had not been a single world but many different ones. In 1800 almost all of the American West, particularly the Plains, the Rockies, inland Alaska, and the kingdom of Hawai'i, was entirely in the hands of native peoples. But by then, everywhere across these enormous expanses, Europeans had intruded themselves into the local economies and ecologies of the native people, diverting their activities, especially their trapping, fishing, and hunting, into the global market. In Hawai'i Europeans had assisted native leader Kamehameha I in his plan to unify the islands. In Alaska the Russian American Company had founded posts and established Greek Orthodox Christianity among the coastal peoples from the Aleutian Islands to northern California. Farther south, in California and in northern New Mexico and Texas, Spanish missions and presidios had dotted the landscape – towns like Santa Fe, in New Mexico, were already two centuries old by 1800 – but almost seemed to exist at the sufferance of local bands of Indians. English traders from Canada skirted the edges of the Plains and Northern Rockies with seductive industrial goods. But in 1800 the natural-resource-based economies of the West, which centered on bison and elk and caribou, fur seals and sea otters, beaver populations in the mountains, whales and sandalwood in the Pacific, were all still in place.

But by 1900, with passage of a mere century, ownership of this enormous region had passed into the hands of the United States. Only a last few marginal areas, mostly in desert and semiarid regions in the Southwest and on the Northern Plains, remained to be settled by American homesteaders in the first decades of the twentieth century. Furbearers and whales, precious metals, Polynesian plantations, and the lowly homestead had drawn American populations to virtually every far corner of the West, and with them had come a massive reduction. The great natural wealth that had attracted the attention of the global economy in the nineteenth century now seemed like the faint images of a dream. Buffalo, sandalwood, fur seals, and several species of whales were all but gone. With the assistance of a federal agency called Animal Damage Control (ADC), livestock interests had pushed for a literal war on predators, targeting wolves, grizzlies, cougars, even coyotes and magpies with poison, bounties, and government hunters; big predators would be locally extirpated across much of the West within four decades of 1900. Salmon runs on the Pacific Coast, the objects of a new cannery industry based on immigrant (mostly Chinese) labor, were already so exploited that their dwindling numbers were alarming the industry by 1910. Even the West's iconic extractive industry, mining, by 1900 had turned to shocking environmentally destructive practices like stream dredging and was eying cyanide treatment for gold, and open-pit mining for copper. Between 1890 and 1907 the great petroleum discoveries in California, Texas, and Oklahoma were making those states some of the wealthiest in the country and by 1911 the West was producing 75 percent of the country's oil and gas. Even the uncomprehended grassland riches of the Great Plains, Intermountain West, and the Big Island of Hawai'i were already suffering from overgrazing by the 1900. And having mostly overcut forestlands in the Upper Midwest, the timber industry was commencing its work in the towering old-growth forests of the Pacific Northwest, and would soon be eying the forests of the Rockies. By 1905 Frederick Weyerhauser had made Washington, Oregon, and California the leading lumber states in the nation, and his subsidiaries (like Potlatch) were moving inland to Idaho and Montana.

To the environmentally acute observer of the early-twentieth-century West, to those like Sierra Club founder John Muir or Mabel Osgood Wright of the Audubon Society, the future of nature in the West thus looked fairly bleak. The natural world that native people had worshiped and that had been celebrated by Romantic Age explorers, writers, and artists – from Lewis and Clark and Captain Cook to Albert Bierstadt and Thomas Moran – seemed to teeter on a black hole of exploitation. With the perspective of distance, however, the environmental history of the twentieth century intrigues us because of the persistence of this natural world and the dogged-ness with which reformers pushed for protections, even for philosophical shifts in the way Americans thought about animals, plants, and landscapes. Despite the capitalist and utilitarian sentiments so deeply ingrained in American and western traditions, new developments like conservation, preservation, wildlife management, and even ecocentric ideas would come to play major roles in the twentieth century environmental history in the West. Indeed, by the end of the twentieth century, political life in the West would come to center around such issues.

Unquestionably, one of the reasons this happened was because turn-of-the-century history determined that the West would be unlike every other region in the United States in one extremely important respect. Despite the homestead laws and the nineteenth-century momentum behind privatization, which as late as 1860 seemed to envision every last piece of the West as destined for private ownership, not every last parcel ended up privatized. A peculiarly American idea called the National Park system, with origins in the nineteenth-century Romantic belief that America held sublime "wilderness" landscapes that were literally sacred, was already in place at the beginning of the century, and steadily folding into it some of the most dramatic (and, through no accident, economically limited) places in the West. And from late-nineteenth-century concerns about protecting watersheds in the arid West, the concept of the Forest Reserve system – federal retention of environmentally sensitive mountainous regions – emerged in 1891 and would influence ownership and land-use in every mountain range of the region.

In other words, in the West a system of federally managed commons was taking form in the early twentieth century. To be sure, this was a different kind of com-mons from the local mountain commons of the Pueblo or Shoshone Indians, or Kamehameha's royal lands in Hawai'i, even the land-grant *ejidos* of Hispanic settlers in New Mexico and California. The entire public, wherever they lived, not just the locals, owned these new federal commons. And a coterie of new federal agencies administered from Washington managed them. But amidst the rush to settle and pri-vatize the West in the nineteenth century, parks and forest reserves were proof that the commons idea had not died entirely. These public lands became the axle around which Western environmental history would spin.

Historians looking back on environmental history have seen three principal periods during the twentieth century when environmental concerns dominated national attention. For the American West, the most critical of these was the first. The Progressive Movement, long debated amongst political historians, who from different perspectives see it as a triumph of democracy, a triumph of conservatism, or in environmental historian Samuel Hays' view (1959), a triumph of efficiency, laid down the foundations for subsequent history in the West. In part this was because of the elaboration Progressivism gave to existing federal programs like the Forest Reserve and National Park systems. But there was also personality to consider. Progressivism's first great president, Republican Theodore Roosevelt, was at heart a westerner, at least symbolically. Like so many upper-class men from the East, as a young man he had gone west, hunting buffalo and grizzlies and buying a pair of ranches in North Dakota, where he attired himself in cowboy gear and tried to recapture the masculine life associated with the Old West, which he and all his contemporaries were convinced was vanishing before their eyes. Roosevelt and others of his generation and class were the ideal audience for historian Frederick Jackson Turner's Darwinian argument that a new habitat (the American wilderness, or "frontier") had shaped an existing type (the European) into something entirely new under the sun (the American). As a historian, ex-rancher and founding member of the Boone & Crockett Club, the new president believed he understood the importance of the West in American history, and he and his compatriots were determined to "save" the region so that its positive influences on America would not be lost to future generations.

That, it so happened, dovetailed with another of Progressivism's missions, which was to curb the excesses of nineteenth-century laissez-faire capitalism and the dangerous power of corporations by intruding the state (essentially the federal government) into economic life so as to protect the public from capitalism's excesses. This philosophical shift from nineteenth century thinking was of course the beginning of a steadily enlarged role for the federal government, trackable across much of twentieth-century American history. Roosevelt himself, looking back on the arc of the period from 1901–9, argued that the origins of this sea change lay in his policies towards the West:

> It was important, indeed, to know the facts so that we could take proper action toward saving the timber still left to the public. But of far more importance was the light that this history (and the history of other resources) throws on the basic attitude, tradition, and governmental beliefs of the American people. The whole standpoint of the people toward the proper aim of government, toward the relation of property to the government, were brought out first by this conservation work (Cutright, 1985: 217–18).

As Roosevelt related here, the first stimulus to scientific conservation came from nineteenth-century fears of forest degradation, brought on by increased consumption and the loss of scores of millions of acres of American woodland to agricultural conversion. Carl Schurz, a German-American Secretary of Interior familiar with the forestry practices of his ancestral country, had argued in the 1870s that America was "a spendthrift people recklessly wasting its heritage, a government careless of its future" (Nash, 1982; Turner, 1985: 306–7). But there was yet another reason to protect mountain forests. In his landmark book, *Man and Nature* (1864), George Perkins Marsh had used deforested mountains in Southern Europe and upland Asia as cautionary examples of the threats to civilization occasioned by environmental destruction to sensitive landscapes. Marsh provided the scientific underpinnings for a connection between mountain forests and streamflow later echoed by the American Forestry Association and the American Association for the Advancement of Science. How to protect that critical linkage? As Marsh had put it, "It is, perhaps, a misfortune to the American Union that the State Governments so generally disposed of their original domain to private citizens" (1864: 263). At a time when eight European nations had already reserved their mountains as public commons, this connection between highlands and streamflow became the rationale for America's move to set aside the ranges of the Rockies, the Sierra Nevada, and Cascades, and the mountains of Alaska and some of those in Hawai'i, as Forest Reserves.

When Roosevelt assumed office in 1901, he inherited a certain momentum – from government bureaus like the US Geological Survey, the Department of Forestry, the Biological Survey, even the General Land Office – favoring new ideas about resources and government. Borrowing the term "conservation" from the General Land Office, the Roosevelt administration made scientific study and government management and regulation the linchpins of a planned, rational Progressive world. Natural resources, these Progressives argued, could be used and conserved at the same time. The result, famously, would be "the greatest good for the greatest number over the longest period of time."

Republican Theodore Roosevelt's programs changed the country, and particularly the West. Under Forest Reserve legislation dating from 1891, Roosevelt's predecessors had already set aside 34 million acres of the mountainous West, and in the Forest Management Act of 1897 had implemented a use program for the reserves. Roosevelt's conservation program, however, went far beyond those steps. Acting on the advice of his German-educated Chief Forester, Gifford Pinchot, in 1905 Roosevelt transferred the existing reserves from Interior to the Department of Agriculture, renamed them National Forests, and under federal management opened them to "multiple use" (watershed and wildlife protection, stock grazing, logging, mining, and recreation) under a formula of permits and, for some uses, fees. And Roosevelt and Pinchot dramatically expanded the system, which by 1907 totaled 151 million acres and 159 national forests. More than any other act of the twentieth century, the National Forest program made the West a public lands region, and thus distinctive in the United States.

The Progressives did not stop here. One powerful stimulus of the age was a sense, shared particularly by men of the elite class in both America and Europe, that urban and industrial civilization in the new century threatened to thwart the masculine virtues to which the "Old West" had given free rein. Lacking Frederick Jackson Turner's "frontier," many wondered how American characteristics would be perpetuated in the new century. These sentiments would fuel a form of turn-of-the-century "primitivism" that was expressed in organizations like the Boy Scouts. For grown men of the elite classes there was the Boone & Crockett Club, which used its considerable clout to push for both state and federal legislation to manage populations of sport fishes and huntable wildlife. In hindsight, the new restrictions on market and "pot" hunting appear to have privileged urban-based sport hunting while regulating rural and ethnic hunters and fishers particularly (Warren, 1997). The shift in consciousness with respect to wildlife also translated into a federally sponsored system of National Wildlife Refuges, which for the American West rested symbolically on refuges set aside for bison. The market hunt during the nineteenth century had driven the numbers of this iconic Great Plains species from millions to fewer than 500 in both Canada and the US at the beginning of the twentieth. With President Roosevelt's backing, the American Bison Society and the New York Zoological Park acquired sufficient buffalo for three new national bison ranges in Oklahoma, Montana, and South Dakota, as well as an augmented herd in Yellowstone Park. In contrast to their plans for deer, elk, and antelope – whose numbers also were astonishingly low early in the century – Progressive-era wildlife restoration did not envision a place on the West's public lands for buffalo as a wild species, however (Isenberg, 1997).

Nor did the federal government's Biological Survey (forerunner of the Fish and Wildlife Service) or state wildlife managers envision a future for predators in the West. In the tradition of the Audubon Society's model bird law, which 28 states had passed by 1905, wildlife management made a distinction between "valuable" (translated: huntable) species and "varmints" that were a threat to "game" and livestock. Throughout the first three decades of the century, the federal Animal Damage Control units waged an unrelenting trapping, poisoning, and shooting war against predators (particularly grizzly bears, mountain lions, wolves, and coyotes) and "varmints," including even historic western species like prairie dogs and magpies. From 1921–4 alone, ADC estimated that it killed 395,359 predators. The result was a more civilized West, but also a biodiversity and ecological disaster that saw continental grizzly populations, once as high as 100,000, shrink (outside Alaska) to just two pockets in the Northern Rockies. Wolves were gone from the Yellowstone ecosystem by 1930, and Mexican wolves – the last wolves remaining in the American West – had been entirely erased from the Southwest by 1970. As for the predator–prey balance, sport hunting emerged as the management tool of choice to control deer and elk herds in a predator-less west.

Within this program and other Progressive projects for the West, forward-looking as they appeared at the time, lay seeds that would eventually threaten the western environment and arouse passionate opposition. To much fanfare in 1902, Progressives had passed the Newlands Reclamation Act creating the Bureau of Reclamation. Its set task – with early projects like Roosevelt Dam on Arizona's Salt River (which boomed Phoenix), Arrowrock Dam on the Snake (which created Idaho's potato boom), and the Imperial Dam on the Lower Colorado (fashioning California's Imperial Valley) – became remaking the arid West into a passable facsimile of the Eastern Seaboard. Essentially a massively funded continuation of John Wesley Powell's nineteenth-century Irrigation Survey, the Bureau of Reclamation under Arthur Powell Davis set about plotting dams, irrigation projects, water manipulation, and interstate water compacts on virtually every major river and tributary in the west, eventually carrying out seventy-five *thousand* dam projects. No federal agency better exemplified the Progressives' optimism about correcting nature's error in the West, and no agency was fated to collide with grass-roots environmentalists – in the form of John Muir's "preservationists," a loosely knit national collection of "short-haired women and long-haired men" who hoped to preserve western wild lands for their recreational and spiritual value – more quickly.

With the possible exception of Edward Abbey, no figure in a western environmental history resonates with the kind of charisma John Muir continues to project across the years. Muir stands for many things to many people, but he is probably best seen as transition figure linking the Romanticism of Emerson and Thoreau with the more science-based, biocentric environmental movement that flowered in the latter half of the twentieth century. As founder of the Sierra Club and self-professed advocate of renewal in "God's Wilds," he personified a new type of amateur environmentalist, who articulated an aesthetic and spiritual vision for the west. The Muir vision and the utilitarian Progressive one finally, famously, collided over the federal government's plans, in the wake of the San Francisco earthquake and fire of 1906, to create a municipal water supply for that city by damming the Hetch Hetchy Canyon, a white-granite marvel within Yosemite National Park. In the first great amateur environmental campaign of the century, Muir organized women's clubs, scientists, and a handful of writers against the dam, a fight that raged on for nearly six years between 1908 and 1914 (Fox, 1981; Merchant, 1984; Nash, 1982).

Muir's campaign on behalf of Hetch-Hetchy failed, but both man and canyon emerged as martyrs in the environmental history on the West. For one thing, out of the ashes of the struggle. Progressives fashioned one last great foundation in the federal environmental infrastructure. In 1916 Congress gave birth to the National Park Service (NPS) to administer and add to the existing national parks. The NPS also got jurisdiction over another category of lands called national monuments, created by presidential proclamation under the Antiquities Act of 1906, whose purpose had been protection of archaeological and geologic treasures on the western public lands. To the first NPS director, Stephen Mather, Congress turned over management of 16 national parks and 18 national monuments, virtually all of them in the West and, given the Hetch Hetchy experience, none of them (apparently) off limits to delisting by political winds at a moment's notice.

This did not deter Mather from growing the system dramatically, or from upgrading several national monuments (starting with the Grand Canyon) to full national park status. By the time Mather stepped down in 1932 he administered 22 parks and 36 monuments. Among the new additions were several stunning crown jewel western parks – Zion and Bryce Canyon in Utah, Kings Canyon in California, Haleakala and Volcanoes in Hawai'i, and McKinley in Alaska – along with a national monument (Dinosaur) that was soon to become the next great conservation battleground in the West. Ecological considerations and boundaries had played no role in the creation of these parks and monuments, however, and that was another problem that would surface later in the century. Still another was the NPS's overemphasis on monumental alpine or canyonated scenery as its sole criteria for park site evaluation. This left the low-elevation desert and plains West woefully underrepresented in the NPS system. A final problem was that by the 1930s the public lands had mostly been scoured for park sites. As had been the case with national parks in the East, many of the remaining potential park sites in the West after 1935 were at least partially on private lands. And the NPS had no acquisition budget for acquiring such properties, which (as ecology began to play a role in determining national park choices) made rounding out the system to make it more representative of western ecosystems increasingly difficult.

Meanwhile, by the 1930s much of the western economy had taken on a modern look. As resource apparatus for the rest of the country, the West's extractive industries produced great wealth – much of which went outside the region – and tremendous environmental devastation, which stayed at home. In states like Alaska and Montana, mining companies now extracted already dwindling precious metals mostly using the cyanide heap-leaching method, which was terrible in its impact on riparian areas. Companies like Phelps Dodge, Anaconda, and Kennecott pulled copper ore – a boon to electrifying the country – from mines in Arizona, Montana, and Utah using the new open-pit technique, setting yet another stage for future environmental disasters. And from pineapple and sugar plantations in Hawai'i to wheat on the Northern Plains and in the Palouse country, to potatoes in the Snake River Plain and fruit and vegetables in mild climates as far-flung as South Texas, the Willamette in Oregon, and California's Central Valley, western agriculture was becoming agribusiness, with powered equipment, capital investment, and ever-larger land holdings.

One western region where the spread of agriculture notoriously confronted a marginal natural world, with disastrous ecological and social results, was the Southern Great Plains, centering upon the region where the borders of Texas, Oklahoma, Kansas, Colorado, and New Mexico join. With both government and private encouragement (via the Enlarged Homestead Act of 1909 and the sale of gigantic private ranches like the XIT in the Texas Panhandle), homesteader-farmers flocked to this region in the 1920s in the West's last significant land-rush of the twentieth century. Although homesteader efforts to settle a similar semiarid landscape in Montana and the Dakotas were already unraveling, tens of thousands of farming families took up farms on the Southern High Plains, breaking out tough buffalo and grama grasses that had functioned as part of the Great Buffalo Belt since the Pleistocene. With few regional rivers from which to irrigate, this was a dry farming boom, its wheat and cotton expected to survive (as the grasslands had) on whatever moisture fell from the skies.

Unfortunately, the agricultural transformation of this delicate shortgrass ecology coincided with the onset of one of the multiyear droughts that visited the Southern Plains on a 20-to-30-year cycle. The result was infamous in the history of the West, the country, and the world: the Dust Bowl, often cited as one of the three most serious human-caused environmental collapses in modern world history. The onset of subnormal rainfall on the Southern High Plains began in 1933 and lasted until 1940, and the result was catastrophic. High winds and blowing dust are endemic to this region even in the best of years, but in the drought of the 1930s and with its grass cover removed and topsoil plowed and exposed, the ecoregion literally fell apart. By 1938 10 million acres had lost at least five inches of topsoil, as the plains country collapsed. One dust storm in May 1934 put 350 million tons of soil aloft; Texas dust settled on ships 300 miles into the Atlantic. Social dislocation was enormous: drifts derailed trains; people, wildlife, and livestock died of dust pneumonia. Farm losses by 1935 reached $25 million a day. Nearly half-a-million "exodusters" (including more than 18 percent of Oklahoma's population) had abandoned the plains by 1940, tens of thousands of the refugees fleeing to the West Coast in a western folk migration made famous by songwriter Woody Guthrie, novelists John Steinbeck and Erskine Caldwell, and photographer Dorothea Lange.

The Dust Bowl's causes may have been misunderstood by the farmers themselves, who tended to blame the drought, but federal officials in Franklin Roosevelt's New Deal quickly apprehended that encouraging homesteaders onto the marginal western lands of the remaining public domain was a mistake. In 1934, after 150 years of land privatization policies, the Taylor Grazing Act ended homesteading in the West. It created an agency initially called the Grazing Service (renamed the Bureau of Land Management [BLM] in 1960) to manage the 142 million acres of public domain remaining. New Dealers even moved to reacquire more than 11 million homesteaded acres across the Great Plains, fashioning from them another subset of western public lands eventually called National Grasslands, administered by the Forest Service. To re-habilitate the acreage remaining in private hands, the New Deal created the Soil Conservation Service, directed by Hugh Bennet, whose lessons in scientific agronomy – coupled with generous New Deal agricultural subsidy programs and the famous "Shelterbelt" tree-planning program – renewed the country's commitment to making the Great Plains function as an agricultural region. This federal bailout pumped $43 million into the Southern Plains between 1935 and 1942. Even so, Southern Plains agriculture might have collapsed under the weight of an even more severe dry pulse in the 1950s had backyard mechanics not figured out a decade earlier how to utilize V-8 automobile engines to tap into the Ogallala aquifer. With an ocean of freshwater beneath it, the Southern High Plains embarked on four decades of agricultural success undreamed for what had once been the "Great American Desert," only to confront a new edge-of-the-world environmental problem as the century drew to an end: depletion of the aquifer, its only water source (Worster, 1979; Green, 1973; Bowden, 1977; Flores, 1990).

Environmental history commonly considers the New Deal to follow the Romantic and Progressive periods as a third major era of environmental concerns in American history. For the West, specifically, however, the New Deal's environmental legacies were significant yet problematic at the same time. Its agricultural programs and dam-building projects propped up western agricultural economies while simultaneously sacrificing prairie and riverine landscapes across the West. The Bureau of Reclamation grew from 2,000 to 20,000 employees during the New Deal, finished off Hoover Dam/Lake Mead on the Colorado in 1936, and launched Grand Coulee, Bonneville, and the Missouri River dams in the late 1930s. In 1940 the bureau had 81 western dams in its planning docket. Meanwhile, the Civilian Conservation Corps, which between 1935 and 1942 employed three million workers doing at least some ecological restoration, introduced tens of thousands of young men to a western world they fell in love with at once. Their experiences – and those of servicemen stationed in places like San Diego, Anchorage, and Honolulu during World War II – served to boom western populations like never before once the war was over. Between 1940 and 1950 another great wave of "homesteaders" settled on the West, this time not on its rural landscapes but in cities like Los Angeles, San Francisco, Seattle, Portland, Salt Lake, Dallas/Ft Worth, and Denver. The West grew its population by eight million in that decade alone. What drew these "first amenity migrants" was not just the defense spending the federal government lavished on the region, but access to the public lands that made the West unique among American places.

This population shift and its recreation/leisure interests helped push the West to the forefront of a complex of issues that launched modern environmentalism in the United States. While many of the issues of the "Age of Ecology" emerged from the postwar economic boom's effect on urban eastern settings, it was western issues – dam building, threats to (and/or management of) the public lands, the creation of a wilderness system, and eventually endangered species recovery questions – that became the most galvanizing hot-button environmental issues in the country.

The event that launched the modern environmental movement, for instance, was a classic western battle, with more than a few echoes of Hetch Hetchy. It emerged – paradoxically – from zealous prosecution of a set piece Progressive conservation mission: the reclamation of arid western landscapes through dam building. But this time the dams were not just slated for the West's most storied rivers, but for some of its most stupendous canyon landscapes, which happened already to be protected by park or monument status. The galvanizing issue was the division of precious Colorado River water between the states of Wyoming, Utah, Colorado, New Mexico, Arizona, Nevada, and California via the Bureau of Reclamation's billion-dollar Colorado River Storage Project, an outgrowth of the Colorado River Compact of 1922. Among the planned 10 major dams were several that inflamed the environmental community to launch a protracted battle that lasted 15 years, from 1950 to 1965. At issue in the beginning was a nonchalant Bureau decision to build two dams – Split Mountain and Echo Park – that would have backed reservoir waters into Dinosaur National Monument's Yampa River Canyon. By the time the battle subsided, environmentalists had managed to strike those dams from the project and save Dinosaur, but had inadvertently condemned underappreciated Glen Canyon in southern Utah to a high dam that buried a national treasure – and eventually a cause célèbre for western environmentalists – beneath the waters of a reservoir called Lake Powell. And they had left open a door for the Bureau to propose Marble Canyon and Bridge Canyon dams, which would have flooded portions of the Grand Canyon itself until Secretary of Interior Stuart Udall famously floated the Grand Canyon and turned thumbs-down on the dams.

In many ways the struggle over western dams that would have compromised the national parks/monuments system (others, including an Army Corps of Engineers' proposal for a dam that would have flooded a piece of Glacier National Park, waited in the wings) was a coming of age for the West. But the fight was also a portent of new divisions between its rural and urban residents. While rural Westerners at midcentury had mostly attracted attention for the so-called "Sagebrush Rebellion," the first attempt (of many to come) to transfer title of the public lands from federal to state or private interests, many urban Westerners found common cause with environmentalists from across the country in opposing dams in park system holdings. The battles simultaneously gave environmentalism, which, frankly, up to this point had mostly attracted upper-middle-class whites of elite backgrounds, a new credibility and tens of thousands of new converts. The dam controversies also pushed environmentalists like David Brower and the Sierra Club and Howard Zahniser and the Wilderness Society to discover a new country, the canyons and deserts of the West. And they gave voice to a new generation of western Thoreaus, the amateur environmentalist writers Bernard DeVoto, Wallace Stegner, and – for a different generation – Edward Abbey.

Environmentalism, in the form of the "Age of Ecology," aided not inconsiderably by the counterculture's Age of Aquarius, emerged as one of the most potent new social and political movements to survive the 1960s and take root as an essential part of American life thereafter. In some ways, as historian Samuel Hays argues, environmentalism is a natural consequence of maturation in a modern society that is successful in providing its citizens the basic necessities of life. In the post-World War II United States, environmental thinking was a natural product of ordinary Americans' new-found leisure, and of their awakening to the consequences of industrial capitalism, population growth, and urban sprawl. By 1970 many of those consequences – health-threatening air and water, looming species extinctions, even an oil spill off the coast of trendy Santa Barbara – were becoming part of everyday life and everyday news headlines. And again, largely because of the existence of its public lands with their rich store of resources and their charismatic fauna – for which all Americans felt some ownership and responsibility – the West seemed to be the flashpoint for one defining late-century environmental issue after another.

It was *wilderness* – the legislative preservation of it, simply the very idea of it – that became the most critical western environmental issue in the second half of the century. Wilderness became synonymous with the West in part because of demographics: while the West was the fastest growing region of the country from midcentury on, many parts of the West seemed relatively uninhabited by eastern standards. And, of course, the only wilderness areas that federal or state governments *could* set aside were out of the public lands. Finally, there was western history itself. The shaping influences of the wild continent on America's character, via Frederick Jackson Turner's "frontier thesis," lingered on well into the second half of the century. In a very real sense the 1964 Wilderness Act, establishing a nine million acre beginning of the Wilderness Preservation System, was Turner's character-shaping frontier perpetuated. This is what Aldo Leopold, father of the first Primitive Areas within the National Forests, had envisioned for the American wilderness system before his death in 1949 (Leopold, 1991).

The Wilderness Act was a linchpin of the "Environmental New Deal," a hugely significant body of environmental legislation that began for the West with the Multiple-Use Act in 1960 (which codified all Pinchot's "uses" for the public lands on an equal footing) and concluded with the landmark Alaska Lands Bill of 1980. While the West benefited along with the rest of the country from the clean air and clean water initiatives that defined the era, along with the creation of the National Environmental Policy Act (which created the Environmental Protection Agency, as well as mandating environmental impact studies for all projects involving federal funds) some key legislation had an especially critical impact on the region. The Land and Water Conservation Fund, established in 1964 and at last giving the National Park Service an acquisitions budget for the creation of new parks, was one. Another was the 1968 Wild and Scenic Rivers Act, which protected 26 rivers in Alaska alone. The 1973 Endangered Species Act (ESA), establishing the basis not just for protecting threatened and endangered species (and their habitats) but their *restoration*, was one more manifestation of Aldo Leopold's influence. His "Land Ethic," extending the philosophy of the "greatest good for the greatest number" to nonhumans, became a hallmark of biocentric policy like the ESA. Posthumously, Leopold – the one-time wolf hunter – had managed to think endangered wolves, grizzlies, eagles, ferrets, and swift foxes back into the West.

In many ways, the Alaska National Interest Lands Conservation Act (ANILCA) of 1980 was the crowning achievement of the period for the West. Alaska's environmental history since its statehood had featured a litany of mind-boggling proposals, from Rampart Dam that would have created the largest reservoir in the world out of the Yukon River (scrapped in 1967), to a bizarre proposal to use nuclear devices to create a deep-water port, along with at least one world-class environmental disaster, the oil spill resulting from the *Exxon Valdez* sinking in Prince William Sound in 1989. The passage of ANILCA first required that Alaskan natives' own lands claims be settled, which happened in 1971. Designating 56.7 million acres as wilderness and another 48 million as national monuments, national wildlife refuges, and national preserves, the ANILCA in one stroke trebled the size of the wilderness system and doubled NPS acreage. But it also guaranteed both natives and white Alaskans subsistence hunting and fishing rights on most categories of federal lands. To those looking for a perpetuation of the frontier into the twenty-first century, the Alaska Lands Bill seemed the ultimate package (Nash, 1982: 296–307; Worster, 1992: 154–224).

Wilderness elsewhere in the West remained a hot-button issue for the rest of the century, particularly after the Sierra Club, supported by other environmental groups, opposed the guidelines of two RARE (roadless area review evaluation) federal programs for adding to the wilderness system. Court cases in 1972 (*Sierra Club v. Butz*) and 1982 (*California v. Block*) had the net effect of throwing wilderness designation into state legislatures. Meanwhile the Federal Lands Policy Management Act of 1976 had extended multiple use, including wilderness review, to millions of acres of BLM lands in the West, magnifying the issue. While some western states (like Colorado) moved expeditiously to determine which federal lands within their boundaries should be included in the wilderness system, others – notably Utah and Montana – reached century's end still unable to agree on wilderness bills for their roadless lands.

The principal reason places like the Colorado Plateau and the Northern Rockies were unable to resolve many critical issues was because these western regions, and others, had become nationally significant to environmentalism. And in the last two decades of the twentieth century, environmentalism had become a sharply divisive and politicized issue. From the time of Teddy Roosevelt through the 1970s, environmentalism had largely been nonpartisan. But the emergence of the New Right within the Republican Party, with its assumptions that much environmentalism was a threat to free enterprise and represented middle-class gains detrimental to both business elites and blue-collar workers, launched an new era that made the West into a political battleground. To Ronald Reagan's Secretary of the Interior, James Watt, western public lands were socialized lands that he hoped to turn over to private or state interests. Environmentalism, meanwhile, took its own radical turn when Dave Foreman and a handful of other "Rednecks for Wilderness" formed Earth First! to do battle with the new corporate/government alliance. Neither the New Right or Earth First! was long-lived, but their legacy – in the form of grass-roots "enviros" and lingering Wise-Use and County Sovereignty groups – was a western populace giving full vent to its democratic right to disagree. And what it seemed to disagree about most was environmentalism's role in the region. Democratic decisions, like Bill Clinton's moves to uphold ESA protection of the spotted owl and thus slow logging of old-growth forests in the Pacific Northwest, or his creation of a slew of new national monuments in the West, struck rural and working-class westerners as outrageous blows at economic opportunity. And Republican moves, such as George W. Bush's hopes to drill for oil in Alaska's Arctic National Wildlife Refuge, galvanized urban and middle-class environmentalists to defend the western public lands legacy.

At century's close, two issues more than any others seemed to be shaping the West as its environmental history unspooled into the future. The most visible centered around the hopes many environmentalists and native people had of using the ESA's species recovery mandates to effect a restoration of the West. Restoration projects dominated the news in the West at the turn of the millennium: returning wolves to the Northern Rockies and Desert Southwest, restoring viable populations of grizzlies in the Bitterroot Mountains, returning black-footed ferrets, swift foxes, and (with the promotion of a 1990s group called the Inter-Tribal Bison Cooperative) buffalo to the Great Plains, even studies on dismantling many of the dams – once central to Progressive and New Deal conservation – that have so altered western rivers, and driven spawning salmon to the point of disappearing. Environmentalist and Indian initiatives like these, along with new conservation-biology-driven ecosystem management (like the Greater Yellowstone Ecosystem) and transnational hopes for new "cores-and-corridors" (the Yukon-to-Yellowstone wildlife migration plan) to help the charismatic big animals make a comeback, seem to show that even a century after the "Old West" ended, the imagery of its nineteenth century condition has never ceased to inspire us. The 1996 return of wolves to Yellowstone Park, after an absence of almost three-quarters of a century, was the first great success of this new restoration theme (Fischer, 1995). Even returning fires as a natural process to western forests was part of the restoration vision (Flores, 2001; Keiter, et al., 1991).

The second end-of-century issue, however, may prove a more formidable opponent than any legislator or Wise-User who ever lived. In the aftermath of the tremendous environmental losses of the nineteenth and twentieth centuries, the West was silently invaded. As western societies have argued about dams and wilderness, exotic species of all kinds – plants and animals both, from salt-cedars to mongooses, spotted knapweed to cheatgrass – have quietly been devouring much of the western landscape. While every western state and ecoregion has been affected by this phenomenon, states like California (with more than half its species now nonnatives) and Hawai'i have experienced a phenomenal transformation. Because of the effects of island biogeography, Hawai'i is a special case, yet its transformation by invading exotics lays out a worrisome twenty-first century path for much of the rest of the West. The process began in Hawai'i with the initial human colonization 15 centuries ago, but accelerated remarkably over the past 200 years. The result now is not just ecologies entirely remade with accidental (and many deliberate) species from India, China, Europe, Africa, but massive extinctions as well. All of Hawai'i's 20 species of flightless birds have become extinct, as well as half the flying ones. One-sixth of the islands' native plants are gone and almost a third (700 altogether) of the remaining ones are threatened. An ecotourist hoping to see some semblance of the original Polynesian world of the islands now finds virtually no native species below 1,000 feet elevation, the rich surrounding bird life a smorgasbord of global exotics. This assault, awaiting the rest of the West with gleaming teeth, threatens obliteration of the grand, longue-durée results of evolution and diversity across the region.

Anyone with a sense of those forces, and of the West's environmental history, dreads those consequences. Because if western environmental history instructs us in anything, it is that the vast assemblage of ecoregions we call "the West," which gleams so brightly in the sunshine of the American past, is not so difficult to make over into some new image in our imaginations. The hope is that we will do justice to all these remarkable places, and create sensitive societies to match the astonishing scenery.

REFERENCES

Bowden, Charles: *Killing the Hidden Waters* (Austin: University of Texas Press, 1977).

Cutright, Paul Russell: *Theodore Roosevelt: The Making of a Conservationist* (Urbana and Chicago: University of Illinois Press, 1985).

Davis, Gavan: *Shoal of Time: A History of the Hawaiian Islands* (Honolulu: University of Hawaii Press, 1968).

Dunlap, Thomas: *Saving America's Wildlife* (Princeton: Princeton University Press, 1982).

Farmer, Jared: *Glen Canyon Dammed: Inventing Lake Powell and the Canyon Country* (Tucson: University of Arizona Press, 1999).

Fischer, Hank: *Wolf Wars: The Remarkable Inside Story of the Restoration of Wolves to Yellowstone* (Helena: Falcon Press, 1995).

Flores, Dan: *Caprock Canyonlands: Journeys into the Heart of the Southern Plains* (Austin: University of Texas Press, 1990).

Flores, Dan: *Horizontal Yellow: Nature and History in the Near Southwest* (Albuquerque: University of New Mexico Press, 1999).

Flores, Dan: *The Natural West: Environmental History in the Great Plains and Rocky Mountains* (Norman: University of Oklahoma Press, 2001).

Flores, Dan: "The West that Was and the West that Can Be: Western Restoration and the 21st Century." In Dan Flores *The Natural West: Environmental History in the Great Plains and Rocky Mountains* (Norman: University of Oklahoma Press, 2001).

Fox, Stephen: *John Muir and His Legacy: The American Conservation Movement* (Boston: Little, Brown and Co., 1981).

Green, Donald: *Land of the Underground Rain: Irrigation on the Texas High Plains, 1910–1970* (Austin: University of Texas Press, 1973).

Harvey, Mark: *A Symbol of Wilderness: Echo Park and the American Conservation Movement* (Albuquerque: University of New Mexico Press, 1994).

Hays, Samuel P.: *Conservation and the Gospel of Efficiency: The Progressive Conservation Movement, 1890–1920* (Cambridge, MA: Harvard University Press, 1959).

Hays, Samuel P.: *Beauty, Health, and Permanence: Environmental Politics in the U.S., 1955–1985* (New York: Cambridge University Press, 1987).

Ise, John: *Our National Park Policy: A Critical History* (Baltimore: John Hopkins University Press, 1961).

Isenberg, Drew: "The Returns of the Bison: Profit, Nostalgia, and Preservation." *Environmental History* 2 (April 1997), 179–96.

Keiter, Robert and Mark S. Boyce (eds.): *The Greater Yellowstone Ecosystem: Redefining America's Wilderness Heritage* (New Haven: Yale University Press, 1991).

Leopold, Aldo: "Wilderness as a Form of Land Use." In Susan Flader and J. Baird Callicott (eds.) *The River of the Mother of God and Other Essays* (Madison: University of Wisconsin Press, 1991).

McEvoy, Arthur. *The Fisherman's Problem: Ecology and Law in the California Fisheries, 1850–1980* (New York: Cambridge University Press, 1986).

McNeil, J. R.: *Something New Under the Sun: An Environmental History for the Twentieth-Century World* (New York: W. W. Norton, 2000).

Malone, William and Richard Etulain: *The American West: A Twentieth-Century History* (Albuquerque: University of New Mexico Press, 1989).

Marsh, George Perkins: *The Earth as Modified by Human Action: A New Edition of Man and Nature* ([1864], reprinted New York: Arno Press and the New York Times, 1970).

Merchant, Carolyn: "Women of the Progressive Conservation Movement, 1900–1916," *Environmental Review* 8 (Spring 1984), 57–86.

Nash, Roderick: *Wilderness and the American Mind*, 3rd edn. (New Haven: Yale University Press, 1982).

Powell, Peter: *Sweet Medicine*, 2 vols. (Norman: University of Oklahoma Press, 1969).

Righter, Robert: "National Monuments to National Parks: The Use of the Antiquities Act of 1906." *Western Historical Quarterly* 13 (August 1989), 281–301.

Rothman, Hal: *Preserving Different Pasts: The American National Monuments* (Urbana: University of Illinois Press, 1989).

Rothman, Hal: *The Greening of America? Environmentalism in the United States Since 1945* (New York: Harcourt Brace, 1997).

Runte, Alfred: *National Parks: The American Experience*, 2nd edn. (Lincoln: University of Nebraska Press, 1987).

Shelford, Victor: "Preservation of Natural Biotic Communities." *Ecology* 14 (1933), 240–5.

Turner, Frederick Jackson: *Rediscovering America: John Muir in His Time and Ours* (San Francisco: Sierra Club Books, 1985).

Warren, Louis: *The Hunter's Game* (New Haven: Yale University Press, 1997).

Wilkinson, Charles: *Crossing the Next Meridian: Land, Water, and the Future of the West* (Washington, DC: Island Press, 1992).

Wilkinson, Charles: *Eagle Bird: Mapping a New West* (New York: Pantheon, 1992).

Williams, Ted: "Killer Weeds." *Audubon* 99 (March–April 1997), 22–8.

Woodcock, Deborah: "Of Posterosional Landscapes, Arrivals, and Extinctions: A Natural History of O'ahu." in D. W. Woodcock (ed.) *Hawai'i: New Geographies* (Honolulu: University of Hawai'i, 1999).

Worster, Donald: *Dust Bowl: The Southern Plains in the 1930s* (New York: Oxford University Press, 1979).

Worster, Donald: "Alaska: The Underworld Erupts." In Donald Worster (ed.) *Under Western Skies: Nature and History in the American West* (New York: Oxford University Press, 1992).

CHAPTER FIFTEEN

Where to Draw the Line?
The Pacific, Place, and the US West

CHRIS FRIDAY

With a few notable exceptions, most historians' conceptions of the US West come to a screeching halt on the western shore of the continent. For those scholars, that body of saltwater marks the end of US "expansion" into contiguous territories and, as further expansion would have to be labeled colonialism and imperialism, they balk at extending that reach. American involvement in the Pacific following the 1898 Spanish–American War was an aberration, a benign uplift experiment, and above all a separate period from the 1890s "closing" of the frontier. These scholars conceive of the Pacific as a vast, cultureless *space* sparsely dotted with islands between the western shore of the United States and the Far East and Latin America. They thus constitute the Pacific as a *very* thick frontier line distinguishing the US, and more broadly European American continental expansion, from Asia. Whether they openly and consciously espouse this particular vision or not, these scholars ultimately fall into the trap of denying and obscuring the colonial and imperialist attempts at conquest that were at the very heart of the creation of the US West. This is perhaps easier to pinpoint if one looks at the inverse proposition: That American colonialist and imperialist expansion did not stop at the water's edge, but instead knit the western portion of the continent into a broader global fabric of which a significant portion overlay the Pacific.

This was not simply a sequential development of an ever-advancing westward march of the "frontier line" as Frederick Jackson Turner proposed or even of empire. Instead, it was a roughly simultaneous development involving the continent and the ocean. One conquest could not proceed without the other. Both were part of a capitalist world system, which involved nationalist triumphs over transportation and communication along with varying degrees of the subjugation and integration of Native peoples. In fact, the two only became different *places* when the United States increasingly gained political and economic control of one section – the western portion of the continent – and never fully controlled the other – the Pacific.

While other essays in this volume address the continent, it remains worthwhile to recall that it took many years for American claims to the West to materialize. In fact, as Richard Maxwell Brown suggests, only a "war of incorporation" could secure the territory (1994). Casting this "incorporation" broadly, it is possible to see the military campaigns against American Indians and the legal efforts to wrest property from

Mexican Americans as simultaneous and similar "wars." Yet full extinguishment of land title took another half century. Not until the 1920s had American Indians and Mexican Americans been fully dispossessed of their lands and directed into the lower tier of the wage labor market in the West, which was itself part of a capitalist hinterland. How these groups responded to those long struggles, their triumphs and defeats, is a complicated story well beyond the pale of this present essay. What remains clear, however, is that by the 1920s, as Thomas Biolsi suggests, the "technologies of control" were in place and constructions of race and class were key components in the state of dependency and underdevelopment in which American Indians and Mexican Americans found themselves (1992).

American attempts to conquer the Pacific were even more complex and, ultimately, less successful. Contests with Asian and Pacific Island peoples partially explain why. But American division over how to approach the Pacific and its peoples were also significant factors. The historic shifts in these conflicts and perspectives suggest how interconnected the "West" and "Pacific" were and why, perhaps, we as scholars have such difficulty seeing the relationships. A review of how scholars have characterized the relationship of the West and the Pacific followed by some possible ways to re-integrate and envision the relationships may well spark anew a very old debate, not only about the role of the Pacific, but about the nature of the frontier in American and world history.

Before delving into the historiography, however, it is important to distinguish place from space. Space, as cultural geographer Yi-fu Tuan notes, is an open, unclaimed nothingness (1977). Like the proverbial tree falling in the forest with nobody to hear it, space has no cultural expectations projected onto it. Place, by contrast, is some-thing in which people invest cultural meaning albeit potentially ambiguous and contradictory. As Katherine Morrissey so astutely argues, definition of place seldom emerges out of unquestioned consensus. In such a hegemonic order there would be no need to define it, for all would accept the fundamental assumptions about its char-acter. Instead, these "mental territories" are a result of conflicting cultural ideas and social relations about who can claim and define a place. The Pacific is a prime example of such a *place*. Examining how select scholars have characterized it allows not only for a joint discussion of the West and the Pacific, but also for a new lens through which to view the "West."

History and Historiography

The mere presence of the Pacific has posed a significant set of questions for histo-rians and historical observers alike. Both have tended to perceive the ocean and the North American West as either distinctly related or distinctly disconnected. Among the early American observers to the Pacific Coast, Richard Henry Dana, Jr., clearly experienced a California woven into Spanish imperial influences and American eco-nomic activities during the 1830s. He aptly noted that the Pacific Islanders with whom he spent much time on the shores of California were integral as laborers to the success of whaling and the hide and tallow trade as they were to mercantile and missionary ventures (1964: 137–42).

Less than a decade later, Lieutenant Charles Wilkes envisioned an American role in the Pacific and the North American West. On his 1841 expedition, Wilkes vested potential American prominence in the great harbors of San Francisco Bay and the Puget Sound. Their potential trading partners included "the whole of Polynesia, as well as the countries of South America on the one side and China, New Holland [Australia], and New Zealand on the other. Among the latter, before many years, may be included Japan." And, he reflected, "[s]uch various climates will furnish the materials for a beneficial interchange of products and an intercourse that in time must become immense" (Schafer, 1922: 284).

Mark Twain, as much as any contemporary author, treated the Pacific and the American West as the same place. In *Roughing It*, his classic account of his 1860s tours through the American West, Twain portrayed the Pacific and most of the American West between the oases of settlement as a large wasteland of either desert or "watery solitude" (1980: 339). One could easily substitute Twain's descriptions of vast stretches of the Pacific for the flat lands of Montana or the landscape of the Great Basin. In both places rising mountains – islands or not – were replete with splendiferous sunsets. Scattered settlements abounded with annoying immigrants alongside exotic and sometimes noble savages. Twain conceived of the territory as a larger whole in spite of apparent differences.

It is difficult to speculate based on these few exceptional authors, but their works do indicate at least one potent strain of thought in American society that bound the Pacific and the West into a larger whole sharing Native inhabitants, vast resources, capitalist ventures, and missionary activities. Migrants to the area lived in far-flung population clusters, whether these were the forts and small towns of the West, or the port towns of the Pacific. So long as continental expansion accompanied American expansion, piecemeal though it may have been, into the Pacific, the question of imperialism and colonialism never registered in ways that would fully separate this informal American Empire into two pieces.

While Frederick Jackson Turner's geographic determinism and particular vision of American society never compelled him, at least in his now famous "frontier thesis," to consider the Pacific as part of the American West, his contemporary and popular historian rival Hubert Howe Bancroft did not shy away from it. In 1899, only a year after the United States acquired Hawaii, Guam, and the Philippines in the Spanish–American War, Bancroft published *The New Pacific* followed by a revised edition in 1913. In the preface to the latter, Bancroft opined, "The occupation of the Pacific by the world's foremost civilization will prove the most absorbing problem of the coming centuries. . . . [T]he untouched wealth of the Pacific is vastly superior," he noted, to that of the Mediterranean or Atlantic world, or even the North American continent. It was entirely "natural and inevitable" for Americans as a "race" to bring to the Pacific "a culture and development such as the world has never imagined." It would otherwise take "many centuries" for the area that was "for the most part lightly held by inferior peoples" to develop. The Pacific "invites the presence of the strong and dominant. The great ocean has waited long for fit occupancy and ownership," and Americans were ideally suited to the task (1913: vii–viii).

Not only would such an arrangement be good for the Pacific, Bancroft continued, it would also be good for Americans. "Here is room to spread out," he waxed poetic, "with ocean air and frontage enough for all, and with endless facilities for many small cities instead of a few large ones." Clearly the rise of urban centers and industrial class relations and mass immigration from "less desirable" nations troubled Bancroft.

The Pacific offered a solution for the "American mechanic" and merchant who stood to gain from American expansion into the Pacific. Because half the world's population fronted that body of water, he believed it a ripe source of raw materials and markets for finished goods. This would be "an industrial conquest such as never seen before" (ibid.: 9–10).

Bancroft was explicit about the relationship of the Pacific to the West. "We have no longer a virgin continent to develop," he explained, "pioneer work in the United States is done, and now we must take a plunge into the sea. . . . The Pacific, its shores and islands, must now take the place of the great west, its plains and mountains, as an outlet for pent-up industry" (ibid.: 13). According to Bancroft, however, Americans were reluctant imperialists. "It is not so much a question as to the will of the people as of the destiny of the people whether or not the United States, in the Westward march of progress, will step forth into the sea. . . . Surely it was a mistake on the part of the United States to permit expansion to present dimensions if we are not prepared to go forward in the path of progress and perform our duty as one of the dominating influences in the world." The Spanish–American War he justified as driving medieval tyranny from the Americas and the Pacific. If the United States was to become a "world power" it must "accept the labor and responsibilities thence arising. Thus the old society passes away; behold a new America appears, and her face is toward the Pacific" (ibid.: 12–14).

Even Bancroft noted, however grudgingly, that the Pacific held challengers. While he belittled the "tropical islander" as even less a threat to American dominance than "the American aboriginal" (whom he and many other Americans assumed to be a "vanishing race" by the turn of the century), both China and Japan posed problems. Japan was already an economic force and threat, particularly in its rivalry to American merchant ships and seamen. But above all others, he feared China, which he believed was waking from a long sleep and whose citizenry threatened to "swarm upon the sea like bees in a field of flowers" (ibid.: 3, 9–10).

Bancroft looked back to William Seward, who in 1852 argued that the Pacific would "become the chief theatre of events in the world's great hereafter." While he saw this early thought as prescient, he implied that Americans were not quite ready to take on the full responsibility of conquering the Pacific. For him, this was a sequential development. First the western reach of the continent, then the Pacific. In taking this stance, Bancroft built on ideas so well formulated by Turner – the sequential development of the West – and those increasingly articulated by American intellectuals and policy makers during the 1890s. With the frontier closed, they believed American democracy was potentially threatened. Only through further expansion could it possibly be maintained. This "psychic crisis" helped to justify continued policies of expansion.

Bancroft was not alone in such racialist and nationalist fervor about the US role in the Pacific. In 1915, a year after the opening of the Panama Canal, San Francisco hosted the Panama International Exposition to boost San Francisco as a world-class port city. Its organizers arranged a special meeting of the American Historical Association – the Panama-Pacific Historical Congress – in the city to mark the celebration. Although more muted than Bancroft, Association President H. Morse Stephens portrayed the history of the Pacific in four stages, each of which revolved around some aspect of European or American influences. As a *place*, he argued, the Pacific had no history before Europeans. "It was," extolled Stephens to the Panama-Pacific Historical Congress, "reserved for European peoples to traverse those wastes of water and to establish regular communities" (Stephens and Bolton, 1917: 25). First Spanish and then Dutch and British forces sought control of the Pacific. For him, European conflict ended with the completion of North American territorial expansion in the 1840s, thus beginning a third stage of American dominance for the remainder of the century. Like Bancroft, Stephens looked to the rise of Japan and the "regeneration" of China along with the growth of Latin American Nation states to produce potential new rivals to American dominance at the beginning of the twentieth century. For the moment, he argued, the Pacific was primarily "American" and secondarily "Asiatic," but he also suggested that the completion of the Panama Canal promised to end "the old isolation of . . . the Pacific" and to reintroduce European nations into the competition to control it (ibid.: 17).

Other luminaries at the meeting, such as former Secretary of State William Jennings Bryan, Stanford University President David Starr Jordan, US Navy League officer James B. Bullit, and renowned historian of the Americas Herbert Eugene Bolton were also in attendance. While they concurred with at least portions of Stephens' remarks, they probably remained skeptical about the likelihood of a European resurgence. Other lesser figures, however, had strikingly different visions to offer. Rudolf J. Taussig's sketch of the Panama Canal revealed a long and rather sordid history of US involvement in Latin America (1917). From the 1840s, various US governmental, mercantile, and industrial interventions, even if inconsistent, preceded the wresting of the "Republic of Panama" from Columbia in order to build the canal. While Taussig hoped to use the history of American involvement to justify American actions, for readers in this day and age his efforts indicate a long-term American imperialist presence along the Pacific Coast.

Oregon delegate Joseph Schafer was a prominent American and regional historian, who had trained at Wisconsin and then became Head of the History Department at the University of Oregon. Schafer tied the otherwise isolated Oregon's success and development directly to the Pacific. In Bancroftian terms, he explained that the Pacific started as a "highway of commerce of all sorts based on furs" and that Oregon and its promoters saw the state as "the future home of the power that is to rule the Pacific . . . for the Anglo-Norman race." The Pacific would "furnish the materials" for a vast capitalist engine and Oregon would become the manufacturing, transportation, and communication nexus for this new empire that linked the North American continent and the Pacific. Citing Wilkes' 1841 expedition, Schafer argued that this vision was not new to the twentieth century but had existed since the beginning of American exploration and settlement (1917). Schafer oversold Oregon at the expense of California and Washington. Yet his portrayal of the state and its residents as aspirant capitalists ran athwart a strong effort on the part of the Oregon Pioneer Association and later the Oregon Historical Society to cast Oregon history as solely that of hardy, yeoman (subsistence) pioneers. Only at the end of the twentieth century would historian William G. Robbins go back to embrace that vision, albeit from the opposite side of the coin with capitalism not as Schafer's great developer but as a great engine pulverizing the landscape as well as its peoples (1997).

As intriguing as those voices were, the visions of J. MacMillan Brown of New Zealand (1917) and Naojiro Murakami of Japan (1917) offer glimpses into other hopeful imperialists in the Pacific. Brown embraced the notion that the Pacific had recently surpassed the Mediterranean and Atlantic worlds. This new prominence along with innovations such as steamers and the telegraph, he argued, meant that New Zealand and Australia could be injected "into the history" of the world. His vision foreshadowed the postcolonial arguments that some Americans were making: Now free of the force of despotic and outmoded European dominance, these former colonies were poised to make the Pacific their own and to take a seat at the imperial dining table.

Murakami had a different take. He argued for a revisionist counter to most of the histories told at the Congress. Murakami acknowledged some validity in current Western academic thought regarding Japan's isolation and stagnation during the Tokugawa period (c. 1600–1867), but also sought to portray Japan's presence in the Pacific as a reexpansion, not a new arrival. In effect, his history made Japanese claims to the *place* as old as that of the Spanish and well prior to any that Americans could offer. For Murakami, like the other delegates, history was a tool to claim the Pacific. Such challenges to American claims on the Pacific continued through the 1920s and persist to the present.

Throughout the 1920s, the connection between American expansion across the continent and subsequently into the Pacific continued to be drawn by many in academia and the general public. Beginning in the 1930s, though, a growing discomfort with the consequences of imperialism created in the United States what has sometimes been characterized as "isolationism." That combined with the discrediting of the assertions and methods of Turner, especially by social scientists, relegated much in western American History to parochialism and the Pacific to a question of America's benign and uplifting presence there. The question of the relationship between the West and the Pacific dropped from sight. In the meantime, historians, especially those of the American West, moved away from virulent expansionist positions like Bancroft's. While Bolton continued to write about "the Americas,", he did little with the Pacific. By the 1950s, Bernard DeVoto had risen to prominence as perhaps *the* popularizer of the history of the US West. DeVoto portrayed the American "empire" as absolutely tied to its continental boundaries. DeVoto boldly started his preface to *The Course of Empire* (1952) with: "One of the facts which define the United States is that its national and its imperial boundaries are the same" (1952: xxxii). This was the intellectual and interpretive framework DeVoto applied. (The book lacked anything that might be called a conclusion and DeVoto's focus was as much on building a narrative as explicitly establishing an interpretation.) Much later in the volume he claimed that the "attainment of their Pacific boundary by the American people . . . [was the] the completion of the continental unit" and the end of American expansion (ibid.: 540). In *The Course of Empire*, DeVoto remained content to glorify exploration and to highlight early American presence on and claims to the western shores of the North American continent. He admitted his West was the "Passage to India." Americans were intent on establishing a continental claim in order to attain a "national homestead" not to create colonies overseas. In this context, DeVoto treated the Pacific, or "Western Ocean" during Spanish conquest, as merely a route of transport to the continent. While the European nations may have had designs on the areas around its rim, Americans were, in his vision, only intent on reaching it in order to stake a claim to the continent, which was ultimately their destiny. The subtitle to a 1960 paperback edition of the book, emblazoned only on the cover, is most telling: "A history of three centuries in which a new race engulfed a continent." DeVoto's decision to end this grand, three-volume narrative with the Lewis and Clark Expedition necessarily limited his ability to speak to much more than "American continentalism."

Contemporary to DeVoto's final volume, other American historians, especially those investigating international relations, engaged in a heated debate – some upholding "American continentalism" and others arguing that American expansion and even imperialism, not continentalism, defined nineteenth- and twentieth-century American history. Norman A. Graebner, following DeVoto's lead, argued that "the Pacific Ocean . . . determined the territorial goals of all American Presidents from John Quincy Adams to Polk" (1955: vi). American interests were, according to Graebner, only vested in "control of the great harbors of San Francisco, San Diego, and Juan de Fuca Strait. With their acquisition, expansion on the coastline ceased" (ibid.: vi). The expansion across the continent was not about Manifest Destiny, or some "natural urge to . . . expand," but was instead about acquiring lands as a "right of way to ocean ports. . . . Westward expansion beyond Texas is meaningless unless defined in terms of commerce and harbors" (ibid.: 218, 226).

Graebner did not directly engage history after the 1850s, but other historians took the debate into the second half of the century. Searching for economic, material justifications for American expansion, William Appleman Williams challenged the idealist orthodoxy that DeVoto and other adherents to "American continentalism" represented (1955). Williams argued that Frederick Jackson Turner had done more than simply reveal the sources of American democratic ideas to Americans, he "had explained the past and implied a program for the present. Materialistic individualism and democratic idealism could be married and maintained by a foreign policy of expansion" (1955: 385). Using the ideas promoted by behind the scenes politico Brook Adams, American politicians and ultimately the public came to believe that only expansion into the Pacific and Asia could sustain American Democracy *and* that it would simultaneously bring racial and economic uplift to the colonized. Williams suggests that the turn-of-the-century transformation and justification of imperialism was only a shift in ideological explanation for expansion, not a change in the root cause – a quest for materials and markets. Pointing to Walter Prescott Webb's *The Great Frontier*, Williams quotes the phrase that Americans saw the frontier and the Pacific "not as a line to stop at, but as an area inviting entrance" (1955: 394).

Frightened by what American expansion had wrought, especially in the technology of the arms race of the Cold War, Williams apocryphally noted that the United States had "finally caught up with History. Americans," he explained, "were no longer unique. Henceforward they, too, would share the fate of all mankind. For the frontier was now on the rim of hell, and the inferno was radioactive" (ibid.: 395). Williams' jeremiad aside, his ideas about American imperialism were quite influential. Charles Vevier (1960) and especially Walter LaFeber (1962) drew on Williams' ideas to argue that American continentalism and the expansion into the Pacific of the second half of the nineteenth century were part and parcel of an American search for markets. They, and Williams, argued that while Americans never systematically established widespread colonies or settler societies, Americans were clearly an imperial power in the Pacific. LaFeber noted that "mercantilists wanted colonies as sources of raw materials, markets for surplus goods, and as areas for the settlement of a surplus or discontented population. . . . Historically defined, this policy resembled traditional colonialism much less than it did the new financial and industrial imperialism of the 1850–1914 period" (1962: 681–2).

Williams and LaFeber measured their work against the "consensus" historians of Cold War America who looked to an American tradition of liberal democratic idealism as the driving historical force. The latter harkened back to American continentalism and separated territorial settlement, which they refused to consider as imperialist much less expansionist, from the Pacific. Representing the consensus response to Williams and LaFeber, Akira Iriye argued that the "westward movement was a self-contained phenomena, unrelated to Asia or the Pacific" (1967: 4). Frontier settlement was, to him, part of the expansion of agricultural idealism – Jeffersonian yeomanry. Beginning in the 1850s, Americans did begin to think about trade with Asia and thence about Pacific ports but missionary and "uplift" impulses tempered mercantile lusts. While America did become a "Pacific nation," its interests were not just economic. There was, he explained, "a desire for friendly relations reinforced by a sense of mission, which was often related to the image of America's future as a Pacific nation." The opening of Asia was a "mission and . . . [a] natural right." Americans embraced the idea that "trade would serve as a harbinger of change . . . to enlighten the hitherto dormant populations" of the Pacific (ibid.: 17). These factors impelled America and Americans into the "diplomacy of imperialism" between 1880 and the 1940s that represented the shift from "informal" to "modern" empire. While imperialism was an attempt "to extend . . . economic and political influence," he contended in a direct reference to Williams and LaFeber, "Marxist Leninist interpretation" does not work to explain American motives. The relations were "between nations, not classes; and no class concept can explain them adequately." International relations were not guided by "economic laws" but by a "series of incidents with many causes – not all of them rational, and not all economic" (ibid.: 56–7).

Iriye also adds that an American presence in the Pacific served to protect against the domestic threat posed by Asia and its peoples. Americans feared a "complete Orientalization of the Pacific Coast." An 1890s editorial comment in the *Coast Seamen's Journal*, he believed, epitomized that protective position: "Never in history had the Caucasian won out in competition with the Oriental. . . . [T]he Aryan always disappeared before the Mongolian" (ibid.: 105). Their experiences between World War I and World War II, however, convinced most Americans to avoid imperialism. Diplomacy was about trade, not, at least for Iriye, about imperialism.

Iriye had not intended to write about the relationship between the American West and the Pacific, but instead focused on World War II and American policy toward Asia through the emergence of the Vietnam War. Still, his rejection of Williams' materialist explanations for American expansion and claims to a multicausal and ultimately benign American imperialism represented a lasting and nearly dominant vision that persists to the present. As recently as 1993, David Wrobel has argued that there is "no overriding, frontier-based argument for expansion" (1993: 54). For him, American expansion is a product of the 1890s, not earlier forces of frontier expansion. Anxiety about the apparent closure of the frontier clearly existed, but drawing causal links between such "currents of thought and concrete foreign policy" is unwise (ibid.: 56). This refusal to link, even if sequentially, the nineteenth-century American frontier to twentieth-century US imperialism has been a trademark of most historians of the US West. Most have remained content to focus on continental frontier processes, or more simply upon a geographic area simply assumed to be exceptional and largely disconnected from the main currents of American history.

Ironically, the search for greater meaning among western historians for their field has compelled them to continually expand their vision. For a time, a handful of historians engaged in comparative frontier studies, measuring the American West against the Canadian West, Australia, portions of Latin America, and even Siberia. Others sought to knit many of these frontier locations together as part of what some labeled the Pacific Basin or Pacific Rim. In 1976 Arrell Morgan Gibson edited a special issue of the *Journal of the West* that marked the beginnings of a new discussion on the relationship of the Pacific to the US West. Gibson explained to readers that he wanted to "integrate the Pacific Basin Frontier with the context of Anglo-American frontiers." The area had "great natural and human diversity" with some of the "most exotic and variegated geography and ethnography" imaginable. In spite of highlighting such differences, Gibson noted that the "imperial contest for supremacy in the Pacific Basin has been a long and troubled process. . . . In the march of Anglo-American civilization across the continent, native peoples were prime casualties of this national expansion. . . . [It was] a near calculated genocide of these unfortunate people and their life style" (1976: 2). For Gibson and the contributors to this special issue, there were other contenders. Aside from the Spanish, Russians garnered attention as European competitors to American interests. Yet fundamentally Gibson and the others characterized America and Americans as the central players in the story. As Blue Clark noted in a bibliographic contribution to the issue, "[g]radually, through history, Americans have attempted to understand and dominate parts of that region." In spite of the fact that Clark conceded that "the world's three greatest military powers border the Pacific" and that "America's most costly and divisive wars have engaged her in that tangled skein of troubled countries," this remained a story about America and the Pacific as an extension of the West (1976: 125).

The focus on the Pacific as an *American* frontier dominated Gibson's final and ultimately posthumously published study, *Yankees in Paradise: The Pacific Basin Frontier* (1993). Gibson promised to "demonstrate that the frontier expansion processes and agents at work on the continent were also present in this maritime realm; thus Americans reaching the Pacific shore, rather than marking the end of westward expansion, pressed into the adjacent water hemisphere, representing a continuum of this nation-building process" (1993: 6). Ultimately, American domination was "attributable largely to geographic propinquity" and was an "inadvertent" but still "virtually an inevitable process" (ibid.: 9, 10). Unlike Bancroft's celebratory and racist visions of that expansion and integration, however, Gibson argued that the Pacific provided "instructive vistas on the true character of the westward movement of the American nation and the very certain work of its expansion process. . . . [I]t is the setting where presumptive, ethnocentric American goals for unlike peoples and cultures have been increasingly rejected" with Korea and Vietnam as the prime examples. John Whitehead, who assisted in the posthumous publication of Gibson's study, added in his conclusion that the American frontier in the Pacific never closed (1993: 411–420).

In the 1990s, Gibson and Whitehead were not alone in reviving the connections between America's westward expansion and the Pacific. Arthur Power Dudden

offered his explanation that the Oregon Treaty of 1846 in which England relin-
quished its claim to the jointly held Oregon country to the United States "signaled
the transcontinental triumph of manifest destiny . . . [and the] American Pacific
empire commenced at the moment of the Oregon Treaty's ratification." Indeed, the
Treaty of Guadeloupe Hidalgo only confirmed and boosted the Pacific Empire (1992:
xix). Indian fighting in the West, suppression of the Boxers in China, and then the
war to subdue rebellious Filipinos amply demonstrated that continuum for Dudden.
The problem for Dudden was that modern "Americans hesitate even to admit the
existence of an American empire. They were regularly exhorted to remember Japan's
attack on Pearl Harbor, but never expected to understand it" (ibid.: xviii). For as
much as Gibson and Dudden linked the continent and the Pacific, they both portrayed the Pacific as inevitably or naturally dominated by American interests. Gibson
put a rather thin veneer on it, while Dudden remained much more critical of
American actions.

The "New Western History" that emerged in the late 1980s and early 1990s
embraced a much more critical rendering of American expansion than most western
historians of several preceding decades. When Patricia Nelson Limerick penned
Legacy of Conquest (1987), she created one of the foundational texts of that New
Western History. In it, she sought to "contribute to the cause of freeing the history
of the American West from the grip of American exceptionalism and [restore] it
to a position of significance in the global history of European expansion" (10).
Limerick opened a discussion about the American West, not as the birthplace of
American democratic ideals, but instead as a site of intense cultural conflict and
oppression. While that early work of hers did not directly address the Pacific, she did
ultimately make links to the West and the Pacific in attempting to address how
Chinese and Japanese immigrants to the American West perceived the environment
and society to which they had immigrated (1992a). In earlier Western histories, Asian
Americans usually appeared as the objects of discrimination or as voiceless sojourners.
They simply had no lasting place in the earlier triumphal narratives of expansion.

Limerick has traveled far and wide across the literary landscape of the West. Related
to her promotion of Asian American studies with western history, she has also encouraged the consideration of Hawaii as part of the West (1992b). In doing so, she joins
a very small phalanx of western historians willing to cast the region's boundaries to
such noncontiguous locales as Hawaii and Alaska (Whitehead, 1992; Wyatt, 1994;
Deutsch, Sanchez, and Okihiro, 1994). Those authors typically point to the investment of capital, a common labor market, the presence of American missionaries, and
the political, military, and cultural attempts to subjugate Native peoples as characteristics that make those territories part of the American West. In doing so, they place
themselves squarely within the context of the New Western History.

Practitioners of the "Old Western History," Western Americana buffs, and readers
in the general public have had many and varied reactions to the willingness of New
Western historians to see colonialism and imperialism where many of their predecessors has seen only continental expansion. Some have been quite receptive; others have
spared no vitriol. In a good-natured reminiscence about the latter, Limerick noted
that the "American public audience gets prickly, defensive, and unhearing if you put
what they know of as the frontier or westward expansion into the category of colonialism and imperialism." Most American audiences "reject [this proposition] at first

hearing," she notes. One might add that they continue to do so even after repeated hearings. American audiences seem, she adds, to hold a "persistent . . . yearning to be removed from, declared innocent of, exonerated from the big patterns of history" (2001: 21). Their history, especially their version of American Western history, is fundamentally celebratory, presentist, and tautological.

The current state of western history thus offers students three visions of the Pacific. First is that portrait of American continentalism: The United States emerged out of the westward expansion of American institutions and peoples. For some scholars, this remains an irreversible, inevitable process that in some form or another ends up embracing earlier ideas of Manifest Destiny. In this version, the West is part of a domestic story and the Pacific is part of foreign policy. A second, alternate version makes the Pacific into simply a final frontier zone in that process. A few scholars see this as relatively benign, while most see some degree of coercion (Native suppression, exploitation of the environment, and a wage-labor frontier) and conquest. This latter group creates a third position from which to view the Pacific. Like Limerick, they do not always portray the frontier as an ever-westward advancing line, but see the possibility for simultaneous and disjointed conquests from all directions.

Pacific Predicaments

Arif Dirlik offers a very different perspective on the Pacific. He flatly states: "The Pacific region, *as* a region, is a Euro-American invention." It began "with the global expansion of Europe . . . [and] emerged in historical consciousness as an extension of the conquest and consciousness of the Americas" (1998: 22–3). It did not "exist as an entity in human consciousness," he explains, "until only about two hundred years ago." Prior to Euro-American interventions, it was a realm of "fragmentation" rather than "unity" (ibid.: 3, 6). As European and American influences consolidated the idea of the Pacific, they also "incorporated the region's peoples . . . [and] bound them together in a regional structure." While this was accomplished in a "haphazard fashion," Dirlik notes that the "logic" of capitalism provided the structure (ibid.: 23, 24).

At first glance, this perspective appears little different than Limerick's ideas of conquest or those of Gibson and other advocates of the "Pacific Basin" as a part of America's westward expansion. Yet Dirlik's analysis differs on two key points. First, he suggests how the Pacific world, once it emerged as a regional construct or structure, differed from the Atlantic. "Ties across the Atlantic," he explains, "have derived their perceived cohesiveness ultimately from assumptions about a metahistorical affinity between the United States and Europe" whereas the Pacific has always stood as the marker between European Americans and Asian "others" (ibid.: 294). It was a defensive barrier against "Orientals," "Mongolians," "Asiatics," and "Island Natives," while it stood as a place for cultural, political, and economic conquest for those same reasons.

Second, Dirlik places the peoples and nations of the Pacific in an active role "decentering" and defining the region. While European Americans initiated the creation of the region, Asians and Pacific Islanders incorporated that construct and offered their own competing versions. In aboriginal systems and local cosmologies the presence of Asia always decentered the Pacific. Rather than a series of "lakes" first

Spanish, then British, and finally American, the Pacific emerged as a site of contradictions that challenged such simple hegemonic notions. Resistance movements, rebellions, and outright war were partial reminders, but so too was cultural adaptation. Charismatic leaders influenced by Christianity, from rebels in China to Filipinos in Hawaii, turned European American constructs to their own end and offered challenges to European American assumptions about cultural superiority. As critical were the structures of the world capitalist system and the international labor migrations to which they gave rise and which, in turn, provided a medium for further migration. In other words, the "ties between . . . localities" within the Pacific created by migrations affected the historic, evolutionary construction of the Pacific as a region, *as a place* (ibid.: 287).

In this context, Evelyn Hu-DeHart offers an assessment of the early plantation economies of Latin America as dependent upon Asian labor, particularly after the abolition of slavery. Those labor migrations then "contributed to the formation of a 'Pacific' and encouraged further flows of population." Historically, Latin America, Asia, and the American West all became part of a regional site of capitalist transformation in which capitalism itself migrated to produce a "maquila-driven . . . economy" in the borderlands of northern Mexico and the US Southwest, the "Asian 'tigers' big and small," and NAFTA (1998: 276). Transnational labor and capitalism continue to reinforce the structure of the Pacific region even as the contests to redefine it as more, or less, "Asian" continue.

Hu-DeHart and others who speak to a borderland do not do so in the same manner as many Western historians. Amy Kaplan argues that the emergence of "borderlands studies" offers a powerful critique of binary relations reproduced in "frontier" literature. This is not simply a line between savagery and civilization ("others" and "Americans") or the periphery and core. It is not even the site of cultural contact and creative hybridity that are all too devoid of "the imperial dimensions of power and violence." Instead, the idea of borderlands developed by scholars in Chicano Studies encompasses "multidimensional and transterritorial" relations that cut through and across various peripheries and cores (1993: 16–17).

Lisa Lowe (1996) and Homi K. Bhabah (1994) broaden borderlands beyond *El Norte* and argue that "in the emergence of the interstices" we are able to locate the ways in which societies and cultures are structured. The Pacific and the West are two, perhaps even one, such place. They *have* been created and conceptualized as different *places*; the West as an *American* place and the Pacific as a *different*, non-American place. Still, their interlocking structures of power are intimately related. The borderlands of the Southwest and indeed the Pacific Northwest, along with California, the Great Basin, and the Rockies have all emerged in the context of the Pacific as much as the American West. By investigating the connections and contests that emerge between the Pacific and the West, we have an opportunity to gaze through a window and see the structures of power at work. By drawing on Katherine Morrissey's discussion of regions and "ghost regions" mapped as "mental territories," we can use conflicts to understand how many different people defined their position within their imagined regions (1997). We should ask not where to draw the line, but instead seek to erase the line and to use the idea of the Pacific to inform our reconstruction of what the West has been and continues to be. This will be a fundamentally different task than simply extending the West into the Pacific.

REFERENCES

Adelman, Jeremy and Stephen Aron: "From Borderlands to Borders: Empires, Nation-States, and the Peoples in Between in North American History." *American Historical Review* 104, 3 (1999), 814–41.

Bhabha, Homi K.: *The Location of Culture* (London and New York: Routledge, 1994).

Bancroft, Hubert Howe: *The New Pacific*, rev. edn. (New York: The Bancroft Company, 1913).

Billington, Ray Allen: *America's Frontier Heritage* (Albuquerque: University of New Mexico Press, 1963).

Biolsi, Thomas: *Organizing the Lakota: The Political Economy of the New Deal on the Pine Ridge and Rosebud Reservations* (Tucson: University of Arizona Press, 1992).

Boxberger, Daniel L.: *To Fish in Common: The Ethnohistory of Lummi Indian Salmon Fishing* (Seattle: University of Washington Press, 2000).

Brokes, Jean Ingram: *International Rivalry in the Pacific Islands, 1800–1875* ([1941], reprinted New York: Russell and Russell, 1972).

Brown, J. MacMillan: "New Zealand and the Pacific Ocean." In H. Morse Stephens and Herbert E. Bolton (eds.) *The Pacific Ocean in History* (New York: MacMillan, 1917).

Brown, Richard Maxwell: "Violence." In Clyde A. Milner, II, Carol A. O'Connor, and Martha A. Sandweiss (eds.) *The Oxford History of the American West* (New York: Oxford University Press, 1994).

Caughey, John W.: "Herbert Eugene Bolton." In Wilber R. Jacobs, John W. Caughey, and Joe B. Franz (eds.) *Turner, Bolton, and Webb: Three Historians of the American Frontier* (Seattle: University of Washington Press, 1965).

Clark, Blue: "Bibliographic Essay: Pacific Basin Sources and Literature." *Journal of the West* 15, 2 (1976), 117–25.

Cronon, William: "Turner's First Stand: The Significance of Significance in American History." In Richard W. Etulain (ed.) *Writing Western History: Essays on Major Western Historians* (Albuquerque: University of New Mexico Press, 1991).

Cronon, William: *Nature's Metropolis: Chicago and the Great West* (New York: W.W. Norton, 1991).

Dana, Richard Henry, Jr.: *Two Years Before the Mast* (New York: Houghton Mifflin Co., 1964).

DeVoto, Bernard: *The Course of Empire* (Cambridge, MA: Riverside Press, 1952).

Deutsch, Sarah: *No Separate Refuge: Culture, Class, and Gender on an Anglo-Hispanic Frontier in the American Southwest, 1880–1940* (New York: Oxford University Press, 1987).

Deutsch, Sarah, George J. Sanchez, and Gary Y. Okihiro: "Contemporary Peoples, Contested Places." In Clyde A. Milner II, Carol A. O'Connor, and Martha A. Sandweiss (eds.) *The Oxford History of the American West* (New York: Oxford University Press, 1994).

Dirlik, Arif: "The Asia-Pacific Idea: Reality and Representation in the Invention of a Regional Structure." In Arif Dirlik (ed.) *What is in a Rim? Critical Perspectives on the Pacific Region Idea*, 2nd edn. (Lanham, MD: Rowman and Littlefield, 1998).

Dudden, Arthur Power: *The American Pacific: From the Old China Trade to the Present* (New York: Oxford University Press, 1992).

Eagleton, Terry, Frederick Jameson, and Edward W. Said: *Nationalism, Colonialism, and Literature* (Minneapolis: University of Minnesota Press, 1990).

Friday, Chris: *Organizing Asian American Labor: The Pacific Coast Canned-Salmon Industry, 1870–1942* (Philadelphia: Temple University Press, 1994).

Friday, Chris: "Recasting Identities: American-born Chinese and Nisei in the Era of the Pacific War." In Richard White and John M. Findlay (eds.) *Power and Place in the North American West* (Seattle: University of Washington Press, 1999).

Gibson, Arrell Morgan: "The Pacific Basin Frontier." *Journal of the West* 15, 2 (1976), 1–4.

Gibson, Arrell Morgan: *Yankees in Paradise: The Pacific Basin Frontier*, completed with the assistance of John S. Whitehead (Albuquerque: University of New Mexico Press, 1993).

Graebner, Norman A.: *Empire on the Pacific: A Study in American Continental Expansion* (New York: Ronald Press, 1955).

Gutierrez, David G.: *Walls and Mirrors: Mexican Americans, Mexican Immigrants, and the Politics of Ethnicity* (Berkeley: University of California Press, 1995).

Haas, Lisbeth: *Conquests and Historical Identities in California, 1769–1936* (Berkeley: University of California Press, 1995).

Hoxie, Frederick E.: *Parading Through History: The Making of the Crow Nation in America, 1805–1935* (New York: Cambridge University Press, 1995).

Hu-DeHart, Evelyn: "Latin America in Asia-Pacific Perspective" In Arif Dirlik (ed.) *What is in a Rim? Critical Perspectives on the Pacific Region Idea*, 2nd ed. (Lanham, MD: Rowman and Littlefield, 1998).

Iriye, Akira: *Across the Pacific: An Inner History of American–East Asian Relations* (New York: Harcourt Brace Jovanovich, 1967).

Jackson, W. Turrentine: "A Brief Message for the Young and/or Ambitious: Comparative Frontiers as a Field for Investigation." *Western Historical Quarterly* 9, 1 (1978), 4–18.

Kaplan, Amy: "Left Alone with America: The Absence of Empire in the Study of American Culture." In Amy Kaplan and Donald E. Pease (eds.) *Cultures of United States Imperialism* (Durham, NC: Duke University Press, 1993).

Kushner, Howard I.: "The Russian–American Diplomatic Contest for the Pacific Basin and the Monroe Doctrine." *Journal of the West*, 15, 2 (1976), 65–80.

LaFeber, Walter: "A Note on the 'Mercantile Imperialism' of Alfred Thayer Hahan." *The Mississippi Valley Historical Review* 48, 4 (1962), 674–85.

LaFeber, Walter: "The Tensions Between Democracy and Capitalism during the American Century." *Diplomatic History*, 23, 2 (1999), 263–84.

Lamar, Howard and Leonard Thompson: "Comparative Frontier History." In Howard Lamar and Leonard Thompson (eds.) *The Frontier in History: North America and Southern Africa Compared* (New Haven, CT: Yale University Press, 1981).

Limerick, Patricia Nelson: *The Legacy of Conquest: The Unbroken Past of the American West* (New York: W.W. Norton, 1987).

Limerick, Patricia Nelson: "Disorientation and Reorientation: The American Landscape Discovered from the West." *Journal of American History*, 79, 3 (1992a), 1021–49.

Limerick, Patricia Nelson: "The Multicultural Islands." *American Historical Review*, 79, 1 (1992b), 121–35.

Limerick, Patricia Nelson: "Going West and Ending Up Global." *Western Historical Quarterly*, 32, 1 (2001), 5–23.

Lowe, Lisa: *Immigrant Acts: On Asian American Cultural Politics* (Durham, NC: Duke University Press, 1996).

Morrissey, Katherine G.: *Mental Territories: Mapping the Inland Empire* (Ithaca, NY: Cornell University Press, 1997).

Murakami, Naojiro: "Japan's Early Attempts to Establish Commercial Relations with Mexico." In H. Morse Stephens and Herbert E. Bolton (eds.) *The Pacific Ocean in History* (New York: MacMillan, 1917).

Nugent, Walter: "Frontiers and Empires in the Late Nineteenth Century." In Patricia Nelson Limerick, Clyde A. Milner, II, and Charles E. Rankin (eds.) *Trails: Toward a New Western History* (Lawrence: University of Kansas Press, 1991).

Pease, Donald E.: "New Perspectives on US Culture and Imperialism." In Amy Kaplan and Donald E. Pease (eds.) *Cultures of United States Imperialism* (Durham, NC: Duke University Press, 1993).

Peterson, Charles S.: "Hubert Howe Bancroft: First Western Regionalist." In *Writing Western History*, 43–70.

Pitt, Leonard: *The Decline of the Californios: A Social History of the Spanish-speaking Californians, 1846–1890* (Berkeley, University of California Press, 1966).

Robbins, William G.: *Colony and Empire: The Capitalist Transformation of the American West* (Lawrence: University Press of Kansas, 1994).

Robbins, William G.: *Landscapes of Promise: The Oregon Story, 1800–1940* (Seattle: University of Washington Press, 1997).

Sahlins, Marshall: "Cosmologies of Capitalism: The Trans-Pacific Sector of 'The World System'." In Marshall Sahlins (ed.) *Culture in Practice: Selected Essays* (New York: Zone Books, 2000).

Schafer, Joseph: *A History of the Pacific Northwest* (New York: MacMillan Company, 1922).

Schafer, Joseph: "The Western Ocean as a Determinant in Oregon History." In *The Pacific Ocean in History*, 287–97.

Sharp, Paul F.: "Three Frontiers: Some Comparative Studies of Canadian, American, and Australian Settlement." *Pacific Historical Review* 24, 4 (1955): 369–77.

Stephens, H. Morse and Herbert E. Bolton (eds.) *The Pacific Ocean in History* (New York: MacMillan, 1917).

Svensson, Frances: "The Final Crisis of Tribalism: Comparative Ethnic Policy on the American and Russian Frontiers." *Ethnic and Racial Studies* 1, 1 (1978), 100–23.

Taussig, Rudolf J.: "The American Inter-Oceanic Land: An Historical Sketch of the Canal Idea." In H. Morse Stephens and Herbert E. Bolton (eds.) *The Pacific Ocean in History* (New York: MacMillan, 1917): 114–36.

Twain, Mark: *Roughing It* (New York: Houghton Mifflin Co., 1980).

Tuan, Yi-fu: *Space and Place: The Perspective of Experience* (Minneapolis: University of Minnesota Press, 1977).

Vevier, Charles: "American Continentalism: An Idea of Expansion, 1845–1910." *American Historical Review* 65, 2 (1960), 323–35.

Webb, Walter Prescott: *The Great Frontier* (Boston: Houghton Mifflin, 1952).

White, Richard: *"It's Your Misfortune and None of My Own": A History of the American West* (Norman: University of Oklahoma Press, 1991).

Whitehead, John S.: "The Frontier Legacy in the Pacific Basin." In Arrell Morgan Gibson (ed.) *Yankees in Paradise: The Pacific Basin Frontier* (Albuquerque: University of New Mexico Press, 1993).

Whitehead, John S.: "Hawai'i: The First and Last Far West?" *Western Historical Quarterly* 23, 2 (1992): 153–77.

Williams, Walter L.: "United States Indian Policy and the Debate over Philippine Annexation: Implications for the Origins of American Imperialism." *Journal of American History*, 66, 4 (1980): 810–31.

Williams, William Appleman: "The Frontier Thesis and Foreign Policy." *Pacific Historical Review* 24, 4 (1955) 379–95.

Wills, Morris W.: "Sequential Frontiers: The Californian and Victorian Experience, 1850–1900." *Western Historical Quarterly* 9, 4 (1978): 483–94.

Wrobel, David M.: "External Solutions: New Frontiers." In David M. Wrobel (ed.) *The End of American Exceptionalism: Frontier Anxiety from the Old West to the New Deal* (Lawrence: University Press of Kansas, 1993).

Wyatt, Victoria: "Alaska and Hawai'i." In Clyde A. Milner, II, Carol A. O'Connor, and Martha A. Sandweiss (eds.) *The Oxford History of the American West* (New York: Oxford University Press, 1994).

CHAPTER SIXTEEN

Religion and the American West

PHILIP GOFF

Just when Frederick Jackson Turner declared the physical frontier closed, another frontier was officially announced as open. Across the Grand Pool that marked the 1893 Chicago World's Exposition as the American cultural event of the century, Hindu philosopher Swami Vivekananda stood before his largely Christian audience and proclaimed the United States as the great new edge, the place where very different religious people from around the world would meet. His language, laced with a spiritualized Manifest Destiny, set the stage for religion in modern America. "It was reserved for America to call, to proclaim to all quarters of the globe that the Lord is in every religion," claimed the founder of the American Bramo-Samaj. "May he who is the Brahma of the Hindus, the Ahura Mazda of the Zoroastrians, the Buddha of the Buddhist, the Jehovah of the Jews, the Father in Heaven of the Christians, give strength to you to carry out your noble idea. . . . Hail Columbia, mother-land of liberty! . . . It has been given to thee to march at the vanguard of civilization with the flag of harmony" (Vivekananda, 1893, 2: 977–8).

It is not surprising that Vivekananda said this, having traveled east to Chicago for the World Parliament of Religions. His American dream was formed as he crossed the American West. For the past two centuries, as eastern religious traditions moved west, and western religious traditions moved east, they met, fought, ignored one another, and synthesized practices and beliefs (often all at once) to create the most religiously diverse region in the world. New religious movements grew out of this ferment and went out around the globe as witnesses to new faiths. Clearly, if there is an arena for analysis of religion in the modern world, it is the American West.

Missing in Action

Given the simultaneous rise of the "New Western History" and the explosion of work on American religion by historians and sociologists, one might expect there to be numerous studies of religion in the American West. But, disappointingly, that has not occurred. Despite recent forays into the topic, religion – in its various forms – remains largely uncultivated by western historians, and the West remains too unexplored by most scholars of American religion. As Ferenc Szasz remarked, "A person who reads only recent works might well conclude that the modern American West has evolved into a thoroughly secular society" (2000: xiii).

He is right. While New England has seen its share of religious histories dating back to Cotton Mather's *Magnalia Christi Americana* and stretching to Perry Miller's magisterial two-volume *New England Mind (1953)*, and the American South has been rewarded over the past thirty years with dozens of monographs about its religious faiths and practices, the American West remains a secular enigma if one mistakes the dearth of literature on religion to mean there is nothing to study. Despite a number of edited volumes containing fresh essays by top scholars of the West, religion there remains shadowy at best, and usually only appears when discussing an individual (whose religion is part of something more significant) or Mormon exceptionalism. Such is the case with a number of otherwise fine studies of the western past, including *A Society to Match the Scenery* (Holthaus, Wilkinson, Limerick, 1991); *Under an Open Sky* (Cronon, Miles, Gitlin, 1992); *A New Significance* (Milner, 1996); *Many Wests* (Wrobel and Steiner, 1997); and *Over the Edge* (Matsumoto and Allmendinger, 1999).

Religious historians have been just as guilty of neglecting the American West as western historians have been in ignoring religion. In truth, the problem is less neglect than a failure to reassess appropriately the role of religion in the West since "church historians" defined the relationship between the two in the early twentieth century. This has enabled a "frontier" mindset to continue its reign in classroom interpretations of American religious history despite the challenges to that way of thinking by the New Western History. A study of contemporary syllabi indicates that while Puritans have been removed as the overarching thesis in the metanarrative, issues surrounding the western movement remain deeply embedded in the way America's religious past is taught. The relationship of religion to democracy, the rights of women, and perfectionism, among a number of other themes, are still tied to Turner's thesis revived wholesale for various religious bodies.

Clearly, it is time to reassess how western historians and religious scholars talk about one another's topics. Like a Venn diagram, the overlap is undeniable. It also proves important. This essay, then, is built largely upon those whose work has come from the religious end of things; that is, I will seek to lay out previous lines of thinking by looking at those interested in religion, first and foremost, as it plays out in the American West. But as the lines of inquiry between the two fields narrow, I will place increasing emphasis on those historians now turning to religion as a means of studying society and culture. In the end, I hope to point out future lines of analysis for this significant and growing field.

Models in Action

Over the past seventy years of scholarship in which religion has been studied in its American West context, three models have been developed. And while the evolution of the field has yielded ever more understanding of the topic, one should not mistake the descriptions below as normative judgments of the efficacy of each model. For while there is a chronological aspect to this evolution, I am not arguing by the calendar – that is, that recent developments are necessarily better than earlier ones. Indeed, we must recognize that the third model rides on the back of the second, and both of the latter models assume the first.

Religion "into" the West

Religion's relationship to the West was first defined in scholarship by William Warren Sweet, a former student of Frederick Jackson Turner, and long-time professor of American church history at the University of Chicago. Not surprisingly, he coupled religion and the Turner thesis to create a sense of faith as a civilizing force in barbaric conditions. "In the task of building this new society in the West the religious forces played a large and essential part," he claimed. "In this uncouth and raw frontier society there was much irreligion and scoffing at the things of the Spirit." Fortunately, there were several "religious forces which were available to meet this crisis" (1947: 35, 37). Ignoring the long tradition of Roman Catholicism in the West, to say nothing of indigenous faiths, Sweet pronounced the Baptists, Presbyterians, and Methodists – American Protestants all – as those who created civilization in the region by joining in the national migration.

Indeed, to Sweet's thinking, the response to the population shift westward "was to determine which of the churches were to become large and which were to remain small; which were to be sectional and which were to be national." Those who failed to recognize the significance of the westward movement, most especially the Congregationalists and Episcopalians, were doomed to remain regional denominations without national influence by the end of the nineteenth century. Baptists, Methodists, and Presbyterians – which Sweet called "the churches of the poor" – "made the greatest impact upon the first two generations of the American frontier" (1947: 38, 40–1). Each brought certain talents to its "frontier task": Baptist farmer-preachers lived among the people; Presbyterian ministers served as school teachers; Methodist circuit riders moved in organized step to cover the region with their version of the gospel. By 1850, Methodists, Baptists, and Presbyterians ranked, respectively, as the three largest denominations in America.

Sweet's contributions to religious scholars' understanding of religion in the American West cannot be overestimated. Throughout his long career he continually turned the attention of church historians, who were centered in elite eastern universities, to the other side of the Mississippi. His four-volume *Religion on the American Frontier* (1931, 1936, 1939, 1946), a reader of important institutional documents that also included his interpretation of the significance of each, placed into the hands of subsequent scholars the notion of frontier Christianity pushing ever westward. Clearly, Robert Samuel Fletcher's review of the third volume in 1940 proved prescient: "Professor Sweet is opening a gate through which many succeeding scholars will gratefully pass."

Even to this day, the four major texts for courses in "American Religious History" across the nation use the West as the stage upon which the story of the growth of American denominations takes place. Following Sweet's interest in national churches, each of the authors of these fast-selling textbooks, while nuancing the story to fit more recent interests in scholarship, still keeps the focus on faith movements that transformed the lives of those on the frontier and were, in turn, changed by the frontier experience. Winthrop Hudson's longtime best-seller places the narrative and analysis within the context of "Protestant Expansion and Consolidation" (1999). Edwin Gaustad, who actually taught for years in the West and generally pays more attention to movements originating there, nonetheless followed suit with "Freedom and the Frontier" (1990). Even the more avant-garde volumes by Catherine L. Albanese (1981) and Peter Williams (1990) confine the West to merely the place where largely eastern religious traditions play out their stories, without taking the region seriously as a place in which innovative sacred beliefs and rituals are developed. Of course, the one exception for each of these authors is Mormonism. But even here, their stories tend to end once the Latter-day Saints reach Utah. While "New England" and "the South" as religious regions are used as either analytic or organizing categories in all four of these text books, "the West" as a religious region is completely ignored for its use as a stage for important national developments.

Of course, there is little hope for telling the story of religion in the American West without this aspect of "into." After all, it is a region of incredible migrations over the past two centuries. Most of the faiths currently residing in the West were carried there at some point. Because of that, each of the succeeding models continued to employ the migratory pattern of analysis. The difference is, of course, that they do not stop there: they continue to press the issues of transformation and innovation. Moving from an interest in national religious movements and denominational growth to distinct regional faiths, a number of authors (including some of those mentioned above) increased our understanding of religion "in" the American West.

Religion "in" the West

A number of developments pushed scholarship in this direction. First of all, the development of less Christian-committed scholarship in American religious history, through the development of "Religious Studies" curricula in state-sponsored universities across the country, opened the door for more serious analyszes of religion in various regions without the need for a metanarrative that emphasized the development of national denominations. Alongside the growth of social history in the 1970s and cultural history in the 1980s, these new religious-studies-type historians took more seriously issues of race, class, and gender as they worked their way out through religious expressions. And while this moved historians of religion away from an intellectually based New England hegemony in telling the story of faith in America, and while it opened new paths of inquiry especially into religion in the South (largely because of a new interest in African American and cross-cultural histories), it did not immediately change the paradigm for understanding religion in the American West. Eventually, with social and cultural historians turning their attention to Native populations, religious historians began to take seriously the scholarly trends that helped create the New Western History. This development is still young and its fruit is yet unripened. But the trickle of studies has clearly turned into a stream, and may prove a healthy river on which careers can be based.

One category in this model of the religious West is the atlas. Several attempts have been made to understand the intersection of regions and institutional faiths. The first, and to date the most influential, was Edwin Gaustad's *Historical Atlas of Religion in America* (1962). Its approach corresponded to Gaustad's textbook mentioned previously. A search for "west" in the index turns up "Westward expansion. See Frontier." The implications are obvious: religion in the West came *from* the East, and it followed Turner's thesis. "The most obvious and the most heroic factor," wrote Gaustad about the first of five dynamics shaping American religion from 1800 to

1960, "is an oft-told tale: *the conquest of the West*" (1962: 37). Sounding very much like Sweet a generation earlier, he promoted a familiar story. "While descriptions of the churches of the frontier are myriad and far from consistent, religion in the West does seem to have had some general characteristics. Novelty was no sin, tradition no burden. Improvisation was the rule in doctrine, in polity, and in morality – not to mention architecture and hymnology. . . . Related to the acceptance of and indulgence in novelty was the loss of authority; the latter, indeed, is the obverse of the former. Recognizing no ecclesiastical, creedal or political authority, the frontiersman – churchman or no – proudly asserted, even flaunted, the liberty which was for him a daily experience" (ibid.: 37). Throughout, the West provided for Gaustad the backdrop for the growth of religious bodies, just as in his popular textbook.

Still, while Gaustad's historical interpretation explicitly took part in the "religion *into* the West" approach, the series of maps he painstakingly pieced together went beyond that and created new inroads for understanding religion in the West. By consistently underscoring the growth of Roman Catholicism not only in the Northeastern states (from whence then-President Kennedy hailed), but also in the American Southwest, he highlighted the significance of the largest Christian group in a culturally Christian nation, as Protestant hegemony continued its retreat. The fold-out, color-coded national map included in the back of the volume drove home just how different the West proved from the rest of the nation: dominated by Catholics from southwest Texas arcing northwest through northern California, with a large pocket of Latter-day Saints in Utah, eastern Nevada, and southern Idaho, a sprinkling of Lutherans among the Catholics in Montana, and a number of Catholics among the non-religious in the Northwest.

Gaustad's atlas remained the touchstone for regional studies for over thirty years. Only recently have others attempted to update his numbers or challenge his conclusions. Bret E. Carroll's *The Routledge Historical Atlas of Religion In America* (2000) is the most recent entry. But while Gaustad's intricate mapping implicitly moved the field beyond primary concerns with religious traditions and took regions more seriously, Carroll's book remains at the level of traditions and movements playing out their stories with region as merely the backdrop. Chapters are divided into particular groups and movements, while the maps are not complicated enough to couch regional issues into the argument in any effective way. Only in an epilog, "American Religious Regions," does Carroll directly confront the issue. Questioning if mass media and interregional migrations will quash regional distinctions, he wondered "whether future atlases like this one treat American religious regions as anything more than a matter of historical interest" (2000: 131). Certainly that is a legitimate question. But it should not deflect us from the task of taking seriously religion and region here and now.

William Newman and Peter Halvorson, who have thought long and hard about regional distinctions in culture over the past two decades, more effectively take up the challenge left for American religious scholars after Gaustad's initial venture into mapping. Subtitling their *Atlas of American Religion* (2000) as "The Denominational Era, 1776–1990," the focus is still placed on traditions. But their utilization of census data for 1850, 1890, 1952, and 1990 – particularly the numerical charts for every county in the nation – gives a richer map of religious culture in the United States than scholars have ever enjoyed. And while one cannot find in the book a section dedicated to the West, per se, readers can nonetheless study the maps of thirty-nine religious traditions to see not only who is present where, but even watch the growth of religions in the West by using "Geographic Change by County" maps for many of the groups.

For instance, one may not be surprised to see a heavy and longtime presence of Catholics in the Southwest; but the growth of Southern Baptists in Arizona and Southern California since 1952 is astounding. In fact, one can easily trace the western migration of these conservative Protestants from 1850 to 1990, and see how their presence is being felt now in the mountain West in places it was not in 1952. Presbyterians, meanwhile, clearly enjoy relative strength along the Pacific coast, the fruit of "home missionary" labors between 1850 and 1890. Ultimately, Newman and Halvorson have used religious mapping to create a debatable fivefold typology (national denominations, multiregional denominations, multiregional sects, classic sects, and national sects). That, they believe, is the point of their book. But, like Gaustad's 1962 atlas, their book's influence will be in both wider and deeper understandings of regional religion rather than in the formation of yet another means to segregate organizations.

Most recently, historian Philip Barlow revised Gaustad's volume, creating the most massive documentation yet of the religious West, along with the other national regions (Gaustad and Barlow, 2001). Better incorporating Native Americans, Jews, and African Americans into the main story, the volume bespeaks the directions American religious studies has traveled since Gaustad's initial volume in 1962. Barlow added two entirely new sections, including three denominational case studies – one of which focuses on the Latter-day Saints – and a new concentration on geographic space and its relation to religion. Not surprisingly, then, the West comes into play more often in this version of religious mapping. For example, while Gaustad's "oft-told tale of the conquest of the West" still makes it to the page, Barlow (and, presumably, Gaustad, who took part in the revision) calls into question the imperial hues of that narrative. "Such unidirectional accounts seem to derive from a parochial majority when one considers the Asian immigrants who arrived in the twentieth century and looked eastward across America from the Pacific Rim" (ibid.: 55). Likewise, the accounts ignore the Russian Orthodox, who migrated south from Alaska, as well as the Spanish Jesuits and Franciscans who long preceded Anglo-Protestants in the West. The West, then, plays a far greater role in this volume through individual chapters on Native Americans, Roman Catholics, Eastern Orthodox, and Asian traditions.

A different sort of cultural mapping of the West can be found in Peter Williams' *Houses of God: Region, Religion and Architecture in the United States* (1997). Unlike his popular textbook discussed above, this work takes very seriously the issues of "region" and "place" in American religious life. Partitioning the nation into seven cultural regions (New England, Mid-Atlantic, South, Old Northwest, Great Plains and Mountains, Spanish Borderlands, and Pacific Rim), Williams has produced an exciting venue to examine the built environment of American religion. And while his treatment of the Spanish borderlands is confined to the history of the missions, he finds the Plains, the mountain West, and the Pacific Rim significant to the American story of religious architecture.

Williams argues that the region between the Mississippi and the Rocky Mountains, contrary to Turner's image of a "safety valve for the pent-up energies of the congested east," is instead satisfied to "follow rather timidly the eastern region of the nation in the realm of both religion and architecture" (1997: 223). While its early days were marked by such creativity as mud houses for worship and evangelization trains, its mainstay was "Prairie Gothic," utilizing Greek revival and other Victorian themes, regardless of the denomination or ethnic group. And while these buildings eventually became part of the national imagination – with their clapboard sides, gabled roofs, and steeples – through "heartland" photography, they distinguish little about those who inhabited them for generations. The exception, of course, is the Latter-day Saints. Building "temples" rather than churches, homes to secret rites open only to Mormon family, these mammoth Gothic structures carry celestial and Masonic images that are meaningful to that faith community. But Latter-day Saints did not stop with their houses of worship and ritual; they imprinted their culture on the "Mormon corridor" running from Salt Lake City to San Diego. Williams repeats Richard Francaviglia's (1978) helpful traits of these towns:

1.   Wide streets, an amenity called for by Smith himself;
2.   Roadside irrigation ditches, part of Young's program to make the dessert blossom;
3.   Barns and granaries located in the town itself;
4.   Open landscape around each house, with houses located in the town rather than on outlying farmland;
5.   The central-hall plan house, a carry-over from the Ohio-Illinois days of origin;
6.   A high percentage of solidly built brick houses, reflecting communal values of endurance and permanence;
7.   The hay derrick, a simple frame device for lifting bales of hay;
8.   The "Mormon fence," an unpainted picket fence made up of assorted pieces of leftover lumber;
9.   Unpainted farm buildings, reflecting communal values of practicality and scorn for unnecessary ornament; and
10. An LDS chapel, in recent years usually of simple Georgian revival design, often with a small steeple topped with a needle-shaped spire "resembling an inverted tuning fork," which serves the religious and social needs of a community in which religious pluralism is virtually unknown.

Even so, Williams finds the Mormon church falling into step with their prairie and mountain West neighbors in the architecture of the wards that dot the landscape. Drawing from eastern styles, they too much resemble the "Prairie Gothic" churches that are so ubiquitous to the region.

The Pacific Rim, however, is a different story. "Unlike the Plains and the Mountain West," Williams claims, "the Pacific Rim has been both pluralistic and innovative" (ibid.: 269). Needless to say, Los Angeles proves the most assorted, but one must view the range in its stages of development since the city, itself, is one layer of culture atop another. Early on, Victorian religious architecture dominated the city, which Reyner Banham described as "the Middle West raised to a flashpoint" (1973: 25). The 1920s saw the arrival of westward and eastward migrants, alongside Moderne (or Art Deco) architecture in Pacific Palisades and Silver Lake. As the Spanish mission past became immortalized, numerous churches and theaters were built along those romantic lines. Meanwhile, Romanesque worship sites, replete with Moorish elements, showed up in Long Beach, Westwood, and MacArthur Park. In time, new American styles found expression in Garden Grove's "Crystal Cathedral" and Frank Lloyd Wright's "Wayfarer's Chapel" in Palos Verdes. "From the early health-seekers who came for the salubrity of the climate to Hollywood's fans, Schuller's worshippers, Disney's vacationeers [sic], Eaton's dear departed, Southern California has occupied a special place in the American imagination" (Williams, 1997: 269–74).

Williams next moves north to the San Francisco Bay area and Seattle. And while San Francisco often remains true to the Classical and medieval revival styles, there are three characteristics of religious architecture that tether the two cities: "wood as a basic material, Arts and Crafts movement-inspired love of detail, and an aesthetic compounded of indigenous Modern influences as well as ideas imported from traditional Japan and contemporary Scandinavia" (Williams, 1997: 279). These influences found their highest expression in Italian-born and Portland-based architect Pietro Bulluschi, who designed San Francisco's New Saint Mary's Cathedral and several notable Oregon religious structures, including the Morninglight Chapel and the Saint Thomas More Catholic Church in Portland. Folding into his aesthetic "Bernard Maybeck and the Arts and Crafts movement, Frank Lloyd Wright and Prairie School modernism, Zen Buddhism, and the contemporary Finnish designers Alvar Aalto and the Saarinens," Williams claims that Belluschi brought together both austerity and natural materials through geometric shapes to create harmony with the Pacific environment. His designs helped synthesize great American architectural traditions with Asian influences and Pacific materials, and in doing so influenced at least the next generation of religious structures.

In all, Williams finds the eclectic nature of the Pacific Rim's architecture to mimic the region itself (285):

> In southern California, the Crystal Cathedral represents the erosion of the lines between sacred and secular and the movement of traditional religion into an alliance with worldly forces that promise escape from mortality and redemption from finitude in a "virtual" reality of natural beneficence and human manufacture. Northern California and the Pacific Northwest share many characteristics. For them, San Francisco's Grace Cathedral might be taken as a symbol of urban Victorian civic presence and power, while Pietro Belluschi's First Presbyterian stands for a more modest quest for harmony with nature and responsibility toward the social order.

The West, through eastern and western migrations of architectural patterns, as well as use of materials from its unique environment, found its greatest expression in religious architecture along its eclectic Pacific Rim.

Two things can be learned from these atlases. First, that early forays into cultural mapping of religion (sans Williams' work) remained too concerned with traditions and denominations – a strange result for self-proclaimed atlases. While the best of these studies have taught us much about faith in the American West (who is where? how long have they been there? who is moving in or starting up now?), these important regional distinctions are picked up by reading between – if not beyond – the lines. We can only continue to hope for future studies in cultural mapping that take regional religion into account more thoroughly, so we can study these important questions directly rather than indirectly. Second, that religious diversity in the West is difficult to study en masse, that is, there is real efficacy in monographs and specific studies about distinct regional faiths.

Indeed, this is where considerable efforts have been placed in recent years. The variety and sheer number of microstudies of religion in specific places or aspects of religion in more than one locale make it impossible to review them all here. Still, their aggregate punch is very significant to the task of understanding religion in the West. Carl Guarneri and David Alvarez's edited volume of essays (1987) is but the largest collection of a growing number of articles and monographs dedicated to particular groups and regions in the American West. Numerous books commissioned and published by discrete traditions lie strewn throughout the West, and while they vary in quality and methodological rigor, they invariably offer a wealth of information for those seeking a synthetic account of religion in the region. For insights into regional Catholicism, for example, readers should consult Bradley and Kelly's Idaho study (1953); Casper's work on Nebraska (1966); Castaneda's seven volume Texas study (1936–58); or Duratschek's look at the high plains (1943).

As religion has increasingly been seen as important aspects of social and cultural history, more significant monographs have appeared. The works of Michael Engh (1992, 1997, 2001), Laurie Maffly-Kipp (1994, 1997), and Randi Jones Walker (1999) are good examples. Engh has built a strong reputation with his dedicated study of religion in Los Angeles as it relates to migrations, class struggle, and urban development. Maffly-Kipp opened new fields of inquiry in both region and gender in regard to religion in the West with her study of early gold mining communities. Walker, meanwhile, has used themes from American civil religion to look anew at Native peoples of the West.

The most sustained examination of the topic is Ferenc Morton Szasz's *Religion in the Modern American West* (2000). Divided into three sections (1890s to 1920s, 1920s to 1960s, and 1960s to the present), the book offers the best overview of twentieth-century religion in the region. Early on, churches and synagogues acted as the glue that kept lonely ethnic groups together. By the turn of the twentieth century, Protestant, Catholic, and Jewish cooperation in the West had become a model of the "social gospel" adapted to regional needs. In fact, Szasz claims that, "Unlike their northern or southern counterparts, from the 1890s to the World War I era the forces of organized religion in the West essentially created the institutional infrastructure for their subregions" (2000: 21). This proved especially true in education and health care. Religious groups sponsored nearly all the non-state-supported colleges throughout the West. And not only did Roman Catholics enjoy a high level of success at that level of education, they also founded a matrix of parochial schools as a separate track throughout the West. They also founded numerous hospitals. Together, Protestants, Catholics, and Jews cooperated to create a social structure through the West that was progressive and tolerant.

The mid-twentieth century saw continued cooperation. Despite early Catholic leadership, the clear healthcare leaders of the West were the Latter-day Saints who would go on to create a social welfare system in subsequent years that few today rival. In all, the period saw a "fourfold" mainstream develop, as Mormons joined mainline Protestants, Catholics, and Jews. And while the West suffered from some of the culture wars surrounding the rise of Fundamentalism during the 1920s, the Great Depression cured the region of any ongoing poisonous relations, as all fought together to survive economic woes. Postwar building campaigns indicated the growing stature of organized religion in these parts, as spires reached ever upward and walls expanded ever outward. By 1952, outsider groups wanted to get in on the action, as Southern Baptists voted to put greater energies into evangelizing the West, yet another "into the West" chapter that would eventually be part of the "religion in the West" story.

After 1960 everything changed, when, as Szasz entitles it, "Western Religion Confronts the Modern World." Already holding the reputation of religious creativity, it was as if those living in the region not only shook up the puzzle box but even added a number of new pieces and still expected them all to fit together. They didn't. By 1990, those in the West responding to a poll indicated "no religion" twice as often as those in other regions. In fact, of the ten highest states on the "no religion" scale, the West boasted nine. Still, pockets of intense religious devotion were easy to discern, particularly in Texas/Oklahoma and Utah. As he writes (2000: 132–3):

> Except for Utah and parts of Oklahoma, most areas of the West show a weakened religious cultural influence. Many regions, especially the Pacific Northwest and California, contain large bodies of nonbelievers. Simultaneously, however, all areas of the West have become home to significant neo-evangelical movements, claiming perhaps 26 percent of the population, who are turning to the political system, usually via the Republican Party, to voice their opinions.

The question was quickly becoming how to make sense of the many religious (or nonreligious) regions within the West.

And this is where, for all the good Szasz's synthesis does, we find ourselves still overwhelmed by the topic. His attempt to bring order to such chaos is apparent in a schema that focuses primarily on religious institutions and secondarily on significant individuals. Dividing each of the three sections into three chapters (the first two descriptive of institutional life within some cultural shifts, the third devoted to religious personalities during that period) clearly brings order to the book, but not to such an unwieldy subject. The "lived religion" of millions of believers and practitioners cannot be captured in either the institutional or important individual stories Szasz pieces together – the natural result of a valiant attempt to bring order to chaos, to decipher the symphony in the midst of a cacophony.

From these atlases, essays, and monographs, we have a much better sense of religion "in" the American West. In other words, we know more today than ever before about which traditions took hold after they came "into" the region, and how they managed to acclimatize to the physical landscape and surrounding diversity. Meanwhile, we have a much greater appreciation for the longtime Native traditions that have adapted and survived as religions "in" the region without having moved into it. And these studies have taught us how syntheses develop within diversity, and how "pluralism" evolves as a philosophy, especially in the urban West where diversity is often celebrated, not just tolerated.

Religion "from" the West

Some of those who have taken most seriously the "in" aspect of religion in the West have begun to push the issue yet further. If, in fact, religion has an important (and at times original) role in the American West, it can be exported. In many ways, this was a natural result of the larger scholarship about the region. As academics, journalists, and cultural critics have increasingly written about the West as the new harbinger of things to come for the rest of the nation, religion has taken its place alongside eclectic fashion, fusion cuisine, and intercultural lifestyles as an export of the American West, particularly the Pacific coast. The region has been a site of cultural encounters and exchanges for centuries, and only now are we beginning to realize the religious significance of that fact.

In many ways, the starting point for this line of thought is Laurie F. Maffly-Kipp's 1997 essay, "Eastward Ho! American Religion from the Perspective of the Pacific Rim." She rewrote the religious history of the region by putting the American westward migration in its historic context as but one of the many migrations into the area. Layering the cultural additions and mixtures – European colonization from 1513 to 1821, American empire-building from 1820 to 1898, and Asian and Latin American migrations from 1851 to the present – enables us to comprehend much better not only the wrongheadedness of a simple "westward" migration of religion, it helps us to understand how religion, as an aspect of culture, adjusts itself to shape the moral and physical landscape of a region, and then a nation.

Maffly-Kipp challenged not just the status quo regarding scholarship on religion in the West, but also the entire field to begin thinking anew about religion and region, imperialism, and culture. Admitting that any narrative is incomplete, she admonished scholars to move beyond merely tacking on the diverse and eclectic West to the older paradigms. The old stories must be rethought, not retold with a twist.

> Phrased more optimistically, however, this new illumination, rather than placing in shadow the older narratives of the westward course of Christianity and empire, will help us to see those stories in a new light by juxtaposing them to other movements, other ways in which the landscape of the United States has been mapped, imagined, and inhabited. Multidirectional and multicultural contacts have shaped the American religious experience on the Pacific from its beginnings (1997: 147).

Indeed, when we understand that West Coast Japanese settlers have moved eastward to once-Puritan New England and that an entire "border culture" has been created along the southern United States that finds cultural sustenance in both Mexican and American traditions, we will stop telling a story of western importation. "Then," she concludes (ibid.: 148), "with Opukahaia, with eighteenth-century Spanish Jesuits, with Russian fur traders, with indigenous Hawaiians, and others, we can discern the eastward, northward, southward, and westward paths that have contributed to our present religious situation."

Eldon Ernst recently took up Maffly-Kipp's charge. "The Emergence of California in American Religious Historiography" argues that recent scholarship underscoring new religious movements originating in the West and older Asian traditions arriving along the Pacific Coast portend that "California's religious heritage might become relevant to contemporary national themes" (2001: 33). Indeed, this new religious "discovery" of California brought together emerging topics in American religious history: the importance of the postwar period for American religion, the significance of region, and a growing recognition of diversity and pluralism.

Shifting political and cultural terrains following World War II shaped religion in the American West both indirectly and directly. "Globally, the immediate postwar years witnessed violent shuffling of political-racial-ethnic alignments and interactions in the Atlantic and Pacific, and in the northern and southern hemispheres," Ernst argues. "Within these sociopolitical upheavals burst forth a global great awakening – a resurgence of cultural-religious consciousness with varieties of Jews, Muslims, Hindus, Buddhists, and Christians asserting their identities in changing regional expressions and dynamic interaction" (ibid.: 33). While the result of much of that dynamism would be delayed until immigration laws changed, a parallel rise in ethnic religious awareness came of age in the American West. This was expressed most readily in increased discussions of religious pluralism.

By turning his attention to California, particularly, Ernst has at his disposal the largest and most colorful canvas on which to paint a portrait that challenges the usual United States' "east to west" story religious historians have repeated since Sweet. He proposes a new narrative consisting of five chapters, "molded by continuous migrations of peoples from all parts of the world – dislocated from where they came and relocated in a new foreign land" (ibid.: 36). Attempting to transplant the old ways in new soil, they added to an ever-changing crop that mutated and migrated as religious cultures interacted and moved about.

The story develops along predictable lines, given advances in the cultural history of the West written over the past decade. Still, Ernst does a service by limiting himself to a particular region and, in doing so, dismantling the old paradigm. The first chapter, he claims, should conclude at the acquisition of the territory by the United States. Up to that point, the religious landscape was dominated by Native faiths and the Catholic Church, but they shared the land with others, particularly the Russian Orthodox who migrated south from Alaska. With the discovery of gold in 1848, the second chapter begins the process that would witness one of the greatest religious migrations in history. Part of this was internal to the nation, as demands to "Americanize" the region failed to take into account the fact that religious diversity ruled the nation – there was no state church to move in and offer religious stability. What Northern California witnessed, instead, was an unheard-of array of religious migrants:

> The Mormons arrived first, unsure whether California or Utah would be the headquarters of their Zion in the wilderness. Following them appeared various Baptist, Congregational, Methodist, Presbyterian, Lutheran, Reformed, Disciples of Christ, Quaker, Episcopal, Roman Catholic, Unitarian, Seventh-Day Adventist, Swedenborgian, and Spiritualist churches, plus the Russian-Greek Slavonic Orthodox Church and Philanthropic Society, Jewish synagogues, and Chinese temples representing mixtures of popular religions and Buddhism, Taoism, and Confucianism (ibid.: 38).

The interaction among these groups proved alternately harmonious, indifferent, and sometimes downright violent. Many were deprived of rights because of their ethnicities, despite sporadic religious concord.

Chapters three through five, according to Ernst, would lead us past the urbanization and industrialization of the state through the Progressive period to today's postwar California that marks a new level in religious and ethnic diversity in world history. With new forms of communication and transportation, California's religious diversity exploded beginning in the late nineteenth century. Much of this came from new movements originating along the coast, including the effervescent Pentecostal faction of Protestant evangelicalism. From a tiny makeshift church in 1906 Los Angeles holding several dozen who believed speaking in tongues marked the indwelling of the Holy Spirit, there swelled a mighty movement which, by some estimates in the 1990s, had spread into most forms of Christianity worldwide to the tune of 450 million adherents.

But California's role in the "out of the West" thesis is much larger than modern glossalalia. For the religious influence that would eventually percolate throughout the rest of the country, and even the globe, needed more than merely internal migration, it needed the immigration of altogether different religions. To be sure, the West Coast already had a greater share of Asian religious traditions than elsewhere in the country due to its proximity to China, Japan, Korea, and India; and its long history as a Mexican territory left a lingering Catholic presence. But none of that foretold the story of the immigration influx that marked the century, as Catholic Mexican and South American migrant workers moved into the American Southwest during the agricultural boom at mid-century and Asians streamed to the urban Pacific after the Immigration Act of 1965. These, along with continued migrations by Atlantic-coast Protestants, Catholics, and Jews in the 1920s, dust-bowl victims from Oklahoma, Arkansas, Texas, and Missouri during the Great Depression, the wartime growth of West Coast cities involved in building war materials during the 1940s, made for a situation that, if it were not qualitatively different from previous migrations to a region (and arguments can be made it was), then it was quantitatively so.

Ernst concludes that, "In this ethos, California's peculiar religious history now appears illuminating to the nation's spiritual heritage overall, and perhaps to global trends as well" (ibid.: 45). Indeed, he links his coastal story to Michael Malone's and Richard Etulain's remark that, "Nothing better illustrates the modern West's evolution from a colonial region – looking elsewhere for its cultural cures – into a pacemaking, trendsetting, postregional culture than does California, with its diverse, chaotic, always invigorating panoply of religious denominations, associations, sects, and cults" (1989: 205).

Among the most significant books to argue the "out of the West" thesis is Donald E. Miller's *Reinventing American Protestantism: Christianity in the New Millennium* (1997). A sociological study of the Calvary Church, Vineyard Fellowship, and Hope Chapel movements, he argues that a "new style of Christianity is being born in the United States, one that responds to fundamental cultural changes that began in the mid-1960s." These "new paradigm churches" have thrown off many of the characteristics of established churches through contemporary worship styles, restructuring denominational hierarchies to a more autonomous polity, and further democratizing the already democratic principle of the "priesthood of all believers."

While they have outgrown their American West nursery, indeed they have been transplanted across the country and around the world, their roots still show an emphatically western spirit. "The Jesus movement of the 1960s was long over," Miller admits. "Although some of these churches had their roots in that movement, they were decidedly part of the 1990s. Gone were the religious hippies, and in their place were young parents trying to make sense out of the urban environment in which they were rearing their children." Much like the "third way" politics preached during that decade, a triangulation of religious traditions created a new path. "These churches preached an old-fashioned gospel, but their music and form of worship were radically contemporary, and their mood was quite different from that of the typical evangelical and fundamentalist churches . . ." (1997: 7)

The three largest of these loosely affiliated movements are Calvary Chapel (founded by Chuck Smith), Hope Chapel (founded by Ralph Moore), and The Vineyard Fellowship (founded by John Wimber). All three of these groups formed in California, in the same cultural milieu that must be seen as an outgrowth of the free-spirited "Jesus movement" of the 1960s. Affected by Pentecostal style and doctrine but not part of the classical Pentecostal movement, these churches have used a laid-back manner of worship and Bible instruction to become national, even international in scope. Meeting inner needs that many mainline denominations seem unable to address, particularly the alienation caused by modern urban life, these churches provide an informal style of Christianity that has begun to influence other denominations.

Miller argues that this movement coming out of the West lassoed three particular elements of the counterculture days. The first is the *therapeutic* aspect. While excoriating the narcissistic values so prominent in American life, they appreciate and encourage openness and tolerance among their religious colleagues who make themselves vulnerable by opening up to one another. "These are the same values that blossomed in the encounter groups of the sixties and proliferated in various schools of psychotherapy, self-help books, and talk show gurus," writes Miller. At the same time, these church members emphasize *individuality*, especially in regard to reading the Bible and interpreting it for themselves, and private devotions to advance their "relationship" to God. Out are denominational rules and heavy-handed ministers. It is a strong sense of Protestant individualism balanced by personal accountability. That characteristic reveals the third cultural survivor of the counter-culture movement: *anti-establishment*. "Members of new paradigm churches tend to be hostile to institutions, bureaucracies, and routinized aspects of organizational life," he adds (ibid.: 21, 22). With buildings stripped of symbolism and a lean, effective pastoral staff, the physical elements of this faith are reminiscent of a Pacific-Coast-based dot-com headquarters.

While Miller's interest is not to characterize religion in the American West, his work has done much to help in that effort. The influence of the Pacific Coast is not, after all, relegated to computer systems, motion pictures, coffee houses, and extreme sports. Miller has revealed an aspect of religious life in this environment that is quintessentially West Coast – and it is spreading fast. By the mid-1980s the three movements had branches throughout the western mountain states. Now there are not only thousands of branches throughout the country, but evangelical and mainline Protestant denominations, even Catholic churches, have incorporated much of the singing and informal worship styles into their congregational life. Throughout the country now there sit advertisements outside churches distinguishing "contemporary" and "traditional" services meeting at different hours on the same Sunday morning in the same building.

Future Possibilities: Religion "and" the West

Clearly our understanding today of religion in the American West proves more complex than it was under William Warren Sweet. But even the most complicated analyzes assume the "religion into the West" model at some level, because migrations are such an important part of the story. Now that our appreciation for religion "in" and "from" the West has grown considerably, where do we go from here? What model might move us forward, taking with us the best of the insights we' have gained over the past seventy years?

We must take more seriously the task of defining our subject – or subjects, as the case may be. The "West" is no less an ambiguous category of analysis than "religion." So lumping them together in an attempt to discuss "religion in the West" only complicates matters exponentially. Is "West" a place? a direction? an idea? all of these things at once? Is "religion" a belief? a behavior? an experience or a social construct? or, like "West," perhaps all of these things simultaneously? Leaving the two categories at the level of the Supreme Court's old definition of pornography – "I'll know it when I see it" – only serves to make serious, substantial, and sustained debate about the role of religion in the American West that much more difficult.

So where do we begin a discussion about how to identify and track the intersection of these two concepts? Laurie Maffly-Kipp's instructive essay points (1997) to the most fruitful route: By paying closer attention to cultural geography, especially as Yi-Fu Tuan depicts it, as "how mere space becomes an intensely human place" through "the nature of experience, the quality of the emotional bond to physical objects, and the role of concepts and symbols in the creation of place identity" (1976: 269). In other words, by looking more closely at the perception and utilization of space, we can learn a great deal about both the power of religious beliefs and the behaviors that define a specific space – personal, home, village, city, or nation. Maffly-Kipp thus joins Thomas Tweed (1997) in calling for greater attention to be paid to geographic placement as AN "important factor in understanding religious behaviors and beliefs."

Some will protest that in doing so, we who write American religious history have made religion merely a component of culture. But if Emile Durkheim taught us anything, it is that culture owns "social facts" that exert compelling power over individuals. These surface as a collective consciousness unique to that society. Religion is its most characteristic product, but still must be seen within the broader "social facts" of law, morals, and economics. Thus, as we look at local societies in their geographic contexts, particularly in the American West, we can look at regional religion as that society's mores writ large. Still, we need not confine our definition of religion to the sociological realm. Beliefs and behaviors are highly personal, even if they are public. Even if events, movements, or individual efforts do not reveal the "social facts" of a region, they constitute another important part of the story of religion in the West. Thus a continued emphasis on monographic studies of, say, Southern Baptists in the 1960s Mountain West, or Catholic and Jewish cooperation in 1920s Los Angeles, remains necessary.

But such studies can still beg the question – what is "religion in the West?" Again, our answers will be predicated on what we mean by the terms. Ultimately, we must get beyond using "religion" and "West" in their most general senses if we hope to gain anything resembling specific answers. We know, for instance, that there are many religions and that there are many Wests. Yet too often we continue to use the terms as if they represented single entities. Thus scholars flock to the crunched numbers of the Glen Mary Research group and tout the "secular" nature of the West, especially the Northwest. For while San Antonio (64 percent), Omaha (55 percent), and Los Angeles (55 percent) enjoy religious adherence rates similar to those cities east of the Mississippi, Portland and Seattle (33 percent), Sacramento (39 percent), and Redding, CA (25 percent) lag far behind. But these conclusions reflect traditional understandings of religious adherence, based upon European Christian models of religious behavior. What happens if we stop to recognize the growing influence of Asian traditions (including New Age appropriation of aspects of Asian religions) in the Northwest's cultural milieu – if we recognize that other faith groups that shape a region's "social facts" do not adhere to traditional modes of religious behavior, particularly adherence to and attendance in a particular congregation? By acknowledging the spiritual aspects of the Northwest's concern for the environment and distrust for corporate monopolies, we can move beyond "religion" in general as measured by church adherence to understand the deeply religious social movements that shape what is often called the most secular region in the country.

From Tai Chi to chai tea, the American West is leading the way in the exportation of these nontraditional religious beliefs and practices. Along these lines, we must begin to understand the religious economy of the West as beliefs and practices either indigenous to the region or transplanted there first are finding their way into the lived religion of millions. The *Yoga Journal*, for instance, began, unsurprisingly, in California in 1975 as 300 copies of a ten-paged newsletter distributed by the California Yoga Teachers Association. By 1990, its distribution was up to 55,000. During the 1990s, a decade in which Pan-Asian influences, poured through the sieve of urban California, Oregon, and Washington, reached a national audience, subscriptions to *Yoga Journal* exploded to 230,000, with an estimated readership of 700,000. With such monthly departments as "Om Page," "Well-Being," "Eating Wisely," "Dharma Wisdom," "Awakened Athletes," "Asana," "Guided Meditation," "Mixed Media," and "Centering," the publication drew together the inward concerns of those very much involved in the New Economy but unsatisfied with even the new brand of traditional faiths that Don Miller describes. The growth of the publication fit the times in more ways than just that, however. Much must be attributed to its "new look" after John Abbott purchased the magazine. A former investment banker for Citicorp, he brought in an experienced team to publish a slick yet true-to-its-purpose magazine that could rival its neighbors on the magazine rack for look and feel. It has helped yoga enter the mainstream of American publishing, and, likewise, the mainstream of American life.

There are, of course, many "out of the West" impulses that need to be tracked in the coming years. More importantly, we must begin to ask ourselves what is particularly "Western" about these movements. Is it just that the West is the stage upon which new and important movements take place? Is it an accident of history and migration patterns that the West has taken on such importance to American religious studies? Too many would answer affirmatively and continue to see study only the phenomenon rather than the context from which it sprung. But if scholars had used that approach when studying religious phenomena in the American South, we would have no sense of it as a distinct religious region.

Thus we come full circle, attempting to argue for serious inquiries into religion in the West as an important field of study in its own right – not just as it relates to national trends or nonreligious categories of analysis of the region. Whether it is religion into the West, in the West, or out of the West, we need to develop categories for analysis that fit its historical context, just as those who study religion in the South have accomplished. Concentrating on space, symbolic representation of the region, and migration patterns – though these are not new as categories – will provide the next generation of scholars studying religion in the West with the best map across the region.

REFERENCES

Albanese, Catherine L.: *America, Religions and Religion* (Belmont, CA: Wadsworth Publishing Company, 1981).

Banham, Reyner: *Los Angeles: The Architecture of Four Ecologies* (Harmondsworth: Penguin, 1973).

Bradley, Cyprian and Edward Kelly: *History of the Diocese of Boise, 1863–1952* (Boise: n.p., 1953).

Carroll, Bret E.: *The Routledge Historical Atlas of Religion in America* (London: Routledge, 2000).

Castaneda, Carlos: *Our Catholic Heritage in Texas, 1519–1936,* 7 vols. (Austin, TX: Von Boeckmann-Jones, 1936–58).

Casper, Henry: *History of the Catholic Church in Nebraska,* 3 vols. (Milwaukee: Bruce/Catholic Life, 1966).

Cronon, William, George Miles, and Jay Gitlin (eds.) *Under an Open Sky: Re-thinking America's Western Past* (New York: Norton, 1992).

Duratschek, M. Claudia: *The Beginning of Catholicism in South Dakota* (Washington, DC: Catholic University of America Press, 1943).

Engh, Michael E.: *Frontier Faiths: Church, Temple, and Synagogue in Los Angeles, 1846–1888* (Albuquerque, NM: University of New Mexico Press, 1992).

Engh, Michael E.: "A Multiplicity of Diversity of Faiths: Religion's Impact on Los Angeles and the Urban West, 1890–1940." *Western Historical Quarterly* 28 (Winter 1997), 463–92.

Engh, Michael E.: "Practically Every Religion Being Represented". In William Deverell and Tom Sitton (eds.) *Metropolis in the Making: Los Angeles in the 1920s* (Berkeley: University of California Press, 2001).

Ernst, Eldon E.: "The Emergence of California in American Religious Historiography." *Religion and American Culture: A Journal of Interpretation* 11, 1 (2001): 33–45.

Fletcher, Robert Samuel: "Review of William Warren Sweet *Religion on the American Frontier: The Congregationalists.*" *Mississippi Valley Historical Review* 26: 568–69.

Francaviglia, Richard V.: *The Mormon Landscape: Existence, Creation, and Perception of a Unique Image in the American West* (New York: AMS Press, 1978).

Gaustad, Edwin Scott: *Historical Atlas of Religion in America* (New York: Harper & Row, Publishers, 1962).

Gaustad, Edwin Scott: *A Religious History of America,* 4th ed. (San Francisco: Harper, 1990).

Gaustad, Edwin Scott and Philip Barlow: *New Historical Atlas of Religion in America* (New York: Oxford University Press, 2001).

Guarneri, Carl and David Alvarez (eds.): *Religion and Society in the American West: Historical Essays* (Lanham, MD: University Press of America, 1987).

Holthaus, Gary, Charles F. Wilkinson, and Patricia Nelson Limerick (eds.) *A Society to Match the Scenery* (Niwot: University Press of Colorado, 1991).

Hudson, Winthrop S. and John Corrigan: *Religion in America: An Historical Account of the*

Development of American Religious Life, 6th edn. (Upper Saddle River, NJ: Prentice Hall, 1999).

Maffly-Kipp, Laurie F.: *Religion and Society in Frontier California* (New Haven, CT: Yale University Press, 1994).

Maffly-Kipp, Laurie F.: "Eastward Ho! American Religion from the Perspective of the Pacific Rim." In Thomas A. Tweed (ed.) *Retelling U.S. Religious History* (Berkeley: University of California Press, 1997).

Malone, Michael P. and Richard W. Etulain: *The American West: A Twentieth-Century History* (Lincoln: University of Nebraska Press, 1989).

Matsumoto, Valerie J. and Blake Allmendinger (eds.): *Over the Edge: Remapping the American West* (Berkeley: University of California Press, 1999).

Miller, Donald E.: *Reinventing American Protestantism: Christianity in the New Millennium* (Berkeley: University of California Press, 1997).

Miller, Perry: *The New England Mind: From Colony to Province.* (Cambridge, Harvard University Press, 1953).

Milner, Clyde A., II (ed.): *A New Significance: Re-envisioning the History of the American West* (New York: Oxford University Press, 1996).

Newman, William H. and Peter L. Halvorson: *Atlas of American Religion: The Denominational Era, 1776–1990* (Walnut Creek, CA: Altamira Press, 2000).

Seager, Richard Hughes: *The World's Parliament of Religions: The East/West Encounter, Chicago, 1893* (Bloomington: Indiana University Press, 1995).

Sweet, William Warren: *Religion on the American Frontier: The Baptists, 1783–1830* (New York: Henry Holt & Co., 1931).

Sweet, William Warren: *Religion on the American Frontier: The Presbyterians, 1783–1840* (New York: Harper Brothers, 1936).

Sweet, William Warren: *Religion on the American Frontier: The Congregationalists, 1783–1850* (Chicago: University of Chicago Press, 1939).

Sweet, William Warren: *Religion on the American Frontier: The Methodists, 1783–1840* (New York: Henry Holt & Co., 1946).

Sweet, William Warren: *The American Churches, An Interpretation* (New York: Abingdon-Cokesbury Press, 1947).

Szasz, Ferenc Morton: *Religion in the Modern American West* (Tucson: The University of Arizona Press, 2000).

Tuan, Yi-Fu: "Humanistic Geography," *Annals of the Association of American Geographers* 66, 2 (June 1976), 266–76.

Tweed, Thomas A.: "Introduction: Narrating U.S. Religious History." In Thomas A. Tweed *Retelling U.S. Religious History* (Berkeley: University of California Press, 1997).

Vivekananda: "Hinduism." In John Henry Barrows (ed.) *The World's Parliament of Religions: An Illustrated and Popular Story of the World's Parliament of Religions, Held in Chicago in Connection with the World's Columbian Exposition*, 2 vols. (Chicago: Parliament Publishing Co., 1893).

Walker, Rander Jones: "Liberators for Colonial Anahuac: A Rumination on North American Civil Religions." *Religion and American Culture: A Journal of Interpretation* 9, 2 (1999), 183–203.

Williams, Peter W.: *America's Religions: Traditions and Cultures* (New York: MacMillan Publishing Company, 1990).

Williams, Peter W. *Houses of God: Region, Religion and Architecture in the United States* (Urbana, IL: University of Illinois Press, 1997).

Wrobel, David M. and Michael C. Steiner (eds.): *Many Wests: Place, Culture, and Regional Identity* (Lawrence: University Press of Kansas, 1997).

CHAPTER SEVENTEEN

Transients and Stickers: The Problem of Community in the American West

ANNE HYDE

Two Places

Behind thick walls of adobe, a community began its morning routine. Owl Woman kept her eyes closed for a minute. She knew it was early because her husband and her children still slept beside her on the floor, wrapped in soft hides against the chill that came off the river in the early fall. She listened to the sounds of the fort awakening: Mexican and Indian women arguing over spots at the creek, Mexican men taking horses outside to graze, English, French, Spanish, and Russian cursing as teamsters began to load their wagons, reveille from the American military camp just outside the fort. When she opened her eyes she noted the breeze blowing across her delicate Victorian desk and ruffling the brocade curtains hanging over adobe windows and she wondered if the linen shirts, leggings, and moccasins that she had laid out for her sons to wear would be warm enough. They planned to join her father's Cheyenne family for a fall hunt, along with the other boys who lived in the fort.

Owl Woman, the wife of William Bent and the daughter of both Cheyenne and Arapaho leaders, lived in a distinctive world. Bent's Fort, along the Arkansas River in what is now southeastern Colorado, though isolated from the centers of American economic power in the 1830s, had every luxury from fine wines to soft beaded moccasins to elegant china to Mexican silver, all which got used daily in the fort's trading and dining rooms (Lavender, 1954: 166–8). The fort, and the people who lived in it, mixed cultural practices to create a particular kind of community that characterized a long period in the American West. The world of William Bent and Owl Woman represented a moment and a place where economic and political power depended upon cultural adaptability and upon communities that supported this complexity. William Bent, from a wealthy family in St Louis, slept on a buffalo hide on the floor but understood that he needed to have silver cigar clamps and a French writing desk as well. Owl Woman knew that diplomacy was at the center of her marriage and that Bent's Fort and the trade it supported depended on her skills. The great adobe walls and wooden gates of Bent's fort demonstrated the solidity of this place, but also its fragility.

Nearly fifty years later, an Italian miner living in Leadville, Colorado, awoke to an entirely different community. The walls that surrounded him, muslin stretched over wooden frames, hardly muffled the sounds of snores of eighteen sleeping men. The miner listened to his landlady prepare breakfast, which he knew would be oatmeal, rancid bacon, and coffee made from yesterday's grounds. Because he dreaded the foreign breakfast and the work that faced him in the Chrysolite mine that day, he decided to flee the boarding house for the refuge of Joe Soretti's bar, which served beer, strong coffee, and Italian bread at all hours of the day. As the miner walked along the streets of Leadville that day in 1884, he took pride in the grand hotels, saloons, shops, and dance halls that lined Harrison Avenue, but he worried about the rumors of layoffs at the mine because he knew that Italians and Austrians were always the first to go. His wife and children, in transit from Italy, would need more than a boarding house room when they arrived in Leadville, but he never seemed able to save enough to rent a house. However, the stale, smoky odor of the bar comforted him, as did the sight of a crucifix that hung in an alcove. He called out a morning greeting in Italian to the miners coming off shift, crossed himself and prayed for his family in Italy, and ordered a coffee and a beer (Leadville *Daily Democrat*: August 20, 1884 and September 14, 1884).

The miner, though he had intended to come to Leadville only to make money, had immersed himself in a community, one every bit as complicated as Owl Woman's. But the central purpose of both of these settings was profit, cold hard cash made as part of an international capitalism that depended on complex trade and the hard work of exploitable people. The gritty, dangerous, industrial world of Leadville's mines could only be made bearable with the help and support of friends and family, making ethnic enclaves essential to every mining town. Behind the flimsy walls of boarding houses, saloons, and churches, a powerful community emerged in spite of itself. People clung together in made-up families, formed fraternal organizations in an effort to protect themselves from the centrifugal power of the mining industry. But suicide, accident, and child abandonment rates indicated that they were not always successful. Community seemed ironic in places like Bent's Fort or Leadville, where people gathered from all over the world to escape the economic and social bonds of their past lives and to remake themselves.

This essay examines some patterns in places people chose to settle and in spots they found themselves during the nineteenth century in the American West. These patterns raise questions about what community means in a region designed to exploit natural resources in imperial economies and about how the people who lived there used these places to serve varied interests. To knit functional relationships out of extremely disparate groups of people, community had to do a special kind of "work" in the nineteenth-century West. Whether they simply wanted to conduct trade or produce something, entrepreneurs and settlers had to build the means to do so. In a setting where people often spoke different languages and had radically different social and cultural practices, like fur-trading fort or a mining town, community had to do the job of making daily life possible which, in turn, made economies functional and profitable. People living in these places had to create community in active ways because they had few institutions to do it for them.

The role of community depends on power relations and intentionality. Community looks different if you own the mine rather than working in it, or if you have a family and ambitions of stability and are not just passing through. We can probe these questions by using three kinds of communities and their surrounding regions as examples: the fur and trading enterprises at Fort Vancouver and Bent's Fort, the intentional agricultural settlements around Salt Lake City, and the "accidental" industrial world of Leadville and the Rocky Mountain mining region.

If Walls Could Talk: Western Communities

As markers of community, walls and fences have always been at the center of political debate in the American West. Whether a white picket fence, strands of barbed wire, or a solid adobe wall, these indicators of human presence send out mixed signals in the region. They can mean settlement, freedom, war, or imprisonment. Cutting a fence or building a wall can be heroic or criminal depending on the time and place. Walls and fences are built to demarcate ownership or the lack of it, to separate humans from animals, or to keep some people in and others out. In 1811 the crew of the ship *Tonquin* built Fort Astoria from the great trees that lined the Columbia River and they felt as much satisfaction about their accomplishment as did Dakota homesteaders in the 1870s, stringing wire to indicate land had been settled (Ronda, 1990: 201; Raban, 1996: 116–21). Both efforts, though ephemeral, represented crucial moves toward individual, corporate, and national profits, as well as toward community. The walls of a fort protect some people from the attacks of unfriendly people and beasts, but they also incarcerate others. Good fences make good neighbors except in places where folks use fences to take land illegally or to keep their neighbors from using water. Fences and walls are crucial to the development of communities but can be destructive as well.

Thinking about the question of the role of community in the American West presents two basic difficulties. One is disciplinary. Because American history and especially western American history has centered on the history of exploration, migration, growth, and movement, and because historians generally concern themselves with change, we may have underestimated the significance of continuity and community. Stories of people who stayed in western places because they were tired of moving, too poor to leave, lacked the ambition to reach for the brass, gold, or copper ring, or were simply satisfied with the place they had found, are the antithesis of the national story. In the American national story we often talk about community values, but most often we celebrate individual action, especially in the nineteenth century when personal ambition became nearly a fetish. Fence builders and fence cutters are heroic because their actions are dramatic, but the stories of the people who do the slow and often dull work of mending and maintaining fences often do not get told (Stegner, 1992: 4–18).

The other problem is more visceral: communities in the American West look different from those in other parts of the country. To continue with the fence analogy, western communities, instead of being neatly tucked behind white picket fences or charmingly surrounded by low stonewalls, mark themselves with barbed wire and tumbleweeds, weed-infested ditches, or high stockades. They have often been isolated, windswept, disorganized, ugly, temporary, and, often, unpleasant and dangerous to live in. Mining towns, Indian reservations, ranching towns, trailer parks, wagon trains, fur trading forts, and ski towns all exhibit social pathologies that keep teams of sociologists and public officials well occupied. Largely, this is because western communities were mostly "unintentional." No one intended to build them, no one intended to stay, and no one intended to build lasting bonds, all of which affected the location, appearance, and operation of these places. People assembled such communities more often to convenience distant economic forces than to enhance the quality of human life.

Despite this, community is important. We humans need communities to raise children into healthy and productive adults, to give meaning and definition to our lives, and generally to make the human project go forward. Even in the grimmest mining town or the most isolated ranching community, people gathered to discuss their ambitions, fears, work, and family life, and they set up structures that allowed them to practice religion, to educate children, and to protect themselves from the fates of the economy, the weather, or human personality. These discussions and structures, whether they emerged out of saloons or churches or union halls or brothels, form the bedrock of community. However, communities in the West have often lacked the "social glue" to attach much that was lasting or helpful to this bedrock.

One of the ironies about thinking about community in the West is that the region has always been, at the same time, the most isolated and the most urban part of the nation. Partly because of the landscape and partly because of the isolation, people settled in tightly bound communities. Forts, mining towns, clusters of tepees, ranching and cattle towns, pueblos, and railroad towns all pack people in fairly densely. The pattern of widely scattered farms that characterized other parts of the nation in the nineteenth century was fundamentally unsuitable for much of the west – as most homesteaders painfully came to understand. But, these dense settlements operated in isolation, cut off from other people by enormous space and austere geographies, making social networks challenging to form and maintain.

Some western communities worked in the ways that social theorists define as healthy; they provided a safe place for families, a source of pride, memory, and tradition, and a sense of group belonging (Hine, 1980: 11–23). And, aspects of all communities provided some of these things for some people. Some pueblos, some Mormon towns, and some agricultural or mining settlements fit standard definitions of community and, ironically, the West hosted numerous utopian experiments in community, most of which failed to live up to their founders' ambitions. And, boosters and speculators in railroad, mining, or agricultural towns after the Civil War boasted, in rather desperate fashion, about the safety, solidity and opportunity present for families (all as a lure for investment) in their respective towns (Wrobel, 1996). On the other hand, a nineteenth-century child growing up in the Santa Cara pueblo, or Provo, Utah, or Salem, Oregon knew that she was part of a functional community that could and would provide support and solace in times of hardship and that expected some loyalty and reciprocity in return.

However, in most of the West for most of the nineteenth century, two kinds of communities characterized the region, neither of which could provide the kinds of support their members needed. The first were multiracial, multinational communities where people connected to conduct business and to extract wealth with little expectation of building anything lasting. These "resource extraction communities" (such as mining camps, fur trading posts, or lumber towns) that emerged in a relative vacuum of political power, appeared most frequently in the first two-thirds of the century, but vestiges of them still linger into the twenty-first century. The second characteristically western community resulted from the clash of industrial capitalism and government power with the isolated west (Robbins, 1994: 22–63). This pattern, in the form of railroad towns, ranching communities, Indian reservations, and mining and smelter towns, dominated the period after the Civil War.

"Walls of Military Precision" or "Mud Castles": The Traders' Communities of Fort Vancouver and Bent's Fort

The world that evolved around the trade in fur and hides required the creation of cosmopolitan communities, which became emblematic of the American West in the nineteenth century. Both Fort Vancouver and Bent's Fort operated as crucial lynchpins in a global economic system. By the beginning of the nineteenth century, fur and its production, transit, and sale had been a central product of international trade for nearly three centuries and was crucial to the economic development of the United States. Fur, like sugar, linked continents, labor systems, and human lives in new and unbreakable ways and it made the western part of North America a locus of international rivalry and intrigue (Hine and Faragher, 2000: 133–51).

The fur trade only functioned, however, because people of different races, classes, and nationalities formed purposeful communities in isolated places. And, the lives they led there required much adjustment in the ways people thought about culture, power, and society. For much of the period, the United States as a political or cultural entity had no special power. Who would control the West remained an open question until the 1850s. The vast region remained a place where a variety of peoples sought new opportunities. Russian, Ute, Mormon, Texan, Cheyenne, Mexican, Apache, Blackfoot, French, African American, Californio, Irish, Yankee, or Lakota, they all moved in and around what we call the West in an uneasy swirl. Race, gender, and ethnicity operated, but had permeable categories and considerable flexibility. International borders had little impact on most westerners' daily lives, but the rhythms of trade, seasonal migration of people and animals, and the conflicts between and among the varied tribes of the region, Anglo, Spanish, and Indian, mattered enormously. The most successful practitioners of this trade operated out of forts, constructing communities that were far from the flimsy and transient entities the term often implies. A symbol of economic power, the fur-trading fort represents a set of imperial dreams and the new cultural arrangements necessary to make them real.

Fort Vancouver, first opened in 1821, claimed the heart of the rich hunting grounds of the Pacific Northwest, grounds that included both sea and land animal pelts. Built on the failure of American, Russian, and Spanish efforts to settle the area, the fort's population reflected this history. Though the behemoth of the fur trade, the Hudson's Bay Company, operated Fort Vancouver, it was unlike their other corporate enterprises. Because of the powerful tribes that surrounded it and the complex international situation that had created it, this fort depended on a much more delicate diplomatic balance (Rich, 1959: 187–96; Dudden, 1992: 7–29). The Scottish "director" and his corps of French-Canadian, British, and Native American clerks, traders, and trappers, lived in a community that depended on cultural flexibility and global economy. The price of fur in Montreal or London dictated as much about the details of daily life in what is now Oregon as did skill and ceremony around tea, tobacco smoking, or flag-raising. It was a region in which no people, nation, or corporate enterprise had uncontested control, so that the peculiar community that lived in and outside of the fort reflected the careful diplomacy and cosmopolitan attitude of a shifting situation.

None of the European powers or the United States had a strong claim (or much of an interest) in that part of the continent while the wars of empire raged over the eastern half of the continent. The English had a weak claim because of the Hudson's Bay Company, which basically said it owned everything anywhere near Canada. The Spanish saw it as an extension of Alta California. The Russians claimed it as part of their interests in Siberia after Vitus Bering sailed south to Alaska in 1741 and began trading for furs (Johansen and Gates, 1957: 10–11). The English got interested in the fur trade potential of the region when Captain James Cook sailed up the west coast in search of the Northwest Passage in 1778. By the 1780s, English and American ships regularly stopped and traded along the coast of what is now Washington, Oregon, and British Columbia, where the local Indians offered Russian and Spanish goods as part of their trade repertoire. However, everyone aspired to trade northwest coast furs in the rapidly opening market in Canton, where perhaps 2.5 million fine furs were sold in the 1780s and 1790s (Johansen and Gates, 1957: 33–74; Lavender, 1961: 66).

The Spanish, who had claimed Nootka Sound in 1774 as a way to prevent Russian incursions into their territory, cared little about otter or beaver pelts but cared a great deal about protecting their claim to the Pacific Northwest and Alta California. Naturally, they found this new international trade activity worrisome and in 1789 a Spanish officer seized four British ships and sent their crews to prisons in Mexico. The British, angry over Spain's action and its efforts to monopolize trade in the region, demanded the creation of a new international treaty. With not much diplomatic or military strength to support its territorial claims, Spain had to agree to the internationally negotiated Nootka Treaty, which gave other nations the right to hunt, trade, and settle along the Northwest Coast, but protected fishing and hunting near areas actually occupied by Spain. Clearly, the message to nations and their traders was that only occupation and settlement could guarantee control of the region. The big winners in this arrangement were the British and, eventually, the Hudson's Bay Company that was inexorably extending its influence south and west from its Canadian stronghold (Johansen and Gates, 1957: 46–51; Ronda, 1990: 63–6).

There were challenges to the supremacy of the Hudson's Bay Company. In 1808, just as Lewis and Clark returned from their epic adventure, an ambitious German immigrant, John Jacob Astor, had already imagined the profits a fort on the Pacific would bring to himself and to the United States. He wrote a letter to President Thomas Jefferson proposing a vast trade network that would link Europe, the American Great Lakes, the Pacific Northwest, Russian America, and China. A combination of federal support, a set of trading posts, and Astor's own entrepreneurial imagination would cement American sovereignty in the fur trade. Jefferson turned him down, but Astor went ahead and created the Pacific Fur Company, which he intended to build into a true competitor for the two great Canadian fur empires, the Hudson's Bay Company and the North West Company. Astor chose to launch the enterprise at a moment when the two giants were locked into mortal combat with each other and the United States and Great Britain were embarking on war over trade issues (Ronda, 1990: 18–33; Phillips, 1961: 119–38).

None of this seemed to worry Astor. He arranged for two expeditions to the mouth of the Columbia, one following the overland route taken by Lewis and Clark and the other by ship around Cape Horn. The ship *Tonquin* arrived first, in March of 1811, and its crew selected a site on the south side of the Columbia River for the new fort and named it Astoria. By the time the overland group arrived in the late winter of 1812, they found an impressive structure. Surrounded by a palisade of Douglas firs, the store, dwelling houses, blacksmith shops, and sheds presaged the great commercial center that the fort would become. The varied group of people who built the fort, tended its gardens, worked to build relationships with local tribes, and who hunted and processed furs modeled the kind of community that the trade in the Far West required. French-Canadians and Mohawk Iroquois, long experienced in the fur trade, offered hunting and diplomatic skills in dealing with the Indians. Iroquois, Chinook, Flathead, and Salish Indians did much of the labor, joined by a contingent of Hawaiians, who had been picked up for a three-year term of service on the trip out. Scotsmen and Anglo-Americans, including Wilson Price Hunt, David and Robert Stuart, and Duncan McDougall, provided much of the leadership (Phillips, 1961: 270–275; Ross, 1849: 2–12).

By 1813, Astoria appeared to be a going concern, though its establishment had been far more work and danger and less profit than the original partners had hoped. When the War of 1812 came to an end and England asserted control over the Pacific Northwest as part of treaty negotiations, Astor lost his gamble. A group of North West Company trappers appeared at the fort in June of 1813 and demanded that the fort be turned over to them. After months of indecision and waiting for official word from New York, the partners on site decided to sell the fort to the North West Company for a mere $80,000, rather than waiting for a British warship to take it from them. In December Fort Astoria became Fort George (Phillips, 1961: 289–91; Ross, 1849: 253).

The coup of the North West Company in seizing control of this piece of the Rocky Mountain fur trade was, however, short-lived. The Hudson's Bay Company, lying in wait, initiated a destructive campaign to destroy its rival, and in an effort to keep the two companies from self-destruction, the British government brokered a deal that merged them. The result, signed in 1821, gave the Hudson's Bay Company a complete monopoly on the fur trade, including the Pacific Northwest. Fort George now became Fort Vancouver, and the Governor, George Simpson of the Hudson's Bay Company, gave the fort a new purpose and new location. Because Simpson knew that his nation's claim on the region could end at any moment, he moved the fort to the north side of the river to bolster England's hope that the Columbia would be the border between the United States. Not being entirely confident of that result, Simpson the businessman also decided to strip the region of furs as quickly as possible (Rich, 1955: 584–87; Pomeroy, 1965: 18–19).

To guide the fort in these economic and nationalistic purposes, Simpson brought in Dr John McLoughlin, an austere and commanding presence, to serve as chief factor of the Columbia district. He stayed in the post until the border issue was settled in 1846. In that twenty-year period, McLoughlin built a community that reached far beyond the walls of the fort itself and that became legendary in the trade. The fort's thorny diplomatic history, its efficient (perhaps ruthless) operation, and the ethnic and racial complexity of its personnel made an indelible mark on the region's development. McLoughlin's Fort Vancouver, with its grand dining hall and thousands of acres of farms, ruled over a community with a distinctive blend of modern capitalism and old world patronage practiced on an improbably diverse group of people.

Such a blend would have looked familiar and practical to William Bent, the *patron* of Bent's Fort. Built only a few years after Fort Vancouver, Bent's Fort served a similar economic and imperial purpose. This fort emerged out of comparable international rivalry with a slightly different cast of characters. Spain, France, and the United States all had interests in the furs located in the southern Rockies and in the increasingly lucrative Taos trade. This region at the border of the United States and Spain, which in the first years of the nineteenth century was located along the Arkansas River, became a center of economic and nationalistic attention. Spain, struggling to maintain its empire and fully aware of the imperial greed of the new United States, policed its borders zealously. In a futile effort to keep American, French, and British traders from horning in on profits, Spain closed off its trade with outsiders. However, with the increasing centrality of St Louis in the fur trade, the overhunting of fur-bearing animals in the northern Rockies, and finally, the Mexican Revolution, Spain lost its control over the region (Adler, 1991: 1–9; Lavender, 1954: 6–10).

When the new Mexican government announced in 1821 that it would open the Santa Fe trade to outsiders, many St Louis entrepreneurs were ready to take advantage of the situation. St Louis, with its enormous geographic advantage of being sited at the confluence of two rivers that drained a vast part of the United States, had become a real competitor to Montreal in the fur trade early in the nineteenth century. Even though the Louisiana Purchase made it an American city, the powerful French and Spanish families who built St Louis continued to dominate trade. As in Montreal or in Fort Vancouver, a cosmopolitan mix of people made the fur trade possible. Traders like Manuel Lisa, Pierre Chouteau, and William Ashley worked with French-Canadian, British, Spanish, and American trappers and their Indian families, to get furs. However, unlike the fur industry in Canada, no large corporate entities emerged to monopolize the upper Missouri and Rocky Mountain trade. Individual trappers and their Indian families watched as a series of trading enterprises attempted to corner the market on furs. The huge distances involved, the powerful Indians who fought the fur trade, and the fickle prices for fur in London, made the Rocky mountain fur trade a risky business.

The Bent and StVrain families, central to the history of the Santa Fe trade, came out of the St Louis fur trade aristocracy. Charles Bent and Ceran St Vrain, working both as independent trappers and as employees and occasionally partners in larger companies, watched the emergence of the new trading network between Santa Fe and St Louis. By the late 1820s both men had concluded that the more diversified Santa Fe trade looked far more promising than the elusive Rocky mountain fur trade. In 1829 Charles Bent and his younger brother, William, used all of their money and more to outfit a caravan filled with trade goods to head out from Missouri along the increasingly heavily traveled Santa Fe trail into Mexico, where they would trade their goods for furs, buffalo hides, blankets, and Mexican silver, which they would carry back to St Louis and sell, if all went well, at a handsome profit. All didn't go well and many of the caravan's men deserted after a series of Indian attacks, but Charles, William, and their goods arrived in Santa Fe intact. They picked up merchandise worth perhaps $200,000 in Missouri, and along with several of their old St Louis fur trade friends, including Ceran St Vrain, prepared for the return trip. William, however, had other ideas. At age 20, he found the actual experience of moving a caravan along the trail tedious and decided to head into the mountains to trap and to trade with the Indians (Lavender, 1954: 99–112; Weber, 1974: 178–81).

This turned out to be a momentous decision for the history of the region. William recognized that the key to success in the trade was developing a more reliable trade with the Indians. Because of their skills in hunting buffalo and in preparing the hides for transport and sale, Native Americans played an essential role in the industry. However, aside from a few individual trappers and traders, few Euro-Americans had developed strong trade relationships with the tribes in the vicinity. Bent's timing mattered because the social and economic changes that brought William Bent to the southern Rockies had also put the world of the southern Plains Indians into flux. Pressure from American settlements in the Mississippi River Valley and in Texas, the official process of removal, and the new possibilities opened by the Santa Fe trade brought new tribes into the region, creating conflict with native peoples with a longer tradition there. The Cheyenne and the Arapahoe in particular were newcomers to the southern plains, looking for ways to increase their horse herds and populations. A chance meeting with William Bent, in which he protected some Cheyenne horse thieves against a group of Comanches, gave the Cheyenne a new ally and Bent an entrée into trade with the Cheyenne (West, 1998; Lavender, 1954: 128–129).

A year or so later, after Charles Bent had made numerous profitable trips back and forth between Santa Fe and St Louis, William introduced high-quality trade goods from St Louis to the Cheyenne, further increasing their interest in trade and their loyalty to him. He built a temporary stockade along the Arkansas to store his goods and soon convinced his brother Charles and their partners, the St Vrain brothers, of the wisdom of building a large and well-stocked permanent fort right on the border. William insisted that such a fort, with an unparalleled supply of goods, would attract traders and Indians to them and they would have a monopoly on everything north of Taos. According to William's son George, who told the story much later, the Bents and St Vrains then consulted their new trading partners, the Cheyenne, as to the proper location of the fort. Yellow Wolf, a chief of the Hairy Rope Clan, advised them to choose a site further out on the plains, a region where Cheyenne, Arapahoe, Ute, Comanche, and Kiowa groups hunted and traded. Construction of the fort began in 1831, with teams of Mexican adobe makers setting up camp on the north side of the Arkansas (Hyde, 1968: 58–60; Comer, 1996: 92–3).

In its own way, Bent's Fort was as impressive as Fort Vancouver. Using adobe rather than the tremendous Douglas firs of the Pacific Northwest, the fort that soon dominated the bluffs overlooking the river covered nearly an acre. The walls, several feet thick, rose from between fifteen and thirty feet above the ground and inclosed enough space to house several hundred people and hundreds of horses and other livestock. In both places, the physically impressive nature of each fort was intended to signal imperial and national power as each fort performed the role of border sentry. However, the fact that private enterprise, rather than the government itself, was policing the border indicates something about the realities of national control of the region.

Neither William Bent nor John McLoughlin worked for the government and in fact, both men ignored the niceties of federal law, borders, and military procedure quite regularly. They operated more like medieval lords, with intricate systems of duty and reciprocity, but immersed in a global system of markets and capital. Managing a far-flung business that depended on the whims of many nations and the skills of a huge variety of cultures and peoples in a setting isolated from commercial and urban entrepots required intelligence, tact, flexibility, and diplomacy. The complexity of cultural connections and the power of the diplomacy that held together the communities McLoughlin and Bent built around trade became evident in the scene presented in the great halls of each fort.

At Fort Vancouver, John McLoughlin presided over the equivalent of state dinners where the aristocracy and peasantry of the fur trade mingled. From his seat at the end of a great table, McLoughlin could see Scottish businessmen, French-Canadian trappers, local Chinook dignitaries, American missionaries, Russian or English ships' captains, Hawaiian laborers, and Iroquois and Shoshone hunters. Many of the men, including McLoughlin and his Scottish and Canadian associates, were married to Indian or métis women, who also sat at the great table (Rich, 1961: 638–43; Holman, 1907: 27–30). As one visitor remembered, "Roast beef, pork, boiled mutton, baked salmon, boiled ham; beets, carrots, turnips, cabbage, and potatoes, and wheaten bread, are tastefully distributed over the table among a set of elegant queen's ware, burnished with glittering glasses and decanters of various-coloured Italian wines. Course after course goes round . . ." (Farnham, 1843: 128). The splendor of the meal, the arrangement of the seating, and the guests invited all reflected the importance of intercultural mixing diplomacy in the operation of the business. Fort Vancouver itself represented an oasis of culture peculiar to the world of the fur trade that dominated the West in that period. The eight hundred people living in or near the fort were part of a much larger community of trappers, traders, hunters, farmers, parents, and business people that enabled the fur industry to operate. Power and influence flowed between and among races and nationalities because of the complexity of the trade. The communities that developed in this world reflected the fur trade's need for cooperation, flexibility, and protection.

William Bent's family, table, and daily life displayed the same cultural practices. His Cheyenne wife, Owl Woman, and his Mexican sisters-in-law helped him to cement trade relationships with various nations, tribes, and governments. These marriages, which many American observers snootily interpreted as casual relationships of "convenience", were long-lasting partnerships that resulted in children, wealth, and power. And, in the first half of the nineteenth century, thousands of families like Bent's made the fur trade operate. Bent's Fort, often described as a "mud castle on the plains," represented a kind of zenith of the culture, where people gathered to live, do business, celebrate, and enjoy the finer things of life: food, drink, conversation and comfort, from a variety of different cultures. (Comer, 1996: 15–28; Lavender, 1954: 103–19) Children from these communities had a special set of skills that included family connections in a range of cultures, languages, and hunting, trading, and business practices, all of which gave them advantages in the world of the fur trade.

These advantages and the communities that granted them, however, did not survive the end of the fur industry and the beginning of the dominance of the United States. The families and children of the fur trade became "squaw men," "half-breeds" and "mongrels" and could find no place in the new communities that developed with

American conquest. Even the power and status of the great enterprises of Fort Vancouver and Bent's Fort could not protect these culturally mixed people from scorn and disaster. John McLoughlin's son was murdered by his employees and McLoughlin spent his last years struggling, and ultimately failing, to maintain his land claims so that his family would have a place in the new American community of Oregon (Rich, 1961: 710–12; Holman, 1907: 96–8). William Bent, watching the fur and hide trades wither away, apparently blew up his great fort after a smallpox epidemic wiped out most of his wife's relatives. He spent his old age watching his children participate in the Sand Creek Massacre, on both the Cheyenne and the United States army sides (Roberts, 2000: 97–8; West, 1998: 246–56). The rich and distinctive communities that characterized the fur trade had clearly been overwhelmed and deliberately destroyed by newer settlements that had different needs and standards.

Building for Eternity: Mormon Communities in Utah

If the community of the fort emerged out of the profit motives and the practical necessities of negotiating the fur trade, another community of lasting significance to the West developed out of a desire to escape exactly that profit-minded and practical bent of the nineteenth-century United States. The Mormons who settled in the Great Basin in the middle of the century, like many utopian communities who headed west, intended to avoid, and perhaps to chastise by example, mainstream American culture. And, in the way they designed and lived in these intentional communities, they both failed and succeeded in their aims.

Now, generalizing about Mormons is particularly hazardous. Infamous for their practice of polygamy as well as for their financial success, the Mormons who arrived in the Great Basin in 1847 have changed in fundamental ways to become the wealthy and powerful group who hosted the 2002 Olympics. The Mormons can be put forward as useful examples of people who held out against the centrifugal forces of the frontier and who built successful and prosperous communities that used land, water, and labor wisely. However, Mormons have also been described as a clannish and dangerous threat to frontier development, as an anti-American aberration in the Great Basin.

The Mormons are neither as good nor as bad as these two sets of images make them out to be. From the beginning, they were far more mainstream than their detractors understood them to be and, at the same time, they were far more radical than their supporters would have them be. The Mormons set out to be distinctive, failed in their most radical efforts at difference, but discovered a successful compromise with American culture in those failures (Arrington, 1958: Arrington, Fox, and May, 1992). Mormon communities, in their spectacular successes and failures, do stand as examples of the wide variety of utopian experiments that ventured west in the nineteenth and early twentieth centuries.

Mormonism evolved out of the tumult of American religion that burned most fiercely across the interior of the eastern United States in the 1820s and 1830s. Joseph Smith's dissatisfaction with the acquisitive, individualistic culture he found himself surrounded by was not at all uncommon in that time and place and neither was his 1831 revelation about building a new religion. Concern over market pressures and the disruptions they created drove many people to question the basic precepts of

American culture and to experiment with new forms of community and religion. Smith and his Latter-day Saints, as directed by the Angel Moroni and the Book of Mormon, differed only in the number of converts they attracted, the range of social mores they challenged, and the reaction they got from the people who lived around them (Hansen, 1981: 114–25; Shipps, 1985: 5). Like many of the other communitarian experiments, such as the Shakers, Oneida, and Amana, Smith wanted to build an egalitarian society that actively made its members equal before God. The new social and economic order, codified in 1831 as "the Law of Consecration and Stewardship," emerged as central to Mormon doctrine. It required giving up material possessions, status, and worldly attachments and developing a truly cooperative style that assured sustenance but not comfort for all (Arrington, Fox, and May, 1992: 2). The Mormons never quite lived up to this egalitarian ideal, but it remained central to their behavior.

Driven out of the Mississippi River Valley by violence, persecution, and the murder of Joseph Smith, the Mormons ended up in the Salt Lake Valley by a series of accidents. In their attempt to escape from the United States, a large group of Saints led by Brigham Young planned to migrate west into what was Mexican territory to build a new Zion. As he planned the mass exodus from his "Winter Quarters" in Iowa, Young did not know whether he would settle in California or some place further east; he simply wanted an isolated and fertile spot far from the gaze of government. Demonstrating the organizational skill and the cooperative ethos that would come to characterize Mormon communities, in 1847 Young led nearly two thousand people to an isolated mountain valley on the western slope of the Wasatch Mountains. In short order the Saints built a fort and laid out a city, began farming using crude irrigation, and organized another mass migration. And they did this not as individuals, but as a group that agreed to put their "mites together for that which is the best for every man, woman, and child" (Quoted in Arrington, 1958: 45).

The distinctive qualities of Mormon settlement were evident from the beginning as they developed practices and laws to divide up land, water, and labor. With specific instructions from the Council of Twelve that formed the church leadership, Mormon pioneers plowed, fenced, and irrigated one "Big Field," devised a system of building houses on evenly spaced city blocks, and gave out farm lots with the idea that they would be "equal according to circumstances, wants, and needs" (Arrington, 1958: 47). Some of this cooperative effort came out of necessity in the first desperate need to feed and shelter a large group of people in an unfamiliar environment. But its success and its continuity came out of religious conviction and the desire to live up to Joseph Smith's vision of an egalitarian kingdom on earth. Because of their early experience and deeply held belief in communal effort, the Mormons succeeded where other groups could not.

The Mormons practiced real cooperation, especially during the long and important years of Brigham Young's Presidency. Their experiences in Missouri, Illinois, and Iowa had made long-term experiments difficult, but had only increased their determination to succeed in Utah. In the decades after they arrived in Utah, the Mormon faithful signaled their difference from mainstream American culture by attempting to farm, merchandise, and manufacture with commonly owned and worked lands, products, and cash. Everything from railroad building, banking, stock grazing, sugar production, and lumbering was undertaken with two related goals: to make the

Mormons entirely self-sufficient so that they could cease all contact with the unfriendly United States and so that they could create the Kingdom of God on earth where all people shared according to their abilities and needs in work, profits, and grace (Arrington, 1958: 7–10; Campbell, 1988: 140–3).

These two goals, and the fact that few Mormons had much cash, made many of these early cooperative experiments successful. Some of this success had practical reasons. Because no one had enough capital to start manufacturing enterprises or to build irrigation systems, people had to pool resources. Several theological practices made this easier. Mormons believed that they all served as stewards of the Church's wealth and that basically everything, in the end, belonged not to individual Mormons, but to the Church as a whole. While the law of stewardship was not always fully lived, every Mormon understood that the practice of tithing took its place and observed it very seriously. At least a tenth of every person's product and labor went directly to the Church, so that people spent every tenth day working on Church building projects such as forts, meetinghouses, roads, and other public works. The produce and stock donated to the church required that each community and ward set up a tithing house to store, sort, grow, and redistribute this increasingly significant source of wealth. The Mormon leadership invested this wealth in a variety of enterprises from a church-owned telegraph company, to iron mills, newspapers, sugar-beet processing companies, and finally to the Zion Cooperative Mercantile Institution that became a long-lasting and successful merchandising cooperative with branches in every community and a set of major department stores by the end of the century (Campbell, 1988: 135–8; Anderson, 1942: 364). Two examples indicate the significance of this cooperation to Mormon culture and economic success: the Perpetual Emigrating Fund and the practice of irrigated agriculture.

Serious about, as Brigham Young put it, their "one great work – the building up of the Kingdom of God of Earth," the Mormons faced some disadvantages in terms of their location. Getting new converts, who tended to be the poor and dispossessed of the new commercial industrial world of eastern America and Western Europe, to the isolation of the Great Basin Kingdom cost a lot of money. Few emigrants could pay their own passage from Europe, much less the cost of emigrating across the Great Plains, and even fewer had the means to set themselves up in business or as farmers in such a forbidding setting as Utah. To solve this problem, Young and the Council of Twelve came up with the concept of the Perpetual Emigrating Fund in 1849. It would operate out of voluntary contributions of church members, repayments by those assisted by the Fund, and with interest accrued on loans given, and it would exist purely to fund the emigration of poor Mormons to Utah. As soon as Young announced the plan, Utah Mormons raised five thousand dollars and sent it east with an agent instructed to make the money stretch as far as he could by providing only minimal supplies and homemade wagons. This maximized the numbers of new converts while tempering their faith with hardship on the trail (Arrington, Fox, and May, 1992: 43; Stegner, 1964: 208).

Upon arrival in Utah, new Saints received land or employment through the new Office of Public Works created out of the wealth accumulating in tithing houses. Throughout the 1850s, hundreds of men worked as blacksmiths, carpenters, painters, adobe-makers, and stone-cutters building the infrastructure of Salt Lake City. With their wages or their farm produce, some emigrants managed to pay back the

Perpetual Emigrating Fund, but most of the money came from more established Mormons. In fact, most beneficiaries of the Fund never paid it back and by 1880 owed it nearly $2,000,000. As a nod to the fiftieth year Jubilee of the Church, its leaders decided to forgive the debts in 1880 and cleared the books, declaring the experiment a grand success, as the Fund eventually brought more than 10,000 Saints to Utah (Arrington, Fox, and May, 1992: 43–5; Campbell, 1988; 140).

Irrigation, famously, represented another success for Mormon settlements. The combination of practical need and theocratic principle made irrigation work. The Mormons recognized instantly that water stood as the most precious commodity in Utah and that only communal effort and ownership would protect this resource. Wilford Woodruff recorded in his 1847 diary that within two days of arriving in the Salt Lake Valley, the first group of Saints had planted potatoes, only possible because "the brethren had dammed up one of the creeks and dug a trench, and by night nearly the whole ground, which was found very dry, was irrigated" (Arrington, Fox, and May, 1992: 49). Within a year, ward bishops had become watermasters so that control of water remained within the Church hierarchy.

Within a few years, Mormons had figured out the organizational and agronomic skills necessary to irrigated agriculture. Canals, ditches, gates, and the equitable apportionment of water became part of the Mormon social fabric and tasks to maintain the system were part of a bishop's duty and of Sunday services. Water doled out equally by fractions of stream flow so that no one could use water at the expense of someone else reflected Mormon ideals of fairness and cooperation. Such practices stood in opposition to the system that developed in much of the rest of the West and that rewarded early comers and allowed single owners to use all the water in a stream. The unique Mormon system, codified into the Utah Irrigation District Act of 1865, superseded all traditions of both riparian water law and Colorado Water Law. It encouraged the development of small farms, gathered around tightly knit villages, where the work on canals and gates could be easily supervised and organized. And, irrigation enthusiasts like John Wesley Power and Elwood Mead singled out the Mormons as examples of how it should be done (Sadler and Roberts, 1994: 2–21; Arrington and May, 1975: 3–11).

Though by many measures the Mormons succeeded, they did not create an egalitarian kingdom, something deeply important to Brigham Young and many early leaders in the Church. This goal and its ultimate failure was showcased in the story of the United Order of Enoch, which grew out of the Mormon's long history of cooperation. As the Mormon state grew and prospered, and as American culture in the form of the Gold Rush, debates over state leaders, and the transcontinental railroad both threatened and strengthened the Kingdom, Brigham Young continued to see Joseph Smith's Law of Consecration and Stewardship as an ideal. Every cooperative experiment could be seen as a step toward the goal of a society of cooperating Saints, all united in the single purpose of sharing wealth to create God's kingdom on earth. Tithing, cooperative sugar mills and department, communal farming practices, water rights, cattle herds, and road-building teams, were only steps to a purely communitarian society (Arrington, Fox, and May, 1992: 135–36; Anderson, 1942: 301).

In the early 1870s, Young apparently decided that the Saints were ready for the final stage. He announced a new structure, the United Order of Enoch, that would take over all private property in Mormon communities, and initiated a great religious revival. The preamble to the articles of the United Order, which contained specific instructions on how to manage community land, bees, tools, stock, and profit, also indicates the kinds of pressures Young felt to create "a closer union and combination of our labor for the promotion of our common welfare" (Anderson, 1942: 375). He implored his followers to take up simple habits, to give up extravagance, and to have energetic and faithful dealings. He began in St George, in southern Utah, and worked his way north, demanding that all good Mormons surrender their private property and combat the "feeling of Mine," thus avoiding the dangers of "grasping individualism" that Young feared had taken over the hearts of many Saints (Hine, 1980: 212; Hansen, 1981: 128). In Young's vision, each community would be entirely self-sufficient and entirely without private enterprise, with the ultimate belief that "to be friends of God we must become friends and helpers of each other" (Anderson, 1942: 376).

The revival ended in a grand fizzle. Though many communities initially responded to Young's pleas with enthusiasm, only a very few could live up to his standards. By 1880 only the town of Orderville, formed out of a nucleus of families who left failed United Order communities to band together, remained to practice Young's principles (Hine, 1980: 212). The economic success of the Mormons, their central location on the railroad, and their importance in the growing mountain west region made cooperation obsolete. Brigham Young was right – the Mormon community had succeeded too well. Most Mormons, though they had intended to sequester themselves from the grasping and profane culture of the United States, had come to share mainstream economic values. Mormon religious ideals would continue to make their quest for community distinctive, and the Mormon village pattern with its neat fields, houses, and meeting houses would represent something unique among western communities, but they would never again challenge the basic economic tenets of American society. Ironically, ditches and fences served to integrate the Saints into American culture, rather than to separate them. Intentional community had created a strong individualism.

Babylon At 10,000 Feet: Leadville's Mining Community

Mining towns operated differently, but equally ironically. Built for purely individualistic, selfish reasons, mining towns had few of the ingredients of Mormon communities, but, in spite of themselves, developed strong communities. Like most mining towns, Leadville appeared unintentionally, achieving permanence after a few sputters. Initially, a group of prospectors avoiding the crowds on Cherry Creek in the spring of 1860 organized a mining district on the upper Arkansas River. Ever optimistic about the big strike, they called it California Gulch and lured thousands of hopeful people to the district that summer. Two stores, owned by Abel Lee and Horace and Augusta Tabor, provided the anchors of the community, called Oro City in those first days.

Though prospectors called the region a good "poor man's camp," meaning that a single miner with a pick and a pan could earn a living, the major claims in California Gulch concentrated into the hands of those who had the capital and organizational skills to dam the river, build sluices, process the gravel, and assay the resulting gold. Even so, the initial placer gold quickly petered out, and by 1865 the district had only a few hundred residents, all frustrated by the sticky black mud that clogged their rockers and Long Toms. In 1874, two investors with metallurgy training, William H. Stevens and Alvinius B. Wood, recognized the black mud as lead carbonate containing significant amounts of silver, and began a hydraulic mining operation. With an investment of $50,000, they quietly bought up all the claims they could before the news of a silver strike leaked out (Griswold and Harvey, 1951: 1–22; Blair, 1980: 8–9).

In 1876, the silver rush began. Eager prospectors raced into the region accompanied by big capitalists who smelled a real bonanza. With the presence of big money, the town exploded. Its bustling business row, however, belied the reality of Leadville: a slapdash collection of buildings that no one cared about. Filthy boarding houses, hard work in the damp, cold ground, streets filled with a foul combination of snow, sewage, and mud could all be ignored. Real Leadville operated under the ground and in the stock market and banks. Daily reports of new silver strikes and frenzied stock transactions kept people focused on the future, the moment they too would join the ranks of the instantly wealthy. Even the poorest day laborer could watch wealth pouring out of the ground and imagine that he too could have a share of it by investing in stock or by staking a claim. An early observer noted with some surprise that, "Not only your banker, but your baker and grocer, and the man who saws your wood, has some cash interest in the silver diggings . . . He discounts his chances though, and in his self-importance, fancies himself a capitalist already" (Ingersoll, 1879: 820). The spectacle of instant urbanization and constant discoveries of vast riches kept people in places like Leadville. Their discomfort and poverty were only temporary, they told themselves.

The community was characterized by large numbers of very rich and very poor residents, with a thin layer of middle class business owners sandwiched between them. In Leadville, investors with names like Simon Guggenheim, Marshall Field, Jerome Chaffee, and John D. Rockefeller expressed interest in a region that was producing $15,000,000 a year. The streets were not paved with silver, but the pockets of wealthy mine and mill owners were. By 1880, the town had an opera house, several glamorous theatres, a railroad service, a telegraph service, offices of New York and Chicago banks, mansions for its old and new rich, and balls and masquerades during the fashionable season. Just beyond the splendor of State Street, however, was a world of squalor. Workers lived in overcrowded boardinghouses or shacks, ate and drank in dirty saloons, and toiled underground or in ore refining facilities for low and uncertain wages.

However, Leadville offered a messy combination of bluster and optimism, suffering and desperation, and to understand the culture that developed there and in other Rocky Mountain communities, one has to see how those two facets nurtured each other. Success and failure literally lived next door to each other in early Leadville. The streets of the town mixed opera houses and hovels, grand mercantile establishments with unheated prostitutes' cribs. Every citizen every day saw examples of sudden wealth and abject poverty and only luck seemed to separate the two. The ebullient editorial prose of the newspaper expressed it best: "This is a fast place in a fast country. In this country everyone has his hope. The drunkard in the gutter when approached on the subject will say, 'Well I'll straighten up and strike it yet'"

(Carbonate *Weekly Chronicle*, 1880). The illusion of the ease of wealth was crafted and the presence of misery and poverty only served to make the illusion more appealing. If you didn't believe it, you didn't have a hope of achieving it. Admitting failure meant it existed.

The newspapers reflected both these hopes and fears in the very structure of the paper. Every issue of the paper began with a report on the mines: who was producing what, how much ore was shipped out, the exploration going on, and optimistic forecasts of future wealth. Each day, Leadvillians could read, in black and white, about the promise of wealth right under their feet. Front-page reports entitled "Mining Notes" or "Our Mines" signaled the universal expectation that wealth was imminent as new lodes appeared and new smelters opened. The right hand side of page one often told a different story. Here, explosions, suicides, murders, and labor troubles vied for the reader's attention – literally the mirror image of wealth pouring out of the mines (Carbonate *Weekly Chronicle* and Leadville *Herald Democrat*, 1879–80).

Subsequent pages show a similar pattern, combining boastful stories about new civic achievements with sordid stories of child abandonment, death by exposure, and horrific living conditions. Nearly every day's local news combined items like the following in the Leadville *Daily Democrat* of April 13, 1880. Page one reported on the huge number of people pouring into Leadville, perhaps 100 to 200 a day, and the greatness that the new railroad would bring to the city. The local news section contained two articles describing mine accidents and an item about an attempted suicide. "Mrs James Inglis who manages a laundry while her husband mines tried to commit suicide yesterday. The husband is prosperous and her reason for wanting to die remains unknown." The combination of great expectations, transiency, and grim living and working conditions made Leadville a difficult place to live.

Though the local paper hesitated to speculate on the reasons for Mrs Inglis' suicide attempt, just imagining the realities of her daily life in Leadville makes her apparent desperation understandable. It is likely that Mrs Inglis was recently transplanted to Leadville, and without a network of family and friends. She found herself in a largely male community, isolated by the climate and fevered transience of the place. Her husband, a miner, worked in an industry that was unsteady at best and deadly at worst. An editorial in the *Mining and Scientific Press* noted that "it required the highest moral courage to be a miner's wife, for every farewell kiss reminds her that he might return a cripple or a corpse, torn and bleeding from some accident" (Lingenfelter, 1974: 9). The Leadville newspaper may have described her husband as "prosperous," but the fact that she ran a laundry suggested otherwise. If she was like most people in Leadville, she lived in a tiny, drafty shack and did the brutal work of washing clothes in a mountain climate at 10,000 feet. In April, snow, alternating with mud, covered the streets, making a laundress's work nearly impossible. After a long winter of severe weather, deep snow, and difficult daily living conditions, the mud that signaled the beginning of spring could inspire thoughts of suicide in a lonely laundress.

Housing and health issues occupied a great deal of space in the Leadville newspapers and in people's lives. In the boom years in Leadville, huge numbers of people poured into the community before permanent structures could even be built. Single men had two choices; they could get room and board in barn-like boarding houses for seven to fifteen dollars a week or they could join in with a couple of other men and build a cabin, providing they had the capital to buy boards, blankets, and coal oil. John Larsh, who came to Leadville to gamble in saloons rather than in the mines, stayed in one of the legendary giant boarding houses in that first winter of 1878. Here, some five to eight hundred men could rent beds by the eight-hour shift. The journalist Ernest Ingersoll described the Mammoth Sleeping Palace in the summer of 1879, "as a rule at least one of the pair in the first bed above you will be sick, two by your head and by your feet drunk, five hundred will be swearing, the rest saying their prayers" (Ingersoll, 1879: 805). Larsh endured that first winter and laid away enough cash to build a two-room cabin on West Second Street. By the next winter, he had his fiancée, his brother, his three sisters, and two of their husbands-to-be all living in the tiny cabin (Larsh and Nichols, 1993: 31–32). No one worried much about such crowded conditions because no one really expected to stay long.

Shocked by the lack of planning and city services, C. C. Davis, the editor of the *Evening Chronicle*, began a crusade to bring order to Leadville. From the pages of the paper, he berated the mayor and the city council for the "huge stacks of waste, animal, and vegetable matter." He noted the first evidence of spring that year: "The weather is delightful and hundreds of garbage piles in back alleys commence to throw off an odor which smells to the mountain summits" (Leadville *Evening* Chronicle, February 7, 1879). Finally, the city council purchased a single garbage cart to haul off the offensive trash, but such services remained secondary to the business of mining and attracting investors.

Though Leadville maintained its mining town values, by 1880 it had the aura of a viable community. Larger than Denver, the "Cloud City" was the largest in Colorado. Twenty thousand people lived in Leadville and perhaps ten thousand more in the surrounding area counted on the town for goods and services. The arrival of the railroad in July of that year solved many of the problems of transportation and supply. A fire alarm system and a water system abated the danger of fire that haunted towns built nearly entirely of wood. Telegraph and telephone service connected the city to the world outside, while gas lights and sturdy sidewalks made Leadville itself easier to navigate (Blair, 1980: 141–45).

Despite such outward indications of urban order, the "Cloud City" continued to have distinctive priorities. The business of mining took precedence over everything. When citizens complained that the smelters were poisoning the city water supply in 1881, the Superintendent of one of the companies wrote a letter in the *Leadville Herald Democrat* defending his position: "I acknowledge the importance of the citizens of Leadville being supplied with pure water, but I also recognize the fact that the prosperity of the city is dependent on the mines from which she receives her existence." He concluded that it should be obvious to everyone that it would "be better for the town that a portion of her citizens should leave Leadville than her ore output should be reduced" (Leadville *Herald Democrat*, January 11, 1881). The old adage "What was good for business was good for Leadville," appeared in the spatial arrangements of the town as well. While miners and speculators carefully mapped mining claims, the town itself developed with no planning on muddy lots 25 feet wide.

Newspaper editors gloated over the fine buildings springing up, but also noted serious problems. Most miners still lived in boarding houses that rented beds by the shift, giving Leadville an odor of desperation under the glamour of State Street. Articles pointed out the wealth pouring out of the mines, but also reported that only

400 out of an estimated 1200 children in town attended school. The rest were kept home because of lack of clothing or because they worked in the mines. The editors commented disapprovingly on the increasing number of prostitutes and infanticides, even dubbing one street "Stillborn Alley" (*Weekly Herald*, Oct. 15, 1880). Several articles noted the unpleasant sight of drunks frozen to death in the streets. Nearly every issue of the paper also reported at least one death in the mines – by falls, explosions, etc. and a suicide or suicide attempt. Another story reported: "A local alcoholic, John Cain, took a break yesterday from beating his wife in a terrible manner to vandalize the school and shoot at students. After quite a fracas, Cain spent the evening in jail" (*Herald Democrat*, July 10, 1891).

The slightly humorous tone in the papers indicates that Leadvillians tolerated such behavior because it was so common, and because they saw it as part of the mining town ethos, something that would fade with settlement. However, what is disturbing about Leadville, and other mining towns, is that these drinking patterns and their results seem permanent. Long after the supposedly "taming" influences of women, families, churches, and schools arrived, drinking and public drunkenness were huge problems. In Leadville, long after the disorganization of the late 1870s, newspapers regularly reported stories of assaults, rapes, murders resulting from heavy drinking in the saloons on State Street and Harrison Avenue. So common were these crimes that the police dockets listed in the newspapers used the abbreviation "d. & d." for drunk and disorderly. And arrests in this category were as common in the early 1890s as they were in 1879.

As Leadville matured, its residents did try to mitigate some of its boomtown roughness. Churches, schools, hospitals, civic and social organizations provided protection against the high cost of failure. The first churches in Leadville were the Methodist and Catholic Churches and each of these had large congregations, impressive buildings, and social outreach programs. The Sisters of Charity from Leavenworth, Kansas founded St Vincent's Hospital early in 1879 and dedicated their services to the poor and sick in the community. The Leadville Order of B'nai B'rith, described in the local paper as "the Jewish Charitable Organization for the care of the sick, widowed, and orphaned" began raising money and providing services in 1879. A similar Catholic organization, St George's Brotherhood, recognized the dangers of being sick, injured, and single in Leadville, and its members signed pledges to provide nursing care, medicine, and burial costs for each other (Griswold and Harvey, 1951: 252–6).

Fraternal organizations, central to working- and middle-class culture in the nineteenth century, arrived with first hopeful miners. These organizations provided important connections for a transient society as well as crucial social services. The Masons, Odd Fellows, Ancient Order of Hibernians, Emerald Benevolent Society, the Elks, the Deutsches Casino, the Knights of Pythias, the Turnverein, the Ancient Order of United Workmen, the Union Veteran Association, the Leadville Miners and Traders' Mutual Benefit Association, and the Good Samaritan Association were among the dozens of organizations that appeared early in Leadville. Organized along a variety of class and ethnic divisions, they all claimed to offer friendship, aid in times of sickness and need, and to educate and foster moral growth. Military companies, volunteer fire brigades, merchants' organizations supported the community in other ways. The Wolfe Tone Guards, the Carbonate Rifles, and the Tabor Highland Guards all trained as militia groups. Local police, entirely overwhelmed by a transient and restless male population, relied on these private organizations for help in protecting and policing the inhabitants. Most importantly, however, these fraternal organizations provided safe places to gather, like-minded men to talk to, and generally, communal anchors in the chaotic world of a mining town.

The 1880 census describes Leadville at perhaps its greatest population and boomtown demographic status. With a population of nearly 15,000 people within the city limits and another 8,000 living within Lake County depending on it as an economic and social hub, Leadville was among the biggest cities in the Rocky Mountains. Only Denver and Salt Lake City could claim bigger populations. Few cities in the entire United States had a more diverse population. With nearly a third of its population (7088 out of 23,513) described as "foreign-born," Leadville and its environs resembled an eastern mill, steel or coal town. And this foreign-born population was strikingly male. Of a total population of over 23,000, only just over 5,000 were women. But among the foreign-born population, only one in ten was a woman.

Such a male, immigrant population skewed social arrangements in Leadville. Large concentrations of Irish, English, Canadian, German, and Scandinavian men crowded into the city, followed by smaller numbers of Scottish, French, and Swiss immigrants. Most of them concentrated in boarding houses with other men from similar ethnic backgrounds. The typical household in Leadville followed one of three patterns: single "family" homes made up of husbands, wives, and children (the rarest arrangement); single "family" homes made up of between three and six unrelated men; or boarding houses made up of a man or a man and his wife providing housing for somewhere between eight and twenty men, usually from the same ethnic group.

This diverse population, however, spent most of its time doing similar kinds of work. Leadville was, of course, a mining town, and a heavily industrialized one from the very start. The yellow pall, created by a dozen smelters, that hung over the town as early as 1880 and the constant booming and shaking from dynamite blasts in a hundred mines below the streets gave Leadville a clear identity. Every step of this operation involved danger, from falling down a shaft to a mistimed explosion to unexpected rockfalls. According to the 1880 census, western miners worked in the most dangerous industry in the nation. Accidents disabled one out of thirty miners every year and killed one out of eighty. With statistics like these, a miner who made a career from mining could expect at least one serious injury and chances were good that his family would be left without his earning power at some point. If an accident did not fell a miner in the short run, silicosis or "miner's consumption" would. Silicosis, caused by breathing the fine silica or quartz dust created by blasting and drilling, affected nearly everyone who worked in a deep mine for any extended period, causing impaired breathing and eventually, death. Another common occupational disease for the silver-lead miners of Leadville was lead poisoning, which caused abdominal pains, shakiness, and dizziness at first, and later internal bleeding and neurological damage (Derickson, 1988: 39–51).

The Leadville newspapers reflected the ubiquity of this danger. While reports of stock prices, profits, and potential riches headlined every issue, the second and third pages nearly always contained evidence of the price of these profits. Small items like "Down to Death," "Killed by Rockfall," "Several Miners Lose Limbs," "Another

Accident," appeared with heartbreaking regularity. Big fires and explosions, which occurred with less certainty, received more coverage in the papers. Articles described the course of the disaster, which often took place over several days, the daring rescues, the injuries and deaths, the characters of the men killed, and recounted the sad situation of families and friends left behind with sympathy and pathos. However, no one seemed to think such accidents were preventable; they were simply a cost to be borne by the miners.

For this difficult and dangerous work, miners received from $2 to $4 a day. Surface workers and smelter workers earned slightly less, about $1.75 to $3 daily. With Leadville's inflated housing and food costs, such wages barely covered basic needs, even if a miner worked regularly. The regularity of work varied according to the season and the output of the mines, but few workers worked a full 24 or 28-shift month. Illness, injury, or company work stoppages affected all miners or smelter workers at some point, casting them on the wrong side of poverty's edge (Larsh and Nichols, 1993: 154; Carbonate *Weekly Chronicle*, Feb. 21, 1880).

Living that close to poverty felt especially poignant in a place where fortunes could be made at any moment. Most miners, especially in the early years, came to Leadville hoping to strike it rich, or at least to make enough to break out of trap of working for someone else. Few managed this, but the exceptions like Horace Tabor, who went from struggling storekeeper to millionaire with some luck and a few smart investments, kept the possibility alive. The breathless boosterism of local papers, the glittery façade of saloons and hotels, the heady world of stock speculation all stood in stark opposition to the daily reality of working in a dark, cold mine for a daily wage. In the face of such a flood of wealth, their three dollars, or less, a day seemed an insulting pittance. Many people moved on, but others, caught in the hopeful snare of easy wealth, stayed, and unintentionally created community.

A combination of businessmen's desire to make Leadville attractive to investors, the miners need to protect themselves against accident, death and disease, and the connections that people made at work, and in saloons, dancehalls, and ethnic organizations did work to build community in Leadville. The patterns were surely different in Leadville, but the ethnic mixing had a whiff of Bent's fort, and very occasionally people cooperated like the Mormons. A fitting symbol for the ephemeral kind of community that Leadville and most other western mining towns spawned could be seen in the 1896 ice palace. Part splendor, part disaster, it demonstrated the grandiose dreams built on weak foundations that mining towns often were.

As in most mining towns, real estate speculators, mine owners, and working people all hoped the boom would last forever. They built hotels, opera houses, railroads, and homes signaling their confidence in the veins underneath the ground and the world economy that drove the search for silver. However, a crash in silver prices that accompanied a world-wide depression came as a huge shock. In 1890, Leadville, or the "Cloud City" as its boosters called it, had nearly ninety producing mines with a payroll of more than 6,000 men. By the summer of 1893 only 18 mines remained open and 90 percent of the workforce was idle. By 1895, Leadville appeared to be on the road to recovery. However, it was clear to anyone who was really paying attention that the economy was soft at best and fading at worst. Prices for silver never really recovered. As the mines got deeper, the costs increased and so did the challenge of keeping water out of the shafts. More unsettling, the population of the community kept dropping, businesses continued to close, and big capital seemed leery of investing in Leadville (Blair, 1980: 175).

In this atmosphere of nervous recovery, a group of local boosters came up with a scheme to show the world that Leadville was as vibrant as ever. Following the lead of other cities that had developed festivals celebrating their natural wonders, a corn palace in Des Moines, a mineral palace in Pueblo, and ice palaces in Montreal and St Paul, these boosters proposed building the biggest ice sculpture in the world (Coquoz, 1969: 4–13; Weir, 1994: 16). The pitch made by fundraisers was twofold. The Ice Palace would attract thousands of people to Leadville who would come on special trains, fill hotels and restaurants, and spend money in local stores. Equally significantly, it would showcase the community for new investment in the mines and in the development of Leadville as part of the growing tourist trade on the railroads. Promoters promised groups of miners, store owners, and fraternal organizations that the Ice Palace would be a year-round benefit to the community. Because of Leadville's altitude, the core of the structure would not melt, and the wooden parts of the building could serve as a dance hall and theater in the summer. By buying $5 shares in the Ice Palace, went the pitch, the citizens of Leadville could demonstrate their faith in the town and ensure their own futures (*Leadville Herald Democrat*, Sept. 29, 1895; Coquoz: 1969, 9–11).

So, with $50,000, thousands of tons of ice, and the labor of nearly a thousand people, Leadville built an ice palace. Modeled on a Norman castle, the structure covered three acres, had the world's largest ice-skating rink, two heated dining rooms, and enormous exhibition halls of ice sculptures and displays. Its ninety-foot towers could be seen from all parts of the city, especially from the railroad depot, where tourists did, initially, pour in to see the ice wonder. It opened on January 3, 1896 with a grand parade and Winter Carnival. Throughout the winter, the city hosted a series of special days to attract various groups of visitors: miners, farmers, insurance salesmen, stockbrokers, members of various fraternal organizations. Tourists did come, but they came only for the day, and they came bearing picnic baskets so that hotels and restaurants did not enjoy the boom they had expected. Underemployed miners and smelterworkers, who had built the Palace, enjoyed the wages they earned during the frenzy of work to build the structure, but they suffered from low wages and frequent periods of no work during the winter season. As a result, the recently organized the Cloud City Miners' Union, a local of the Western Federation of Miners, swelled with new members.

In March, the fragile façade of Leadville's recovery crumbled, or more accurately, melted. During an usually warm spell of March weather, the Ice Palace began to melt, far more rapidly than anyone had imagined. The dining rooms and skating rinks were awash with water, damaging the wooden parts of the building irreparably. Promoters scheduled a few more events there, but as the newspapers reported, rather tersely, these were poorly attended. By the end of the spring, the grand structure that signaled Leadville's new future had dissolved into a few dripping towers of ice and a lot of soggy wood. By summer, when the Cloud City Miners' Union went out on strike, the site of the Ice Palace became Camp McIntyre, where the National Guard set up camp to do battle with the miners (Leadville *Herald Democrat*, March 24, 1896; Coquoz, 1969: 24–7; Blair, 1980: 187–9). The place intended to unite and reinvigorate the community of Leadville became site of its unraveling.

The melting of Leadville's Ice Palace and the blowing up of Bent's Fort represented the most dramatic examples of what could happen to western communities
in the nineteenth century. The deep changes engendered by the long period of international rivalry and the imposition of a global economy brought crisis to some communities and prosperity to others, but they did not promote stability. Community,
as the Mormons discovered, operated against the gale force winds of Anglo-American
individualism. Community also provided some protection against the storms of a
boom-bust economy, as members of ethnic enclaves in mining towns experienced it,
but not nearly enough. For Indian people, caught between the various disasters of
conquest, community may have been a comfort, but a cold one. Communities like
Fort Vancouver or Santa Fe or Leadville served to bring people together to experiment with the new cultural relations necessary to make a new economy and polity
operate, but in the isolation of the nineteenth American West, these places were mere
flashes in the pan. Community became a servant to national, corporate, and personal
wealth, and in that role much was lost.

REFERENCES

Adler, Jeffrey S.: *Yankee Merchants and the Making of the Urban West* (Cambridge: Cambridge
    University Press, 1991).
Anderson, Nels: *Desert Saints: The Mormon Frontier in Utah* (Chicago: University of Chicago
    Press, 1942).
Arrington, Leonard J.: *Great Basin Kingdom: An Economic History of the Latter-Day Saints,
    1830–1900* (Cambridge, MA.: Harvard University Press, 1958).
Arrington, Leonard J., Feramorz Y. Fox, and Dean L. May (eds.) *Building the City of God:
    Community and Cooperation Among the Mormons* (Urbana and Chicago: University of
    Illinois Press, 1992).
Arrington, Leonard J. and Dean May: "A Different Mode of Life: Irrigation and Society in
    Nineteenth Century Utah." *Agricultural History* 49,1 (1975), 3–11.
Blair, Edward: *Leadville: Colorado's Magic City* (Boulder: Pruett Publishing, 1980).
Campbell, Eugene: *Establishing Zion: The Mormon Church in the American West, 1847–1869*
    (Salt Lake City: Signature Books, 1988).
Coquoz, Rene: *King Pleasure Reigned in 1896: The Story of the Fabulous Leadville Ice Palace*
    Boulder, CO: Johnson Publishing Co, 1969.
Comer, Douglas: *Ritual Ground: Bent's Old Fort, World Formation, and the Annexation of the
    Southwest* (Berkeley: University of California Press, 1996).
Derickson, Alan: *Workers' Health, Workers' Democracy: The Western Miners' Struggle, 1891–
    1925* (Ithaca: Cornell University Press, 1988).
Dudden, Arthur Power: *The American Pacific: From the Old China Trade to the Present* (New
    York: Oxford University Press, 1992).
Emmons, David and William G. Robbins: *Colony and Empire: The Capitalist Transformation
    of the American West* (Lawrence: University of Kansas Press, 1994).
Farnham, Thomas Jefferson: *Travels in the Great Western Prairies, the Anahuac and Rocky
    Mountains, and in the Oregon Territory* (New York: Greeley & McElrath, 1843).
Griswold, Don L. and Jean Harvey: *A Carbonate Camp Called Leadville* (Denver: University
    of Denver Press, 1951).
Hafen, LeRoy (ed.): *Mountain Men and the Fur Trade of the Far West*, 8 vols. (Glendale CA:
    A. H. Clark Co., 1965–72).

Hansen, Klaus J.: *Mormonism and the American Experience* (Chicago: University of Chicago Press, 1981).

Hine, Robert: *Community on the American Frontier: Separate But Not Alone* (Norman: University of Oklahoma Press, 1980).

Hine, Robert V. and John M. Faragher: *The American West: A New Interpretive History* (New Haven: Yale University Press, 2000).

Holman, Frederick V.: *Dr. John McLoughlin, the Father of Oregon*. (Cleveland, OH: The Arthur H. Clark Company, 1907)

Hyde, George E. (ed.): *A Life of George Bent Written From His Letters* (Norman: University of Oklahoma Press, 1968).

Ingersoll, Ernest: "Ups and Downs in Leadville." *Scribner's Monthly* 18 (May through October 1879).

Johansen, Dorothy O. and Charles M. Gates: *Empire of the Columbia: A History of the Pacific Northwest* (New York: Harper and Brothers, 1957).

Larsh, Edward B. and John Nichols: *Leadville, U.S.A.* (Boulder: Pruett Publishing, 1993).

Lavender, David: *Bent's Fort* (Lincoln, NE: Bison Books, 1954).

Lavender, David: *The Fist in the Wilderness*, (Garden City, NJ: Doubleday, 1964).

Lecompte, Janet: *Pueblo, Hardscrabble, and Greenhorn: Society on the High Plains, 1832–1856* (Norman: University of Oklahoma Press, 1978).

Lingenfelter, Richard E.: *The Hardrock Miners: A History of the Mining Labor Movement in the American West, 1863–1893* (Berkeley: University of California press, 1974).

Magoffin, Susan: *Down the Santa Fe Trail and Into Mexico* (New Haven: Yale University Press, 1926).

Mann, Ralph: *After the Gold Rush: Society in Grass Valley and Nevada City, California, 1849–1870* (Stanford: Stanford University Press, 1982).

May, Dean: *Three Frontiers: Family, Land and Society in the American West, 1850–1900* (London: Cambridge University Press, 1994).

Mead, Elwood and R. P. Teele: *Report of Irrigation Investigations in Utah*, (Washington, DC: US Government Printing Office, 1903).

Morgan, Dale L.: *The Great Salt Lake* (New York: Bobbs-Merrill Company, 1947).

Phillips, Paul C.: *The Fur Trade*, vol. 2 (Norman, OK: University of Oklahoma Press, 1961).

Pomeroy, Earl: *The Pacific Slope: A History of California, Oregon, Washington, Idaho, Utah, and Nevada* (New York: Alfred A. Knopf, 1965).

Raban, Jonathan: *Bad Land: An American Romance*, (New York: Pantheon Books, 1996).

Rich, E. E.: *Hudson's Bay Company, 1670–1870* (New York: Macmillan Books, 1961).

Robbins, William: *Colony and Empire: The Capitalist Transformation of the American West* (Lawrence, KS: University Press of Kansas, 1994).

Roberts, David: *A Newer World: Kit Carson, John C. Fremont, and the Claiming of the American West* (New York: Simon and Schuster, 2000).

Robertson, R. G.: *Competitive Struggle: America's Western Fur Trading Posts, 1764–1865* (Boise: Tamarack Books, 1999).

Ronda, James: *Astoria and Empire*, (Lincoln: University of Nebraska Press, 1990).

Ross, Alexander: *Adventures of the First Settlers on the Columbia River* (London: Smith, Elder, and Co., 1849).

Sadler, Richard W. and Richard C. Roberts: *The Weber River Basin: Grass Roots Democracy and Water Development*, (Logan: Utah State University Press, 1994).

Shipps, Jan: *Mormonism: The Story of A New Religious Tradition* (Urbana: University of Illinois Press, 1985).

Smythe, William: *The Conquest of Arid America*. (New York: The Macmillian Company, 1905).

Stegner, Wallace: *The Gathering of Zion: The Story of the Mormon Trail* (New York: McGraw Hill, 1964).

Stegner, Wallace: *Marking the Sparrows Fall: The Making of the American West* (New York: Henry Holt, 1998).

Stegner, Wallace: *Where the Bluebird Sings to the Lemonade Springs: Living and Writing in the American West* (New York: Henry Holt, 1992).

Van Alstyne, Richard: *The Rising American Empire* (New York: Oxford University Press, 1960).

Weber, David: *The Taos Trappers: The Fur Trade in the Far Southwest, 1540–1846* (Norman: University of Oklahoma Press, 1971).

Weir, Darlene Godat: *Leadville's Ice Palace: A Colossus in the Colorado Rockies* (Lakewood, CO: Ice Castle Editions, 1994).

West, Elliott: *The Contested Plain: Indians, Goldseekers, and the Rush to Colorado* (Lawrence: University of Kansas Press, 1998).

Wrobel, David: *The End of American Exceptionalism: Frontier Anxiety from the Old West to the New Deal* (Lawrence: University Press of Kansas, 1993).

CHAPTER EIGHTEEN

American Indians in the Twentieth Century

PETER IVERSON

The story seemed to end at Wounded Knee. That terrible event in December of 1890 in which members of the US Seventh Cavalry slaughtered hundreds of Lakota children, women, and men symbolized the place of American Indians in American society and American history. Historians grew accustomed to telling a tale noteworthy for its tragic dimensions. They featured Crazy Horse and Chief Joseph and Geronimo in their chronicles. In these accounts the Indians always lost. Their resistance always ended in defeat – in death or exile, in the forfeiture of power and homeland. The history of Native peoples became subsumed in a larger, triumphant narrative – of Anglo-American progress, of demographic expansion, of conquest. After all, we were told, 1890 also marked the end of the American frontier.

The story included some Indians but not others. It featured those who fought and especially those who fought for a long time. The more trouble they caused the bigger stars they became in the melodrama. Those who fought later generally gained more attention than those whose resistance had come earlier. Those whose defiance had been of another sort disappeared. Thus in the Southwest the Apaches earned more scrutiny than did the Navajos, while the Yavapais and Tohono O'odham vanished from view. Historians took their cue from the photographer Edward Curtis, who had pictured Indians as a vanishing race and from sculptor James Fraser, who had portrayed Indians as being at the end of the trail. Indians became hurdles in the way of white advancement and progress; they were heroic but doomed victims whose days of glory were now but distant memories. Native experiences in the twentieth century, if deemed worthy of comment at all, received a quick, dismissive footnote, which inevitably stressed poverty and despair. Observers equated reservations with ghettoes; they depicted Indians who somehow had made their way to the city as vanishing once again, this time as victims of assimilation or alcoholism. Such a sad, insignificant story paled in comparison to the heroic defiance of Native peoples on the northern plains.

Of course not all subscribed to this construction, least of all the Indians themselves. One of them, D'Arcy McNickle (Salish-Kutenai), published a book in 1973 whose title and contents offered an alternative perspective on Native history. In *Native American Tribalism: Indian Survivals and Renewals* McNickle reminded his readers that Indians had not disappeared nor were they necessarily destined by definition for poverty and obscurity. "Only the Indians," he wrote, "seemed unwilling to accept oblivion as an appropriate final act in their role in the New World drama." "The Indians lost," he added, "but they were never defeated." (McNickle, 1973: 4)

Two dramatic recent developments, indeed, had demonstrated that indeed loss should not be equated with defeat. In 1969 Vine Deloria, Jr. (Standing Rock Sioux) published his "Indian manifesto": *Custer Died For Your Sins*. He informed his readers that Indians today had "little in common with the Mohicans." The final ringing sentence of that extraordinary book asserted, "It is up to us to write the final chapter of the American Indian on this continent" (Deloria, 1969: 27, 279). *Custer Died For Your Sins* gained a new audience for the telling of Indian history as an ongoing story. A few months later, the occupation of Alcatraz Island by Native individuals protesting contemporary policies and problems underlined the continuing presence of Indian peoples.

Just as the civil rights movement helped fuel the writing of a new African American history, developments in Indian country in the 1960s and 1970s encouraged the crafting of a new American Indian history. The fishing rights protests in the Pacific Northwest and the protests against the strip mining of coal on Black Mesa in Arizona, the occupations of Alcatraz, Bureau of Indian Affairs offices in Washington, DC, and Wounded Knee, the creation of the National Indian Youth Council and the American Indian Movement, the founding of Rough Rock Demonstration School, Navajo Community College, and other institutions that exemplified self-determination in Indian education, all testified to people who were determined to gain greater control over their lands and lives.

In another parallel to the civil rights movement, the presence of television brought these stories into millions of homes. Moreover, new publications like *Akwesasne Notes* (from a Mohawk community in upstate New York) and *Wassaja*, published by Rupert Costo (Cahuilla) and Jeannette Henry (Eastern Cherokee) in San Francisco, gave extensive coverage to the latest news from Indian country. N. Scott Momaday (Kiowa) received the Pulitzer Prize for fiction for *House Made of Dawn* (1968). Momaday's success helped open the door for other Native writers, including James Welch (Blackfoot-Gros Ventre) and Leslie Marmon Silko (Laguna Pueblo), who also earned critical praise and a wide readership for novels furnishing decidedly unromantic portraits of the recent past and present. Buffy Sainte-Marie (Cree) and Floyd Westerman (Lakota) through their music addressed an Indian world "now that the buffalo's gone." Indian rock bands like Redbone and XIT followed. Painters such as T. C. Cannon (Kiowa-Caddo) and Fritz Scholder (Luiseno) brought to their canvases wonderful expressions of irony and social commentary.

A rather unlikely location, the Newberry Library in Chicago, also became an important force in shaping a new vision of Indian history. The Newberry was one of the few remaining private research libraries in North America and possessed impressive collections with considerable material about American Indians and the American West. Library director Lawrence W. Towner wanted more scholars to take advantage of such material and therefore decided to establish a new center for American Indian history. At least two major obstacles loomed. The rigid, formal environment appeared less than welcoming and the collections were rooted almost entirely in the years before 1900. However, with the appointment in 1972 of McNickle as its first director and the establishment of some generous doctoral and postdoctoral fellowships, the Center began to attract scholars. Nevertheless, during its first years, the Center struggled to find its place, both within the library and within the larger world of Indian history.

In time the Center outgrew its awkward beginnings and in time it clearly played a vital role in developing new approaches to writing and teaching Indian history. Fellows benefited from McNickle's presence and from their access to members of the Center's distinguished advisory council. These senior scholars provided advice and encouragement and helped the fellows become part of a national network of people with shared interests. David Warren (Santa Clara-Ojibwe) and Robert Dumont (Cree) spoke about Indians as continuing peoples. Although their work had emphasized federal policy and the era before 1900, non-Indian scholars such as William T. Hagan (1961) and Francis Paul Prucha (1977) recognized the need to pay more attention to the twentieth century and began to probe the often murky waters of the modern era. Another advisory council member, Robert F. Berkhofer, Jr., wrote a particularly influential essay in 1971, advocating a new approach, which he termed "Indian-centered" history.

The D'Arcy McNickle Center for American Indian History, as the Center was eventually renamed, realized its full potential during the period from 1984 to 1994, when Frederick Hoxie served as its director. Under Hoxie's leadership the Center sponsored conferences on the impact of Indian history on the teaching of American history and on "Indian voices in the academy." Using the themes of leadership, local history, and the construction of gender and the experience of women, the "Indian voices" sessions brought together individuals who taught at the various tribal colleges with instructors from other colleges and universities. Through its Occasional Papers in Curriculum series as well as other publications by university presses, the McNickle Center brought the results of these conferences to a wider audience (D'Arcy McNickle Center 1986, 1994; Hoxie and Iverson, 1998).

The writing of modern American Indian history thus began to be transformed. By the 1990s more universities, especially public universities in the West, had developed outstanding programs for graduate study in the field. These programs attracted an unprecedented number of students, including a small but gradually increasing contingent of Native scholars who promised to have a dramatic impact upon how Indian history is constructed, written, and taught. Prior to the 1980s nearly all academic students of western American Indian history had entered through the door of western United States history. They were almost always trained by western historians. Almost inevitably, their work reflected the notion that Indian history constituted a subfield of western history. Given the preoccupation of western historians with the history of the westward movement and the close of the frontier, Indian history had been condemned to being a narrative that concluded at Wounded Knee. These histories generally portrayed whites as the victors and Indians as the vanquished. Within the past generation Indian history emerged as a field of its own, increasingly able to ask its own questions. In the process Indians moved from the periphery to center stage of an ongoing drama.

The transformation of the field can be examined by analyzing some examples of its main forms and themes. This essay considers the following topics: (1) writing Indian history, (2) surveys of twentieth century Indian history, (3) federal policy and

Indian-White relations, (4) tribal, group and area history, (5) biography and life history, (6) education, (7) culture and economy, and (8) sovereignty. These areas obviously overlap and their full concerns cannot be covered entirely here.

Writing Indian History

How should Indian history be written? Who should write it?

Until the early 1970s such central questions went largely unasked and unanswered. Few Native scholars had been trained. Anthropologists and an occasional historian addressed the writing of Indian history from time in the 1950s and 1960s in the pages of the journal of the American Society for Ethnohistory, *Ethnohistory*. However, even if scholars like William Fenton, Arrell M. Gibson, Charles Hudson, Nancy Lurie, William Sturdevant, and Wilcomb Washburn had some important things to say, few heard them. They largely preached to the converted – those few people who read the journal in the first place. Other than the young iconoclast Jack Forbes (Powhatan-Lenape), almost no one tackled the question of who should write Indian history, because, again, American Indian history consisted almost entirely as the history of Indian–White relations. Forbes did raise the issue in a series of articles, but apparently without much response (Forbes, 1959).

The publication in August 1971, of the special issue of the *Pacific Historical Review* devoted to American Indian history marked the field's maturation. The issue included not only Berkhofer's essay but also articles by Hagan and Lurie and Wilcomb Washburn's "status report" on the writing of Indian history (Washburn, 1971). Berkhofer's important analysis of the images of American Indians (Berkhofer, 1977) also reflected the evolution of the field. By the time *The American Indian and the Problem of History* (Martin, 1987) gained publication in 1987, considerable headway had been achieved. This somewhat idiosyncratic volume contained some searching, even poignant essays. Some prominent non-Indian scholars and noteworthy Native scholars – Deloria, Michael Dorris, Henrietta Mann, Momaday, and Gerald Vizenor – offered their thoughts. However, the editor puzzled aloud in the introduction why others had been unwilling to contribute and then in a rambling epilogue attacked some of those who had contributed – in the process probably answering his own question. Nonetheless, some of the writers raised fundamental points about some of the alternative approaches one might embrace in seeking alternative ways to present the Native past. Robin Ridington, for example, spoke of the tendency of scholars to see myth only as "flawed history" and to define history as a resource only "to be mined from lodes of artifacts and documents." "History," he wrote," was dead and gone from the breath of experience. It was about a past that would not return to life." Yet to write the history of people like the Dunne-za of western Canada, historians "must find ways of recognizing the validity of personal experience without violating their own scholarly traditions of obtaining valid information about the past" (Martin, 1987: 128, 135).

During the 1980s and 1990s more Native scholars completed PhDs in history and anthropology and joined departments representing those disciplines or formed or augmented departments or programs in American Indian studies. In time how Indian history should be written and who should write it increasingly became linked. Two significant volumes edited by Native historians in the late 1990s addressed these questions from a number of different vantage points. Those providing essays for the book edited by Donald L. Fixico (Shawnee, Sac and Fox, Seminole, and Muscogee Creek) emphasized the need for rethinking how Indian history should be written, while those who furnished essays for the book edited by Devon A. Mihesuah (Oklahoma Choctaw) addressed more directly the matter of Native authorship (Fixico, 1997; Mihesuah, 1998). Although Fixico and Angela Cavender Wilson (Wahpatonwan Dakota) authored essays in both volumes, only American Indians contributed to *Natives and Academics: Researching and Writing About American Indians*. As Mihesuah emphasized in her introduction, their perspectives varied considerably. Duane Champagne (Turtle Mountain Ojibwe) argued that American Indian studies were for every one, but Karen Gayton Swisher (Standing Rock Sioux) contended that only Indians should write about Indian education. By the first years of the twenty-first century, then, how Indian history should be written and who should write it had become major points for discussion and debate. The continuing development of American Indian studies programs and the growing number of Native graduate students promised to influence future developments.

Another example of revisionist scholarship emerged in 2002. Native American history had generally remained atheoretical. *Clearing a Path: Theorizing a Past in Native American Studies* furnished a useful overview of new or revisionist approaches. Editor Nancy Shoemaker divided this volume into four sections (narrative and storytelling, social and cultural categories, political economy, and tribal and indigenous histories). In addition to Shoemaker, Julie Cruikshank, Leanne Howe, Gunlog Fur, Patricia Albers, Jacki Thompson Rand, Craig Howe, and James Brooks contributed essays to this important book.

Surveys of the Twentieth Century

Few historians have been unwise enough to attempt a synthesis surveying the history of Indians in the twentieth-century American West. However, as the secondary literature has developed and the field of Indian history has matured, such syntheses have become somewhat more feasible. Even so, given the number and diversity of Native communities and all of the complex questions these communities have confronted, any person foolish enough to take on this assignment is bound to have not only second but third thoughts about it.

James S. Olson and Raymond Wilson (1984) merit praise for writing the first overview. The authors did enter the turbulent waters of the twentieth century with understandable hesitation; three of the eight chapters in *Native Americans in the Twentieth Century* dealt with the period before 1900. Once they finally waded in, Olson and Wilson made a good effort to tell their national story. They could not address developments after the early 1980s, of course, and their synthesis inevitably reflected an evolving literature's emphasis on victimization. At the same time, the authors recognized the roles of many important Native organizations and individuals and their final chapters took on a somewhat optimistic tone.

The one book centered exclusively in the region, *Indians and the American West in the Twentieth Century* (Parman, 1994) moved expeditiously into the 1900s. However, Donald L. Parman chose to present Indian history in the context of regional development. Parman's book appeared in a series on the American West in the twentieth century, edited by Martin Ridge and Walter Nugent, and mirrored the editors' conviction that Indian history represented a subfield of western history. Therefore although Parman made a conscientious effort, his overview had curious omissions because certain topics did not fit this format. So a book about Indians in the twentieth century somehow avoided discussion of the Native American Church. Only two American Indian women, Alice Jemison (Seneca) and Ada Deer (Menominee) surfaced in the text, with a third, Helen Peterson (Northern Cheyenne) included in the section of photographs.

The most recent volume, *"We Are Still Here": American Indians in the Twentieth Century*, (Iverson, 1998) appeared just before century's end. It tried to do too much in too little space, but it brought the story up to the late 1990s, incorporated cultural history, and offered revisionist interpretations of key eras.

Federal Policy and Indian–White Relations

Although analyses of federal policy and White–Indian relations no longer dominate the writing of Native history, these subjects remain of great interest to many historians. As previously noted, the work of Francis Paul Prucha has been enormously important in regard to these two topics. Some critics chastised Prucha for being too uncritical of federal policy-makers, but he steadfastly maintained that historians should not judge but rather should explain why individuals and institutions acted in particular ways. He took pride in, as he phrased it, "boldly" taking his history of the United States government and American Indians to 1980, "for historical studies of Indian affairs have for too long emphasized events of the nineteenth century." (1984: xxix)

Among the countless students of federal policy and Indian–White relations, six others will be mentioned here: Alison Bernstein, Vine Deloria, Jr., Donald L. Fixico, Frederick E. Hoxie, R. Warren Metcalf, and Kenneth R. Philp. These scholars were particularly important in revising perspectives about crucial eras and subjects. In *A Final Promise: The Campaign to Assimilate the Indians, 1880–1920* (1984), Hoxie offered a darker view of the workings of federal policy than had been presented by Prucha. He argued that, by roughly the turn of the century, policy-makers succumbed to a less optimistic view of the potential of Native people to adjust to changing times and to a more insistent refrain from western politicians and developers that Indian lands and resources must be exploited by non-Indian interests. Trained more as an American historian than an American Indian historian, Hoxie was especially interested in the larger context of Native history. One had to understand the transition in federal policy, he suggested, in the light of changes in American political culture; one had to read Indian history informed by one's knowledge of Anglo-American responses to massive immigration and the newly established order of "separate but equal" in the American South (Hoxie, 1984).

Deloria joined with political scientist Clifford Lytle to dissect the campaign by Commissioner of Indian Affairs John Collier to inaugurate a "new deal" for American Indians during the years of the Franklin D. Roosevelt administration. Deloria and Lytle delineated in painstaking detail the dichotomies between what Collier initially proposed and what Congress ultimately was willing to accept in the form of the Indian Reorganization Act of 1934 (Deloria and Lytle, 1984). Additional insight into this era is afforded by the best study of Collier and his career: *John Collier's Crusade for Indian Reform, 1920–1954* (Philp, 1977). Kenneth Philp furnished valuable details about Collier's experiences before he became commissioner and offered perceptive judgments about his performance during the Indian New Deal.

If one of his predecessors had solemnly proclaimed it time to "make the Indian at home in America," then Collier sought to reaffirm the Native right to a different kind of residence. At one level Collier appeared to be the very embodiment of cultural pluralism; he pushed for bilingual and bicultural education in the Bureau schools, advocated religious freedom for Indian communities, and sought to create more independent tribal governments. But, as Philp revealed in his biography of Collier and in a new study of the roots of both the movement for termination and the drive for Indian self-determination (Philp, 1999), Collier under certain circumstances seemed as likely to impose his will when he deemed it necessary for Indian well-being. For example, Collier concluded that the Navajos, the Tohono O'odham, and other Indian nations needed to reduce drastically their livestock holdings, even if the peoples themselves did not agree with this radical prescription. The heavy-handed nature of the Collier commissionership fueled both a reactionary movement by those who wanted to "liberate" individual Indians from federal "controls" and a parallel movement by those Natives who sought to achieve self-determination by their communities. In the years following the World War II, members of the US Congress would seize upon "liberation" for their own purposes and seek, once again, to make Indians at home in America. The achievements of Indian soldiers and the contributions made by other Native persons to off-reservation war industries made it seem all the more feasible to withdraw federal trusteeship. Alison Bernstein's study of Indians during the 1940s helps us understand the transition to termination (1991). Bernstein affirmed that the war experience had expedited rather than retarded the movement, both imposed and voluntary, of Indians to off-reservation towns and cities. Donald L. Fixico (1986) also echoed these sentiments in his examination of the federal policies of termination and relocation. Fixico documented the deleterious impact of withdrawing federal protection and support of reservations singled out for termination. He told of rural people forced into an unfamiliar urban environment filled with new and difficult demands, expectations, and complications. This significant work remains all too rare a consideration of this vitally important subject. However, another study published in 2002, Metcalf's *Termination's Legacy: The Discarded Indians of Utah*, furnished both a thorough analysis of Utah Senator Arthur Watkins, who championed termination in Congress, as well as of the impact of this policy on different Native communities in Watkins' home state.

Tribal, Group, and Area Histories

For much of the twentieth century, historians employed tribal histories as a standard means, for relating the experiences of Native peoples in the United States. The University of Oklahoma Press's long-established series, entitled the Civilization of the American Indian, was constructed on this foundation. Nevertheless, the notion of "tribe" has long been critiqued as artificial and as an imposed concept. As Alexandra Harmon contends in her brilliant history of Indian communities of the Puget Sound (1998), the entities can be formed at different points in time. Indian identity is not dependent by definition on an existing reservation land base. Even though we appreciate such distinctions among Indian nations, we can also acknowledge that as the twentieth century progressed many Indian communities transformed the meaning and the possibility of reservations. Over time land bases took on new layers of experience and offered new teachings. Reservations often started as prisons and eventually became homes. So reservation and tribal histories remain significant. In addition, given the shifting circumstances of twentieth-century American Indian life, it has also been useful to consider relations between neighboring groups of people or to ponder the overall status of Native groups within a defined geographic region.

Morris Foster (1991), Loretta Fowler (1982 and 1987), Hoxie (1995), Iverson (1983), Paul Robertson (2002), Joe S. Sando (Jemez Pueblo) (1982), and Veronica Velarde Tiller (Jicarilla Apache) (1983) were among those who authored such histories. Stephen Crum (Duck Valley Shoshone) (1994), Martha Knack (2002), and Angie Debo (1972) are representative of those who furnished significant studies of Indian groups and works by Harmon and Stephen Trimble (Trimble, 1993) exemplify volumes encompassing geographic areas.

Most of these studies, in fact, are not limited to the twentieth century. However, all recognize Indian history as a continuing story and, with the exception of Hoxie, all bring their presentations up to the present. Debo certainly stressed victimization, but given the machinations she uncovered in Oklahoma, one can understand why she chose "The Betrayal of the Five Civilized Tribes" as the subtitle for her classic study of the Five Tribes. It is important to remember that *And Still the Waters Run* did not exactly sprint into print. Debo's portrayal of how various civic leaders had defrauded Native communities unnerved her prospective publisher. The University of Oklahoma Press wilted under severe local pressure and reneged on its contract. Eventually Princeton University Press published the manuscript – her first book. Debo's courage and determination did not gain proper appreciation until late in her remarkable life; an "American Experience" documentary completed shortly after her death revealed the nature of her perseverance. When *And Still the Waters Run* finally saw the light of day, Angie Debo barely paused to celebrate. This indefatigable scholar kept on writing about Oklahoma's Indian peoples and other subjects. She had the pleasure of seeing her final book come out in time for her eighty-sixth birthday. As most of her other work had been, *Geronimo: The Man, His Time, His Place* was published by the University of Oklahoma Press.

The volumes included here generally shared a common understanding about the resilient, adaptive nature of Indian nations. They reflected the authors' realization that Indian communities could and did defy that conventional wisdom about ultimate disappearance. They also began to call attention to the efforts of latter-day heroes who believed that their people could build better futures for their children and grandchildren and were determined to resist the policies and individuals who kept trying to evict them from their homes. Crum, Sando, and Tiller wrote as members of the Indian communities that they chronicled, and, even though their methodology remained quite conventional, their overall presentations were clearly enhanced. In the same sense, Paul Robertson's marriage to an Oglala Lakota and his extended residence at Pine Ridge centrally affected what he wanted to say and how he wanted to say it. One also had to be impressed at the willingness of Crum, Sando, and Tiller to convey a sense of their people's past, given the less than universal desire on the part of their peers in the community for one of their own to publish such analyzes. In addition, Foster, Fowler, Harmon, Iverson, Knack, and Trimble all spent very extended periods of time in the communities they portrayed and all employed oral histories and personal interviews to obtain a firsthand sense of how different peoples saw their lands and their histories. Hoxie furnished particularly searching discussions about Crow families, religious pluralism, leadership, and economy; *Parading Through History* did not minimize the pressures against the Crows as it underlined that "outsiders could not remake the community's habits of mind, erase its collective memory, or obliterate its values" (Hoxie, 1995: 167).

With the exception of works by Trimble and Iverson, these histories tell their stories almost entirely through text. Even though they lived in an increasingly visual society, most scholars persisted in relying on their talents as writers to convey their ultimate meanings and messages. And even though most of them were, indeed, able writers, their reluctance to add a visual component to their overall presentation became increasingly counterproductive. Two decades after writing a history of the Navajo nation noteworthy for its complete neglect of visual images, Iverson finally realized that photographs would make a major contribution to the story he was trying to tell (2002a). Even more fortunately, a leading Native American photographer, Monty Roessel (Navajo), agreed to collaborate on this project and contributed two 16-page color photo essays and eight of the 57 black and white photographs in the book. He also served as photo editor for a complementary volume of Navajo speeches, letters, and petitions that brought forth previously unpublished indigenous perspectives relating to land, community, education, rights, government, and identity (2002b). Trimble, by contrast, understood the need for illustrations. A first rate photographer, he used dozens of his own photographs as well as the work of others to create a far more attractive and engaging book.

Biography and Life Histories

Most students of twentieth-century Indian history have balked at biography and hesitated about life histories. Historians have continued to create portraits of Tecumseh and Sitting Bull, but have rarely attempted comparable depictions of major figures of the 1900s. More than twenty years ago, anthropologist Alfonso Ortiz (San Juan Pueblo) bemoaned the lack of biographies that focused on those whom he termed (in contrast to the spate of biographies about Native war leaders) "peace chiefs" – Native leaders who had made a difference for their peoples during the past hundred years. Unfortunately, Ortiz's counsel has gone largely unheeded, even though biography is a valuable vehicle through which to address not only an individual life but also the life of one or more communities.

A welcome exception to this generalization is Hagan's biography of the Comanche leader Quanah Parker (1993). In this volume written for the Oklahoma western biographies series, Hagan completed a compelling study of a complicated and charismatic individual whose life and career inform us about the Comanches in a transitional era. Two other biographies are centered in the same period. Their subjects are two Native MDs who worked as cultural brokers: Charles Eastman (Wilson, 1983) and Carlos Montezuma (Iverson, 1982). These life stories bring forth considerable information about reservation circumstances and the workings of such organizations as the Society of American Indians. Two other studies of twentieth-century Native individuals are Greg Sarris' (Pomo-Miwok) compelling portrait of Native artist and religious healer Mabel McKay (1994) , and editor R. David Edmunds's anthology, *The New Warriors* (2002), that profiled fourteen 20th century indigenous leaders, including five women: Ada Deer (Menominee), LaDonna Harris (Comanche), Wilma Mankiller (Oklahoma Cherokee), Janine Pease Pretty On Top (Crow), and Zitkala-Sa (Yankton Dakota).

There are a handful of other biographies and a larger number of articles and chapters that furnish shorter sketches, but all in all we have not heeded Ortiz's counsel. Life histories can yield information and insight that cannot emerge through other forms of communication. Charlotte Frisbie's exceptional collaboration with Rose Mitchell (2002) demonstrated the possibilities of this genre.

There may be understandable concern about having any one person fully stand for any one community and additional pause about appearing to make one person more important than she or he actually may have been. Although any biographer can volunteer cautionary tales the opportunities and obligations in this regard clearly outweigh the liabilities. To tell the story of western Indian America in the twentieth and twenty-first centuries, biography and life history are tools that must be more fully utilized.

Education

Scholars have been more willing to explore this terrain. Education, of course, comprised one of the primary means through which federal officials, missionaries, and others attempted to change the values and goals of Native peoples. Yet it also constituted one of the ways through which Indian individuals and communities sought to obtain better futures for the young and thus for all. Education affords a telling example of how misguided policies do not always bring only negative results; through the decades Indians have attempted to utilize imposed educational systems for their own purposes. For the first half of this century, public schools were not available to a great many Indian children. If a child were to gain instruction that would better equip her or him for the rigors of the future, then that acquisition often had to occur in the confines of a Bureau of Indian Affairs (BIA) or church school. Such institutions could produce results other than what their founders and directors had intended. The schools were supposed to assimilate and acculturate, but attending multitribal boarding schools frequently increased the student's sense of tribal and Indian identity. This, after all, is not surprising. Identity is often enhanced or reinforced not through isolation but through contact and conflict. Being with individuals from other communities could simultaneously add to one's appreciation of one's own nation even as one began to recognize common ground with other Native entities. At such schools in the 1910s, 1920s, and 1930s, more than a few Native people had their first contact with peyote and the teachings of the Native American Church. This is not exactly what the founder of Carlisle Indian Industrial School, Richard Henry Pratt, had in mind.

Through their accounts of particular schools and the process of Indian education scholars have thus told a progressively more comprehensive and complicated story. They have moved from a simple tale of victimization to a more nuanced rendition of Native experiences. They have been able to offer perceptive and significant analysis of gender, identity, and community. They have acknowledged that institutions, including schools and reservation communities, do not remain static but change over time.

Margaret Connell-Szasz's pathbreaking book on Indian education in the twentieth century opened the door to this area of inquiry. Published in 1999 in its third edition, *Education and the American Indian* provided a sensitive and perceptive overview of its subject. Brenda J. Child (Red Lake Ojibwe) furnished a searching consideration of students, families, and the schools in *Boarding School Seasons* (1998). Another volume (Archuleta, Child, and Lomawaima, 2000), inspired by an impressive exhibit at the Heard Museum in Phoenix, employed striking visual images. A series of institutional studies produced additional insights into the nature of Indian boarding schools. Clyde Ellis (1996) described the Rainy Mountain school in Oklahoma; Sally Hyer, (1990), the Santa Fe Indian School, K. Tsianina Lomawaima (Creek), the Chilocco Indian Industrial School (1994), Scott Riney (1999), the Rapid City Indian School, and Robert A. Trennert (1984), the Phoenix Indian School. These volumes tell us a great deal about Native people during the early twentieth century. Historians and other scholars have just started to examine in detail the more recent past, including community schools, tribal colleges and public schools. Careful consideration of these and other developments in this era will add a vital chapter to our understanding of American Indians in this century.

Culture and Economy

This broad category covers many key issues in American Indian life, from religious belief to work. Few historians have been willing to delve into many subjects relating to culture and economy. This hesitation mirrors the lack of attention that cultural history receives from most western historians. It also reflects the disinclination of many historians to do oral history and field research. Gender, for example, has remained a category of analysis infrequently employed by students of Indian history. Fortunately, there are signs that these tendencies are beginning to be eroded, in part because more women are now entering the field of American Indian history.

These studies are crucial because we need to gain a more thorough understanding of the internal workings and priorities of Indian societies. Historians must find ways to articulate how and why Native communities make choices and determine their destinies. This means taking Native languages seriously, regarding traditional Indians teachings with respect, and appreciating more fully the power of Native landscapes.

The work of anthropologist Keith Basso demonstrates the utility of gaining more than a passing understanding of Native languages, teachings, and landscapes. *Wisdom Sits in Places: Landscape and Language Among the Western Apache* revealed how "Apache constructions of place reach deeply into other cultural spheres, including conceptions of wisdom, notions of morality, politeness and tact in forms of spoken discourse, and certain conventional ways of imagining and interpreting the Apache tribal past" (Basso, 1994: xv).

L. G. Moses' characterization of Indian participation in the Wild West (1996) represents another example of the value of cultural history. *Wild West Shows and the Images of American Indians, 1883–1933* demonstrated convincingly that this story was far more complicated than a simple tale of exploitation. Graced with some stunning illustrations, the book provided a perceptive reinterpretation that enhanced our understanding of Native agency during a transitional era.

Other subjects await the attention of historians. The Native American Church, for example, is an extremely important institution in twentieth-century American Indian life, yet historians have almost entirely ignored it. Anthropologists have studied the Native American Church (NAC), but even the best overview could be considerably more cohesive. Wade Davies' recent book on Navajo healthcare (2001) does offer a thorough discussion of the NAC within a broader context. Basso's work or the writings of Julie Cruikshank about Native women elders of the Canadian Yukon furnish an exciting reminder of the potential benefits to be gained. A few studies have focused on economic development and cultural concerns that attend such development. In 1990 journalist Marjane Ambler wrote of Indian efforts to control development of energy resources on their lands. More recently Donald L. Fixico offered case studies of a century-long struggle over natural resources on Indian lands (1998). Iverson probed the cultural and economic meanings of Native involvement in the cattle industry (1994). The ongoing importance of subsistence and the campaign to exploit mineral resources in Alaska prompted several volumes, of which two of the most engaging were by Canadian jurist Thomas R. Berger (1985) and by James H. Barker (1993). Berger presented an indictment of the Alaska Native Claims Settlement Act, while Barker explained the functioning of the Yup'ik traditional economy. Barker's magnificent photographs furnished another pertinent example of the value of visual images.

Several younger scholars have recognized the significance of Native cultural and economic history. Brian Hosmer's *American Indians in the Marketplace* presented a thoughtful and thoroughly researched analysis of the economies of the Menominees in Wisconsin and the Metlakakans in Alaska (1999). Although the Menominees have the misfortune to live outside of the West, the book deserves citation here for its balanced account of Native initiatives in the face of adversity.

Although we may assume that such accounts are centered in rural surroundings, the steady movement of indigenous individuals into urban settings has inspired new work about Indian residence in metropolitan areas, including Fixico's ambitious overview (2000) and James LaGrand's perceptive examination of life in Chicago (2002).

Sovereignty

If anthropologists have dominated considerations of culture, then attorneys have monopolized the discussion of Indian efforts toward self-determination. Felix Cohen provided a major voice, authoring many important articles as well as a landmark volume, *Handbook of Federal Law* (1942). Cohen often wrote for a broader audience, but many attorneys have chosen to write for each other. Their writings are important but not necessarily easily appreciated nor fully understood by those not blessed with legal training. University of Colorado law school professor Charles Wilkinson is a happy exception to the rule; most writing about sovereignty tends to be as tedious as it is tendentious. At this very moment there are hundreds of lawyers out there making new verbs out of old nouns.

One of the few historians to venture into this arena, John Wunder, earned his PhD after receiving his law degree. This kind of behavior ought to be rewarded and in this instance it has. Wunder's history of Indians and the Bill of Rights (1994) weighed Indian rights in modern America. Another important book, *Braid of Feathers*, by University of South Dakota law school professor Frank Pommersheim, measured the impact of the law on contemporary tribal life (1995). Lumbee political scientist David Wilkins has written a series of valuable studies, one of them co-authored with Tsianina Lomawaima (Wilkins, 1997; Wilkins and Lomawaima, 2001).

Throughout the twentieth century Indians in the West fought for water, hunting, and fishing rights. These battles have often been waged in the courts, with the Supreme Court often serving as final arbiter of crucial issues. Lloyd Burton completed a useful introduction to the murky matters of Indian water rights (1991), while Alexandra Harmon's *Indians in the Making* (1998) dealt with fishing rights in the Pacific Northwest. Much remained to be considered. A more detailed analysis of the impact of organizations such as the Native American Rights Fund, attorneys for the various tribes, and legal services programs, would be most welcome. A sample of what might be unearthed could be observed in Wilkinson's memoir. *Fire on the Plateau* (1999) provided information about the beneficial impact of the Native American Rights Fund; it also unearthed the grimy details of Hopi tribal attorney John Boyden's duplicitous dealings with the Peabody Coal Company.

Contemporary Indian movements have focused much of their energy and attention on matters relating to sovereignty. One of the most provocative and engaging discussions of recent years was written by journalist Paul Chaat Smith (Comanche) and English professor Robert Warrior (Osage) (1996). The two presented an often pointed discussion of the Indian movement from Alcatraz to Wounded Knee. This is in many ways a landmark book: a provocative examination of the recent past by Native writers willing to take a critical view of their subject. *Like a Hurricane* is complemented by other perspectives on the events and leaders of this era, such as Troy R. Johnson's consideration of the Alcatraz occupation (1996).

The evolution of the gaming industry in many Indian communities in the past generation has provoked central questions about the nature of Indian sovereignty. To what extent can or should the state or the federal government regulate such enterprise within the boundaries of Indian nations? This is one of a number of remarkable stories waiting to be told by historians willing to address controversial dimensions of the recent past.

Conclusion

This essay often has suggested avenues for further research. In fact the list is considerably longer than this presentation could accommodate. Urbanization, for example, is a major dimension of modern Indian life, yet historians have paid precious little attention to it. Books by Donald Fixico (2000) and James LaGrand (2002) are rarer exceptions to this generalization; Myla Vincenti-Carpio has also recently completed a dissertation that considers Indian communities in Albuquerque (2001). These scholars do not deserve this kind of scholarly solitary confinement. In addition, few historians have paid sufficient attention to urbanization on reservations, a development that has had major social and cultural consequences.

In marked contrast to a century ago, relatively few Americans now harbor illusions about Indians being vanishing peoples. Throughout the past one hundred years, countless Native women and men have struggled and sacrificed so that their communities could continue. More historians are finally realizing the richness, the complexity, and the significance of twentieth-century Indian history and many able young scholars, Native and non-Native, are entering the field. Nevertheless, we have not paid sufficient attention to this subject. Although we have made a beginning, we have a lot of work to do.

REFERENCES

Ambler, Marjane: *Breaking the Iron Bonds: Indian Control of Energy Development* (Lawrence, KS: University Press of Kansas, 1990).

Archuleta, Margaret L., Brenda J. Child, and K. Tsianina Lomawaima (eds.): *Away from Home: American Indian Boarding School Experiences, 1879–2000* (Phoenix: Heard Museum, 2000).

Barker, James H.: *Always Getting Ready: Yup'ik Eskimo Subsistence in Southwest Alaska* (Seattle: University of Washington Press, 1993).

Basso, Keith H.: *Wisdom Sits in Places: Landscape and Language Among the Western Apache* (Albuquerque: University of New Mexico Press, 1996).

Berger, Thomas R.: *Village Journey: The Report of the Alaska Native Review Commission* (New York: Hill and Wang, 1985).

Berger, Thomas R.: *Village Journey: The Report of the Alaska Native Review Commission*, rev. edn. (New York: Hill and Wang, 1995).

Berkhofer, Robert F., Jr.: "The Political Context of a New Indian History." *Pacific Historical Review 40* (August 1971), 357–82.

Berkhofer, Robert F., Jr.: *The White Man's Indian: Images of the Indian From Columbus to the Present* (New York: Alfred A. Knopf, 1977).

Bernstein, Alison R.: *American Indians and World War II: Toward a New Era in Indian Affairs* (Norman: University of Oklahoma Press, 1991).

Burton, Lloyd: *American Indian Water Rights and the Limits of Law* (Lawrence: University Press of Kansas, 1991).

Child, Brenda J.: *Boarding School Seasons: American Indian Families, 1900–1940* (Lincoln: University of Nebraska Press, 1998).

Cohen, Felix: *A Handbook of Federal Indian Law* (Washington, DC: Government Printing Office, 1942).

Connell-Szasz, Margaret: *Education and the American Indian: The Road Toward Self-Determination* (Albuquerque: University of New Mexico Press, 1990).

Cruikshank, Julie: *The Social Life of Stories: Narrative and Knowledge in the Yukon Territory* (Lincoln: University of Nebraska Press, 1997).

Crum, Stephen K.: *The Road on Which We Came: Po'i pentun tammen Kimmappeh: A History of the Western Shoshone* (Salt Lake City: University of Utah Press, 1994).

D'Arcy McNickle Center for American Indian History: *The Impact of Indian History on the Teaching of United States History* (Chicago: Newberry Library, Occasional Papers in Curriculum Series, no. 5, 1986).

D'Arcy McNickle Center for American Indian History: *The Struggle for Political Autonomy* (Chicago: Newberry Library, Occasional Papers in Curriculum Series, no. 11, 1989).

D'Arcy McNickle Center for American Indian History: *Teaching and Writing Local History: The Crows* (Chicago: Newberry Library, Occasional Papers in Curriculum Series, no. 18, 1994).

Davies, Wade M.: *"Healing Ways": Navajo Health Care in the 20th Century* (Albuquerque: University of New Mexico Press, 2001).

Debo, Angie: *And Still the Waters Run: The Betrayal of the Five Civilized Tribes* (Princeton: Princeton University Press, 1972).

Deloria, Vine, Jr.: *Custer Died For Your Sins: An Indian Manifesto* (New York: Macmillan, 1969).

Deloria , Vine, Jr. and Clifford Lytle: *The Nations Within: The Past and Future of American Indian Sovereignty* (New York: Pantheon, 1984).

Edmunds, R. David (ed.): *The New Warriors: Native American Leaders Since 1900* (Lincoln: University of Nebraska Press, 2001).

Ellis, Clyde: *To Change Them Forever: Indian Education at the Rainy Mountain Boarding School, 1893–1920* (Norman: University of Oklahoma Press, 1996.)

Fixico, Donald L.: *Termination and Relocation: Federal Indian Policy, 1945–1961* (Albuquerque: University of New Mexico Press, 1986).

Fixico, Donald L.: *The Invasion of Indian Country in the Twentieth Century: American Capitalism and Tribal Natural Resources* (Niwot: University Press of Colorado, 1998).

Fixico, Donald L.: *Rethinking American Indian History* (Albuquerque: University of New Mexico Press, 1997).

Fixico, Donald: *The Urban Indian Experience in America* (Albuquerque: University of New Mexico Press, 2000).

Forbes, Jack D.: "The Indian in the West: A Challenge for Historians." *Arizona and the West* 1 (Winter 1959), 206–15.

Foster, Morris W.: *Being Comanche: A Social History of an American Indian Community* (Tucson: University of Arizona Press, 1991).

Fowler, Loretta: *Arapahoe Politics, 1851–1978: Symbols in Crises of Authority* (Lincoln: University of Nebraska Press, 1982).

Fowler, Loretta: *Shared Symbols, Contested Meanings: Gros Ventre Culture and History, 1778–1984* (Ithaca, NY: Cornell University Press, 1987).

Fowler, Loretta: *Tribal Sovereignty and the Historical Imagination: Cheyenne–Arapahoe Politics* (Lincoln: University of Nebraska Press, 2002).

Hagan, William T.: *American Indians* (Chicago: University of Chicago Press, 1961).

Hagan, William T.: *Quanah Parker, Comanche Chief* (Norman: University of Oklahoma Press, 1993).

Harmon, Alexandra: *Indians in the Making: Ethnic Relations and Indian Identities around Puget Sound* (Berkeley: University of California Press, 1998).

Hosmer, Brian: *American Indians in the Marketplace: Persistence and Innovation Among the Menominees and Metlakatlans, 1870–1920* (Lawrence: University Press of Kansas, 1999).

Hoxie, Frederick E.: *A Final Promise: The Campaign to Assimilate the Indians, 1880–1920* (Lincoln: University of Nebraska Press, 1984).

Hoxie, Frederick E.: *Parading Through History: The Making of the Crow Nation in America, 1805–1935* (New York: Cambridge University Press, 1995).

Hoxie, Frederick E. and Peter Iverson (eds.) *Indians in American History*, 2nd edn. (Wheeling, IL: Harlan Davidson, 1998).

Hyer, Sally: *One House, One Voice, One Heart: Native American Education at the Santa Fe Indian School* (Santa Fe: Museum of New Mexico Press, 1990).

Iverson, Peter: *Carlos Montezuma and the Changing World of American Indians* (Albuquerque: University of New Mexico Press, 1982).

Iverson, Peter: *The Navajo Nation* (Albuquerque: University of New Mexico Press, 1983).

Iverson, Peter: *"We Are Still Here": American Indians in the Twentieth Century* (Wheeling, IL: Harlan Davidson, 1998).

Iverson, Peter: *When Indians Became Cowboys: Native Peoples and Cattle Ranching in the American West* (Norman: University of Oklahoma Press, 1994).

Iverson, Peter: *Dine: A History of the Navajos* (Albuquerque: University of New Mexico Press, 2002a).

Iverson, Peter: *"For Our Navajo People": Dine Letters, Speeches, and Petitions, 1900–1960* (Albuquerque: University of New Mexico Press, 2002b).

Johnson, Troy R.: *The Occupation of Alcatraz Island: Indian Self-Determination and the Rise of Indian Activism* (Urbana: University of Illinois Press, 1996).

Knack, Martha C: *Boundaries Between: The Southern Paiutes, 1775–1995* (Lincoln: University of Nebraska Press, 2001).

LaGrand, James B.: *Indian Metropolis: Native Americans in Chicago, 1945–75* (Urbana: University of Illinois Press, 2002).

Lomawaima, K. Tsianina: *They Called It Prairie Light: The Story of Chilocco Indian School* (Lincoln: University of Nebraska Press, 1994).

Martin, Calvin (ed.) The *American Indian and the Problem of History* (New York: Oxford University Press, 1987).

McNickle, D'Arcy: *Native American Tribalism: Indian Survivals and Renewals* (New York: Oxford University Press, 1973).

Metcalf, R. Warren: *Termination's Legacy: The Discarded Indians of Utah* (Lincoln: University of Nebraska Press, 2002).

Mihesuah, Devon A. (ed.): *Natives and Academics: Research and Writing About American Indians* (Lincoln: University of Nebraska Press, 1998).

Mihesuah, Devon A.: *Indigenous American Women: Decolonization, Empowerment, Activism* (Lincoln: University of Nebraska Press, 2003).

Mitchell, Rose: *Tall Woman: The Life Story Rose Mitchell, a Navajo Woman*, ed. Charlotte Frisbie (Albuquerque: University of New Mexico Press, 2003).

Moses, L. G.: *Wild West Shows and the Images of American Indians, 1883–1933* (Albuquerque: University of New Mexico Press, 1996).

Olson, James S. and Raymond Wilson: *Native Americans in the Twentieth Century* (Provo: Brigham Young University Press, 1984).

Parker, Dorothy R.: *Singing an Indian Song: A Biography of D'Arcy McNickle* (Lincoln: University of Nebraska Press, 1992).

Parman, Donald L.: *Indians and the American West in the Twentieth Century* (Bloomington: Indiana University Press, 1994).

Philp, Kenneth R.: *John Collier's Crusade for Indian Reform, 1920–1954* (Tucson: University of Arizona Press, 1977).

Philp, Kenneth R.: *Termination Revisited: American Indians on the Trail to Self-Determination, 1933–1953* (Lincoln: University of Nebraska Press, 1999).

Pommersheim, Frank: *Braid of Feathers: American Indian Law and Contemporary Tribal Life* (Berkeley: University of California Press, 1995).

Prucha, Francis Paul: (*A Bibliographical Guide to the History of Indian–White Relations in the United States* (Chicago: University of Chicago Press, 1977).

Prucha, Francis Paul: *The Great Father: The United States Government and American Indians*, 2 vols. (Lincoln: University of Nebraska Press, 1984).

Ridington, Robin: *"Fox and Chickadee."* In Calvin Martin (ed.) *The American Indian and the Problem of History* (New York: Oxford University Press, 1987).

Riney, Scott: *The Rapid City Indian School, 1898–1933* (Norman: University of Oklahoma Press, 1999).

Robertson, Paul: *The Power of the Land: Identity, Ethnicity, and Class among the Oglala Lakota* (New York: Routledge, 2002).

Sando, Joe S.: *Nee Hemish: A History of Jemez Pueblo* (Albuquerque: University of New Mexico Press, 1982).

Sarris, Greg: *Mabel McKay: Weaving the Dream* (Berkeley: University of California Press, 1994).

Shoemaker, Nancy (ed.): *Clearing a Path: Theorizing a Past in Native American Studies* (New York: Routledge, 2002).

Smith, Paul Chaat and Robert Warrior: *Like a Hurricane: The Indian Movement From Alcatraz to Wounded Knee* (New York: Basic Books, 1996).

Tiller, Veronica Velarde: *The Jicarilla Apache Tribe: A History, 1846–1970* (Lincoln: University of Nebraska Press, 1983).

Trennert, Robert A., Jr.: *The Phoenix Indian School: Forced Assimilation in Arizona, 1891–1935* (Norman: University of Oklahoma Press, 1984).

Trimble, Stephen: *The People: Indians of the American Southwest* (Santa Fe: School of American Research Press, 1993).

Vicenti-Carpio, Myla Thyrza: "'Let Them Know We Still Exist': Indians in Albuquerque." (PhD dissertation, Arizona State University, 2001).

Washburn, Wilcomb E.: *"The Writing of American Indian History: A Status Report." Pacific Historical Review* 40 (August 1971), 261–81.

Wilkins, David E.: *American Indian Sovereignty and the U.S. Supreme Court: The Masking of Justice* (Austin: University of Texas Press, 1997).

Wilkins, David E. and K. Tsianina Lomawaima: *Uneven Ground: American Indian Sovereignty and Federal Law.* Norman: University of Oklahoma Press, 2001).

Wilkinson, Charles: *Fire on the Plateau: Conflict and Endurance in the American Southwest* (Washington, DC: Island Press, 1999).

Wilson, Raymond: *Ohiyesa: Charles Eastman, Santee Sioux* (Urbana: University of Illinois Press, 1983).

Wunder, John R.: *"Retained By the People": A History of American Indians and the Bill of Rights* (New York: Oxford University Press, 1994).

CHAPTER NINETEEN

The New Deal's West

KAREN R. MERRILL

Most accounts of the New Deal in the West begin from the vantage point of the dry plains, turned parched and cracked from the drought that, in a case of tragically poor timing, coincided with the deepest depression in the nation's history. But so much of the West's fate lay in Washington during those years that we could also begin there and with a scene that seemed to take its script from a classic confrontation in a western film. That scene was of a resignation, but a resignation in which both parties involved were anything but resigned. In 1938 the Secretary of the Interior, Harold Ickes, forced the head of the department's Grazing Division, Farrington Carpenter, to leave his position. Harold Ickes was a formidable presence in the New Deal administration: intensely loyal to Franklin Roosevelt and to what he interpreted as Roosevelt's mission, he was also pugnacious and outspoken and an irritant in many a legislator's side. Ickes had had trouble with Farrington Carpenter since Carpenter had joined the Interior Department in 1934 to start up the department's management of grazing on its public lands: among other things, he thought Carpenter (a politically active rancher from Colorado) an inept administrator who simply kowtowed to the prevailing powers in the western livestock associations, with little thought of the reputation and purposes of the Interior Department's work. In 1936, for instance, Ickes wrote an acerbic 11-page letter to Carpenter, raking him over the coals for both small and grand matters having to do with his policy decisions, his public statements, his seemingly never ending trips to the West, and his general indifference to, well, Harold Ickes. Carpenter responded with a 42-page reply that attempted to set the record straight for Ickes, which it did at best temporarily.

Their relationship deteriorated quickly after that, and thus, the day after election day in 1938, Ickes asked for Carpenter's resignation. Carpenter wasn't averse to resigning, although he knew that, as a presidential appointee, he could not be forced to resign except as requested by Roosevelt. Moreover, he wanted to be sure that he could get a letter of commendation from Ickes, testifying to his good work as the head of the Grazing Division. Days went by as Ickes refused to write such a letter, and Carpenter refused to hand in his resignation. Finally, Carpenter was brought into Ickes's office by an administrative assistant who promised Carpenter that Ickes had written a very nice commendation letter for him. However, Ickes would not let him read it until he had Carpenter's letter in hand. By this point, Carpenter was so convinced that Ickes and his assistant were trying to trick him – indeed, that they would literally try to change his commendation letter to a condemnation letter, if given the chance – that they all agreed to bring in the Assistant Secretary of the Interior, Oscar Chapman, to help break the stalemate. "Finally," recalled Carpenter in a written recollection some years later, the assistant "asked how I would trade [the letters] and I said, 'you go over in one corner and Chapman in another and leave Ickes's letter on the desk and I'll open [it] and read it and if it is o.k., I'll hand you my resignation.' They did that and I read it and it was o.k. and I handed him my letter."[1]

On the one hand, the viewer of this scene can interpret it as simply the workings of two very politically astute men, each concerned with protecting his own reputation and deploying what power was available to him. And it is a scene of simple incompatibility: Ickes and Carpenter had grown to dislike each other deeply, and the politics of their personalities often got in the way of their land management work in the Interior Department. But their parting of ways was also perfectly emblematic of the gulf in their understandings of what the New Deal's job in the West should be. Carpenter deeply feared that the increasing power and oversight of the federal government over the West would stanch westerners' political freedom, while Ickes believed that federal power was the only thing that could save the West's natural resources from complete exhaustion. Thus, they each proposed a fundamentally different political relationship between the West and Washington, and although Ickes won their particular battle, public land historians have long believed that Carpenter may have won the war. Local control in federal programs was indeed a reality throughout the New Deal's operations in the region. Of course, their disagreements reflected the enormous divide among westerners over the New Deal, which in turn reflected an even larger conflict among Americans over the course of governmental power in the 1930s.

From the moment that Franklin Delano Roosevelt began experimenting with government programs in 1933, the New Deal has been under the microscope, and in the decades since the end of his administration, historians have largely focused on three questions: what was the New Deal, where did it come from, and what did it do? As for the first question, conclusions have ranged from William Leuchtenberg's early assessment (Leuchtenberg, 1999) that it constituted a "half-way revolution" to Barton Bernstein's claim (Bernstein, 1999) that it was a conservative response to economic crisis that served to bolster the corporate liberal regime already in place. Recent scholars (Skocpol and Finegold, 1982) have given more theoretical shading to the question, by trying to analyze how responsive the structures of the federal government were to the Great Depression and the extent to which institutions and actors within the state were able to chart their own paths – in particular away from the demands and desires of powerful, capitalist interests (Brinkley, 1998). As for the second question, a great deal of scholarship has shown how much the New Deal drew on antecedents in the past; historians have long known, for instance, that the National Industrial Relations Board was drawn from the model of the War Industries Board of World War I, and recently Daniel Rodgers (1998) has richly shown the degree to which New Deal leaders drew from a wealth of social experiments both in the past and in other countries.

But it is the third question that in many ways has formulated how both historians and the lay public have understood the New Deal: the New Deal was as the New

Deal *did*. One very good reason for such a focus, particularly among historians, is the difficulty of summing up the New Deal as a whole. It was such a messy conglomeration of programs, impulses, and motivations that it is simply very hard to characterize. And, of course, the New Deal has long been taught as "alphabet soup," where high school teachers and professors expect their students to recite what the N. R. A. was, the A. A. A., the C. C. C., the W. P. A., and so on. The particularization of the New Deal in terms of its programs is paralleled in the historical profession by the particularization of scholarship around the effects of the New Deal. For instance, two anthologies of essays about the New Deal (Hamilton, 1999; Sitkoff, 1985) both have sections that look at the effects of the New Deal on specific groups, such as African Americans, women, and workers. To ask therefore about the relationship between the New Deal and the West is to risk falling into just such a pattern, that is, to ask what the New Deal *did* for the West.

It should come as no surprise to say that it did a lot, and plenty of scholarship in western history has shown just how much. Works that have ranged over a number of topics, from water and public land management to Indian policy, show that the federal government clearly took an active interest in the West during the 1930s. And yet relatively few historians have looked directly at what happened to the West as a region with the New Deal. Richard Lowitt's *The New Deal and the West*, published in 1994, was the first book-length work to explore the question, and it remains the only comprehensive account today – although comprehensive in a very particular way. Lowitt looked at the New Deal's impact on the West largely through the lenses of two federal agencies, the Department of Agriculture and the Department of the Interior, whose programs were focused greatly on the West. In the case of the former department, that focus fell on the plains states and California; in the case of the latter, largely on the mountain states and the Pacific Northwest. Taken as a whole, agricultural and land planners in the 1930s saw the West as a vast arena for government intervention, to restructure what social order was left after the ravages of the depression, especially on the plains, and to reenvision a new relationship between people and land use.

In concrete terms, the New Deal, in Lowitt's words, "left a legacy of constructive government accomplishments in conservation, public power, and natural resource use" (1994: 228). But it was a mixed legacy in a couple ways. First, historians, including Lowitt, have questioned just how well the federal government both during the New Deal and following it was able to sustain these achievements. The case of water management is perhaps the most illustrative. While the West's most prominent dam was finished during the New Deal – bearing the name of the president whom Roosevelt defeated – it and the other massive water projects are now seen as producing countless environmental problems. Not only did they simply flood significant parts of the western landscape, but they also destroyed local ecosystems and encouraged urban and agricultural growth that, in turn, took their tolls on the environment. New Deal land management has also come under sharp attack. Historians have long considered the signal legislative act meant to save the western rangelands, the Taylor Grazing Act, as simply a sell-out to the ranching industry, despite the official aims of the act to rehabilitate public grazing lands. In the last thirty years scholars and environmental activists have given a detailed look at the tremendous environmental costs of that legislation, for by essentially making ranchers partners in setting government policy for the range, domesticated cattle and sheep have caused tremendous ecological damage, particularly in delicate riparian areas (Donahue, 2000; Merrill, 2002). Even New Deal policies for Native Americans have come under criticism. While Bureau of Indian Affairs chief John Collier did depart from the disastrous course of the nineteenth century, his emphasis on tribal sovereignty was still laced with a strong dose of governmental paternalism.

Thus, what kind of legacy the New Deal left behind in the West is still up for considerable debate. And while the New Deal clearly ushered in large, federal programs, such as those in water management, that helped prop up local economies, it is unclear just how important these ultimately were in shoring up the region's economy. Here, the historical work on the New Deal and the West parallels the conclusions drawn about the New Deal generally, which hold that it really was World War II that pulled the nation out of its depression, and that the war years and not the New Deal years shaped federal officials' understandings of the government's role in economic planning. Gerald Nash has repeatedly reached this conclusion in his works: while the New Deal helped break the West from its colonial relationship to Eastern and international capital, he argues, it was the World War II that charted the future of the region, in particular by making large population segments dependent on defense contracts (Nash, 1999).

What we are left with, then, are conclusions that echo the main conclusions about the New Deal in the United States: the programs had high aims that they often did not meet, and World War II was really the event that most transformed the region. But such conclusions are deeply unsatisfying – and are, in fact, misleading. As David Kennedy has written, "When the war brought recovery at last, a recovery that inaugurated the most prosperous quarter century America has ever known, it brought it to an economy and a country that the New Deal had fundamentally altered" (1999: 363). That transformation did not occur simply through launching a multitude of new federal programs; it also happened because the experience of the depression and the New Deal itself changed government planners' ideas about what liberal reform meant. As the New Deal wore on, the most influential of them found themselves scaling back their goals and increasingly speaking of the government's "responsibility less as a commitment to restructure the economy than as an effort to stabilize it and help it grow" (Brinkley, 1995: 7). That ideological shift within the New Deal would, of course, help shape postwar economic planning with its emphasis on fueling consumption. As well, both ordinary Americans and those involved at all levels of government understood that something profound had happened in their relationship to the federal government and in the government's place in the nation during the New Deal. Westerners were no different. When journalist Anna Louise Strong set out to examine the impact of the New Deal in just one county of California (Lowitt, 1984: 175), she practically gave up after ten days because the job was so large. Whether westerners welcomed or derided governmental intervention, be that in the form of grazing permits under the Taylor Grazing Act or of migratory labor camps or of acreage-reduction payments under the Agricultural Adjustment Act, westerners stood in a different relationship to Washington in 1940 than they had in 1932.

Moreover, despite its contradictions and its tendency to go in ten different directions at the same time, the American New Deal did represent a truly flourishing time of experimentation. Daniel Rodgers (1998) has noted, for instance, that in the 1930s

European countries cast their gaze at American political changes, rather than the other way around, as Roosevelt's administration enlisted political talents in a panoply of policy arenas – agriculture, finance, labor relations, social insurance, conservation, and electrification. Much of what these reformers attempted to put in place was based on ideas that had, in fact, been around since the Progressive period – ideas that themselves had been drawn from European experimentation in the late nineteenth and early twentieth century. Even some of the plans that affected seemingly the most American parts of the country – the problems of southern agriculture and western land use – had distant roots in what Rodgers calls the "Atlantic crossings" of reformist ideas. Since the turn of the century, for example, rural planners in Washington had looked to countries like Ireland and Denmark, which had embarked on trying to bring the countryside and the city into better balance, and where farmers did not feel the press of a market economy with such terrible force. For New Deal agricultural planners, the entire American countryside was in desperate need of help: they believed that farmers had to gain better purchasing power, they needed to overcome their socially atomistic ways, and the land required expert attention to make it more productive.

The New Deal's agricultural program was central to the entire nation and points to the importance of not setting "the New Deal West" apart from other regions of the country. That separation is in part the effect of such accounts as Lowitt's, which emphasizes the programs that focused, as one reviewer (Malone, 1984) phrased it, "more or less exclusively on the West." *And yet*, the logic of governmental activity makes it difficult to avoid such separation. First, as Leonard Arrington discovered in 1983, the federal government contributed more per capita to the West than to any other region in the country. Even more importantly, Arrington also shows that New Deal agencies became attached to particular regions, such as the Interior Department's deep connection to the intermountain West, where so much public domain land was left. Lowitt had good cause, in other words, to focus on the Departments of Agriculture and Interior to investigate what the New Deal did in the West. Or to state it more specifically: investigating those departments shows us in detail how the federal government defined the West and the West's problems. For while federal relief programs were spread across the country, it was the work of agricultural and land planners that distinguished how the New Deal envisioned the West's future relationship to the federal government.

But how did the New Deal *see* the West? By asking that question I mean to use that word *see* as literally as it may be stretched to talk about the way an entire bureaucratic apparatus conceived of the region and of its work in the region. To ask how the American state saw the West takes us beyond simply the question of what conditions it found when it turned its gaze west of the Missouri; it takes us to the very essence of statecraft itself. To "see like a state," as James C. Scott (1998) has argued, is to make the social and natural world "legible" to the state. It means taking profoundly complex interactions among people and between people and their environment and reducing them to often radically simpler forms. Of course, by the time of the New Deal, government reformers had accomplished much of this work. The American landscape had long been surveyed and divided into 640-acre units; nomadic peoples such as certain Native American tribes had been forced into a sedentary existence; a property regime embracing freehold tenure was firmly in place; and decennial censuses provided the federal government with detailed information about the American population. These accomplishments can all be traced to early modern state formation in Western Europe and England, which saw, as Michel Foucault (1991) has noted, an "explosion" of interest in the "art of government." What marked the New Deal as such a distinctive period in American political history was that it sought to extend further than had ever been done before the art of government, to extend it to include the reformation of American society, *particularly in the West and the South*. Federal planners believed that those two regions had some of the most marginal lands and the most marginal rural folk in the country. Restructuring the West's economy, and its people, to the land was one of the New Deal's central projects; in setting that goal, New Deal agencies clearly drew on historical antecedents, but they also involved the government more directly in the region than had ever happened before.

To say that land and agricultural planners had a deep interest in centralizing their management in Washington does not mean either that they wanted to create an all-powerful state or that they succeeded. In fact, as in other areas of the New Deal, those officials involved with land use struggled over how to balance centralization with democratic participation, and many of their ideas to implement greater governmental oversight never made the light of day. And as Rodgers notes, "[I]t's hard not to be struck by the decentralist elements in the New Deal political imagination" (1998: 448). All across the New Deal agricultural and land programs, one can see the government building not only institutional authority in Washington, but also decision-making structures that involved local people. Can the New Deal in the West therefore be said to contain both centralizing and decentralizing elements? That's one way to understand it – and certainly the most straightforward. But in fact the impulse within federal agencies was more than just "both/and," for in a number of projects the decentralization was framed by the expansion of federal power. That is, what the New Deal saw as the fulfillment of democratic promise, whether that meant ranchers' voting for herd reductions or a migrant labor camp's governing itself, in fact only held meaning through the government's increased authority. Returning to the opening figures of this essay, then, we might say that neither Harold Ickes' nor Farrington Carpenter's beliefs prevailed, either during the New Deal or afterwards. Rather, federal grazing management perfectly embodies the features of "the New Deal's West," as Carpenter's vision of local control emerged within the framework of Ickes's desire for administrative expansion.

Such a political development left a significant legacy in the region. And perhaps the most dramatic avenue to begin examining that relationship is through the documentary photography produced by the Farm Security Administration (FSA) in the 1930s, which more than anything dramatized the visual "legibility" of the region. Given that the FSA's collection holds over 160,000 photographs by a number of different photographers, it is impossible, of course, to generalize about either what the photographers intended to show in making the images or how their audiences interpreted those images. Nonetheless, these photographs can help us to see the tensions within the New Deal's relationship to the West, whereby ordinary people were constituted simultaneously as the focus of socioeconomic reform and the legitimate foundation for state power.

Like the other states in the country, the western states were overwhelmed by the scale of immiseration during the Depression and by their inability to provide relief, and the desperation of the people was anything but unique to the region. But one thing did distinguish the Depression in the western states from other areas in the nation, and that was its place within the national consciousness about the Depression. For by the eve of World War II, the image of the so-called Okies would dominate Americans' understanding of what had befallen them. As Charles J. Shindo has written, "Images and descriptions of the dust bowl migrants proliferated in literature, music, newspapers, magazines, photo collections, films and onstage. The dust bowl migration to California evokes the Great Depression perhaps more than any other event of the 1930s, not only because of its pervasiveness but because of its representational possibilities" (1997: 2). Among those possibilities, the photographic images that were produced out of the Historical Section of the Farm Security Administration helped to define the West of the Great Depression.

The FSA photography did not operate only west of the Mississippi, of course; as famous as the dust bowl photographs were, other images of poor southern farmers and sharecroppers also broadcast the social dislocation in the American countryside. But the meanings that the dust bowl photographs were both infused with and generated were profoundly different than their southern counterparts. On the one hand, as Shindo (ibid.: 51) has argued, the FSA documentary project produced what has now become the most recognized icon of the Great Depression: Lange's 1936 *Migrant Mother*. By focusing so tightly on the mother's anxious face and by removing all clues to the family's specific location, Lange created an image that universalized particularly the white experience of suffering during the 1930s. When the photograph first appeared in *Midweek Pictorial*, it clearly caught the general mood of the depression and was pitched in that way. As the magazine noted, "This woman is watching something happen to herself and her children who are part of America" (Shindo: 53).

On the other hand, if the westward migration of the "Okies" represented something that seemed to be quintessentially American about the experience of the depression, it also played on images and narratives that themselves were rooted deeply in American understandings of the West. This was evident in the instructions or "shooting scripts" that Roy Stryker, the head of the documentary program for the FSA, gave to his photographers. For example, to Marion Post Wolcott, who was heading for the plains, Stryker noted that he hoped for the following:

1. Shots which give the sense of great distance and flat country. House, barn and windmill on horizon, lots of sky. Row of telephone poles.
2. Wheat. YOU MUST BE IN KANSAS FOR A WHILE DURING THE WHEAT HARVEST. Get the sense that there is nothing in the world that matters very much but wheat. Wheat and wheat just as far as the unaided eye can see.
3. Search for ideas to give the sense of loneliness experienced by the women folks who helped settle this country. This idea might be developed around an abandoned dwelling on a plains homestead.[2]

Such evocations of the enormous space of the West had a long history, going back at least to Leatherstocking's near speechlessness in the face of the endless expanse of the plains; having never seen anything like it, the only metaphor he could reach for was the sea: "The earth was not unlike the ocean, when its restless waters are heaving heavily, after the agitation and fury of the tempest have begun to lessen" (Cooper, 1985: 630). Representing the vast expanse of land was central not simply to the FSA photography of the dust bowl West but to that of the West generally, and that vastness could be put to different uses. The image of the individual man against the backdrop of the immense western landscape had long been a heroic one; indeed, those valences still infused the FSA photography. However, the tragedies of the Great Depression placed a different interpretive lens on that image. Dust Bowl migrants could seem just as easily dwarfed and overwhelmed by the landscape as uplifted by it. The FSA project also effectively fused the landscape with particular interpretations of what had gone wrong on the plains. Lange, for instance, understood the dust bowl migration as the consequence of agricultural mechanization – and of the mechanization of modern society generally. Her 1938 photograph "Tractored Out, Childress County, Texas," featuring an abandoned house surrounded by cultivated rows represented, as Shindo notes, just one of many such photographs that showcased her conviction that agricultural technology had set the westward migration in motion.

Indeed, mechanization had profoundly dislocating effects on the agriculture of all the plains states. In his study of Texas cotton culture in the early twentieth century, for instance, Neil Foley (1997: 165) writes that "[t]he efficiency of power farming came with the social costs of a throng of homeless and underemployed farm laborers." But mechanization was not simply the "push" factor of the dust bowl migrants of the thirties; much more significantly, as Foley argues, it reshaped the class and racial hierarchies of Texas cotton culture, which, earlier in the century, was an industry where white tenants could distinguish themselves from poorer black and Mexican sharecroppers and migrant workers:

> In the new farm order of the New Deal, tenants and sharecroppers had become anachronistic and inefficient producers, while migrant cotton pickers . . . were essential to more profitable and efficient agricultural production. . . . Capitalist transformation in the countryside during the New Deal thus restructured class hierarchies and racialized group relationships, especially as poor white tenants were systematically excluded from the rights and privileges accorded the higher class of white landowners (ibid.: 164).

Foley's reference to "the new farm order of the New Deal" is important, because mechanization was not the only cause of rural social disruption; particularly as the decade wore on, New Deal agricultural policy itself was restructuring the countryside. That restructuring could be seen perhaps most dramatically within the cotton cultures of the South and the Southwest, which had relied so heavily on tenancy and sharecropping. With Congress's passing of the Agricultural Adjustment Act (AAA) in 1933, the owners of cotton plantations were paid to reduce the amount of acreage they had under production. Knowing that this reduction would certainly put tenants and sharecroppers out of work, federal agricultural planners expected landlords to divide their payment with those who worked for them. Not surprisingly, however, landlords in central Texas found numerous ways to pocket the checks. With painstaking attentiveness to the social and political forces weighed against black, white, and Mexican cotton workers, Foley (ibid.: 172) details how "[t]he cotton contract . . . fundamentally served to transfer government money to landowners, who often evicted unprofitable and expendable tenant farmers and their families." As these families fell into a downward economic spiral, propelled by the AAA, they landed at the doorstep of any one of several New Deal relief agencies, such as the Federal Emergency Relief Administration (FERA) or its state equivalent (SERA).

For some tenants and sharecroppers, the experience of getting government relief involved more than just receiving help; it thrust them into an entirely different set of government impulses than those that drove the AAA. Roosevelt's agricultural policy had a kind of schizophrenic personality to it; while agricultural planners connected to the AAA built the program around those farmers who could afford the new technologies of cultivation and large-scale production, another cadre of planners – more radical and idealistic than those associated with the AAA – sought to create a new agricultural society out of the displacement of marginal farmers in the countryside. A number of the latter projects could be found in the West. For instance, in 1935 the Resettlement Administration launched two migrant labor camps in California to house the rural white migration swelling in the state. As with other resettlement programs, camp administrators attempted to create communities founded on citizen democracies, in part because there was great fear that these camps would spawn radical activities and in part because administrators genuinely believed in the ideals of the New Deal that put great stock in the value of self-government. But it was at best half an attempt. While campers were expected to produce constitutions for their camps, in fact the constitutions were fill-in-the-blank models created for them by government officials. Thus, the canned preamble (as noted in Shindo: 28) read as follows:

> We the people of the _____ Migratory Labor Camp, in order to form a more perfect community, promote the general welfare, and insure domestic tranquility, do hereby establish this constitution for the _____ Migratory Labor Camp.

While the camps were a relatively minor feature of the California landscape, they assumed an almost emblematic place in the most important cinemagraphic portrait of the dust bowl migration, John Ford's *Grapes of Wrath*, which bore similarities to Steinbeck's 1939 novel but in no way simply reproduced it. After having experienced one trial after another in their journey from Oklahoma to southern California, the Joad family arrives finally at a neat and orderly government camp. The sign above the entrance to the Farmworkers' Wheat Patch Camp indicates that it's run by the Department of Agriculture, and, clearly, this is a different community than any they've encountered on the road. The camp manager explains that the Camp Committee would be paying them a visit and informs Ma Joad that the sanitary units have running water. Though concerned at first that such a good deal might involve the ubiquitous "cops," Tom (Henry Fonda) nonetheless registers them at the camp, still not quite believing that such a camp – clean and orderly and seemingly self-governing – is real: "Who runs this place?" he finally asks the manager. "The government," replies the manager. "Why ain't there more like it?" Tom asks. "You find out. I can't."

Needless to say, Tom is getting a mixed message here. On the one hand, the government's presence and power is overwhelming; in the sign that announces the camp, in the high quality "sanitary" facilities, in the protection that it offers workers from strikebreaking thugs, in the medical attention it promises the family, in its very embrace of the workers' self-government – all these things signal an authority above and beyond the local authorities and above and beyond what the people can muster on their own. On the other hand, the manager seems to be saying that such camps can only be formed from the will of the people, that government has no power outside the political desires of such regular folks as Tom Joad.

The work of the FSA photographers and representations more generally of dust bowl migrants gave Americans iconic images of both the universal, human toll of the depression, as well as the specific suffering experienced in the West, where past narratives of westward migration for white families were turned on their head: instead of that migration bringing independence and land ownership, it brought dispossession and proletarianization instead. For government administrators in particular, these images were given a certain legibility through the notion, deeply held by agricultural and land planners, that these were marginal farmers on marginal or "submarginal" lands.

"Marginality" was a powerful term. When used to describe people, it could mean a number of things: these were rural folk who were just barely hanging on, who, in the larger socioeconomic picture, stood at the boundary of modern agricultural production. Without government help, the implication went, they could not be brought into the modern economy; without government guidance, they would fall from the margins to the very brink. And what of marginal lands? In a sense, the lands like the people who worked them had not yet been brought into modern production. That is, they were lands that had stood at the margins of expert, agricultural knowledge. They had been farmed when they should not have been farmed, or farmed in the wrong way, or grazed far beyond what the growing number of range managers would deem appropriate. Marginal lands, like marginal people, required the guiding hand of the state to bring them into the modern economy. This did not always mean putting the lands into production, however. Areas of the plains which had seen most of their topsoil blown away required rest, as did much of the public rangeland.

For good reason, environmentalists have praised many of the efforts of these agricultural and land planners. In one of the most recent assessments, law professor and wildlife biologist Debra Donahue (2000) sees the 1930s as a time when environmental concerns came to the fore in government planning. Among other things she points to the Forest Service's 1936 Report, *The Western Range*, as an "epochal work" that for the first time in the twentieth century catalogued the abuses on the western rangelands and proposed far-reaching solutions. The abuses would strike us as familiar today: millions of acres of overgrazed lands, in both private and public hands, erosion and the consequent silting of streams and rivers, all due to decades of largely unregulated domestic livestock grazing. As for proposals, this 600-page document called for a very active governmental program to rehabilitate western grazing land, including more regulatory oversight of the land and the acquisition of more private land as a safeguard against overgrazing. Undergirding the report was a firm belief that placing grazing land in public ownership and federal management would save it far better than allowing individuals to alienate it. Of course, such a notion went back to the Progressive period, when the modern Forest Service was born. What marked the significance of *The Western Range*, however, was the scale of the Forest Service's ambition, as the Forest Service (which was in the Department of Agriculture) foresaw an aggressive program of government land acquisition and managerial expansion that is almost impossible to imagine today (Merrill, 2002).

Since Gifford Pinchot had launched the Forest Service in 1905, the agency had a reputation for being bold and confident, but its recommendations for land acquisition fell in line with a growing belief among some planners in the US Department of Agriculture (USDA) that increased public land ownership would happen alongside increased government oversight of private land. For instance, while Rexford Tugwell was certainly one of the most radical voices in the Roosevelt administration (he was identified strongly, and often disparagingly, with his previous job as an economics professor at Columbia University), his public articulations of New Deal policy not only captured the ideas that the USDA embraced during the 1930s; they also captured the spirit and enthusiasm that agricultural planners felt for their work. Addressing the annual meeting of the American Farm Economics Association in 1933, for instance, Tugwell was crystal clear about the role of the federal government in land planning:

> It will directly hold and administer, as public forests, parks, game preserves, grazing ranges, recreation centers and the like, all areas which cannot at the time be effectively operated under private ownership. And it will control the private use of the areas held by individuals to whatever extent is found necessary for maintaining continuous productivity. It is only by conceiving the Government in this double active and supervisory role that we can expect to attain a permanent system of agriculture (Quoted in Tugwell, 1935: 143).

Certainly, the New Deal accomplished some of these goals: it put the last of the public domain in federal management with the Taylor Grazing Act; the government did acquire millions of acres of land; the centerpiece of New Deal agricultural policy – the Agricultural Adjustment Act – involved farmers in federal regulation that they had never before experienced; and even the community programs, which aimed literally to *resettle* farmers and industrial workers on the land, were a profoundly radical attempt to put the government at the center of agricultural production in this country. But, of course, this was not Soviet collectivization either. American agricultural planners deeply believed that their work was part of an American democratic tradition, albeit a departure from the individualistic methods of the past. If anything, they believed they were helping to save democracy in America. Though Tugwell was to the left of most New Dealers, many others in the USDA would have joined his sentiments that under the New Deal agricultural program, "the threads which run backward and forward between the county associations and the administration in Washington are sensitive to local wishes," and that this backing-and-forthing was "a democratic process revised to meet the necessities of a world economic system" (Tugwell, 1935: 198, 199).

Such an assessment would have found very mixed support among westerners. As numerous scholars have pointed out over the years, westerners (like many Americans) wanted government help but not government oversight, and particularly as the New Deal wore on, western politicians pulled away from the New Deal. But Tugwell was right in this respect: the New Deal did encourage westerners – some westerners – to participate in setting up federal programs, which were also explicitly structured to include certain local groups as part of the administration. The AAA, for instance, involved the advisory boards of the American Farm Board Federation. And as Brian Q. Cannon (2000) has shown, the Rural Electrification Administration (REA) –

which probably had the most concrete effect on the lives of rural westerners, as it brought electricity to most of them for the first time – fully brought western citizens into the administration of the program. While the Rural Electrification Administration supervised the local planning committees, Cannon notes, its "control over the rural electrification process in the West was sharply limited in practice." And the REA in Cannon's opinion was not a unique case. Other New Deal programs, particularly in agriculture, were also "committed to grass-roots organization and participation." From the Soil Conservation Service districts to the Agricultural Adjustment Administration, Cannon argues, "the New Deal empowered westerners rather than deprived them of their initiative or agency" (2000: 159–60).

As already noted, not all westerners were included in this democratic project, however. The political structure of the big-ticket items in the agricultural New Deal – the AAA and the Taylor Grazing Act – were directly built upon local structures that left out many farmers and ranchers. To be sure, these structures were *decentralized*, but they were decidedly undemocratic because they did not involve smaller farmers and ranchers. As Theda Skocpol and Kenneth Finegold (1982: 258) have written about the AAA, "[C]ommercial farmers were ultimately able to use well-institutionalized farm programs to beat back all challenges from the agricultural underclasses and to gain an enduring governmental niche within the post-New Deal political economy." Likewise, public grazing management in the Department of the Interior largely involved only the most prominent and politically active ranchers in local policy decisions.

But the New Deal's concern for small-scale democratic process was not just idle political rhetoric, and it signaled a deeper issue at work. Federal officials were clearly concerned with figuring out what constituted the source of the government's sovereignty during this period of increased administrative authority. That is, as the federal government's scope of powers expanded, particularly in the executive branch, what legitimated the use of those powers? Was it, as Tugwell (1935: 197) wrote, that "[t]he sovereignty of the American people is the real source of this administration's power"? Or was it, as many critics noted – and many of those critics were in the West – that in fact the people's sovereign power was being undermined by New Deal programs?

What constituted sovereignty was a tricky issue, and no area proved that more than Indian affairs. The legal relationship between the United States government and Indian tribes had long been a thorny one, centering around the degree to which Indians had the right to self-government. In 1832 Chief Justice John Marshall held that Indian tribes had "limited sovereignty," which meant in practice that for some years "government officials negotiated with Indian tribes as corporate bodies." Indians occupied a wholly anomalous situation of having been granted "quasi-international status" at the same time that they were seen as wards of the state (Prucha, 1994: 3–5). By the late nineteenth century, however, reformers pushed to assimilate Indians more fully in American society and succeeded in passing the Dawes Severalty Act in 1887, which divided up tribal lands into 160 acres plots, which were then allotted to the heads of Indian families. Instead of helping Indians to assimilate into mainstream American society, however, the act largely succeeded in divesting Indians of their lands, as millions of acres passed into the hands of whites. By 1932 the amount of land in Indian hands had decreased from 139 million acres to 48 million acres. It was this devastation that the "Indian New Deal" hoped to turn around.

The man most associated with the Indian New Deal was the head of the Bureau of Indian Affairs (BIA) during the Roosevelt administration, John Collier, who had come to his position through Indian reform circuits and through his skillful political lobbying on behalf of Indian interests. At the urging of Collier, other bureau officials, reformers, and legislators, Congress passed the Wheeler-Howard Act, or the Indian Reorganization Act of 1934. The act initiated a number of reforms in Indian policy, but at its core "were the development of Indian economic resources and the restoration of Indian self-determination through the revival of tribal governments" (Taylor, 1980: x). Self-determination did not mean complete autonomy, however. Lawyers for the Department of the Interior, where the BIA was housed, understood Indians' tribal sovereignty to still be limited. The tribes did not have "external sovereignty" and could not be recognized as separate nations under international law. But they did have "internal sovereignty" in relationship to the United States government, possessing "the right to organize their own local self-government, except where the latter powers were limited by express act of Congress" (Taylor, 1980: 95–96).

In fact, the conflict between Indian internal sovereignty and the prerogatives of the bureau was profound. Once tribes had accepted the terms of the Reorganization Act, the Interior Department provided tribal leaders with a template of a constitution, which they would use to draw up their own constitution in conversation with bureau officials, much as the Resettlement Administration provided constitutions for migrant labor camps. Indians and non-Indians alike criticized such a procedure. As the 1944 Senate Committee on Indian Affairs noted, in a statement that embodies the very paternalism that it also criticizes,

> The Indians were supposed to write their own constitutions but they had no experience in such matters; besides they did not know what the Bureau wanted them to want. . . . Using standard forms a constitution could be pieced together in conference with the Indians by allowing them to fill in the blank forms as suggested, between the items required by the Bureau. Some constitutions when completed contained more Bureau required or suggested matter than matter that was used to fit them to the actual situation (Quoted in Taylor: 97).

They did not know what the Bureau wanted them to want. This is a remarkable statement. Of course, given their history, many American Indians likely knew quite specifically what the Bureau wanted them to want. But the statement also captures the new political relationship between so many westerners and the federal government. While New Deal officials genuinely sought to foster local participation in land, agricultural, and Indian programs – and, indeed, saw the government's legitimacy in part as deriving from the people – they nonetheless built and articulated the terms of that participation from the foundation of federal power. Some might understandably interpret this link as unmasking the New Deal's desire to control certain populations (such as Indians or migrant workers) who could cause trouble, and undoubtedly federal officials' interest in constitution-making for these groups had a much more paternalistic edge than their encouraging the participation of well-established farmers or ranchers. As Charles Shindo (1997: 35) has written of the New Deal farmworkers' camps in California, "The creation of a farmworkers' community was not a spontaneous gathering of concerned citizens who decided to write a constitution for the governance of their community; it was a carefully planned endeavor in which the government preprinted a constitution for the migrants and placed numerous restrictions over the migrants' control of the camps." But the New Deal's attempts at social control only tell part of the story. Much more compelling for historians is to understand how its officials gave political expression to what it was doing, how they sought to legitimate the federal government's power in light of their ideas about popular sovereignty. Of course, the West was not the only place where citizens and federal officials forged a new relationship that entailed a local governance given shape by Washington's expanded authority. But what does make the West stand out is the variety of ways that this relationship unfolded – in AAA contracts, in Taylor Grazing allotments, in resettlement camps, in Indian reorganization. In all these areas westerners had to figure out what the federal government wanted them to want. Needless to say, not even officials in federal agencies always knew or agreed on the answers to that question.

In the end, it is easy to imagine that many westerners got the same kind of mixed message that Tom Joad did – one that highlighted the new-found powers of the state at the same time that it embedded those powers in notions of popular sovereignty. What westerners *did* with that mixed message is a story that can perhaps illuminate the volatile politics of the postwar West.

NOTES

1   For this account, see "The Taylor Grazing Act: The Story of Its Early Operation in the Far Western 'Public Land States,'" Box 2, Farrington R. Carpenter Papers, Denver Public Library.
2   Quoted in Bill Ganzel, *Dust Bowl Descent* (Lincoln: University of Nebraska Press, 1984: 8). Stryker wrote to Russell Lee in the northern plains that Arthur Rothstein's "pictures of the dust and its effects on farm buildings and land are very excellent, but we do need an addition of more pictures of people, their homes, and their children" (p. 7).

REFERENCES

Agee, James and Walker Evans: *Let Us Now Praise Famous Men: Three Tenant Families* (Boston: Houghton Miflin, 1941).

Arrington, Leonard: "The Sagebrush Resurrection: New Deal Expenditures in the Western States, 1933–39." *Pacific Historical Review*, 52 (February 1983), 1–16.

Bernstein, Barton J.: "The Conservative Achievement of New Deal Reform." In David E. Hamilton (ed.) *The New Deal* (Boston: Houghton Mifflin company, 1999).

Brinkley, Alan: *The End of Reform: New Deal Liberalism in Recession and War* (New York: Alfred A. Knopf, 1995).

Brinkley, Alan: *Liberalism and Its Discontents* (Cambridge, MA: Harvard University Press, 1998).

Cannon, Brian Q.: "Power Relations: Western Rural Electric Cooperatives and the New Deal." *Western Historical Quarterly*, 31 (Summer 2000): 159–60.

Cohen, Lizabeth: *Making a New Deal: Industrial Workers in Chicago, 1919–1939* (Cambridge: Cambridge University Press, 1990).

Cooper, James Fenimore: "The Prairie: A Tale." In James Fenimore Cooper *The Leather-stocking Tales*, vol. 1 ([1827], New York: Library of America, 1985).

Donahue, Debra L.: *The Western Range Revisited: Removing Livestock from Public Lands to Conserve Native Biodiversity* (Norman, OK: University of Oklahoma Press, 2000).

Foley, Neil: *The White Scourge: Mexicans, Blacks, and Poor Whites in Texas Cotton Culture* (Berkeley, CA: University of California Press, 1997).

Foucault, Michel.: "Governmentality." In Graham Burchell, Colin Gordon, and Peter Miller (eds.) *The Foucault Effect: Studies in Governmentality* (Chicago: University of Chicago Press, 1991).

Ganzel, Bill: *Dust Bowl Descent* (Lincoln: University of Nebraska Press, 1984).

Gelber, Steven: "The Eye of the Beholder: Images of California by Dorothea Lange and Russell Lee." *California History* 64, 4 (1985) 264–71.

Hamilton, David E. (ed.) *The New Deal* (Boston: Houghton Mifflin company, 1999).

Kennedy, David: *Freedom from Fear: The American People in Depression and War, 1929–1945* (New York: Oxford University Press, 1999).

Lange, Dorothea and Paul Taylor: *An American Exodus: A Record of Human Erosion.* (New York: Reynal and Hitchcock, 1939).

Leuchtenberg, William E.: "The Triumph of Liberal Reform." In David E. Hamilton (ed.) *The New Deal* (Boston: Houghton Mifflin company, 1999).

Lowitt, Richard: *The New Deal and the West* (Bloomington, IN: Indiana University Press, 1984).

McConnell, Grant: *Private Power and American Democracy* (New York: Random House, 1966).

Malone, Michael: "Review of Lowitt *The New Deal and the West.*" *New Mexico Historical Review* 59 (October 1984): 415–18.

Merrill, Karen R.: *Public Lands and Political Meaning: Ranchers, the Government, and the Property Between Them* (Berkeley: University of California Press, 2002).

Nash, Gerald: *Federal Landscape: An Economic History of the Twentieth Century* (Tucson, AZ: The University of Arizona Press, 1999).

Prucha, Francis Paul: *American Indian Treaties: The History of a Political Anomaly* (Berkeley, CA: University of California Press, 1994).

Rodgers, Daniel T.: *Atlantic Crossings: Social Politics in a Progressive Age* (Cambridge, MA: Harvard University Press, 1998).

Scott, James C.: *Seeing Like a State: How Certain Schemes to Improve the Human Condition Have Failed* (New Haven: Yale University Press, 1998).

Shindo, Charles J.: *Dust Bowl Migrants in the American Imagination* (Lawrence, KS: University Press of Kansas, 1997).

Sitkoff, Harvard (ed.) *Fifty Years Later: The New Deal Evaluated* (New York: Alfred A. Knopf, 1985).

Skocpol, Theda and Kenneth Finegold: "State Capacity and Economic Intervention in the Early New Deal." *Political Science Quarterly*, 97, 2 (Summer 1982). 255–78.

Taylor, Graham D.: *The New Deal and American Indian Tribalism: The Administration of the Indian Reorganization Act, 1934–45* (Lincoln: University of Nebraska Press, 1980).

Tugwell, Rexford G.: *The Battle for Democracy* (New York: Columbia University Press, 1935).

CHAPTER TWENTY

Art, Ideology, and the West

DOUGLAS R. NICKEL

History abhors determinism but cannot tolerate chance. – Bernard DeVoto

Anyone who studies the American West must at some moment confront the Cartesian question from which all such inquiry stems: what is "the West," and how does it constitute itself as a distinct intellectual subject? Attempts to define the region politically, demographically, or geographicly must at length accede to the realization that the West is not so much a physical place as a series of abstractions, of overlapping and occasionally conflicting rhetorical constructions. Indeed, when we use the term what we are ultimately referring to is a collection of representations, transmitted variously through popular culture, legal documents, oral histories, written narratives, scholarly research, literature, and the arts. While cultural objects from these various spheres of activity usually appear to answer their own local needs and contexts, when it comes to those portraying the American West, a remarkable homogeneity and diachronic consistency may be observed. From Frederic Remington sketches to John Ford movies, Teddy Roosevelt to the Marlboro Man, Karl May to Louis L'Amour, western types and locales have proven abidingly evocative in the creation of a potent national myth, one so embedded in our collective consciousness that its demystification seems accompanied only with a high psychic toll. As a symbolic space, the West has had more than two centuries of elaboration, first having been imagined, then explored, then settled by white Americans in the eighteenth and nineteenthcenturies, only to be reinvented and romanticized in the aftermath of its demise as a site of actual experience. Already in 1893 F. J. Turner noted how the frontier acted as a kind of screen – for the projection of social ideals, national identity, and economic self-reliance. But by that time even Turner realized that the frontier ideals of rugged individualism and self-government had outlived their usefulness and, in an urbanizing world, required replacement with a more practical creed of social accommodation. That we as a nation have as yet failed to evolve beyond the logic of individual entitlement and nature-as-endless-resource is reflected in areas as diverse as our gun laws, road rage, the single-family home, our policies on water, energy, and global warming, and the perennial misfortunes of collective bargaining in the United States.

The sanctity of the western myth was never more in evidence than in 1991, when the National Museum of American Art in Washington, DC presented a revisionist art exhibition, "The West as America," to investigate the idea of the American frontier as one such set of representations. The project brought together 164 historical works – paintings, sculpture, watercolors, photographs and prints – by major and minor figures alike working in the years between 1820 and 1920, each depicting the life and landscape of the West and the process of its settlement. According to William Truettner, the exhibition's lead curator, the "embracing factor" motivating the project was the concept of ideology. "Ideology functions smoothly and effectively in these images to justify the headlong rush across the continent . . . In each image it serves to extol progress, 'authorizing' westward expansion as a beneficial national undertaking" (1991b: 40). To clarify the thesis, the installation was organized into six thematic sections, under headings like "Repainting the Past," "Picturing Progress," and "Inventing the Indian." In its ample catalog, and most conspicuously in its lengthy and pointed wall texts, "The West as America" argued against either a celebratory function for depictions of the frontier or a naive understanding of such images as neutral historical documents. It instead wanted to illustrate western art's complicity in the dirty work of empire-building. The controversy the show generated at the time, and the interpretive challenges it continues to extend, dramatize the intellectual stakes of what all historians of the American West do when they make choices about what or what not to admit into their field of vision.

That the exhibition happened at all is remarkable. As cultural institutions, museums of art tend to function in alignment with the various elite interests that typically support them – corporations, wealthy trustees, government- and foundation-based funders – and in the service of popular taste. Professional intellectuals do not make up a large segment of that audience. Consequently, "critical" or revisionist art histories, however commonplace now in academic circles, rarely find much acceptance in the museum world; those amounting to a critique of ideology are less welcome still. In fact, the museum itself has become one of the principal targets of recent academic criticism: its investments in naturalizing the economic status quo, in valorizing nationalism and the romantic figure of the artist, in creating a vision of the past that is stable and eternal have all figured in the analysis (Wallach, 1998). Where the typical museum exhibition implicitly or explicitly promotes the notion of art's universality – its ability to speak across time and cultural barriers – revisionist exhibitions often underscore art's temporal specificity, its operation within a set of social relations extant at a precise historical moment. It comes as no surprise therefore if we find the museum usually resistant to perspectives that touch on its (or its supporters) long-standing complicity in buttressing an unreconstructed system of values, even as part of a scholarly exercise. "The West as America" amounts to a watershed in thinking about the relationship between representation and ideology in American art to no small degree because it dared to bring what might otherwise have been a debate among academics to a broad and general audience – and did it in the nation's capital, no less.

The organizers of the exhibition scarcely set out to foment controversy, though they knew theirs was an unconventional approach to the materials. "We were aware that the art had come to be accepted as just comfortable, regional pictures of the Old West," recalled Elizabeth Broun, the museum's director. "We felt we needed to say emphatically that this art is something else. It was necessary to say, as we did, that ours is an alternative reading. . . . It is *not* a balanced point of view, but then the traditional point of view had held sway for more than 50 years" (1991: 77–78). From Broun's vantage, at least some of the antagonism to this corrective could be ascribed to bad timing: the show opened amid the patriotic mood of Desert Storm, an event held by many to be expiation for Vietnam and occasion for unbridled national pride. An exhibition that regarded the history of American westward expansion as the lopsided contest of Anglo-Europeans (backed by a military) over sovereign Native people in order to displace them and lay claim to their natural resources might well have suggested a parallel too immediate for comfort. Those across the political spectrum found cause for concern with the project. Lynne Cheney, chairperson of the National Endowment for the Humanities, cited "The West as America" as evidence that the disease of political correctness had spread from university campuses to other civic institutions. Former Librarian of Congress Daniel Boorstin called it "a perverted, historically inaccurate exhibition." Historian Simon Schama described it as "a relentless sermon, phenomenally condescending to both the painters and the painted." The controversy soon moved to the halls of Congress, when Republican Senator Ted Stevens of Alaska publicly humiliated Smithsonian secretary Robert McAdams at an Appropriations Committee hearing, condemning the show and alleging "leftist influence" in the museum administration. His threatened cuts in Smithsonian funding never materialized. (Wallach 1998: 109–111.) However, to understand the controversy in these proximate terms misses the planners' real transgression, which was to question the very basis for nationalism and the molding of national identity through official history.

Specifically, the organizers took on the doctrine of Manifest Destiny, the nineteenth-century belief, promulgated in countless high school textbooks, that the United States was impelled to expand westward by divine providence and natural right. As Howard Lamar notes in his contribution to the catalog, the idea was long resident in the American psyche – Benjamin Franklin brought an image of the West as a farmer's paradise, with the capacity to feed a flourishing middle-class population, with him to the Treaty of Paris in 1782, decades before journalist John L. O'Sullivan invented the phrase for the 1845 *Democratic Review* (Lamar, 1991). The continent's size and emptiness mandated settlement, it was thought; "taming the wilderness, Christianizing the savages, spreading the gospel of democracy and freedom" were construed as good, rational, necessary goals (Broun, 1991: viii). John Quincy Adams designated the Pacific Coast the nation's "natural" boundary in the 1820s, though most of this feature happened then to belong to Mexico; in 1844 James Polk won the presidency on a Manifest Destiny platform, declared war on Mexico, and in 1853 signed the Gadsden Purchase, which, along with the 1846 Oregon Territory treaty, satisfied the will of geography in filling out the country between two oceans. As the exhibition proposed, Manifest Destiny was intimately linked to the Victorian ethos of *progress*, a secular faith in the future that understood personal ambition as directly reflecting some larger human drive towards social improvement. Its favorite metaphor was the path, leading through hardship and uncertainty from the imperfect present to the Promised Land ahead.

"The West as America" wanted to examine Manifest Destiny as an ideology. It argued that period narrators describing settlement as the heroic adventure of white

Christians were simultaneously and purposefully drawing a veil over those parts of the story that were "unsavory or equivocal or simply mundane. Artists skated over the low points of the historical record – economic disasters, mining busts, droughts, depredations of the land, decimation of the buffalo herds, near obliteration of Indian culture – with a consoling rhetoric of grand purpose" (Broun, 1991: viii). The real frontier was in truth not a racial melting pot, not a New Jerusalem of equal opportunity where anyone willing to work hard and take risks was rewarded for their entrepreneurial zeal, not a place where the land's assets could forever be consumed with impunity. Period images engendered an imaginary West, the show proposed, noticeably unencumbered by the contradictions and harsh realities that informed most occupants' daily existence. The mythic ideal of personal freedom identified by Turner with trappers, cowboys, and homesteaders served not only those who had financial interests in "taming" the West, but also the later industrialists, developers, and politicians for whom the myth became an expedient abstraction. Ideology, if understood to be the set of interlinked symbols and beliefs by which a culture seeks to perpetuate itself, here serves to obscure the actual racism, sexism, greed, brutality, and genocide that characterized the western experience. The exhibition hoped to look beyond the surface of frontier images and illuminate those who might today mistake ideology for historical fact.

By proposing this concept as its point of departure, however, the survey entailed intellectual complexities that resound beyond the scope of its original ambitions. What is ideology, actually? If ideology is an attribute of, for instance, a painting, how does it get into the painting? Why can't everyone always see it? As interpreters of these cultural productions, are historians or institutions ever free of their own, contemporary ideological filters? Should we suppress them, or, as the Smithsonian curators did, put them stridently on display?

The first problem is that the term has acquired over time some rather contradictory meanings. The more prevalent is also the more recent: "ideology," as the word is employed in colloquial discourse, is often used to suggest a rigidly held system of political beliefs. One "has" an ideology in this usage, where, conversely, the majority is imagined to be free from it. The designation is thus pejorative, identified with those who would press an abstruse or extreme viewpoint (from either the left or right) upon a mainstream, pragmatic, nonideological middle. To the formalist critic, the ideological aspects of a work of art or literature are seen as outside, and frequently a distraction from, its aesthetic value. Put simply, it is regarded as the trespass of doctrine or political opinion into the otherwise autonomous realm of the imagination. Such understanding of the word in any case implies a distortion of common sense and reason, a synthetic and deceptive rendering of reality.

This now fashionable version of the term does not accord with its original meaning, though, nor does it properly reflect the way the concept of ideology is discussed in contemporary critical theory. After the French Revolution, rationalist philosophy took an eager interest in examining the roots of knowledge – in liberating thought from inherited prejudices and superstitions, especially the sort associated with the church. To the *philosophes*, any dogma that preached material sacrifices in this world for spiritual benefits in the next was more medieval than enlightened; the power-interests of church and state jointly regulating the masses through the inculcation of metaphysical belief systems needed serious questioning. Destutt de Tracy

(1754–1836), the first author to use the word *ideology*, rallied his compatriots with the sentiment that universal education was the key to overcoming idolatry and political repression. In his *Éléments d'idéologie* (1817–1818) he argued for a new science of ideas, one that would systematically overcome traditional errors and apply philosophy to moral questions with the precision of the natural sciences. De Tracy's "idéologues" were those who shared his Enlightenment ideal that only reason could lead to justice and general happiness. The term was coined, then, with clearly positive intent, as urging a progressive sociology of knowledge with widespread, altruistic ambitions. Revolution in the streets was not possible without first a revolution of the mind, a critique of ideas its authors referred to as ideology.

Strangely enough, history credits Napoleon Bonaparte with transforming this positive conception into something negative. As a fellow of the Institut de France, the young Napoleon shared de Tracy's goals of social reform and popular literacy. But as his despotic tendencies emerged, he grew disillusioned with his former associates' "ideological" tendencies, labeling them doctrinaire and out-of-step with political necessity (or his view of it at least). After his defeat by the Russians, Napoleon blamed *idéologues*: "It is to ideology, that sinister metaphysics, that we must attribute all the misfortune of our beloved France. Instead of adapting the laws to knowledge of the human heart and the lessons of history, ideology seeks to base the legislation of nations on those first principles into which it so subtly inquires." (Larrain, 1979: 215, n. 38) The modern, derogatory sense of the word thus derives from an inversion of its original logic: an ideologue became someone *overly* attached to ideas, who placed the realization of utopian goals ahead of immediate practical needs. Already by 1813 John Adams could erroneously report, "Napoleon has lately invented a word, which perfectly expresses my opinion. He calls the project ideology" (John Adams, *Works*, quoted in the *Oxford English Dictionary*, compact edition, vol. I. Oxford: Oxford University Press, 1971. p. 1368).

As the nineteenth century unfolded, the concept became influential, especially through the writings of Marx and Engels. In *The German Ideology*, first published in 1845, the authors criticized the political philosophy of the day, and recast the term in a newly negative light. Ideas, in particular the ideas of the ruling class, were to them nothing more than an idealization of the prevailing material (i.e., economic) relationships of any epoch – material relations parading as ideas. (These ideas, largely the product of elite professional thinkers, took the form of images, representations, beliefs; philosophy and religion are apt examples.) Ideology is what happens when one fails to grasp this upside-down projection of reality, which they famously compared to the working of the camera obscura. It is an error of thinking to see ideas as determining historical change, and not vice versa. Such ideas seem to arise spontaneously and to follow their own laws; one is conscious of them, but only as what Engels calls "false consciousness." Thus it follows that, as a kind of mental activity, ideology functions only when one is unaware of its operations as such. Yet ideological forms are not just illusions, for they express real changes in economic conditions, being symptoms, as it were, of the conflicts these changes inevitably produce.

In a subtle way, Marx's conception straddled the two seemingly contradictory aspects the word had acquired by that point. Ideology could be thought of as the mistakes we make in understanding our actual situation in the social arena; it could also be seen as the way a social class collectively thinks about itself, and the beliefs it

propagates based upon such thinking. This latter, more neutral sense yields specialized descriptions – "bourgeois ideology" or "the ideology of the proletariat," for
example – to denote systems of ideas appropriate to each group. Insofar as one takes
a position in the class struggle, of course, it requires only a short step back to see a
particular ideology as correct and another as backward, repressive, or deceptive.

Modern critical theory has endeavored to make sense of the wide-ranging
implications of the Marxian formulation. Marx himself had relatively little to say
about culture and its products, so a great deal has had to be extrapolated from his
original diagram of ideology – a term that for Marxists crucially relates the spheres
of culture and political economy. As a comprehensive social theory, Marxism is
concerned before all else with the way a society is defined by its class structure, and
the way this structure is kept stable and productive of wealth. Antonio Gramsci
(2000) once noted how there are two mechanisms available to manage the tensions
between the dominant and subordinate classes – that prevent the latter from rising
up against the former, in other words. The first will be obvious: coercion, the use of
armies, police, the courts, and so on to quell unrest. But this method by itself is
expensive for the state, both in terms of money and lives. The second and more
effective mechanism is what Gramsci calls hegemony. If everyone (both dominant
and subordinate classes) understands the prevailing order of social relations to be
essentially fair, or better than any alternative, or even simply impossible to change, it
is unlikely open rebellion will ever be considered an option to begin with. Here ideology, rather than force, is used to manage class tensions; bourgeois cultural hegemony is the apparatus that constructs individuals as social beings and projects the
values of the dominant class as natural or "common sense" for their internalization.
The masses repress themselves, through popular consent, and buy into the system,
or else convey dissatisfaction through easily controlled, culturally sanctioned chan-
nels, leaving the privileged secure in the knowledge that their wealth and power are,
in the end, justified.

Gramsci's deliberation on ideology leads away from the determinisms of "vulgar"
Marxism – of ideology as mere deception – towards a more sociological formulation.
In the 1970s, the French structuralist Louis Althusser (1984) offered an even richer
account of ideology's hand in the shaping of political consciousness. How is it exactly,
he asked, that the oppressed individual willingly submits to the dominant ideology
of his or her society? His answer was that one's experience of individuality is itself an
effect of ideology. From society's perspective, any single individual is utterly expendable. But if individuals collectively are to remain productive and docile, we each need
to grasp our identity as if we were free, self-determining beings in the process of
crafting unique and socially meaningful lives. Althusser speaks of the individual's
"lived experience of the real" as that of tacit significance, of having a purposeful relationship to the world at large: of the world, in a fashion, being centered on the individual. Ideology is the force that does this centering and binds the individual to the
social structure. It is more pervasive and complex than a set of political ideas – it is
reflected in everything from one's choice for president to one's choice of hair products. Ideology transforms human beings into subjects, giving them an image of coherent selfhood by maintaining their experience of reality as something essentially
private, rather than something socially determined. Material relations – the unequal

distribution of wealth, for example – become very difficult to "see" through the filters of this reigning, seductive subjectivity.

In such a scheme, ideology plays a big role in forming the picture of society people carry around in their heads, and of their place in it. Where traditional Marxism stressed the importance of class difference, contemporary thinking on the matter now recognizes that as social subjects we infer our identities through a whole network of differences, including gender, race, ethnicity, age, education, religion, nationality, even birth order. Culture and politics can no longer be removed to separate realms: ideology is not an either/or, a detectable extrinsic presence, but always there, always in action, whether recognized or not, and far more powerful than the politics of governments. Critical theory therefore uses the term to discuss the systems of representations that relate the individual (his or her lived experience) to some sociohistorical context. What keeps it from becoming social psychology is the inherently complicated ways ideology works through specific kinds of cultural artifacts – movies, advertisements, art, the essays in this book – to define the "real" or the "normal" or the "accepted" and thus constitute us socially as viewers or readers.

Given the ways "The West as America" handled the issue of ideology, many of the objections raised might well have been anticipated. The most predictable sort challenged the motives for organizing such an exhibition in the first place. "Men do not care to have beliefs to which they attach great moral significance examined dispassionately, no matter for how pure a purpose," the anthropologist Clifford Geertz once observed. "And if they are themselves highly ideologized, they may find it simply impossible to believe that a disinterested approach to critical matters of social and political conviction can be other than a scholastic scam" (1973: 195). Conservative commentary on the show made this very point: that the curators were biased, that their own political leanings inflected their interpretations, or that they started with their revisionist thesis already formulated and went out searching for frontier images that might serve as illustrations of it, rather than starting with the artworks and letting the interpretation follow from the problems they seem to pose – art history's conventional way of thinking about what it does. Yet the organizers made no pretense to disinterestedness. As Truettner acknowledged, "Thematic categories . . . proved to be the most effective means of returning images to a context in which ideology prevailed, although admittedly the process has a bias of its own. One cannot discount the objectivity of past historical studies while claiming the unassailability of contemporary standards of scholarship. But establishing thematic categories is not the same as discovering the 'reality' of an earlier age. It is, rather, a means of using historical data to identify and interpret expansionist rhetoric, a process that is safer, if still a bit like proceeding through a minefield" (Truettner, 1991b: 40–1). A variant of the conservative argument denies the possibility of analysis by invoking a kind of relativism – you have your subjective view of history and I have mine – or plays it out on the field of emotions. (The organizers targeted the western myth as "comfortable" and "consoling"; some viewers believed their motive was to elicit diametrical feelings of "shame" and "guilt" in their white audience.) On the whole, this brand of criticism marshals the concept of ideology in its more quotidian, journalistic form, as self-interested distortion, proposing that the Smithsonian project did nothing more than displace the charged rhetoric of Manifest Destiny with the equally charged rhetoric

Figure 1   William S. Jewett, *The Promised Land—The Grayson Family*, 1850, oil on canvas, Terra Foundation for the Arts, Daniel J. Terra Collection.

of political correctness. As Geertz suggests, interpretation ends up being staged as a question of morality rather than of reason.

But however tendentious an approach to western history the exhibition may have taken, its authors appreciated some of the special interpretive problems that visual art entails, and endeavored to speak directly to the function of pictorial images in the creation of expansionist ideology. The catalog prided itself on its "readings" of specific pictures, offering to "decode" the latent ideological messages at work within them. For example, Patricia Hills describes William S. Jewett's 1850 painting *The Promised Land – The Grayson Family* (Figure 1), commissioned by the Missouri land-speculator Andrew Jackson Grayson to commemorate his family's arrival in California four years earlier, as a modern Flight into Egypt:

> Drawing on the legacy of conversation pieces – family scenes of eighteenth-century English gentry posed before their country manors – Jewett painted a group portrait blending biblical allusion with landscape and history painting to validate western expansion as enlightening and ultimately rewarding. A Holy Family image has been modified for the occasion: Grayson dons a buckskin coat and leggings over his starched white

shirt and cravat; Mrs. Grayson wears a dress appropriate to a middle-class parlor while holding her son on her knee; and their son sports a regal, ermine-trimmed robe. The costumes announce a metaphoric message: Grayson is prepared to deal with city affairs (starched shirt and cravat) but equally at home on the frontier (buckskin, telescope, gun and dead game); his wife will bring gentility and nurturing ways to the new settlement (her sober dress, shawl, and maternal gesture); and the son, the next generation, will be heir to that wealth (the red, ermine-trimmed robe). The parents survey the distant valley with its golden meadows; their view commands not their personal property but the limitless horizon of California. The son, on the other hand, gazes at the painter. It is Jewett, after all, who gives visual permanence to the memory and the scene (Hills, 1991: 98).

The painting is thus seen to meld contemporary western iconography with traditional motifs from European art of the Renaissance and Regency periods; it historicizes the pioneer Grayson family through a combination of accurate detail (the painter accompanied Grayson as he retraced his steps to the spot in the Sierra where he first beheld the Sacramento Valley) and ahistorical symbolism. The ideological message of the picture – "the future of American progress," in Hills' telling – betokens the "deep well of economic and expansionist interests" that "permeated" western image-making in the 1840s and 1850s (ibid.: 100). Stylistic overlays from past art are themselves seen as ideological: an ordinary family is made sacred by association with the poses and composition of earlier Italian painting, while a nod towards the English conversation piece associates Jewett's work with a genre that, in the end, celebrates the possession of wealth and property.

But how is it that ideological messages come to "permeate" images? An earlier generation of scholars might have proposed that, like style, ideology reflects "the spirit of the age," the *zeitgeist*. For Heinrich Wölfflin, Alois Riegl, and other German-speaking art historians at the beginning of the twentieth century, this Hegelian concept explained why it was that disparate cultural objects (say, spired Gothic cathedrals and pointy medieval shoes) appeared stylistically of a whole: each culture or period had a spirit, or feeling, which found expression in the individual products of that culture or period. The spirit of "progress," "expansion," and Manifest Destiny certainly seems like the kind of shared belief that could align disparate artworks from nineteenth-century America into a consistent worldview, but as the catalog authors realized, this breed of explanation is circular, never really addressing the issue of agency. We cannot demonstrate the existence of the age's spirit except so far as it shows itself in works – the object embodies the culture that explains the object. Such accounts reduce the artist to the status of mouthpiece, passively or unconsciously articulating the will of his or her era, and reduce ideology to a kind of disembodied sociopolitical thought, largely removed from the life circumstances of those it affects. If artworks are to be treated as a barometer of the dominant ideological patterns of a culture, we are still left to identify what *direct* forces incline the needle and induce artists to paint this way or that.

Truettner offers one solution to this difficulty: artistic patronage. Citing the work of historian Richard Slotkin (1986), Truettner proposes that mid-century expansionist rhetoric be understood as the consequence of a geographic and cultural bifurcation, a dynamic between the open West (the "Wilderness") and the settled East (the "Metropolis") (1991b: 30–1). For urban industrialists and financiers in, mostly, eastern cities, the West stood for cheap land, abundant resources, relative lawlessness, and freedom from labor unrest – a veritable dreamworld of economic possibilities that in their minds contrasted with the immediate limitations upon growth they faced at home. Western types became for them their colonialist Other, living out a bourgeois fantasy of unregulated capitalism. Key to this dialectic is the metropolis, where the patrons and critics of frontier art dwelled, where almost every one of its important artists had their studios, and where the actual business of selling the West was conducted. Slotkin contends (*contra* Turner) that it is to entrepreneurial land companies in major urban centers that we owe settlement, and cites the 1860 census to show that most of what we call westward migration involved "pioneers" moving to the state immediately adjacent to the one in which they were born (Slotkin, 1986: 38). Manifest Destiny is here cast not as a broad cultural imperative but as the rhetoric of a mass-media marketing campaign involving an elite group of real-estate speculators, railroad companies (who needed passengers and freight), mining and farming interests (who needed labor), and a federal government intent on settling the interior for purposes of national security. Eastern-based artists obliged their influential Eastern-based patrons – the ones backing the railroads, mines, farms, and land-grabs – with a West redacted to their liking, a psychic space of reverie uncomplicated by the realities of their everyday urban situation.

This reasoning goes some distance in explaining why an artist like Jewett might paint his patron Grayson as if arriving upon his Promised Land, or why contemporaries would suffer the railroad tracks that unrepentantly despoil so many landscape views of the time (Figure 2). Within the patronage network where it most effortlessly operated, ideology was not a latent subtext of the work – it is hegemonic, unremarkable (and hence unremarked on) simply because it was taken for granted as the cultural *lingua franca* of artist, critic, and patron alike. Albert Bierstadt, the wealthiest American painter of his generation, need hardly have been (as he was) an actual landholder and investor in the developing West to share the values of his sponsors; when railroad baron Collis P. Huntington advised Bierstadt where to stand along the Central Pacific's right-of-way to compose *Donner Lake from the Summit* (1873 – Figure 3), he, like Grayson, was not so much imposing a vision on his votary as joining with him in one (Anderson, 1991). The lived experience of the real they had in common was hardly a choice; their subjectivity – the picture of the world they carried around in their heads – knew no other reality, let alone what subsequent history would make of this reality. Patronage networks reveal a certain fluidity between the realms of popular and high art – between, for instance, the motifs of oil paintings, engravings after those paintings, and advertisements based on both – though the ideological links obviously become more difficult to substantiate the broader a hypothetical lay audience becomes. It also suggests that patrons not be caricatured as shameless and deliberate purveyors of propaganda, working for themselves against the interests of others, but that an ideological agenda be more generally spread across the culture, flowing from multiple seats of interest and power.

If one indulges the "permeation" premise, however, it is important to recognize the inseparability of ideology from style: style and ideology commingle as form and content, alloyed carriers of a work's meaning. *The West as America* maintained this correlation as a background inference, but a sister publication, exactly contemporaneous with the Smithsonian project, makes the reciprocity of style and ideology its

Figure 2   Carleton E. Watkins, *Cape Horn near Celilo*, 1867, mammoth plate albumen print from glass negative, Gilman Paper Company Collection.

central thesis. As its title indicates, *The Magisterial Gaze: Manifest Destiny and American Landscape Painting c. 1830–1865* by Albert Boime (1991) overlaps significantly in theme and chronology with *The West as America*. Boime's study wished to isolate a feature of many nineteenth-century American depictions of scenery in both East and West: the landscape's orientation from an elevated vantage point, looking down on a panoramic vista below. The view from the mountain allowed the landscape to embrace visual information that for Boime also carries deeper meaning. "This Olympian bearing metonymically embraced past, present, and future, synchronically plotting the course of empire," the author writes; such a viewing position facilitates what he terms "the magisterial gaze." "There is an American viewpoint in American landscape painting that can be identified with this characteristic line of vision, and this peculiar gaze represents not only a visual line of sight but an ideological one as well" (1991: 1–2). Accordingly, the commanding view in works like *The Promised Land – The Grayson Family* or *Donner Lake from the Summit* derives its ideological force from a visual penetration of the countryside that stands for socioeconomic ingress as well. And as a variant, Watkins' photographic view of the Columbia River gorge, with its railway tracks rendered compositionally as plunging

Figure 3   Albert Bierstadt, *Donner Lake from the Summit*, 1873, oil on canvas, Collection of the New-York Historical Society.

orthogonals, becomes in this reading "the material realization of the magisterial gaze," an emblem of futurity that makes literal a metaphoric path of progress traced first with the eyes and then with commerce (Boime, 1991: 99). Physically, the railroad was engineered to run as flat and as straight as possible – to disregard or overcome geographic irregularity – a mechanical feature that carries ideological weight when showcased by a picture. Boime's analysis hinges upon an identity of content in a visual representation with the stylistic modes by which that content is transmitted, an imbrication of meaning and style.

But discussing cultural objects as products of ideological permeation courts the danger of suggesting that ideology is somehow inherent in the image, and strictly historical, in that it is supposed to be planted there at the time of object's making. What is overlooked here is the activity of the critic and viewer, the ways meaning is made to adhere to the work as a consequence of ideological analysis. Meaning is not imminent: it is the confluence of manifest codes and stylistic properties in a work and a perceiver who can articulate what these codes and properties signify within specific contexts. Historians habitually bolster the rhetorical force of their analyzes with the fiction that their interpretation is an intrinsic artifact of the work and not of their description of it. Yet, as we can now surmise, confusing the program of the reader with the affective properties of the work is an act that itself can only be regarded as ideological. This was the greatest weakness of the approach adopted by "The West as America" project. Take the wall text for Charles Russell's painting *Carson's Men* (1913), for example:

The three men, with their halo-like hats, are situated above a bison skeleton that recalls the skulls of Golgotha. Russell may also intend a play on Carson's first name, *Christopher*, and on his crossing of the river, to convey the Christian meaning of the explorer's mission . . . (Wallach, 1991: 114).

Such manner of interpretation clearly overreaches in its authors' desire to discover Christian iconography resident in Russell's work, in a way that the analysis of Jewett's *Promised Land*, with its historicized account of the landscape's title, commission, and reception, does not. The job of the historian is much like that of a lawyer in court: to apply deductive logic to the available evidence, construe motives, and make the most convincing case possible to account for acts or events that transpired in the past. As critical readers, we are like members of the jury, deciding which elements of the case speak to history – to the evidence of or surrounding the work – and which speak more to the solicitor's talent for selective argumentation. The lawyer or historian confuses fact and interpretation at their own peril, as we the jury often prove better at detecting pettifoggery than they might imagine.

Measured by its own ambitions, "The West as America" fell far short of its goals, not because it espoused a faulty or distorted understanding of American history, but rather because it became entangled in its hermeneutic maneuvers. The project's weaknesses stemmed from its authors' oversimplified model of the ways artworks communicate messages, and their inability to develop anything but a narrow critical framework for understanding the relationship between ideology and social hegemony. It betrayed a wholesale indifference to its own ideological operations – to its appropriation of traditional art historical methods and modes of explanation, for instance, or its uncritical willingness to speak in and through the authoritative and hegemonic voice of the institutional art museum. The exhibition's self-righteous condescension towards its materials undermined what would otherwise be important lessons to be learned about how ideology has worked throughout the historiography of the West to constitute what is and is not thought to be its purview, what history's omissions mean, and the ways historians positively or negatively identify with their chosen subjects. The interpretative issues raised by the project can be applied to a much broader range of materials – the way images from the surface of the moon or Mars extend survey photography's investments in Manifest Destiny is but one example – so as students of history, we might best regard the exhibition as a shaky first step in the right direction. Anyone who studies the history of the West is a product of, and productive of, ideology, stands in some relation to nationalism, and responsible for the way that history is crafted through images. The best history will invariably come from those who recognize the consequences of their methods.

REFERENCES

Althusser, Louis: *Essays on Ideology* (London: Verso, 1984).
Anderson, Nancy K.: "'The Kiss of Enterprise': The Western Landscape as Symbol and Resource." In William H. Truettner (ed.) *The West as America: Reinterpreting Images of the Frontier, 1820–1920* (Washington, DC: Smithsonian Institution Press, 1991).
Bercovitch, Sacvan: "The Problem of Ideology in American Literary History." *Critical Inquiry* 12 (Summer 1986), 635.

Boime, Albert: *The Magisterial Gaze: Manifest Destiny and American Landscape Painting c. 1830–1865* (Washington and London: Smithsonian Institution Press, 1991).

Broun, Elizabeth: "The Story Behind the Story of *The West as America*." *Museum News*, 70, 5 (September/October 1991), 77–8.

Davis, John: *The Landscape of Belief: Encountering the Holy Land in Nineteenth-Century American Art and Culture* (Princeton: Princeton University Press, 1996).

Eagleton, Terry: *Literary Theory: An Introduction* (Minneapolis: University of Minnesota Press, 1983).

Geertz, Clifford: *The Interpretation of Cultures* (New York: Basic Books, 1973).

Gramsci, Antonio: *The Gramsci Reader: Selected Writings, 1916–1935* ed. David Forgacs (New York: New York University Press, 2000).

Hills, Patricia: "Picturing Progress in the Era of Westward Expansion." In William H. Truettner (ed.) *The West as America: Reinterpreting Images of the Frontier, 1820–1920* (Washington, DC: Smithsonian Institution Press, 1991).

Kavanagh, James H.: "Ideology." In Thomas McLaughlin and Frank Lentricchia (eds.) *Critical Terms for Literary Study* (Chicago: University of Chicago Press, 1995).

Lamar, Howard: "An Overview of Westward Expansion." In William H. Truettner (ed.) *The West as America: Reinterpreting Images of the Frontier, 1820–1920* (Washington, DC: Smithsonian Institution Press, 1991).

Larrain, Jorge: *The Concept of Ideology* (London: Hutchinson and Co., 1979).

Marx, Karl and Friedrich Engels: *The German Ideology* (New York: International Publishers, 1972).

Mitchell, W. J. T.: *Iconology: Image, Text, Ideology* (Chicago and London: University of Chicago Press, 1986).

Nemerov, Alex: "Doing the 'Old America': The Image of the American West, 1880–1920." In William H. Truettner (ed.) *The West as America: Reinterpreting Images of the Frontier, 1820–1920* (Washington, DC: Smithsonian Institution Press, 1991).

Slotkin, Richard: *The Fatal Environment: The Myth of the Frontier in the Age of Industrialization, 1800–1890* (Middletown, CT: Wesleyan University Press, 1986).

Truettner, William H. (ed.): *The West as America: Reinterpreting Images of the Frontier, 1820–1920* (Washington, DC: Smithsonian Institution Press, 1991).

Truettner, William H.: "Ideology and Image: Justifying Westward Expansion." Introduction to William H. Truettner (ed.) *The West as America: Reinterpreting Images of the Frontier, 1820–1920* (Washington, DC: Smithsonian Institution Press, 1991b).

Truettner, William H.: "Prelude to Expansion: Repainting the Past." In William H. Truettner (ed.) *The West as America: Reinterpreting Images of the Frontier, 1820–1920* (Washington, DC: Smithsonian Institution Press, 1991c), 55–96.

Wallach, Alan: "The Battle over 'The West as America.'" In Alan Wallach *Exhibiting Contradiction: Essays on the Art Museum in the United States* (Amherst: University of Massachusetts Press, 1998).

Williams, Raymond: *Keywords: A Vocabulary of Culture and Society* (New York: Oxford University Press, 1985).

Winter, Irene J.: "The Affective Properties of Styles: An Inquiry into Analytic Process and the Inscription of Meaning in Art History." In Caroline A. Jones and Peter Galison (eds.) *Picturing Science, Producing Art* (New York and London: Routledge, 1998).

CHAPTER TWENTY-ONE

"The West Plays West": Western Tourism and the Landscape of Leisure

MARGUERITE S. SHAFFER

In the summer of 1915 Mary Roberts Rinehart, a popular writer famed for her short stories, comedies, and mystery thrillers, traveled through Glacier National Park with the noted western outdoorsman and dude rancher, Howard Eaton. Rinehart and forty-one other "adventurers" packed three hundred miles across the park from the Glacier Park Hotel up along the spine of the continental divide through mountain passes and glacial valleys to Lake McDonald on the west side of the park. Rinehart published her account of the Eaton expedition in a series of articles for *Collier's* magazine in April, 1916. She described her outdoor experience in rhapsodic terms. "If you are normal and philosophical," she wrote; "if you love your country; if you like bacon . . . ; if you are willing to learn how little you count in the eternal scheme of things; if you are prepared, for the first day or two, to be able to locate every muscle in your body . . . , go ride in the Rocky Mountains and save your soul" (Rinehart, 1983: 4).

For Rinehart the park represented true wilderness and the "real" West. "I object to the word 'park,' especially in connection with the particular National Reserve in northwestern Montana known as Glacier Park," she wrote. "A park is a civilized spot connected in all our minds with neat paths and clipped lawns." Glacier was the antithesis of these civilized city oases in Rinehart's perspective. "It is the wildest part of America." Glacier offered trails of adventure, wild animals, and wild flowers: "Here is the last stand of Rocky Mountain sheep, the Rocky Mountain goat. Here are antelope and deer, black and grizzly bears, mountain lions and trout . . . Here are trails that follow the old game trails along the mountain side; here are meadows of . . . a thousand sorts of flowers beside snow-fields. Here are ice and blazing sun, vile roads, and trails of a beauty to make you gasp" (ibid.: 5). This pristine wilderness was inseparable from its western context. Rinehart described her arrival at Glacier: "West. Still west. An occasional cowboy silhouetted against the sky; thin range cattle; impassive Indians watching the train go by; a sawmill, and not a tree in sight over the vast horizon!. . . . Then, at last, at twilight, Glacier Park Station, and Howard Eaton on the platform, and old Chief Three Bears, of the Blackfeet, wonderfully dressed and preserved at ninety-three" (ibid.: 7) The cowboy and the Indian, the prairies and the mountains, the camp fire and the game trail embodied Rinehart's image of Glacier National Park and the West. However, she lamented, "There is little of the old West left" (ibid.: 14). Settlement and civilization, railroads and automobiles were rapidly replacing the picturesque open spaces and romantic characters that shaped western history. She admonished her readers, "Now is the time to see it – not from a train window; not if you can help it from an automobile, but afoot or on horseback, leisurely, thoroughly" (ibid.: 85).

In recounting her experiences, Rinehart provides one of the more eloquent and culturally charged descriptions of the tourist's West. Her articles and serials published in popular magazines such as *Collier's* and *The Saturday Evening Post* reached a large audience and were widely read. Stories such as "My Country Tish of Thee" (1916) and "The Family Goes A-Gypsying" (1918) along with books such as *Out Trail* (1923) and *Tenting Tonight* (1918) popularized western wilderness and encouraged tourists to reenact the nation's frontier past by camping and hiking in western parks and nature preserves. What her Glacier narrative, and many others like it, suggest is that during the late nineteenth and into the twentieth century, as America emerged and matured as a modern consumer culture, the mythic frontier provided the basis for a landscape of leisure that reshaped spaces and places throughout the American West both physically and symbolically.

As western historian Ann Fabian has argued, "In a peculiar way in the West, legend actually *becomes* fact. Producers of mass culture have kept right on turning popular legend into social and economic facts of the living present" (1992: 227). However the interplay between legend and fact moves beyond the popular stories and imagery of the frontier that vie with the realities of western history. Western legend and the commercial culture that sustains it have also spawned an array of real places – tourist landscapes – that objectify the evolving popular mythology of the frontier. These frontier playgrounds define the economic, social, and ecological relations of communities across the West. The tourist's West unites myth and region within the larger historical framework of advanced corporate capitalism. Defined by the social, cultural and economic infrastructures of tourism and consumption, these places challenge our established conceptualization of western regionalism and frontier mythology. In this essay I explore how the tourist's West as it evolved from the turn of the century through the post-World War II era reveals this complex interplay between fantasy and reality, myth and region, process and place. These western tourist landscapes suggest that our understanding and definition of the American West as a distinct region and geography need to be reconsidered in light of the larger historical and cultural frameworks of commerce, leisure, mobility, and consumer desire.

The history of tourism in the West is a relatively new topic of study. Earl Pomeroy's *In Search of the Golden West: The Tourist in Western America* ([1957], 1990), charted the field, but few scholars followed his lead in the ensuing decades. Pomeroy traces the development of tourism in the West from the 1870s to the 1950s detailing the tourist experience as it evolved from an elite pastime to a middle-class entitlement. More recently, Hal K. Rothman has provided another broad overview of western tourism in his book *Devil's Bargains: Tourism in the Twentieth-Century American West* (1998). Rothman focuses more closely on the economic and social impact of tourism in the West from the turn of the twentieth century to the present. In many ways these two books reveal the larger narratives that frame the history of western tourism. In focusing on the way tourists and tourism imagined the West, Pomeroy builds on the myth and symbol school of western history, linking tourism to frontier imagery and experience. Rothman, on the other hand, defines (1998: 11) tourism as "the most colonial of colonial economies," thus connecting tourism with a long history of extractive industry in the West that has been central to the process of conquest. As with much of western history, these narratives reveal that, through the lens of tourism, the West can be understood as both image and region, process and place.

Recent trends in the New Western History have focused on demythologizing western history, rejecting or at least questioning the idea of the frontier and addressing more disturbing issues of power, race, ethnicity, gender, and the environment. Specifically, scholars have debunked Frederick Jackson Turner's frontier thesis for romanticizing the West as frontier – a mythological experience on the boundary between civilization and wilderness – and thus overlooking the more sordid and complicated side of western history. As the new western historians have revived western history in the past decade, scholars have rejected Turner's thesis as a nationalistic myth in favor of more concrete and complex social, cultural, and environmental issues that are played out in complicated ways across the West. As Donald Worster (1991: 7) has written, "For this region that was once so lost in dreams and idealization, we have been creating a new history demythologized and critical." Yet in doing so, many of these assessments have overlooked the fact that the myth of the frontier has spawned its own reality across the West, a reality that has its own history and landscape. National Parks, mountain resorts, dude ranches, preserved Indian ruins, historic frontier towns, casinos, theme parks, and an array of roadside kitsch reveal a landscape of leisure steeped in the mythology of the frontier. In fact one might argue that the mythic West vies with the real West for space and place across the western landscape.

This mythic western frontier made manifest deserves critical exploration. The frontier thesis was more than a nationalist manifesto celebrating the frontier, it was also a lament, a eulogy for the passing of the frontier. In this sense Turner's essay might be understood as an expression of what anthropologist Renato Rosaldo has termed "imperialist nostalgia": an innocent yearning for what one has helped intentionally to efface or destroy. It was this nostalgia, I would argue, that helped to reshape particular places across the West as frontier dreamscapes – landscapes of leisure dependent on an array of "western" texts and images available for consumption. Turner's eulogy for this mythic frontier was articulated at a moment when technological, economic, political, and social change was transforming the United States into a modern urban-industrial consumer society. In many ways, one could argue that this nostalgia for the frontier resulted from the transformation taking place in American culture. The intersection of imperialist nostalgia and the mechanisms of the emerging consumer culture recast Turner's mythical frontier into a real place – the tourist's West.

The presence of Buffalo Bill's Wild West show camped on the perimeter of the Chicago World's Fair grounds where Turner first presented his frontier thesis in 1893 reflects the link between Turner's nostalgia for the frontier and the commercial popularization of the frontier myth. Buffalo Bill's Wild West Show offers just one example of the way in which the West was symbolically reimagined as a mythic leisure commodity, paving the way for the creation of a full-fledged tourist landscape. By the late nineteenth century a vast array of imagery including dime novels, photographs, Wild West shows, and travel accounts, as well as landscape paintings and panoramas, had popularized the West as a romantic landscape – a pristine wilderness peopled by cowboys and Indians, mountain men and pioneers. This popular western imagery prefigured the tourist's West; it defined what might best be understood as a "third nature" in opposition to the "first" and "second" nature of westward expansion. If "first nature" describes undeveloped land and a preindustrial landscape, and "second nature" embodies an environment transformed by the technologies and economics of industrialization and commercial capitalism, "third nature" represents a romantic ideal tinged with nostalgia and fantasy. Classic western histories such as Henry Nash Smith's *Virgin Land* (1950) and Richard Slotkin's *Regeneration Through Violence* (1973) and *The Fatal Environment* (1985) have examined the creation and dissemination of this mythic West. However, their work focuses on intellectual and popular imagery, stopping short of exploring how this powerful cultural imagery shaped physical and imaginary geographies throughout the West. In codifying the West as a fantasy dreamscape, in presenting the West as a subject for popular entertainment, in romanticizing the West as an escape from urban-industrial living, popular western imagery not only laid the ground work for a western landscape of leisure, it also created a desire and a set of expectations about what the tourist's West would offer. In other words, dime novels, Wild West shows, western travel accounts, and landscape paintings, among the abundance of visual, verbal, and dramatic spectacles celebrating the mythic West were important in that they informed potential tourist's expectations about the West and also influenced tourist promoters in their shaping of the tourist landscape. They provided the substance and framework for consumer desires that centered on the mythic West. As scholars of consumption have argued, consumer products – both goods and experiences – generate desire because they are linked with self-fulfilling fantasy and daydreams based on popular stories, films, and photographs. Although a number of scholars have explored the popular mythology of the West, few have examined the role played by popular western imagery in shaping consumer desire, exploring this imagery as a kind of first step toward the production and consumption of the West as a landscape of leisure. Yet, the development of tourism in the West reveals that popular western imagery played a central role in shaping and defining tourist landscapes throughout the region.

   In the aftermath of the Civil War, the transcontinental railroads began to transform the West into a commodified landscape. But this was not simply a landscape filled with natural resources to be mined and harvested, it was also a symbolic landscape available for consumption. Not only did railroads support and reinforce the production of popular western imagery to lure passengers to travel cross-continent, but they also went about objectifying the mythic West in stations, hotels, and tourist attractions across the West. In 1871, noted landscape painter Thomas Moran accompanied the Hayden survey to the Yellowstone region under the financial backing of Jay Cooke and the Northern Pacific Railroad. Moran worked with photographer William Henry Jackson to document the Yellowstone landscape. Moran's paintings and Jackson's photographs popularized the West as a vast unpeopled wilderness to an increasingly curious eastern audience. Other major railroads followed suit, commissioning painters and photographers to document and dramatize the western scenic wonders along their lines. Railroads reproduced these images in promotional brochures and guidebooks, which were widely distributed in stations and railroad offices throughout the East. Railroads also distributed a slew of brochures and guidebooks publicizing the tourist's West – a West of pristine wilderness populated by

rugged individuals and picturesque Indians. But railroads did more than just subsi-
dize the distribution of imagery that popularized a mythic ideal of the West, they
also marketed and constructed a mythic West at stations and stopping points along
their lines.

A number of scholars have examined what Marta Weigle and Kathleen Howard
(1996) have termed the "corporate dominion" established by the Santa Fe Railway
and the Fred Harvey Company in the southwestern United States. The Santa
Fe/Harvey conglomeration not only constructed a tourist infrastructure that linked
the railroad to hotels and tourist attractions, but they also framed and marketed the
tourist experience by distributing promotional material, sponsoring artistic render-
ings of the landscape, and selling souvenirs and art. Santa Fe/Harvey packaged such
attractions as the Grand Canyon, the Painted Desert, and various southwestern
Indian pueblos, building an elaborate tourist infrastructure and defining a unique
southwestern style and ambiance that celebrated the region as a land of enchantment
replete with sublime scenery, domesticated Indians, and frontier romance. At the
Grand Canyon, Santa Fe/Harvey's brand-name tourist destination, a series of structures were designed to objectify the southwestern tourist experience. The Harvey
Company contracted with Mary Colter, a young architect from St Paul, Minnesota,
who had designed the interior of the Indian Building at the Alvarado Hotel in
Albuquerque, to design a similar structure for the Grand Canyon. The result was the
Hopi House completed in 1905, which was modeled after traditional Hopi dwellings
at Oraibi, Arizona. Santa Fe promotional material likened Hopi House to a miniature Indian pueblo. Although Colter modified the traditional Hopi dwelling to
address its function as a commercial space, she intended Hopi House to be a recreation and celebration of the distinct Native American culture of the Southwest.
Colter went on to design a number of additional structures at the canyon for the
Harvey Company in a similar vein, all of which helped to frame the Grand Canyon
as an icon of the southwestern tourist landscape. As Leah Dilworth (1996: 78–9) has
argued, the Fred Harvey Company and the Santa Fe Railway constructed a tourist
landscape that "fostered a remarkably coherent – and persistent – version of the
Southwest as a region inhabited by peaceful, pastoral people, 'living ruins' from
the childhood of civilization," all of which extended from notions of the primitive.
The work of the Santa Fe Railway and the Harvey Company reveals the very concrete ways in which a mythology of the West was used not only to create an
imaginary geography of the West, but also to map that mythology onto the built
environment and landscape.

Although the promotional work of Santa Fe/Harvey has been the most thoroughly documented, other major railroad corporations also promoted and constructed tourist landscapes throughout the West that capitalized on the mythology
of the frontier. Northern Pacific developed and promoted Yellowstone as "Wonderland," and the Great Northern designed and marketed Glacier as the "Crown of the
Continent." From the trademark yellow "tally-ho" stagecoaches that met passengers
at the Gardiner Station to the distinctive design of the Old Faithful Inn, Northern
Pacific interests packaged Yellowstone Park's sublime scenery and geothermal
wonders as an extension of the process of westward expansion. Similarly, Great
Northern combined Swiss chalets with rustic log palaces to frame the Rocky Mountain landscape of Glacier National Park, promoting tourism in the park as a vicarious

frontier wilderness experience. Through careful design and marketing, transcontinental railroads created scripted western landscapes, mixing together an eclectic range of references that blended sublime scenery and civilized taste and style with frontier imagery and a benign version of Manifest Destiny. By World War I, these iconographic western landscapes – Yellowstone, Glacier, Yosemite, and the Grand Canyon being the most prominent – had been transformed into brand-name tourist attractions that offered the mythic frontier West up for display and pleasure.

The promotional work of transcontinental railroads set off a flurry of tourist development throughout the West as they incorporated the region into the national infrastructure and spread the materials and desires of commerce across the continent. As the railroads shrank distance and time, the tourist's West became readily accessible, and what had begun as a transcontinental railroad promotional strategy became a viable economic enterprise across the West. The western landscape of leisure dramatically expanded as tourism diversified into a spate of recreational activities that included hunting, fishing, hiking, camping, autotouring, and skiing. In the interwar period, as a corporate consumer culture solidified, national parks and dude ranches, autocamps and ski resorts emerged to satisfy the urge to experience and consume the mythic West.

The 1915 Panama Pacific International Exposition marked a turning point for the development of tourism in the West. Opening in San Francisco in the wake of the closing of European borders, the exposition provided tourist industries and organizations with an opportunity to celebrate the wonders of the western tourist landscape. Exposition promoters touted the extensive tourist opportunities available to visitors traveling to or from the exposition. Railroads offered special fares and tickets that allowed for unlimited stopovers and variable routes. Exposition exhibits and events also celebrated western tourist attractions. The major transcontinental railroads all mounted elaborate displays of the scenic wonders along their lines. In addition, a number of railroads, most notably the Union Pacific and the Santa Fe set up concessions in the commercial section of the fair that promoted re-created touring experiences for fair goers. The Union Pacific went so far as to reconstruct the major attractions of Yellowstone National Park in miniature: the Golden Gate of Yellowstone, Eagle Nest Rock, Hot Springs Terrace, Old Faithful Geyser, and the "crowning feature" of the concession, the Old Faithful Inn. Similarly, the Santa Fe railway constructed a miniature model of the Grand Canyon for fairgoers to explore, including a replica of the El Tovar Hotel and a model Indian pueblo. In advocating domestic tourism and exhibiting western tourist attractions, the Panama Pacific International Exposition showcased the culmination of decades of work to develop and promote the tourist infrastructure throughout the West. Just as the declaration of war closed European borders, the exposition helped to make western tourism fashionable for American tourists.

The automobile, however, made western tourism increasingly feasible and helped to further legitimize and expand the tourist spectacle of the mythic West as a viable middle-class consumer experience. In 1908, the Ford Motor Company first began to sell the Model T for $850. Designed as the "car for the great multitude," it was sturdily built with a high wheel base for rough terrain and a two-speed transmission (forward and reverse) for case of handling. By 1914, the Ford Company had perfected the assembly line system that allowed for the production of one car every hour and a half. That year the company sold 260,720 Model T's at almost half the original price. Other automobile manufactures struggled to keep pace. Between 1914 and 1917 the production of automobiles in the United States soared from a little over half a million to almost two million (Rae, 1965). No longer a novel luxury, the automobile was quickly becoming a popular consumer product.

The affordable automobile transformed western tourism by placing added emphasis on outdoor recreation and therapeutic escape. In contrast to confining train schedules and standardized destinations, the automobile brought tourists into the landscape allowing them to move beyond the passive act of viewing to experience the West firsthand. Not only did western tourist destinations promise an escape from the social confines and the monotonous routines of urban industrial living, but poor roads and unpredictable automobiles challenged tourists to embrace primitive conditions and strenuous action. Braving difficult roads, camping out in the open landscape, and assuming sole responsibility for their machines, automobile tourists played pioneer and Indian, imagining themselves at the boundaries of civilization and seeking out the vigor of nature and the promise of the American West. Frederick Van de Water, who autocamped cross-continent with his family in the 1920s, commented in his published touring narrative (1927: 393) that they arrived in San Francisco "thin" and "tanned, brown as Indians." Automobile touring, thus, became a recreational sport. The West now offered more than scenic views, it offered a venue for camping, hiking, riding, and fishing – a glimpse of the strenuous life and an opportunity for regenerative play. In this way, touring came to be understood as a much more athletic and authentic experience; and in the process, western tourist attractions became recreational and therapeutic spaces that extended from the western frontier past.

As tourists in the West sought out opportunities to play cowboy and Indian, pioneer and mountain man, established tourist destinations and emerging tourist resorts sought to fuse a frontier mythology that celebrated strenuous action and rugged individualism with western landscapes that offered remote solitude and rugged natural landscapes. The national parks were promoted as national "playgrounds." There tourists were encouraged to hike, fish, ride, and camp – to regenerate city-softened muscles and minds numbed by overwork. As wilderness advocate John Muir (1898: 15) wrote, "Thousands of nerve-shaken, overly civilized people are beginning to find out that going to the mountains is going home, and that mountain parks and reservations are useful not only as fountains of timber and irrigating rivers, but as fountains of life." Dude ranches, which began to flourish throughout the mountain West during the interwar period, offered tourists the chance to rough it in style. Places like Eatons and the Bar BC encouraged tourists to temporarily refashion themselves as cowboys and ranch hands living a self-sufficient life close to nature, far removed from the humdrum of the modern city. Guests wrangled cattle and rode fence lines; they hunted and camped; they enjoyed the simple pleasures of rough-hewn cabins that let in the cold night air and meals cooked over an open fire. In this way tourists were free to engage in bounded fantasies, imagining themselves as cohorts of Zane Grey's Lassiter and Jane or Owen Wister's Virginian, vicariously experiencing life on the open frontier. The lens of consumption allowed them to see and experience this mythic frontier as a real place connected to an authentic western past.

Similarly, skiing, which began to emerge as a popular and viable recreational sport in the West during the 1930s with the development of resorts in places like Steamboat Springs, Colorado, Sun Valley, Idaho, and Mt Hood, Oregon, further added to the western tourist experience by allowing tourists to pit individual strength and endurance against winter wilderness, thus reenacting and reframing the classic frontier myth. Replicas of Bavarian ski lodges and Swiss chalets, along with European ski instructors and imported skiwear did not simply seek to tap into the cachet of the Old World; this imagery encouraged elite tourists to imagine themselves as Anglo-European aristocrats ensconced in the American wilderness testing the self against the environment and re-enacting a particular version of the civilizing process of the mythic western frontier.

The growing popularity of skiing in the post-World War II era along with other forms of recreational tourism helped to spawn an array of extreme wilderness sports ranging from mountain climbing and river running to mountain biking and backpacking. Although less invasive than the infrastructure required for downhill skiing, these sports also rely on high-tech gadgets and specialized gear that reveals their integral connection to modern corporate consumer culture. And, like skiing, they also depend on the promises of western wilderness and frontier adventure. Whether scaling a sheer Rocky Mountain cliff, careening down a class five rapid on the Colorado River, trekking into the back country of Glacier National Park, or negotiating a field of powdered snow in the Alaskan wilderness, extreme sports tourists both consciously and unconsciously embrace frontier mythology that celebrates rugged individualism, strenuous action, and wilderness adventure.

During the postwar boom years, American tourists inundated highways, resorts, and roadside attractions. In 1949, 6.3 million new motor vehicles came off American assembly lines. By 1950 there were over 40 million automobiles registered in the United States – approximately one car for every three people. In 1948 a little over half of American families owned one or more automobiles. By 1965 over three quarters of American families owned one or more automobiles. At the same time that automobile use and ownership increased, so too did the construction of new roads. In 1945 the federal highway system encompassed approximately 300,000 miles; by 1965 the number of miles had tripled to over 900,000. In an effort to promote and expand the development of national interstate highways, Congress passed the Interstate Highway Act, which provided federal funding for the construction of 41,000 miles of national highways. Simultaneously, work time was decreasing while vacation time was increasing. In 1950, American workers spent approximately 40 hours per week on the job; a decade later those hours had decreased to 37.5. In addition, American companies increasingly began to institutionalize the paid vacation. Almost half of American wage earners had some form of paid vacation plan by the early 1940s. Despite the fact that paid vacations remained a privilege rather than an entitlement after World War II, by 1949 93 percent of all union contracts included some provision for a paid holiday.

With increased automobile use and ownership, along with federally funded highway construction and the expansion of leisure time, tourism emerged as a central social and economic force in the postwar West. For example, in Southern California, where tourism provided the second largest source of income behind the aircraft industry, tourists spent approximately $457 million dollars in 1949. Between 1950 and 1960, in San Diego County alone, tourist revenues more than doubled, rising from $60 million to over $150 million. And tourist revenues in places like Southern California only continued to increase as the tourist infrastructure expanded during the postwar decades. Tourism to the national parks and monuments rose from 3.2 million in 1929 to 65.9 million in 1960: a twentyfold increase. The park service, in an attempt to address the infrastructural needs for rising numbers of tourists adopted the Mission 66 program, which contained provisions for new and improved visitor facilities, including the construction and maintenance of roads and trails, campgrounds and visitors centers, as well as expanded visitor services and programs. Thus, throughout the West, established tourist destinations and new tourist attractions emerged to satisfy the rising demand in the postwar era.

The rise of mass tourism in the West ushered in a new phase of tourist development and a whole new category of tourist landscapes emerged throughout the region that epitomized the promises of post-World War II abundance. Two tourist destinations in particular defined this new phase of tourist development – Disneyland and Las Vegas. Although both Disneyland and Las Vegas capitalized on direct references to the Wild West, they also transcended the literal link to frontier imagery and tapped into an expanded version of the western mythology spawned by Los Angeles boosters and spread by the celebrity of Hollywood. Extending from the popular imagery associated with Southern California, this particular version of western mythology helped shape the tourist's West as an earthly paradise, a land of perpetual sunshine and temperate climate where dreams come true and desire is actualized.

Between 1938 and 1942, as reform-minded Los Angeles politicians clamped down on illegal gambling and prostitution while soldiers and defense workers inundated the region, Las Vegas began to emerge as a casino gambling mecca. Fremont Street in downtown Las Vegas soon sported an array of gambling clubs – the Boulder, the Pioneer, and the Frontier, among others – that defined the city as wild western outpost that offered free-flowing liquor, accommodating women, and unlimited legal gambling. In 1940. California hotelman Thomas Hull expanded and transformed this frontier image by building the first casino resort on what would come to be known as the Las Vegas Strip. Constructed in the Spanish Mission style, the El Rancho was a sprawling hacienda that housed a casino, restaurant, Opera House Showroom, shops, and guest rooms situated amid lush gardens with a large pool. The El Rancho's success sparked a flurry of casino development in Las Vegas; and in 1947 the opening of the lavish Flamingo resort and casino, which had been financed by mob money and spearheaded by Los Angeles syndicate boss Bugsy Seigel, marked the emergence of Las Vegas as a glamorous resort city.

With its three-story waterfall, nine-hole golf course, swimming pool, stables, and trapshooting range, in addition to its posh casino and guest rooms along with health club, gym, steam rooms, and tennis courts, the Flamingo brought cosmopolitan style and exotic luxury to the Las Vegas Strip while liberating the city from its Wild West image. Instead, the Flamingo and the resorts that followed it – the Desert Inn, the Thunderbird, the Dunes, the Tropicana, and the Stardust – capitalized on the eclectic fantasy, romance, luxury, and celebrity associated with Hollywood and Beverly Hills and extending to Monte Carlo, Miami Beach, Palm Springs, and Havana. The national advertising firm of J. Walter Thompson promoted the city as a desert paradise – a place where leisure, luxury, promiscuity, and possibility were all rolled into one. Offering the allure of gambling along with the promise of opulent relaxation, Las Vegas came to epitomize the possibilities of postwar abundance, a kind of hedonistic libertarianism that celebrated unrestricted, individualized leisure and pleasure.

As Las Vegas flourished in the postwar era another novel tourist destination also emerged in the West. In 1955, on the outskirts of the sprawling Los Angeles metropolitan region in Anaheim, California, Walter Elias Disney Enterprises (WED) opened Disneyland, a modern-day theme park and resort. As a compliment to ABC's television series of the same name, Disneyland gave physical form to the Magic Kingdom, which included a series of distinct places – "Main Street," "Fantasyland," "Frontierland," "Adventureland," Tomorrowland" – that corresponded to ongoing Disney projects such as the Mickey Mouse cartoon characters, westerns like *Davy Crockett*, nature documentaries like *Seal Island*, and Disney's overriding interest in modern technology. As narrated space, Disneyland mirrored its television program, offering viewers the opportunity to become characters in an array of well-known Disney productions. Extending from the illusion of Hollywood, the park reflected an abstracted frontier promise of abundance and individual fulfillment.

However, the allure of Disneyland was also rooted in a more direct reference to an idealized West. Based on Walt Disney's romantic recollections of his boyhood home in Marceline, Missouri and given visual form by Harper Goff, who grew up in Fort Collins, Colorado, Main Street and the Disneyland railroad, along with the pedestrian plan of the park, reflected a sanitized image of a small midwestern or western railroad town. With its scaled down railroad station, town hall, barber shop, opera house, emporium, ice cream parlor, and specialty shops, Main Street represented an "architecture of reassurance," according to cultural historian Karal Ann Marling (1997: 86–7, 89). It offered all the conveniences of modern America in a colorful, harmonious, and reassuring Victorian package. In following the prescribed walk through the turnstile, under the railroad station, down Main Street, visitors entered a scripted landscape that forced them to reenact a daily ritual that took place in small towns across America at the turn of the century. "Main Street was for pedestrians," Marling explains. "Lookers in windows. Sniffers of aromas: chocolate from the candy shop, coffee, and fresh-baked rolls. People who strolled and fingered the merchandise and savored the glint of gold-leaf letters on a polished window pane." Visitors entered a movie set that told "a story about the wondrousness of pressing one's nose to a store window, or rubbing elbows with one's fellow creatures, of taking a walk in a place that bathes the senses in unalloyed charm." Through this process, Disney sought to reaffirm a frontier vision of democratic community and face-to-face interaction and exchange. As a combination fantasy toyland and shopper's paradise, the park catered to the desires of middle-class suburban families, promising good, clean fun embodied by this image of small-town America.

Representing two sides of the same coin, Disneyland and Las Vegas have set the standard for tourist destinations throughout the United States in the postwar era. Despite their eclectic imagery, I would argue that they are both quintessentially western in nature, reflecting the most recent intersection of postmodern consumer culture and western mythology. The frontier West they embody extends beyond the cliché cowboy and Indian to embrace the even larger frontier promise of unlimited abundance and individual fulfillment.

What this brief survey reveals is that in places across the West the mythic frontier in its myriad of forms has become a landscape of leisure made real through the economic, technological, social, and cultural framework of consumption. Whether it is Glacier National Park or Disneyland, Sun Valley or Las Vegas, the tourist's West offers an array of places where, to use Earl Pomeroy's (1990: 225) phrase, the "West plays West." In the process, myth and region are synthesized to create a hyper-reality that fuses cowboys and Indians, abundance and opportunity, wilderness and perpetual sunshine with consumer desire. Although new western historians have sought to juxtapose frontier and region, opposing process and place, myth and history, the realities of the tourist's West and the rapid expansion of it suggest that we need to look more closely at the complex intersection between these two historical frameworks. The tourist's West challenges the seemingly fixed boundaries of the region, revealing the larger more malleable forces of culture. For many, the West as place, region, and geography depends on the myth, fiction, and desire generated by the transnational historical framework of advanced corporate capitalism. The longing for the physical and imaginary geography of the multifaceted mythical western frontier embodied by cowboys and Indians, wilderness and sunshine, abundance and leisure might best be understood as a regional extension of modern consumer culture. In promising leisure, escape, pleasure, and self-fulfillment, the tourist's West helped to give shape and meaning to the frontier West. From this perspective the opposition between the mythic narrative and the regional narrative makes little sense. We need to come to terms with the ideological implications of consumer desire defined in terms of western frontier mythology. We also need to address the social, political, economic, and environmental relations that underlie the tourist's West. Scholars will find a rich and largely unexplored topic in the recognition that for many Americans, be they tourists, boosters, neo-natives or retirees, the mythic West is the real West.

REFERENCES

Allen, John B.: *From Skisport to Skiing: One Hundred Years of an American Sport* (Amherst: University of Massachusetts Press, 1993).

Aquila, Richard (ed.): *Wanted Dead or Alive: The American West in Popular Culture* (Urbana: University of Illinois Press, 1996).

Athearn, Robert G.: *The Mythic West in Twentieth-Century America* (Lawrence: University Press of Kansas, 1986).

Baranowski, Shelley and Ellen Furlough (eds.): *Being Elsewhere: Tourism, Consumer Culture, and Identity in Modern Europe and North America* (Ann Arbor: University of Michigan Press, 2001).

Barringer, Mark Daniel: *Selling Yellowstone: Capitalism and the Construction of Nature* (Lawrence: University Press Of Kansas, 2002).

Bartlett, Richard A.: *Yellowstone: A Wilderness Besieged* (Tucson, AZ: University of Arizona Press, 1985).

Belasco, Warren James: *Americans on the Road: From Autocamp to Motel, 1910–1945* (Cambridge, MA: MIT Press, 1981).

Benson, Jack A.: "Before Aspen and Vail: The Story of Recreational Skiing in Frontier Colorado." *Journal of the West*, 22, 1 (1983), 52–61.

Bold, Christine: *Selling the Wild West: Popular Western Fiction, 1860–1960* (Bloomington: University of Indiana Press, 1987).

Borne, Lawrence R.: *Dude Ranching: A Complete History* (Albuquerque: University of New Mexico Press, 1983).

Braun, Bruce and Noel Castree (eds.) *Remaking Reality: Nature at the Millenium* (London: Routledge, 1998).

Butchart, J. Harvey: "Summits Below the Rim: Mountain Climbing in the Grand Canyon." *Journal of Arizona History* 17, (1976), 21–38.

Campbell, Colin: *The Romantic Ethic and the Spirit of Modern Consumption* (Oxford: Basil Blackwell, 1987).

Christenson, Bonnie: *Red Lodge and the Mythic West: Coal Miners to Cowboys* (Lawrence: University Press of Kansas, 2002).

Coleman, Annie Gilbert: "The Unbearable Whiteness of Skiing." *Pacific Historical Review* 65 (November 1996) 583–614.

Coleman, Annie Gilbert: *Skiing Colorado: A History of Sport, Landscape, and Identity* (Lawrence: University Press of Kansas, 2004).

Constiguglia, Georgiana: "Ski Tracks: A Century of Skiing in Colorado." *Journal of the West* 30, 4 (1991), 82–6.

Cross, Gary S.: *Time and Money: The Making of Consumer Culture* (New York: Routledge, 1993).

Davis, Clark: "From Oasis to Metropolis: Southern California and the Changing Context of American Leisure." *Pacific Historical Review* 61 (June 1992), 357–86.

Davis, Susan G.: "Landscapes of Imagination: Tourism in Southern California." *Pacific Historical Review* 68 (May 1999), 173–92.

Degenhart, Stella: "The Mountaineers: Pioneers of Recreational Skiing in the Pacific Northwest." *Columbia* 9 (Winter 1995–6), 6–10.

Dilworth, Leah: *Imagining Indians in the Southwest: Persistent Visions of a Primitive Past* (Washington DC: Smithsonian Institution Press, 1996).

Eaton, Howard: "Birth of Western Dude Ranching." *American West* 16 (Winter, 1979), 18–22.

Etulain, Richard: *Telling Western Stories: From Buffalo Bill to Larry McMurtry* (Albuquerque: University of New Mexico Press, 1999).

Fabian, Ann: "History for the Masses: Commercializing the Western Past." In William Cronon, George Miles, and Jay Gitlin (eds.) *Under an Open Sky: Rethinking America's Western Past* (New York: W. W. Norton and Company, 1992).

Fay, Abbot: *Ski Tracks in the Rockies: A Century of Colorado Skiing* (Denver: Cordillera Press, 1984).

Fifer, J. Valerie: *American Progress: The Growth of Transport, Tourist, and Information Industries in the Nineteenth-Century West* (Chester, CN: Pequot Press, 1988).

Findlay, John M.: *Magic Lands: Western Cityscapes and American Culture after 1940* (Berkeley: University of California Press, 1992).

Fisher, Robert Colin: "Frontiers of Leisure: Nature, Memory, and Nationalism in American Parks, 1850–1930." (PhD dissertation: University of California, Irvine, 1999).

Fischman, Lisa Anne: "Coonskin Fever: Frontier Adventures in Postwar American Culture." (PhD dissertation: University of Minnesota, 1996).

Flink, James: *The Car Culture* (Cambridge, MA: MIT Press, 1975).

Fogelson, Robert M.: *The Fragmented Metropolis: Los Angeles, 1850–1930* (Cambridge, MA: Harvard University Press, 1967).

Francaviglia, Richard V.: "Main Street USA: A Comparison/Contrast of Streetscapes in Disneyland and Walt Disney World." *Journal of Popular Culture* 15 (Summer 1981), 141–56.

Goetzmann, William H.: *The West of the Imagination* (New York: Norton, 1986).

Grattan, Virginia L.: *Mary Colter: Builder Upon the Red Earth* (Flagstaff, AZ: Northland Press, 1980).

Green, Harvey: *Fit For America: Health, Fitness, Sport and American Society* (New York: Pantheon Books, 1981).

Haines, Aubrey L.: *The Yellowstone Story: A History of Our First National Park*, 2 vols. (Yellowstone National Park, WY: Yellowstone Library and Museum Association in cooperation with Colorado University Press, 1977).

Hales, Peter B.: *William Henry Jackson and the Transformation of the American Landscape* (Philadelphia: Temple University Press, 1988).

Howard, Kathleen L. and Diana F. Pardue: *Inventing the Southwest: The Fred Harvey Company and Native American Art* (Phoenix, AZ: The Heard Museum, 1996).

Hugill, Peter J.: "The Rediscovery of America: Elite Automobile Touring." *Annals of Tourism Research* 12, 3 (1985): 435–47.

Hyde, Anne Farrar: *An American Vision: Far Western Landscape and National Culture* (New York: New York University Press, 1990).

Interrante, Joseph Anthony: "A Movable Feast: The Automobile and the Spatial Transformation of American Culture, 1890–1940." (PhD dissertation: Harvard University, 1983).

Jakle, John: *The Tourist: Travel in Twentieth-Century North America* (Lincoln, NE: University of Nebraska Press, 1985).

King, Margaret J.: "Disneyland and Walt Disney World: Traditional Values in Futuristic Form." *Journal of Popular Culture* 15 (Summer 1981), 56–62.

Kinsey, Joni Louise: *Thomas Moran and the Surveying of the American West* (Washington, DC: Smithsonian Institution Press, 1992).

Klein, Kerwin L.: "Frontier Products: Tourism, Consumerism, and the Southwestern Public Lands, 1890–1990." *Pacific Historical Review* 62 (February 1993), 39–71.

Klein, Kerwin L.: "Reclaiming the F Word: Or Being and Becoming Postwestern." *Pacific Historical Review* 65 (May 1996), 179–215.

Limerick, Patricia Nelson, Clyde A. Milner, II, and Charles E. Rankin, (eds.): *Trails: Toward a New Western History* (Lawrence, KS.: University Press of Kansas, 1991).

McLuhan, T.C.: *Dream Tracks: The Railroad and the American Indian, 1890–1930* (New York: Harry N. Abrams, 1985).

McQuaid, Matilda and Karen Bartlett: "Building an Image of the Southwest: Mary Colter, Fred Harvey Company Architect" In Marta Weigle and Barabar Babcock (eds.) *The Great Southwest of the Fred Harvey Company and the Santa Fe Railway* (Phienix: The Heard Museum, 1996).

Magoc, Chris J.: *Yellowstone: The Creation and Selling of an American Landscape, 1870–1903* (Albuquerque, NM: University of New Mexico Press, 1999).

Marling, Karal Ann: *As Seen On TV: The Visual Culture of Everyday Life in the 1950s* (Cambridge: Harvard University Press, 1994).

Marling, Karal Ann: (ed.) *Designing Disney's Theme Parks: The Architecture of Reassurance* (Montreal: Canadian Center for Architecture, 1997).

Milner, Clyde A., II (ed.): *A New Significance: Re-Envisioning the History of the American West* (New York: Oxford University Press, 1996).

Moehring, Eugene P.: *Resort City in the Sun Belt: Las Vegas, 1930–1970* (Reno: University of Nevada Press, 1989).

Mrozek, Donald J.: "The Image of the West in American Sport." *Journal of the West* 17, 3 (1978), 2–15.

Muir, John: "Wild Parks and Forest Reservations of the West." *Atlantic Monthly* 81 (January 1898), 15.

Nash, Roderick: *Wilderness and the American Mind* (New Haven: Yale University Press, 1967).

Neel, Susan Rhoades (ed.): "Tourism and the American West." Special Issue, *Pacific Historical Review* 65 (November 1996).

Neumann, Mark: *On the Rim: Looking for the Grand Canyon* (Minneapolis: University of Minnesota Press, 1999).

Norris, Scott (ed.): *Discovered Country: Tourism and Survival in the American West* (Albuquerque, NM: Stone Ladder Press, 1994).

Patrick, Kevin: "Mountain Bikes and Baby Boomers." *Journal of American Culture* 11, 2 (1988), 17–24.

Philpott, William: "Visions of a Changing Vail: Fast-Growth Fallout in a Colorado Resort Town." (Master's thesis: University of Wisconsin, Madison, 1994).

Pomeroy, Earl: *In Search of the Golden West: The Tourist in Western America* ([1957], reprinted Lincoln: University of Nebraska Press, 1990).

Prown, Jules David, Nancy K. Anderson, William Cronon, Brian W. Dippie, Martha A. Sandweiss, Susan Prendergast Schoelwer, and Howard R. Lamar: *Discovered Lands, Invented Pasts: Transforming Visions of the American West* (New Haven: Yale University Press, 1992).

Rae, John B.: *The American Automobile: A Brief History* (Chicago: University of Chicago Press, 1965).

Rae, John B.: *The Road and the Car in American Life* (Cambridge, MA: MIT Press, 1971).

Rinehart, Mary Roberts: "My Country Tish of Thee." *Saturday Evening Post* (1 April 1916), 3–6, 54–5, 58–9, 62, 65–6; (8 April 1916), 19–22, 43, 47, 50–1.

Rinehart, Mary Roberts: "On the Trail in Wonderland II." *Wide World* (November 1916), 59–68.

Rinehart, Mary Roberts: *Tenting Tonight* (Boston: Houghton Mifflin, 1918).

Rinehart, Mary Roberts: "The Family Goes A-Gypsying." *Outlook* (12 June 1918), 263–6.

Rinehart, Mary Roberts: *The Out Trail* (New York: George H. Doran, 1923).

Rinehart, Mary Roberts: *Through Glacier National Park in 1915,* reprint (Boulder, CO: Roberts, Rinehart, Inc., 1983).

Rosaldo, Renato: "Imperialist Nostalgia." *Representations* 26 (Spring 1989), 107–22.

Rothman, Hal K.: *Devil's Bargains: Tourism in the Twentieth-Century American West* (Lawrence, KS: University Press of Kansas, 1998).

Rothman, Hal K.: *Neon Metropolis: How Las Vegas Started the Twenty-First Century* (New York: Routledge, 2002).

Rothman, Hal K.: (ed.): *The Culture Of Tourism, The Tourism Of Culture* (Albuquerque, NM: University of New Mexico Press, 2003).

Runte, Alfred: *Trains of Discovery: Western Railroads and the National Parks* (Niwot, CO: Roberts Rinehart, 1994).

Schmitt, Peter J.: *Back to Nature: The Arcadian Myth in Urban America* (Baltimore: Johns Hopkins University Press, 1990).

Schwantes, Carlos A.: *Railroad Signature Across the Pacific Northwest* (Seattle: University of Washington Press, 1993).

Sears, John F.: *Sacred Places: American Tourist Attractions in the Nineteenth Century* (New York: Oxford University Press, 1989).

Shaffer, Marguerite S.: *America First: Tourism and National Identity, 1880–1940* (Washington, DC: Smithsonian Institution Press, 2001).

Slotkin, Richard: *Regeneration Through Violence: The Mythology of the American Frontier, 1600–1860* (Middletown, CT: Wesleyan Press, 1973).

Slotkin, Richard: *The Fatal Environment: The Myth of the Frontier in the Age of Industrialization, 1800–1890* (New York: Atheneum, 1985).

Slotkin, Richard: *Gunfighter Nation: The Myth of the Frontier in Twentieth-Century America* (New York: Atheneum, 1992).

Slotkin, Richard: "Buffalo Bill's 'Wild West' and the Mythologization of the American Empire." In Amy Kaplan and Donald E. Pease (eds.) *Cultures of United States Imperialism* (Durham, Duke University Press, 1993).

Smith, Henry Nash: *Virgin Land: The American West as Symbol and Myth* (New York: Vintage, 1950).

Sorkin, Michael: "See You in Disneyland." In Michael Sorkin (ed.) *Variations on a Theme Park: The New American City and the End of Public Space* (New York: Hill and Wang, 1992).

Steiner, Michael C.: "Frontierland as Tomorrowland: Walt Disney and the Architectural Packaging of the Mythic West." *Montana* 48 (Spring 1998), 2–17.

Truettner, William H. (ed.): *The West as America: Reinterpreting Images of the Frontier* (Washington, D.C.: Smithsonian Institution Press, 1991).

Turner, Frederick Jackson: "The Significance of the Frontier in American History." In John Mack Faragher (ed.) *Rereading Frederick Jackson Turner: "The Significance of the Frontier in American History" and Other Essays* (New York: Henry Holt and Co., 1994).

Van de Water, Frederic F.: *The Family Flivvers to Frisco* (New York: D. Appleton & Company, 1927).

Wallace, Mike: "Mickey Mouse History: Portraying the Past at Disney World." In Mike Wallace *Mickey Mouse History and Other Essays on American Memory* (Philadelphia: Temple University Press, 1996).

Watts, Steven: *The Magic Kingdom: Walt Disney and the American Way of Life* (Boston: Houghton Mifflin, 1997).

Weigle, Marta: "From Desert to Disney World: The Santa Fe Railway and the Fred Harvey Company Display the Indian Southwest." *Journal of Anthropological Research* 45 (1989), 115–37.

Weigle, Marta: "Southwest Lures: Innocents Detoured, Incensed, Determined." *Journal of the Southwest* 32 (1990): 499–540.

Weigle, Marta: "Exposition and Mediation: Mary Colter, Erna Fergusson, and the Santa Fe/Harvey Popularization of the Native Southwest, 1902–1940." *Frontiers: A Journal of Women Studies* 12 (Summer 1991), 117–50.

Weigle, Marta: and Kathleen L. Howard: "'To *experience* the real Grand Canyon': Santa Fe/Harvey Panopticism, 1910–1935". In Marta Weigle and Barbara Babcock (eds.) *The Great Southwest of the Fred Harvey Company and the Santa Fe Railway* (Phoenix: The Heard Museum, 1996).

Weiner, Lynn Y.: "There is Great Big Beautiful Tomorrow: Historic Memory and Gender in Walt Disney's Carousel of Progress." *Journal of Popular Culture* 20, 1 (1997): 111–16.

Weinstein, Raymond M.: "Disneyland and Coney Island: Reflections of the Evolution of the Modern Amusement Park." *Journal of Popular Culture* 26, 1 (1992), 131–64.

Weiselberg, Erik Lawrence: "Ascendancy of the Mazamas: Environment, Identity and Mountain Climbing in Oregon, 1870 to 1930." (PhD dissertation: University of Oregon, 1999).

Worster, Donald: "Beyond the Agrarian Myth." In Patricia Nelson Limerick, Clyde A. Milner, II, and Charles E. Rankin (eds.) *Trails: Toward a New Western History* (Lawrence, KS: University Press of Kansas, 1991).

Wrobel, David M.: "Beyond the Frontier-Region Dichotomy." *Pacific Historical Review* 65 (August 1996), 401–29.

Wrobel, David M. and Patrick T. Long (eds.): *Seeing the Being Seen: Tourism in the American West* (Lawrence, KS: University Press of Kansas, 2001).

Wrobel, David M. and Michael C. Steiner (eds.) *Many Wests: Place, Culture, and Regional Identity* (Lawrence: University Press of Kansas, 1997).

Zimmerman, Tom: "Paradise Promoted: Boosterism and the Los Angeles Chamber of Commerce." *California History* 44 (Winter 1985), 22–33.

Chapter Twenty-Two

Hispanics and Latinos

Ramón A. Gutiérrez

The July 12, 1999 issue of *Newsweek* magazine had as its cover story "Latin U.S.A." (Larmer, 1995). "On the last Independence Day of the millennium, a new nation is being born," the story announced. Never mind that the Fourth of July had already passed. Since the beginning of a millennium had not, *Newsweek* offered some apocalyptic prophecies about this new Latino nation. The year 2000 would bring a Latino population explosion, "ground zero for a demographic upheaval," the magazine warned. Chronicling transformations wrought by immigration and high reproductive rates, *Newsweek* described a national geometry of culture, politics, and money radiating from Miami, Los Angeles, and Chicago, from Houston, New York, and San Jose. "By 2005, Latinos will be the largest US minority; they're already shaping pop culture and presidential politics. The Latin wave will change how the country looks – and how it looks at itself." As a diasporic nation, diverse and dispersed, with multiple population hubs, extensive networks, and switching points, Latino America was not neatly territorially bound. Calling the residents of "Latino USA." Hispanics and Latinos interchangeably, *Newsweek* proclaimed, "Hispanics are hip, hot and making history" (Larmer, 1999: 85).

When *Newsweek* announced that "Hispanics are hip, hot and making history," simultaneously expressing fear that the United States was "ground zero" for a cataclysmic "Latino" population explosion, the magazine summarized what are two long stereotypes about Mexicans in the United States. Since at least the late nineteenth century, when American historians have wanted to depict Mexicans in a positive and heroic light, as bearers of civilization, they have called them Hispanic or Spanish-American, pointing to their Christian religion, European language, culture, ancestry, and legal institutions, and white racial origin. This tradition is called Hispanophilia. Hispanophobia, its Janus face, is just as antique, but much more virulent. Fear of things Hispanic has manifested itself discursively through an emphasis on the Indian and African origins of Mexicans; viewing their religious lives as ordered by Indian and African cults; noting that their racial histories are stories of mongrelization as *mestizos* (mix of Spaniard and Indian) and *mulatos* (mix of Spaniard and African); and concluding that they were born of illegitimate unions, are intellectually inferior and racially depraved, and that, if their passions are left unfettered, they will destroy Anglo-Protestants' purity. Such have been the rhetorical excesses

Hispanophobes have deployed, particularly in moments of national anxiety whatever their source (Weber 1992: 335–60; Woll 1997).

This essay explores the historiographic traditions that developed in the United States about the nation's Hispanic peoples, focusing as well on their own identities and self-fashioning. During the sixteenth century Spain claimed as its immense colonial empire the lower half of what is now the United States, but effectively settled only parts of Georgia, Florida, Louisiana, Texas, New Mexico, Arizona, and California.

Throughout much of the eighteenth and nineteenth centuries, Spain saw this territorial expanse severely shrink, losing control of large areas first to Mexico; Mexico in turn losing them to the United States. The process began at the beginning of the eighteenth century when Spain formally ceded Florida, Georgia, and Louisiana to the United States. Mexican and Latin American independence movements by 1821 had reduced Spain's American possessions to Cuba and Puerto Rico. With the Texas Revolution in 1836, the US–Mexican War in 1846, and the Gadsden Purchase in 1853, Mexico lost over a third of its national territory, along with roughly 50,000 inhabitants.

By 1900 there were approximately 100,000 individual of Spanish and Mexican origin living in the United States. Most of these residents traced their ancestral roots in Arizona, California, New Mexico and Texas to colonization under Spanish and later Mexican rule. Starting in 1900, older residents of the Southwest, some tracing their Spanish ancestry in the Southwest as far back as 1598, were joined by massive numbers of Mexican immigrants. Fleeing poverty and those social dislocations that fueled the 1910 Mexican Revolution, these immigrants found work constructing the railroad lines that began to crisscross the Southwest, extracting minerals, and transforming arid fields into productive agricultural plots. Between 1911 and 1920, 219,000 Mexican immigrants "officially" entered the United States. Between 1921 and 1930, 459,287 more arrived, along with countless others never enumerated.

The arrival of such a large numbers of Mexican nationals in the Southwest created tensions between the long-time residents and recent arrivals. Not wishing to be confused as citizens of another country and hoping to avoid the most egregious forms of racism and discrimination then being heaped on Mexican immigrant laborers, by about 1915 the older residents began calling themselves *Hispanos*, Spanish-Americans, and Latin Americans, depending on their locale, particularly when speaking English, the dominant language. Calling someone a Mexican in English was an insult, usually because of the intonation with which it was uttered, the adjectives that often preceded it (dirty, greasy, filthy, stinking), the expletives that attached to it, and the linguistic corruptions of the word that were bantered just as coarsely (Mex, Meskin, Skin, Skin diver) (Paredes 1978). When speaking Spanish among members of their own group, it was common for both older Spanish/Mexican residents and recent Mexican immigrants to all call themselves *mexicanos* in recognition of their common language and Mexican culture on both sides of the border (Gonzales 2001; Gutiérrez 1986).

Except perhaps among elites and in the most polite of conversations, the dominant Anglo-American population of the Southwest did not appreciate the distinction between those who called themselves Spanish Americans and those who were truly Mexican nationals. In the early 1920s Anglo-Americans tended to view all Spanish-speakers as Mexicans, associating them rather uniformly with cheap, unskilled labor.

Mexicans were viewed as a mongrel race of low intelligence and this precisely was the Hispanophobic response that Spanish Americans and Latin Americans hoped to counter with these defensive personal identities (Hernandez, 1974: 37; Paredes, 1978: 36; Gonzalez, 1969: 33; Fergusson, 1964: 34).

The Spanish Borderlands and the Romantic Tradition

While the presence of ethnic Mexicans grew exponentially between 1900 and 1930, the dominant cultural trend in the United States was to deny Mexico's proximity, previous ownership, and continuing impact on the Southwest. What was celebrated instead was Spain's imperial past, its European culture, institutions, religion and language. In historical writing this trend was particularly apparent in the works of Herbert Eugene Bolton, who spent much of his career at the University of California, Berkeley. There he constructed a romantic tradition for Spain's presence in the United States that was full of majesty, heroism, and intrigue. Bolton called the area he studied the Spanish Borderlands, encompassing those areas presently in the United States previously under Spain's colonial control. Here was a true "American epic," claimed Bolton. Its history began in 1492 and neatly ended with Mexican Independence in 1821.

Bolton thought of his project as disrupting those late-nineteenth-century histories that depicted the development of the United States in linear and monolithic terms. As a student and protegé of Frederick Jackson Turner, Bolton chronicled the distinctiveness of those areas of the United States that Spain once claimed. The history of the United States had, until then, Bolton explained, been written "almost solely from the standpoint of the East and of the English colonies," largely by New Englanders, most of whom had been trained at Harvard (Bolton 1911: 3). The Berkeley history department was uniquely positioned geographically to change this and to chronicle the Spanish frontier in North America. Needed were documentary collections through which the Spanish legacy could be reconstructed. Toward this goal he gathered Spanish documents and published transcriptions in accessible form. So that the Spanish language did not become an obstacle to scholarship, he prepared documentary translations. He edited guides to archival collections and wrote numerous works detailing how Spain had explored, conquered, and colonized its various borderlands (Bolton 1907; Bolton 1910; Bolton 1913).

Bolton's ideas received their fullest articulation in his 1921 book, *The Spanish Borderlands: A Chronicle of Old Florida and the Southwest*, which showed how the area had been profoundly shaped by interactions among Spanish colonial institutions and personnel, indigenous populations, and colonial rivals. This "epic" was marked by "Spanish exploration and conquest; the Spanish mission, presidio, pueblo, mine, and ranch; Anglo-American trappers, explorer, contraband trader, and filibuster within the Spanish domain; revolution from Spain and development under Mexican rule; and finally, Anglo-American settlement, diplomacy, and conquest" (Bolton 1911: 2). This became the thematic grid for Spanish Borderland scholarship, a framework some 300 Bolton students ultimately sketched.

Bolton learned to think spatially about American historical development from his teacher, Frederick Jackson Turner. If Turner's frontier moved from east to west, Bolton's looped from south to north with Florida, Georgia and Louisiana settled and governed from Cuba, and New Mexico, Texas, and California founded by people and institutions moving northward from central Mexico (Bolton, 1946).

While Bolton clearly embraced and complicated his teacher's spatial developmental model, on the relationship between humans and their environments they differed. Spanish institutions, culture, and personnel had forged the frontier in Spain's own hierarchical image, Bolton maintained. The Hapsburg monarchs had profoundly stifled local initiative, personal liberty, and self-government throughout most of the Spanish Empire, save in remote California where a moderate climate, rich land, and docile Indian labor had bred a "mellower spirit" (Bolton 1921: 294).

Bolton advanced this interpretation primarily by documenting the lives of important leaders, both civic and religious, and the baroque intrigues of European imperial rivalries in the Americas. The indefatigable friars who endured all sorts of hardships to plant Christianity in the Americas were true saints in Bolton's mind. They were textually animated only by the most heroic and roseate verbs from his pen. The role of the missionaries and soldiers in establishing the missions and the *presidios* (colonial forts), the two frontier institutions that brought "civilization" to the most remote areas of the empire, were the topic of Bolton's most important essays. The missions and the presidios, and occasionally towns, figured large in his histories (Bolton, 1917; Bolton, 1930). As a great Hispanophile, Bolton gave inordinate attention to the Spanish language, architecture, religion, law, festivals, and archival records. Scant mention was made of the Native American cultures and of the considerable racial mixture that had occurred. Despite the considerable differences and complexity that existed among Native peoples at the time of Spanish exploration, conquest, and settlement, Native Americans in Bolton's writings were simple, monolithic passives. The brutality of the wars of blood and fire the Spaniards wreaked on the Indians and the impact of the confinement of Indians in Spanish missions went largely unnoted. Bolton's goal was to counter the Black Legend. Logically, violence, death, disease, and destruction had little place in such a romance. Writing in a period of intense Hispanophobia provoked by the rising number of Mexican immigrants in the Southwest also meant that the largely *mestizo* character of the Spanish Borderlands escaped notice in favor of pure Spanish types (Bolton, 1917; Bolton, 1930).

Starting in the late 1940s, Bolton's cherished missions and missionaries came under searing historiographic attack from demographers and anthropologists who chronicled the devastating impact of the missions on the Indians (Cook, 1940, 1941, 1943a, 1943b). In 1770 California's Indian population numbered about 133,500, estimated Sherburne F. Cook. By 1870 this number had fallen to 20,000. Much of the decline had to be blamed on the Spanish policy of gathering Indians into mission communities where they suffered extensive malnutrition and starvation. Their confinement in close quarters created fertile breeding grounds for the rapid spread of disease. Forced labor demands, excessive punishment for crimes against morality, and imposed celibacy dispirited the Indians and led to their rapid numeric decline (Cook, 1976).

The Natives Talk Back

By the mid-1960s the mute and largely stoic Indians of the Boltonian imagination started to talk back. Bolton and his students saw the Indians as the Spaniards themselves had once imagined them, as little more than "savages," possessing no significant civilization, ensnared in superstitions not religion, as participants in anarchy rather than true government. When Indians talked back as Native Americans, writing about their own lives, memories, and histories, they recounted stories of indigenous heroism, of native struggle and resistance, and of endurance, despite scholarly and popular tracts lamenting their demise. Native Americans had not vanished and in the 1960s became outspokenly militant about their right to preserve their languages, lands, and cultures. As participants in the worldwide movement of egalitarian aspirations sparked by students, racial minorities, and women in the 1960s, Native Americans began to demand self-determination. Vine Deloria Jr., Jack Forbes, and Peter Blue Cloud were but a few of the Native American scholars who wrote histories of Indian activism and resistance. As these scholars so correctly pointed out, histories of Indian passivity and extinction were themselves the toxic products of colonial domination (Blue Cloud, 1972; Deloria, 1969, 1970; Forbes, 1960, 1965).

Similar political mobilization occurred among the children of ethnic Mexicans in the United States. Defiantly calling themselves Chicanos, these children of assimilated Mexican Americans identified with the oppressed, and in solidarity with Native Americans, laid claim to their own repressed and forgotten Indian ancestry. They putatively discovered direct genealogical links to the Aztecs, the fiercest warriors that had ever roamed the Americas. They claimed the Southwest was Aztlán, their ancestral homeland, and demanded its independence from the United States as a sovereign nation. Though these militant Chicanos may have been the remote descendants of the Spanish soldiers that had once conquered the Southwest, of whom Bolton had waxed so lyrical, Chicanos wanted no part of this European Spanish heritage. Instead they proclaimed working-class origins, celebrated Mexican national roots, and were quick to point to their *mestizo* heritage as products of racial and cultural mixing between Spaniards and Indians. Chicanos were a hybrid people. They had never crossed a border. The border crossed them. For Chicano activists and scholars in the late 1960s and 1970s, Spain had indeed established the institutions of colonial domination in North America, but that legacy was not a particularly heroic or romantic one. It was a history of plunder, rape, and destruction, or so they opined (Muñoz, 1989: 92; Valdez and Steiner, 1972: 93).

The Mexican-American parents and grandparents of Chicanos were largely unaccepting of this newly found political identity. For them the term Chicano had long been a derogatory in-group Spanish-language term for a person of dubious character and for a recent immigrants of lower-class standing. The word etymologically derived from *chinaco*, which means "tramp" or "guttersnipe." Much as Negroes began identifying as black during the 1960s, so too militant Chicanos embraced this once derogatory class identity, inverting its meaning, and using it instead as a badge of ethnic pride. Examining the social origins of those who then called themselves Chicanos reveals that they were young, largely of working-class origin, politically militant, harboring an oppositional stance toward the dominant society and toward assimilation. Chicano was a generational identity. Within a single extended household one could thus find Spanish-speaking monolingual grandparents who identified as *mexicanos*, their bilingual Mexican American and *mexicano* children, and their Chicano monolingual English-speaking grandchildren. Of note too is the fact that Chicano was a Spanish-language word that was being proclaimed defiantly as an identity in English-dominant contexts (Gutiérrez, 1986, 1989).

Border Studies

In 1965 the United States Congress passed a number of amendments removing the so-called National Origins Quotas, which since 1924 had severely restricted the number of immigrant entrants. Chinese immigrants formerly barred under the Chinese Exclusion Act (1881), Japanese excluded by the Japanese Gentlemen's Agreement (1907), Mexicans restricted by caps on the number of western hemisphere immigrants (1924), and previously excluded Africans and South Asians were now granted admission. The impact of this legal change was quite dramatic. While between 1941 and 1960, only 3,550,000 immigrants had gained legal entry, in the next forty years more than 20 million immigrants arrived; Mexicans representing roughly 25 percent of the total (US Department of Commerce, 1999: 71, 11).

The desire to understand these Mexican immigrants, along with a host of subsidiary themes – US–Mexico border control, trade, and immigrant pathologies such as crime, drug use, welfare dependence – led to the development of Border Studies as a distinct academic field in the late 1960s (Stoddard, 1974: 47; García, 1981: 2; de León, 1982: 3; Acuña, 1981: 6). The Association of Borderlands Scholars was begun around 1981, publishing the first issue of their *Journal of Borderlands Studies* in 1986, and two years later a massive bibliographic guide (Stoddard and Nostrand, 1983).

Unlike Bolton's fuzzy Spanish Borderlands, this border was conceived as two abutting spaces joined by the international boundary separating Mexico and the United States. How far north and south of the legal line the border zone actually extended was left opaque, but its temporal scope was not. Its focus was 1900 plus, the period of massive Mexican migration to the US border.

For Bolton, Spanish culture and institutions were strongest and most vibrant in colonial centers, becoming weaker and anemic as one moved outward to the Spanish Borderlands, to the margins of empire. Border Studies scholars likewise thought of places like Mexico City, Guadalajara, Los Angeles, and Dallas as dynamic centers of cultural generation. Located far from these centers, the border was thus little more than a contact zone where the wretched and mongrel cultural forms of two nations met, producing abominations and pathologies of every sort. Twin border towns such as Tijuana/San Diego, Ciudad Juárez/El Paso, were imagined as ugly places of decadence and debauchery (de Baca, 1991; Vila, 1994).

Whereas Bolton always gave attention to the constant circulation of products and personnel along a south/north axis, border scholars imagined a much more unilinear trajectory of development. Mexican immigrants moved from a weak Mexico in the south to a powerful United States in the north; traditional Mexican peasants migrated to the modernity of the United States and there assimilated to a purity of form. The reality of return trips, of cultural mixing, of complicated exportations, was of little theoretical import for these scholars who mostly lived and worked in the United States.

Border Studies was largely dominated by one theme: Mexican emigration to the United States. Hundreds of books and essays were written on the topic. While subtlety and nuance can sometimes be found in this literature, much of it was ideological, imagining Mexicans in Manichean terms: good/bad, asset/problem, citizen/alien. As a "problem," Mexicans threatened the racial, hygienic, social and economic basis of life in the United States (Bamford, 1923; Jenks, and Lauck 1971). As an asset, they contributed to American prosperity, performing tasks at wages that citizen workers would not accept, and paying taxes they rarely benefited from (Borjas, 1990). Advocates of the former position have generally demanded severe immigration restrictions, particularly in moments of economic depression. Their opponents have favored higher levels of immigration, particularly in times of economic prosperity when cheap labor has been in short supply. Mexicans workers have been desired because they are said to be "docile, patient, usually orderly in camp, fairly intelligent under competent supervision, obedient, and cheap" (Clark, 1908: 496). Those eager to restrict their numbers have deplored Mexicans as "human swine . . . plastered with flies, disease, lice, human filth, stench, promiscuous fornication, bastardy, lounging, apathetic peons and lazy squaws, beans and dried chili, liquor, general squalor, and envy" intent on destroying the racial purity of the United States (Garis, 1930: 436).

Arguments for and against Mexican immigrants have not changed much whether one studies the year 1900 or 2001. Peter Brimelow's *Alien Nation* is rather typical of anti-immigrant tracts produced during the economic recession of the early 1990s. "The American nation has always had a specific core. And that core has been white," wrote Brimelow. Americans had a right to demand that their government stop shifting the nation's racial balance, he insisted. "Indeed, it seems to me that they have a right to insist that it be shifted back" (Brimelow, 1995: 45: 10, 265 (??)). Similar sentiments from the extreme political right are found in Lawrence Auster's *The Path to National Suicide: An Essay on Immigration and Multiculturalism* (1990: 48), and Richard D. Lamm and Gary Imhoff's, *The Immigration Time Bomb* (1985: 47), as well as from the liberal left, such as Arthur Schlesinger, Jr.'s *The Disuniting of America* (1992: 46). Even racist ideas about the relationship between race and intelligence, dismissed a century ago, reemerged in the 1990s. In their 1994 book, *The Bell Curve*, Richard J. Herrnstein and Charles Murray claimed that on the average, Latinos scored nine percent lower than whites on IQ tests. Such disparity, they warned, would lower the overall intelligence of the United States, and ultimately lead to crime, women on welfare, and single-parent households (1994: 49, 362–65). Anthropologist Leo R. Chavez excellently surveys these themes in his recent book, *Covering Immigration* (Chavez 2001).

Chicano Studies

Border Studies and Chicano Studies developed almost simultaneously in the academy during the mid-1960s and often had overlapping membership. But, unlike Border Studies, which focused on public policy and grew into a vibrant field because of ample federal research dollars, Chicano Studies grew out of the civil rights movement of the late 1950s and 1960s with specific political demands – racial equality and full participation in American society. Feeling themselves stigmatized by their race, segregated spatially in many urban and rural settings, denied access to educational opportunities and employment, Chicanos fashioned a racialized political identity to overcome these obstacles. Some militated for assimilation, others for national self-determination, and some for social revolution and socialism. As participants in the worldwide decolonization movement, Chicanos found inspiration for their own struggles in the Mexican, Algerian, Chinese, and Cuban revolutions, borrowing ideas from Emiliano Zapata, Frantz Fanon, Mao Tse-Tung, and Ernesto "Che" Guevara to address their oppression in the United States.

Like Border Studies, Chicano Studies preoccupied centrally with Mexican immigration. The experiences of Mexican immigrant men were the primary curricular objects of study. They were imagined as heroic, indefatigable men, struggling against an exploitative capitalist labor regime. Never mind that more than half of all Mexican emigrants to the United States since 1945 had been women. This demographic reality rarely precipitated much scholarly reflection. "Man" as the universal subject of historical inquiry, men as the persons who populated the professorate dictated who and what was worthy of study as Chicano.

Four major interpretive frameworks emerged in these histories written from a Chicano Studies perspective, each pivoting on different factors to explain Chicano poverty and second-class status in American society. Were Chicanos an oppressed class? Was their race the principal cause of lower status? Were their experiences, comparable to those of other European immigrant groups, improving generation by generation? Where did women's experiences fit into the phallocentric interpretations? Did Chicanas suffer different forms of oppression? These were the burning questions Chicano Studies scholars grappled with, yielding different answers and political courses of action.

Bear in mind while reading this discussion that the major interpretations I have organized for theoretical clarity into five, were, in fact, much more complexly intertwined. There were significant theoretical and empirical overlaps and fuzzy edges, prompted by life experiences, personal epiphanies, ideological shifts, retractions, modifications, and later repudiations of earlier work.

Let us begin with the bourgeois interpretation of Chicano history, one in which the economy was seen as the motor of change, "pushing" and "pulling" Mexicans out of their homeland and into the United States. Found in a number of popular textbooks, this framework is most readily evident in Matt S. Meier and Feliciano Rivera's *The Chicanos: A History of Mexican Americans*, and James Diego Vigil's, *From Indians to Chicanos: The Dynamics of Mexican American Culture*. For Meier and Rivera, Chicano history was an "epic" that began "50,000 years" ago with Asian migration across the Bering Straits and culminated with the Chicano protest of the 1960s. Constant "resurgence" and "regeneration" were the themes of Mexican participation in the American economy. Discrimination and segregation reduced *la raza* (the people) to "a minority position of second-class citizenship", which they constantly resisted, finally rising like a phoenix as Chicanos during the civil rights movement, and thus gaining access to education, housing, and employment (Meier, 1972: 78: 3, xiv, 189–90). In *From Indians to Chicanos: The Dynamics of Mexican American Culture*, anthropologist James Diego Vigil takes readers on a similar odyssey from the Ice Age to the 1960s. The Chicano's life cycle is said to have begun with "embryonic life and infancy" between 30,000 BC and 1519, and finally reached "adulthood" in the 1960s. Racism, argued Vigil, was an important determinant of this history, but one that "obscured the real problem source – economic competition" (Vigil, 1980: 128).

The immigrant paradigm of American social science has had a number of Chicano devotees. Here the story is of Mexican peasants transformed into immigrants and into Mexican-American and Chicano workers in the cities of the United States and in its "factories in the field," as Carey McWilliams called them (McWilliams, 1971). Mario García's *Desert Immigrants: The Mexicans of El Paso, 1880–1920* stands as an exemplar of this perspective. The Mexican "saga" in the United States is "the immigrant story commencing in the late nineteenth century . . . linked with the growth of American industrial capitalism," noted García. "Mexican immigrants . . . shared a common tie with the larger wave of Eastern and Southern European immigrants . . . [and] may have experienced less economic and social advances owing to persistent racial and cultural discrimination, yet they were significant additions to an expended multiracial American working class by World War I." By embracing the European immigrant analogy, García and a number of other historians of the Mexican experience in the United States simply echoed the regnant 1950s social science faith in assimilation as the route to upward mobility and full incorporation into American life (Gamio, 1930; García, 1981:1, 233; Martinez, 1972; Reisler, 1976).

Many of the of the historians who wrote self-consciously as Chicanos were themselves of Mexican working-class origin, and this understandably led them to embrace a theory of history propelled by class struggle. Like the bourgeois interpretation of the Chicano past, the proletarian model was anchored to a linear and progressive historical trajectory. Whether capitalists were grabbing for markets or workers were militating for better wages and work conditions, the narrative logic of these histories was evolutionary, originating in a bleak past that led to a bountiful future; from feudalism, to capitalism, to socialism. Historian Juan Gómez-Quiñones and the cadre of doctoral students he trained at UCLA are most identified with this model. Much of Juan Gómez-Quiñones' own writing has been on Mexican workers on both sides of the border, particularly their heroic attempts to unionize. These histories chronicle worker radicalism, labor unionization and strikes, the relationship between Mexican workers and state authorities, political organizations on both sides, and the culture of Mexican workers and Chicanos (Gómez-Quiñones, 1972, 1975, 1977, 1982 1990). An analysis of class formation has been the central unifying thread in this work. Racism, while an important theme to Gómez-Quiñones and his students, has been deemed of lesser import, viewed as false consciousness, an ideological ploy of the ruling class used to divide workers. If workers were truly to improve their station and seize state power, it would only be accomplished by organizing strictly along class lines (Arroyo, 1975; Balderrama, 1982; Weber, 1994).

Further to the political left, eschewing assimilation, even class struggle, have been the Chicano nationalist historians. Rodolfo Acuña's 1972, *Occupied America* is typical of this perspective; the book's subtitle cogently expressing its narrative goal – "*The Chicano's Struggle Toward Liberation*" (Acuña, 1972). Inspired by Latin American theories of internal colonialism diffused in the United States first by the black power movement and transferred from them to the Chicano student movement, the argument proclaims that Chicanos suffer the yoke of "domestic colonialism", which will only be overthrown by revolutionary nationalist struggle (Muñoz, 1989). Internal colonialism, as Acuña and others employed the idea, was most extensively elaborated by Berkeley sociologist Robert Blauner (1969, 1972) and by his then graduate student Tomás Almaguer. Almaguer gave the model its fullest substantiation, arguing that Chicanos were an internally colonized population stigmatized by color, economically and culturally subordinated, and segregated by whites (Almaguer, 1971, 1974, 1975). Almaguer later repudiated much of this work from his graduate student days (Almaguer, 1989), but it nevertheless provided the theoretical framework for works by Rodolfo Acuña (1972), Albert Camarillo (1979: 1?), Richard Griswold del Castillo (?1979), and Ricardo Romo (1983) in history, Joan W. Moore in sociology (1970), and Mario Barrera, Carlos Muñoz, and Charles Ornelas in political science (Barrera, 1979; Barrera Muñoz, and Ornelas, 1972).

Born of personal politics and feminist critique of male chauvinism within the Chicano Movement, a fifth interpretive thread came into its own around 1969, as Chicanas drew attention to their triple oppression by race, class, and sex. They questioned the movement's nationalist rhetoric, saying that true personal liberation could not be won while *machismo* (hypervirility) dominated gender relations within the movement (Hancock García, 1971; Longauex y Vásquez, 1970; Rodarte, 1973; Valdes Fallis, 1974; Vidal, 1971). The Chicana feminist project was to re-vision the past, ordering it by a sense of place and time that pivoted around events of gender and sexual oppression (Mirandé and Enriquez, 1979; Sweeney, 1977). Eschewing 1848 (the end of the Mexican War) as the beginning of Chicano history, Chicana feminists began their "herstories" with 1519, focusing on the Spanish conquest of Mexico's Indian women and most particularly on Doña Marina, Hernán Cortés' Indian mistress, translator, and confidante who facilitated the defeat of the Aztecs. In Mexican history Doña Marina, or la Malinche, had long been a symbol of Indian betrayal in nationalist rhetoric (Alarcón, 1983; Del Castillo, 1977; Messinger Cypess, 1991; Mirandé and Enriquez, 1979; Phillips, 1983). The Chicana historical project began by rehabilitating Malinche, seeing in her the primordial source of *mexicanidad* (the unity of Mexican culture on both sides of the border) and *mestizaje* (miscegenation), and thus significantly expanding the terms of political debate in the Chicano Movement. Sexism was gradually, if grudgingly, given equal importance to racism. *Carnalismo*, the ethos of brotherhood so central to Chicano nationalism was thus complicated, giving attention to women's role in the reproduction of the hybrid *mestizo* nation.

Despite the rhetoric that the "New Chicana" was shattering cultural stereotypes and defining herself, those definitions, at least at the scholarly level, were highly constrained by the then still hegemonic immigrant and proletariat models of history. Mexican immigrant women were important, men explained, but theirs was a much shorter, less significant chapter in the larger book of the struggles men had waged. The feminist retort was that, while they had escaped historical note, their presence was significant nonetheless. For example, of the 311,717 Mexicans deported from the United States between 1930 and 1933, two-thirds had been women (Carreras de Velasco, 1974). Studies estimated that, since 1945, slightly more than one half of all Mexican immigrants have been women, and since 1990, particularly in Los Angeles County, women constituted the bulk (Cardenas and Flores, 1986; Cornelius, 1999(?); Ruiz and Tiano, 1987). While focused initially on the experiences of female immigrants, feminist-inspired scholarship expanded to women's work, rates of labor force participation, comparable worth, occupational preferences, their roles in secondary labor markets, the production and reproduction of material life, gender ideology, and family, kinship, and sexuality (Cardenas, 1982; Cooney, 1975; Cravey, 1998; Fernández-Kelly, 1983; Gutman, 1996; Hondagneau-Sotelo, 1994; Kossoudji and Ranney, 1984; Mirandé, 1997; Romero, 1992; Ruiz, 1987; Zavella, 1987).

Latinos and Border Hybridity

Our discussion of Bolton's Spanish Borderlands noted that ethnic Mexicans in the United States had created the terms Spanish American and Latin American as defensive identities during the 1920s. Starting in the 1940s the appellation Latin American increasingly appeared translated into Spanish as *Latinoamericano*, and then shortened simply as *Latino*. Not until the 1970s did the word Latino begin to denote a nonwhite panethnic identity composed of Mexicans, Cubans, Puerto Ricans, and Central and South Americans, which was racially located between blacks and whites.

Why Latino identity emerged requires some explanation. Immigrants of Spanish and Latin American origin have resided in what is now the United States for more than 400 years. The US Census enumerated Mexicans, Cubans, Puerto Ricans, and Latin Americans by country of origin since 1880. Counting the children and grand-children of these immigrants required a number of surrogate categories. "Spanish surname" was used from 1950 to 1980, "Spanish mother tongue" from 1940 to 1970, and finally "Hispanics" in 1980. Fearing that their national identities would be forgotten and erased, many persons of Latin American origin aggressively resisted Hispanic as an English-language identity imposed by government from above, calling themselves Latinos instead, a word from the subordinate language Spanish.

There are approximately 31 million Latinos in the United States today, constitut-ing roughly 12 percent of the total population, and projected to represent 18 percent in the year 2025, and 25 percent by 2050. Already in states like California, Texas, Florida, and New York, the Latino proportion of the total population is much higher. In 1998 they accounted for 40 percent of New Mexico's population, 31 percent of California's, 30 percent of Texas's, 15 percent of Florida's, and 14 percent of New York's. The population in the former three states is largely of Mexican origin, while the latter two are Cuban and Puerto Rican. These proportions are even higher in specific metropolitan areas. El Paso in 1997 was 75 percent Latino, San Antonio 53 percent, Fresno 42 percent, Albuquerque 39 percent, Los Angeles 39 percent, and Miami-Fort Lauderdale 37 percent (US Department of Commerce, 1999).

Latinos are extremely diverse. Most of the 1.2 million Cubans fled Cuba in the early 1960s and came from educated, middle-class and professional families. They were joined in 1980 by a group of lower-class origin known as the Marielitos. Puerto Ricans are US citizens. Of the 2.4 million currently living on the mainland, most emigrated from the island between 1945 and 1960; they arrived poor, and few have improved their lot. Mexicans are complexly stratified by class, race, ethnicity, and date of entry. The original Spanish and Mexican settlers of the Southwest were joined by wave after wave of compatriots in every decade since the 1880s. Mexican emigration to the United States never stopped. To this mix add emigrants from the Caribbean, Central and South America, and the complexity of Latino identity becomes appar-ent (Moore and Pachón, 1985; Oboler, 1995).

Latinos are largely concentrated at the bottom of the socioeconomic ladder. Very few have managed to ascend into the ranks of the rich. When *Hispanic Business* identified the richest "Hispanics" in the United States in 1995, it listed 75, out of a population of roughly 30 million. The majority of these, 27, were Cuban Americans; 25 were Mexican Americans, 8 were Spaniards, 7 were Puerto Rican (5 lived in the US and 3 on the island), and one each from Chile, Columbia, Costa Rica, the Dominican Republic, Ecuador, Uruguay, and Venezuela (*Hispanic Business,* 1996).

The number of Latinos in the corporate elite is just as small. Again, *Hispanic Business* reported that between 1990 and 1995, the number of Hispanics on the boards of directors of *Fortune* 1000 companies did not exceed 1 percent of all corporate directors. In 1990 they numbered 40, and in 1995, 51, with roughly one out of every five of these a Latina. Analyzing the personal histories of these individuals, sociologists Richard L. Zweigenhaft and G. William Domhoff found that most had been born into well-connected middle-class families with access to elite education, and included very few rags-to-rich stories (Zweigenhaft and Domhoff, 1998: 124, 126).

Economist Elías López, heading a California Research Bureau team in 1998 reported that *Latinos* had the state's lowest median wages. The median wage for California's 15.6 million workers was $21,000; for whites it was $27,000, for Asians $24,000, for blacks $23,000, and for Latinos $14,560. Holding all other factors constant, such as immigrant status and length of time in the United States, most of the wage disparity could be explained by level of educational achievement. Only 7 percent of white workers lacked a high school diploma. Seven percent of black workers had failed to reach this basic benchmark, 12 percent of Asians, and 45 percent of Latinos. Only 8 percent of Latinos had a bachelor's degree or higher. 24 percent of black workers had this level of education, as did 33 percent of whites, and 43 percent of Asians. Projecting the size and composition of California's population forward to the year 2025, López predicted dire fiscal consequences for the state if investments in Latino educational achievement were not radically increased. In 2025, Latinos would constitute 43 percent of the population. If roughly 50 percent of Latinos continued to drop out of high school, this would account for about a fourth of the state's population (López, Ramirez, and Rochin, 1999).

What other economists have also found particularly worrisome about this wage and employment pattern is that over the last decade Latino males have had the highest rates of labor force participation. In 1990, 85 percent of age-eligible Latinos worked, while only 77 percent of Anglos did. What these statistics show is a pattern of working poverty, not joblessness, due to low levels of educational achievement and limited social networks for acquiring better-paid work (Hayes-Bautista, 1993; Melendez, 1993; Pastor, 1995).

A number of factors explain Latino working poverty. In his study of Mexican emigration to the United States, sociologist Douglas Massey and a group of researchers found highly developed "bonding" networks that connected Mexicans in their country to work in the United States (Massey et al., 1987). In San Diego and Los Angeles, 70 percent of Mexican immigrants found work through such ties. These networks provided steady access to work, but it was poorly paid, nonunionized work in services and light manufacturing sectors that often provided no benefits and offered little possibilities for upward mobility. To expand their economic opportunities Mexican immigrants needed "bridging" networks, ties that cut across geography, class, and ethnicity to offer access to higher-paid work. For, as economist Manuel Pastor has argued, when communities are boxed in by residential segregation, racial discrimination, and weak educational structures, broadened opportunities develop only through the construction of bridging networks in the form of community-based employment and training agencies (Pastor, 2000: 12).

Much of the recent scholarship on Mexicans in the United States has focused largely on the second and third generations, on Mexican Americans and on Chicanos, on marital and linguistic assimilation, on the determinants of intergenerational mobility, and on educational attainment and occupational patterns. Important as this work has been, much more attention must be given to the first generation and particular on ways of improving their wages. We know for fact that English-language proficiency is the major determinant of wage level for Mexican immigrants. The challenge is how to teach adult immigrants English. Second-generation pathologies – juvenile crime, poor health, and poor school performance – are largely based on the low and unstable incomes of first-generation parents. If we bear in mind the feminization of Mexican immigration over the last two decades, the monumentality of the challenge becomes even more pressing (Cornelius, 1999).

The racialization of Latinos as nonwhites has also been a significant barrier to upward mobility for some. Latin American societies have long been extremely color-conscious, recognizing fine gradations of mixture between Africans, Europeans, and Indians. In the United States these complex racial classifications have been reduced to three categories – black, white, and nonwhite – based primarily on visual assessments of a person's color. Take Cubans for example. Many of those in the middle-class easily pass for white in the United States and blend into the dominant population without notice. But those who are dark, who in Cuba would not be considered black, are so judged in the United States and suffer all the consequences. No one color or phenotype characterizes Mexicans and Puerto Ricans. Immigrants of Indian origin from the Mexican states of Oaxaca and Yucatan are very dark. Most Mexican *mestizos* run the gamut of color. A few can pass as white in the United States. The majority cannot, and have been racialized as nonwhite, suffering the disabilities such an assessment brings: lower wages, occupational segregation, fewer educational opportunities, racial profiling by the authorities, and residential segregation (Arce, Murguía and Frisbie, 1987; Telles and Murguía, 1990).

Sociologists David López and Yen Espiritu have analyzed the structural and cultural forces that account for the development of panethnic identities such as Latino and argue that they emerge when members of different nationalities share a common structural relationship to race, class, generation and geography. If subethnicities "look alike" to dominant outsiders and are the targets of racial discrimination, panethnic solidarity is likely to develop. A shared class position, a high level of residential proximity, and several generations of residence in the United States has often led marginalized ethnic/national groups to enhance their power through ethnic alliances. Cultural factors, such as common language and religion, are also important but not determinative (López and Espiritu, 1990).

While recognizing that Latino identity has, on occasion, played an important political role, such as that described in Chicago by Felix Padilla (Padilla, 1985), López and Espiritu do not believe that it will ever be a structurally significant identity because of the racial, class, and generational diversity it subsumes. Sixty percent of all Mexicans are geographically concentrated in California and the Southwest. The majority of Puerto Ricans on the mainland live in New York and New Jersey. Cubans reside primarily in South Florida. Each group has different political priorities, histories, memories, and objective class interests not easily abandoned in the name of Latino identity goals (López and Espiritu, 1990).

A common language (Spanish) and religion (Catholicism) certainly create strong affective ties at the cultural level among Latinos, argue López and Espiritu. But these are not structurally significant. For if one looks at the popular manifestations of Latino identity in the United States today, they are primarily at the cultural level of consumption: shared language, religion, literature, and music. Cuban American Gloria Estefan sings in her popular 1993 song *Hablemos el mismo idoma* (Let's Speak the Same Language), that "Latinos" must put aside their differences, stand united, speak their shared Spanish language, proud of being Latinos, regardless of national origin. *Newsweek*'s "Latino USA." issue, while suspicious of the political implications of the rising demographic numbers (Hispanophobia), did celebrate rising Latino cultural influence (Hispanophilia) in the music of Ricki Martin, Marc Anthony, Junot Diaz, Shakira, the popularity of boxing champion Oscar de la Hoya and baseball player Alex Rodriguez, and in the sexiness of Latino media stars.

One finds in the academy a similar cultural celebration of Latinos for their cultural hybridity and diasporic past. Code switching back and forth between English and Spanish, as bilingual Puerto Ricans often do in their speech, New Yorican poet Tato Laviera writes about his island's tortured history, neither state nor colony, a dependent commonwealth of the United States, with a long history of exploitation by colonial rivals (Laviera, 1985). Laviera insists that America has become AmeRíca, and by Latinizing, accentuating, and syncopating the word America, he draws our attention to AmeRíca's hybridity, to its heterogeneity, and to its profound history of miscegenation. AmeRíca is complex. AmeRíca is centerless. No existing notion of Americanness can possibly contain the cultural changes wrought in the United States by Latino by immigrants since 1965, Laviera tells us.

Performance artist Guillermo Gómez-Peña makes a similar point when he asks us to imagine a new cartography of American possibilities in *The New World Border: Prophecies, Poems & Loqueras for the End of the Century*. A modernist map of America with hermetically sealed borders does not square with reality. One needs "a more complex system of overlapping, interlocking, and overlaid maps," he explains, which acknowledge intercultural translators, political tricksters, nomadic chroniclers, members of multiple communities who "trespass, bridge, interconnect, reinterpret, remap, and redefine" (Gómez-Peña, 1996: 169: 6, 12). In her highly influential book, *Borderlands/La Frontera: The New Mestiza*, Gloria Anzaldúa argues that people living along the US–Mexico border have developed a *mestizo* consciousness that allows them to inhabit multiple cultures simultaneously. "Cradled in one culture, sandwiched between two cultures, straddling all three cultures and their value systems, *la mestiza* [the hybrid woman] undergoes a struggle of flesh, a struggle of border, an inner war . . . a cultural collision" that exists not only spatially but metaphorically as well (Anzaldúa, 1987: 78, 194).

The works of Laviera, Gómez-Peña, and Anzaldúa prod us to reexamine modernist assumptions about the unity of nation-states, the coherence of national languages, the consistency of communities, and the complexity of personal subjectivities. From such a vantage point the border becomes a liminal zone, a space of cultural hybridity and transculturation, where peoples, cultures, and ideas circulate in complicated ways, mirroring the very logic of the new global economy, and thus defying the linearity by which Herbert Bolton and Border Studies scholars understood space and culture.

Anthropologist Roger Rouse splendidly elaborates this new cultural geography by studying the transnational migration circuit from the Mexican township of Aguililla, Michoacán, to Redwood City, California. Rouse shows how Mexican laborers, though separated from their natal community by thousands of miles, remain active participants in the economic, political, and cultural life of Aguililla, through telephone links, remittances, and information obtained from travelers. Mexicans working in Redwood City struggled to get permanent resident status in the US as Mexican citizens so that they could go back and forth across the border, have their children educated in Mexico, thereby acquiring the bilingual and bicultural skills necessary to operate successfully in both countries. Rouse notes that just as the movement of labor defies simple border dichotomies, so too do the enterprises that employ Mexican labor in the United States. The owners do not belong to a single national community, do not speak a single national language, and owe no particular nation-state more allegiance than any other. They are truly global capitalists, just as the migrants are cosmopolitan internationalists (Rouse, 1991).

Indeed, much of the new cultural studies scholarship follows Rouse's lead, complicating our understanding of the circulation of people, money and ideas in ways that defy the simplistic dualities that structured Bolton's imaginary Spanish Borderlands and the iconic fence that so informed the organizational principles of Border Studies (Aparicio and Chávez-Silverman, 1997; Goldman, 1994; Gómez-Peña, 2000; Lipsitz, 1986, 1994, 1998; Saldívar, 1997). As scholars and activists imagine alternative futures for Latinos, clearly income inequality, working poverty, the feminization of the immigrant work force, and residential segregation remain the most pressing issues of the day (Browne, 1999; Hondagneu-Sotelo, 2001; Lamphere et al., 1993). These are the themes that help explain the second-class citizenship that most Latinos experience in the United States, be they *mexicanos*, Mexican Americans, Chicanos, Puerto Ricans or Peruvians. The recent study of inequality in Los Angeles headed by sociologist Lawrence D. Bobo is exemplary. *Prismatic Metropolis* is the first benchmark work to compare wage differentials, residential and occupational segregation, and racial discrimination among blacks, whites, Asians, and Latinos in Los Angeles (Bobo et al., 2000). This type of comparative empirical work is a wonderful antidote to the ethnic exceptionalist arguments that so colored past scholarship.

Exciting new scholarship is being produced on the historical racialization of ethnic Mexicans and other Latinos as non-whites (Foley, 1997, 1998; Haney López, 1998; Hurtado, 1996; Martinez, 1997; Rodríguez, 2000), their experiences of miscegenation (Moran, 2001), and the changing nature of assimilation among the second and third generation immigrants (Portes, 1996; Portes and Rumbaut, 2001). Rising anti-immigrant sentiment in the United States has resulted in important studies on this theme (Chavez, 2001; Perea, 1997), the politics of anti-immigrant initiatives in California (Chávez, 1998), and a broader understandings of formal and cultural forms of citizenship (Flores and Benmayor, 1997; Torres, Mirón and Inda, 1999). These then are the themes that are at the cutting edge of the study of Hispanics and Latinos in the United States. They are recurring themes that were as salient in the nineteenth century as they are today.

REFERENCES

Acuña, Rodolfo: *Occupied America: The Chicanos Struggle Toward Liberation*, 2nd ed. (San Francisco: Canfield, 1972).

Acuña, Rodolfo: *Occupied America: A History of Chicanos*. New York: Harper and Row, 1981).

Alarcón, Norma: "Chicana's Feminist Literature: A Re-Vision through Malintzin or La Malinche; Putting Flesh Back on the Object." In Cherrie Moraga and Gloria Anzaldúa (eds.): *This Bridge Called My Back: Writings by Radical Women of Color* (New York: Kitchen Table, Women of Color Press, 1983).

Almaguer, Tomás: "Toward the Study of Chicano Colonialism." *Aztlán* 2, 1 (1971), 7–21.

Almaguer, Tomás: "Historical Notes on Chicano Oppression: The Dialectics of Racial and Class Domination in North America." *Aztlán* 5, 1–2 (1974), 27–56.

Almaguer, Tomás: "Class, Race, and Chicano Oppression." *Socialist Revolution* 25 (1975), 71–99.

Almaguer, Tomás: "Ideological Distortions in Recent Chicano Historiography." *Aztlán* 18, 1 (1989), 7–27.

Anzaldúa, Gloria: *Borderlands/La Frontera: The New Mestiza* (San Francisco: Aunt Lute Books, 1987).

Aparicio, Frances R. and Susana Chávez-Silverman (eds.): *Tropicalizations: Transcultural Representations of Latinidad* (Hanover, NH: University Press of New England, 1997).

Arce, Carlos H., Edward Murguía, and W. Parker Frisbie: "Phenotype and Life Chances Among Chicanos." *Hispanic Journal of Behavioral Sciences* 9, 1 (1987), 19–32.

Arroyo, Luis: "Notes on Past, Present and Future Directions of Chicano Labor Studies." *Aztlán* 6, 2 (1975), 137–50.

Auster, Lawrence: *The Path to National Suicide: An Essay on Immigration and Multiculturalism* (Monterey, VA: American Immigration Control Foundation, 1990).

Balderrama, Francisco: *In Defense of La Raza: The Los Angeles Mexican Consulate and the Mexican Community, 1929–1936* (Tucson: University of Arizona Press, 1982).

Bamford, E. F.: "The Mexican Casual Problem in the Southwest." *Journal of Applied Sociology* 8 (1923), 364–71.

Barrera, Mario: *Race and Class in the Southwest: A Theory of Racial Inequality*. (Notre Dame, IN: Notre Dame University Press, 1979.)

Barrera, Mario, Carlos Muñoz, and Carlos Ornelas: "The Barrio as Internal Colony." *Urban Affairs Annual Reviews* 6 (1972), 465–98.

Blauner, Robert: "Internal Colonialism and Ghetto Revolt." *Social Problems* 16, 4 (1969), 393–408.

Blauner, Robert: *Racial Oppression in America* (New York: Harper and Row, 1972).

Blue Cloud, Peter: *Alcatraz Is Not an Island* (Berkeley: Wingbow Press, 1972).

Bobo, Lawrence D., Melvin L. Oliver, James H. Johnson, Jr., and Abel Valenzuela, Jr. (eds.): *Prismatic Metropolis: Inequality in Los Angeles*. (New York: Russell Sage Foundation, 2000).

Bolton, Herbert Eugene: "Spanish Records at San Antonio." *Texas State Historical Association Quarterly* 10 (April 1907), 297–307.

Bolton, Herbert Eugene: "Records of the Mission of Nuestra Señora del Refugio." *Texas State Historical Association Quarterly* 14 (October 1910), 164–66.

Bolton, Herbert Eugene: *Need for the Publication of a Comprehensive Body of Documents Relating to the History of the Spanish Activities within the Present Limits of the United States*. Bolton Papers: (Bancroft Library, University of California, Berkeley, 1911).

Bolton, Herbert Eugene: *Guide to Materials for the History of the United States in the Principal Archives of Mexico* (Washington, DC: Carnegie Institution of Washington, 1913).

Bolton, Herbert Eugene: "The Mission as a Frontier Institution in the Spanish-American Colonies." *American Historical Review* 23 (October 1917), 42–61.

Bolton, Herbert Eugene: *The Spanish Borderlands: A Chronicle of Old Florida and the Southwest* (New Haven, CT.: Yale University Press, 1921.)

Bolton, Herbert Eugene: "Defensive Spanish Expansion and the Significance of the Borderlands." In James Field Willard and Colin Brummitt Goodykoontz (eds.) *The Trans-Mississippi West: Papers Read at a Conference Held at the University of Colorado, June 18–June 21, 1929* (Boulder: University of Colorado Press, 1930).

Bolton, Herbert Eugene: *The Northward Movement in New Spain* (Berkeley: University of California Press, 1946).

Borjas, George J.: *Friends or Strangers: The Impact of Immigration on the U.S. Economy* (New York: Basic Books, 1990).

Brimelow, Peter: *Alien Nation: Common Sense about America's Immigration Disaster* (New York: Random House, 1995).

Browne, Irene (ed.): *Latinas and African American Women at Work: Race, Gender, and Economic Inequality* (New York: Russell Sage Foundation, 1999).

Camarillo, Albert M. *Chicanos in a Changing Society: From Mexican Pueblos to American Barrios in Santa Barbara and Southern California, 1848–1930* (Cambridge, MA: Harvard University Press, 1979).

Cardenas, Gilberto: "Undocumented Immigrant Women in the Houston Labor Force." *California Sociologist* 5, 2 (1982), 98–118.

Cardenas, Gilberto and Estevan Flores: *The Migration and Settlement of Undocumented Women* (Austin: Mexican American Studies Center Publications, 1986).

Carreras de Velasco, Mercedes: *Los Mexicanos que devolvio la crisis, 1929–1932* (Mexico City: Secretaría de Relaciones Exteriores, 1974).

Chávez, Lydia: *The Color Bind: California's Battle to End Affirmative Action* (Berkeley: University of California Press, 1998).

Chavez, Leo R.: *Covering Immigration: Popular Images and the Politics of the Nation* (Berkeley: University of California Press, 2001).

Clark, Victor S.: "Mexican Labor in the United States." *United States Bureau of Labor Bulletin* 78 (1908), 450–503.

Cook, Sherburne F.: "Population Trends Among the California Mission Indians." *Ibero-Americana* 17 (1940), 1–48.

Cook, Sherburne F.: "The Mechanism and Extent of Dietary Adaptation Among Certain Groups of California and Nevada Indians." *Ibero-Americana* 18 (1941), 1–59.

Cook, Sherburne F.: "The Indian versus the Spanish Mission." *Ibero-Americana* 21 (1943a), 1–194.

Cook, Sherburne F.: "The Physical and Demographic Reaction of the Nonmission Indians in Colonial and Provincial California." *Ibero-Americana* 22 (1943b), 155.

Cook, Sherburne F.: *The Conflict Between the California Indian and White Civilization* (Berkeley: University of California Press, 1976).

Cooney, R. S.: "Changing Labor Force Participation of Mexican-American Wives: A Comparison with Anglos and Blacks." *Social Science Quarterly* 56 (1975), 252–61.

Cornelius, Wayne A.: "Trends in Mexican Migration to California: Implications for Politics and Research in the 21st Century." Unpublished paper (1999).

Cravey, Altha J.: *Women and Work in Mexico's Maquiladoras.* Lanham, MD: Rowman & Littlefield Publishers, 1998.

de Baca, Vincent Z. C.: "Moral Renovation of the Californias: Tijuana's political and economic role in American–Mexican Relations, 1920–1935." University of California, San Diego, 1991.

Del Castillo, Adelaida. "Malintzin Tenepal: A Preliminary Look into a New Perspective." In

Rosaura Sánchez (ed.) *Essays on La Mujer* (Los Angeles: UCLA Chicano Studies Research Center Publications, 1977).

de León, Arnoldo: *The Tejano Community, 1836–1900* (Albuquerque: University of New Mexico Press, 1982).

Deloria, Vine, Jr.: *Custer Died for Your Sins: An Indian Manifesto* (New York: Macmillan, 1969).

Deloria, Vine, Jr.: *We Talk, You Listen: New Tribes, New Turf* (New York: Macmillan, 1970).

Fergusson, Erna: *New Mexico: A Pageant of Three Peoples* (New York: Knopf, 1964).

Fernández-Kelly, Maráa Patricia. *For We Are Sold, I And My People: Women and Industry in Mexico's Frontier* (Albany: State University of New York Press, 1983).

Flores, William and Rena Benmayor (eds.) *Latino Cultural Citizenship: Claiming Identity, Space, and Rights.* Boston: Beacon, 1997.

Foley, Neil: *The White Scourge: Mexicans, Blacks, and Poor Whites in Texas Cotton Culture* (Berkeley: University of California Press, 1997).

Foley, Neil: "Becoming Hispanic: Mexican Americans and the Faustian Pact with Whiteness." In Neil Foley (ed.) *Reflexiones 1997: New Directions in Mexican American Studies* (Austin: Center for Mexican American Studies Books, 1998).

Foley, Neil: "Partly Colored or Other White: Mexican Americans and Their Problem with the Color Line." Unpublished paper presented at the Organization of American Historians annual meeting *in St Louis* (2000).

Forbes, Jack D.: *Apache, Navaho and Spaniard* (Norman: University of Oklahoma Press, 1960).

Forbes, Jack D.: *Warriors of the Colorado* (Norman: University of Oklahoma Press, 1965).

Gamio, Manuel: *Mexican Immigration to the United States: A Study of Human Migration and Adjustment* (Chicago: University of Chicago Press, 1930).

García, Mario T.: *Desert Immigrants: The Mexicans of El Paso, 1880–1920* (New Haven, CT: Yale University Press, 1981).

Garis, Roy L.: *Mexican Immigration: A Report by Roy L. Garis for the Information of the Members of Congress* (United States House of Representatives, 1930).

Goldman, Shifra M.: *Dimensions of the Americas: Art and Social Change in Latin America and the United States* (Chicago: University of Chicago Press, 1994).

Gómez-Peña, Guillermo: *The New World Border: Prophecies, Poems & Loqueras for the End of the Century* (San Francisco: City Lights, 1996).

Gómez-Peña, Guillermo: *Dangerous Border Crossers* (New York: Routledge, 2000).

Gómez-Quiñones, Juan: "The First Steps: Chicano Labor Conflict and Organizing 1900–1920." *Aztlán* 3, 1 (1972), 13–50.

Gómez-Quiñones, Juan: "Piedras contra la luna, México en Aztlán y Aztlán en México: Chicano–Mexican Relations in the Mexican Consulates, 1900–1920." In *Contemporary Mexico: Papers of the IV International Congress of Mexican History in Mexico City* (El Colegio de México 1975).

Gómez-Quiñones, Juan: "On Culture." *Revista Chicano-Riqueña* 5, 2 (1977), 35–53.

Gómez-Quiñones, Juan: *Development of the Mexican Working Class North of the Rio Bravo: Work and Culture among Laborers and Artisans, 1600–1900* (Los Angeles: UCLA Chicano Studies Research Center Publications, 1982).

Gómez-Quiñones, Juan: *Chicano Politics: Reality and Promise, 1940–1990* (Albuquerque: University of New Mexico Press, 1990).

Gonzalez, Nancie H.: *The Spanish-Americans of New Mexico: A Heritage of Pride* (Albuquerque: University of New Mexico Press, 1969).

Gonzales, Phillip B: *Forced Sacrifice as Ethnic Protest: The Hispano Cause in New Mexico and the Racial Attitude Confrontation of 1933* (New York: Peter Lang, 2001).

Griswold del Castillo, Richard: *The Los Angeles Barrio, 1850–1890: A Social History* (Berkeley: University of California Press, 1979).

Gutierrez, David G.: "Ethnicity, Ideology, and Political Development: Mexican Immigration as a Political Issue in the Chicano Community, 1910–1977." (PhD dissertation: Stanford University, 1988).

Gutierrez, David G.: *Walls and Mirrors: Mexican Americans, Mexican Immigrants, and the Politics of Ethnicity* (Berkeley: University of California Press, 1995).

Gutiérrez, Ramón A.: "Unraveling America's Hispanic Past: Internal Stratification and Class Boundaries." *Aztlán* 17 (1986), 70–101.

Gutiérrez, Ramón A.: "Changing Ethnic and Class Boundaries in America's Hispanic past." In Sucheng Chan (ed.) *Social and Gender Boundaries in the United Sates* (Lewiston, NY: Edwin Mellen Press, 1989).

Gutman, Mathew C.: *The Meanings of Macho: Being a Man in Mexico City* (Berkeley: University of California Press, 1996).

Hancock García, Velia: "La Chicana: Chicana Movement and Women's Lib." *Chicano Studies Newsletter* (February–March 1971).

Haney López, Ian F.: "Race and Erasure: The Salience of Race to Latinos/as." In Richard Delgado and Jean Stefancic (eds.) *The Latino/a Condition: A Critical Reader* (New York: New York University Press, 1998).

Hayes-Bautista, David E.: "Mexicans in Southern California: Societal Enrichment or Wasted Opportunity?" In Abraham F. Lowenthal and Katrina Burgess (eds.) *The California-Mexico Connection* (Stanford: Stanford University Press, 1993).

Hernandez, Philip A.: *The Other North Americans: The American Image of Mexico and Mexicans, 1550–1850* (PhD dissertation: University of California, Berkeley, 1974).

Herrnstein, Richard J. and Charles Murray: *The Bell Curve: Intelligence and Class Structure in American Life* (New York: Free Press, 1994).

HispanicBusiness: "Emerging Wealth: The Hispanic Business Rich List." *Hispanic Business* (1996) 18.

Hondagneu-Sotelo, Pierrette: *Gendered Transitions: Mexican Experience of Immigration* (Berkeley: University of California Press, 1994).

Hondagneu-Sotelo, Pierrette: *Doméstica: Immigrant Workers Cleaning and Caring in the Shadows of Affluence* (Berkeley: University of California Press, 2001).

Hurtado, Aida: *The Color of Privilege: Three Blasphemies on Race and Feminism* (Ann Arbor: University of Michigan Press, 1996).

Jenks, J. W. and W. J. Lauck: *The Immigrant Problem: A Study of American Immigration Conditions and Needs* (New York: Funk and Wagnalls, 1971).

Kossoudji, S. A. and S. I. Ranney: "The Labor Market Experience of Female Immigrants: The Case of Temporary Mexican Migration to the United States." *International Migration Review* 18, 3 (1984), 1120–43.

Lamm, Richard D. and Gary Imhoff: *The Immigration Time Bomb: The Fragmenting of America* (New York: Truman Talley Books, 1985).

Lamphere, Louise, Patricia Zavella, Felipe Gonzales, and Peter B. Evans (eds.) *Sunbelt Working Mothers: Reconciling Family and Factory* (Ithaca: Cornell University Press, 1993).

Larmer, Brook: "Latin U.S.A." *Newsweek* 134, 2 (1999).

Laviera, Tato: *AmeRícan* (Houston: Arte Público Press, 1985).

Lipsitz, George: "Cruising Around the Historical Bloc: Postmodernism and Popular Music in East Los Angeles." *Cultural Critique* 5 (1986), 157–77.

Lipsitz, George: *Dangerous Crossroads: Popular Music, Postmodernism, and the Poetics of Place* (New York: Verso, 1994).

Lipsitz, George: "Their America and Ours: Intercultural Communication in the Context of 'Our America'." In Jeffrey Belnap and Raúl Fernández (eds.) *José Martí's "Our*

America": From National to Hemispheric Cultural Studies (Durham: Duke University Press, 1998).

Longauex y Vásquez, Enriqueta: "The Mexican-American Woman." In Robin Morgan (ed.) *Sisterhood is Powerful* (New York: Random House, 1970).

López, David and Yen Espiritu: "Panethnicity in the United States: A Theoretical Framework." *Ethnic and Racial Studies* 13, 2 (1990), 198–224.

López, Elias, Enrique Ramirez, and Refugio I. Rochin: *Latinos and Economic Development in California*, CRB-99-008 (California Research Bureau, 1999).

Martinez, George A.: "The Legal Construction of Race: Mexican Americans and Whiteness." *Harvard Latino Law Review* (1997).

Martinez, John: *Mexican Emigration to the United States* (San Francisco: R&E Research Associates, 1972).

Massey, D., R. Alarcón, J. Durand, and H. González. *Return to Aztlán: the Social Process of International Migration from Western Mexico* (Berkeley: University of California Press, 1987).

McWilliams, Carey: *Factories in the Field* (Santa Barbara, CA.: Peregrine, 1971).

Meier, Matt S. and Feliciano Rivera: *The Chicanos: A History of Mexican Americans* (NewYork: Hill and Wang, 1972). Melendez, Edwin: "Understanding Latino Poverty." *Sage Relations Abstracts* 18, 2 (1993).

Messinger Cypess, Sandra: *La Malinche in Mexican Literature: From History to Myth* (Austin: University of Texas Press, 1991).

Miller, Beth (ed.): *Women in Hispanic Literature: Icons and Fallen Idols* (Berkeley: University of California Press, 1983).

Mirandé, Alfredo: *Hombres y Machos: Masculinity and Latino Culture* (Boulder: Westview Press, 1997).

Mirandé, Alfredo and Evangelina Enriquez: *La Chicana: The Mexican-American Woman* (Chicago: University of Chicago Press, 1979).

Moore, Joan and Harry Pachón: *Hispanics in the United States*. Englewood Cliffs, NJ: Prentice-Hall, 1985.

Moore, Joan W.: "Colonialism: The Case of the Mexican Americans." *Social Problems* 17, 4 (1970), 463–72.

Moran, Rachel F.: *Interracial Intimacy: The Regulation of Race and Romance*. Chicago: University of Chicago Press, 2001.

Muñoz, Carlos: *Youth, Identity, Power: The Chicano Movement* (New York: Verso, 1989).

Oboler, Suzanne: *Ethnic Labels, Latino Lives* (Minneapolis: University of Minnesota Press, 1995).

Padilla, Felix M.: *Latino Ethnic Consciousness* (Notre Dame: University of Notre Dame Press, 1985).

Paredes, Américo: "The Problem of Identity in a Changing Culture: Popular Expressions of Culture Conflict Along the Lower Rio Grande Border." In Stanley R. Ross (ed.) *Views across the Border: The United States and Mexico* (Albuquerque: University of New Mexico Press, 1978).

Pastor, Manuel, Jr.: "Economic Inequality, Latino Poverty and the Civil Unrest in Los Angeles." *Economic Development Quarterly* 9, 3 (1995).

Pastor, Manuel, Jr.: "The California Economy: Servant or Master?" In David López (ed.) *Latino Inequality: California's Challenge* (Berkeley: California Policy Seminar, 2000).

Perea, Juan F. (ed.): *Immigrants Out: The New Nativism and the Anti-Immigrant Impulse in the United States* (New York: New York University Press, 1997).

Phillips, Rachel: "Marina/Malinche: Masks and Shadows." In Beth Miller (ed.) *Women in Hispanic Literature: Icons and Fallen Idols* (Berkeley: University of California Press, 1983).

Portes, Alejandro (ed.): *The New Second Generation* (New York: Russell Sage Foundation, 1996).

Portes, Alejandro and Rubén G. Rumbaut: *Legacies: The Story of the Immigrant Second Generation* (Berkeley: University of California Press, 2001).

Reisler, Marc: *By the Sweat of Their Brow: Mexican Immigrant Labor in the United States* (Westport, CT: Greenwood Press, 1976).

Rodarte, Irene: "Machismo vs. Revolution." In Dorinda Moreno (ed.) *La mujer en pie de lucha* (Mexico City: Espina del Norte Publications, 1973).

Rodríguez, Clara A.: *Changing Race: Latinos, the Census, and the History of Ethnicity in the United States* (New York: New York University Press, 2000).

Romero, Mary: *Maid in the U.S.A* (New York: Routledge, 1992).

Romo, Ricardo: *East Los Angeles: The History of a Barrio* (Austin: University of Texas Press, 1983).

Rouse, Roger: "Mexican Migration and the Social Space of Postmodernism." *Diaspora* 1, 1 (1991), 8–23.

Ruiz, Vicki L.: *Cannery Women, Cannery Lives: Mexican Women, Unionization, and the California Food Packing Industry, 1930–1950* (Albuquerque: University of New Mexico Press, 1987).

Ruiz, Vicki L. and Susan Tiano: *Women on the U.S.–Mexico Border: Responses to Change* (Boston: Allen and Unwin, 1987).

Saldívar, José David: *Border Matters: Remapping American Cultural Studies* (Berkeley: University of California Press, 1997).

Schlesinger, Arthur, Jr.: *The Disuniting of America* (New York: W. W. Norton, 1992).

Stoddard, Ellwyn R. *U.S.–Mexico Borderlands Studies: An Inventory of Scholars, Appraisal of Funding Resources, and Research Prospects* (El Paso: Univerisyt of Texas at El Paso, Center for Inter-American Studies, 1974).

Stoddard, Ellwyn R. and Richard L. Nostrand (eds.) *Borderlands Sourcebook: A Guide to the Literature on Northern Mexico and the American Southwest* (Norman: University of Oklahoma Press, 1983).

Sweeney, Judith: "Chicana History: A Review of the Literature." In Rosaura Sánchez (ed.) *Essays on La Mujer* (Los Angeles: UCLA Chicano Studies Research Center Publications, 1977).

Telles, Edward A. and Edward Murguía: "Phenotypic Discrimination and Income Differences Among Mexican Americans." *Social Science Quarterly* 71 (1990), 682–96.

Torres, Rodolfo D., Louis F. Mirón, and Jonathan Xavier Inda (eds.) *Race, Identity, and Citizenship: A Reader* (Malden, MA: Blackwell Publishers, 1999).

US Department of Commerce. *Statistical Abstract of the United States, 1999* (Washington, DC: US Government Printing Office, 1999).

Valdes Fallis, Guadalupe: "The Liberated Chicana: A Struggle against Tradition." *Women: A Journal of Liberation* 3, 4 (1974), 20–21.

Valdez, Luis and Stan Steiner (eds.): *Atzlan: An Anthology of Mexican American Literature* (New York: Knopf, 1972).

Vidal, Mirta: *Chicanas Speak Out* (New York: Pathfinder Press, 1971).

Vigil, James Diego: *From Indians to Chicanos: The Dynamics of Mexican American Culture* (St Louis: C.V. Mosby Co., 1980).

Vila, Pablo Sergio: "Everyday Life, Culture, and Identity on the Mexican-American Border: the Ciudad Juárez-El Paso Case." (PhD Thesis, University of Texas, 1994).

Weber, David J.: *The Spanish Frontier in North America* (New Haven: Yale University Press, 1992).

Weber, Devra: *Dark Sweat, White Gold: California Farm Workers, Cotton, and the New Deal* (Berkeley: University of California Press, 1994).

Woll, Allen J.: *The Latin Image in American Film* (Los Angeles: UCLA Latin American Center Publications, 1997).

Zavella, Patricia: *Women's Work and Chicano Families: Cannery Workers of the Santa Clara Valley* (Ithaca: Cornell University Press, 1987).

Zweigenhaft, Richard L. and G. William Domhoff: *Diversity in the Power Elite: Have Women and Minorities Reached the Top?* (New Haven: Yale University Press, 1998).

CHAPTER TWENTY-THREE

City Lights: Urban History in the West

ROBERT O. SELF

Born in Chicago, at the boundary of the West, urban history grew up on the streets of that burgeoning metropolis. The publication in 1925 of *The City* by Robert E. Park and Ernest W. Burgess, which distilled social ecology, economic determinism, and structural geography into an account of the rise of the industrial city, brashly made Chicago the normative American urban place. With its concentric zones of economic functionality, its dense geometric neighborhoods of immigrants, factories, and commerce, its hinterland, and its resume of social problems, Chicago seemed systematically knowable, especially to the University of Chicago sociology department. Graduate students under Park dissected the city for decades and exerted an intellectual and institutional sway now legendary in the academy. Some seventy-five years later, Los Angeles's astonishing rise in the twentieth century as the nation's most conspicuous and controversial metropolis has given urban history another paradigmatic city on western soil. And the Sunbelt's spectacular emergence as a mainspring of American politics, culture, and urban design in the decades since World War II has cemented the West as the archetypal postwar region, its cities prologues to the nation's multicentered metropolitan future. A new generation of urbanists now asserts its own brash claim that Los Angeles embodies American urbanization writ large. The story of western urban history, and historiographical traditions of the urban West, thus lie in a tracking between Chicago and Los Angeles, between the West's most influential city in the nineteenth century and its most influential in the twentieth.

As pivots of western urban history, Chicago and Los Angeles make a strong case for their centrality to national historical narratives. Chicago sutured together the emerging postbellum nation state with its railroads, commodity markets, industrial production, and vast merchandising reach. Its class warfare and immigrant cultural politics, too, stood for the nation as a whole across the turn of the century. Los Angeles has more recently come to stand for the nation. From the city's 1965 riot and rebellion and its suburban politics of property and white privilege to its multi-centered patterns of development and post-1965 immigration, Los Angeles has come to embody the spatial politics increasingly associated with late-twentieth-century capitalist urbanism in the United States. At the same time, however, without Chicago and Los Angeles where would western urban history be? Outside of those cities, there is often little to unite the various studies of the urban West. Furthermore, historians rarely see Chicago history as *western* – unless, as in William Cronon's *Nature's Metropolis* (1991), the hinterland or frontier is at stake – and a still large number of American historians regard Los Angeles as an outlying, not representative, American city, an antipode to what they consider real cities to be. Alternately, Los Angeles is seen as hyper-American and thus divorced from its regional context. In such cross-currents it has been difficult to discern a distinctive western urban history at all. This essay is at once a description of western urbanization, an analysis of key books and authors, and an exhortation to western historians to produce a richer regional urban history, more theoretically provocative, synthetic, and aggressive in its analysis of cities *as* cities.

With the above in mind, I offer this essay in four parts, each corresponding to a major set of interpretive trends within western urban history. Along the way, I intervene in the existing literature and suggest potentially profitable new directions. The first part addresses the long tradition of scholarship on the spatial economy of western cities. The nineteenth-century "instant cities" of booster imaginings gave way, in the telling summarized by this body of work, to the rationalizing efforts of engineers, planners, and other progressives after the turn of the century and eventually to the transformative economic influences of mobilization for World War II and the Cold War. In this extensive literature, economy and space, especially the relationship of cities to distant markets and resources, form the critical axes of interpretation. The second part deals with histories of the urban public. This literature focuses on the boundary between public and private resources and amenities in the process of urbanization as well as contests over the meaning of and inclusions in the "public" itself. In a third tradition of western urban history, scholars have examined the "white republic" and its legacies, beginning with the formation of early *barrios* and *colonias* in the Southwest, through the ghettoization of Chinese in the late nineteenth century, and to the complex racial hierarchies and white supremacy preserved and defended in western cities well into the twentieth century. Finally, western urbanists have increasingly turned their attention to a metropolitan history, a history of the city–suburb relationship in all of its economic, political, racial, and spatial elaborations. Here, historians have joined a long line of geographers and other social scientists who have made understanding the twentieth-century metropolis as a social and political formation their preeminent concern. These categories are intended to be descriptive, not proscriptive – the field needs more innovation not adherence to traditional forms and paradigms.

Freed from both Turnerian shackles and the disciplinary battles waged a decade ago over the New Western History, an emerging generation of historians is positioned to offer a history of cities in the West with fresh perspectives on urbanism, region, citizenship, and nation that will draw attention across fields and disciplines. Instead of seeing western cities as merely abstract entities or the *sites* of the dramatic action, these historians are poised to present "the urban" as a set of relationships and urban history as the study of process. Patterns of human work and residence, capital flow, and property value extend within, across, and around city boundaries, which are themselves social and ideological as well as material. The "solid" parts of cities, their most visible and characteristic features, as geographer David Harvey (1997) reminds us, form the "basis of daily material existence." But cities are not willful and have no subjectivity – they are made. Urbanization is ultimately a relational process, set into motion by capitalism, contested in politics local and national, and constantly transformed through the social dynamics of class, gender, and race. Above all, urbanization is produced through human choices and human politics. The cities we have are the cities our choices have produced. This essay is, in part, an urging to western urbanists to take up the study of those choices.

To do that, we must see western cities in both regional and national contexts. The urban West is inseparable from the region itself. Its cities are embedded in a shared history. Western urbanization was linked to conquest and empire. Western cities have played an enormously important role in extractive economies, as hinterlands of resource exploitation fed urbanization in dramatic cycles in both the nineteenth and twentieth centuries. The federal government shaped cities as it shaped the region, its disproportionate influence in the West a constant feature of urban economic and spatial development. Western urbanization unfolded on a complex national and racial terrain that included Euro-Americans, ethnic Mexicans, Native Americans, Chinese, Japanese, Filipinos, African Americans, and others. Cities in the West, like the region as a whole, have historical and contemporary relationships of great significance with Pacific-rim Asia and the Mexican borderlands. And western cities have been products of wars, hot and cold, and of a regional economy generally weaker in manufacturing than in services, including leisure, tourism, retirement, real estate, transportation, and government. Simultaneously, the urban West is urban America. To act as if western cities can be isolated in a regional exceptionalism is to endorse both a parochialism and a pretension. The western metropolis emerged from and contributed to a national process of urbanization, a national process of city-building – indeed, of colonial conquest and nation-building – stretching from the mid-nineteenth century in an unbroken, if varied and uneven, arc to our own day. From the moment that Euro-American colonizers pushed over the Appalachian Mountains into the Ohio River valley and established urban settlements at Pittsburgh and Cincinnati, and from the moment that Anglo-America replaced the Republic of Mexico (which had replaced Spain) in the urbanizing regions of what became the states of New Mexico, Texas, and California, urban history in the North American West was intimately linked to a national colonial project.

The Spatial Economy of Western Cities

"Economically and culturally," Earl Pomeroy wrote of the West, "the most significant divisions were not state boundaries but the watersheds of urban allegiance and control" (1965: 120). Scholars of western cities have mostly agreed. The significance and reach of cities has been one of the region's defining characteristics. Cites are bounded communities, but urbanization and urban influence cross scales and geographies, making cities the architects of the countryside. Adherents of the Chicago School model of social ecology have typically gazed inward at the structures and competitive relationships of the urban maelstrom, the urban interior. Conflicts over the organization of urban space, social mobility, and the distribution of institutions and services within municipal boundaries have occupied their attention. But the Chicago School also saw the city organizing its periphery, shaping hinterlands from the center. More often than their counterparts studying other regions, western urban historians have borrowed from the latter approach, turning their gaze outward toward the connections between the city and rural hinterlands, between the city and extended networks of power, between the city and the region itself. This has particularly been the case for studies of the nineteenth century, when the West's extractive economy churned at a furious pace, and urban fortunes rose and fell in conjunction with the vicissitudes of an unregulated economy and its cycles of natural resource extraction.

Ironically, this approach owes something to the frontier. It was Richard Wade's effort in the 1950s to reinsert the urban into frontier historical scholarship that led him to conceive of western cities as capital and credit markets, processing centers, and marketing hubs for developing rural areas in the nineteenth century. Other scholars followed, making the city–hinterland model of urban development something of a western specialty. River cities like St Louis on the border of the West, cattle towns on the prairie like Kansas City, port cities like San Francisco on the "Pacific Slope," lumbering cities like Minneapolis and St Paul, the cotton, timber, and ultimately oil city of Houston, and mining cities like Denver in the mountain West all received their due as urbanization writ regional capitalism. The drive to turn land into capital had long been the foundation of the capitalist city, but in the American West that drive reached a fevered pitch in a zero-sum competition over hinterlands and their elusive resources. Western populations have always been more urban than rural, the family farm limited largely to the grassland prairies. The real business of westerners has been city-building. The "instant cities" of the nineteenth-century West, to borrow an expression from Gunther Barth (1975), developed in dependent association with their resource hinterlands. "The history of Los Angeles," Carey McWilliams suggested in an observation equally applicable to dozens of western cities, "is the history of its booms" (1946: 114).

Integral to the hinterland and "instant city" models of nineteenth-century western urban history has been the figure of the urban booster. Cities in the west have been promoted, hawked, and downright lied about on a scale rarely matched elsewhere in the nation. Boosters in cities on the make – Chicago in the mid-nineteenth century, San Francisco in the 1860s, Denver in the 1880s, Seattle in the 1900s, Los Angeles and Oakland in the 1920s – spared little effort in luring the investment capital, industry, and residents necessary to ensure sustained economic development. Western boosters and their allies engaged in what one historian calls "urban imperialism," an endless quest for control of the markets and economic bonanzas that guaranteed real estate profits. Booster scholarship has tended to focus on the art of promotion and to see cities as products less of social construction than of capitalist fantasies. But behind boosters is the most interesting feature of western cities: urban growth as an end in itself, an economic logic fundamental to capitalism, was elevated by western boosters to the level of civic religion. In some cities, for instance, space was rarely scarce but capital was. In places like Los Angeles and later Dallas and Phoenix this led boosters to cultivate real estate markets and encourage an urban morphology that spread development horizontally across vast distances. In other cities, an opposite geography was at work, and a great deal of scarce capital went into creating very expensive space. In Seattle, Portland, and San Francisco immense amounts of capital were devoted to filling tidelands and wetlands that allowed the cities to grow. From the selling of a single plot of land to the retailing of an entire urban concept, boosters in western cities were enormously important to a critical process: attracting the eastern and midwestern capital and migrants necessary for urban survival.

The hinterland, instant cities, and booster literatures, all standards of western urban history, received abundant new life, and substantial rethinking, in William Cronon's study of Chicago (1991). In a book that now claims an astonishing commentary, Cronon cast Chicago in its old role as paradigmatic urban system but told his narrative of urban growth through an exquisite parsing of nature, market, and region. *Nature's Metropolis* does not just turn its gaze outward; the gaze extends all the way to the Pacific. As the center of the "Great West," Chicago shaped an economic and ecological terrain from the Michigan peninsula and Ohio Valley across the prairie and Rockies and beyond the Sierra and Cascades to the port cities of the West Coast. In this vast terrain, "city and country formed a single commercial enterprise" where "to speak of one without the other made little sense" (Cronon, 1991: 47). But Cronon does more than reiterate the urban frontier and hinterland models of western history. Through his rendering of commodity markets, wholesaling, and agricultural production he conveys the "logic of capitalism" that drew city and countryside tightly together and then "concealed the very linkages" on which such markets and other activities were constructed. In the end, Chicago emerges as a grand illusionist that caused the "economic point of production" to grow "ever more remote from the economic point of consumption" (ibid.: 340). In his stitching together of environmental and urban history, Cronon reinserted geography into western studies and provoked a wide-ranging debate over nature, culture, human labor, urbanization, and economic value that has engaged scholars of cities across disciplines. Cronon's argument about Chicago, no matter what its shortcomings, is about the centrality of urban life in understanding a vast area in and beyond the city.

Nature's Metropolis came in for substantial criticism, but together the book and its commentary have cleared fertile ground for future scholarship. Cronon's concern with the regional exploitation of nature and his reliance on neo-Turnerian perspectives led him to obscure other elements of Chicago's development, including industrial class relations, manufacturing, local real estate markets, and international capital. But such oversights translate readily into fresh new avenues of research and theorizing. Chicago is too complex a city to capture in a single narrative, and the paths that Cronon laid out, as well as those he overlooked, deserve following. Historians of the urban West should take regional flows of capital, raw materials, goods, and "first" and "second" nature seriously, and environmental historians should pay more attention to urban markets and the urban underpinnings of the transformation of nature. At the same time, unlike Cronon, urban historians in the West must keep their eyes focused on human exploitation, both in terms of conquest and labor, and must follow capital accumulation as much as capital flow. Western urbanists must learn to act more like geographers in exploring the spatial extension of urbanization across multiple scales – regional, national, and international – and under multiple guises, including transportation, technologies of labor process, energy production, and communication, and the location and development of factories and labor markets. Finally, the regional hinterland conception of western urbanism, largely limited to nineteenth-century historiography, must begin to converse with the twentieth century and its complex production of horizontal metropolitan forms, including intensive residential and industrial suburbanization.

By the end of the nineteenth century, according to the interpretive trend within western history of which *Nature's Metropolis* is the preeminent example, the West was home to a range of cities attached on the one hand to local and regional extractive economies and on the other by transcontinental rail to Chicago and the Northeast. A Pacific Coast tier stretched from Seattle in the north to Los Angeles in the south, dominated by San Francisco, which at the turn of the century had partially escaped dependence on eastern capital, owing to the fabulous wealth generated by the Gold Rush. The queen city of the Pacific, San Francisco had three times the population of its nearest rival, Denver, and exerted extraordinary influence over the vast interior valleys of California, the mining regions of the Sierra, and even the timber country of the Pacific Northwest. Los Angeles would not experience its population explosion until the first decades of the twentieth century and its heaviest industrialization until the mid-twentieth century, when it emerged as the West's dominant metropolis. Denver and Salt Lake City in the Rocky Mountains, Minneapolis on the northern plains, and Houston on the Gulf of Mexico each claimed spheres of influence. Dallas, Kansas City, Portland, Seattle, and Spokane had also developed as substantial population centers and concentrated nodes of economic activity by the turn of the century. Historians emphasize that western cities as a group remained in this period dependent on both eastern capital and extractive resources and bound to subregional hinterlands and markets. But the West's future nonetheless lay in its cities. Already more urban than the nation as whole in 1900, the West would only grow more so, its cities in the twentieth century powerful engines of economic growth and magnets for migrants from across the US and immigrants from Latin America, Asia, and Europe.

Since Gerald Nash (1977) called the urban West an "oasis civilization," historians have been tempted to see the region – with its rugged mountains, massive rural valleys, and vast desert land area in between major cities – through metaphors of urban isolation. Provocative as Nash's concept may be, the West is both more and less than he would have it, and the metaphor leaves us bereft of useful analytical purchase on the region. Nash's West looks like a series of urban oases because he adopts the perspective of an exhausted traveler longing for rest, but this is an inadequate metaphor for understanding the deep interpenetration of urban and rural in western history. One need only consult Richard White's book on the Columbia River (1995) or William Kahrl's on the Owens Valley (1982) to understand that someone standing in a dry creek bed in central Washington state or near Mono Lake in California, not a city in sight, would nonetheless occupy land profoundly shaped by urbanization. Indeed, urban penetration of the countryside has been the thrust of the hinterland scholarship. The West is less than Nash's metaphor implies because, unlike the imagined oasis, western cities have only rarely been fully self-sufficient. The urban West was long dependent on networks of power outside the region, from eastern and international capital to the railroads and the federal government. Visual metaphors for western urbanization like Nash's are often misleading – "sprawl," for instance, is another problematic term – because so much of what matters to urbanization remains invisible. David Harvey's (1997) notion of "urbanization as process" comes closer because it redirects our attention away from the physical manifestations of cities to their underlying relationships. It helps us understand how thirst in the desert can be an artifact of the city.

Hinterlands, boosters, and instant cities have been good to western historians. As Cronon and more recently David Igler (2001) and Matthew Klingle (2001) have shown, these cornerstones of western urban history have retained sharp and compelling interpretive possibilities. But the field also begs for an expanded range of analytical frameworks. Before they were competing cities on the make, for instance, many western urban settlements were imperial outposts or trading centers in the forward national territories of Spain, Mexico, and the United States. Along the Pacific Coast, San Francisco, San Jose, Santa Barbara, Los Angeles, and San Diego formed a network of political, commercial, and religious entrepôts in Spanish and then Mexican territory in the late eighteenth and early nineteenth centuries. So too did Albuquerque, Santa Fe, El Paso, and San Antonio. On the Anglo side, Chicago, St Louis, and Omaha served as trading centers, merchandising hubs, and staging grounds for the United States military occupation of Indian lands further west. All of these cities played some role in the US–Mexican War and in subsequent wars of conquest prosecuted by the US against Indian nations in the decades between the 1840s and 1870s. Western urbanists have left this military terrain almost entirely to scholars of empire and native people, and there has been no systematic study of these early proto-city networks from an urban development standpoint. This is unfortunate, because ties between imperial projects, militarism, and urbanization were important features of transnational regions across the globe, from the US West to Central Europe, South America, and Southeast Asia.

Few urban historians have ventured outside the hinterland, booster, and instant city paradigms to tackle broad questions of western urbanization in regional, national, or international comparative perspective for the nineteenth century. Relationships between cities, patterns of population growth and decline, capital networks between cities (rather than between cities and hinterlands), and relationships between western urban networks and the American Midwest and East, as well as Mexico and Asia, to name only a few topics, remain untouched or concentrated on one or two cities. These broader issues of urban space-economies have been left to geographers and global systems theorists, but the historian's deft touch and empirical orientation remain much needed; we need a transnational history of western cities. Moreover, aside from Carl Abbott (1981, 1993), few western urbanists have asked what may be either uniquely regional or comparatively "American" about western cities. Further research on these questions may very well provide a useful path out of the place-versus-process debate within western historiography, because surely western urbanization, as I have strongly implied here, has been some combination of both a national colonial project and a regional process of development. Cities are embedded in the distinct regional features and history of the west, but they cannot be divorced from national processes of capital mobility, political culture, urban planning, demographic trends, and the like. To take just one twentieth-century example, Pacific Coast cities were sites of "branch plant" industrialization – the expansion of subsidiaries of eastern and midwestern firms to the West to be nearer consumer markets – beginning in the interwar period, a process driven by regional conditions (including cheaper labor, lower taxes, and consumer market growth) as well as national dynamics (mass production of consumer durables and Fordist production strategies).

The historiography of hinterlands and instant cities tends to focus on the nineteenth century. When work does carry the story into the twentieth, it typically marks

World War II as an epochal transition. That World War II and its federally directed wartime economy created the modern urban West has become so familiar a claim to students and scholars of the West that it hardly bears repeating. Therefore, allow me a caveat or a corrective to the rehearsed. The war dramatically accelerated processes already underway in western cities. Industrialization had proceeded on a limited, but still significant, basis on the Pacific Coast, especially in Seattle, San Francisco, Oakland, and Los Angeles. The region had already proved to be attractive to migrants. Depression-era federal spending in the West, along with the federal government's long-standing control of much of the rural West, had established a precedent for state-sponsored development. The fragmentation of cities into multi-centered metropolitan regions, especially in California, had a nearly twenty-year history by the 1940s. The war did not initiate these processes. But it gave them new long-term momentum, a vast infusion of capital and people, and new reach into parts of the interior West and the Southwest. Despite precedents, the West had seen nothing like the federal government's wartime investment. With millions of dollars in military contracts, hundreds of thousands of migrants, and hundreds of new factories, expanded airports, and new suburbs, western cities led the nation in rates of population and industrial growth during the 1940s.

The unprecedented prosperity and economic growth that attended the war, and the centrality of the urban West to wartime production, represented industrialization on a scale the region had never seen. The consolidation of war-related manufacturing power in metropolitan areas like Los Angeles-Long Beach, Seattle-Tacoma, San Francisco-Oakland, and Dallas-Ft Worth reiterated a western pattern: the federal state, not private capital, would spur development. But private capital followed, and the West began to leave behind its dependence on extractive economies and their frustrating elliptical cycles. Moreover, the war brought hundreds of thousands of rural and small-town Americans – a huge proportion, African American and white, from the South – to Pacific Coast cities.Mexican immigration to the Southwest accelerated as well. Following the war, national industry decentralized and patterns of national capital investment and human migration and immigration shifted to the West, prompted by Cold War fears of nuclear attack and the growing clout of congressional delegations from the South and West. In addition, federal tax policy and public works expenditures, particularly on highways and airports, facilitated industrial dispersion to the West. Local and state governments also encouraged capital mobility by recruiting firms with advertisements about their comparative advantages such as low taxes and low wages. These dramatic movements of people and capital to and through the region constituted far more than a brief "gold rush." Rather, they represented new national trends in which western cities would sustain their place as magnets of population growth and investment.

Ironically, the World War II narrative challenges the hinterland–booster–instant cities paradigms, as well as their Chicago School origins, in ways that western urbanists have yet to explore. Can those interpretations of urbanization explain the massive state-led transformation of an entire urban region? In particular, is the urban–hinterland model of urbanization a useful framework in which to understand the emergence of a regional urban military-industrial complex? Or the massive suburbanization of the west after 1945, what one historian has called the "suburban-industrial complex"? Do the differences between nineteenth-century Chicago and post-1945

Los Angeles, for instance, suggest merely their vastly different historical circumstances or do they argue for rethinking how urbanists conceive of cities more fundamentally? These are open questions and they await a rigorous historical treatment, one the so-called LA School of geography and cultural studies has yet to provide.

The Urban Public

In the late nineteenth- and early twentieth-century west, efforts to rationalize the economy and social order brought conflict over the public interest to the core of urban life and politics. Such conflicts were part of national patterns, but they developed a special urgency and ferocity in the West – and ultimately a peculiarly western pattern. Western cities were dependent on outside capital and the ceaseless booster-ism that accompanied competition for economic development. In this context, the quest for reliable sources of water, electricity, transportation, infrastructure investment, and tax revenue generated intense debate over the boundaries between public and private resources. Accompanying these developments, and often related to them, were struggles to define "the public" itself in an increasingly complex urban world marked by gender, class, and racial hierarchies and floods of new immigrants. Each of these dimensions of western urbanization had been present since the 1850s, but between the turn of the century and the World War II they acquired greater signifi-cance, as western urban populations expanded dramatically, as the power of concen-trated capital grew larger, and as reform movements emerged from both middle- and working-class urban communities. Historians of the urban West have developed no single framework for understanding the interpenetrating tendencies of this period and, like their counterparts who study other regions, have engaged in long debates about the meaning of *progressivism*. Still, well-worn paths of inquiry stand out in the scholarship: most follow economic influence and political power and their relation-ship to conceptions of the public.

Few technologies and resources mattered more to western cities than railroads, water, and electricity. Few have attracted more scholarly attention. As the offspring of eastern (and often European) capital and the federal government, railroads bedev-iled western cities. Subsidized by public land giveaways on a massive scale, railroads made possible the spectacular rise of the urban West in the nineteenth century. The same power and reach that delighted boosters, however, provoked reformers and their allies, who opposed the railroads' monopoly rate-setting, vast property-holdings, and their "octopus"-like control over municipal government and state legislatures. The most compelling battles, however, were often those that pitted reformers against reformers. Most famously, San Francisco progressives battled John Muir and his plucky preservationist colleagues over water in the Hetch Hetchy Valley of Yosemite National Park. The city won, secured cheap water from federal land, and eliminated the tricky problem of, in Michael Kazin's words, "essential public resources in private hands" (1987: 189). But even in public hands, western water did not always benefit a broad "public." To secure water for Los Angeles in the first decade of the twen-tieth century, the LA Department of Water and Power destroyed the Owens Valley through deception, collusion with the Bureau of Reclamation, and violence. Average Angelenos benefited, but so did those who amassed fortunes speculating in San Fernando Valley land.

In these battles over the public domain, outcomes were always mixed. The inventive, but often rapacious, engineers and politicians who scrambled for the deals that would bring the cheapest water to their metropolis, often carried out callous theft in the name of progressive objectives. As with water, so too with electric power. A strong public power movement in Seattle successfully created a municipal electrical system by damming one of Washington's most salmon-stocked rivers, along which numerous Northwest Indian tribes still lived and fished. But urban engineers and their political patrons were not their own worst enemy. They encountered massive opposition from far more privilege places. Following Seattle, Denver and Kansas City also developed versions of public utilities. But as other cities went down the path of municipal utility ownership, private companies and their political friends fought back. San Francisco remained beholden to its private power company, and across the West gas, telephones, and urban transportation remained in private hands through the first half of the twentieth century. Urban historians have understood these conflicts as part of a larger western concern: who and what belongs to the public and under what terms? Reformers may have presented the question in bald terms – were cities to be forums for the accumulation of vast wealth in the hands of a few or spaces where citizens could come together to protect a democratic "public" interest? – but the resolutions were hardly so clear cut.

Conflict over railroads, water, and electric power put middle-class reformers in a position to articulate their vision of the public good and the appropriate relationship between urban growth and capitalist markets. Western urban workers shared elements of various middle-class visions, but in the main they imagined a narrative of progress with their own institutions at the center. Key chapters of that narrative unfolded in Seattle and San Francisco, where AFL labor movements demonstrated a proletarian solidarity, inventiveness, and cooperation (and success) rarely seen in eastern and other western cities. As Dana Frank and Michael Kazin have shown, from workers' consumer cooperatives to political parties, laborers in both cities stood at the forefront of attempts to improve the life chances of a broadly conceived urban "producing class" in the period before World War I. They sought to offset the power of capital and to guarantee the "working man" full participation in economic and political affairs. In alliance with other progressives, both trade union movements supported public utilities and won strong labors laws from their state legislatures before seeing their fortunes fall in the business counteroffensive of the 1920s. Attempts to duplicate these successes in Los Angeles called forth one of the nation's most vicious and conspicuously violent rejoinders by private capital that secured an open shop in Southern California and shaped that city's political economy and political culture for decades. These working-class efforts, no less than those emerging from the rapidly expanding western bourgeoisie, had profound consequences for *urban* history – because trade union strength affected municipal politics, patterns of investment, and political culture in far reaching ways.

In the end, these western urban reformers limited the political power of the railroads, produced the nation's strongest public power movement, anchored one of the nation's most inventive and influential labor movements in two of its premier cities, and reengineered western water. However, as William Deverell and Tom Sitton have argued (1994), the early twentieth century in California and the West cannot be reduced to a morality-tale struggle between the powerless and the powerful.

Conflicts, contenders, and resolutions were rarely so neatly delineated. Reformers attacked large concentrations of capital and fought for public ownership of essential urban services and resources, true. But reform activists left a much more mixed legacy. Led by middle-class urban progressives, for instance, westerners nearly destroyed the political party system and called forth a radical experiment in direct democracy with long-term unintended consequences. Determined to expand the public's power through direct primaries, direct legislation, recall, and nonpartisan elections, reformers across the west thoroughly weakened parties and in doing so ironically enhanced the power of the special interests they sought to contain. And they set western urban politics on a course dramatically different from that of eastern and midwestern cities like New York, Chicago, Philadelphia, and Boston. Contests to define the public interest in the early-twentieth-century urban West were often an expression of raw class conflict, but, as Deverell and Sitton have noted, reform efforts were just as often "a weird amalgam of self-defense and selfless reform" with unanticipated consequences (1994: 6).

Western urbanists have devoted significantly less attention to the role of women as a group and gender as a category of power in contests over the urban public. The few studies we have, those by Sarah Deutsch (1987), Peggy Pascoe (1990), and Janis Appier (1998), for instance, demonstrate the enormous potential of joining the study of urbanization to women's history. But few urbanists have followed these examples, even as research on eastern and midwestern cities, including Deutsch's new work on Boston, has produced fascinating studies of prostitution and sex work, gender and policing, leisure and urban consumption, family and labor, women reformers, and low-wage service work, to name only a handful of topics. California, in particular, with its rapid urbanization, industrialization, and in-migration in the first decades of the century would seem an ideal place to investigate the women's complicated relationships to various aspects of urban life. Furthermore, studies of gender more broadly (including masculinity) in the urban West are practically nonexistent, creating a major gap in the field. This is an unfortunate, even unexpected, oversight, given how crucial the "West," both mythic and real, was to constructions of masculinity and gendered forms of cultural power in the first decades of the twentieth century.

The multiple struggles over public and private rights and resources, class power, and the role of large concentrations of capital and the federal state came together powerfully in the rise of organized labor in western cities during the 1930s. Following the interregnum of business ascendancy in the 1920s, the American Federation of Labor (AFL) rebuilt strongholds in major western cities, especially San Francisco, Oakland, Seattle, and even Los Angeles, and in smaller cities closer to the heart of extractive economies. In the middle 1930s, the Congress of Industrial Organizations (CIO) also began organizing in the west. Led by Harry Bridges and the San Francisco-based International Longshoremen's and Warehousemen's Union (ILWU), the California CIO emerged during the depression as a force for class solidarity and limits on the power of employers. Another CIO stalwart, the United Cannery, Agricultural, Packing, and Allied Workers of America (UCAPAWA), organized ethnic Mexican and Filipino cannery workers and was among the few industrial unions consistently to organize women workers. AFL and CIO unions embraced a wide range of ideological and political commitments, and the region as a whole remained dominated by the moderate-to-conservative AFL, but together the two organizations constituted a major corrective to the historic power of employers in the western urban economy. Backed by new federal labor laws under the New Deal state, organized labor formed coalitions with liberals, African Americans, and, though more rarely, ethnic Mexicans in municipal and statewide elections between 1936 and the 1950s in California and Washington. In California, such a coalition erected one of the nation's most comprehensive extensions of the welfare state, including the country's premier open-access college and university system and generous health, labor, and welfare laws. Only their concentration in cities on the Pacific Coast, combined with postwar red scares, kept unions from becoming a broader, region-wide power.

The federal government gave its backing to organized labor in the 1930s, but of comparable long-term importance to western cities and the urban public was Congress's depression-era public works projects, the beginning of more than two decades of federal investment in western infrastructure and industrial capacity. Massive federal building in the *rural* West dwarfed relief efforts in urban centers, but the real benefits to cities were measured in kilowatts, water, and contracts. The Bureau of Reclamation spent the greater part of the 1930s building the Hoover Dam on the Colorado River, the Grand Coulee Dam on the Columbia, and the Central Valley Project on the Shasta in California. These "rivers of empire" made an enormous federal bureaucracy, the Bureau of Reclamation, even more powerful and encouraged the concentration of western agriculture in fewer and fewer corporate hands. On the urban side, however, the dams meant abundant new sources of cheap, federally subsidized electricity that would in subsequent decades feed residential and industrial development in virtually every major metropolitan area in the West. Contracts for dam construction went to major western firms, especially the so-called Six Companies directed by Henry J. Kaiser, which would play an enormous role in western urban development after the 1930s. The kind of public–private economic partnership, anchored by federal bureaucracies, that characterized the West during the Depression would increasingly define development in the region in subsequent years. Always capital poor, the West and its cities had rediscovered an old, if ambivalent partnership with the federal state.

Despite the foregoing, American historians still look east to understand modernity in the first half of the twentieth century. A weird western exceptionalism persists. For definitive studies of the American labor movement, immigration, political reform, landscape architecture, urban planning, first wave feminism, the birth of the New Man and New Woman – in short, for the lengthy list of phenomena that constituted the American metropolis in its myriad forms in the first half of the twentieth century – the profession seems barely to notice the West. Los Angeles may be heralded as the shock city of the *second* half of the century, but between 1920 and 1930 alone its population doubled to well over one million, and by 1945 its industrial capacity made it one of the five most productive cities in the nation. It was not home to the same number of European immigrants as eastern cities, but it was among the most ethnically, racially, and nationally diverse cities in the nation, with large populations of African Americans, ethnic Mexicans, Japanese, Chinese, Filipinos, and enough Southern and Eastern Europeans to dispel the persistent myth that the Euro-American component of the city remained entirely WASP throughout this period. There are few reasons why Los Angeles at midcentury should not attract the same scholarly attention that Chicago famously has. And this is not to mention San

Francisco, Oakland, Denver, and Houston. It is not simply a matter of stating the obvious, that we need more studies of western urban labor, gender, politics, city-building, tax structures, culture, and the state. It is also to note that western cities in this era may have *more* to say about certain aspects of modernity than their eastern counterparts. Western cities, for instance, experienced their greatest development in the twentieth century, after the suburb had already become a major feature of American urbanization; during periods of intensive federal state-building and bureaucratization; in conjunction with eras of widespread political reform; and during the long battle over the urban sociospatial color line. As the next historiographical wave crests, western cities should be in full dialogue with their eastern, southern, and midwestern counterparts on questions of the American modern moment.

This raises the more fundamental question of what urban history is and should be. Most studies of progressivism, public culture, labor, and reform in the West do not explicitly engage urban history. On the other hand, many studies of labor or politics receive honorary inclusion in "urban history" simply because they are located in large cities – Chicago, for instance. Policing the boundaries of subfields is both uninteresting and unnecessary. However, a more lively and engaged western urban history requires that students of the urban public take urbanization as a process more seriously. We know that urbanization – and urban voters, urban workers, urban social problems, urban "vice," etc. – was central to how the national public came to be contested and defined in the decades between the late nineteenth century and World War II, just as suburbanization was central to how that public came to be defined in the decades after the war. Too much historical scholarship takes cities for granted or treats cities as mere locations, when critical urban processes often underlie the topics at hand. This is not a call for an imperial urban history, gobbling up every subfield. It is a call for a more critical and self-aware western urbanism.

The Urban White Republic and Its Legacies

Race was central to how the urban public was defined both before and after World War II. Western cities were born in the age of the "white republic," an era extending from the late nineteenth century through the middle of the twentieth during which a colonial settler mentality and culture held sway among whites. In this context, urbanization in the west was largely a matter of consolidating markets in land, labor, capital, and resources, and restricting access to those markets. Among the most prominent markers of restriction was race. Ideologies of racial hierarchy and cultures of racial superiority were fundamental dimensions of nineteenth-century urbanization. In many cities, Los Angeles, San Francisco, San Antonio, and Tucson for instance, white racial and US national projects were embedded in the process of city-building itself, as imperial nationalism and white/Anglo racial supremacy overlapped and interpenetrated. In others, like Seattle, Portland, and Denver, white racial projects emerged at key moments, often violently, to shape labor markets and patterns of residence. The ghettoization of urbanizing Chinese miners and railroads workers across the West in the 1850s and 1860s, the Alien Land Laws that forbade Japanese ownership of property, and the incorporation of ethnic Mexican *barrios* and *colonias* into expanding Anglo cities at distinct disadvantage, among dozens of other possible examples, represented on a human and community scale the vastly unequal terms on which non-Euro-Americans were incorporated into civic life in western cities. Racial hierarchies, dual labor markets, and a real estate industry determined well before official government red-lining to preserve homogenous white/Anglo districts stacked the deck of most cities against people denied access to the benefits of whiteness.

Western urban history has been immeasurably enriched, if perhaps not yet transformed, by the scholarship on race in the West. Not all of this scholarship has adopted an explicitly urban focus or cast itself as urban history, but the meeting ground of urban and race studies is one of the most fertile and productive within western historiography. It is increasingly impossible for western urbanists to write as if racial hierarchies, white supremacy, and the transnational and transracial character of western communities were or are merely "phenomena" of urban histories. They are much more: embedded in the process of urbanization itself, determining and shaping urban growth, development, markets, residence, morphology, politics, power, and reform. Western urban history was first led in this direction by the internal colonial model of scholarship within Chicano history in the late 1970s, which inspired the first generation of *barrio* studies. These have given way in the intervening decades to an enormous range of theoretical approaches to race in the urban West, many of which – like the emerging literature on transnationalism or recent work on the rise of the New Right in California – promise a conceptual transformation in western urban studies.

In nineteenth-century western cities, the racialized dual labor market met the white republican ideology of "free labor." The mix was potent. Employers self-consciously capitalized on what Ronald Takaki (1989) has called the "yellow proletariat" and Neil Foley (1998) found Texans calling "greasers" and "the little brown man" – a marginalized pool of nonwhite workers that kept labor costs low and hiring and firing flexible. Labor exploitation at the hands of employers and little possibility of advancement meant that these workers and their families lived barely outside of poverty and could afford only second-rate housing on marginal land in and around cities. At the same time, as Alexander Saxton (1971), Tomás Almaguer (1994), and Gary Okihiro have shown, Euro-American workers in the West invested in definitions of whiteness that emphasized free, productive, and manly labor, an ideology of work, masculinity, and color pervasive in the US beginning in the mid nineteenth century. "California is the white man's country," a San Francisco labor newspaper, *Organized Labor*, openly declared in 1907 (quoted in Kazin, 1987: 145). Whenever possible, white Euro-American workers sought to exclude "nonwhites" from the most remunerative employment, apprenticeships, and crafts and from labor unions. Trapped in a dual labor market enforced by both employers and white laborers, workers of color in the West who migrated from rural to urban places found work in the city as onerous and poorly compensated as in agriculture, railroading, and extractive industries. In addition, many of these workers were immigrants who could not vote, giving them no voice in city politics and providing established leaders with little reason to court them. Economic and political marginalization in the urban milieu translated into unreliable and substandard city services, low property values, and no patronage or political favors for *barrios* and for Japanese, Chinese, and later Filipino neighborhoods.

If the dual labor market and the ideology of whiteness embedded in notions of "free labor" were pervasive in the urban west, racial discrimination in practice was nonetheless a variable phenomenon. "One key aspect of the racial formation process in California," Tomás Almaguer has observed, "was the differential racialization of the various cultural groups that settled within this geographic region." These differences have enormous implications for urbanists, because the varied inflections of white supremacy shaped the terms under which ethnic, national, and racial groups were incorporated into and marginalized from urban life and politics. For ethnic Mexicans, to take one instance, legacies of conquest structured urban space into distinct Anglo and "Mexican" or "Spanish" districts, while Anglos stripped Californios and other ethnic Mexicans in the Southwest of hundreds of thousands of acres of land. Tens of thousands of working-class ethnic Mexicans, however, lived in semi-rural *colonias,* communities linked to rural labor markets. Encroaching suburbanization and industrialization enveloped many of these communities in the twentieth century, with new Anglo subdivisions literally surrounding aging and deteriorating *colonias.* In still other cases, expanding cities looked to annex inexpensive *colonia* land in order to clear and redevelop it for industry, a not uncommon process that sent tens of thousands of ethnic Mexicans looking for housing in postwar California. Stephen Pitti's (2003) study of San Jose chronicles this history of ethnic Mexican land occupation and its relationship to Anglo-led economic development.

For Japanese and Chinese immigrants, to take a different instance, land ownership itself was contested by the native white majority. Alien Land Laws and restrictive covenants either denied property ownership outright to immigrants or segregated them in discrete urban neighborhoods. Many of these neighborhoods – the numerous "Chinatowns" across the West the most obvious examples – emerged by the turn of the century as dense urban districts forged in part by the necessity of community self-defense and in part by white-enforced quarantine. In San Francisco, especially, white workers and public health reformers constructed racialized definitions of hygiene, disease, and citizenship that contributed to the balkanization of Chinese residential districts (Shah, 2001). Indeed, a central element of both white working- and middle-class definitions of the public interest and the "producing classes" was the mystification and subjugation of Japanese, Chinese, and Filipino laborers and communities – the consequences of which were the denial of citizenship rights along with labor exploitation and exclusion from most trade unions. These patterns of mystification and subjugation did more than define certain groups *out* of urban public life; they defined the ideological boundaries of whiteness to determine who was allowed *in.*

Emerging western cities disadvantaged those denied access to whiteness, Anglo-ness, citizenship, and English as a first language. But there is much left to know, much left to do. We know less about the opportunities cities offered. Western cities in the nineteenth and early twentieth centuries were, as work by David Montejano (1987), George Sánchez (1993), and Yong Chen (2000) demonstrates, transnational. Both migrants and their earnings traveled between Latin America, Asia, and the urban US West, as did culture. Western urbanization offered jobs, resources, and the possibility of class advancement, however small, in addition to threats, dangers, and marginalization. The "white republic" and the internal colonial model of racial exploitation have exerted an understandably strong hold on western scholarship, but new interpretive frameworks stand ready to offer fresh insights. The recent surge in borderlands scholarship and transnational studies, in particular, promises a set of perspectives on US imperialism, cross-border human and capital migration, urbanization, science, and race that highlights racial and community formation along with overlapping forms of both oppression and liberation. Still other paths remain open. Western historians of a generation ago produced a variety of ethnic, religious, and national community studies among urban Euro-Americans and European immigrants, from the Irish in Butte, Montana (Emmons, 1989), to Italians in San Francisco (Cinel, 1982) and Jewish residents of Portland (Toll, 1982). These have yet to be followed up by studies of racial and ethnic projects across both time and space and by deeper research into whiteness in the urban West. And we still have far too few studies of gender politics and race in the urbanizing nineteenth-century West, where Protestant Victorian womanhood, "manly" laborite working-class culture, Catholic traditions across the class spectrum from both Europe and Mexico, and immigrants from Asia encountered one another in a variety of contexts.

Confined to the "peripheries of power" on the one hand, ethnic Mexicans, various Asian-origin groups, and African Americans in the urban West nonetheless forged dynamic and highly differentiated communities in the first half of the twentieth century. Even as racial hierarchies and the legacies of the white republic drew restrictive boundaries around a normative white/Anglo "public," these communities constructed public cultures of their own in which more than assimilation into the white mainstream was at stake. In their ground-breaking studies of ethnic Mexicans in the west, David Gutiérrez (1995) and George Sánchez (1994) reveal the rich traditions and debates that framed Mexican American urban life. The economic and political dilemmas faced by Mexican Americans were shaped by Anglo racism, but also by internal class differentiation, the Mexican Revolution, immigration, Mexican nationalism and the "new nationalism" among Los Angeles Mexicans, suburbanization, rural-urban migration, and generational divides. All of this played out in the context of a Mexican Great Migration in which more than one million Mexican citizens came to the United States between 1900 and 1930, the vast majority to the West. In Chinese, Japanese, and Filipino American urban communities as well, dynamic political and economic cultures emerged in the first half of the twentieth century. These cultures cannot be reduced solely to reflexive responses to racial marginalization. Recent work by Judy Yung (1995), David Yoo (2000), and Dorothy Fujita Rony (forthcoming) illustrates that transnational migration, gender and familial conflicts and traditions, and economic entrepreneurship, among other influences, gave form to urban Asian communities in the west. There are parallel developments among urban Indians, though a great deal more scholarship is required to understand the experience of Native communities in cities across the west. None of this scholarship on ethnic and national communities in western cities denies the power of racial hierarchies or white racial supremacy. Rather, a new generation of western historians has opened a set of vistas on urban life that illuminates multiple public cultures in constant conversation and interaction, as well as in conflict.

In the middle twentieth century, the politics, activism, and organizing of the West's communities of color and immigrants forced the gradual retreat of the white republic and its most explicit and raw forms of white supremacy. In its place, they forged a version of racial liberalism. But racial subordination remained embedded institutionally – especially in urban housing markets, education, and labor markets – and in more subtle and resistant forms. Moreover, by the 1960s, a new and powerful challenge to racial liberalism had taken hold among whites. This challenge did not take the form, in the main, of a return to claims of white superiority and supremacy. Instead, its adherents adopted rights-based claims that sought to defeat or weaken racial liberalism's objectives – such as fair employment, fair housing, access to citizenship for immigrants, and bilingual education, among others – in the name of putatively "race neutral" or "colorblind" criteria. Both the development of racial liberalism in the West and its subsequent challenge by organizations and movements deploying a rights discourse had enormous consequences for western cities and for urbanization as a process. As new studies by Lisa McGirr (2001) Becky Nicolaides (2002), myself (2003a), Mark Brilliant (forthcoming), Lon Kurashige (2002), and others demonstrate, urban history in the last two-thirds of the twentieth century was inextricably bound up in the struggle of people of color against the white republic, the fight for racial liberalism (and, in myriad forms, nationalism and radicalism), and the challenges posed to the latter.

Among African Americans, the struggle for racial justice in the urban West was neither derivative of the southern black civil rights movement nor a denouement to the fight against southern Jim Crow. It had its own logic, obstacles, and trajectories. Between the 1930s and the late 1960s, African American-led political movements challenged white supremacy in the name of racial liberalism. Local activists targeted liberal mayors and city councils, rallied against urban renewal, challenged workplace discrimination, and fought for incorporation on school boards, city councils, union headquarters, and on social welfare and social service agencies. In particular, a combination of protest politics, grassroots mobilizations, traditional Democratic party-building, and political street theatrics led by groups as diverse as the Brotherhood of Sleeping Car Porters, CORE, the National Welfare Rights Organization, and the Black Panther Party successfully built both a black electoral base and a political leadership class that would reshape city government. At the same time, a new generation of grassroots African American insurgents took to the streets in hundreds of violent uprisings or riots (still greatly understudied by historians) during the "long hot summers" from 1964 to 1968, further undermining confidence in liberalism on both the left and right. In this developing narrative, western cities are understood not as places where civil rights organizing failed, but as places where the postwar black freedom movement took unique forms and trajectories and where African American politics overlapped with the logic of race-inflected urban industrial and postindustrial capitalism.

The black–white civil rights axis was hardly the only, or even the most prominent, focal point of struggle against the legacies of the white republic in the urban West, however. Mexican immigrants and Mexican Americans brought to western cities a complicated range of social protest, political mobilization, and ideologies of liberation. Fair employment and housing were important to ethnic Mexican political organizations like the Community Services Organization (CSO) and the Mexican American Political Association (MAPA), but on a scale of priorities they often came after citizenship and immigration reform, language rights, and the organization of trade unions. Nevertheless, ethnic Mexicans moving from rural-agricultural labor to urban-industrial labor – an extensive process unfolding across most of the twentieth century – dramatically affected patterns of residence and labor markets in both older cities and newer suburbs. We know far too little about the nature of this process.

Isolated studies of places like San Jose and East Los Angeles are of critical impor-
tance, but comparative, region-wide studies are necessary to understand ethnic
Mexican urbanization (including its differences from African American and Asian
American urbanization). The latter is crucial, because Mexican Americans and
Mexican immigrants were the most rapidly urbanizing social group in the second half
of the twentieth century in the West, and ethnic Mexicans now make up between
thirty and fifty percent of many of the West's major cities, including Los Angeles,
Long Beach, Fresno, Bakersfield, Dallas, Houston, San Antonio, Albuquerque, and
Denver, and in a handful are the majority, including El Paso and San Antonio (and
twenty percent in a handful of others, including Oakland, Sacramento, San Diego,
and Phoenix).

Again we might ask whether the scholarship on race in the West may rightly be
called urban history. Some may, but certainly not all. The longer answer leads back
to the Chicago School of urbanism. For all of their racial paternalism and class condescension, Park and his contemporaries nonetheless placed the city itself at the center
of their understanding of race and nation. In their view, the city was important precisely because its cycles of interethnic and ultimately interracial conflict, accommodation, and acculturation produced the modern urban public: a rational, modernized
citizenry with bourgeois WASP values and behavior led by elites. Though the Chicago
School interpretive framework persisted in the academy for decades, scholars have
wisely rejected this "modernization theory" as a basis for studying race, ethnicity,
and nationality. But in throwing out modernization theory, we may well err and
throw out the *urban* with it. Contemporary approaches to race and nation now draw
from a plethora of theoretical orientations – from racial formation scholarship in
sociology, from cultural studies, from neo-Marxist materialism, and liberal multiculturalism, among others. But urban history and the history of race and of racial and
national groups remain intimately linked, neither one fully comprehensible without
the other. Scholarship on the urban West does not in the main reflect this interpenetration, a shortcoming that leaves the door open for new and innovative work.

The Metropolitan West

Increasingly, western urban historiography focuses on metropolitan growth and differentiation: the spatial and political process of multicity development within a single,
continuous *urban* landscape. The subjects of this diverse and broad literature vary:
from urban morphology, planning, industrial location, and housing to politics and
race, but they are united by a concern with the spatial political economy of the
western metropolis. True to their Chicago School origins, historians of the metropolitan West track between urban form and social and political contest, between
spatial patterns and culture. But these historians have also rejected the Chicago
School's functionalism, its faith in predictable geometry, and its urban teleology.
Instead, urbanists like Greg Hise, Becky Nicolaides, Eric Avila, and Phil Ethington
have begun to place Los Angeles at the center of an eclectic new urban history that
is, if you will, decentered. Within geography, a "Los Angeles" school has emerged
at the same time to set a new agenda for critical urban studies. However, scholars
associated with this literature, such as Edward Soja, Allan Scott, and Michael Dear,
have yet to make a convincing historical case for their approach, which has

constrained their influence. Both groups are seeking a metropolitan perspective on urbanism, one that moves beyond fixed binaries – center and periphery, ethnic conflict and assimilation, and industrialization and deindustrialization. Still very much in infancy, both the metropolitan historiography and the broader LA school of critical studies deserve close watching in the next generation. They may in time represent the most dynamic and productive locus of thinking about the urban west.

Since the Depression, western metropolitan areas have shared a great deal with those of the rest of the nation: federal sponsorship of white homeownership and its spur to suburbanization; deindustrialization and the shift to services at the core of the urban economy; and the emergence of new forms of racial segregation. But the western metropolis has also exhibited profound regional characteristics. The so-called urban crisis took distinct forms (or was absent) in the West, suburban city-building emerged earlier than in the rest of the nation as an engine of economic growth, and the New Right was largely a phenomenon of western cities and suburbs prior to its emergence nationwide, to take three prominent examples. The study of the western city as *metropolis*, then, is a useful way to group a wide-ranging urban scholarship. It is now commonplace to talk about the postwar United States in terms of urban decline and crisis. We possess an extensive popular and academic vocabulary to describe the features of post-1945 urban transformation: the racialization and deindustrialization of cities, suburban growth, urban decay, the weakening of unions and working-class consciousness, the increasing mobility of capital, and the rise of a politics focused on private property. But because these processes exhibited profound regional, and even intraregional, variations, western cities have not shared a single postwar history with the nation. Some older cities, such as Portland and Oakland, were struck hard by deindustrialization and capital flight in the 1950s and 1960s. Others, like San Jose, Phoenix, and Dallas, experienced dynamic economic and population booms in those same decades. Still others, such as Long Beach, Sunnyvale, San Diego, and Houston, grew ferociously in tandem with the federal military bases and defense or government contractors located in or near them. No single narrative captures the complexity of postwar urban history in the West, but distinct regional patterns have given western urbanists important guideposts. Western cities were reshaped by massive migrations: the migration of southern blacks and whites to the cities of the Pacific Coast and Texas; the mass movement of whites to suburban places; the migration of people from all regions to California, Texas, and Arizona; the rural-urban and cross-border migrations of ethnic Mexicans; and the post-1965 immigration from Southeast Asia. Accompanying these population shifts was a remapping of American capitalism, as the commerce and manufacturing that drove postwar consumerism grew increasingly mobile. Economic restructuring drained older eastern and midwestern cities of industrial jobs and made emerging western metropolitan corridors the primary engines of postwar employment and economic growth.

How historians write about metropolitanization, suburbanization, and the "multicentered metropolis" matters a great deal. "Sprawl," a favorite of urban design critics in the 1960s, has achieved a kind of popular resonance, but, as Greg Hise has emphasized, it obscures much of the reality of postwar city-building. By the 1930s, if not the 1920s, few planners or city-builders thought of the urban landscape in terms of core and periphery – the "inner city" and "suburbia" enshrined in our contemporary language. Instead, they imagined and built cities where industrial and residential proximity were intentional and complementary design elements. Workers would live, work, shop, and play in a single city. Suburban communities remained connected to their larger neighbors in important ways, but they were not shaped by the "center" as the older logic of the Chicago School imagined. In this process of "suburbanization as urbanization," suburban cities emerged less as oases of middle-class commuters than as mixed-class nodes of development embedded in a larger metropolitan system. Hise and other western urbanists have drawn our attention to postwar greater Los Angeles because it exemplifies a long-term trend in twentieth-century American urbanization – the dispersal of industry and residence across space without a dominant "center." This city-building did not produce the geometric spatial logic that Chicago had embodied at the turn of the century.

Since the appearance more than a decade ago of Kenneth Jackson's seminal work of suburban history (1985), it has become commonplace to understand suburbanization as a consolidated form of consumption, driven by two impulses. The first is the broad, but ideologically erased, subsidizing of the American middle class by the federal government in the post-World War II decades. The second is the privatization of the public sphere in which suburban landscape architecture, detached single-family homes, and property-centered politics conspired to accelerate the erasure of civic culture by the private spaces of the nuclear family, automobile, and shopping mall. Both impulses powerfully shaped the postwar western urban and suburban terrain. Forms of residence (like "lifestyle" communities, retirement complexes, and entire suburban districts), entertainment (from Disneyland to Sea World), and municipal governance all yielded in the postwar decades to various formulas of private design and management. This was a national process, but led by Sunbelt entrepreneurs who invented entire cityscapes from whole cloth and created vast horizontal urban expanses served by little or no public transportation. This large-scale privatization reflected westerners' historic distaste for public institutions, yet continued to mask the ways in which western urban landscapes were shaped by extensive public intervention in the private economy. Military installations, federal military contractors, the interstate highway system, and federal housing policies constituted unprecedented government subsidies for urban and suburban development, unprecedented even in a region long accustomed to reliance on the federal government.

Two postwar trends, regional industrial dispersal and suburbanization, came together powerfully in the rise of the Sunbelt after 1945. Stretching from California across the Southwest to Texas, the Sunbelt experienced decades of rapid population growth and exhibited patterns of urbanization that looked, to observers from other parts of the nation, like suburbanization. Following a distinctly twentieth-century pattern of development, these new metropolitan areas were characterized by highly dispersed, low-density neighborhoods and decentralized commerce and industry. Most Sunbelt cities lacked the densely populated downtowns of older cities; many grew up along interstate highways rather than on the waterways and railways that had shaped nineteenth-century western urbanization. Residence and industry were spread over large territories. Sunbelt cities grew according to a very American form of civic imperialism, annexation. And low property taxes, anti-union right-to-work laws, and cheap land, in addition to federal military-industrial investment, provided the structural basis for a postwar industrial boomlet in many parts of the region. Carl Abbott, the leading western historian of the Sunbelt, has called the "multicentered metropolis" characteristic of this region "a new urban form that had to be judged on its own terms" (1993).

The federal government directly or indirectly underwrote much of the economic and population growth of postwar western cities and suburbs, but private entrepreneurs placed their own indelible stamp on urbanization. In particular, service industries that had been part of western urbanization for decades – leisure, tourism, and retirement especially – became phenomenal poles of growth in the postwar decades. Cities in the Southwest specialized in such service economies, in which deserts begat golf courses, retirement complexes like Sun City, and gateway communities to mountain, river, and canyon tourism. Las Vegas embodied this accelerated economy, as two generations of entrepreneurs produced the nation's most elaborately imagined community in a scratchy desert valley – drawing on heavily subsidized water and electric power. But these new urban inventions were far from alone. San Francisco transformed its once working waterfront and port into a tourist attraction, its downtown into a collection of hotels and convention spaces. Vast sections of Los Angeles and Orange County did the same. And across the West's second and third tiers of cities, postwar urban development shifted local economies from resource extraction to tourism. Entrepreneurs, real estate speculators, and pro-growth political coalitions also built urban economies based on government services, and the FIRE complex (finance, insurance, and real estate), transforming downtowns, warehouse districts, and rail yards into office high rises and networks of white-collar employment in places like Denver, Houston, San Francisco, and Los Angeles.

The dramatic expansion of western cities, however, left the governing metropolitan structures largely intact. Growth did not address the fragmented nature of metropolitan politics and the relative autonomy of local governments. By 1960, the United States had 91,186 local governments. In most parts of the United States, and the West was no exception, localities controlled education, public works, and social services and paid for goods and services through local taxes. Municipal governments also controlled land use through zoning laws and other local regulations. The fragmentation of government reinforced inequalities by race and class. Municipal boundaries determined access to fundamental public goods and services. As population, commerce, and industry fled cities, restructured, and settled in other places, older communities often saw their tax bases diminish, while their suburban counterparts were flush with new tax revenue. The interconnection between local government, property taxes, and public goods created a feedback loop that compounded urban disadvantage. Depopulation and decentralization ravaged urban property tax bases, which in turn lowered the quality of city services and education, which spurred further population loss and capital flight. As a consequence, by the 1960s and 1970s many major western cities teetered on the brink of bankruptcy, while their suburban neighbors prospered. Oakland and Los Angeles nearly went bankrupt in the mid 1970s, while their adjoining suburbs boasted of world-class school districts, lush municipal golf courses, and low demand for social services for the poor and elderly.

The consolidation of postwar consumption in a private physical and cultural geography contributed to a conscious economic and political project of reimagining western American civic space – as the suburban home became the center of national life – and to a major realignment of electoral coalitions and political culture. Western cities pushed American politics in profoundly new directions. In particular, the rise of the New Right originated in the disaffection and political mobilization of a generation of white American metropolitan residents who believed that taxes were too high and that the liberal state had created, not ameliorated, the problems of core cities by catering to the poor. Postwar conservatives mobilized a constituency whose politics were shaped by the rise of a new white middle class whose concerns revolved around private property and the extent to which it could and should be harnessed to the provision of social resources. Animated by what Lisa McGirr (2001) has called "suburban warriors," the postwar right challenged New Deal liberalism, grafting the politics of tax revolt and racial resentment onto older strains of religious and anti-statist conservatism. Western conservatives, based in postwar metropolitan corridors like Los Angeles, Orange, Ventura, Riverside, and Santa Clara counties in California, Maricopa and Pinal counties in Arizona, and Dallas-Ft Worth and the Houston metropolitan areas in Texas, helped to change the face of American politics. By the time that Ronald Reagan took advantage of regional and metropolitan political realignments to win the Presidency in 1980, high taxes, and their symbolic identification with liberal "big government" social programs, had a proven track record as a core conservative issue in the west.

These politics, in keeping with western tradition, underestimated or ignored the extent to which class privilege had been achieved with public subsidy. Among whites, suburbanization was driven by the politics of making markets in property and in maintaining exclusionary access to those markets. The New Deal state's broad embrace of white uplift enabled white homeowners – with Federal Housing Administration (FHA) and Veterans Administration (VA) mortgage guarantees in hand – to erect suburban cities along with high-walled barriers that excluded others based on both class and race. Far from the crucible of republican independence its apologists claimed, postwar suburban housing was among the most state-subsidized features of the postwar western economy. Nonetheless, white homeowners across the West increasingly adopted a political discourse of property rights – one drawn from both western traditions of antistatism and libertarian populism – to rationalize segregation.

Together, these broad shifts in metropolitan political culture and economy redefined the meaning of race and citizenship in the West, as in the nation. Increasingly, in a variety of contexts race came to be defined spatially and embedded in the structural inequalities of urban America, even as the nation as a whole embraced civil rights laws. African Americans had long claimed that full citizenship required economic opportunity not simply civil equality. Postwar urban black political movements, from the Brotherhood of Sleeping Car Porters to the Black Panther Party, continued to articulate this message, albeit with different ideological and strategic accents. Mexican Americans had long asserted that citizenship, language, and labor rights were fundamental to their own full participation in American life. Among whites, a sometimes unspoken, sometimes explicit racial identity and set of privileges coalesced around property rights, taxes, and the spatial exclusion of black people from whole spheres of social and political activity. These developments had roots in older American racial politics that focused on biological and cultural notions of racial hierarchy, but they quickly developed a powerful life of their own in the second half of the twentieth century. Race was coded in the language and structures of metropolitan access, opportunity, and space, rather than in the paranoia of miscegenation or the brutal rhetoric of Jim Crow, anti-Mexican, and cultural inferiority. But the new arrangements proved no less onerous and taxing – on American cities, public and political culture, and individual lives.

The urban West offers a unique perspective on the historiographical paradigm now ascendant in postwar US urban history: the urban crisis. The paradox of western cities has always been that despite the power of racism and the legacies of the white republic, the urban West has been, on the whole, much less segregated than the North and South. Indices of segregation for the postwar decades suggest that San Francisco, Los Angeles, Denver, and Houston have looked more like each other than they have like Detroit, Milwaukee, and Philadelphia (Much more research is required to determine if this is a difference in kind or simply degree, and in any case segregation has remained a fundamental part of western urbanization). The pace and scale of African American and ethnic Mexican suburbanization in many western metropolitan regions, coupled with the early decentralization of industry, make rust-belt models of inner-city segregation less useful than they might seem. Furthermore, because deindustrialization was such an uneven process in the West, the "urban crisis" in places like Los Angeles looked little like that in Detroit – the Alameda Corridor, one of Los Angeles County's principal industrial districts, has never stopped being an engine of job creation. Finally, the biracial model of poverty and ghetto-formation that has dominated studies of the Midwest and Northeast is not broadly applicable across the urban West. Indeed, if the principal victims of the urban crisis in the rust belt were blue-collar African Americans, they were joined in western cities by ethnic Mexicans, Filipinos, and many post-1965 Southeast Asian immigrants, who endured a long, continuous, and difficult adjustment to blue-collar urban labor markets in the postwar period. All of this points in profitable new directions for additional and comparative research on the metropolitan West.

Western urban history has shortcomings that have opened up a research agenda with vast areas of yet untapped subject matter. The most pressing direction for new work lies in the area of gender, culture, and power. The urban West contains far more stories about masculinity, femininity, and queer history than have been written. The great postwar migration of African Americans and white southerners and midwesterners to western cities awaits its historian. This migration, one of the great demographic transformations of the twentieth century – and as important as earlier urban immigrations – remains in the literature largely a macrosocial phenomenon, understood strictly in broad terms. The cultural and social dimensions of white suburban flight also remain poorly documented and understood, even as historians evoke "suburbanization" to explain a variety of phenomena. New work on both types of migration will enrich the field by placing the urban crisis literature in a fresh context, perhaps modifying the crisis paradigm's reliance on violence as a controlling metaphor. Finally, if western urban historians of the first two postwar decades have traced the relationship between political economy and race in the context of the postindustrial city and African American freedom movement, historians of the period after 1965 surely will find a natural epilog in the emerging multiracial global western city. Post-1965 immigration transformed the western American metropolis again, bringing enormous new waves of immigrants from Latin America and Asia who have remapped neighborhoods, commerce, and politics in *both* city and suburb. Likewise, globalization and accompanying reorganizations of capital accumulation on national and transnational scales have brought new stresses and opportunities to the western metropolitan system. Exploring the narratives of these changes must be part of any new research agenda in western urban history.

At the core of western urban history, indeed of all urban history, are questions of economy, space, and power. Cities are shaped by modes of production and structures of accumulation and have long been places of consumption and of the generation of capital and labor. Cities have also given shape to, inspired, and constrained politics, culture, and identities in ways that have far-reaching consequences for our understanding of the region and nation as a whole. Cities are more than mere stages of dramatic action or abstract objects of argument. Cities are far more than containers or empty vessels. Neither are they sets of teleological processes and impersonal structures. Cities are less static containers of action than constitutive historical subjects that act on and through the social and political landscape of the nation. Metaphorically, they work less as stages or containers and more as multidimensional terrains, simultaneously produced by, shaping, and constraining political and economic options and choices. As the historiography of western urban America develops, urban historians must continue to explode artificial boundaries between varieties of history – from labor, planning, and political to cultural, gender, and Mexican American – that are accustomed to telling stories separately. Continuing to push past those boundaries, to reveal the power of place within the landscape of regional history, will enrich and invigorate urban, western, and US history. Western history may have unfolded "under an open sky," but, like the story of Charlie Chaplin's tramp, its dramas, wonders, and relationships, its flesh and blood, its achievements and betrayals all, were illuminated by "city lights." In both the illuminated spaces and the shadows, western urban historians are finding narratives of city-building, power, and space that, together, have made the West a region of cities, the nation a continuous landscape of city lights.

REFERENCES

Abbott, Carl: *The New Urban America: Growth and Politics in Sunbelt Cities* (Chapel Hill: University of North Carolina Press, 1981).

Abbott, Carl: *Portland: Planning, Politics, and Growth in a Twentieth-Century City* (Lincoln: University of Nebraska Press, 1983).

Abbott, Carl: *The Metropolitan Frontier: Cities in the Modern American West* (Tucson: University of Arizona Press, 1993).

Abu-Lughod, Janet: *New York, Chicago, Los Angeles: America's Global Cities* (Minneapolis: University of Minnesota Press, 1999).

Adler, Jeffrey S.: *Yankee Merchants and the Making of the Urban West: The Rise and Fall of Antebellum St Louis* (New York, 1991).

Almaguer, Tomás: *Racial Fault Lines: The Historical Origins of White Supremacy in California* (Berkeley: University of California Press, 1994).

Appier, Janis: *Policing Women: The Sexual Politics of Law Enforcement and the LAPD* (Philadelphia: Temple University Press, 1998).

Avila, Eric: *Chocolate Cities and Vanilla Suburbs: Popular Culture in the Age of White Flight* (Berkeley: University of California Press, forthcoming).

Baldassare, Mark: *Trouble in Paradise: The Suburban Transformation of America* (New York: Columbia University Press, 1986).

Barrera, Mario: *Race and Class in the Southwest: A Theory of Racial Inequality* (Notre Dame: University of Notre Dame Press, 1979).

Barth, Gunther: *Instant Cities: Urbanization and the Rise of San Francisco and Denver* (New York: Oxford University Press, 1975).

Blackford, Michael: *The Lost Dream: Businessmen and City Planning on the Pacific Coast, 1890–1920* (Columbus: Ohio State University Press, 1993).

Blackhawk, Ned: *Violence Over The Land: Colonial Encounters In The American Great Basin* (Cambridge, MA: Harvard University Press, forthcoming).

Bluestone, Barry and Bennett Harrison: *The Deindustrialization of America: Plant Closings, Community Abandonment, and the Dismantling of Basic Industry* (New York: Basic Books, 1982).

Brechin, Gray: *Imperial San Francisco: Urban Power, Earthly Ruin* (Berkeley: University of California Press, 1999).

Bridges, Amy: *Morning Glories: Municipal Reform in the Southwest* (Princeton, NJ: Princeton University Press, 1997).

Brilliant, Mark: *Color Lines: Struggles for Civil Rights on America's "Racial Frontier," 1945–1975* (New York: Oxford University Press, forthcoming).

Broussard, Albert S.: *Black San Francisco: The Struggle for Racial Equality, 1900–1954* (Lawrence, KS: University of Kansas Press, 1993).

Brown, Kate: "Gridded Lives: Why Kazakhstan and Montana are Nearly the Same Place." *American Historical Review* 106 (Spring 2001), 17–48.

Browning, Rufus P., Dale Rogers Marshall, and David H. Tabb: *Protest is Not Enough: The Struggle of Blacks and Hispanics for Equality in Urban Politics* (Berkeley: University of California Press, 1984).

Bulmer, Martin: *The Chicago School of Sociology: Institutionalization, Diversity, and the Rise of Sociological Research* (Chicago: University of Chicago Press, 1984).

Camarillo, Albert: *Chicanos in a Changing Society: From Mexican Pueblos to American Barrios in Santa Barbara and Southern California, 1848–1930* (Cambridge, MA: Harvard University Press, 1979).

Chávez, Miroslava: *Mexican Women and the American Conquest in Los Angeles: From the Mexican Era to American Ascendancy* (PhD dissertation: University of California, Los Angeles, 1998).

Chen, Yong: *Chinese San Francisco, 1850–1943: A Trans-Pacific Community* (Stanford: Stanford University Press, 2000).

Cinel, Dino: *From Italy to San Francisco: The Immigrant Experience* (Stanford: Stanford University Press, 1982).

Coclanis, Peter A.: "Urbs in Horto." *Reviews in American History* 20 (March 1992), 14–20.

Cronon, William: *Nature's Metropolis: Chicago and the Great West* (New York: W.W. Norton, 1991).

Cronon, William: *Nature's Metropolis.* A Symposium." Special issue of *Antipode* 26 (April 1994).

Cronon, William, George Miles, and Jay Gitlin (eds.): *Under An Open Sky: Rethinking America's Western Past* (New York: W.W. Norton, 1992).

Daniels, Roger: *Asian America: Chinese and Japanese in the United States Since 1850* (Seattle: University of Washington Press, 1988).

Davis, Mike: *City of Quartz: Excavating the Future in Los Angeles* (London: Verso, 1990).

Davis, Susan: *Spectacular Nature: Corporate Culture and the Sea World Experience* (Berkeley: University of California Press, 1997).

Dear, Michael (ed.): *From Chicago to L.A.: Making Sense of Urban Theory* (Thousand Oaks, CA: Sage Publications, 2001).

Dear, Michael, Eric Schockman, and Greg Hise (eds.): *Rethinking Los Angeles* (Thousand Oaks, CA: Sage Publications, 1996).

Delgado, Grace: *In the Age of Exclusion: Race, Religion, and Chinese Identity in the Making of the Arizona-Sonora Borderlands, 1863–1943* (PhD dissertation: University of California, Los Angeles, 2000).

Deutsch, Sarah: *No Separate Refuge: Culture, Class, and Gender on an Anglo-Hispanic Frontier in the American Southwest, 1880–1940* (New York: Oxford University Press, 1987).

Deutsch, Sarah: *Women and the City: Gender, Space, and Power in Boston, 1870–1940* (New York: Oxford University Press, 2000).

Deverell, William: *Railroad Crossing: Californians and the Railroad, 1850–1910* (Berkeley: University of California Press, 1994).

Deverell, William and Tom Sitton: *California Progressivism Revisited* (Berkeley: University of California Press, 1994).

Dykstra, Robert: *The Cattle Towns* (New York: Alfred A, Knopf, 1968).

Emmons, David: *The Butte Irish: Class and Ethnicity in an American Mining Town* (Urbana: University of Illinois Press, 1989).

Escobar, Edward: *Race, Police, and the Making of a Political Identity: Mexican Americans and the Los Angeles Police Department, 1900–1945* (Berkeley: University of California Press, 1999).

Ethington, Philip: *The Public City: The Political Construction of Urban Life in San Francisco, 1850–1900* (New York: Cambridge University Press, 1994).

Ethington, Philip and Martin Meeker: "Saber y Conocer: The Metropolis of Urban Inquiry." In Michael Dear, Eric Schockman, and Greg Hise (eds.) *Rethinking Los Angeles* (Thousand Oaks, CA: Sage Publications, 1996).

Feagin, Joe R.: *Free Enterprise City: Houston in Political-Economic Perspective* (New Brunswick, NJ: Rutgers University Press, 1988).

Findlay, John: *Magic Lands: Western Cityscapes and American Culture After 1940* (Berkeley: University of California Press, 1992).

Foley, Neil: *The White Scourge: Mexicans, Blacks, and Poor Whites in Texas Cotton Culture* (Berkeley: University of California Press, 1998).

Frank, Dana: *Purchasing Power: Consumer Organizing, Gender, and the Seattle Labor Movement, 1919–1929* (New York: Cambridge University Press, 1994).

Fraser, Steve and Gary Gerstle (eds.): *The Rise and Fall of the New Deal Order* (Princeton, NJ: Princeton University Press, 1989).

Frug, Gerald E.: *City Making: Building Communities Without Building Walls* (Princeton, NJ: Princeton University Press, 1999).

García, Mario: *Desert Immigrants: The Mexicans of El Paso, 1880–1920* (New Haven: Yale University Press, 1981).

Gelfand, Mark: *A Nation of Cities: The Federal Government and Urban America, 1933–1965* (New York: Oxford University Press, 1975).

Gomez-Quinones, Juan: *Roots of Chicano Politics, 1600–1940* (Albuquerque: University of New Mexico Press, 1994).

Gutierrez, David: *Walls and Mirrors: Mexican Americans, Mexican Immigrants, and the Politics of Ethnicity* (Berkeley: University of California Press, 1995).

Guy, Donna J. and Thomas E. Sheridan (eds.): *Contested Ground: Comparative Frontiers on the Northern and Southern Edges of the Spanish Empire* (Tucson: University of Arizona Press, 1998).

Haas, Lisbeth: "Grass-Roots Protest and the Politics of Planning: Santa Ana, 1976–1988." In Rob Kling, Spencer Olin, and Mark Poster (eds.): *Postsuburban California: The Transformation of Orange County Since World War II* (Berkeley: University of California Press, 1991).

Hartman, Chester: *The Transformation of San Francisco* (Totowa, NJ: Rowman & Allenheld, 1984).

Harvey, David: *Justice, Nature, and the Geography of Difference* (Cambridge, MA: Blackwell, 1997).

Hayden, Dolores: *The Power of Place: Urban Landscapes as Public History* (Cambridge, MA: MIT Press, 1995).

Hays, Samuel P.: *Conservation and the Gospel of Efficiency* (Cambridge, MA: Harvard University Press, 1959).

Hise, Greg: *Magnetic Los Angeles: Planning the Twentieth Century Metropolis* (Baltimore: Johns Hopkins University Press, 1997).

Horne, Gerald: *Fire This Time: The Watts Uprising and the 1960s* (Charlottesville: University Press of Virginia, 1995).

Hughes, Thomas: *Networks of Power: Electrification in Western Society, 1880–1930* (Baltimore: Johns Hopkins University Press, 1983).

Ichioka, Yuji: *The Issei: The World of First Generation Japanese Immigrants, 1885–1924* (New York: Free Press, 1988).

Igler, David: *Industrial Cowboys: Miller & Lux and the Transformation of the Far West, 1850–1920* (Berkeley: University of California Press, 2001).

Issel, William and Robert Cherney: *San Francisco, 1865–1932: Politics, Power, and Urban Development* (Berkeley: University of California Press, 1986).

Jackson, Kenneth: *Crabgrass Frontier: The Suburbanization of the United States* (New York: Oxford University Press, 1985).

Johnson, Marilyn: *The Second Gold Rush: Oakland and the East Bay in World War II* (Berkeley: University of California Press, 1993).

Jolly, Michelle: *Inventing the City: Gender and the Politics of Everyday Life in Gold-Rush San Francisco, 1848–1869* (PhD dissertation: University of California, San Diego, 1998).

Kahn, Judd: *Imperial San Francisco: Politics and Planning in an American City, 1897–1906* (Lincoln: University of Nebraska Press, 1979).

Kahrl, William: *Water and Power: The Conflict Over Los Angeles' Water Supply in the Owens Valley* (Berkeley: University of California Press, 1982).

Kazin, Michael: *Barons of Labor: The San Francisco Building Trades and Union Power in the Progressive Era* (Urbana: University of Illinois Press, 1987).

Kimeldorf, Howard: *Reds or Rackets?: The Making of Radical and Conservative Unions on the Waterfront* (Berkeley: University of California Press, 1988).

Klingle, Matthew: *Urban by Nature: An Environmental History of Seattle, 1880–1970* (PhD dissertation: University of Washington, 2001).

Kurashige, Lon: *Japanese American celebration and conflict: A History of Ethnic Identity and Festival, 1934–1990* (Berkeley: University of California Press, 2002).

Larsen, Laurence: *The Urban West at the End of the Frontier* (Lawrence: University Press of Kansas, 1978).

Leclerc, Gustavo, Raúl Villa, and Michael J. Dear (eds.): *La vida latina en L.A.: Urban Latino Cultures* (Thousand Oaks, CA: Sage Publications, 1999).

Lemke-Santangelo, Gretchen: *Abiding Courage: African American Migrant Women and the East Bay Community* (Chapel Hill: University of North Carolina Press, 1996).

Leonard, Kevin: *The Battle for Los Angeles: Race, Politics and World War II* (Albuquerque: University of New Mexico Press, forthcoming).

Lipsitz, George: *The Possessive Investment in Whiteness: How White People Profit From Identity Politics* (Philadelphia: Temple University Press, 1998).

Locke, Mary Lou: "Out of the Shadows and into the Western Sun: Working Women of the Late Nineteenth-Century Urban Far West." *Journal of Urban History* 16, 2 (1990), 175–204.

Lotchin, Roger (ed.): *The Martial Metropolis: US Cities in War and Peace* (New York: Praeger, 1984).

Lotchin, Roger: *Fortress California, 1910–1961: From Warfare to Welfare* (New York: Oxford University Press, 1992).

Lotchin, Roger: "The Impending Western Urban Past: An Essay on the Twentieth Century West." In Gerald D. Nash and Richard Etulain (eds.) *Researching Western History: Topics in the Twentieth Century* (Albuquerque: University of New Mexico Press, 1997).

Lotchin, Roger, Walter Nugent, and Martin Ridge (eds.): *The Bad City in the Good War: San Francisco, Oakland, and San Diego* (Indiana University Press, 2003).

Luckingham, Bradford: *The Urban Southwest: A Profile History of Albuquerque, El Paso, Phoenix, Tucson* (El Paso: Texas Western Press, 1982).

McDonald, Terrence: *The Parameters of Urban Fiscal Policy: Socioeconomic Change and Political Culture in San Francisco, 1860–1906* (Berkeley: University of California Press, 1986).

McGirr, Lisa: *Suburban Warriors: The Origins of the New American Right* (Princeton: Princeton University Press, 2001).

McKenzie, Evan: *Privatopia: Homeowner Associations and the Rise of Residential Private Governments* (New Haven, CT: Yale University Press, 1994).

Mahoney, Timothy: *River Towns in the Great West: The Structure of Provincial Urbanization in the American Midwest, 1820–1870* (New York: Cambridge University Press, 1990).

Mallery, James: *From a Dangerous to a Dependent and Defective Group of Men: Social Policy, Urban Space, and the Masculinity of Hoboes in San Francisco, 1848–1917* (PhD dissertation: University of California, Los Angeles, 1999).

Markusen, Ann, Scott Campbell, Peter Hall, and Sabrina Deitrick: *The Rise of the Gunbelt: The Military Remapping of Industrial America* (New York: Oxford University Press, 1991).

Marquez, Benjamin: *Power and Politics in a Chicano Barrio: A Study of Mobilization Efforts and Community Power in El Paso* (Lanham, MD: University Press of America, 1985).

Massey, Douglas S. and Nancy A. Denton: *American Apartheid: Segregation and the Making of the Underclass* (Boston: Harvard University Press, 1993).

Moehring, Eugene P.: *Resort City in the Sunbelt: Las Vegas, 1930–1970* (Reno: University of Nevada Press, 1989).

Mollenkop, John H.: *The Contested City* (Princeton, NJ: Princeton University Press, 1983).

Monkkonen, Eric H.: *America Becomes Urban: The Development of US Cities and Towns, 1780–1980* (Berkeley: University of California Press, 1988).

Montejano, David: *Anglos and Mexicans in the Making of Texas, 1836–1986* (Austin: University of Texas Press, 1987).

Moore, Shirley A.: *To Place Our Deeds: The African American Community in Richmond, California, 1910–1963* (Berkeley: University of California, 2000).

Mumford, Kevin T.: *Interzones: Black/White Sex Districts in Chicago and New York in the Early Twentieth Century* (New York: Columbia University Press, 1997).

Mumford, Lewis: *The Culture of Cities* (New York: Harcourt, Brace, and Company, 1938).

Nash, Gerald: *The American West in the Twentieth Century: A Short History of an Urban Oasis* (Albuquerque: University of New Mexico Press, 1977).

Nash, Gerald: *The American West Transformed: The Impact of the Second World War* (Bloomington, IN: Indiana University Press, 1985).

Nash, Gerald: *World War II and the West: Reshaping the Economy* (Lincoln: University of Nebraska Press, 1990).

Nelson, Bruce: *Workers on The Waterfront: Seamen, Longshoremen, and Unionism in the 1930s* (Urbana: University of Illinois Press, 1988).

Nicolaides, Becky: *My Blue Heaven: Life and Politics in the Working Class Suburbs of Los Angeles, 1920–1965* (Chicago: University of Chicago Press, 2002).

O'Connor, Alice A.: *Poverty Knowledge: Social Science, Social Policy, and the Poor in the Twentieth Century* (Princeton, NJ: Princeton University Press, 2001).

Okihiro, Gary Y.: *Margins and Mainstream: Asians in American History and Culture* (Seattle: University of Washington Press, 1994).

Park, Robert E. and Ernest W. Burgess: *The City: Suggestions for Investigation of Human Behavior in the Urban Environment* (Chicago: University of Chicago Press, 1925).

Pascoe, Peggy: *Relations of Rescue: The Search for Female Moral Authority in the American West, 1874–1939* (New York: Oxford University Pres, 1990).

Peiss, Kathy: *Cheap Amusements: Working Women and Leisure in Turn-of-the-Century New York* (Philadelphia: Temple University Press, 1986).

Phelps, Robert: "The Search for a Modern Industrial City: Urban Planning, the Open Shop, and the Founding of Torrance, California." *Pacific Historical Review* 64, 4 (1995): 503–35.

Pierce, Bessie Louise: *A History of Chicago*, vol. 1, *The Beginning of a City* (New York: Knopf, 1937).

Pitti, Stephen: *The Devil in Silicon Valley: Northern California, Race, and Mexican Americans* (Princeton: Princeton University Press, 2003).

Pomeroy, Earl: *The Pacific Slope: A History of California, Oregon, Washington, Idaho, Utah, and Nevada* (New York: Alfred A. Knopf, 1965).

Putnam, John: *The Emergence of a New West: The Politics of Class and Gender in Seattle, Washington, 1880–1917* (PhD dissertation: University of California, San Diego, 2000).

Rieff, David: *Los Angeles: Capital of the Third World* (New York: Simon and Schuster, 1991).

Rome, Adam: *Bulldozer in the Countryside: Suburban Sprawl and the Rise of American Environmentalism* (New York: Oxford University Press, 2001).

Romo, Ricardo: *East Los Angeles, History of a Barrio* (Austin: University of Texas Press, 1983).

Rony, Dorothy Fujita: *Facing America: Filipina/o Seattle, 1919–1941,* (Berkeley: University of California Press, forthcoming).

Rose, Mark: *Interstate: Express Highway Politics, 1941–1956* (Lawrence: University Press of Kansas, 1979).

Rothman, Hal K.: *Devil's Bargains: Tourism in the Twentieth-Century American West* (Lawrence: University Press of Kansas, 1998).

Rothman, Hal K.: *Neon Metropolis: How Las Vegas Started the Twenty-First Century* (New York: Routledge, 2002).

Ruiz, Vicki: *Cannery Women, Cannery Lives: Mexican American Women, Unionization, and the California Food Processing Industry* (Albuquerque: University of New Mexico Press, 1987).

Sánchez, George: *Becoming Mexican American: Ethnicity, Culture and Identity in Chicano Los Angeles, 1900–1945* (New York: Oxford University Press, 1993).

Sassen, Saskia: *Globalization and Its Discontents: Essays on the New Mobility of People and Money* (New York: New Press, 1998).

Saxton, Alexander: *The Indispensable Enemy: Labor and the Anti-Chinese Movement in California* (Berkeley: University of California Press, 1971).

Saxton, Alexander: *The Rise and Fall of the White Republic: Class Politics and Mass Culture in Nineteenth-Century America* (London: Verso, 1990).

Schulman, Bruce: *From Cotton Belt to Sunbelt: Federal Policy, Economic Development and the Transformation of the South, 1938–1980* (New York: Oxford University Press, 1990).

Scott, Allen J. and Edward Soja (eds.): *The City: Los Angeles and Urban Theory at the End of the Twentieth Century* (Berkeley: University of California Press, 1996).

Self, Robert: *American Babylon: Race and the Struggle for Postwar Oakland* (Princeton, NJ: Princeton University Press, 2003a).

Self, Robert: "California's Industrial Garden: Remaking Postwar Oakland and the Greater Bay Area." In Jefferson Cowie and Joseph Heathcott (eds.) *Beyond the Ruins: Deindustrialization and the Meanings of Modern America* (Ithaca: Cornell University Press, 2003b).

Shah, Nayan: *Contagious Divides: Epidemics and Race in San Francisco's Chinatown* (Berkeley: University of California Press, 2001).

Shoemaker, Nancy: "Urban Indians and Ethnic Choices: American Indian Organizations in Minneapolis, 1920–1950." *Western Historical Quarterly* 19 (November 1988), 431–48.

Simpson, Lee Michelle: *Selling the City: Women and the California City Growth Games* (PhD dissertation: University of California, Riverside, 1996).

Smith, Duane: *Rocky Mountain Mining Camps: The Urban Frontier* (Bloomington: Indiana University Press, 1967).

Starr, Kevin: *Material Dreams: Southern California Through the 1920s* (New York: Oxford University Press, 1990).

Stern, Alexandra: *Eugenics Beyond Borders: Science and Medicalization in Mexico and the United States West, 1900–1950* (PhD dissertation: University of Chicago, 1999).

Takaki, Ronald: *Strangers From a Different Shore: A History of Asian Americans* (Boston: Little, Brown and Company, 1989).

Taylor, Quintard: "Blacks and Asians in a White City: Japanese Americans and African Americans in Seattle, 1890–1940." *Western Historical Quarterly* 22, 4 (November 1991) 401–29.

Taylor, Quintard: *The Forging of a Black Community: Seattle's Central District, from 1870 through the Civil Rights Era* (Seattle: University of Washington Press, 1994).

Taylor, Quintard and Shirley A. Moore: *African American Women in the American West* (Norman: University of Oklahoma Press, 1999).

Toll, William: *The Making of an Ethnic Middle Class: Portland's Jewry over Four Generations* (Albany: State University of New York Press, 1982).

Truett, Samuel: *Neighbors by Nature: The Transformation of Land and Life in the United States–Mexico Borderlands, 1854–1910* (PhD dissertation: Yale University, 1997).

van der Woude, A. M., Akira Hayami, and Jan de Vries (eds.): *Urbanization in History: A Process of Dynamic Interactions* (New York: Oxford University Press, 1990).

Viehe, Fred: "The First Recall: Los Angeles Urban Reform or Machine Politics?" *Southern California Quarterly* 70 (1988), 1–28.

Wade, Richard: *The Urban Frontier: The Rise of Western Cities, 1790–1830* (Cambridge, MA: Harvard University Press, 1959).

Weber, David J.: *The Mexican Frontier, 1821–1946: The American Southwest Under Mexico* (Albuquerque: University of New Mexico Press, 1982).

Wheeler, Kenneth: *To Wear a City's Crown: The Beginnings of Urban Growth in Texas, 1836–1965* (Cambridge: Harvard University Press, 1968).

White, Richard: *The Organic Machine: The Remaking of the Columbia River* (New York: Hill and Wang, 1995).

Wiley, Peter and Robert Gottlieb: *Empires in the Sun: The Rise of the New American West* (Tucson: University of Arizona Press, 1982).

Wilson, William: *Hamilton Park: A Planned Black Community in Dallas* (Baltimore: Johns Hopkins University Press, 1998).

Worster, Donald: *Rivers of Empire: Water, Aridity, and the Growth of the American West* (New York: Pantheon, 1985).

Yoo, David: *Growing Up Nisei: Race, Generation, and Culture Among Japanese Americans of California, 1924–49* (Urbana: University of Illinois Press, 2000).

Yung, Judy: *Unbound Feet: A Social History of Chinese Women in San Francisco* (Berkeley: University of California Press, 1995).

CHAPTER TWENTY-FOUR

Politics and the Twentieth-Century American West

WILLIAM DEVERELL[1]

How to Organize a Century of Politics and Political Behavior?

Politics in the twentieth-century American West: where to begin? It may be but envious hindsight to suggest that students of the same topic in the nineteenth century West often – albeit appropriately – hang similar inquiries on a small number of critical moments of legislative action or political themes. Undoubtedly the juggernaut of the coming Civil War offers an obvious organizing principle though which to grapple with western politics from at least the 1830s forward. Territorial acquisition, political maturation, statehood, western violence spawned of disputes over the expansion of slavery – each of these important themes can be analyzed from the scholarly vantage of the coming crisis, and scholars have ably mined such fields for more than a century.

Manifest Destiny, too, can and has operated as a fundamental historiographical theme in this regard. But casting the *antebellum* history of the West more in the direction of the coming of the war, provided the scholarship sails hard away from the dangers of reading the historical record backward as an exercise in inevitability, has been an especially fruitful way by which to approach nineteenth-century politics and political history in and of the region. Through the opening salvos of sectional conflict, Congressional (read Republican Party) action regarding the West – especially the Pacific Railroad bills and homestead legislation – present other key moments by which to organize critical aspects of western American political history.

Following the war, and up to the end of the century, three political themes of great importance stand out as crucial to an understanding of the region's ultimate incorporation into the nation. One, federal action in response to the environmental challenges of settlement and development played a manifestly important role in the ways in which the now-states of the American West were fully woven, however unevenly, into the national fabric during Reconstruction and beyond. Such seemingly arcane – but actually very significant – actions such as the various desert and timber acts enacted by the US Congress, as well as federal efforts to address western aridity, further clarified the expanding role Washington would play in the nation's western states and few remaining territories. Two, the final, violent burst of Native American resistance to coerced assimilation within American culture and American jurisdictions offers another galvanizing moment of unquestionable political importance. Scholars of the West can scrutinize President Ulysses S. Grant's hapless 1860s "Peace Policy" ambitions and come to the sad conclusion that Reconstruction in the West failed as miserably as it did in the South. And last, the resistance, violent and otherwise, especially of industrial workers and farmers, in league with political idealists and opportunists both, to the tectonic changes in the nation's political economy so characteristic of the Populist Era have critical ties to the West and to western politics, and many an important work of national or regional historical analysis has focused directly upon the American West in this regard.

Now cross the divide separating the nineteenth from the twentieth-century West. Organization of inquiries around western politics seemingly becomes a more difficult task. The tragic convenience of the sectional conflict no longer exerts dominance as the central organizing feature of any chronologically broad investigation. And what had just recently been such a momentous and politically divisive regional theme as Populism had, at least by the time William Jennings Bryan's presidential ambitions sputtered – again – in the 1900 election, lost much of its salience, a downturn in part tied to Bryan's loss in the preceding campaign of 1896.

This lack of organizational clarity is itself a clarion for scholarly production and imagination. The field is in short supply of ambitious synthetic studies of twentieth-century western politics – books and essays that tackle the region's political history, its legislation and legislative issues, its voters and vote-getters, its parties and realignments, and the complex relationship between region and nation spanning the eras between self-conscious (if not actual) westerners Theodore Roosevelt on one end and Ronald Reagan and George W. Bush on the other. Attempts at distilling a century's worth of political activity and political behavior into thesis and theme-driven monographs or essays are few and far between, and the western American scholarly field is worse off for it. In the late 1980s, the historians Gerald Nash and Richard Etulain noted that western political history of the twentieth century had as yet been "largely unwritten" (1989:293). Historian Robert Cherny, in his especially helpful overview of the topic in 1997, concluded similarly. The case is largely the same today.

Yet salient themes do stand out, many of which are held over from nineteenth-century – and earlier – processes of regional incorporation into broader frameworks of governance and economic rationalization and into the political economy of the nation. For example, the political history of the twentieth-century American West is marked by the continuity of an often peculiar, to say nothing of turbulent, relationship to the federal government and to bureaucratic and agency structures (and individuals) in Washington. This relationship is largely shaped by the West's continued efforts to harness federal resources to address regional environmental assets or deficits of one form or another; the eccentricities of the relationship spring especially from the West's uneven record of wanting federal intervention in some arenas and fighting hard against it in others. Of long-standing importance and continuity, too, are time-worn struggles over grassroots issues of democracy and political participation. Demographic upheaval and change are hardly new phenomena in the American West. Nor are the questions such change inevitably provokes. Who in the West is allowed unhindered access to the rights and privileges, the goods and services, not to mention the protections, of citizenship in the region, in the nation? Who decides? Who votes?

While this essay will not remedy the lack of scholarly synthesis in twentieth-century western politics, I will try to sketch out some of these broad ways in which scholars have contemplated the topic through focus on several of these themes and, as the essay closes, offer some suggested avenues for further research.

We turn first to the supposedly discrete historical period known as the Progressive Era. The complex political legacies of this period suggest lines of inquiry for scholars to follow forward much further into the twentieth-century American West.

Progressivism and Its Legacies

Within the litany of greater and lesser western political issues, themes, and movements of the last century, the region's embrace of progressivism and progressive reform through the coming of the 1920s is an undeniably important chapter in the political history of the entire nation. And yet it is a curiously understudied topic at the broadest regional level. American historical scholarship sorely needs a scholar, or set of scholars, to tackle "progressivism and the American West."

But, as suggested above, we need as well to track the endurance of Progressive Era concerns about the very nature of politics and political relationships, and broad-brush case studies of the American West would offer excellent starting points for such work. For the political questions that most vexed progressives, a loosely confederated but nonetheless grouped set of diverse political actors and audiences, continue to be central issues in American public and political life to this day. At heart a political and cultural struggle over the exact nature of the public realm and any given individual's relationship to it, progressivism was marked, perhaps especially in the West, by a reformist program seeking nothing short of the "betterment" of the polity and the people who defined it. Progressives, and the movement they inspired, aimed to perfect the nation for the new century through programs and policies of moral uplift, political housecleaning, bureaucratic regulation of corporate interests, and expanded participation in public affairs and life.

More than simply chronologically appropriate as an introduction to the political history of the twentieth century, progressivism offers a perhaps idiosyncratic jumping-off point for thinking through an entire century of politics and political behavior. While progressivism may have a lifespan that scholars confidently expect to identify (the formerly firm bracket of 1900–20 has been pushed backwards and forwards in time, but not by much), the era's concerns did not fade when 1920 ended. The continuity of Progressive Era issues is a political legacy worth investigating at the regional level. Scholars would do well to explore possible analytical linkages between the progressives, their programs, and their anxieties and more recent periods. The questions the progressives asked in themselves suggest lines of possible continuity. How can politics and business be kept free from corruption? How can the public good be sustained? How can democratic institutions and democratic principles be invigorated in a weary polity? Look to the American West of today, and such hearty challenges as these are yet rendered in high relief. Tracing progressivism forward in time from its regional highwater mark early in the twentieth century could conceivably yield new ways to think about an entire century of western political history.

More important, historians increasingly recognize that many of the Progressive Era's uglier impulses regarding social and political reform gained momentum and adherents as the century advanced. Where scholars were formerly apt to draw a line at the point when political extremism appeared in the late 1910s and 1920s – this *cannot* be progressivism – they now recognize the darker subtleties within a movement embracing broad and even competing understandings of just what constituted "reform."

The foundations for more ambitious studies of progressivism and progressive legacies already exist. The lack of a regional synthesis notwithstanding, historians have done important work in addressing the movement's rise in the American West. Any national study of the era and its reform look and feel would necessarily place a great deal of attention on western states, western politicians, and western voters. Though beholden to Populism's ideological frameworks, progressives flattened Populism's generally radical stance towards concentrations of capital and corporate power. Progressives attempted to chart a more moderate, centrist course through the political economy of the early twentieth century. Often attacking powerful railroad corporations as dire threats to the public good, the West's nascent progressive politicians lashed out – in thought and word, if not always deed. A favorite target was the behemoth Southern Pacific Railroad, the biggest corporate entity (by far) in the entire region. Progressives insisted that arrogant rail corporations like the S.P. controlled western politics at the local and state levels, and they were not shy about insinuating that Washington might be at railroad beck and call as well. In sometimes consciously modeling their platforms, speeches, and even comportment after the national standard for progressive engagement, Theodore Roosevelt, western reform-minded activists and office-seekers promised little less than the fundamental reorganization of the polity through the elimination of corrupt business practices in political affairs.

Such claims were generally over the top. Progressives in the West, more likely to be elected if they emerged out of reform wings of the regionally dominant Republican Party, generally did not earn trust-busting or anticorporate credentials on a grand scale. Legislative revision of the government's relationship to conglomerates of capital and technology had little of the more radical "pop" of previous decades or of reform movements to the left of the progressives (like, for example, the not inconsequential Socialist Party of the era). Outside of important examples of public ownership of utilities and even a state-owned bank in North Dakota, it is best to think of the progressive approach to corporations as a regulatory one, of greater or lesser stringency, than as the frontal attack that progressives claimed to be mounting from their bully pulpits and in their campaign speeches.

This is not to suggest that progressives accomplished little once they began to win elected office. The regulatory frameworks that western progressives erected help define legal and economic relationships between corporations, the state, and the public to this day (Mowry, 1951). Establishment of such measures was often hard fought. At a more grassroots level, progressives, with westerners at the vanguard, sponsored sweeping changes in the relationships between voters, public officials, and laws. Beginning at the very end of the nineteenth century, western municipalities and a few states began experimenting with various forms of "direct legislation" and "direct democracy" as ways to put the voting public more in touch with legislation and public officials. Designed generally as antidotes to political corruption in one form or another (and again rail corporations were the favored target), the tools of direct democracy included the initiative, the referendum, and the recall. The first two allowed voters to cast ballots potentially creating or nullifying specific pieces of legislation (if majority figures were met), and the recall offered voters the chance to remove public officials from office (again, dependent upon voting percentages). These political innovations spread across the United States in the first decades of the twentieth century, but they were doubtless peculiarly western tools (Cherny, 1997: 96–97; Sitton, 1992). They remain so to this day. In a momentous contemporary example, California voters contemplate the state's first gubernatorial recall election in the fall of 2003, just as this essay goes to press.

The stated goals behind adoption of the initiative, referendum, and recall were to widen political participation and thus encourage democratic impulses to wash away corruption and the stains of entrenched corporate power in everyday life. It would be fair to ask scholars and others to consider if such goals have been met in the hundred years since Los Angeles became the nation's first municipality to adopt the recall. It may be that, as has often been charged, special interests able to marshal resources to mount an expensive initiative campaign now dominate a process once championed as explicitly *anti*-special interest. We may in fact not know enough as yet; much more work remains to be done on the regional level to see if the progressives' democratic glee upon numerous state adoptions of the tools rings hollow a century later, though important initial forays have been undertaken (Allswang, 2000).

While the ultimate benefits of "direct democracy" may remain in question, progressives did nonetheless preside over an unquestionably fundamental expansion of democracy through women's suffrage. The West again played the key trailblazing role. A number of western states allowed women to vote long before the 1920 passage of the Nineteenth Amendment granted that right to women across the nation. Historians continue to puzzle over the reasons why western states were so far ahead of the rest of the nation regarding women's suffrage. Scholars once expected that answers could be found in close study of the social and political consequences of the West's skewed gender ratios. But it may be more fruitful to analyze western suffrage leadership and campaign tactics. Suffrage activists in the West may have proven better at keeping the issue away from harmful (from a voting standpoint) linkages with other issues or competing progressive initiatives; it may have also been significant that western suffrage was not expected to (nor did it) alter regional racial hierarchies (White, 1991:356–9; Mead, 2004). One thing is certain: despite the West's strong support for suffrage in the years leading up to the Nineteenth Amendment, the victories were hard fought on the ground. Opponents who insisted, as did one prominent westerner, that equal suffrage was simply "evil to the cause of good government," generally attacked the idea either by arguing that women were incapable of handling the obligations of full citizenship or by asserting that women must be protected from the hurly burly of politics for their own physical, mental, or moral good (Deverell and Hyde, 2000: 120). Or they lumped their opposition: women's suffrage would prove as deleterious to the body politic as it would to the bodies of women. Proponents persevered. Propelled by the West's domino effect of state by state adoption of suffrage through the first decade and a half of the twentieth century, the issue soon became law throughout the nation.

Consideration of the political and other linkages between the suffrage amendment and its immediate constitutional precursor brings us again directly to the American

West. The Eighteenth Amendment prohibited the manufacture, distribution, or sale of alcoholic beverages. Like suffrage, the issue had deep western roots, and it is difficult to imagine the prohibition movement reaching its 1919 constitutional destination without the significant role played by the region. Prohibition offers a particularly apt case study for revealing the complexities of the West's Progressive Era political climate.

Tied to progressive concerns about individual and society-wide morality, and probably linked to the increase in civic or electoral participation by women in the West, prohibition carried the day in a number of western states through the early 1910s. Home to such famous zealots as Kansas's saloon-busting Carrie Nation, the West undoubtedly helped put a face (if not a hatchet) on the issue for the rest of the nation. But prohibition's roots in the West ran far deeper than the individual notoriety of key soldiers in the battle against drink. Religious opposition to liquor, including that of the Mormon Church and fundamentalist or simply conservative Protestants prompted many a western town, county, or entire state to "go dry" in the period leading up to the amendment's passage; many western towns had been dry since the late nineteenth century. Westerners who couched their support in less religious terms wanted to believe that prohibition could lessen (if not eliminate) poverty, crime, class conflict, and homelessness. Like their counterparts elsewhere in the nation, many westerners voted for local, regional, or national prohibition because they hoped the ban on alcohol would foster the return of their town, state, or region to a simpler, idealized time where moral righteousness and, implicit to many of these hopes, Anglo-Saxon purity held unquestioned sway (Ostrander, 1957; Clark, 1965; Franklin, 1971; Gould, 1973).

It should not be hard to discern the outlines of deeper complexity here, and scholars have probed the topic with interest (Timberlake, 1963; Bader, 1986). Out to remake America, progressives embraced prohibition as an important milestone on an ambitious journey to the perfectible future. But popular, progressive opposition to liquor meant far more than the clumsy and ultimately disastrous Eighteenth Amendment and Volstead Act. Prohibition gathered up strains of opinion, thought, and behavior that had less to do with antagonism to booze than they did with racial, ethnic, and religious antipathies.

Prohibitionists were probably as interested in controlling drinkers as they were in controlling drink. As in other parts of the United States, the West had strains of anti-German, anti-Italian, and anti-Irish discrimination, antipathy, and stereotype. When "dry" westerners of white, northern European origin squared off against Irish, German, Italian, and other "wets," prohibition offered supposedly high moral ground upon which uglier impulses could congeal. Mixing humanitarian concerns with ideas about social control, ethnocentrism, and religious antipathy, among others, prohibition was a complex political brew all by itself. Once the United States entered World War I, patriotism offered up yet another potential excuse for supporting prohibition's attack on, for example, German American breweries and beer halls. Anti-Catholicism undoubtedly played its part here as well, as Protestant "drys" took on Catholic "wets" in a few key local western battles over prohibition measures. Outnumbered and outspent, "wets" almost always lost.

We should not be surprised that so-called ethnocultural issues – those that divide a given population along lines of ethnicity, national background, or culture – played a role in the ways in which the progressives imagined the future and used politics and political action to get there. Nor should we accept the old-fashioned notion that prohibition was somehow not a progressive issue at all, but was instead a weird and extreme example of moral policing unconnected with the body of progressive reform.

Ethnocultural concerns haunted western progressives. While it is intriguing to note that ethnocultural concerns or allegiances seem not to have divided western voters along party lines as they did so prominently elsewhere in the country (Kleppner, 1989), ideas and fears about ethnic, racial, and cultural differences nonetheless informed progressive programs to a large degree. Americanization efforts at the heart of the progressive reform package were nothing if not ethnoculturally imagined and promulgated, a sort of social alchemy designed to turn immigrants into white, Christian (Protestant, preferably), and eventually middle-class stalwarts of the republic. And Americanization ideas were at the soft edge of an ethnocultural worldview. Progressives could just as easily play even dirtier. Progressive darling Hiram Johnson of California, elected governor in 1910 on an antirailroad ticket through the reform wing of the state's Republican Party, with an Anti-Saloon League running mate, had few qualms about presiding over a resurgence of anti-Japanese legislation early in his term (Lower, 1993). Ethnocultural issues may not have cleaved western voters in the way they did easterners, but they nonetheless played an important role in the very ways in which progressives refashioned western politics and the West itself, and those legacies endure.

It should not be surprising that the resurgent Ku Klux Klan, taking Americanization, anti-Catholicism, and a retrogressive view of an idealized past before western voters in the 1920s, briefly took over the state governments of Colorado and Oregon by effectively centering political debate on "religion, ethnicity, and associated 'moral' issues." (White, 1991: 384). The Klan's influence extended beyond electoral success in the Rockies, the Pacific Northwest, or Southern California (where Klansmen captured the government of Orange County as well). As historians Michael Malone and Ross Peterson have argued, the Klan of the 1920s "reached into every corner of the Far West" (Malone and Peterson, 1994: 513), precisely because the organization adhered to a set of ideas about "reform" that could be found without much difficulty in more mainstream progressive programs or pronouncements. To be sure, progressive reform made a hard right turn in cases where the Klan rose to prominence (and the specific nature of *every* Klan political victory in the West deserves close study), but it is important that students and scholars of the West consider the likelihood that the very roots of such extremism came from the progressive movement itself. It would be wrong to isolate the 1920s Klan at the fringes, far removed from mainstream politics. Better to view the Klan and its worldview as more "enthusiastic" expressions of enthnocultural anxieties exuding from within, if not from the very heart of, the western progressive moment *writ large*. From progressive-sponsored anti-Asian acts of the 1910s (legislative prohibitions on, among other things, Japanese or Japanese American land ownership), like those endorsed by Governor Johnson of California, it is not far down the discriminatory legal path to the coercive travesty of massed internment of western American people of Japanese descent in the early years of the World War II (Daniels, 1962; Saxton, 1971; Takaki, 1989). A likely scholarly connection between such moments as illustrative of the enduring political will of the majority population of the West – across supposedly disparate historical periods – might be further enhanced by inclusion of the coerced repatriation of ethnic Mexican and Mexican American people from the region during the Great Depression. And what might an enterprising scholar make of the possible ideological connections between the fluorescence of eugenics and politically sanctioned "social hygiene" programs of the Progressive Era West (centered in California) and contemporary debates on a wide variety of genetic or human reproduction issues?

The point is a simple one: historians and other scholars must continue to look closely for possible continuities across the formerly strict chronological, legislative, or programmatic boundaries of the Progressive Era. Only then will the enduring influence of the political activism of the early twentieth century, for better or ill, be fully understood. That work ought to begin with a critical, even skeptical, reception of what progressives themselves claimed about political motives and the meanings, if not the very definitions, of political reform.

Divided Loyalties and the Federal West

In disarmingly optimistic and ultimately naïve efforts to perfect their world, progressives believed firmly that government was both a powerful tool and an ally. Consequently, an obvious political feature of the Progressive Era concerns various attempts on the part of progressives to lasso government (at all levels) and bring it to bear on regional problems and programs. In the most general sense, the American West proved no different in this regard than other regions of the country: progressives across America believed that efficient governmental and bureaucratic institutions and their personnel existed at the heart of meaningful reform.

But particular aspects of the West's relationship to government, the federal government in particular, merit emphasis here, beginning with the most salient. The federal government owns, and has long owned, much of the American West. That fact alone imparts a peculiar dynamism to the entire subject of federalism, especially in the related realms of environmental issues and development of natural resources.

Through the last third of the nineteenth century, federal action in regard to the western lands had a baseline aim of rationalizing the landscape so as to make it into a vast quilt of discrete parcels of productive, arable (if often wishfully so), land. The Homestead Act, the various Pacific Railroad bills, and the Dawes Severalty Act (which clumsily attempted to make small farmers out of tribal Native Americans) – diverse acts of legislation – nonetheless shared fundamental, old-fashioned assumptions about the West as an idealized republic of independent yeomen.

By the twentieth century, such hopes had proven wishful and misplaced. The West of the twentieth century would not be some sort of Jeffersonian paradise. It did not have enough water, for one, or at least did not have enough water in the "right" places. More to the point, western political and economic elites, along with key agencies and individuals in the federal government, were far more interested in large-scale industrial and urban development than they were in dreamy notions of small independent farmers spread out in tiny towns throughout the landscape.

What the West wanted, and what the West got, was federal help in reshaping the landscape through huge reclamation projects that benefited the region's agribusinesses and cities and city people far more than they did the by now almost mythical collection of small western farmers.

For their part, westerners – politicians and the public alike – did express political and other antagonisms towards Washington when they viewed the developing relationship as a colonial one. Despite a rising, early-twentieth-century appreciation of the aesthetic and other merit of preserved landscapes in the form of national parks and monuments, westerners reacted with hostility when federal conservation restrictions on timber, grazing, or other lands conflicted with regional expectations regarding rapid and unfettered development of western resources. It is probably safe to assume that in many such early-twentieth-century instances of regional ire lie the seeds of the West's now flourishing strains of antigovernment thought and behavior. Looking at the historical landscape, it is not hard to spot angry westerners shouting at the government in the first decades of the twentieth century to butt out of western affairs. But what usually happened at that time was that their voices were drowned out by those of neighbors and other westerners eager for federal "interference" in the shape of the aid and money starting to pour into the West to address various regional infrastructural deficits – none of which was more pressing than the lack of enough water to sustain western urban, suburban, or farmland expansion at the scale western dreamers envisioned.

Through innumerable federal New Deal programs, big western projects during the Great Depression rendered the number and scale of earlier federally sponsored internal improvements puny. Previous regional partnerships with the government ("partnerships" suggests perhaps greater equity between region and Washington than is merited) often, given the challenges of western aridity, focused on strategies of water distribution, containment, and storage. Federal largess and federal expertise were imperative in mounting projects with complex engineering, jurisdictional, or financial challenges. But even very ambitious Progressive Era projects look tiny when compared with the extraordinary public works efforts of the New Deal, with its web of dams, aqueducts, and other landscape projects. The huge Boulder Dam project on the Colorado River outside of Las Vegas – President Franklin D. Roosevelt called it "a twentieth century marvel," and he was right – was the first giant project completed in the New Deal, and it is fitting that it was done in the West (Deverell and Hyde, 2000: 179).

There is no doubt that Roosevelt's New Deal forever changed the West's relationship to the federal government. Not only did federal resources and programs reshape the western environment and the lives of westerners, the bureaucratic and agency structures (and individuals attached to them) likewise altered the political balance of power in towns, cities, counties, and states across the entire region. Federal agencies and bureaucrats had shaped the Progressive Era West, as historian Samuel P. Hays demonstrated in his 1959 study of conservation policies and programs, but the New Deal was an entirely new ballgame. In essence, the New Deal pioneered connections between region and nation that only grew and expanded with the coming of World War II. We know the federal presence in the West during the war assumed extraordinary proportions through defense spending and establishment of military installations (Lotchin, 1992; Nash, 1985; Nash, 1990). We know less about the connections and possible continuities, in personnel or otherwise, between the New Deal's federal presence in the West and the War Department's ensuing arrival in very large terms. A region-wide study linking the Depression decades with the wartime period, one that had as its primary objective an analysis of the impact and nature of federal programs in the West, would be a welcome addition to the political history literature of the modern period. Scholarly work has begun to address the impact of the Cold War on politics in the region (Fernlund, 1998; McGirr, 2001), especially in terms of the West's fervent anticommunist impulses, and biographical portraits of especially charismatic or notorious western political figures of the war and postwar era have been or are being written (Mitchell, 1998). But it would be well to carry the investigations back before US entry into World War II. It would be especially fruitful if scholars uncovered ideological or other links between anticommunist activities and ideologies of the 1940s and 1950s and the West's powerful strains of antigovernment attitudes dating well back in the early century.

Some important scholarly work has been done which analyzes the political ramifications of wartime and postwar migrations to the West. Both in terms of internal group dynamics (of, for example, racial and ethnic groups) within western cities and in broader arenas of political activity, the arrival of new westerners from all over the United States and across the world shifted political debates and political loyalties in the 1940s and 1950s (Sides, 2003; Bernstein, 2003). But we know less about the political impact of broader demographic shifts of long-standing duration in the twentieth century West, movements of people in which the wartime migrations are but part of a larger whole. Western historians have tracked the astonishing rural to urban demographic drain in the region, a pattern of now more than a century's duration, and Walter Nugent's magisterial 1999 book *Into the West* is comprehensive in this regard. But we know less about the political ramifications of that transition, either at the voting booth or within the realm of decision-making by state, local, or federal governments.

In similar terms, ambitious studies that contemplate the political meanings of momentous demographic trends regarding the population of Mexican and Latino peoples of the West and nation have only recently begun to emerge (Gutierrez, 2004). A few years ago, federal census data revealed that Latinos constituted the largest minority group within the US population. That feature alone is of doubtless political magnitude. Scholars would do well to embark upon long-range studies of the differential political impact of, for example, the West's Mexican American population through key moments of political fluorescence and quiescence. What such studies uncover regarding demographic connections to shifting ideas about citizenship and civic participation (and the limits of both) may suggest analytical frameworks for other investigations of the some of the most pressing questions regarding identity and civil rights in contemporary America.

Conclusion: Research Opportunities and Gaps

Historian Robert Cherny, who has written extensively on western politics from the age of William Jennings Bryan forward, concluded his 1997 review of regional political history with a helpful section addressing gaps in our collective knowledge of the political history of the modern West (103–5). Imagine twentieth-century western politics as a scholarly topic divided into three overlapping cells containing issues, actors (voters, politicians, constituent groups), and decision-making structures. Conceived thus, it is not difficult to see where gaps appear when scholars pose questions across Cherny's grid. Especially glaring are those holes in our understanding of major events as refracted or experienced through the lives, thoughts, and behavior of nonwhites. What do we know, for example, about the ways in which the anti-Catholicism of Progressive Era prohibitionists reinforced regional western antipathies towards ethnic Mexicans, immigrant or otherwise? Not much, I would suggest. What do we know about region-wide African American response to the Americanization programs and ideologies of the Progressive Era? How would scholars begin to assess the ways in which twentieth-century federal land policy and federal oversight of western lands differentially affected (if indeed it did) various ethnic groups? Could a similar analysis be explored with respect to differential impacts across gender? As Cherny implicitly notes, western historians have been far too content to write about political themes and issues with regard to traditional understandings of the dynamics between political groups, actors, and the decision-making apparatus. Part of the challenge (and opportunity) regarding the political history of the modern American West is simply to ask bold, even unusual, questions.

One approach is to bring forward political themes from the nineteenth century to the twentieth. For example, historians of the nineteenth-century West know well the impact of the United States military on western politics before, during, and after the Civil War. But the political ramifications – at the local, state, and regional levels – of the United States military on the twentieth-century West is little understood and little studied, despite the continued presence of many western military installations, and the western residency of large numbers of both active-duty and retired military personnel. Nor do we know much about the political consequences of military base closures that have taken place throughout the West in recent decades. The region's economic reliance upon defense spending, as well as the cultural ramifications of that relationship, has begun to receive scholarly attention (Markusen, et al., 1991), but the expressly political, and often highly localized, ramifications have gotten far less scrutiny.

It may be that the influential resurgent conservative politics of the West, a topic of great scholarly interest in recent years, has important connections to the West's military history. What is clear is that the rise of New Right politics has significant western American roots planted deep in the region's suburbs and conservative Protestant churches (McGirr, 2001). Important scholarly work has gotten underway investigating conservative and far Right western politics (which need not necessarily be viewed as the same thing, but rather as "tree" and "branch") of the second half of the Cold War, and some of the findings may alter conventional understandings of, for instance, the public and political role of women activists in fostering a conservative groundswell in places like Southern California where Richard Nixon and Ronald Reagan first came to prominence during the Cold War period (Nickerson, 2003). What remains tantalizing from a scholarly point of view are the ways in which the modern expressions and antagonisms of far Right politics in the West may link up with much earlier, pre-World War II, even Progressive Era examples of similar outlook.

In the broadest of brush strokes painted across the whole period, it is possible to describe the twentieth-century political history of the West as a fundamental transition "from seeing government as Savior to seeing it as Satan" (Cherny, 1997:103). The West's progressive leaders did not shy away from the use of government to achieve political and societal goals, believing that government at all levels was of key importance to their work. That faith (especially that faith in federal government) does not characterize western political outlook any longer.

How did that happen? And can the roots of this very important transition be found and analyzed through case-study work on particular themes or moments? In this vein, historians and other scholars have begun to take up the challenge of drawing meaningful connections between the various "sagebrush rebellion" outbursts of westerners throughout the twentieth century who rebelled against federal bureaucratic supervision of western lands (Cawley, 1993; Klyza, 1996; Robbins and Foster, 2000). Karen Merrill's recent book *Public Lands and Political Meaning* (2000) looks closely at New Deal-era western ranchers and the federal agents and institutions that control access to grazing lands, and what she has uncovered suggests meaningful, enduring continuities across historical periods (see also Arrington, 1983).

Any discussion of the ways in which westerners interact with the federal government must contemplate Native America and Native Americans. No other group in the West (or throughout American history) has had a more complex or fraught connection to the federal government. Of course, the political history of the Native American populations of the West in the twentieth century is a topic rich in historical irony. At the beginning of the century, the prevailing assumption on the part of non-Indians was that the region's Native Americans would simply pass away, either assimilated into the dominant society or rendered extinct by their inability to compete with white America. Time has of course proven that racist assumption blatantly false, just as the passage of a century has seen the uneven rise in the political and economic power of some tribal entities over others, differential patterns now further exacerbated by the phenomenon of Indian gaming. As the historian Peter Iverson points out in his contribution to this volume, the recent history of western Native Americans, tribal and otherwise, must be incorporated into wider streams of scholarly analysis. One particularly apt case-study approach to such incorporation would be region-wide examinations of the changing political fortunes of the native peoples of the West through comparison to other western populations. What has a "federal West" meant to Native Americans, and how do experiences and histories vary across region or tribal and non-tribal affiliations?

One of this essay's major thrusts has been to urge that western historians pull strands of early-twentieth-century politics and ideas forward and across what may turn out to be arbitrary boundaries. But we might learn as much if we cast our scholarly nets backwards as well. For example, as others have also suggested, what might an enterprising scholar tell us about the West's changing relationship with the federal government through a comparative analysis of transportation history, one that examined railroads in the mid-nineteenth century and freeways in the mid-twentieth? (Cherny, 1997:85).

In similar fashion, scholars might take up the history of the Mormon Church in the West sometime in the mid to late nineteenth century and carry it forward, through the Progressive Era, past the Depression, and into more recent times. The political impact and influence of the Mormon Church is a topic of unquestioned importance in twentieth-century western history, and there remains much work to do in this area. The political affinities of devout Mormons need to be better understood, as does the political power of the church itself, in Utah and throughout the greater West and Southwest (and beyond). At heart of such investigations is a perplexing scholarly mystery: how, in a century's time, have the Mormon Church and its adherents transitioned from being the ideal types of "un-American" characteristics to their position now as wholesome, conservative representations of "all-American" traits? What political trajectories from the Mormon Church to the Republican Party, and back, await further explication from scholars of the American West?

Beyond a litany of topics like those suggested in the above paragraphs, it should be made clear as well that historians of western American politics must think broadly about evidence and method; obviously there are questions about political behavior and political impacts which can be attacked by other than conventional or usual historical means. Political historians would do well to enlist the collegial aid of political scientists, for example, as they contemplate issues, methods, and data in their own work. Perhaps such a collaborative project could begin with that sorely needed, multivolume study: the history of progressivism in the American West.

NOTE

1   I am grateful to David Wrobel for several sustained discussions about this topic.

REFERENCES

Abbott, Carl: *Portland: Planning, Politics, and Growth in a Twentieth Century City* (Lincoln: University of Nebraska Press, 1983).

Allswang, John: *The Initiative and Referendum in California, 1898–1998* (Stanford: Stanford University Press, 2000).

Ambrecht, Biliana C. S., and Harry P. Pachon: "Ethnic Political Mobilization in a Mexican American Community: An Exploratory Study of East Los Angeles, 1965–72." *Western Political Quarterly* 21, 3 (September 1974), 500–19.

Arrington, Leonard: "The Sagebrush Resurrection: New Deal Expenditures in the Western States, 1933–1939." *Pacific Historical Review* 52 (February 1983), 1–16.

Bader, Robert S.: *Prohibition in Kansas: A History* (Lawrence: University Press of Kansas, 1986).

Baldassare, Mark: *Trouble in Paradise: The Suburban Transformation of America* (New York: Columbia University Press, 1986).

Bernard, Richard M. and Bradley R. Rice (eds.): *Sunbelt Cities: Politics and Growth since World War II.* (Austin: University of Texas Press, 1983).

Bernstein, Shana Beth: "Building Bridges at Home in a Time of Global Conflict: Interracial Cooperation and the Fight for Civil Rights in Los Angeles, 1933–1954." (PhD dissertation: Stanford University, 2003).

Blocker, Jack S., Jr.: *Retreat from Reform: The Prohibition Movement in the United States, 1890–1913* (Westport, CT: Greenwood Press, 1976).

Bridges, Amy: *Morning Glories: Municipal Reform in the Southwest* (Princeton: Princeton University Press, 1997).

Brilliant, Mark: "Color Lines: Civil Rights Struggles on America's 'Racial Frontier,' 1945–1975." (PhD dissertation: Stanford University, 2002).

Burton, Robert E.: *Democrats of Oregon: The Pattern of Minority Politics, 1900–1956* (Eugene: University of Oregon Press, 1970).

Cawley, R. McGreggor: *Federal Land, Western Anger* (Lawrence: University Press of Kansas, 1993).

Clark, Norman H.: *The Dry Years: Prohibition and Social Change in Washington* (Seattle: University of Washington Press, 1965).

Cherny, Robert W.: *Populism, Progressivism, and the Transformation of Nebraska Politics, 1885–1915* (Lincoln: University of Nebraska Press, 1981).

Cherny, Robert W.: "Research Opportunities in Twentieth-Century Western History: Politics." In Gerald Nash and Richard Etulain (eds.) *Researching Western History: Topics in the Twentieth Century* (Albuquerque: University of New Mexico Press, 1997).

Cocoltchos, Christopher N.: "The Invisible Government and the Viable Community: The Ku Klux Klan in Orange County, California during the 1920s." (Ph.D. dissertation: University of California, Los Angeles, 1979).

Coggins, George C., Parthenia Blessing Evans, and Margaret Lindberg-Johnson: "The Law of Public Rangeland Management: The Extent and Distribution of Federal Power." *Environmental Law* 12 (1982), 535–621.

Cornell, Stephen: *The Return of the Native: American Indian Political Resurgence* (New York: Oxford University Press, 1988).

Daniels, Roger: *The Decision to Relocate the Japanese Americans* (Philadelphia: J. B. Lippincott Company, 1975).

Daniels, Roger: *The Politics of Prejudice: The Anti-Japanese Movement in California and the Struggle for Japanese Exclusion* (Berkeley: University of California Press, 1962).

Deloria, Vine and Clifford M. Lytle: *The Nations Within: The Past and Future of American Indian Sovereignty* (New York: Pantheon, 1984).

Deverell, William: *Railroad Crossing: Californians and the Railroad, 1850–1910* (Berkeley: University of California Press, 1994).

Deverell, William and Anne F. Hyde: *The West in the History of the Nation: Since 1865* (Boston: Bedford/St. Martin's, 2000).

Deverell, William and Tom Sitton (eds.): *California Progressivism Revisited* (Berkeley: University of California Press, 1994).

Elkind, Sarah S.: *Bay Cities and Water Politics: The Battle for Resources in Boston and Oakland.* (Lawrence: University Press of Kansas, 1998).

Feinman, Ronald L.: *Twilight of Progressivism: The Western Republican Senators and the New Deal* (Baltimore: Johns Hopkins University Press, 1981).

Fernlund, Kevin (ed.): *The Cold War American West, 1945–1989* (Albuquerque: University of New Mexico Press, 1998).

Fisher, Sethard: *Black Elected Officials in California* (San Francisco: R & E Research Associates Inc., 1978).

Flamming, Douglas: *A World to Gain: African Americans in Los Angeles, 1890–1940* (Berkeley: University of California Press, 2004).

Foss, Phillip O.: *Politics and Grass: The Administration of Grazing on the Public Domain* (Seattle: University Press of Washington, 1960).

Franklin, Jimmie Lewis: *Born Sober: Prohibition in Oklahoma, 1907–1959* (Norman: University of Oklahoma Press, 1971).

Garcia, Juan R.: *Operation Wetback: The Mass Deportation of Mexican Undocumented Workers in 1954* (Westport, CT: Greenwood Press, 1980).

Goble, Danney: *Progressive Oklahoma: The Making of a New Kind of State* (Norman: University of Oklahoma Press, 1980).

Goldberg, Robert A.: *Hooded Empire: The Ku Klux Klan in Colorado* (Urbana: University of Illinois Press, 1981).

Goldberg, Robert A.: *Barry Goldwater* (New Haven: Yale University Press, 1995).

Gottlieb, Robert: *Forcing the Spring: The Transformation of the American Environmental Movement* (Washington, DC: Island Press, 1993).

Gould, Lewis L.: *Progressives and Prohibitionists: Texas Democrats in the Wilson Era* (Austin: University of Texas Press, 1973).

Graf, William L.: *Wilderness Preservation and the Sagebrush Rebellions* (Savage, MD: Rowman & Littlefield, 1990).

Gullett, Gayle: *Becoming Citizens: The Emergence and Development of the California Women's Movement, 1880–1911* (Urbana: University of Illinois Press, 2000).

Gutierrez, David G.: *Walls and Mirrors: Mexican Americans, Mexican Immigrants, and the Politics of Ethnicity* (Berkeley: University of California Press, 1995).

Gutierrez, David G. (ed.): *The Columbia History of Latinos in the United States, 1960 – Present* (New York: Columbia University Press, 2004).

Gutierrez, David G.: "Editor's Introduction." In David G. Gutierrez (ed.) *The Columbia History of Latinos in the United States, 1960–Present* (New York: Columbia University Press, 2004).

Hays, Samuel P.: *Conservation and the Gospel of Efficiency: The Progressive Conservation Movement, 1890–1920* (Cambridge: Harvard University Press, 1959).

Heale, M. J.: "Red Scare Politics: California's Campaign Against Un-American Activities, 1940–1970." *Journal of American Studies* 20 (April 1986), 5–32.

Hennings, Robert E.: *James D. Phelan and the Wilson Progressives of California* (New York: Garland, 1985).

Hundley, Norris, Jr.: *Water and the West: The Colorado River Compact and the Politics of Water in the American West* (Berkeley: University of California Press, 1975).

Hundley, Norris, Jr.: *The Great Thirst: Californians and Water, 1770s–1990s* (Berkeley: University of California Press, 1992).

Issel, William and Robert W. Cherny: *San Francisco, 1865–1932: Politics, Power, and Urban Development* (Berkeley: University of California Press, 1986).

Iverson, Peter: *The Navajo Nation* (Westport, CT: Greenwood Publishing, 1981).

Iverson, Peter: *Barry Goldwater: Native Arizonan* (Norman: University of Oklahoma Press, 1997).

Iverson, Peter: *The Din é: A History of the Navajos* Albuquerque: University of New Mexico Press, 2002).

Jenkins, J. Craig: *The Politics of Insurgency: The Farm Worker Movement in the 1960s* (New York: Columbia University Press, 1985).

Kazin, Michael: *Barons of Labor: The San Francisco Building Trades and Union Power in the Progressive Era* (Urbana: University of Illinois Press, 1987).

Kelley, Robert: *Battling the Inland Sea: American Political Culture, Public Policy, and the Sacramento Valley, 1850–1986* (Berkeley: University of California Press, 1989).

Kleppner, Paul: "Politics Without Parties: The Western States, 1900–84." In Gerald Nash and Richard Etulain (eds.) *The Twentieth-Century West: Historical Interpretations* (Albuquerque: University of New Mexico Press, 1989).

Kling, Rob, Spencer Olin, and Mark Poster (eds.): *Postsuburban California: The Transformation of Orange County since World War II* (Berkeley: University of California Press, 1991).

Klyza, Christopher M.: *Who Controls Public Lands? Mining, Forestry, and Grazing Policies, 1870–1990* (Chapel Hill: University of North Carolina Press, 1996).

Lamb, Karl A.: *As Orange Goes: Twelve California Families and the Future of American Politics* (New York: Norton, 1974).

La Forte, Robert S.: *Leaders of Reform: Progressive Republicans in Kansas, 1900–1916* (Lawrence: University Press of Kansas, 1974).

Limerick, Patricia N.: *The Legacy of Conquest: The Unbroken Past of the American West* (New York: W. W. Norton, 1987).

Lotchin, Roger: *Fortress California, 1910–1961: From Warfare to Welfare* (New York: Oxford University Press, 1992).

Lower, Richard Coke: *A Bloc of One: The Political Career of Hiram W. Johnson* (Stanford: Stanford University Press, 1993).

Lowitt, Richard: *Bronson M. Cutting: Progressive Politician* (Albuquerque: University of New Mexico Press, 1992).

Lowitt, Richard: *The New Deal in the West* (Bloomington: Indiana University Press, 1984).

Markusen, Ann, Peter Hall, Scott Campbell, and Sabina Deitrick: *The Rise of the Gunbelt: The Military Remapping of Industrial America* (New York: Oxford University Press, 1991).

McGirr, Lisa: *Suburban Warriors: The Origins of the New American Right* (Princeton: Princeton University Press, 2001).

McKinley, Charles: *Uncle Sam in the Pacific Northwest* (Berkeley: University of California Press, 1952).

Mead, Rebecca: *How the Vote was Won: Woman Suffrage in the Western United States, 1868–1914* (New York: New York University Press, 2004).

Merrill, Karen R.: *Public Lands and Political Meaning: Ranchers, the Government, and the Property Between Them* (Berkeley: University of California Press, 2002).

Merrill, Karen R.: "In Search of the 'Federal Presence' in the American West." *Western Historical Quarterly* 30 (Winter 1999), 449–73.

Malone, Michael P. and F. Ross Peterson: "Politics and Protests." In Clyde A. Milner, II, Carol A. O'Connor, and Martha Sandweiss (eds.) *The Oxford History of the American West* New York: Oxford University Press, 1994).

Milner, Clyde A., Carol A. O'Connor, and Martha Sandweiss (eds.): *The Oxford History of the American West* New York: Oxford University Press, 1994).

Mitchell, Gregg: *The Campaign of the Century: Upton Sinclair's Race for Governor of California and the Birth of Media Politics* (New York: Random House, 1992).

Mitchell, Gregg: *Tricky Dick and the Pink Lady: Helen Gahagan Douglas, Sexual Politics, and the Red Scare, 1950* (New York: Random House, 1998).

Modell, John: *The Economics and Politics of Racial Accomodation: The Japanese of Los Angeles, 1900–1942* (Urbana: University of Illinois Press, 1977).

Montejano, David: *Anglos and Mexicans in the Making of Texas, 1836–1986* (Austin: University of Texas Press, 1987).

Morlan, Robert L.: *Political Prairie Fire: The Non-Partisan League, 1915–1922* (Minneapolis: University of Minnesota Press, 1955).

Mowry, George: *The California Progressives* (Berkeley: University of California Press, 1951).

Nash, Gerald: *The American West Transformed: The Impact of the Second World War* (Bloomington: Indiana University Press, 1985).

Nash, Gerald: *World War II and the West: Reshaping the Economy* (Lincoln: University of Nebraska Press, 1990).

Nash, Gerald and Richard Etulain (eds.): *The Twentieth Century West: Historical Interpretations* (Albuquerque: University of New Mexico Press, 1989).

Nickerson, Michelle: *"Domestic Threats: Women, Gender and Conservatism in Cold War Los Angeles, 1945–1966."* (PhD Dissertation, Yale University, 2003).

Nobles, Melissa: *Shades of Citizenship: Race and the Census in Modern Politics* (Stanford: Stanford University Press, 2000).

Nugent, Walter T. K.: (*Into the West: The Story of Its People* New York: Knopf, 1999).

Olin, Spencer C.: *California's Prodigal Sons: Hiram Johnson and the Progressives, 1911–1917* (Berkeley: University of California Press, 1968).

Ostrander, Gilbert: *The Prohibition Movement in California, 1848–1933* (Berkeley: University of California Press, 1957).

Peffer, E. Louise: *The Closing of the Public Domain: Disposal and Reservation Policies, 1900–1950* (Stanford: Stanford University Press, 1951).

Perry, David C. and Alfred J. Watkins (eds.): *The Rise of the Sunbelt Cities* (Beverly Hills, CA: Sage, 1977).

Pisani, Donald J.: *From the Family Farm to Agribusiness: The Irrigation Crusade in California and the West, 1850–1931* (Berkeley: University of California Press, 1984).

Pisani, Donald J.: *Water, Land, and Law in the West: The Limits of Public Policy, 1850–1920* (Lawrence: University Press of Kansas, 1996).

Putnam, Jackson K.: *Old-Age Politics in California from Richardson to Reagan* (Stanford: Stanford University Press, 1970).

Rice, Ross R.: *Carl Hayden: Builder of the American West* (Lanham, MD: University Press of America, 1994).

Robbins, William G. and James C. Foster (eds.): *Land in the American West: Private Claims and the Common Good* (Seattle: University of Washington Press, 2000).

Rogin, Michael P. and John L. Shover: *Political Change in California: Critical Elections and Social Movements, 1890–1966* (Westport, CT: Greenwood Press, 1970).

Rowley, William D.: "The West as a Laboratory and Mirror of Reform." In Gerald Nash and Richard Etulain (eds.) *The Twentieth-Century West: Historical Interpretations* (Albuquerque: University of New Mexico Press, 1989).

Sarasohn, David: "The Election of 1916: Realigning the Rockies." *Western Historical Quarterly* 11 (July 1980), 285–306.

Saxton, Alexander: *The Indispensable Enemy: Labor and the Anti-Chinese Movement in California* (Berkeley: University of California Press, 1971).

Scales, James R. and Danney Goble: *Oklahoma Politics: A History* (Norman: University of Oklahoma Press, 1982).

Schusky, Ernest L.: *Political Organization of Native North Americans.* (Washington, DC: University Press of America, 1980).

Sears, David O. and Jack Citrin: *Tax Revolt: Something for Nothing in California* (Cambridge, MA: Harvard University Press, 1982).

Sides, Josh *L. A. City Limits: African American Los Angeles from the Great Depression to the Present* (Berkeley: University of California Press, 2003).

Sitton, Tom: *John Randolph Haynes: California Progressive* (Stanford: Stanford University Press, 1992).

Sonenshein, Raphael: *Politics in Black and White: Race and Power in Los Angeles* (Princeton: Princeton University Press, 1993).

Starr, Kevin: *Endangered Dreams: The Great Depression in California* (New York: Oxford University Press, 1996).

Starr, Kevin: *The Dream Endures: California Enters the 1940s* (New York: Oxford University Press, 1997).

Takaki, Ronald: *Strangers from a Different Shore* (Boston: Little, Brown and Company, 1989).

Taylor, Graham D.: *The New Deal and American Indian Tribalism: The Administration of the Indian Reorganization Act, 1934–1945* (Lincoln: University of Nebraska Press, 1980).

Thomas, Clive S. (ed.): *Politics and Public Policy in the Contemporary American West* (Albuquerque: University of New Mexico Press, 1991).

Timberlake, James: *Prohibition and the Progressive Movement, 1900–1920.* (Cambridge, MA: Harvard University Press, 1963).

White, Richard: *"It's Your Misfortune and None of My Own": A History of the American West* (Norman: University of Oklahoma Press, 1991).

Wickens, James F.: *Colorado in the Great Depression* (New York: Garland, 1979).

Wiley, Peter and Robert Gottlieb: *Empires in the Sun: The Rise of the New American West.* (Tucson: University of Arizona Press, 1985).

Worster, Donald: *Rivers of Empire: Water, Aridity, and the Growth of the American West.* (New York: Pantheon, 1985).

Wrobel, David M.: *The End of American Exceptionalism: Frontier Anxiety from the Old West to the New Deal* (Lawrence, KS: University Press of Kansas, 1993).

CHAPTER TWENTY-FIVE

The Literary West and the Twentieth Century

DAVID M. WROBEL

Introduction

Regardless of the common East Coast critical laments concerning the provincialism of western American literary writing, the last century witnessed an abundance of memorable western works by novelists, poets, short story writers, historians, journalists, travel writers, and various cultural critics. The list of Pulitzer-Prize-winning western novelists alone is impressive: Willa Cather, H. L. Davis, John Steinbeck, A. B. Guthrie, Jr., N. Scott Momaday, Wallace Stegner, and Larry McMurtry. What is more, the late twentieth century witnessed a scholarly renaissance in western literary studies, with the formation of the Western Literature Association in the mid-1960s and the publication of its journal, *Western American Literature*. Since then, scores of important books and articles on western letters have appeared. In recent years major commercial publishers have taken western writers far more seriously, and scholars of western letters have gained increasing critical respect.

Making sense of the veritable mass of writings by members of diverse western culture groups in the twentieth century, discerning overarching patterns or themes, is no easy task. At the most elemental level of analysis, it is worth noting that two seemingly contradictory processes have marked western writing in the twentieth century. First, there has been a movement away from the largely white, male, rural, romantic, and morally simplistic "Old" nineteenth-century West of mythology, toward a more inclusive, complex, and ultimately more interesting set of stories about men and women of all races and about rural, urban, and suburban places in the "New West." The second trend, strangely contradictory as it may seem, has been the dogged persistence, indeed, the remarkable endurance, of the very same old western "frontier mythology" on more subliminal levels throughout American popular culture.

The popular frontier writing of the late eighteenth and nineteenth centuries was primarily a literature of escape and adventure, but it always had national audiences and spoke to national concerns (or at least to the concerns of the white majority). If much of the early writing about the West presented it as a place for white Americans to escape *to*, it was because of the growing sense of the increasingly urbanized and industrialized East as a place to escape *from*. The literary West in this early period, as the late Henry Nash Smith showed so memorably in his seminal work *Virgin Land*

(1950), was presented by popular writers as a wilderness to test the acumen of rugged frontiersmen and as an agrarian utopia, the "Garden of the World."

In the twentieth century, western writing was increasingly marked by a stark realism and by the presence of a multitude of diverse voices; in short, it echoed the complex issues relating to race relations and the environment that faced the nation then and now. But the mythic, frontier, rugged, white, male, and rural West has not disappeared from the scene, perhaps because of the continued cultural need for the West as a place of mental escape. The frontier West has not gradually subsided in concordance with the ascendancy of the "real West"; the processes of life and literature are rarely so neat. As historian Robert Athearn reminded us: "there is no real conflict between the [mythic West and the actual West]. We live with both quite comfortably – one world filled with immediate problems at hand, the other serving as a spare tire, a numbered emotional bank account, a fall back position that is reassuring, comforting" (1986: 274). The frontier West remains a feature in some western writing and it surfaces frequently in popular music, film, journalism, and in radio and television advertising. The demographically and geographically diverse and complex West where real people live coexists with the stereotyped West of the imagination; the two are not in a state of diametrical opposition. These two Wests –mental and actual – interact in complex ways that often belie the neat categorizations of scholarly writing in the field.

This essay does not provide a systematic, chronologically organized overview of modern western writing; instead, it explores some of the organizational categories that have been used in analyzes of that writing. It argues that, while western writing has reflected the complexities of the region, including the nuanced relationships between mental Wests and actual Wests, writing *about* western literature (namely, literary history and criticism) has often constructed overly comfortable categorizations of periods and subgenres, and has dichotomized works that are fundamentally interrelated. The essay also offers a tentative model for cross-chronological and cross-cultural comparative analysis of twentieth-century western works.

While the focus here is largely on literary works, it is important to recognize that in the field of modern western letters the lines between fiction and nonfiction, literature and history are often rather blurry. As literary critic Gary Scharnhorst (1999: 346) has noted, "western writers are regional historians," and, conversely, western historians are regional writers, as are journalists, magazine editors, and others. Furthermore, much of the output of western writers, even those who are classified as novelists and short story writers, is actually nonfictional (travel narratives are a good example of this).

Since the West is so tied, through mythology and migration, to the nation, analyzes of western writing should (in addition to including works of fiction and nonfiction) include both writers native to the region as well as those who reside outside of the West but choose it as their subject. The commonly made claim that real western literature comes from natives of the region and that mythic, or fake, western literature comes from outsiders (read: easterners), draws the lines between westerners and nonwesterners too sharply. Literary scholar David Fine (1995) notes that much of the best fiction centered in Los Angeles has been written by newcomers and recent arrivals, hence by people who are not deeply rooted in the place. Indeed, Fine adds, "the [LA] landscape offered itself readily to a vision of being cut off from a familiar sense of place" (1995: 10). The traditionalist might contend that the absence of a strong sense of place renders such LA writing (by Nathaniel West, Joan Didion, Thomas Pynchon, Evelyn Waugh, Aldous Huxley, and others) "nonwestern." However, such contentions rest on a bed of assumptions concerning the presence of an elevated regional consciousness in the West. Since the vast majority of western residents have arguably not been in the region long enough to develop any such heightened consciousness of place, claims that westerners are more rooted than residents of other American regions seem at best dubious and at worst parochial. Such claims certainly limit the number of "real westerners" to a very select and small group. This essay seeks to broaden our conception of the parameters of "western" writing.

Continuing the trend of broad and inclusive categorizations, "westerners" are defined here simply as "those who reside in the area of the United States stretching from the Pacific Coast to the eastern edge of the Plains," California included. This is a definition that also gives short shrift to claims to elevated westernness based on primacy. There is no suitable yardstick for measuring "westernness," not even the length of time of residence. Claims to heightened regional affiliation – the "I've been here longer and know and appreciate the place better than you ever can" school of thought – should certainly not be viewed as markers of "real" western writing. Westerners' literary expressions are viewed here simply as examples of "interior regionalism" – reflections of a relationship to place, or of a *sense of place*. Nonwesterners' writings on the West are viewed as examples of "exterior regionalism" – reflections of their *sense of the place*, which have also played a role in shaping western identities. Neither of the two categories, "interior regionalism" or "exterior regionalism," can be presumed to have greater inherent value; both interior and exterior forces have combined together in complex ways to shape regional identities across the West. Similarly, western literature rooted in the land is deemed no more authentic, no more intrinsically western, than western literature rooted in cities, where the vast bulk of westerners now reside, and have done throughout much of the twentieth century. No western subregion's writers or residents are deemed to have any greater claims to "westernness" than those of any other subregion. The definition of western writing that is offered here is simple and inclusive: "writing centered on the West or some part/s of it."

Place, of course, is central to this writing, but *genius loci* (spirit of place) is not, for all people who reside in or visit the West, necessarily the same as "westernness." Indeed, an effort is made here to try and strike beyond the limiting parameters of "westernness" as a thematic construct for examining the region's writing. Since western mythology has traditionally been white-centered and land-centered, the concept of "westernness" has been of less significance to peoples of color, and to the urban places that lie between the West's wide open spaces, than to white westerners in rural places. The writers who center their stories on the rural West are the ones most likely to acquire the label of "western writer"; yet the label is in need of some expansion. For "westernness" to retain any usefulness as a thematic construct it will need to be applicable to more than just the West's white rural minority.

Categorizing Modern Western Writing: Existing Frameworks

A number of organizational frameworks have proven helpful for examining the diverse mass of twentieth-century western writing. Scholars and general readers are indebted to these models, which have functioned as important road maps for traversing western literary landscapes. Acts of framework construction are generally more intellectually demanding and time-consuming than acts of literary deconstruction, and so critiques of existing frameworks should be offered with that understanding in mind. A few of these frameworks are outlined and examined here as a prelude to a proposed alternative model.

In his work *Re-Imagining the Modern American West: A Century of Fiction, History, and Art* (1996), historian Richard Etulain constructs a tripartite division of modern western history, art, and literature, into works linked thematically by the categories of frontier (1890–1920), region (1920 to roughly World War II), and postregion (from the transformations of World War II and the 1960s to the present). Etulain's sweeping, detailed and insightful work of synthesis constitutes an effective framework for comparative analysis across literary, historiographic, and artistic borders. His categories of "to-the-West" (frontier), "in-the-West" (regional), and "beyond-the-West" (postregional) works bring some order to a tremendous range of subgenres, individuals, and works. Writers included in the frontier category include Owen Wister and Zane Grey; among the regionalist writers covered are Mary Austin, Charles Fletcher Lummis, Davis, Cather, and Steinbeck. Etulain's postregionalists are a diverse group, including Stegner, Momaday, McMurtry, Marilynne Robinson, Leslie Marmon Silko, Amy Tan, and Rudolfo Anaya.

Etulain's framework is characterized more by contrast than continuity among these three bodies of western writing. In his model, western literature moves through quite distinct stages of development – frontier, region, and postregion – that might be equated with stages of human life: youth (adolescence), middle age (maturity), and old age (wisdom). The comparison with stages of human development is instructive since Etulain emphasizes that modern western literature has grown out of one stage and into the next. There is, however, some fluidity to Etulain's categories; he does point to early examples of one stage of western writing occupying the chronological terrain of later stages, and he does see holdovers from earlier stages appearing in later periods.

The broad parameters of this framework are also evident in Etulain's more recent book, *Telling Western Stories: From Buffalo Bill to Larry McMurtry* (1999), which uses the categories of "Creation Stories" (including Buffalo Bill's creation of western mythology), "Untold Stories" (by Mary Hallock Foote, Geronimo, and Mourning Dove, and about Calamity Jane), "Traditional Stories" (by Wister, John Ford, and Louis L'Amour, and about Billy the Kid), and "New Stories" (by Stegner, Momaday, Silko, McMurtry, and historian Patricia Limerick). The book explores the theme of continuity between the different kinds of western stories and Etulain places heavier emphasis on the crossovers between the various categories than he did in *Re-Imagining the Modern American West*. Still, the basic contours of the "to-the-West," "in-the-West," "beyond-the-West" framework are still very much evident in his later more synchronic approach.

Historian Elliott West, in his humorous and insightful treatment of western "Stories" (1995) divides western writing and storytelling into two broad categories: firstly, pioneer literature – the literature of "placelessness" or "no place", also known as "old geezer fiction" – and, secondly, the literature of place – stories of "places known from the ground up." The literature of placelessness category includes travel writers from Sir Richard Francis Burton in the late nineteenth century to Dayton Duncan, Ian Frazier, and Kathleen Norris in the late twentieth. The place category includes most Native American writing, along with the works of Gary Paul Nabhan, William Kittredge, Stegner, and other European American writers. Elliott West's structure is similar to Etulain's in its juxtaposition of process and place, of "to-the-West" writing with "in-the-West" writing. However, West, more so than Etulain, emphasizes that some writers have produced a wide range of works that are not confined to just one of the categories; his framework is more fluid than Etulain's. It is important to note, though, that both of these historians view regional literature as being generally more mature than frontier or process-oriented writing.

Etulain draws on the theme of postregion to capture the growing diversity of western American literature in the second half of the twentieth century, including the emergence of writers of color exploring ethnic themes, and the presence of more urban and suburban settings in western writing. For Etulain, the category of regionalism no longer holds up as a viable unit for analysis of more recent works, since they are increasingly marked less by an emphasis on place than by issues of ethnicity and complexities of character (a point we will return to later). West's less rigid designations of "place" and "placelessness" enable him to incorporate a diverse range of literary voices into just those two categories.

Literary scholar Thomas J. Lyon, in a wide-ranging essay on "The Literary West" in *The Oxford History of the American West* (1994), presents a model that partially parallels those of Etulain and West by dividing western literature into "frontier and postfrontier mentalities." Lyon notes that "a complex self-consciousness stands behind [the] more mature regional literature," to which he also gives the designation "postfrontier" (708). This is similar to West's emphasis on the greater maturity of western literature written "from the ground up," and of Etulain's preference for "in-the-West" and "beyond-the-West" writing over "to-the-West" works. Lyon treats Native American literature as an add-on to his model, rather than fully incorporating it into the framework. He also adds a category titled "Other Contemporary Trends," which is reminiscent of Etulain's postregion category, in that it comprises those works that do not really fit his (Lyon's) two main categories of frontier and postfrontier (frontier and region for Etulain).

More recently, in his similarly detailed introductory essay, "The Conquistador, the Lone Ranger, and Beyond," to his edited collection *The Literary West: An Anthology of Western American Literature* (1999), Lyon divides the West and its literary outpourings into the categories of "the mythic West" and "the real West." This second effort at model building is more complete (with coverage of Chicana/o writing and environmental writing), more integrated, and more convincing; nonetheless, the dichotomy remains. Lyon writes somewhat dismissively about the "mythic West" writings and uses the terms "serious" western literature and "real" western literature in a way that is reminiscent of Elliott West's use of the terms mature and immature. Etulain, West, and Lyon provide us, then, with three quite similar metaframeworks or macromodels for organizing modern western writing. They successfully provide some sense of order and shape to a massive and varied body of writings. To some degree, all three – but especially Etulain and Lyon – construct progressive models marked by movement from one stage of western writing to the next higher stage. They essentially chart a shift from lamentably simplistic and

Eurocentric beginnings to culturally rich and diverse and structurally complex contemporary works.

Problematizing Categories

There are, of course, serious departures from the models of Etulain, West, and Lyon. In his recent book *Ten Most Wanted: The New Western Literature* (1998), Blake Allmendinger launches an animated attack on western American literary criticism, characterizing it as inherently conservative and unimaginative. He introduces queer theory into the discussion of the fictional West, arguing that same-sex male relationships "occur more frequently, consistently, and explicitly in westerns than they do elsewhere in literature" (154). In addition, Allmendinger provides western readings of works that are not generally considered to be westerns, including Pearl Buck's Pulitzer-Prize-winning *The Good Earth (1931)*, Truman Capote's *In Cold Blood* (1966), and David Lynch's postmodern cult television series *Twin Peaks* of 1990–1991.

The effect of Allmendinger's approach is to broaden the parameters and the horizons of the field in some ways; yet, on some level, the alternative framework he offers is marked by limitations similar to those of the models discussed earlier. Elsewhere, in a recent essay, Allmendinger (1999) amplifies his model by discussing the need to highlight in the classroom both utopian and dystopian narratives, to engage in celebration as well as exposé in order to balance what he views as conservative and unimaginative western literature and literary criticism with more critical writings and insightful readings. This advice is sound enough for the most part, except that it has the effect of replacing one set of organizational dichotomies – frontier and region – with another equally inflexible set – "chique" and "unchique".

Twentieth-century western writing is marked by a wealth of complexities. Dividing that literary output into clearly prescribed categories certainly helps us make some sense of a disparate mass of writings, for these categorizations bring some order and structure to what can seem like a chaotic swirl of "majority" and "minority" literatures. Yet all these frameworks seem too dualistic in structure, their juxtapositions rigid and contrived. The models seem, infelicitously, to separate the "Old West" from the "New West," memories of the past from the present (which is, after all, shaped in part by those very same memories), rural spaces from the urban places they surround, and white majority literature from multiple minority literatures. The frameworks also seem (and it comes as a revelation of sorts for a historian to admit this) somewhat hidebound by chronology. Writers who are deemed to be ahead of the prevailing cultural currents of their time – Carey McWilliams' 1940s work on race relations would be a good example – come to be seen as precursors of later literary movements or cultural attitudes. Other writers in more recent times, such as Louis L'Amour, who favored "frontier themes," are described as throwbacks to earlier ages or genres. Thus writers are categorized as being ahead of their time, or behind it, which reinforces the notion that certain periods are clearly marked by particular literary genres, rather than by a diverse array of often conflicting voices. Of course there are prevailing literary currents in every period, but the danger is that rigid categorization often devalues, or even ignores, the significance of alternative countercurrents.

The existing analytical models generally emphasize a movement from the immature literary output fueled by frontier mythology to a mature, regionally grounded western literature (a literature of place) that flowered during the interwar years. From there, the common approach is to highlight the range of "minority" literary streams that have complicated the "mainstream" by taking it in a myriad of new directions. It is a kind of "worst" (frontier), "better" (regional), "best" (contemporary, postregional, postwestern) model. However, this model is complicated by the fact that the contours of the final (postregional) category appear largely indefinable, and are deemed meritorious perhaps in part because of their very indefinability, i.e., because they are not definably "western." In other words, the existing frameworks present western writing as being first white and placeless, then remaining white but becoming place-centered (a step, at least, in the right direction), and then finally becoming multicolored and multicentered, or multi-streamed/"unwestern"/"postwestern." Thus, western writers are seen as trapped within the realm of myth in the frontier stage, partially free of the myth in the regional stage, and fully liberated in the postregional phase. Problematically enough, when treated within these kinds of organizational paradigms, the various literary works do not seem to speak to each other across racial and chronological borders. These sorts of models do not hold out the possibility that regional identity, sense of place, or as geographer Yi-fu Tuan puts it (1974), topophilia, can remain just as important even as western places become more diverse. It is assumed that a multicolored West must be a nonregional, postwestern, or "nonwestern" place, that the mythic western heritage is not malleable and cannot become more inclusive over time to better reflect regional demographic realities.

Furthermore, these models for categorizing western writing seem to delineate too strictly between frontier literature and regional literature. Movements *to* places have played a vital role in shaping people's sense *of* places. Frontier process-centered and place-centered regional realities are fundamentally intertwined through the weight of collective memory of earlier times. People move to and adjust to new places, and those processes of movement and adjustment become vital to the process by which regional identity is formed. Similarly, separating the regional literature of the early to mid-twentieth century from the so-called postregional and postwestern literature of the late twentieth century may assume a more significant break than actually exists.

This assumed epistemic break has been influenced, in its turn, by the aesthetic representational shift from the modern to the postmodern that marks the caesura in material output from manufacturing to service economy, electric to electronic, etc. Nonetheless, as British sociologist Mike Featherstone (1991) suggests, a more accurate representational term may be the more inclusive "transmodern," since elements of modernity and postmodernity exist contemporaneously within cultures. Similarly, the West, a culturally diverse place to begin with, has become increasingly diverse, and its already rich and varied literary tradition has become ever more so over time to reflect the evolving cultural and demographic realities of the region; but the mythic West has certainly not disappeared from popular consciousness as a corollary of this movement. The mythic and the actual coexist in western writing, as do the regional and the postregional, much like the modern and the postmodern. Indeed, terms such as "transmythic" and "transregional" or "transwestern" may, for the purpose of discussing issues of identity and cultural expression in the West, be more useful and more accurate than "postmythic" or "postwestern." Whatever the case, it is worth emphasizing that these categories (frontier, region, postregion, etc.), if employed at all, should be treated as fluid, as more likely to merge with one another than to be strictly delineated from one another.

Crossing Canonical Divides

In addition to facilitating cross-cultural, cross-chronological, and urban/suburban–rural comparisons, a more fluid model may help us to move beyond the great divide that seems to separate popular western writing from more "literary" works. In our efforts to illuminate the excesses, oversights, and inadequacies of popular, mythic, frontier, Wild-West conceptions of the West we have been a little too dismissive of expressions of the "to-the-West" mindset. We have imagined a progressive model in which the influence of the popular diminishes as the influence of the literary increases throughout the course of the twentieth century. As noted at the outset, these two seemingly contradictory processes – the rise of a more diverse and demographically representative body of western literature and the persistence of the popular frontier-western literary tradition – have unfolded together.

In charting this ascendancy of so-called "serious" literature and the presumed accompanying decline of "pot-boiler" frontier writing, we have paid a good deal of attention to what we feel merits inclusion in the canon and considerably less attention to what the public reads. Literary scholars tend to presume that figures such as L'Amour are somehow floating in a sea of insignificance, buffeted only by the undiscerning tides of public opinion. But, as Stegner once wittily replied to a probing question concerning the main difference between himself and L'Amour, the answer was "a few million dollars" (Stegner and Etulain, 1996: vi). The point here is not to elevate L'Amour above Stegner, based upon the simplest yardstick of measurement – sales (approximately 250 million copies of L'Amour's works have been sold to date). Rather, it is to emphasize that our existing models may construct the parameters of the literary canon a little too tightly, thereby rendering judgments about the popular and the literary a little too cavalierly, and exaggerating the divisions that exist between "real" and "mythic."

Furthermore, boxing authors into either the "to-the-West" or "in-the-West" category has its dangers, since writers often cross such categories in their careers. Take for example Jack London, whose early "frontier-fiction" phase, featuring most notably *The Call of the Wild* (1903), transitioned into a "regional phase," marked by his California-based novel *The Valley of the Moon* (1913). Similarly, Steinbeck transitioned from "to-the-place" to "in-the-place" writing, moving from the group journey narrative *The Grapes of Wrath* (1939) to the microcosmic study of life in a place in *Cannery Row* (1945). Jack Kerouac moved from the frenetic travel narrative *On the Road* (1957) to the more place-bound and introspective *Big Sur* (1962). A more recent example is William Least Heat Moon, who transitioned from the road book, *Blue Highways: A Journey into America* (1983), to the intensive exploration of place book, *PrairyErth: (a deep map)* (1991), and on to *River-Horse* (1998), which charts his journeys on America's great river systems. Furthermore, western historians as diverse as Frederick Jackson Turner in the 1890s and the first third of the twentieth century, Walter Prescott Webb in the middle third, and Patricia Nelson Limerick in the last two decades, have written about the West as both frontier and region.

Literary scholar Martin Padget, in a recent essay review of current works on the literary West, notes that western American writers have been writing about a land caught up in "the anguish of its own transition" for many years, and that in drawing easy "distinction[s] between Old and New West . . . one runs the risk of drawing arbitrary lines in the sand" (1998: 382–3). Illustrating this point, Padget notes that bestselling western writer Larry McMurtry focused on the nineteenth-century frontier past in *Lonesome Dove: A Novel* (1985), and on "contemporary small town life" in *Texasville* (1987). Moreover, it is worth adding that McMurtry's *The Last Picture Show*, the precursor volume to *Texasville*, and another close exploration of the seamy underside of small-town western "regional" life, was published back in 1966. In later works such as *Buffalo Girls* (1990) and *Anything for Billy* (1988), McMurtry seeks to dismantle the mythology surrounding Billy the Kid, Calamity Jane, and Buffalo Bill Cody. McMurtry has criss-crossed the chronological borders separating the nineteenth- and twentieth-century western landscapes with such frequency that it would be meaningless to divide his work into frontier and regional phases. Etulain views McMurtry as the quintessential example of the "new gray West," of a new western literature that has been increasingly evident since the mid-1960s (Etulain, 1999: 137). Yet, as Etulain himself notes, there are plenty of examples of (or precursors to) this gray West in the early and mid-twentieth century – he cites Cather, Guthrie, Jr., Mari Sandoz, Steinbeck, and Stegner as examples.

The "gray West," it seems, has been a feature in western writing at least as early as Edgar Watson Howe's harrowing and myth-shattering account of agrarian existence *The Story of a Country Town* (1883). Howe's book might be paralleled with Annie Proulx's recent and disturbing collection *Close Range: Wyoming Stories* (1999), which exhibits a deep sense of place unfettered by romantic notions about life in the region. Published more than a century apart, these two books illuminate the connections between works of western writing from different eras and underscore the need to move beyond the boundaries of our own prescriptive analytical modeling. Western historians from Earl Pomeroy in the 1950s and 1960s to Limerick in the 1980s and 1990s have emphasized the theme of continuity between the nineteenth- and twentieth-century Wests. Those connections can clearly be drawn between works of western literature from different periods. Yet, western literary historians and literary critics have generally emphasized not the continuities but the great divides in modern western writing.

Movement & Adjustment: A Model for Cross-Cultural/Chronological Comparison

So how do we begin to dissolve or at least de-emphasize the dichotomies of frontier and region, "to-the-West" and "in-the-West," region and postregion/postwestern in western American literary history and criticism? The recently opened Tate Modern Art Gallery on London's increasingly fashionable South Bank is indicative of a trend in exhibition management that may help provide an answer. At the Tate Modern (housed in a converted power station and designed by Swiss architects Jacques Herzog and Pierre de Meuron) a wondrous array of works of twentieth-century art and sculpture is arranged thematically, not chronologically, or by school, or movement, or style. This arrangement might seem jarring to the viewer at first, and has raised the ire of a number of art critics. But the thematic arrangement of works enables viewers to compare works in broad categories such as "Landscape/Matter/ Environment" and "History/Memory/Society." In the early 1990s, the controversial Smithsonian Institution exhibit "The West as America" (1990–1) also arranged works thematically. Indeed, since thematic arrangement is becoming more and more common in the art world, it can help us to rethink American western writing and draw connections across chronological and cultural divides.

Somehow, in assembling our chronological frameworks the writings of different racial and ethnic groups have become increasingly separated. The autobiographical writings of Mourning Dove in the early twentieth century and Nate Love in the late nineteenth, for example, came to be viewed as precursors of later works by Native Americans, mixed-bloods, and African Americans. We have, in fact, in constructing literary canons, often taken such works out of chronological context in order to place them into cultural groupings. By following a strictly thematic model, one that is neither chronologically hidebound, nor divided up into separate racial and ethnic groupings, we may be able to achieve more meaningful cross-cultural and cross-chronological comparison and synthesis. This involves setting aside our notions of a western mainstream literature broadening to include minority literary streams and consequently becoming postwestern, and thinking instead of a model for western literature more akin to that offered by historian Frederick Jackson Turner for conceptualizing America's separate regions. Turner (1994b) described the nation's regions as "fit rooms in a worthy house." Most existing models, by contrast, construct a "white" thematic superstructure with "colored" additions tacked on. How, then, can we reconceptualize western literature and put all the rooms into a single (if massive) structure, like the works of art at the Tate Modern?

More than a decade ago historian and literary scholar Annette Kolodny (1992) offered some very important clues for disassembling the existing literary puzzle and reassembling a new one. She explained that existing paradigms of literary analysis exhibit a tendency to "obscure any text that cannot be accommodated to whatever are currently accepted as the features of the mature national literary consciousness" (1992: 12) and, as a consequence, tend to promote notions of American cultural and literary exceptionalism." She proposed as an alternative model the "thematizing [of] frontier as a multiplicity of ongoing first encounters over time and land, rather than as a linear chronology of successive discoveries and discrete settlements" (ibid.: 13). This much, she stated, would be necessary for us to "let go our grand obsessions with narrowly geographic and strictly chronological frameworks" (ibid.: 3).

Kolodny's directive is still a tall order given the power of the existing frameworks and the acuteness of our obsession with them. Taking her lead and applying her model to the literature of the American West in the twentieth century is difficult to do, of course, since comparatively narrow geographic parameters and strict chronology are implied in the very phrase "twentieth-century western writing." What is offered here is a diluted application at best, and one that maintains that there are certain themes that, while not unique *to*, are particularly pronounced *in* the western context.

Western writing in the twentieth century, regardless of the subregion, racial and ethnic groupings, or rural or urban locales from which it has sprung, has primarily centered on the topics of "movement" and "adjustment." People have of course migrated to places and adjusted to them in all parts of the West, the nation, and the world since the beginning of human history. The West is not different by nature so much as by degree. The themes of movement and adjustment seem more applicable to this region of the country since the West increasingly became, in the course of the twentieth century, the locus for immigration from all other parts of the country and the world. The movement of Americans of European extraction into the trans-Mississippi West in the second half of the nineteenth century is paralleled by the movements of immigrants from Asian, South American, and Central American countries in the twentieth, particularly since the passage of the Hart-Celler Immigration Act in 1965. Because the rates of migration to the West and within it have been so acute, the processes of adjustment have been particularly pronounced. Highlighting these ongoing processes of movement and adjustment leads to a natural emphasis on certain historical continuities and cultural parallels, as historian Walter Nugent (1999) has recently shown. But the approach of this essay is not intentionally ahistorical or consciously incognizant of the different circumstances experienced by various racial and ethnic groups; rather, it eschews emphasis on those differences in order to draw parallels across boundaries of race/ethnicity and time.

Since the themes of movement and adjustment are so vital to understanding life in the West, it should come as no surprise that twentieth-century western writing is, in turn, so often characterized by these very forms. And, unlike the organizing themes of frontier, region, and postregion, or westernness and postwesternness, mobility and adjustment are themes that apply equally well and at all times to all the peoples within the West. Indeed, these themes may even assist us in going beyond the separatist group-centeredness that currently dominates so much western history and literature. The success of contemporary western authors, from Momaday, Silko, and Tan, to Anaya, Barbara Kingsolver, and others, in reaching large audiences, suggests that powerful writing can cut across ethnic lines to tell human stories about universally vital issues (just as regional writing should transcend the boundaries of a single place to address universal concerns). The list should also remind us that women are at the center of the western literary tradition, and have always been important shapers of it.

Fit Rooms for a Worthy House

So how do we link these various writers together within the thematic framework of mobility and adjustment? Three possible subthemes (fit rooms for a worthy house) within the framework spring to mind: the individual travel narrative, stories of family adjustment and inter-generational tension, and works of autobiography and reminiscence. A few brief examples of cross-cultural literary comparisons are provided, rather than lengthy examinations of any individual works. One suspects that many other examples will spring to readers' minds.

The individual travel narrative is one of the staples of western writing and one that cuts across the categories of interior and exterior expressions of regionalism. Both westerners and nonwesterners have recorded their instant impressions of western places in the course of traveling through them. The tradition stretches back at least as far as Lewis and Clark at the beginning of the nineteenth century. In the closing years of that century the West was still largely unknown terrain for most Americans at the same time that many observers lamented that the frontier's journey across the West was over and that the West was becoming just like the rest of the nation. A multitude of travel narratives appeared to satisfy the reading public's curiosity about the region, including Richard Harding Davis' *The West from a Car Window* (1892), and Charles Fletcher Lummis' account of his 1884 journey on foot from Chillicothe, Ohio to Los Angeles, *A Tramp Across the Continent* (1892). As the West became increasingly well known by the nation during the course of the twentieth century, the travel narrative remained a staple in writings about the West. Even in the closing decades of this last century, the lure of the West has remained strong for travel writers and scores of notable books in the genre appeared, including Robert Kaplan's *An Empire Wilderness: Travel's Into America's Future* (1998), Frazier's *Great Plains* (1989), Duncan's *Out West: An American Journey* (1987) and *Miles from Nowhere: Tales from America's Contemporary Frontier* (1993).

If there is a conclusion that can be drawn from the enduring popularity of such works perhaps it is simply that the West, always at the heart of the nation's creation story, continues to sustain the interest of the reading public, enabling people to visit the place vicariously, even in an age when they can visit it virtually, on line, anytime. Even as we continue to bemoan (as Americans were doing a century ago) the forces of standardization and homogenization that are supposedly sweeping the country, we turn to western travel narratives in the hope that there is still something distinct and exceptional about the nation's newest American region. Western travel literature is worth studying as a genre that may not be entirely unique, but is clearly more prevalent than the travel literature of other American regions. Furthermore, the genre is not neatly divisible into categories of frontier, region, and postregion; rather, it is an enduring and natural cultural element in a region marked by mobility.

Notably, western travel literature, contrary to the expectations one might draw from the writers listed above, is not an exclusively white European American endeavor. We can broaden our canonical horizons to incorporate a wide range of travel writings by peoples of color in the West, writings that serve to illuminate the theme of adjustment and the variety of lived experiences in the region. One thinks here immediately of Chinese American writer Frank Chin's wonderful California travel narrative "Pidgin Contest Along I-5" (1998). Chin recounts the reactions of white Americans – from skinheads to little old ladies – to himself and his son, Sam, as they travel on I-5, "the road between Seattle and LA I've called home for thirty years" (1998: 35–6). The chronological backdrop of Chin's journey narrative is the immediate post-Gulf War euphoria and accompanying heightened jingoism in the white mainstream, which he juxtaposes with the rage and confusion of LA's multiple minorities during the 1992 riots. Chin and his son are made to feel like aliens along I-5 as they are refused service at a restaurant in Northern California; the owners unashamedly tell them that the place (which is filled with white customers) is closed. Then, during the riots, white news anchors and reporters comment on how "most of the looters look like illegal aliens" (ibid: 37); meanwhile the National Guardsmen and Secret Servicemen who descend upon the city seem like alien invaders to the culturally diverse residents of LA.

Chin's "Pidgin Contest Along I-5" is no *Travels With Charley*, and even Jack Kerouac's *On the Road*, with its Benzedrine-fueled prose and wide-eyed dreams of the West, from Denver to San Francisco with Neal Cassady (a.k.a. Dean Moriarty), seems tame and romantic compared with Frank and Sam Chin's observations and experiences. The same could be said for African American Evelyn C. White's essay "Black Women and the Wilderness" (1995) which might be described as an anti-travel narrative of sorts. White describes her reluctance to explore the great outdoors when conducting a writing workshop in the foothills of Oregon's Cascade Mountains. White writes that she experienced "a sense of absolute doom about what might befall me in the backwoods" (1995: 378), but had difficulty articulating those anxieties to students and colleagues. How can one convey to white Oregonians the "genetic memory of ancestors hunted down and preyed upon in rural settings" (ibid.: 378)? White's response to wilderness as she ventures out into one of the West's great "natural wonderlands" departs radically from the standard white "master" narrative of western travel literature. She eventually manages to overcome some of her fears, starts to enjoy wilderness treks, in much the same limited way that Chin enjoys truck stop food bars along I-5 – with the knowledge that white people are staring, wondering what these aliens are doing, in wilderness areas, at truck stops. The addition of Chin, White, and other diverse voices to the western travel literature genre helps us to see the region from vital angles of vision. Indeed, our vision of the West seems rather peripheral without them.

Similarly, one wonders how stories of family adjustment to western places, such as Davis' *Honey in the Horn* (1935), Steinbeck's *The Grapes of Wrath* (1939), or Stegner's *Angle of Repose* (1971), can be categorized separately from works such as Anaya's *Bless Me Ultima* (1972), Tan's *The Joy Luck Club* (1989), or Chin's *Donald Duk* (1991), if we are to envision a western literature that is representative of the region's diverse voices. These are all literary explorations of how families try to orient themselves to new western surroundings and they underscore the centrality of the theme of adjustment in western writing. Yet, while the parallels between these works are obvious, the tendency among literary scholars is still to group together writers such as Steinbeck and Davis as western regionalists, and to view Anaya, Tan, Chin, and a host of other western writers of color as representative voices of their cultural groups or of a broader subaltern west. But surely *The Grapes of Wrath* and Steinbeck's earlier journalistic work on California's white migrant labor force (Steinbeck, 1996) has as much in common with Carlos Bulosan's semi-autobiographical *America is in the Heart* (1946), which traces the experiences of Filipino migrant workers laboring in the fields and canneries from the Mexican border to Alaska in the 1920s and 1930s, as it does with other classics of white western regionalism. Exploring both the parallels and the departures in the experiences of different cultural groups moving into and around and adjusting to various parts of the West is likely to enrich our understanding of all the groups' experiences and of the diversity within each cultural group.

Regarding the third of these fit rooms in a worthy house – works of autobiography and reminiscence: historian Richard Maxwell Brown has written recently (1996) about what he calls "the new western autobiography," citing Ivan Doig's *This House of Sky: Landscapes of a Western Mind* (1978), Mary Clearman Blew's *All But the Waltz: Essays on a Montana Family* (1991), and Kittredge's *Hole in the Sky: A Memoir* (1992), as examples. These are, as Brown makes clear, harrowing works charting various tragedies and failures as families sought to adjust to western places. But, as

Brown further notes, these works "do not leave the reader sunk in pessimism . . . one is left with both purged and purified emotions and with hope" (1996: 60).

We could add a good number of nonwhite western voices to this mix and the same theme of "courage without illusion" would apply. Luis Alberto Urrea's *Nobody's Son: Notes from an American Life* (1998), a memoir of a childhood divided between Tijuana and San Diego, between Mexican roots and "mainstream" American culture, and the search for identity in adulthood, merits inclusion as a vital example of this new western autobiography. Richard Rodriguez's *Hunger of Memory: The Education of Richard Rodriguez* (1981) and his *Days of Obligation: An Argument with My Mexican Father* (1992) explore similar themes of adjustment in a complex multicultural West where simplistic notions of race and identity still prevail. Jeanne Wakatsuki Houston's *Farewell to Manzanar* (1973), coauthored with her husband James D. Houston, also traces the theme of family adjustment, in a World War II internment camp. We could add to the list Chinese-Hawaiian writer Kathleen Tyau's essay "The City I Colored White," an account of the author's and her family's adjustment to her going to university in Oregon in the 1950s (1995). "Oregon," Tyau writes, "was my frontier." But Tyau felt she was "not Chinese enough, yet not truly Hawaiian. I didn't feel like I belonged to either race. . . . So I longed to be *hapa haole*, part white, to merge with white skin and culture" (1995: 370).

And, of course, works by Native American writers such as Mary Brave Bird's *Lakota Woman* (1990) and the mixed-blood Mourning Dove's *Co-ge-we-a, the Half-Blood* (1927) also fit well in Brown's "courage without illusion" category and enrich the genre of modern western autobiography and reminiscence. What is more, it goes without saying that the themes of mobility and adjustment are pervasive in all of these works by western writers of color. Surely, if we consider this vast array of western writings, from those of Doig, Blew, and Kittredge, to those of Urrea, Rodriguez, Houston, Tyau, Mary Crow Dog, Mourning Dove, and many others, our western literary horizons become more challenging and revealing.

Race is, of course, a central issue in these autobiographical accounts of individual and family adjustment to place by western authors of color. The tendency, though, has been to place such writings outside of the framework of western writing. Nonetheless, cross-cultural comparative analysis of travel writings, family adjustment stories, and autobiographies and reminiscences, surely points us toward a western literary canon that better reflects the cultural composition of the region. Furthermore, such a broad and inclusionary framework underscores the importance of the metatheme of mobility and adjustment to western literary expressions.

Conclusion

Various scholars have taken important steps toward the kind of comparative literary analysis that is needed in the field. Elliott West points to some of the possible cross-cultural connections in his treatment of western "Stories" by comparing place-centered Native American narratives with place-centered European-American regionalist narratives. Literary scholar Krista Comer also charts fruitful new directions in her important recent book, *Landscapes of the New West: Gender and Geography in Contemporary Western Women's Writing* (1999). Comer expresses her unwillingness to let western regionalism remain a "white thing" and reconstructs the western literary landscape not to merely accommodate writers of color and the theme of gender, but to make them central to it. One memorable player in Comer's inclusionist paradigm is the black Los Angles poet Wanda Coleman, a woman who ". . . likes cars . . . loves the freeway . . . [and] is thoroughly preoccupied with issues of space and mobility" (1999: 357). Yet our existing strict parameters of literary perception and classification somehow mandate (albeit unofficially) that she falls through the cracks between African American literature, LA writing and western writing. But Coleman writes about black communities in LA, communities undergoing processes of mobility and adjustment, poverty and violence, and doing so in ways more pronounced than those experienced by many westerners. Surely her recordings of those processes are no less a part of the literature of the region than those of the great white western writers who are more commonly associated with it.

Putting Wanda Coleman, along with other writers of color, into the western literary pantheon, has the obvious advantage of giving us a literature that takes us beyond the canonical confines of the western American literary tradition to reflect the demographic realities of the region. Similarly, placing urban literature into "the West," or better, recognizing that it has always been there – from Frank Norris's San Francisco-based novel *McTeague* (1899) at the turn of the century, to Didion's LA-freeway-based *Play It as It Lays* (1970) and in a multitude of works published since then – also reflects the region's demographic and geographic realities.

The price, of course, of adopting this more inclusive model is that not all people of color in the West will want their literature subsumed within the category of "modern western writing" (just as not all rural western writers will want their work categorized together with urban western writing). This reaction notwithstanding, the term "modern western writing" is applied here as a simple descriptor for twentieth-century writings from and about a geographic region lying between the Plains and the Pacific, regardless of the race, ethnicity, or gender of the author. The term is certainly *not* used here as a synonym for writing that reflects the mythic white male and rural literary tradition of "westernness."

Still, there remain obvious advantages to separateness of literary canons for those groups that are underrepresented or unrepresented in the prevailing mainstream canonical tradition. Every racial and ethnic group could argue that it has experienced special circumstances and has had special concerns that render its modes of literary expression distinct from those of other groups. Native American writers might resent comparative analyzes of Indian sense of place and white western sense of place, finding the two sets of cultural traditions essentially incomparable. Native writers might argue that white western writers, while they may have moved from a tradition of "to-the-place" literature to an "in-the-place" literary framework (from frontier to region), are not "of-the-place" in the way indigenous peoples are. Or, again, they might emphasize the incompatibility of Indian oral storytelling traditions and Euro-American literary models. Minority writers and scholars may argue that a literary model that places the majority culture and the minority cultures together, within a single framework, would simply perpetuate the canonical hegemony of the majority and render minority literatures indistinct and unexceptional.

These issues are at the heart of age-old and contemporary debates about race and ethnicity in America, about cultural inclusiveness and individual assimilation versus group-centered collective action and cultural separateness and preservation. What is offered here, of course, is *a* single alternative model, not *the* only viable solution. It is a thematic alternative that might help us reconsider our western literary horizons in some small way. It is not a framework that requires us to ignore issues of racial disparity, or to assume that integration is preferable to cultural separation in every case. Nor does it imply that chronological context is unimportant or deny that deep differences separate rural Wests from western cities. Still, in our thinking about western writing, we have dwelt on the great divides at the expense of the connecting streams, and the latter warrant more attention.

Ultimately, then, we will either have to broaden the concept of westernness and find ways to apply it to *all* the people of the region residing in its many and varied rural, urban, and suburban locales – to make it more inclusive and more reflective of regional realities – or we will have to reject westernness as a construct that is too rigid and simplistic and therefore unfit for a dynamic and complex place. My preference is for following the former course, not the latter. This effort to broaden our conception of westernness as it is applied to western writing may even help point the way. What is certain is that in the light of the many memorable efforts by western writers in the twentieth century to address the key issues that face the nation – including race relations and economic disparities – critical assessments of the provincialism of western writing ring hollow indeed. However, if we continue to divide up the region's literary production in ways that preclude comparison and communication between the works of diverse cultural groups in different periods, western American literary history and criticism will seem provincial indeed in the twenty-first century.

REFERENCES

Allmendinger, Blake: *Ten Most Wanted: The New Western Literature* (New York: Routledge, 1998).

Allmendinger, Blake: "Proposition 2000: Debating California's Sesquicentennial." *Western American Literature* 34 (Summer 1999), 173–7.

Anon: "New Ways of Seeing." *Tate: The Art Magazine* 21 (2000): 48–9.

Anaya, Rudolfo: *Bless Me Ultima* (New York: Warner Books, 1972).

Athearn, Robert G.: *The Mythic West in Twentieth-Century America* (Lawrence: University Press of Kansas, 1986).

Balassi, William, John F. Crawford, and Annie O. Eysturov (eds.): *This is About Vision: Interviews with Southwestern Writers* (Albuquerque: University of New Mexico Press, 1990).

Barnes, Kim and Mary Clearman Blew (eds.): *Circle of Women: An Anthology of Contemporary Western Women's Writing* (New York: Penguin, 1994).

Blackburn, Alexander: "A Western Renaissance." *Western American Literature* 29 (Spring, 1994), 51–62.

Blew, Mary Clearman: *All But the Waltz: Essays on a Montana Family* (New York: Viking, 1991).

Blew, Mary Clearman: *Bone Deep in Landscape: Writing, Reading, and Place* (Norman: University of Oklahoma Press, 1999).

Boag, Peter: "Mountain, Plain, Desert, River: The Snake River Valley as a Western Crossroads." In David Wrobel Michael Steiner (eds.) *Many Wests: Place, Culture, and Regional Identity* (Lawrence: University Press of Kansas, 1997).

Bouldrey, Brian: *Writing Home: Award-Winning Literature from the New West* (Berkeley, California: Heyday Books, 1999).

Boynton, Percy: *The Rediscovery of the Frontier* (Chicago: University of Chicago Press, 1931).

Brave Bird, Mary (with Richard Erdoes): *Lakota Woman* (New York: Grove Weidenfeld, 1990).

Brown, Richard Maxwell: "Courage Without Illusion." In Clyde Milner, II (ed.) *A New Significance: Re-Envisioning the History of the American West* (New York: Oxford University Press, 1996).

Buck, Pearl S.: *The Good Earth* (New York: Grossett & Dunlap, 1931).

Bulosan. Carlos: *America Is in the Heart* ([1946] rpt., Seattle: University of Washington Press, 2000).

Butler, Anne M: "Selling the Popular Myth." In Clyde A. Milner, II, Carol A. O'Connor, and Martha A. Sandweiss (eds.) *The Oxford History of the American West* (New York: Oxford University Press, 1994).

Capote, Truman: *In Cold Blood* (New York: Random House, 1966).

Cather, Willa: *One of Ours* (New York: Knopf, 1922).

Chin, Frank: *Donald Duk* (St Paul, MN: Coffee House Press, 1991).

Chin, Frank: *Bulletproof Buddhists and Other Essays* (Honolulu: University of Hawaii Press, 1998).

Chin, Frank: "Pidgin Contest Along I-5." In Brian Bouldrey (ed.) *Writing Home: Award Winning Literature from the New West* (Berkeley, CA: Heydey Books, 1999).

Comer, Krista: *Landscapes of the New West: Gender and Geography in Contemporary Women's Writing* (Chapel Hill: University of North Carolina Press, 1999).

Comer, Krista: "Revising Western Criticism Through Wanda Coleman." *Western American Literature* 33 (Winter 1999). 356–83.

Davis, H. L.: *Honey in the Horn* (New York: Harper and Brothers, 1935).

Davis, H. L. and James Stevens: *Status Rerum: A Manifesto Upon the Present Condition of Northwestern Literature, Containing Several Near-Libelous Utterances, Upon Persons in the Public Eye* (The Dalles, Oregon: n.p., 1927).

Davis, Richard Harding: *The West from a Car Window* (New York: Harper, 1892).

Didion, Joan: *Play It as It Lays* (New York: Farrar, Straus & Giroux, 1970).

Doig, Ivan: *This House of Sky: Landscapes of a Western Mind* (New York: Harcourt, Brace Jovanovich, 1978).

Duncan, Dayton: *Out West: An American Journey* (New York: Viking, 1987).

Duncan, Dayton: *Miles from Nowhere: Tales from America's Contemporary Frontier* (New York: Viking, 1993).

Egan, Tim: *Lasso the Wind: Away to the New West* (New York: Random House, 1998).

Elliott, Emory (ed.): *Columbia Literary History of the United States* (New York: Columbia University Press, 1988).

Erisman, Fred: "The Changing Face of Western Literary Realism." In Gerald D. Nash and Richard W. Etulain (eds.) *The Twentieth-Century West: Historical Interpretations* (Albuquerque: University of New Mexico Press, 1989).

Erisman, Fred and Richard W. Etulain (eds.): *Fifty Western Writers: A Bio-Bibliographical Sourcebook* (Westport, CT: Greenwood Press, 1982).

Etulain, Richard W.: "The American Literary West and Its Interpreters: The Rise of a New Historiography." *Pacific Historical Review*, 45 (August 1976), 311–48.

Etulain, Richard W.: "Western Fiction and History: A Reconsideration." In Jerome O. Steffen (ed.) *The American West: New Perspectives, New Dimensions* (Norman: University of Oklahoma Press, 1979).

Etulain, Richard W.: "Main Currents in Modern Western Literature." In Richard W. Etulain (ed.) "Cultural History of the American West," Special Issue, *Journal of American Culture*, 3 (Summer 1980), 374–88.

Etulain, Richard W.: *The American Literary West* (Manhattan, KS: Sunflower University Press, 1980).

Etulain, Richard W.: *A Bibliographical Guide to the Study of American Western Literature* (Lincoln: University of Nebraska Press, 1982).

Etulain, Richard W.: *Re-Imagining the Modern American West: A Century of Fiction, History, and Art* (Tucson: University of Arizona Press, 1996).

Etulain, Richard W.: "Research Opportunities in Twentieth-Century Western Cultural History." In Gerald D. Nash and Richard W. Etulain (eds.) *Research Western History: Topics in the Twentieth Century* (Albuquerque: University of New Mexico Press, 1997).

Etulain, Richard W.: *Telling Western Stories: From Buffalo Bill to Larry McMurtry* (Albuquerque: University of New Mexico Press, 1999).

Etulain, Richard W.: "Western Stories for the Next Generation," *Western Historical Quarterly* 31 (Spring 2000), 5–23.

Etulain, Richard W. and N. Jill Howard (eds.): *A Bibliographical Guide to the Study of American Western Literature*, 2nd edn. (Albuquerque: University of New Mexico Press, 1995).

Featherstone, Mike: *Consumer Culture and Postmodernism* (London: Sage, 1991).

Fine, David (ed.): *Los Angeles in Fiction: A Collection of Essays*, rev. ed. (Albuquerque: University of New Mexico Press, 1995).

Frazier, Ian: *Great Plains* (New York: Farrar, Straus Giroux, 1989).

Fussell, Edwin: *Frontier: American Literature and the American West* (Princeton, NJ: Princeton University Press, 1965).

Georgi-Findlay, Brigitte: *The Frontiers of Women's Writing: Women's Narratives and the Rhetoric of Westward Expansion* (Tucson: University of Arizona Press, 1996).

Gorman, Ed and Martin H. Greenberg (eds.): *The Best of the American West* (New York: Penguin/Putnam, 1998).

Gorman, Ed and Martin H. Greenberg (eds.): *The Best of the American West, II* (New York: Berkley Books, 1999).

Guthrie, A. B., Jr.: *The Way West* (Boston: Houghton, Mifflin, 1949).

Hazard, Lucy Lockwood: *The Frontier in American Literature* (New York: Thomas Y. Crowell, Co., 1927).

Heat Moon, William Least: *Blue Highways* (Boston: Little, Brown, 1983).

Heat Moon, William Least: *PrairyErth: (a deep map)* (Boston: Houghton, Miflin, 1991).

Heat Moon, William Least: *River-Horse: The Logbook of a Boat across America* (Boston, Houghton, Miflin, 1999).

Houston, Jeanne Wakatsuki and James Houston: *Farewell to Manzanar* (Boston: Houghton, Mifflin, 1973).

Howe, Edgar Watson: *The Story of a Country Town* (Atchison, KS: Howe and CO., 1883).

Johnson, Michael L.: *New Westers: The West in Contemporary American Culture* (Lawrence: University Press of Kansas, 1996).

Jordan, Teresa and James Hepworth (eds.): *The Stories that Shape Us: Contemporary Women Write About the West* (New York: W. W. Norton, 1995).

Kaplan, Robert: *An Empire Wilderness: Travels Into America's Future* (New York: Random House, 1998).

Kerouac, Jack: *On the Road* (New York: Viking, 1957).

Kerouac, Jack: *Big Sur* (New York: Farrar, Straus and Cudahy, 1962).

Kingston, Hong: *Landscapes of the New West: Gender and Geography in Contemporary Women's Writing* (Chapel Hill: University of North Carolina Press, 1999).

Kittredge, William: *Hole in the Sky: A Memoir* (New York: Knopf, 1992).

Kittredge, William: *The Portable Western Reader* (New York: Penguin, 1997).

Kolodny, Annette: "Letting Go Our Grand Obsessions: Notes Toward a New Literary History of American Frontiers." *American Literature* 64 (March 1992), 1–18.

Kowalewski, Michael. *Reading the West: New Essays on the Literature of the American West* (NY: Cambridge University Press, 1996).

Levine, Lawrence W.: *Highbrow/Lowbrow: The Emergence of Cultural Hierarchy in America* (Cambridge, MA: Harvard University Press, 1983).

Lewis, Merrill and L. L. Lee (eds.): *The Westering Experience in American Literature: Bicentennial Essays* (Bellingham: Bureau for Faculty Research, Western Washington University, 1977).

Limerick, Patricia Nelson: *The Legacy of Conquest: The Unbroken Past of the American West* (New York: W. W. Norton, 1987).

Limerick, Patricia Nelson: "The Adventures of the Frontier in the Twentieth Century." In James Grossman (ed.) *The Frontier in American Culture* (Berkeley and Los Angeles: California University Press, 1994).

Limerick, Patricia Nelson, Clyde Milner, II, and Charles Rankin (eds.): *Trails: Toward a New Western History* (Lawrence: University Press of Kansas, 1991).

London, Jack: *Call of the Wild* (New York: Macmillan, 1903).

London, Jack: *Valley of the Moon* (New York: Macmillan, 1913).

Lummis, Charles Fletcher: *A Tramp Across the Continent* ([1892], reprinted Lincoln: University of Nebraska Press, 1982).

Lyon, Thomas J.: "Beyond the Frontier Mind." In Judy Nolte Lensink (ed.) *Old Southwest, New Southwest: Essays on a Region and Its Literature* (Tucson: Tucson Public Library, 1987).

Lyon, Thomas J. (ed.): *The Literary West: An Anthology of Western American Literature* (New York: Oxford University Press, 1999).

Lyon, Thomas J.: "The Literary West." In Clyde A. Milner, II, Carol A. O'Connor, and Martha Sandweiss (eds.) *The Oxford History of the American West* (New York: Oxford University Press, 1994).

Lyon, Thomas J. and J. Golden Taylor (eds.): *Updating the Literary West* (Fort Worth: Texas Christian University Press, 1997).

McMurtry, Larry: *The Last Picture Show* (New York: Dial Press, 1966).

McMurtry, Larry: *Lonesome Dove* (New York: Simon and Schuster 1985).

McMurtry, Larry: *Texasville* (New York: Simon and Schuster, 1987).

McMurtry, Larry: *Anything for Billy* (New York: Simon and Schuster, 1988).

McMurtry, Larry: *Buffalo Girls* (New York: Simon and Schuster, 1990).

McMurtry, Larry (ed.): *Still Wild: Short Fiction of the American West, 1950 to the Present* (New York: Alfred A. Knopf, 2000).

Martin, Russell (ed.): *New Writers of the Purple Sage: An Anthology of Contemporary Western Writing* (New York: Penguin Books, 1992).

Martin, Russell and Marc Barasch: *Writers of the Purple Sage: An Anthology of Recent Western Writing* (New York: Viking Penguin, Inc., 1984).

Meldrum, Barbara Howard (ed.): *Under the Sun: Myth and Realism in Western American Literature* (Troy, NY: Whitson, 1985).

Momaday, N. Scott: *House Made of Dawn* (New York: Harper & Row, 1968).

Morgan, David, Mark Busby, and Paul Bryant (eds.): *The Frontier Experience and the American Dream: Essays on American Literature* (College Station: Texas A & M University Press, 1989).

Morris, Gregory L.: *Talking Up a Storm: Voices of the New West* (Lincoln: University of Nebraska Press, 1988).

Mourning Dove: *Co-ge-we-a, the Half-Blood: A Depiction of the Great Montana cattle Range* (Boston: The Four Seas Company, 1927).

Nash, Gerald D.: *Creating the West: Historical Interpretations, 1890–1990* (Albuquerque: University of New Mexico Press, 1991).

Norwood, Vera and Janice Monk (eds.): *The Desert is No Lady: Southwestern Landscapes in Women's Writing and Art* (New Haven, CT: Yale University Press, 1987).

Norris, Frank: *McTeague* ([1899], reprinted New York: Norton, 1977).

Nugent, Walter: *Into the West: The Story of Its People* (New York: Alfred A. Knopf, 1999).

Padget, Martin: "Claiming, Corrupting, Contesting: Reconsidering 'The West' in Western American Literature." *American Literary History* 10 (Summer 1998), 378–92.

Pomeroy, Earl: "Toward A Reconsideration of American Western History." *Mississippi Valley Historical Review* 41 (March 1955), 579–600.

Pomeroy, Earl: *The Pacific Slope: A History of California, Oregon, Washington, Idaho, Utah, and Nevada* (Lincoln and London: University of Nebraska Press, 1991).

Proulx, Annie: *Close Range: Wyoming Stories* (New York: Scribner, 1999).

Riley, Glenda: *Women and Nature: Saving the "Wild" West* (Lincoln: University of Nebraska Press, 1999).

Rodriguez, Richard: *Hunger of Memory: The Education of Richard Rodriguez* (Boston: D. R. Godine, 1981).

Rodriguez, Richard: *Days of Obligation: An Argument with My Mexican Father* (New York: Viking, 1992).

Scharff, Virginia: "Mobility, Women, and the West." In Valerie J. Matsumoto and Blake Allmendinger (eds.) *Over the Edge: Remapping the American West* (Berkeley: University of California Press, 1999).

Scharff, Virginia: *Twenty Thousand Roads: Women, Movement, and the West* (Berkeley: University of California Press, 2003).

Scharnhorst, Gary: "In Defense of Western Literary Biography." *Western American Literature*, 33 (Winter 1999), 345–53.

Schlissel, Lillian and Catherine Lavender: *The Western Women's Reader* (New York: Harper Perennial, 2000).

Simonson, Harold P.: *Beyond the Frontier: Writers, Western Regionalism and a Sense of Place* (Fort Worth: Texas Christian University Press, 1989).

Smith, Henry Nash: *Virgin Land: The American West as Symbol and Myth* (Cambridge, MA: Harvard University Press, 1950, 1970).

Snodgrass, Mary Ellen: *Encyclopedia of Frontier Literature* (Santa Barbara, CA: ABC-CLIO, 1997).

Stauffer, Helen Winter and Susan Rosowski: *Women and Western American Literature* (Troy, NY: Whitstone, 1982).

Stegner, Wallace: *Angle of Repose* (New York: Doubleday, 1971).

Stegner, Wallace and Richard W. Etulain: *Stegner: Conversations on History and Literature* (Reno: University of Nevada Press, 1996).

Stegner, Wallace: *Angle of Repose* (New York: Doubleday, 1971).

Steinbeck, John: *The Grapes of Wrath* (New York: Viking, 1939).

Steinbeck, John: *Cannery Row* (New York: Viking, 1945).

Steinbeck, John: *The Harvest Gypsies: On the Road to* The Grapes of Wrath (Berkeley, CA: Heydey Books, 1996).

Tan, Amy: *The Joy Luck Club* (New York: Putnam's, 1989).

Tompkins, Jane: *West of Everything: The Inner Life of Westerns* (New York: Oxford University Press, 1992).

Truettner, William H. (ed.): *The West as America: Reinterpreting Images of the Frontier, 1820–1920* (Washington, DC: Smithsonian Institution Press, 1991).

Tuan, Yi-fu: *Topophilia: A Study of Environmental Perception, Attitudes, and Values* (Englewood Cliffs, NJ: Prentice Hall, 1974).

Turner, Frederick Jackson: "The Significance of the Frontier in American History." In John Mack Faragher (ed.) *Rereading Frederick Jackson Turner: "The Significance of the Frontier in American History" and Other Essays* (New York: Henry Holt and Co., 1994a).

Turner, Frederick Jackson: "Sections and Nation." In John Mack Faragher (ed.) *Rereading*

Frederick Jackson Turner: "The Significance of the Frontier in American History" and Other Essays (New York: Henry Holt and Co., 1994b).

Turner, Frederick Jackson: "The Significance of Sections in American History." In John Mack Faragher (ed.) *Rereading Frederick Jackson Turner: "The Significance of the Frontier in American History" and Other Essays* (New York: Henry Holt and Co., 1994c).

Tuska, Jon and Vicki Piekarski (eds.): *The Frontier Experience: A Reader's Guide to the Life and Literature of the American West* (Jefferson, NC: McFarland and Co., Inc., 1984).

Tyau, Kathleen: "The City I Colored White." In Kathleen Tyau *A Little Too Much is Enough* (New York: Farrar, Straus and Giroux, 1995).

Urrea, Luis Alberto: *Nobody's Son: Notes from an American Life* (Tucson: University of Arizona Press, 1998).

Webb, Walter Prescott: *The Great Plains* (New York: Grosset & Dunlap, 1931).

Webb, Walter Prescott: *Divided We Stand: The Crisis of a Frontierless Democracy* (New York, Toronot: Farrar & Rinehart, 1937).

Webb, Walter Prescott: *The Great Frontier* (Boston: Houghton Mifflin, 1952).

West, Elliott: "Stories." In Elliott West (ed.) *The Way to the West: Essays on the Central Plains* (Albuquerque: University of New Mexico Press, 1995).

West, Elliott: "Selling the Myth: Western Themes in Advertising." *Montana: The Magazine of Western History* (Summer 1996), 36–50.

White, Evelyn C.: "Black Women and the Wilderness." In Teresa Jordan and James Hepworth (eds.): *The Stories that Shape Us: Contemporary Women Write About the West* (New York: W. W. Norton, 1995).

Work, James C. (ed.): *Prose and Poetry of the American West* (Lincoln: University of Nebraska Press, 1990).

Wrobel, David M.: *The End of American Exceptionalism: Frontier Anxiety from the Old West to the New Deal* (Lawrence: University Press of Kansas, 1993).

Wrobel, David M.: "Beyond the Frontier-Region Dichotomy." *Pacific Historical Review* 65 (August 1996), 401–429.

Bibliography

Abbey, Edward: *Desert Solitaire: A Season in the Wilderness* (New York: McGraw-Hill, 1968).

Abbott, Carl: *The New Urban America: Growth and Politics in Sunbelt Cities* (Chapel Hill: University of North Carolina Press, 1981).

Abbott, Carl: *Portland: Planning, Politics, and Growth in a Twentieth-Century City* (Lincoln: University of Nebraska Press, 1983).

Abbott, Carl: *The Metropolitan Frontier: Cities in the Modern American West* (Tucson: University of Arizona Press, 1993).

Abbot, W. W.: "George Washington, the West, and the Union." *Indiana Magazine of History*, 84 (March 1988), 3–14.

Abu-Lughod, Janet. *New York, Chicago, Los Angeles: America's Global Cities* (Minneapolis: University of Minnesota Press, 1999).

Acuña, Rodolfo: *Occupied America: The Chicanos' Struggle toward Liberation*, 2nd edn. (San Francisco: Canfield, 1972).

Acuña, Rodolfo: *Occupied America: A History of Chicanos* (New York: Harper and Row, 1981).

Adams, David Wallace: *Education for Extinction: American Indians and the Boarding School Experience, 1875–1928* (Lawrence: University Press of Kansas, 1995).

Adelman, Jeremy and Stephen Aron: "From Borderlands to Borders: Empires, Nation-States, and the Peoples in Between in North American History." *American Historical Review* 104 (June 1999), 814–41.

Adler, Jacob: "The Oceanic Steamship Company: A Link in Claus Spreckels' Hawaiian Sugar Empire." *Pacific Historical Review* 29 (1960), 257–69.

Adler, Jacob: *Claus Spreckels: The Sugar King in Hawaii* (Honolulu: University of Hawaii Press, 1966).

Adler, Jeffrey S.: *Yankee Merchants and the Making of the Urban West* (Cambridge: Cambridge University Press, 1991).

Adler, Michael A. (ed.): *The Prehistoric Pueblo World, A.D. 1150–1350* (Tucson, AZ: University of Arizona Press, 1996).

Agee, James and Walker Evans: *Let Us Now Praise Famous Men: Three Tenant Families* (Boston: Houghton Miflin, 1941).

Albanese, Catherine L.: *America, Religions and Religion* (Belmont, CA: Wadsworth Publishing Company, 1981).

Albers, Patricia C. and Beatrice Medicine (eds.) *The Hidden Half: Studies of Plains Indian Women* (Latham, MD: University Press of America, 1983).

Albers, Patricia C.: "The Regional System of the Devil's Lake Sioux." (PhD dissertation: University of Wisconsin, Madison, 1974).

Albers, Patricia C.: "Sioux Women in Transition: A Study of Their Changing Status in Domestic and Capitalist Sectors of Production." In Patricia C. Albers and Beatrice Medicine (eds.) *The Hidden Half: Studies of Plains Indian Women* (Latham, MD: University Press of America, 1983).

Aldrich, John. "A New Country for Americans: The West Coast of Mexico." *Overland Monthly* 54 (August 1909), 216–24.

Allen, James B.: " 'Good Guys' vs. 'Good Guys': Rudger Clawson, John Sharp, and Civil Disobedience in Nineteenth-Century Utah." *Utah Historical Quarterly* 48, no. 2. (spring 1980), 148–74.

Allen, John B.: *From Skisport to Skiing: One Hundred Years of an American Sport* (Amherst: University of Massachusetts Press, 1993).

Allen, John L.: *Passage through the Garden: Lewis and Clark and the Image of the American Northwest* (Urbana: University of Illinois Press, 1975).

Allen, John L.: "The Canadian Fur Trade and the Exploration of Western North America." In John L. Allen (ed.) *The Continent Comprehended* (Lincoln: University of Nebraska Press, 1997).

Allen, John L.: "The Invention of the American West: Fur Trade Exploration 1821–1839." In John L. Allen (ed.) *The Continent Comprehended* (Lincoln: University of Nebraska Press, 1997).

Allen, Michael: *Western Rivermen, 1763–1861: Ohio and Mississippi Boatmen and the Myth of the Alligator Horse* (Baton Rouge: Louisiana State University Press, 1990).

Allen, Robert S.: *His Majesty's Indian Allies: British Indian Policy in the Defence of Canada, 1774–1815* (Toronto: Dundern Press, 1992).

Allmendinger, Blake: "Proposition 2000: Debating California's Sesquicentennial." *Western American Literature* 34 (Summer 1999), 173–7.

Allmendinger, Blake: *Ten Most Wanted: The New Western Literature* (New York: Routledge, 1998).

Allswang, John: *The Initiative and Referendum in California, 1898–1998* (Stanford: Stanford University Press, 2000).

Almaguer, Tomás: "Toward the Study of Chicano Colonialism." *Aztlán* 2, 1 (1971), 7–21.

Almaguer, Tomás: "Historical Notes on Chicano Oppression: The Dialectics of Racial and Class Domination in North America." *Aztlán* 5, 1–2 (1974): 27–56.

Almaguer, Tomás: "Class, Race, and Chicano Oppression." *Socialist Revolution* 25 (1975), 71–99.

Almaguer, Tomás: "Ideological Distortions in Recent Chicano Historiography." *Aztlán* 18, 1 (1989), 7–27.

Almaguer, Tomás: *Racial Fault Lines: The Historical Origins of White Supremacy in California* (Berkeley: University of California Press, 1994).

Althusser, Louis: *Essays on Ideology* (London: Verso, 1984).Ambler, Marjane: *Breaking the Iron Bonds: Indian Control of Energy Development* (Lawrence, KS: University Press of Kansas, 1990).

Ambrecht, Biliana C. S., and Harry P. Pachon: "Ethnic Political Mobilization in a Mexican American Community: An Exploratory Study of East Los Angeles, 1965–72." *Western Political Quarterly* 21, 3 (September 1974), 500-19.

Ambrose, Stephen E.: *Crazy Horse and Custer: The Parallel Lives of Two American Warriors* (New York: Doubleday, 1975).

Ambrose, Stephen E.: *Undaunted Courage: Meriwether Lewis, Thomas Jefferson, and the Opening of the American West* (New York: Simon and Schuster, 1996).

Ambrose, Stephen E.: *Nothing Like It in the World: The Men Who Built the Transcontinental Railroad, 1863–1869* (New York: Simon and Schuster, 2000).

Amundson, Michael A.: *Yellowcake Towns: Uranium Mining Communities in the American West* (Boulder: University Press of Colorado, 2002).

Anaya, Rudolfo: *Bless Me Ultima* (New York: Warner Books, 1972)

Anderson, Fred: *Crucible of War: The Seven Years' War and the Fate of Empire in British North America, 1754–1766* (New York: Knopf, 2000).

Anderson, Gary Clayton: *The Indian Southwest, 1580–1830: Ethnogenesis and Reinvention* (Norman: University of Oklahoma Press, 1999).

Anderson, Nancy K.: " 'The Kiss of Enterprise': The Western Landscape as Symbol and Resource." In William H. Truettner (ed.) *The West as America: Reinterpreting Images of the Frontier, 1820–1920* (Washington, DC: Smithsonian Institution Press, 1991).

Anderson, Nels: *Desert Saints: The Mormon Frontier in Utah* (Chicago: University of Chicago Press, 1942).

Angelou, Maya: *I Know Why the Caged Bird Sings* (New York: Random House, 1970; Bantam reissue, 1993).

Anon: "New Ways of Seeing." *Tate: The Art Magazine* 21 (2000): 48–9.

Anzaldua, Gloria: *Borderlands-La Frontera: The New Mestiza* (San Francisco: Spinster/Aunt Lute Book Company, 1987).

Anzaldua, Gloria and Cherrie Moraga (eds.): *This Bridge Called My Back: Writings by Radical Women of Color* (New York: Kitchen Table/Women of Color Press, 1981).

Aparicio, Frances R. and Susana Chávez-Silverman (eds.): *Tropicalizations: Transcultural Representations of Latinidad* (Hanover, NH: University Press of New England, 1997).

Appier, Janis: *Policing Women: The Sexual Politics of Law Enforcement and the LAPD* (Philadelphia: Temple University Press, 1998).

Applegate, Shannon and Terence O'Donnell: *Talking on Paper: An Anthology of Oregon Letters and Diaries* (Corvallis: Oregon State University Press, 1994).

Aquila, Richard (ed.): *Wanted Dead or Alive: The American West in Popular Culture* (Urbana: University of Illinois Press, 1996).

Arce, Carlos H., Edward Murguía, and W. Parker Frisbie: "Phenotype and Life Chances Among Chicanos." *Hispanic Journal of Behavioral Sciences* 9, 1 (1987): 19–32.

Archuleta, Margaret L., Brenda J. Child, and K. Tsianina Lomawaima (eds.): *Away from Home: American Indian Boarding School Experiences, 1879–2000* (Phoenix: Heard Museum, 2000).

Argersinger, Peter H.: *The Limits of Agrarian Radicalism: Western Populism and American Politics* (Lawrence, KS: University Press of Kansas, 1995).

Armitage, Susan: "Through Women's Eyes: A New View of the West." In Susan Armitage and Elizabeth Jameson (eds.) *The Women's West* (Norman: University of Oklahoma Press, 1987).

Armitage, Susan and Elizabeth Jameson (eds.): *The Women's West* (Norman: University of Oklahoma Press, 1987).

Arnold, Morris S.: *Unequal Law Unto a Savage Race: European Legal Traditions in Arkansas, 1686–1836* (Fayetteville, University of Arkansas Press, 1985).

Aron, Stephen: "Lessons in Conquest: Towards a Greater Western History." *Pacific Historical Review*, 63 (May 1994), 125–47.

Aron, Stephen: "Lessons in Conquest: Towards a Greater Western History." *Pacific Historical Review* 63 (1994), 125–47.

Aron, Stephen: *How the West Was Lost: The Transformation of Kentucky from Daniel Boone to Henry Clay* (Baltimore: Johns Hopkins University Press, 1996).

Aron, Stephen: *American Confluence: The Missouri Frontier from Borderlands to Border State* (Bloomington: Indiana University Press, forthcoming).

Arrington, Leonard J. and Dean May: "A Different Mode of Life: Irrigation and Society in Nineteenth Century Utah." *Agricultural History* 49, 1 (1975), 3–11.

Arrington, Leonard J.: *Great Basin Kingdom: An Economic History of the Latter-Day Saints, 1830–1900* (Cambridge, MA.: Harvard University Press, 1958).

Arrington, Leonard J.: "The Sagebrush Resurrection: New Deal Expenditures in the Western States, 1933–39." *Pacific Historical Review*, 52 (February 1983), 1–16.

Arrington, Leonard J., Feramorz Y. Fox, and Dean L. May (eds.). *Building the City of God: Community and Cooperation Among the Mormons* (Urbana and Chicago: University of Illinois Press, 1992).

Arroyo, Luis: "Notes on Past, Present and Future Directions of Chicano Labor Studies." *Aztlán* 6, 2 (1975), 137–50.

Asher, Brad: "Their Own Domestic Difficulties: Intra-Indian Crime and White Law in Western Washington Territory, 1873–1889." *Western Historical Quarterly* 27 (summer 1996), 189–209.

Asher, Brad: *Beyond the Reservation: Indians, Settlers, and the Law in Washington Territory, 1853-1889.* (Norman, OK: University of Oklahoma Press, 1999).

Athearn, Robert G.: *Union Pacific Country* (Chicago: Rand McNally, 1971).

Athearn, Robert G.: *The Mythic West in Twentieth-Century America* (Lawrence: University Press of Kansas, 1986).

Atherton, Lewis. *The Cattle Kings* (Bloomington, IN: Indiana University Press, 1961).

Atkins, Annette: *Harvest of Grief: Grasshopper Plagues and Public Assistance in Minnesota, 1873–1878* (St Paul: Minnesota Historical Society Press, 1984).

August, Ray: "Cowboys v. Rancheros: The Origins of Western American Livestock Law." *Southwestern Historical Quarterly* 96, 4 (April 1993), 475-88.

August, Ray: "Gringos v. Mineros: The Hispanic Origins of Western American Mining Law." *Western Legal History* 9 (summer/fall 1996), 147–75.

Auster, Lawrence: *The Path to National Suicide: An Essay on Immigration and Multiculturalism* (Monterey, VA: American Immigration Control Foundation, 1990).

Avila, Eric: *Chocolate Cities and Vanilla Suburbs: Popular Culture in the Age of White Flight* (Berkeley: University of California Press, forthcoming).

Axtell, James: *The Invasion Within: The Contest of Cultures in Colonial North America* (New York: Oxford University Press, 1985).

Ayers, Edward L.: *Vengeance and Justice: Crime and Punishment in the Nineteenth-Century American South* (New York: Oxford University Press, 1984).

Ayers, Edward: "A Valley Divided." *Humanities* 20 (July/August 1999), 43.

Baade, Hans W.: "The Historical Background of Texas Water Law." *St Mary's Law Review* 18 (1986), 1–98.

Bader, Robert S.: *Prohibition in Kansas: A History* (Lawrence: University Press of Kansas, 1986).

Bailyn, Bernard: *Voyagers to the West: A Passage in the Peopling of America on the Eve of the Revolution* (New York: Knopf, 1986).

Bain, David H.: *Empire Express: Building the First Transcontinental Railroad* (New York: Viking, 1999).

Bakken, Gordon Morris: "Admiralty Law in Nineteenth-Century California." *Southern California Quarterly* 58 (1976), 499-514.

Bakken, Gordon Morris: *The Development of Law on the Rocky Mountain Frontier* (Westport, CT: Greenwood Press, 1983).

Bakken, Gordon Morris: *Rocky Mountain Constitution Making, 1850–1912,* (Westport, CT: Greenwood Press, 1987).

Bakken, Gordon Morris (ed.): *Law in the Western United States,* (Norman, OK: University of Oklahoma Press, 2000).

Balassi, William, John F. Crawford, and Annie O. Eysturov (eds.): *This is About Vision: Interviews with Southwestern Writers* (Albuquerque: University of New Mexico Press, 1990).

Baldassare, Mark: *Trouble in Paradise: The Suburban Transformation of America* (New York: Columbia University Press, 1986).

Balderrama, Francisco: *In Defense of La Raza: The Los Angeles Mexican Consulate and the Mexican Community, 1929–1936* (Tucson: University of Arizona Press, 1982).

Bamford, E. F.: "The Mexican Casual Problem in the Southwest." *Journal of Applied Sociology* 8 (1923), 364–71.

Bancroft, Hubert Howe: *Popular Tribunals*, 2 vols. (San Francisco: A. L. Bancroft & Co., 1887).

Bancroft, Hubert Howe: *The New Pacific*, rev. edn. (New York: The Bancroft Company, 1913).

Banham, Reyner: *Los Angeles: The Architecture of Four Ecologies* (Harmondsworth: Penguin, 1973).

Baranowski, Shelley and Ellen Furlough (eds.): *Being Elsewhere: Tourism, Consumer Culture, and Identity in Modern Europe and North America* (Ann Arbor: University of Michigan Press, 2001).

Barker, James H.: *Always Getting Ready: Yup'ik Eskimo Subsistence in Southwest Alaska* (Seattle: University of Washington Press, 1993).

Barnes, Kim and Mary Clearman Blew (eds.): *Circle of Women: An Anthology of Contemporary Western Women's Writing* (New York: Penguin, 1994).

Barr, Alwyn: *Black Texans: A History of African Americans in Texas, 1528–1995* (Norman, OK: University of Oklahoma Press, 1996).

Barr, Daniel P.: "Contested Ground: Competition and Conflict on the Upper Ohio Frontier, 1744–1784." (PhD dissertation: Kent State University, 2001).

Barrera, Mario: *Race and Class in the Southwest: A Theory of Racial Inequality* (Notre Dame: University of Notre Dame Press, 1979).

Barrera, Mario, Carlos Muñoz, and Carlos Ornelas: "The Barrio as Internal Colony." *Urban Affairs Annual Reviews* 6 (1972), 465–98.

Barringer, Mark Daniel: *Selling Yellowstone: Capitalism and the Construction of Nature* (Lawrence: University Press Of Kansas, 2002).

Barron, Hal S.: *Mixed Harvest: The Second Great Transformation in the Rural North, 1870–1930* (Chapel Hill: University of North Carolina Press, 1997).

Barsh, Russel L.: "The Substitution of Cattle for Bison on the Great Plains." In Paul A. Olson (ed.) *A Struggle for the Land: Indigenous Insight and Industrial Empire in the Semiarid World* (Lincoln: University of Nebraska Press, 1990).

Barth, Gunther: *Instant Cities: Urbanization and the Rise of San Francisco and Denver* (New York: Oxford University Press, 1975).

Bartlett, Richard A.: *Great Surveys of the American West* (Norman: University of Oklahoma Press, 1962).

Bartlett, Richard A.: *The New Country: A Social History of the American Frontier, 1776–1890* (New York: Oxford University Press, 1974).

Bartlett, Richard A.: *Yellowstone: A Wilderness Besieged* (Tucson, AZ: University of Arizona Press, 1985).

Basso, Keith H.: *Wisdom Sits in Places: Landscape and Language Among the Western Apache* (Albuquerque: University of New Mexico Press, 1996).

Basso, Matthew, Laurel McCall, and Dee Garceau (eds.): *Across the Great Divide: Cultures of Manhood in the American West* (New York: Routledge, 2001).

Baxter, John O.: *Dividing New Mexico's Waters, 1700–1912* (Albuquerque, N.M., Universiyt of new Mexico Press, 1997).

Bayer, Laura, with Floyd Montoya and the Pueblo of Santa Ana: *Santa Ana: The People, the Pueblo, and the History of Tamaya* (Albuquerque: University of New Mexico Press, 1994).

Beeton, Beverly: "Woman Suffrage in Territorial Utah." *Utah Historical Quarterly* 46, 2 (1978), 100–20.

Beeton, Beverly: *Women Vote in the West: The Woman Suffrage Movement, 1869–1896* (New York: Garland Publishing, 1986).

Belasco, Warren James: *Americans on the Road: From Autocamp to Motel, 1910–1945* (Cambridge, MA: MIT Press, 1981).

Belue, Ted Franklin: *The Long Hunt: Death of the Buffalo East of the Mississippi* (Mechanicsburg: Stackpole Books, 1996).

Benson, Jack A.: "Before Aspen and Vail: The Story of Recreational Skiing in Frontier Colorado." *Journal of the West*, 22, 1 (1983), 52–61.

Bercovitch, Sacvan: "The Problem of Ideology in American Literary History." *Critical Inquiry* 12 (Summer 1986), 635.

Berger, Thomas R.: *Village Journey: The Report of the Alaska Native Review Commission* (New York: Hill and Wang, 1985).

Berger, Thomas R.: *Village Journey: The Report of the Alaska Native Review Commission*, rev. edn. (New York: Hill and Wang, 1995).

Berk, Gerald: *Alternative Tracks: The Constitution of American Industrial Order, 1865–1917* (Baltimore: Johns Hopkins University Press, 1994).

Berkhofer, Robert F., Jr.: "The Political Context of a New Indian History." *Pacific Historical Review* 40, 3 (August 1971), 357-82.

Berkhofer, Robert F., Jr.: *The White Man's Indian: Images of the American Indian from Columbus to the Present* (New York: Alfred A. Knopf, 1978).

Bernard, Richard M. and Bradley R. Rice (eds.): *Sunbelt Cities: Politics and Growth since World War II*. (Austin: University of Texas Press, 1983).

Bernstein, Alison R.: *American Indians and World War II: Toward a New Era in Indian Affairs* (Norman: University of Oklahoma Press, 1991).

Bernstein, Barton J.: "The Conservative Achievement of New Deal Reform." In David E. Hamilton (ed.) *The New Deal* (Boston: Houghton Mifflin company, 1999).

Bernstein, Shana Beth: "Building Bridges at Home in a Time of Global Conflict: Interracial Cooperation and the Fight for Civil Rights in Los Angeles, 1933–1954." (PhD dissertation: Stanford University, 2003).

Berthrong, Donald J.: *The Cheyenne and Arapahoe Ordeal: Reservation and Agency Life in the Indian Territory, 1875–1907* (Norman: University of Oklahoma Press, 1976).

Bhabha, Homi K.: *The Location of Culture* (London and New York: Routledge, 1994).

Bigler, David L.: *Forgotten Kingdom: The Mormon Theocracy in the American West, 1847–1896*, (Spokane, WA: Arthur Clark Co., 1998).

Billington, Monroe: *New Mexico's Buffalo Soldiers, 1866–1900* (Niwot: University Press of Colorado, 1991).

Billington, Ray Allen: *America's Frontier Heritage* (Albuquerque: University of New Mexico Press, 1963.

Bing, Leon: *Do or Die* (New York: HarperPerennial, 1992).

Biolsi, Thomas: *Organizing the Lakota: The Political Economy of the New Deal on the Pine Ridge and Rosebud Reservations* (Tucson: University of Arizona Press, 1992).

Blackburn, Alexander: "A Western Renaissance." *Western American Literature* 29 (Spring, 1994), 51–62.

Blackford, Michael: *The Lost Dream: Businessmen and City Planning on the Pacific Coast, 1890–1920* (Columbus: Ohio State University Press, 1993).

Blackhawk, Ned: *Violence Over The Land: Colonial Encounters In The American Great Basin* (Cambridge, MA: Harvard University Press, forthcoming) .

Blackwood, Evelyn: "Sexuality and Gender in Certain Native American Tribes." *Signs* 10, 1 (1984): 27–42.

Blair, Edward: *Leadville: Colorado's Magic City* (Boulder: Pruett Publishing, 1980).

Blauner, Robert: "Internal Colonialism and Ghetto Revolt." *Social Problems* 16, 4 (1969), 393–408.

Blauner, Robert: *Racial Oppression in America* (New York: Harper and Row, 1972).

Blew, Mary Clearman: *All But the Waltz: Essays on a Montana Family* (New York: Viking, 1991).

Blew, Mary Clearman: *Bone Deep in Landscape: Writing, Reading, and Place* (Norman: University of Oklahoma Press, 1999).

Blocker, Jack S., Jr.: *Retreat from Reform: The Prohibition Movement in the United States, 1890–1913* (Westport, CT: Greenwood Press, 1976).

Blue Cloud, Peter: *Alcatraz Is Not an Island* (Berkeley: Wingbow Press, 1972).

Bluestone, Barry and Bennett Harrison: *The Deindustrialization of America: Plant Closings, Community Abandonment, and the Dismantling of Basic Industry* (New York: Basic Books, 1982).

Boag, Peter G.: *Environment and Experience: Settlement Culture in Nineteenth-Century Oregon* (Berkeley: University of California Press, 1992).

Boag, Peter: "Mountain, Plain, Desert, River: The Snake River Valley as a Western Crossroads." In David Wrobel Michael Steiner (eds.) *Many Wests: Place, Culture, and Regional Identity* (Lawrence: University Press of Kansas, 1997).

Bobo, Lawrence D., Melvin L. Oliver, James H. Johnson, Jr., and Abel Valenzuela, Jr. (eds.): *Prismatic Metropolis: Inequality in Los Angeles.* (New York: Russell Sage Foundation, 2000).

Boessenecker, John: *Gold Dust and Gunsmoke: Tales of Gold Rush Outlaws, Gunfighters, Lawmen, and Vigilantes* (New York, John Wiley, 1999).

Boime, Albert: *The Magisterial Gaze: Manifest Destiny and American Landscape Painting c. 1830–1865* (Washington and London: Smithsonian Institution Press, 1991).

Bold, Christine: *Selling the Wild West: Popular Western Fiction, 1860–1960* (Bloomington: University of Indiana Press, 1987).

Bolton, Herbert Eugene: "Spanish Records at San Antonio." *Texas State Historical Association Quarterly* 10 (April 1907): 297-307.

Bolton, Herbert Eugene: "Records of the Mission of Nuestra Señora del Refugio." *Texas State Historical Association Quarterly* 14 (October 1910): 164–66.

Bolton, Herbert Eugene: "Need for the Publication of a Comprehensive Body of Documents Relating to the History of the Spanish Activities within the Present Limits of the United States." (Bolton Papers: Bancroft Library, University of California, Berkeley, 1911).

Bolton, Herbert Eugene: *Guide to Materials for the History of the United States in the Principal Archives of Mexico.* (Washington, DC: Carnegie Institution of Washington, 1913).

Bolton, Herbert Eugene (ed.): *Spanish Exploration In The Southwest 1542–1706* (New York: Scribner's 1916).

Bolton, Herbert Eugene: "The Mission as a Frontier Institution in the Spanish-American Colonies." *American Historical Review* 23 (October 1917), 42–61.

Bolton, Herbert Eugene: *The Spanish Borderlands: A Chronicle of Old Florida and the Southwest.* (New Haven, CT.: Yale University Press, 1921).

Bolton, Herbert Eugene: "Defensive Spanish Expansion and the Significance of the Borderlands." In James Field Willard and Colin Brummitt Goodykoontz (eds.) *The Trans-Mississippi West: Papers Read at a Conference Held at the University of Colorado, June 18–June 21, 1929* (Boulder: University of Colorado Press, 1930).

Bolton, Herbert Eugene: *The Northward Movement in New Spain* (Berkeley: University of California Press, 1946).

Boorstin, Daniel J.: *The Americans: The National Experience* (New York: Random House, 1965).

Borjas, George J.: *Friends or Strangers: The Impact of Immigration on the U.S. Economy* (New York: Basic Books, 1990).

Borne, Lawrence R.: *Dude Ranching: A Complete History* (Albuquerque: University of New Mexico Press, 1983).

Bouldrey, Brian: *Writing Home: Award-Winning Literature from the New West* (Berkeley, California: Heyday Books, 1999).

Bowden, Charles: *Killing the Hidden Waters* (Austin: University of Texas Press, 1977).

Bowden, Martyn J.: "The Great American Desert and the American Frontier, 1800-1881: Popular Images of the Plains and Phases in the Westward Movement." In Tamara Hareven (ed.) *Anonymous Americans: Explorations in Nineteenth-Century Social History* (Englewood Cliffs, NJ: Prentice-Hall, 1971).

Boxberger, Daniel L.: *To Fish in Common: The Ethnohistory of Lummi Indian Salmon Fishing* (Seattle: University of Washington Press, 2000).

Boyer, Ruth McDonald and Narcissus Duffy Gayton: *Apache Mothers and Daughters: Four Generations of a Family* (Norman: University of Oklahoma Press, 1992).

Boynton, Percy: *The Rediscovery of the Frontier* (Chicago: University of Chicago Press, 1931).

Brack, Gene M.: *Mexico Views Manifest Destiny, 1821–1846: An Essay on the Origins of the Mexican War* (Albuquerque: University of New Mexico Press, 1990).

Bradley, Cyprian and Edward Kelly: *History of the Diocese of Boise, 1863–1952* (Boise: n.p., 1953).

Bramwell, Lincoln: "Aggressive Fire Suppression: The US Forest Service's 10 AM Policy and Interagency Hotshot Fire Crews." (MA thesis: University of Utah, 2000).

Braun, Bruce and Noel Castree (eds.): *Remaking Reality: Nature at the Millenium* (London: Routledge, 1998).

Brave Bird, Mary (with Richard Erdoes): *Lakota Woman* (New York: Grove Weidenfeld, 1990).

Brebner, John B.: *The Explorers of North America, 1492–1806* (New York: Macmillan, 1933).

Brechin, Gray: *Imperial San Francisco: Urban Power, Earthly Ruin* (Berkeley: University of California Press, 1999).

Bridges, Amy: *Morning Glories: Municipal Reform in the Southwest* (Princeton, NJ: Princeton University Press, 1997).

Brightman, Robert: *Grateful Prey: Rock Cree Human–Animal Relationships* (Berkeley: University of California Press, 1993).

Brilliant, Mark: *Color Lines: Struggles for Civil Rights on America's "Racial Frontier," 1945–1975* (New York: Oxford University Press, forthcoming).

Brimelow, Peter: *Alien Nation: Common Sense about America's Immigration Disaster* (New York: Random House, 1995).

Brinkley, Alan: *The End of Reform: New Deal Liberalism in Recession and War* (New York: Alfred A. Knopf, 1995).

Brinkley, Alan: *Liberalism and Its Discontents* (Cambridge, MA: Harvard University Press, 1998).

Brokes, Jean Ingram: *International Rivalry in the Pacific Islands, 1800–1875* ([1941], reprinted New York: Russell and Russell, 1972).

Brooks, James: *Captives and Cousins: Slavery, Kinship, and Community in the Southwest Borderlands* (Chapel Hill: University of North Carolina Press, 2002).

Brooks, Juanita: *The Mountain Meadow Massacre* (Norman, OK: University of Oklahoma Press, 1991).

Brosnan, Kathleen A.: *Uniting Mountain and Plain: Cities, Law, and Environmental Change along the Front Range* (Albuquerque: University of New Mexico Press, 2002).

Broun, Elizabeth: "The Story Behind the Story of *The West as America.*" *Museum News*, 70, 5 (September/October 1991), 77–8.

Broussard, Albert S.: *Black San Francisco: The Struggle for Racial Equality in the West, 1900–1954* (Lawrence, KS: University Press of Kansas, 1993).

Brown, Dee: *Bury My Heart at Wounded Knee: An Indian History of the American West* (New York: Holt, Rinehart and Winston, 1970).

Brown, Dee: *The Fetterman Massacre: An American Saga* (London: Barrie and Jenkins, 1972).

Brown, J. MacMillan: "New Zealand and the Pacific Ocean." In H. Morse Stephens and Herbert E. Bolton (eds.) *The Pacific Ocean in History* (New York: MacMillan, 1917)

Brown, Jennifer S. H.: *Strangers in Blood: Fur Trade Company Families in Indian Country* (Vancouver: University of British Columbia Press, 1980).

Brown, Kate: "Gridded Lives: Why Kazakhstan and Montana are Nearly the Same Place." *American Historical Review* 106 (Spring 2001), 17–48.

Brown, Richard Maxwell: "Historiography of Violence in the American West" In Michael P. Malone (ed.) *Historians and the American West* (Lincoln, NE: University of Nebraska Press, 1983)

Brown, Richard Maxwell: *No Duty to Retreat: Violence and Values in American History and Society* (New York: Oxford University Press, 1991).

Brown, Richard Maxwell: "Violence." In Clyde A. Milner, II, Carol A. O'Connor and Martha Sandweiss (eds.) *The Oxford History of the American West* (New York: Oxford University Press, 1994).

Brown, Richard Maxwell: "Courage Without Illusion." In Clyde A. Milner, II (ed.): *A New Significance: Re-Envisioning the History of the American West* (New York: Oxford University Press, 1996).

Brown, Ronald C.: *Hard Rock Epic: Western Miners and the Industrial Revolution, 1860–1910* (Berkeley: University of California Press, 1979).

Brown, Ronald C.: *Hard-Rock Miners: The Intermountain West, 1860–1920* (College Station: Texas A&M University Press, 1979).

Browne, Irene (ed.): *Latinas and African American Women at Work: Race, Gender, and Economic Inequality* (New York: Russell Sage Foundation, 1999).

Browning, Rufus P., Dale Rogers Marshall, and David H. Tabb: *Protest is Not Enough: The Struggle of Blacks and Hispanics for Equality in Urban Politics* (Berkeley: University of California Press, 1984).

Brundage, W. Fitzhugh (ed.): *Under Sentence of Death: Lynching in the South* (Chapel Hill, NC: University of North Carolina Press, 1997).

Bryant, Clora: *Central Avenue Sounds: Jazz in Los Angeles* (Berkeley: University of California Press, 1998).

Buck, Pearl S.: *The Good Earth* (New York: Grossett & Dunlap, 1931).

Bulmer, Martin: *The Chicago School of Sociology: Institutionalization, Diversity, and the Rise of Sociological Research* (Chicago: University of Chicago Press, 1984).

Bulosan. Carlos: *America Is in the Heart* ([1946] rpt., Seattle: University of Washington Press, 2000).

Bunch, Lonnie: *Black Angelenos: The Afro-American in Los Angeles, 1850–1950* (Los Angeles: California Afro-American Museum, 1988).

Bunch, Lonnie: "A Past Not Necessarily Prologue: The African American in Los Angeles." In Norman M. Klein and Martin J., Scliesl (eds.) *20th Century Los Angeles: Power, Promotion, and Social Conflict* (Claremont, CA: Regina Books, 1990).

Bunting, Robert: *The Pacific Raincoast: Environment and Culture in an American Eden, 1778–1900* (Lawrence: University Press of Kansas, 1997).

Bunting, Robert: *The Pacific Raincoast: Environment and Culture in an American Eden, 1778–1900* (Lawrence: University Press of Kansas, 1997).

Burnham, Philip: *Indian Country, God's Country: Native Americans and the National Parks* (Washington, DC: Island Press, 2000).

Burton, Lloyd: *American Indian Water Rights and the Limits of Law* (Lawrence: University Press of Kansas, 1991).

Burton, Robert E.: *Democrats of Oregon: The Pattern of Minority Politics, 1900–1956* (Eugene: University of Oregon Press, 1970).

Butchart, J. Harvey: "Summits Below the Rim: Mountain Climbing in the Grand Canyon." *Journal of Arizona History* 17, (1976), 21–38.

Butler, Ann M.: "Still in Chains: Black Women in Western Prisons, 1865–1910." *Western Historical Quarterly* 22. (November, 1991), 18–35.

Butler, Anne M.: "Selling the Popular Myth." In Clyde A. Milner, II, Carol A. O'Connor, and Martha A. Sandweiss (eds.) *The Oxford History of the American West* (New York: Oxford University Press, 1994).

Byrkit, James: *Forging the Copper Collar: Arizona's Labor Management War of 1901–1921* (Tucson, AZ: University of Arizona Press, 1982).

Calloway, Colin G.: *Crown and Calumet: British–Indian Relations, 1783–1815* (Norman: University of Oklahoma Press, 1987).

Calloway, Colin G. (ed.): *New Directions in American Indian History* (Norman: University of Oklahoma Press, 1988).

Calloway, Colin G.: *The World Turned Upside Down: Indian Voices from Early America* (Boston: Bedford/St Martin's Press, 1994).

Calloway, Colin G.: *The American Revolution in Indian Country: Crisis and Diversity in Native American Communities* (Cambridge: Cambridge University Press, 1995).

Calloway, Colin G. (ed.): *Our Hearts Fell to the Ground: Plains Indian Views of How the West was Lost* (Boston: Bedford/St. Martin's, 1996).

Camarillo, Albert: *Chicanos in a Changing Society: From Mexican Pueblos to American Barrios in Santa Barbara and Southern California, 1848–1930* (Cambridge, MA: Harvard University Press, 1979).

Cameron, Ian and Douglas Pye (eds.): *The Book of Westerns* (New York: Continuum, 1996).

Campbell, Colin: *The Romantic Ethic and the Spirit of Modern Consumption* (Oxford: Basil Blackwell, 1987).

Campbell, Eugene: *Establishing Zion: The Mormon Church in the American West, 1847–1869* (Salt Lake City: Signature Books, 1988).

Candelaria, Cordelia: "La Malinche, Feminist Prototype." *Frontiers* 5, 2 (Summer 1980), 1–6.

Cannon, Brian Q.: "Power Relations: Western Rural Electric Cooperatives and the New Deal." *Western Historical Quarterly*, 31 (Summer 2000), 159–60.

Cannon, Kenneth L., II: "Mountain Common Law: The Extralegal Punishment of Seducers in Early Utah." *Utah Historical Quarterly* 51, 4 (Fall, 1983), 308–27.

Cannon, Lou: *Official Negligence: How Rodney King and the Riots Changed Los Angeles and the LAPD* (New York: Times Books, 1997).

Capote, Truman: *In Cold Blood* (New York: Random House, 1966).

Cardenas, Gilberto: "Undocumented Immigrant Women in the Houston Labor Force." *California Sociologist* 5, 2 (1982), 98–118.

Cardenas, Gilberto and Estevan Flores: *The Migration and Settlement of Undocumented Women* (Austin: Mexican American Studies Center Publications, 1986).

Carlson, Leonard A.: *Indians, Bureaucrats, and Land: The Dawes Act and the Decline of Indian Farming* (Westport, CT: Greenwood Press, 1981).

Carreras de Velasco, Mercedes: *Los Mexicanos que devolvio la crisis, 1929–1932* (Mexico City: Secretaría de Relaciones Exteriores, 1974).

Carrico, Richard L.: "Spanish Crime and Punishment: The Native American Experience in Colonial San Diego." *Western Legal History* 3 (Winter 1990–Spring 1991), 21–33.

Carrigan, William D.: "Between South and West: Race, Violence, and Power in Central Texas, 1836–1916." (PhD dissertation: Emory University, 1999).

Carriker, Robert C.: *Father Peter John De Smet: Jesuit in the West* (Norman: University of Oklahoma Press, 1995).

Carroll, Bret E.: *The Routledge Historical Atlas of Religion in America* (London: Routledge, 2000).

Carson, Rachel: *Silent Spring* (Boston: Houghton Mifflin, 1962).

Carter, Edward C. (ed.): *Surveying the Record: North American Scientific Exploration to 1930* (Philadelphia: American Philosophical Society, 1999).

Case, Suzann Espenett: "Almeda Eliza Hitchcock." In Mari J. Matsuda (ed.) *Called From Within: Early Women Lawyers of Hawai'i* (Honolulu: University of Hawaii Press, 1992).

Cash, Joseph H.: *Working the Homestake* (Ames, Iowa State University Press, 1973).

Casper, Henry: *History of the Catholic Church in Nebraska*, 3 vols. (Milwaukee: Bruce/Catholic Life, 1966).

Cassidy, James G.: *Ferdinand V. Hayden: Entrepreneur of Science* (Lincoln: University of Nebraska Press, 2000).

Castañeda, Antonia I: "Gender, Race, and Culture: Spanish-Mexican Women in the Historiography of Frontier California." *Frontiers* 11, 1 (1990), 8–20.

Castañeda, Antonia I.: "Women of Color and the Rewriting of Western History: The Discourse, Politics, and Decolonization of History." *Pacific Historical Review* 61 (November 1992), 501-34.

Castañeda, Carlos: *Our Catholic Heritage in Texas, 1519–1936*, 7 vols. (Austin, TX: Von Boeckmann-Jones, 1936–58).

Cather, Willa: *One of Ours* (New York: Knopf, 1922).

Catton, Theodore: *Inhabited Wilderness: Indians, Eskimos, and National Parks in Alaska* (Albuquerque: University of New Mexico Press, 1997).

Caughey, John W.: "Herbert Eugene Bolton." In Wilber R. Jacobs, John W. Caughey, and Joe B. Franz *Turner, Bolton, and Webb: Three Historians of the American Frontier* (Seattle: University of Washington Press, 1965).

Cawley, R. McGreggor: *Federal Land, Western Anger* (Lawrence: University Press of Kansas, 1993).

Cayton, Andrew R. L. and Fredrika J. Teute (eds.) *Contact Points: American Frontiers from the Mohawk Valley to the Mississippi, 1750–1830* (Chapel Hill, 1998).

Cayton, Andrew R. L.: "'Noble Actors' upon 'the Theatre of Honour': Power and Civility in the Treaty of Greeville." In Andrew R. L. Cayton and Fredrika J. Teute (eds.) *Contact Points: American Frontiers from the Mohawk Valley to the Mississippi, 1750–1830* (Chapel Hill: University of North Carolina Press, 1998).

Cayton, Andrew R. L.: *The Frontier Republic: Ideology and Politics in the Ohio Country, 1780–1825* (Kent, OH: Kent State University Press, 1986).

Cebula, Larry: *Plateau Indians and the Quest for Spiritual Power, 1700–1850* (Lincoln: University of Nebraska Press, 2003).

Chaffin, Tom: *Pathfinder: John Charles Fremont and the Course of American Empire* (New York: Hill and Wang, 2002).

Chamberlain, Charles D.: *Victory at Home: Manpower and Race in the American South during World War II* (Athens, GA: University of Georgia Press, 2003).

Chan, Sucheng: *Entry Denied: Exclusion and the Chinese Community in America, 1882–1943* (Philadelphia: Temple University Press, 1991).

Chan, Sucheng: *This Bittersweet Soil: The Chinese in California Agriculture, 1860–1910* (Berkeley: University of California Press, 1986).

Chan, Sucheng: "Western American Historiography and Peoples of Color." In Sucheng Chan, Douglas Henry Daniels, Mario T. García, and Terry P. Wilson (eds.) *Peoples of Color in the American West* (Lexington, MA: D. C. Heath, 1994).

Chandler, Alfred D.: *The Visible Hand: The Managerial Revolution in American Business* (Cambridge, MA: Harvard University Press, 1977).

Chávez, Lydia: *The Color Bind: California's Battle to End Affirmative Action* (Berkeley: University of California Press, 1998).

Chavez, Leo R.: *Covering Immigration: Popular Images and the Politics of the Nation* (Berkeley: University of California Press, 2001).

Chávez, Miroslava: *Mexican Women and the American Conquest in Los Angeles: From the Mexican Era to American Ascendancy* (PhD dissertation: University of California, Los Angeles, 1998).

Chavez, John R.: *The Lost Land: The Chicano Image of the Southwest* (Albuquerque: University of New Mexico Press, 1984).

Chen, Yong: *Chinese San Francisco, 1850–1943: A Trans-Pacific Community* (Stanford: Stanford University Press, 2000).

Cherny, Robert W.: *Populism, Progressivism, and the Transformation of Nebraska Politics, 1885–1915* (Lincoln: University of Nebraska Press, 1981).

Cherny, Robert W.: "Research Opportunities in Twentieth-Century Western History: Politics." In Gerald Nash and Richard Etulain (eds.) *Researching Western History: Topics in the Twentieth Century* (Albuquerque: University of New Mexico Press, 1997).

Child, Brenda J.: *Boarding School Seasons: American Indian Families, 1900–1940* (Lincoln: University of Nebraska Press, 1998).

Chin, Frank: *Donald Duk* (St Paul, MN: Coffee House Press, 1991).

Chin, Frank: *Bulletproof Buddhists and Other Essays* (Honolulu: University of Hawaii Press, 1998).

Chin, Frank: "Pidgin Contest Along I-5." In Brian Bouldrey (ed.) *Writing Home: Award Winning Literature from the New West* (Berkeley, CA: Heydey Books, 1999).

Christensen, Scott R.: *Sagwitch: Shoshone Chieftain, Mormon Elder, 1822–1887* (Logan: Utah State University Press, 1999).

Christenson, Bonnie: *Red Lodge and the Mythic West: Coal Miners to Cowboys* (Lawrence: University Press of Kansas, 2002).

Christie, John A.: *Thoreau as World Traveler* (New York: Columbia University Press, 1965).

Chuman, Frank F.: *The Bamboo People: The Law and Japanese Americans* (Del Mar, CA: Publisher's Inc., 1976).

Cinel, Dino: *From Italy to San Francisco: The Immigrant Experience* (Stanford: Stanford University Press, 1982).

Clark, Blue: "Bibliographic Essay: Pacific Basin Sources and Literature." *Journal of the West* 15, 2 (1976), 117–25.

Clark, Blue: *Lone Wolf v. Hitchcock: Treaty Rights and Indian Law at the End of the Nineteenth Century* (Lincoln, NE: University of Nebraska Press, 1994).

Clark, Norman H.: *The Dry Years: Prohibition and Social Change in Washington* (Seattle: University of Washington Press, 1965).

Cleland, Robert Glass: *A History of Phelps Dodge, 1834–1950* (New York: Alfred A. Knopf, 1952).

Cleland, Robert Glass: *The Cattle on a Thousand Hills: Southern California, 1850–80* (San Marino, CA: Huntington Library, 1941).

Clifton, James E.: *The Prairie People: Continuity and Change in Potawatomi Indian Culture* (Lawrence: The Regents Press of Kansas, 1977).

Clifton, James E. (ed.): *Being and Becoming Indian: Biographical Studies of North American Frontiers* (Chicago: Dorsey Press, 1989).

Cobb, James C.: *Industrialization and Southern Society, 1877–1984* (Lexington: University of Kentucky Press, 1984).

Cochran, Thomas: *Two Hundred Years of American Business* (New York: Oxford University Press, 1977).

Cochran, Thomas: *Frontiers of Change: Early Industrialism in America* (New York: Oxford University Press, 1981).

Coclanis, Peter A.: "Urbs in Horto." *Reviews in American History* 20 (March 1992), 14–20.

Cocoltchos, Christopher N.: "The Invisible Government and the Viable Community: The Ku Klux Klan in Orange County, California during the 1920s." (Ph.D. dissertation: University of California, Los Angeles, 1979).

Coggins, George C., Parthenia Blessing Evans, and Margaret Lindberg-Johnson: "The Law of Public Rangeland Management: The Extent and Distribution of Federal Power." *Environmental Law* 12 (1982), 535–621.

Cohen, Felix: *A Handbook of Federal Indian Law* (Washington, DC: Government Printing Office, 1942).

Cohen, Lizabeth: *Making a New Deal: Industrial Workers in Chicago, 1919–1939* (Cambridge: Cambridge University Press, 1990).

Cole, Richard P. and Gabriel J. Chin: "Emerging from the Margins of Historical Consciousness: Chinese Immigrants and the History of American Law." *Law and History Review* 17 2 (Summer 1999), 325–64.

Coleman, Annie Gilbert: "The Unbearable Whiteness of Skiing." *Pacific Historical Review* 65 (November 1996), 583–614.

Coleman, Annie Gilbert: *Skiing Colorado: A History of Sport, Landscape, and Identity* (Lawrence: University Press of Kansas, 2004).

Coleman, Michael C.: *American Indian Children at School, 1850–1930* (Jackson: University of Mississippi Press, 1993).

Coleman, William S. E.: *Voices of Wounded Knee* (Lincoln: University of Nebraska Press, 2000).

Collins, Keith: *Black Los Angeles: The Maturing of the Ghetto, 1940–1950* (Saratoga, CA: Century Twenty One Publishing, 1980).

Comer, Douglas: *Ritual Ground: Bent's Old Fort, World Formation, and the Annexation of the Southwest* (Berkeley: University of California Press, 1996).

Comer, Krista: "Revising Western Criticism Through Wanda Coleman." *Western American Literature* 33 (Winter 1999), 356–83.

Comer, Krista: *Landscapes of the New West: Gender and Geography in Contemporary Women's Writing* (Chapel Hill: University of North Carolina Press, 1999).

Conetah, Fred A.: *A History of the Northern Ute People* (Salt Lake City: University of Utah Printing Service for the Uintah-Ouray Ute Tribe, 1982).

Connell-Szasz, Margaret: *Education and the American Indian: The Road Toward Self-Determination* (Albuquerque: University of New Mexico Press, 1990).

Conot, Robert: *Rivers of Blood, Years of Darkness* (New York: Morrow, 1968).

Conrad, Joseph: *Heart of Darkness* ([London, 1902], New York: Dover Publications, 1990).

Constiguglia, Georgiana: "Ski Tracks: A Century of Skiing in Colorado." *Journal of the West* 30 4 (1991), 82–6.

Cook, Sherburne F.: "Population Trends Among the California Mission Indians." *Ibero-Americana* 17 (1940), 1–48.

Cook, Sherburne F.: "The Mechanism and Extent of Dietary Adaptation Among Certain Groups of California and Nevada Indians." *Ibero-Americana* 18 (1941), 1–59.

Cook, Sherburne F.: "The Indian versus the Spanish Mission." *Ibero-Americana* 21 (1943), 1–194.

Cook, Sherburne F.: "The Physical and Demographic Reaction of the Nonmission Indians in Colonial and Provincial California." *Ibero-Americana* 22 (1943), 155.

Cook, Sherburne F.: *The Indian Population of the California Indians, 1769–1970* (Berkeley: University of California Press, 1976).

Cook, Sherburne F.: *The Conflict Between the California Indian and White Civilization* (Berkeley: University of California Press, 1976).

Coolidge, Mary Roberts: *Chinese Immigration.* (New York: H. Holt and Company, 1909).

Cooney, R. S.: "Changing Labor Force Participation of Mexican-American Wives: A Comparison with Anglos and Blacks." *Social Science Quarterly* 56 (1975), 252–61.

Cooper, James Fenimore: "The Prairie: A Tale." In James Fenimore Cooper *The Leatherstocking Tales*, vol. 1 ([1827], New York: Library of America, 1985).

Coquoz, Rene: *King Pleasure Reigned in 1896: The Story of the Fabulous Leadville Ice Palace* Boulder, CO: Johnson Publishing Co, 1969.

Corey, Elizabeth and Philip L. Gerber: *Bachelor Bess: The Homesteading Letters of Elizabeth Corey, 1989–1919* (Iowa City: University of Iowa Press, 1990).

Cornell, Stephen: *The Return of the Native: American Indian Political Resurgence* (New York: Oxford University Press, 1988).

Cornford, Daniel " 'We all live more like brutes than humans': Labor and Capital in the Gold Rush." In James J. Rawls and Richard J. Orsi (eds.) *A Golden State: Mining and Economic Development in Gold Rush California in California History* (Berkeley: University of California Press, 1998/99).

Costo, Rupert and Jeannette Henry Costo (eds.): *The Missions of California: A Legacy of Genocide* (San Francisco: The Indian Historian Press for the American Indian Historical Society, 1987).

Couve de Murville, M. N. L.: *The Man Who Founded California: The Life of Blessed Junipero Serra* (San Francisco: Ignatius Press, 2000).

Cox, Bette Yarborough: *Central Avenue – It's Rise and Fall (1890–c. 1955): Including the Musical Renaissance of Black Los Angeles* (Los Angeles: BEEM Publications, 1996).

Cox, Thomas R.: *Mills and Markets: A History of the Pacific Coast Lumber Industry to 1900* (Seattle: University of Washington Press, 1974).

Cox, Thomas R.: "Changing Forests, Changing Needs: Using the Pacific Northwest's Westside Forests, Past and Present." In Dale D. Goble and Paul W. Hirt (eds.) *Northwest Lands, Northwest Peoples* (Seattle: University of Washington Press, 1999).

Cravey, Altha J.: *Women and Work in Mexico's Maquiladoras.* Lanham, MD: Rowman & Littlefield Publishers, 1998.

Cresswell, Stephen E.: *Mormons & Cowboys, Mooshiners & Klansmen: Federal Law Enforcement in the South and West, 1870–1893* (Tuscaloosa, AL: University of Alabama Press, 1991).

Cronon William: "Revisiting the Vanishing Frontier: The Legacy of Frederick Jackson Turner." *Western Historical Quarterly* 18 (1987), 157–76.

Cronon, William: *Changes in the Land: Indians, Colonists, and the Ecology of New England* (New York: Hill and Wang, 1983).

Cronon, William: "Turner's First Stand: The Significance of Significance in American History." In Richard W. Etulain (ed.) *Writing Western History: Essays on Major Western Historians* (Albuquerque: University of New Mexico Press, 1991).

Cronon, William: *Nature's Metropolis: Chicago and the Great West* (New York: W. W. Norton and Company, 1991).

Cronon, William, George Miles, and Jay Gitlin (eds.) *Under an Open Sky: Re-thinking America's Western Past* (New York: Norton, 1992).

Cronon, William: *Nature's Metropolis.* A Symposium." Special issue of *Antipode* 26 (April 1994).

Cronon, William: "The Trouble with Wilderness; or, Getting Back to the Wrong Nature." *Environmental History* 1 (1996), 7–28.

Cronon, William, George Miles, and Jay Gitlin: "Becoming West: Toward a New Meaning for Western History." In William Cronon, George Miles, and Jay Gitlin (eds.) *Under an Open Sky: Rethinking America's Western Past* (New York: W. W. Norton, 1992).

Cronon, William, Howard R. Lamar, Katherine G. Morrissey, and Jay Gitlin: "Women and the West: Rethinking the Western History Survey Course." *Western Historical Quarterly* XVII, 3 (July 1986), 269–90.

Crosby, Alfred W., Jr.: *The Columbian Exchange: Biological and Cultural Consequences of 1492* (Westport, CT: Greenwood Publishing Co., 1972).

Crosby, Alfred W., Jr.: *Ecological Imperialism: The Biological Expansion of Europe, 900–1900* (New York: Cambridge University Press, 1986).

Cross, Gary S.: *Time and Money: The Making of Consumer Culture* (New York: Routledge, 1993).

Cruikshank, Julie: *The Social Life of Stories: Narrative and Knowledge in the Yukon Territory* (Lincoln: University of Nebraska Press, 1997).

Crum, Steven J.: *The Road on Which We Came, Po'i pentun tammen kimmappeh: A History of the Western Shoshone* (Salt Lake City: University of Utah Press, 1994).

Cuch, Forrest S. (ed.): *A History of Utah's American Indians* (Salt Lake City: Utah State Division of Indian Affairs and Utah State Division of History, 2000).

Cumfer, Cynthia: " 'The Idea of Mankind is So Various': An Intellectual History of Tennessee, 1768–1810." (PhD dissertation: University of California, Los Angeles, 2001).

Cutright, Paul Russell: *Theodore Roosevelt: The Making of a Conservationist* (Urbana and Chicago: University of Illinois Press, 1985).

Cutter, Charles R.: "Judicial Punishment in Colonial New Mexico." *Western Legal History* 8 (Winter 1995–Spring 1996), 114–29.

Cutter, Charles R.: *The Legal Culture of Northern New Spain, 1700–1810* (Albuquerque, NM: University of New Mexico Press, 1995).

Dana, Richard Henry, Jr.: *Two Years Before the Mast* (New York: Houghton Mifflin Co., 1964).

D'Arcy McNickle Center for American Indian History: *Teaching and Writing Local History: The Crows* (Chicago: Newberry Library, Occasional Papers in Curriculum Series, no. 18, 1994).

D'Arcy McNickle Center for American Indian History: *The Impact of Indian History on the Teaching of United States History* (Chicago: Newberry Library, Occasional Papers in Curriculum Series, no. 5, 1986).

D'Arcy McNickle Center for American Indian History: *The Struggle for Political Autonomy* (Chicago: Newberry Library, Occasional Papers in Curriculum Series, no. 11, 1989).

Daniels, Douglas Henry: *Pioneer Urbanites: A Social and Cultural History of Black San Francisco* (Philadelphia: Temple University Press, 1980; reprinted, Berkeley: University of California Press, 1990).

Daniels, Roger: *The Politics of Prejudice: The Anti-Japanese Movement in California and the Struggle for Japanese Exclusion* (Berkeley: University of California Press, 1962).

Daniels, Roger: *The Decision to Relocate the Japanese Americans* (Philadelphia: J.B. Lippincott Company, 1975).

Daniels, Roger: *Asian America: Chinese and Japanese in the United States Since 1850* (Seattle: University of Washington Press, 1988).

Danziger, Edmund J., Jr.: *The Chippewas of Lake Superior* (Norman: University of Oklahoma Press, 1978).

Davies, K. G. (ed.): *Documents of the American Revolution*, 21 vols. (Shannon, Ireland: Irish University Press, 1972–81).

Davies, Wade M.: *"Healing Ways": Navajo Health Care in the 20th Century* (Albuquerque: University of New Mexico Press, 2001).

Davis, Clark: "From Oasis to Metropolis: Southern California and the Changing Context of American Leisure." *Pacific Historical Review* 61 (June 1992), 357–86.

Davis, Gavan: *Shoal of Time: A History of the Hawaiian Islands* (Honolulu: University of Hawaii Press, 1968).

Davis, H. L. and James Stevens: *Status Rerum: A Manifesto Upon the Present Condition of Northwestern Literature, Containing Several Near-Libelous Utterances, Upon Persons in the Public Eye* (The Dalles, Oregon: n.p., 1927).

Davis, H. L.: *Honey in the Horn* (New York: Harper and Brothers, 1935).

Davis, John: *The Landscape of Belief: Encountering the Holy Land in Nineteenth-Century American Art and Culture* (Princeton: Princeton University Press, 1996).

Davis, Mike: *City of Quartz: Excavating the Future in Los Angeles* (New York: Verso, 1990).

Davis, Richard Harding: *The West from a Car Window* (New York: Harper, 1892).

Davis, Susan G.: *Spectacular Nature: Corporate Culture and the Sea World Experience* (Berkeley: University of California Press, 1997).

Davis, Susan G.: "Landscapes of Imagination: Tourism in Southern California." *Pacific Historical Review* 68 (May 1999), 173–92.

Daynes, Kathryn: *More Wives Than One: Transformation of the Mormon marriage system, 1840–1910* (Urbana: University of Illinois Press, 2001).

de Baca, Vincent Z. C.: "Moral Renovation of the Californias: Tijuana's political and economic role in American–Mexican Relations, 1920–1935." University of California, San Diego, 1991.

de Graaf, Lawrence B.: "Negro Migration to Los Angeles, 1930–50" (PhD dissertation: University of California, Los Angeles, 1962).

de Graaf, Lawrence B.: "The City of Black Angeles: The Emergence of the Los Angeles Ghetto, 1890–1930." *Pacific Historical Review* 39 3 (August 1970), 323–52.

de Graaf, Lawrence B.: "Recognition, Racism, and Reflections on the Writing of Black Western History." *Pacific Historical Review* 44:1 (February 1975), 22–51.

de Graaf, Lawrence B.: "Race, Sex, and Region: Black Women in the American West, 1850–1920." *Pacific Historical Review* 49:1 (February 1980), 285–314.

de Graaf, Lawrence B.: "Significant Steps on an Arduous Path: The Impact of World War II on Discrimination against African Americans in the West." *Journal of the West* 35 1 (January 1996), 24–33.

de Graaf, Lawrence B., Kevin Mulroy and Quintar Taylor (eds.): *Seeking El Dorado: African American California* (Seattle: University of Washington Press, 2001).

Dear, Michael (ed.): *From Chicago to L.A.: Making Sense of Urban Theory* (Thousand Oaks, CA: Sage Publications, 2001).

Dear, Michael, Eric Schockman, and Greg Hise (eds.): *Rethinking Los Angeles* (Thousand Oaks, CA: Sage Publications, 1996).

Debo, Angie: *And Still the Waters Run: The Betrayal of the Five Civilized Tribes* (Princeton: Princeton University Press, 1972).

DeBuys, William E.: *Enchantment and Exploitation: The Life and Hard Times of (?) New Mexican Mountain Range* (Albuquerque: University of New Mexico Press, 1985).

DeBuys, William E.: *Salt Dreams: Land and Water in Low-Down California* (Albuquerque: University of New Mexico Press, 1999).

Degenhart, Stella: "The Mountaineers: Pioneers of Recreational Skiing in the Pacific Northwest." *Columbia* 9 (Winter 1995–6), 6–10.

Del Castillo, Adelaida R.: "Malíntzin Tenépal: A Preliminary Look into a New Perspective." In Rosaura Sánchez and Rosa Martínez Cruz (eds.) *Essays on La Mujer* (Los Angeles: UCLA Chicano Studies Center Publications, 1977).

de León, Arnoldo: *The Tejano Community, 1836–1900* (Albuquerque: University of New Mexico Press, 1982).

Delgado, Grace: *In the Age of Exclusion: Race, Religion, and Chinese Identity in the Making of the Arizona-Sonora Borderlands, 1863–1943* (PhD dissertation: University of California, Los Angeles, 2000).

Deloria, Vine, Jr.: *Custer Died For Your Sins: An Indian Manifesto* (New York: Macmillan, 1969).

Deloria, Vine, Jr.: *We Talk, You Listen: New Tribes, New Turf* (New York: Macmillan, 1970).

Deloria, Vine, Jr. and Clifford Lytle: *The Nations Within: The Past and Future of American Indian Sovereignty* (New York: Pantheon, 1984).

Dennis, Matthew: *Cultivating a Landscape of Peace: Iroquois-European Encounters in Seventeenth-Century America* (Ithaca: Cornell University Press, 1993).

Derickson, Alan: *Workers' Health, Workers' Democracy: The Western Miners' Struggle, 1891–1925* (Ithaca: Cornell University Press, 1988).

Deutsch, Sarah: *No Separate Refuge: Culture, Class, and Gender on an Anglo-Hispanic Frontier in the American Southwest, 1880–1940* (New York: Oxford University Press, 1987).

Deutsch, Sarah: *Women and the City: Gender, Space, and Power in Boston, 1870–1940* (New York: Oxford University Press, 2000).

Deutsch, Sarah, George J. Sanchez, and Gary Y. Okihiro: "Contemporary Peoples, Contested Places." In Clyde A. Milner II, Carol A. O'Connor, and Martha A. Sandweiss (eds.) *The Oxford History of the American West* (New York: Oxford University Press, 1994).

Devens, Carol: *Countering Colonization: Native American Women and Great Lakes Missions, 1630–1900* (Berkeley: University of California Press, 1992).

Deverell, William F.: *Railroad Crossing: Californians and the Railroad, 1850–1910* (Berkeley: University of California Press, 1994).

Deverell, William and Douglas Flamming: "Race, Rhetoric, and Regional Identity: Boosting Los Angeles, 1880–1930." In R. White, R. and J. M. Findlay (eds.) *Power and Place in the North American West* (Seattle: University of Washington Press, 1999).

Deverell, William and Anne F. Hyde: *The West in the History of the Nation: Since 1865* (Boston: Bedford/St. Martin's, 2000).

Deverell, William and Tom Sitton (eds.): *California Progressivism Revisited* (Berkeley: University of California Press, 1994).

DeVoto, Bernard: "The West: A Plundered Province." *Harper's* 169 (1934), 355–64.

DeVoto, Bernard: *The Course of Empire* (Boston: Houghton Mifflin, 1952).

Dexter, Franklin B. (ed.): *The Diary of David McClure, Doctor of Divinity, 1748–1820* (New York: Knickerbocker Press, 1899).

Didion, Joan: *Play It as It Lays* (New York: Farrar, Straus & Giroux, 1970).

di Leonardo, Micaela: "The Female World of Cards and Holidays" *Signs* 12 3 (Spring 1987), 440–53.

Dilworth, Leah: *Imagining Indians in the Southwest: Persistent Visions of a Primitive Past* (Washington DC: Smithsonian Institution Press, 1996).

Din, Gilbert C.: *Spaniards, Planters, and Slaves: The Spanish Regulation of Slavery in Louisiana, 1763–1803* (College Station: Texas A&M University Press, 1999).

Dippie, Brian W.: *The Vanishing American: White Attitudes and US Indian Policy* (Middletown, CT: Wesleyan University Press, 1982).

Dippie, Brian W.: *Catlin and his Contemporaries: The Politics of Patronage* (Lincoln: University of Nebraska Press, 1990).

Dirlik, Arif: "The Asia-Pacific Idea: Reality and Representation in the Invention of a Regional Structure." In Arif Dirlik (ed.) *What is in a Rim? Critical Perspectives on the Pacific Region Idea*, 2nd edn. (Lanham, MD: Rowman and Littlefield, 1998).

Djedje, Jacqueline Cogdell: "Gospel Music in the Los Angeles Black Community: A Historical Overview." *Black Music Research Journal* 9, 1 (Spring 1989), 35–77.

Djedje, Jacqueline Cogdell and Eddie S. Meadows: *California Soul: Music of African Americans in the West* (Berkeley: University of California Press, 1998).

Dobyns, Henry F.: "Estimating Aboriginal American Population: An Appraisal of Techniques with a New Hemispheric Estimate." *Current Anthropology* 7 (1966): 395–416, 425–49.

Dobyns, Henry F.: *Their Number Become Thinned: Native American Population Dynamics in Eastern North America* (Knoxville: University of Tennessee Press, 1983).

Doig, Ivan: *This House of Sky: Landscapes of a Western Mind* (New York: Harcourt, Brace Jovanovich, 1978).

Donahue, Debra L.: *The Western Range Revisited: Removing Livestock from Public Lands to Conserve Native Biodiversity* (Norman, OK: University of Oklahoma Press, 2000).

Dowd, Gregory Evans: *A Spirited Resistance: The North American Indian Struggle for Unity, 1745–1815* (Baltimore: Johns Hopkins University, 1992).

Dowd, Gregory Evans: *War Under Heaven: Pontiac, the Indian Nations, and the British Empire* (Baltimore: Johns Hopkins University Press, 2002).

Drago, Harry S.: *The Great Range Wars: Violence on the Grasslands* (Lincoln, NE: University of Nebraska Press, 1970).

Drago, Harry S.: *The Legend Makers: Tales of the Old-Time Peace Officers and Desperadoes of the Frontier* (New York: Putnam, 1975).

Dubofsky, Melvyn: *Industrialism and the American Worker, 1865–1920*. 3rd ed. (Arlington Heights, IL: Harlan Davidson, 1996).

Dubofsky, Melvyn: *We Shall Be All: A History of the Industrial Workers of the World* (Chicago: Quadrangle Books, AHM Publishing Co., 1969).

Ducker, James H.: *Men of the Steel Rails: Workers on the Atchison, Topeka and Santa Fe Railroad, 1869–1900* (Lincoln: University of Nebraska Press, 1983).

Dudden, Arthur Power: *The American Pacific: From the Old China Trade to the Present* (New York: Oxford University Press, 1992).

Duncan, Dayton: *Out West: An American Journey* (New York: Viking, 1987).

Duncan, Dayton: *Miles from Nowhere: Tales from America's Contemporary Frontier* (New York: Viking, 1993).

Dunlap, Thomas: *Saving America's Wildlife* (Princeton: Princeton University Press, 1982).

Dunlay, Thomas W.: *Wolves for the Blue Soldiers: Indian Scouts and Auxiliaries with the United States Army, 1860–90* (Lincoln: University of Nebraska Press, 1982).

Dunlay, Thomas W.: *Kit Carson and the Indians* (Lincoln: University of Nebraska Press, 2000).

Duratschek, M. Claudia: *The Beginning of Catholicism in South Dakota* (Washington, DC: Catholic University of America Press, 1943).

Dykstra, Robert R.: *The Cattle Towns* (New York: Knopf, 1968).

Dykstra, Robert R.: "To Live and Die in Dodge City: Body Counts, Law and Order, and the Case of Kansas v. Gill." In Michael A. Bellesiles (ed.) *Lethal Imagination: Violence and Brutality in American History* (New York: New York University Press, 1999).

Dykstra, Robert R. and Jo Ann Manfra: "The Circle Dot Cowboys at Dodge City: History and Imagination in Andy Adams's *The Log of a Cowboy*." *Western Legal History* 13, 1 (Spring, 2002), 19–40.

Dysart, Jane: "Mexican Women in San Antonio, 1830–1860: The Assimilation Process." *Western Historical Quarterly* 7, 4 (October 1976), 365–75.

Eagleton, Terry: *Literary Theory: An Introduction* (Minneapolis: University of Minnesota Press, 1983).

Eagleton, Terry, Frederick Jameson, and Edward W. Said: *Nationalism, Colonialism, and Literature* (Minneapolis: University of Minnesota Press, 1990).

Eaton, Howard: "Birth of Western Dude Ranching." *American West* 16 (Winter, 1979), 18–22.

Ebright, Malcolm: "Frontier Land Litigation in Colonial New Mexico: A Determinant of Spanish Custom and Law." *Western Legal History* 8 (Summer–Fall 1995), 198–226.

Eccles, W. J.: *The Canadian Frontier, 1534–1760* (New York: Holt Rinehart and Winston, 1969).

Eco, Umberto: *Serendipities: Language of Lunacy* (New York: Harcourt, Brace, 1998).

Edmunds, R. David (ed.): *American Indian Leaders: Studies in Diversity* (Lincoln: University of Nebraska Press, 1980).

Edmunds, R. David: "Native Americans, New Voices: American Indian History, 1895–1995," *American Historical Review* 100, 3 (June 1995), 717–40.

Edmunds, R. David (ed.): *The New Warriors: Native American Leaders Since 1900* (Lincoln: University of Nebraska Press, 2001).

Egan, Ferol: *Fremont, Explorer for a Restless Nation* (Garden City, New York: Doubleday, 1977).

Egan, Tim: *Lasso the Wind: Away to the New West* (New York: Random House, 1998).

Ehle, John: *Trail of Tears: The Rise and Fall of the Cherokee Nation* (New York: Doubleday, 1988).

Einstadter, Walter J.: "Crime News in the Old West." *Urban Life* 8 (1979), 323–30.

Eisenhower, John S. D.: *So Far From God: The U.S. War with Mexico, 1846–1848* (New York: Random House, 1990).

Ekberg, Carl J: *French Roots in the Illinois Country: The Mississippi Frontier in Colonial Times* (Urbana: University of Illinois Press, 1998).

Elkind, Sarah S.: *Bay Cities and Water Politics: The Battle for Resources in Boston and Oakland.* (Lawrence: University Press of Kansas, 1998).

Elliott, Emory (ed.): *Columbia Literary History of the United States* (New York: Columbia University Press, 1988).

Ellis, Clyde: *To Change Them Forever: Indian Education at the Rainy Mountain Boarding School, 1893–1920* (Norman: University of Oklahoma Press, 1996).

Ellis, Joseph J.: *American Sphinx: The Character of Thomas Jefferson* (New York: Alfred A. Knopf, 1997).

Emmerich, Lisa E.: "'Save the Babies': American Indian Women, Assimilation Policy, and Scientific Motherhood, 1912–1918." In Elizabeth Jameson and Susan Armitage (eds.) *Writing the Range: Race, Class, and Culture in the Women's West* (Norman: University of Oklahoma Press, 1997).

Emmons, David M.: *Garden in the Grasslands: Boomer Literature of the Central Great Plains* (Lincoln: University of Nebraska Press, 1971).

Emmons, David M.: *The Butte Irish: Class and Ethnicity in an American mining Town, 1873–1925* (Urbana: University of Illinois Press, 1989).

Emmons, David and William G. Robbins: *Colony and Empire: The Capitalist Transformation of the American West* (Lawrence: University of Kansas Press, 1994).

Engh, Michael E.: "A Multiplicity of Diversity of Faiths: Religion's Impact on Los Angeles and the Urban West, 1890–1940." *Western Historical Quarterly* 28 (Winter 1997), 463–92.

Engh, Michael E.: "Practically Every Religion Being Represented." In William Deverell and Tom Sitton (eds.) *Metropolis in the Making: Los Angeles in the 1920s* (Berkeley: University of California Press, 2001).

Engh, Michael E.: *Frontier Faiths: Church, Temple, and Synagogue in Los Angeles, 1846–1888* (Albuquerque, NM: University of New Mexico Press, 1992).

Erickson, Winston: *Sharing the Desert: The Tohono O'odham in History* (Tucson: University of Arizona Press, 1994).

Erisman, Fred: "The Changing Face of Western Literary Realism." In Gerald D. Nash and Richard W. Etulain (eds.) *The Twentieth-Century West: Historical Interpretations* (Albuquerque: University of New Mexico Press, 1989).

Erisman, Fred and Richard W. Etulain (eds.): *Fifty Western Writers: A Bio-Bibliographical Sourcebook* (Westport, CT: Greenwood Press, 1982).

Ernst, Eldon E.: "The Emergence of California in American Religious Historiography." *Religion and American Culture: A Journal of Interpretation* 11, 1 (2001): 33–45.

Escobar, Edward J.: *Race, Police, and the Making of a Political Identity: Mexican Americans and the Los Angeles Police Department, 1900–1945* (Berkeley, CA: University of California Press, 1999).

Ethington, Philip: *The Public City: The Political Construction of Urban Life in San Francisco, 1850–1900* (New York: Cambridge University Press, 1994).

Ethington, Philip and Martin Meeker: "Saber y Conocer: The Metropolis of Urban Inquiry." In Michael Dear, Eric Schockman, and Greg Hise (eds.) *Rethinking Los Angeles* (Thousand Oaks, CA: Sage Publications, 1996).

Etulain, Richard W.: "The American Literary West and Its Interpreters: The Rise of a New Historiography." *Pacific Historical Review*, 45 (August 1976), 311–48.

Etulain, Richard W.: "Western Fiction and History: A Reconsideration." In Jerome O. Steffen (ed.) *The American West: New Perspectives, New Dimensions* (Norman: University of Oklahoma Press, 1979).

Etulain, Richard W.: "Main Currents in Modern Western Literature." In Richard W. Etulain (ed.) "Cultural History of the American West," Special Issue, *Journal of American Culture*, 3 (Summer 1980), 374–88.

Etulain, Richard W.: *A Bibliographical Guide to the Study of American Western Literature* (Lincoln: University of Nebraska Press, 1982).

Etulain, Richard W.: *Re-Imagining the Modern American West: A Century of Fiction, History, and Art* (Tucson: University of Arizona Press, 1996).

Etulain, Richard W.: "Research Opportunities in Twentieth-Century Western Cultural History." In Gerald D. Nash and Richard W. Etulain (eds.) *Research Western History: Topics in the Twentieth Century* (Albuquerque: University of New Mexico Press, 1997).

Etulain, Richard W.: *Telling Western Stories: From Buffalo Bill to Larry McMurtry* (Albuquerque: University of New Mexico Press, 1999).

Etulain, Richard W.: "Western Stories for the Next Generation," *Western Historical Quarterly* 31 (Spring 2000), 5–23.

Etulain, Richard W.: *The American Literary West* (Manhattan, KS: Sunflower University Press, 1980).

Etulain, Richard W. and N. Jill Howard (eds.): *A Bibliographical Guide to the Study of American Western Literature*, 2nd edn. (Albuquerque: University of New Mexico Press, 1995).

Ewers, John C.: *The Blackfeet: Raiders of the Northwestern Plains* (Norman: University of Oklahoma Press, 1958).

Fabian, Ann: "History for the Masses: Commercializing the Western Past." In William Cronon, George Miles, and Jay Gitlin (eds.) *Under an Open Sky: Rethinking America's Western Past* (New York: W. W. Norton and Company, 1992).

Faragher, John Mack: *Women and Men on the Overland Trail* (New Haven: Yale University Press, 1979).

Faragher, John Mack: *Daniel Boone: The Life and Legend of an American Pioneer* (New York: Henry Holt, 1992).

Farmer, Jared: *Glen Canyon Dammed: Inventing Lake Powell and the Canyon Country* (Tucson: University of Arizona Press, 1999).

Farnham, Thomas Jefferson: *Travels in the Great Western Prairies, the Anahuac and Rocky Mountains, and in the Oregon Territory* (New York: Greeley & McElrath, 1843).

Fay, Abbot: *Ski Tracks in the Rockies: A Century of Colorado Skiing* (Denver: Cordillera Press, 1984).

Feagin, Joe R.: *Free Enterprise City: Houston in Political-Economic Perspective* (New Brunswick, NJ: Rutgers University Press, 1988).

Featherstone, Mike: *Consumer Culture and Postmodernism* (London: Sage, 1991).

Fehrenbach, T. R.: *Lone Star: A History of Texas and the Texans* (New York: Macmillan, 1968).

Feinman, Ronald L.: *Twilight of Progressivism: The Western Republican Senators and the New Deal* (Baltimore: Johns Hopkins University Press, 1981).

Fergusson, Erna: *New Mexico: A Pageant of Three Peoples* (New York: Knopf, 1964).

Fernández-Kelly, Maráa Patricia. *For We Are Sold, I And My People: Women and Industry in Mexico's Frontier* (Albany: State University of New York Press, 1983).

Fernlund, Kevin (ed.): *The Cold War American West, 1945–1989* (Albuquerque: University of New Mexico Press, 1998).

Fernlund, Kevin J.: *William Henry Holmes and the Rediscovery of the American West* (Albuquerque: University of New Mexico Press, 2000).

Fiege, Mark: *Irrigated Eden: The Making of an Agricultural Landscape in the American West* (Seattle: University of Washington Press, 1999).

Fifer, J. Valerie: *American Progress: The Growth of Transport, Tourist, and Information Industries in the Nineteenth-Century West* (Chester, CN: Pequot Press, 1988).

Findlay, John M.: *Magic Lands: Western Cityscapes and American Culture after 1940* (Berkeley: University of California Press, 1992).

Fine, David (ed.): *Los Angeles in Fiction: A Collection of Essays*, rev. edn. (Albuquerque: University of New Mexico Press, 1995).

Finger, John R.: *Tennessee Frontiers: Three Regions in Transition* (Bloomington: Indiana University Press, 2001).

Firmage, Edwin Brown and Richard Collin Mangrum: *Zion in the Courts: A Legal History of the Church of Jesus Christ of Latter-day Saints, 1830–1900* (Urbana, IL: University of Illinois Press, 1988).

Fischer, Hank: *Wolf Wars: The Remarkable Inside Story of the Restoration of Wolves to Yellowstone* (Helena: Falcon Press, 1995).

Fischman, Lisa Anne: "Coonskin Fever: Frontier Adventures in Postwar American Culture." (PhD dissertation: University of Minnesota, 1996).

Fisher, Robert Colin: "Frontiers of Leisure: Nature, Memory, and Nationalism in American Parks, 1850–1930." (PhD dissertation: University of California, Irvine, 1999).

Fisher, Sethard: *Black Elected Officials in California* (San Francisco: R & E Research Associates Inc., 1978).

Fixico, Donald L.: *Termination and Relocation: Federal Indian Policy, 1945–1961* (Albuquerque: University of New Mexico Press, 1986).

Fixico, Donald L. (ed.): *Rethinking American Indian History* (Albuquerque: University of New Mexico Press, 1997).

Fixico, Donald L.: *The Invasion of Indian Country in the Twentieth Century: American Capitalism and Tribal Natural Resources* (Niwot: University Press of Colorado, 1998).

Fixico, Donald: *The Urban Indian Experience in America* (Albuquerque: University of New Mexico Press, 2000).

Flamming, Douglas: *Creating the Modern South: Millhands and Managers in Dalton, Georgia, 1884–1984* (Chapel Hill: University of North Carolina Press, 1992).

Flamming, Douglas: "African Americans and the Politics of Race in Progressive-Era Los Angeles." In William Deverell and T. Sitton (eds.) *California Progressivism Reconsidered* (Berkeley: University of California Press, 1994).

Flamming, Douglas: "A Westerner in Search of 'Negro-ness': Region and Race in the Writing of Arna Bontemps." In V. Matsumoto and B. Allmendinger (eds.) *Over the Edge: Remapping the American West* (Berkeley: University of California Press, 1999).

Flamming, Douglas: "Becoming Democrats: Liberal Politics and the African American Community in Los Angeles." In Lawrence B. de Graaf, Kevin Mulroy, and Quintard Taylor (eds.) *Seeking El Dorado: African American California* (Seattle: University of Washington Press, 2001).

Flamming, Douglas: "The *Star of Ethiopia* and the NAACP: Pageantry, Politics, and the Los Angeles African American Community." In William Deverell and T. Sitton (eds.) *Metropolis in the Making: Los Angeles in the 1920s* (Berkeley: University of California Press, 2001).

Flamming, Douglas: *A World to Gain: African Americans in Los Angeles, 1890–1940* (Berkeley: University of California Press, 2004)

Fletcher, Robert Samuel: "Review of William Warren Sweet *Religion on the American Frontier: The Congregationalists*." *Mississippi Valley Historical Review* 26: 568–69.

Flink, James: *The Car Culture* (Cambridge, MA: MIT Press, 1975).

Flores, Dan (ed.): *Jefferson and Southwestern Exploration: the Freeman & Custis Accounts of the Red River Expedition of 1806* (Norman: University of Oklahoma Press, 1984).

Flores, Dan: *Caprock Canyonlands: Journeys into the Heart of the Southern Plains* (Austin: University of Texas Press, 1990).

Flores, Dan: "Bison Ecology and Bison Diplomacy: The Southern Plains from 1800 to 1850." *Journal of American History* 78, 2 (September 1991), 465–85.

Flores, Dan: "Place: An Argument for Bioregional History." *Environmental History Review* 18 (1994), 1–18.

Flores, Dan: *Horizontal Yellow: Nature and History in the Near Southwest* (Albuquerque: University of New Mexico Press, 1999).

Flores, Dan: *The Natural West: Environmental History in the Great Plains and Rocky Mountains* (Norman: University of Oklahoma Press, 2001).

Flores, William and Rena Benmayor (eds.): *Latino Cultural Citizenship: Claiming Identity, Space, and Rights.* Boston: Beacon, 1997.

Fogelson, Robert M.: *The Fragmented Metropolis: Los Angeles, 1850–1930* (Cambridge, MA: Harvard University Press, 1967).

Foley, Neil: *The White Scourge: Mexicans, Blacks, and Poor Whites in Texas Cotton Culture* (Berkeley, CA: University of California Press, 1997).

Foley, Neil: "Becoming Hispanic: Mexican Americans and the Faustian Pact with Whiteness." In Neil Foley (ed.) *Reflexiones 1997: New Directions in Mexican American Studies* (Austin: Center for Mexican American Studies Books, 1998).

Forbes, Jack D.: "The Indian in the West: A Challenge for Historians." *Arizona and the West* 1 (Winter 1959), 206–15.

Forbes, Jack D.: *Apache, Navaho and Spaniard* (Norman: University of Oklahoma Press, 1960).

Forbes, Jack D.: *Warriors of the Colorado* (Norman: University of Oklahoma Press, 1965).

Ford, Paul Leicester (ed.): *The Works of Thomas Jefferson* (New York and London: G. P. Putnam's Sons, 1905).

Foss, Phillip O.: *Politics and Grass: The Administration of Grazing on the Public Domain* (Seattle: University Press of Washington, 1960).

Foster, Morris W.: *Being Comanche: A Social History of an American Indian Community* (Tucson: University of Arizona Press, 1991).

Foucault, Michel: "Governmentality." In Graham Burchell, Colin Gordon, and Peter Miller (eds.) *The Foucault Effect: Studies in Governmentality* (Chicago: University of Chicago Press, 1991).

Fowler, Loretta: *Arapahoe Politics, 1851–1978: Symbols in Crises of Authority* (Lincoln: University of Nebraska Press, 1982).

Fowler, Loretta: *Shared Symbols, Contested Meanings: Gros Ventre Culture and History, 1778–1984* (Ithaca, NY: Cornell University Press, 1987).

Fowler, Loretta: *Tribal Sovereignty and the Historical Imagination: Cheyenne–Arapahoe Politics* (Lincoln: University of Nebraska Press, 2002).

Fox, Stephen: *John Muir and His Legacy: The American Conservation Movement* (Boston: Little, Brown and Co., 1981).

Francaviglia, Richard V.: *The Mormon Landscape: Existence, Creation, and Perception of a Unique Image in the American West* (New York: AMS Press, 1978).

Francaviglia, Richard V.: "Main Street USA: A Comparison/Contrast of Streetscapes in Disneyland and Walt Disney World." *Journal of Popular Culture* 15 (Summer 1981), 141–56.

Francis, Daniel: *Battle for the West: Fur Traders and the Birth of Western Canada* (Edmonton: Hurtig, 1982).

Frank, Dana. *Purchasing Power: Consumer Organizing, Gender, and the Seattle Labor Movement, 1919–1929* (New York: Cambridge University Press, 1994).

Frank, Ross: *From Settler to Citizen: New Mexican Economic Development and the Creation of Vecino Society, 1750–1820* (Berkeley: University of California Press, 2000).

Franklin, Jimmie Lewis: *Born Sober: Prohibition in Oklahoma, 1907–1959* (Norman: University of Oklahoma Press, 1971).

Fraser, Steve and Gary Gerstle (eds.): *The Rise and Fall of the New Deal Order* (Princeton, NJ: Princeton University Press, 1989).

Frazier's: *Great Plains* (New York: Farrar, Straus Giroux, 1989)

Freehling, William: *The Road to Disunion* (New York: Oxford University Press, 1990).

Freyfogle, Eric: "*Lux v. Haggin* and the Common Law Burden of Modern Water Law." *University of Colorado Law Review* 57 (Spring 1986), 485–525.

Friday, Chris: *Organizing Asian American Labor: The Pacific Coast Canned-Salmon Industry, 1870–1942* (Philadelphia: Temple University Press, 1994).

Friday, Chris: "Recasting Identities: American-born Chinese and Nisei in the Era of the Pacific War." In Richard White and John M. Findlay (eds.) *Power and Place in the North American West* (Seattle: University of Washington Press, 1999).

Friedman, Lawrence M. and Robert V. Percival: *The Roots of Justice: Crime and Punishment in Alameda County, California, 1870–1910* (Chapel Hill, NC: University of North Carolina Press, 1981).

Friend, Craig Thompson (ed.): *The Buzzel about Kentuck: Settling the Promised Land* (Lexington: University of Kentucky Press, 1999).

Fritz, Christian G.: *Federal Justice: The California Court of Ogden Hoffman, 1851–1891* (Lincoln, NE: University of Nebraska Press, 1991).

Fritz, Christian G.: "Popular Sovereignty, Vigilantism, and the Constitutional Right of Revolution." *Pacific Historical Review* 63 (February 1994), 39–66.

Fritz, Christian G.: "The American Constitutional Tradition Revisited: Preliminary Observations on State Constitution-Making in the Nineteenth-Century West." *Rutgers Law Journal* 25 (Summer 1994), 945–98.

Frug, Gerald E.: *City Making: Building Communities Without Building Walls* (Princeton, NJ: Princeton University Press, 1999).

Furtwangler, Albert: *Acts of Discovery: Visions of America in the Lewis and Clark Journals* (Urbana: University of Illinois Press, 1993).

Fussell, Edwin: *Frontier: American Literature and the American West* (Princeton, NJ: Princeton University Press, 1965).

Ganzel, Bill: *Dust Bowl Descent* (Lincoln: University of Nebraska Press, 1984).

Garcia, Juan R.: *Operation Wetback: The Mass Deportation of Mexican Undocumented Workers in 1954* (Westport, CT: Greenwood Press, 1980).

García, Mario: *Desert Immigrants: The Mexicans of El Paso, 1880–1920* (New Haven: Yale University Press, 1981).

Gamio, Manuel: *Mexican Immigration to the United States: A Study of Human Migration and Adjustment* (Chicago: University of Chicago Press, 1930).

García, Mario T.: *Desert Immigrants: The Mexicans of El Paso, 1880–1920.* (New Haven, CT: Yale University Press, 1981).

Garis, Roy L.: *Mexican Immigration: A Report by Roy L. Garis for the Information of the Members of Congress* (United States House of Representatives, 1930).

Garrison, Tim Alan: *The Legal Ideology of Removal: The Judiciary and the Sovereignty of Native American Nations* (Athens, GA: University of Georgia Press, 2002).

Gates, Paul Wallace: *History of Public Land Law Development* (Washington, DC: Public Land Law Review Commission, 1968).

Gates, Paul Wallace: *Landlords and Tenants on the Prairie Frontier: Studies in American Land Policy* (Ithaca: Cornell University Press, 1973).

Gates, Paul Wallace: *Land and Law in California: Essays on Land Policies* (Ames: Iowa State University Press, 1991).

Gaustad, Edwin Scott: *Historical Atlas of Religion in America* (New York: Harper & Row, Publishers, 1962).

Gaustad, Edwin Scott: *A Religious History of America*, 4th edn. (San Francisco: Harper, 1990).

Gaustad, Edwin Scott and Philip Barlow: *New Historical Atlas of Religion in America* (New York: Oxford University Press, 2001).

Geertz, Clifford: *The Interpretation of Cultures* (New York: Basic Books, 1973).

Gelber, Steven: "The Eye of the Beholder: Images of California by Dorothea Lange and Russell Lee." *California History* 64, 4 (1985) 264–71.

Gelfand, Mark: *A Nation of Cities: The Federal Government and Urban America, 1933–1965* (New York: Oxford University Press, 1975).

George, Lynell: *No Crystal Stair: African Americans in the City of Angels* (New York: Anchor Books, 1992).

Georgi-Findlay, Brigitte: *The Frontiers of Women's Writing: Women's Narratives and the Rhetoric of Westward Expansion* (Tucson: University of Arizona Press, 1996).

Gibson, Arrell Morgan: "The Pacific Basin Frontier." *Journal of the West* 15, 2 (1976), 1–4.

Gibson, Arrell Morgan: *The American Indian: Prehistory to the Present* (New York: D. C. Heath, 1980).

Gibson, Arrell Morgan: *Yankees in Paradise: The Pacific Basin Frontier,* completed with the assistance of John S. Whitehead (Albuquerque: University of New Mexico Press, 1993).

Glacken, Clarence J.: *Traces on the Rhodian Shore: Nature and Culture in Western Thought from Ancient Times to the End of the Eighteenth Century* (Berkeley: University of California Press, 1967).

Glenn, Evelyn Nakano: "Racial Ethnic Women's Labor: The Intersection of Race, Gender, and Class Oppression." *Review of Radical Political Economics* 17, 3 (Fall 1985), 86–108.

Goble, Dale D. and Paul W. Hirt (eds.): *Northwest Lands, Northwest Peoples: Readings in Environmental History* (Seattle: University of Washington Press, 1999).

Goble, Danney: *Progressive Oklahoma: The Making of a New Kind of State* (Norman: University of Oklahoma Press, 1980).

Goetzmann, William: *Army Exploration in the American West* (New Haven: Yale University Press, 1959).

Goetzmann, William H.: "Mountain Man as Jacksonian Man." *American Quarterly* 15 (Fall 1963), 402–15.

Goetzmann, William H.: *Exploration and Empire: The Explorer and the Scientist in the Winning of the West* (New York: Knopf, 1966).

Goetzmann, William H.: *When the Eagle Screamed: The Romantic Horizon in American Diplomacy, 1800–1860* (New York: Wiley, 1966).

Goetzmann, William H.: *The West as Romantic Horizon* (Lincoln: University of Nebraska Press, 1981).

Goetzmann, William H.: *Exploring the American West, 1803–1879* (Washington, DC: National Park Service, 1982).

Goetzmann, William H.: *The West of the Imagination* (New York: Norton, 1986).

Goetzmann, William H.: *New Lands, New Men: America and the Second Great Age of Discovery* (New York: Viking Press, 1986).

Goetzmann, William H. and Glyndwr Williams: *Atlas of North American Exploration, from the Norse Voyages to the Race for the Pole* (New York: Prentice-Hall, 1992).

Goldberg, Michael Lewis: *An Army of Women: Gender and Politics in Gilded Age Kansas* (Baltimore: Johns Hopkins University Press, 1997).

Goldberg, Robert A.: *Barry Goldwater* (New Haven: Yale University Press, 1995).

Goldberg, Robert A.: *Hooded Empire: The Ku Klux Klan in Colorado* (Urbana: University of Illinois Press, 1981).

Goldman, Marion S.: *Gold Diggers and Silver Miners: Prostitution and Social Life on the Comstock Lode* (Ann Arbor: University of Michigan Press, 1979).

Goldman, Shifra M.: *Dimensions of the Americas: Art and Social Change in Latin America and the United States* (Chicago: University of Chicago Press, 1994).

Goldy, Samuel N.: *The Era of California's Supreme Industrial Possibilities* (San Jose: Press of Muirson and Wright, 1903).

Gómez-Peña, Guillermo: *The New World Border: Prophecies, Poems & Loqueras for the End of the Century* (San Francisco: City Lights, 1996).

Gómez-Peña, Guillermo: *Dangerous Border Crossers* (New York: Routledge, 2000).

Gómez-Quiñones, Juan: "The First Steps: Chicano Labor Conflict and Organizing 1900–1920." *Aztlán* 3, 1 (1972): 13–50.

Gómez-Quiñones, Juan: "Piedras contra la luna, México en Aztlán y Aztlán en México: Chicano–Mexican Relations in the Mexican Consulates, 1900–1920." In *Contemporary Mexico: Papers of the IV International Congress of Mexican History in Mexico City* (El Colegio de México 1975).

Gómez-Quiñones, Juan: "On Culture." *Revista Chicano-Riqueña* 5, 2 (1977), 35–53.

Gómez-Quiñones, Juan: *Development of the Mexican Working Class North of the Rio Bravo: Work and Culture among Laborers and Artisans, 1600–1900* (Los Angeles: UCLA Chicano Studies Research Center Publications, 1982).

Gómez-Quiñones, Juan: *Chicano Politics: Reality and Promise, 1940–1990* (Albuquerque: University of New Mexico Press, 1990).

Gómez-Quiñones, Juan: *Roots of Chicano Politics, 1600–1940* (Albuquerque: University of New Mexico Press, 1994).

González, Deena J.: "La Tules of Image and Reality: Euro-American Attitudes and Legend Formation on a Spanish–Mexican Frontier." In Adela de la Torre and Beatríz M. Pesquera (eds.) *Building with Our Hands: Directions in Chicana Scholarship* (Berkeley: University of California Press, 1993), reprinted in Vicki L. Ruiz and Ellen Carol DuBois *Unequal Sisters: A Multicultural Reader in US Women's History*, 2nd edn. (New York: Routledge, 1994).

González, Deena J.: *Refusing the Favor: The Spanish-Mexican Women of Santa Fe, 1820–1880* (New York: Oxford University Press, 1999).

Gonzalez, Nancie H.: *The Spanish-Americans of New Mexico: A Heritage of Pride* (Albuquerque: University of New Mexico Press, 1969).

Gonzales, Phillip B: *Forced Sacrifice as Ethnic Protest: The Hispano Cause in New Mexico and the Racial Attitude Confrontation of 1933* (New York: Peter Lang, 2001).

González, Rosalinda Méndez: "Distinctions in Western Women's Experience: Ethnicity, Class, and Social Change." In Susan Armitage and Elizabeth Jameson (eds.) *The Women's West* (Norman: University of Oklahoma Press, 1987).

Goodman, George J. and Cheryl Lawson: *Retracing Stephen H. Long's 1820 Expedition: The Itinerary and the Botany* (Norman: University of Oklahoma Press, 1995).

Gordon, Sarah Barringer: "'The Liberty of Self-Degradation': Polygamy, Woman Suffrage, and Consent in Nineteenth-Century America." *Journal of American History* 83 4 (December 1996), 815–47.

Gordon, Sarah Barringer: *The Mormon Question: Polygamy and Constitutional Conflict in Nineteenth-Century America* (Chapel Hill, NC: University of North Carolina Press, 2002).

Gordon-McCutchan, R. C. (ed.): *Kit Carson: Indian Fighter or Indian Killer?* (Niwot, CO: University Press of Colorado, 1996).

Gorman, Ed and Martin H. Greenberg (eds.): *The Best of the American West* (New York: Penguin/Putnam, 1998).

Gorman, Ed and Martin H. Greenberg (eds.): *The Best of the American West, II* (New York: Berkley Books, 1999).

Gottlieb, Robert: *Forcing the Spring: The Transformation of the American Environmental Movement* (Washington, DC: Island Press, 1993).

Gould, Lewis L.: *Progressives and Prohibitionists: Texas Democrats in the Wilson Era* (Austin: University of Texas Press, 1973).

Graebner, Norman A.: *Empire on the Pacific: A Study in American Continental Expansion* (New York: Ronald Press Co., 1955).

Graf, William L.: *Wilderness Preservation and the Sagebrush Rebellions* (Savage, MD: Rowman & Littlefield, 1990).

Gramsci, Antonio: *The Gramsci Reader: Selected Writings, 1916–1935* ed. David Forgacs (New York: New York University Press, 2000).

Grattan, Virginia L.: *Mary Colter: Builder Upon the Red Earth* (Flagstaff, AZ: Northland Press, 1980).

Green, Donald: *Land of the Underground Rain: Irrigation on the Texas High Plains, 1910–1970* (Austin: University of Texas Press, 1973)

Green, Harvey: *Fit For America: Health, Fitness, Sport and American Society* (New York: Pantheon Books, 1981).

Green, Rayna: "The Pocahantas Perplex: The Image of Indian Women in American Culture." *Massachusetts Review* 16, 4 (1976), 698–714.

Greene, Jerome: *Lakota and Cheyenne: Indian Views of the Great Sioux Wars, 1876–1877* (Norman: University of Oklahoma Press, 1994).

Greene, John C.: *American Science in the Age of Jefferson* (Ames, Iowa: Iowa State University Press, 1984).

Greever, William: *Bonanza West: The Story of Western Mining Rushes* (Norman: University of Oklahoma Press, 1963).

Griswold, Don L. and Jean Harvey: *A Carbonate Camp Called Leadville* (Denver: University of Denver Press, 1951).

Griswold, Robert: *Family and Divorce in California, 1850–1880* (Albany: State University of New York Press, 1982).

Griswold del Castillo, Richard: *The Los Angeles Barrio, 1850–1890: A Social History* (Berkeley: University of California Press, 1979).

Grossman, Lewis: "John C. Fremont, Mariposa, and the Collision of Mexican and American Law." *Western Legal History* 6 (Winter/ Spring, 1993), 16–50.

Guarneri, Carl and David Alvarez (eds.): *Religion and Society in the American West: Historical Essays* (Lanham, MD: University Press of America, 1987).

Guice, John D.: *The Rocky Mountain Bench: The Territorial Supreme Courts of Colorado, Montana, and Wyoming, 1861–1890* (New Haven, CT: Yale University Press, 1972).

Gullett, Gayle: *Becoming Citizens: The Emergence and Development of the California Women's Movement, 1880–1911* (Urbana: University of Illinois Press, 2000).

Gumerman, George J. (ed.): *The Anasazi in a Changing Environment* (New York: Cambridge University Press, 1988).

Guthrie, A. B., Jr.: *The Way West* (Boston: Houghton, Mifflin, 1949).

Gutierrez, David G.: *Walls and Mirrors: Mexican Americans, Mexican Immigrants, and the Politics of Ethnicity* (Berkeley: University of California Press, 1995).

Gutierrez, David G.: (ed.) *The Columbia History of Latinos in the United States, 1960–Present* (New York: Columbia University Press, 2004).

Gutiérrez, Ramón A.: "Unraveling America's Hispanic Past: Internal Stratification and Class Boundaries." *Aztlán* 17 (1986), 70–101.

Gutiérrez, Ramón A.: "Changing Ethnic and Class Boundaries in America's Hispanic past." In Sucheng Chan (ed.) *Social and Gender Boundaries in the United Sates* (Lewiston, NY: Edwin Mellen Press, 1989).

Gutiérrez, Ramón A.: *When Jesus Came, the Corn Mothers Went Away: Marriage, Sexuality, and Power in New Mexico, 1500–1846* (Stanford, CA: Stanford University Press, 1991).

Gutman, Mathew C.: *The Meanings of Macho: Being a Man in Mexico City* (Berkeley: University of California Press, 1996).

Guy, Donna J. and Thomas E. Sheridan (eds.): *Contested Ground: Comparative Frontiers on the Northern and Southern Edges of the Spanish Empire* (Tucson: University of Arizona Press, 1998).

Gyory, Andrew: *Closing the Gate: Race, Politics, and the Chinese Exclusion Act* (Chapel Hill: University of North Carolina Press, 1998).

Haas, Lisbeth: "Grass-Roots Protest and the Politics of Planning: Santa Ana, 1976–1988." In Rob Kling, Spencer Olin, and Mark Poster (eds.) *Postsuburban California: The Transformation of Orange County Since World War II* (Berkeley: University of California Press, 1991).

Haas, Lisbeth: *Conquests and Historical Identities in California, 1769–1936* (Berkeley: University of California Press, 1995).

Hackel, Steven W.: "Land, Labor, and Production: The Colonial Economy of Spanish and Mexican California." In Ramón Gutiérrez and Richard J. Orsi (eds.) *Contested Eden: California Before the Gold Rush* (Berkeley: University of California Press, 1998).

Hafen, LeRoy (ed.): *Mountain Men and the Fur Trade of the Far West*, 8 vols. (Glendale CA: A.H. Clark Co., 1965–72).

Hagan, William T.: *American Indians* (Chicago: University of Chicago Press, 1961).

Hagan, William T.: *United States–Comanche Relations: The Reservation Years* (New Haven: Yale University Press, 1976).

Hagan, William T.: *Quanah Parker, Comanche Chief* (Norman: University of Oklahoma Press, 1993).

Haines, Aubrey L.: *The Yellowstone Story: A History of Our First National Park*, 2 vols. (Yellowstone National Park, WY: Yellowstone Library and Museum Association in cooperation with Colorado University Press, 1977).

Halaas, David F.: *Boom Town Newspapers: Journalism on the Rocky Mountain Mining Frontier, 1859–1881* (Albuquerque, NM: University of New Mexico Press, 1981).

Hales, Peter B.: *William Henry Jackson and the Transformation of the American Landscape* (Philadelphia: Temple University Press, 1988).

Hall, Kermit L.: "Hacks and Derelicts Revisited: American Territorial Judiciary, 1789–1959." *Western Historical Quarterly* 12, 3 (1981), 273–89.

Hall, Thomas D.: *Social Change in the Southwest, 1350–1880* (Lawrence: University Press of Kansas, 1989).

Hamilton, David E. (ed.): *The New Deal* (Boston: Houghton Mifflin company, 1999).

Hamilton, Kenneth Marvin: *Black Towns and Profit: Promotion and Development in the Trans-Appalachian West, 1877–1915* (Urbana: University of Illinois Press, 1991).

Hammond, George P. and Agapito Rey: *Don Juan de Oñate: Colonizer of New Mexico, 1595–1628* (Albuquerque, NM: University of New Mexico Press, 1953).

Hammond, George P. and Agapito Rey (eds.): *Narratives of the Coronado expedition, 1540–1542* (Albuquerque, NM: University of New Mexico Press, 1966).

Hammond, George P. and Agapito Rey (eds.): *The Rediscovery of New Mexico, 1580–1594: The explorations of Chamuscado, Espejo, Castaño de Sosa, Morlete, and Leyva de Bonilla and Humaña* (Albuquerque, NM: University of New Mexico Press,1966).

Hampsten, Elizabeth: *Read This Only to Yourself: The Private Writings of Midwestern Women, 1880–1910* (Bloomington: Indiana University Press, 1982).

Hampton, Edgar L.: "A Day in Camp." *Seattle Mail and Herald*, September 6, 1902.

Haney López, Ian F.: "Race and Erasure: The Salience of Race to Latinos/as." In Richard Delgado and Jean Stefancic (eds.) *The Latino/a Condition: A Critical Reader* (New York: New York University Press, 1998).

Hansen, Klaus J.: *Mormonism and the American Experience* (Chicago: University of Chicago Press, 1981).

Hanson, Jeffrey R.: "Introduction." In Gilbert L. Wilson *Buffalo Bird Woman's Garden* (St. Paul: Minnesota Historical Society Press, 1987).

Harbison, J. S.: "Hohfeld and Herefords: The Concept of Property and the Law of the Range." *New Mexico Law Review* 22 (1992), 459–99.

Harbottle, Garman and Philip Weigand: "Turquoise in Pre-Columbian America." *Scientific American* 266, 2 (February 1992), 78–85.

Hardin, Garrett: "The Tragedy of the Commons." *Science* 162 (December 13, 1968), 1243–8.

Harmon, Alexandra: *Indians in the Making: Ethnic Relations and Indian Identities Around Puget Sound* (Berkeley: University of California Press, 1998).

Harring, Sidney L.: *Crow Dog's Case: American Indian Sovereignty, Tribal Law and United States Law in the Nineteenth Century* (Cambridge, Cambridge University Press, 1994).

Harris, Katherine: *Long Vistas: Women and Families on Colorado Homesteads* (Niwot, CO: University Press of Colorado, 1993).

Hart, E. Richard (ed.): *Zuni and the Courts: A Struggle for Sovereign Land Rights* (Lawrence, KA: University of Kansas Press, 1995).

Hart, E. Richard: *Pedro Pino: Governor of Zuni Pueble, 1830–1878* (Logan: Utah State University Press, 2003).

Hartman, Chester: *The Transformation of San Francisco* (Totowa, NJ: Rowman & Allenheld, 1984).

Harvey, David: *Justice, Nature, and the Geography of Difference* (Cambridge, MA: Blackwell, 1997).

Harvey, Mark: *A Symbol of Wilderness: Echo Park and the American Conservation Movement* (Albuquerque: University of New Mexico Press, 1994).

Hastings, David W.: "Frontier Justice: The Court Records of Washington Territory, 1853–1889." *Western Legal History* 2 (Winter 1989–Spring 1990), 79–87.

Hatley, Thomas: *The Dividing Paths: Cherokees and South Carolinians through the Era of the American Revolution* (New York: Oxford University Press, 1993).

Hayden, Dolores: "Biddy Mason's Los Angeles, 1856–1891." *California History* 68, 3 (Fall 1989), 86–99.

Hayden, Dolores: *The Power of Place: Urban Landscapes as Public History* (Cambridge, MA: MIT Press, 1995).

Hayes-Bautista, David E.: "Mexicans in Southern California: Societal Enrichment or Wasted Opportunity?" In Abraham F. Lowenthal and Katrina Burgess (eds.) *The California-Mexico Connection* (Stanford: Stanford University Press, 1993).

Hays, Samuel P.: *Beauty, Health, and Permanence: Environmental Politics in the U.S., 1955–1985* (New York: Cambridge University Press, 1987)

Hays, Samuel P.: *Conservation and the Gospel of Efficiency: The Progressive Conservation Movement, 1890–1920* (Cambridge, MA: Harvard University Press, 1959).

Haywood, C. Robert: *Cowtown Lawyers: Dodge City and its Attorneys, 1876–1886* (Norman: OK: University of Oklahoma Press, 1988).

Hazard, Lucy Lockwood: *The Frontier in American Literature* (New York: Thomas Y. Crowell, Co., 1927).

Heale, M. J.: "Red Scare Politics: California's Campaign Against Un-American Activities, 1940–1970." *Journal of American Studies* 20 (April 1986), 5–32.

Heat Moon, William Least: *Blue Highways* (Boston: Little, Brown, 1983).

Heat Moon, William Least: *PrairyErth: (a deep map)* (Boston: Houghton, Miflin, 1991).

Heat Moon, William Least: *River-Horse: The Logbook of a Boat across America* (Boston, Houghton, Miflin, 1999).

Henige, David: *Numbers From Nowhere: The American Indian Contact Population Debate* (Norman: University of Oklahoma Press, 1998).

Hennings, Robert E.: *James D. Phelan and the Wilson Progressives of California* (New York: Garland, 1985).

Hernandez, Philip A.: *The Other North Americans: The American Image of Mexico and Mexicans, 1550–1850* (PhD dissertation: University of California, Berkeley, 1974).

Hess, Karl: *Rocky Times in Rocky Mountain National Park: An Unnatural History* (Niwot, CO: University Press of Colorado, 1993).

Hicks, John D.: *The Populist Revolt: A History of the Farmers' Alliance and the People's Party* (Minneapolis: University of Minnesota Press, 1931).

Hietter, Paul T.: "How Wild Was Arizona? An Examination of Pima County's Criminal Court, 1882–1909." *Western Legal History* 12 (Summer–Fall 1999), 183–209.

Hills, Patricia: "Picturing Progress in the Era of Westward Expansion." In William H. Truettner (ed.) *The West as America: Reinterpreting Images of the Frontier, 1820–1920* (Washington, DC: Smithsonian Institution Press, 1991).

Hinderaker, Eric and Peter Mancall: *At the Edge of Empire: The Backcountry in British North America* (Baltimore: Johns Hopkins University Press, 2003).

Hinderaker, Eric: *Elusive Empires: Constructing Colonialism in the Ohio Valley, 1673–1800* (New York: Cambridge University Press, 1997).

Hine, Robert V. and John M. Faragher: *The American West: A New Interpretive History* (New Haven: Yale University Press, 2000).

Hine, Robert: *Community on the American Frontier: Separate But Not Alone* (Norman: University of Oklahoma Press, 1980).

Hirt, Paul W.: *A Conspiracy of Optimism: Management of the National Forests Since World War Two* (Lincoln: University of Nebraska Press, 1994).

Hise, Greg: *Magnetic Los Angeles: Planning the Twentieth Century Metropolis* (Baltimore: Johns Hopkins University Press, 1997).

Hoare, Michael E. (ed.): *The "Resolution" Journals of Johann Reinhold Forster, 1772–1775*, 4 vols. (London: The Hakluyt Society, 1982).

Hoebbel, E. Adamson: "The Political Organization and Law Ways of the Comanche Indians." *Memoirs of the American Anthropological Association* 5 (1940).

Hoffman, Paul E.: *Florida's Frontiers* (Bloomington: Indiana University Press, 2001).

Hoig, Stan: *The Sand Creek Massacre* (Norman, OK: University of Oklahoma Press, 1961).

Holliday, James S.: *The World Rushed In: The California Gold Rush Experience* (New York: Simon and Schuster, 1981).

Holliday, James: *Rush for Riches: Gold Fever and the Making of California* (Berkeley: Oakland Museum of California and University of California Press, 2000).

Hollon, W. Eugene: *The Lost Pathfinder, Zebulon Montgomery Pike* (Norman: University of Oklahoma Press, 1949).

Hollon, W. Eugene: *Frontier Violence: Another Look* (New York: Oxford University Press, 1974).

Hollon, W. Eugene: "Law and Order." In Howard R. Lamar (ed.) *The New Encyclopedia of the American West* (New Haven, CT: Yale University Press, 1998).

Holman, Frederick V.: *Dr. John McLoughlin, the Father of Oregon.* (Cleveland, OH: The Arthur H. Clark Co., 1907).

Holthaus, Gary, Charles F. Wilkinson, and Patricia Nelson Limerick (eds.): *A Society to Match the Scenery* (Niwot: University Press of Colorado, 1991).

Hondagneau-Sotelo, Pierrette: *Gendered Transitions: Mexican Experience of Immigration* (Berkeley: University of California Press, 1994).

Hondagneau-Sotelo, Pierrette: *Doméstica: Immigrant Workers Cleaning and Caring in the Shadows of Affluence* (Berkeley: University of California Press, 2001).

Horne, Gerald: *Fire This Time: The Watts Uprising and the 1960s* (Charlottesville: University Press of Virginia, 1995).

Horsman, Reginald: *Race and Manifest Destiny: The Origins of American Anglo-Saxonism* (Cambridge, MA: Harvard University Press, 1981).

Horsman, Reginald: "Well-Trodden Paths and Fresh Byways: Recent Writings on Native American History." In Stanley I. Kutler and Stanley N. Katz (eds.) *The Promise of American History: Progress and Prospects* (Baltimore: Johns Hopkins University Press, 1982).

Hosmer, Brian: *American Indians in the Marketplace: Persistence and Innovation Among the Menominees and Metlakatlans, 1870–1920* (Lawrence: University Press of Kansas, 1999).

Houck, Louis (ed.): *The Spanish Regime in Missouri*, 2 vols. (Chicago: R. R. Donnelley, 1909).

Houston, Jeanne Wakatsuki and James Houston: *Farewell to Manzanar* (Boston: Houghton, Mifflin, 1973).

Howard, Kathleen L. and Diana F. Pardue: *Inventing the Southwest: The Fred Harvey Company and Native American Art* (Phoenix, AZ: The Heard Museum, 1996).

Howe, Edgar Watson: *The Story of a Country Town* (Atchison, KS: Howe and CO., 1883).

Howell, Anabel: *Ninety Miles from Nowhere* (Peralta, NM: Pine Tree Press, 1987).

Hoxie, Frederick E.: *A Final Promise: The Campaign to Assimilate the Indians, 1880–1920* (Lincoln: University of Nebraska Press, 1984).

Hoxie, Frederick E.: *Parading Through History: The Making of the Crow Nation in America, 1805–1935* (Cambridge and New York: Cambridge University Press, 1995).

Hoxie, Frederick E. and Peter Iverson (eds.) *Indians in American History*, 2nd edn. (Wheeling, IL: Harlan Davidson, 1998).

Hoxie, Frederick E., Peter C. Mancall, and James H. Merrell (eds.): *American Nations: Encounters in Indian Country, 1850 to the Present* (New York: Routledge, 2001).

Hu-DeHart, Evelyn: "Latin America in Asia-Pacific Perspective" In Arif Dirlik (ed.) *What is in a Rim? Critical Perspectives on the Pacific Region Idea*, 2nd ed. (Lanham, MD: Rowman and Littlefield, 1998).

Hudson, Karen E.: *Paul R. Williams, Architect: A Legacy of Style* (New York: Rizzoli, 1993).

Hudson, Winthrop S. and John Corrigan: *Religion in America: An Historical Account of the Development of American Religious Life*, 6th edn. (Upper Saddle River, NJ: Prentice Hall, 1999).

Hughes, J. Donald: *American Indian Ecology* (El Paso: Texas Western Press, 1983).

Hughes, Langston: *The Panther and the Lash: Poems of Our Times* (New York, Knopf, 1967).

Hughes, Thomas: *Networks of Power: Electrification in Western Society, 1880–1930* (Baltimore: Johns Hopkins University Press, 1983).

Hugill, Peter J.: "The Rediscovery of America: Elite Automobile Touring." *Annals of Tourism Research* 12, 3 (1985): 435–47.

Hundley, Norris, Jr.: *Water and the West: The Colorado River Compact and the Politics of Water in the American West* (Berkeley: University of California Press, 1975).

Hundley, Norris, Jr.: *The Great Thirst: Californians and Water, 1770s–1990s* (Berkeley: University of California Press, 1992).

Hurst, James Willard: *Law and the Conditions of Freedom in the Nineteenth-Century United States* (Madison: University of Wisconsin Press, 1956).

Hurst, James Willard: *Law and Economic Growth: The Legal History of the Lumber Industry in Wisconsin, 1836–1915* (Cambridge, MA: Harvard University Press, 1964).

Hurt, R. Douglas: *The Ohio Frontier: Crucible of the Old Northwest, 1720–1830* (Bloomington: Indiana University Press, 1996).

Hurt, R. Douglas: *The Indian Frontier, 1763–1846* (Albuquerque: University of New Mexico Press, 2002).

Hurtado, Aida: *The Color of Privilege: Three Blasphemies on Race and Feminism* (Ann Arbor: University of Michigan Press, 1996).

Hurtado, Albert L.: *Indian Survival on the California Frontier* (New Haven, CT: Yale University Press, 1988).

Hurtado, Albert L.: "Parkmanizing the Spanish Borderlands: Bolton, Turner, and the Historians' World." *Western Historical Quarterly* 26 (Summer 1995), 149–67.

Hurtado, Albert L.: *Intimate Frontiers: Sex, Gender and Culture in Old California* (Albuquerque: University of New Mexico Press, 1999).

Hurtado, Albert L. and Peter Iverson (eds.): *Major Problems in American Indian History* 2nd edn. (Boston: Houghton Mifflin, 2001).

Hutchinson, W.H.: "The Remaking of the Amerind: A Dissenting Voice Raised Against the Resurrection of the Myth of the Noble Savage." *Westways* (October 1972), 94.

Hyde, Anne F.: *An American Vision: Far Western Landscape and National Culture, 1820–1920* (New York: New York University Press, 1990).

Hyde, George E.: *Red Cloud's Folk: A History of the Oglala Sioux Indians* (Norman, OK: University of Oklahoma Press, 1937).

Hyde, George E. (ed.): *A Life of George Bent Written From His Letters* (Norman: University of Oklahoma Press, 1968).

Hyer, Sally: *One House, One Voice, One Heart: Native American Education at the Santa Fe Indian School* (Santa Fe: Museum of New Mexico Press, 1990).

Ichioka, Yuji: *The Issei: The World of First Generation Japanese Immigrants, 1885–1924* (New York: Free Press, 1988).

Igler, David: "When is a River not a River? Reclaiming Nature's Disorder in *Lux v. Haggin*." *Environmental History* 1 (April 1996), 52–69.

Igler, David: "The Industrial West: Region and Nation in the Late Nineteenth Century." *Pacific Historical Review* 69 (2000), 159–92.

Igler, David: *Industrial Cowboys: Miller & Lux and the Transformation of the Far West, 1850–1920* (Berkeley: University of California Press, 2001).

Ingersoll, Ernest: "Ups and Downs in Leadville." *Scribner's Monthly* 18 (May through October 1879).

Ingold, Tim: *Hunters, Pastoralists, and Ranchers: Reindeer Economies and their Transformations* (Cambridge: Cambridge University Press, 1980).

Interrante, Joseph Anthony: "A Movable Feast: The Automobile and the Spatial Transformation of American Culture, 1890–1940." (PhD dissertation: Harvard University, 1983).

Inter-Tribal Council of Nevada: *Newe: A Western Shoshone History* (Reno: Inter-Tribal Council of Nevada, 1976).

Ireland, Robert M.: "Homicide in Nineteenth-Century Kentucky." *Register of the Kentucky Historical Society* 81 (1983), 134–53.

Iriye, Akira: *Across the Pacific: An Inner History of American–East Asian Relations* (New York: Harcourt Brace Jovanovich, 1967).

Irving, Washinton: *Astoria; Or, Anecdotes of an Enterprise beyond the Rock Mountains* (Philadelphia: Carey, Lea, & Blanchard, 1836).

Ise, John: *Our National Park Policy: A Critical History* (Baltimore: John Hopkins University Press, 1961).

Isenberg, Andrew C.: "The Returns of the Bison: Profit, Nostalgia, and Preservation." *Environmental History* 2 (April 1997), 179–96.

Isenberg, Andrew C.: *The Destruction of the Bison: An Environmental History, 1750–1920* (New York: Cambridge University Press, 2000).

Issel, William and Robert Cherney: *San Francisco, 1865–1932: Politics, Power, and Urban Development* (Berkeley: University of California Press, 1986).

Iverson, Peter: *The Navajo Nation* (Westport, CT: Greenwood Press, 1981).

Iverson, Peter: *Carlos Montezuma and the Changing World of American Indians* (Albuquerque: University of New Mexico Press, 1982).

Iverson, Peter: *When Indians Became Cowboys: Native Peoples and Cattle Ranching in the American West* (Norman: University of Oklahoma Press, 1994).

Iverson, Peter: *Barry Goldwater: Native Arizonan* (Norman: University of Oklahoma Press, 1997).

Iverson, Peter: *"We Are Still Here": American Indians in the Twentieth Century* (Wheeling, IL: Harlan Davidson, 1998).

Iverson, Peter: *Diné: A History of the Navajos* (Albuquerque: University of New Mexico Press, 2002).

Iverson, Peter: *"For Our Navajo People": Dine Letters, Speeches, and Petitions, 1900–1960* (Albuquerque: University of New Mexico Press, 2002).

Jackson, Donald (ed.): *The Journals of Zebulon Montgomery Pike, with Letters and Related Documents*, 2 vols. (Norman: University of Oklahoma Press, 1966).

Jackson, Donald (ed.): *The Letters of the Lewis and Clark Expedition with Related Documents, 1783–1854*, 2nd edn., 2 vols. (Urbana: University of Illinois Press, 1978).

Jackson, Donald: *Thomas Jefferson and the Stony Mountains: Exploring the West From Monticello* (Urbana: University of Illinois Press, 1981).

Jackson, Donald and Mary L. Spence (eds.): *The Expeditions of John C. Fremont*, 3 vols. and map portfolio (Urbana: University of Illinois Press, 1970–84).

Jackson, Kenneth: *Crabgrass Frontier: The Suburbanization of the United States* (New York: Oxford University Press, 1985).

Jackson, W. Turrentine: "A Brief Message for the Young and/or Ambitious: Comparative Frontiers as a Field for Investigation." *Western Historical Quarterly* 9, 1 (1978), 4–18.

Jacobs, Margaret D.: "Resistance to Rescue: The Indians of Bahapki and Mrs. Annie E. K. Bidwell." In Elizabeth Jameson and Susan Armitage (eds.) *Writing the Range: Race, Class, and Culture in the Women's West* (Norman: University of Oklahoma Press, 1997).

Jacobs, Wilbur: "The Great Despoliation: Environmental Themes in American Frontier History." *Pacific Historical Review*, 47 (1978), 1–26.

Jakle, John: *The Tourist: Travel in Twentieth-Century North America* (Lincoln, NE: University of Nebraska Press, 1985).

James, Ronald M.: *The Roar and the Silence: A History of Virginia City and the Comstock Lode* (Reno: University of Nevada Press, 1998).

Jameson, Elizabeth: "Women as Workers, Women as Civilizers: True Womanhood in the American West." In Susan Armitage and Elizabeth Jameson (eds.) *The Women's West* (Norman: University of Oklahoma Press, 1987).

Jameson, Elizabeth: "Toward a Multicultural History of Women in the Western United States." *Signs* 13, 4 (1988), 761–91.

Jameson, Elizabeth: *All That Glitters: Class, Conflict, and Community in Cripple Creek* (Urbana, University of Illinois Press, 1998).

Jameson, Elizabeth and Susan Armitage: *Writing the Range: Race, Class, and Culture in the Women's West* (Norman: University of Oklahoma Press, 1997).

Janisch, Hudson: "The Chinese, the Courts, and the Constitution: A Study of the Legal Issues Raised by Chinese Immigrants in the United States, 1850–1902." (JSD dissertation: University of Chicago, 1971).

Jefferson, Thomas: "A Memoir on the Discovery of Certain Bones of a Quadruped of the Clawed Kind in the Western Parts of Virginia." (10 March 1797). In Keir B. Sterling (ed.) *Selected Works in Nineteenth-Century North American Paleontology* (New York: Arno, 1974), reprinted from *Transactions of the American Philosophical Society* 4 (1799).

Jefferson, Thomas: *Notes on the State of Virginia*, ed. William Peden (New York: Norton, 1954).

Jeffrey, Julie Roy: *Frontier Women: The Trans-Mississippi West, 1840–1880* (New York: Hill and Wang, 1979).

Jeffrey, Julie Roy: *Converting the West: A Biography of Narcissa Whitman* (Norman: University of Oklahoma Press, 1991).

Jenkins, J. Craig: *The Politics of Insurgency: The Farm Worker Movement in the 1960s* (New York: Columbia University Press, 1985).

Jenks, J. W. and W. J. Lauck: *The Immigrant Problem: A Study of American Immigration Conditions and Needs* (New York: Funk and Wagnalls, 1971).

Jennings, Francis: *The Invasion of America: Indians, Colonialism and the Cant of Conquest* (Chapel Hill: University of North Carolina Press, 1975).

Jennings, Francis: *The Ambiguous Iroquois Empire: The Covenant Chain Confederation of Indian Tribes with English Colonies from Its Beginnings to the Lancaster Treaty of 1744* (New York: W. W. Norton, 1984).

Jennings, Francis: *Empire of Fortune: Crowns, Colonies, and Tribes in the Seven Years War in America* (New York: W. W. Norton, 1988).

Jensen, Joan M.: *With These Hands: Women Working on the Land* (New York: McGraw Hill, 1981).

Jensen, Joan M.: "'Disenfranchisement Is a Disgrace': Women and Politics in New Mexico, 1900–1940." In Joan M. Jensen and Darlis A. Miller (eds.) *New Mexico Women: Intercultural Perspectives* (Albuquerque: University of New Mexico Press, 1986).

Jensen, Joan M. and Darlis A. Miller: "The Gentle Tamers Revisited: New Approaches to the History of Women in the American West." *Pacific Historical Review* 49, 2 (May 1980), 173–213.

Johansen, Dorothy O. and Charles M. Gates: *Empire of the Columbia: A History of the Pacific Northwest* (New York: Harper and Brothers, 1957).

John, Richard R.: "Elaborations, Revisions, Dissents: Alfred D. Chandler, Jr.'s, *The Visible Hand* after Twenty Years." *Business History Review* 71 (Summer 1997), 151–200.

Johnson, Marilyn: *The Second Gold Rush: Oakland and the East Bay in World War II* (Berkeley: University of California Press, 1993).

Johnson, Michael L.: *New Westers: The West in Contemporary American Culture* (Lawrence: University Press of Kansas, 1996).

Johnson, Susan L.: "Sharing Bed and Board: Cohabitation and Cultural Difference in Central Arizona Mining Towns, 1863–1873." In Susan Armitage and Elizabeth Jameson (eds.) *The Women's West* (Norman: University of Oklahoma Press, 1987).

Johnson, Susan L.: "A Memory Sweet to Soldiers: The Significance of Gender in the History of the American West." *Western Historical Quarterly* XXIV, 4 (November 1993), 495–518.

Johnson, Susan L.: *Roaring Camp: The Social World of the California Gold Rush* (New York: W. W. Norton, 2000).

Johnson, Troy R.: *The Occupation of Alcatraz Island: Indian Self-Determination and the Rise of Indian Activism* (Urbana: University of Illinois Press, 1996).

Johnston, Robert Douglas: "Beyond 'The West': Regionalism, Liberalism, and the Evasion of Politics in the New Western History." *Rethinking History* 2 (Summer 1998), 239–77.

Jolly, Michelle: *Inventing the City: Gender and the Politics of Everyday Life in Gold-Rush San Francisco, 1848–1869* (PhD dissertation: University of California, San Diego, 1998).

Jones, Dorothy V.: *License for Empire: Colonialism by Treaty in Early America* (Chicago: University of Chicago Press, 1982).

Joralemon, Ira B.: *Romantic Copper* (New York: D. Appleton-Century Co., 1936).

Jordan, Teresa and James Hepworth (eds.): *The Stories that Shape Us: Contemporary Women Write About the West* (New York: W. W. Norton, 1995).

Jordan, Terry G. and Matti Kaups: *The American Backwoods Frontier: An Ethnic and Ecological Interpretation* (Baltimore: Johns Hopkins University Press, 1989).

Jordan, Terry G.: *North American Cattle-Ranching Frontiers: Origins, Diffusion and Differentiation* (Albuquerque: University of New Mexico Press, 1993).

Jorgensen, Joseph G.: *The Sun Dance Religion: Power for the Powerless* (Chicago: University of Chicago Press, 1972).

Josephy, Alvin M.: *The Civil War in the American West* (New York: A. A. Knopf, 1991).

Jung, Maureen A.: "Capitalism Comes to the Diggings: From Gold-Rush Adventure to Corporate Enterprise." In James J. Rawls and Richard J. Orsi (eds.) *A Golden State: Mining and Economic Development in Gold Rush California in California History* (Berkeley: University of California Press, 1998/99).

Kahn, Judd: *Imperial San Francisco: Politics and Planning in an American City, 1897–1906* (Lincoln: University of Nebraska Press, 1979).

Kahrl, William: *Water and Power: The Conflict Over Los Angeles' Water Supply in the Owens Valley* (Berkeley: University of California Press, 1982).

Kaplan, Amy and Donald E. Pease (eds.): *Cultures of United States Imperialism* (Durham: Duke University Press, 1993).

Kaplan, Robert: *An Empire Wilderness: Travels Into America's Future* (New York: Random House, 1998).

Karamanski, Theodore J.: *Fur Trade and Exploration: Opening the Far Northwest, 1821–1852* (Norman: University of Oklahoma Press, 1983).

Katz, Ellen D.: "The Six Companies and the Geary Act: A Case Study in Nineteenth-Century Civil Disobedience and Civil Rights Litigation." *Western Legal History* 8, 2 (Summer–Fall, 1995), 227–71.

Katz, William Loren: *The Black West* (Garden City, NY: Doubleday, 1971; rev. edn., Seattle: Open Hand Publishing, 1987).

Kavanagh, James H.: "Ideology." In Thomas McLaughlin and Frank Lentricchia (eds.) *Critical Terms for Literary Study* (Chicago: University of Chicago Press, 1995).

Kavanagh, Thomas W.: *Comanche Political History: An Ethnohistorical Perspective, 1706–1875* (Lincoln, NE: University of Nebraska Press, 1996).

Kazin, Michael: *Barons of Labor: The San Francisco Building Trades and Union Power in the Progressive Era* (Urbana: University of Illinois Press, 1987).

Keiter, Robert and Mark S. Boyce (eds.): *The Greater Yellowstone Ecosystem: Redefining America's Wilderness Heritage* (New Haven: Yale University Press, 1991).

Keller, Robert H., Jr.: *American Protestantism and United States Indian Policy, 1869–82* (Lincoln: University of Nebraska Press, 1983).

Keller, Robert H. and Michael F. Turek: *American Indians and National Parks* (Tucson: University of Arizona Press, 1998).

Kelley, Robert L.: *Gold vs. Grain: The Hydraulic Mine Controversy in California's Sacramento, Valley* (Glendale, CA: A. H. Clark Co., 1959).

Kelley, Robert L.: *Battling the Inland Sea: American Political Culture, Public Policy, and the Sacramento Valley, 1850–1986* (Berkeley: University of California Press, 1989).

Kelly, Robin D. G.: *Race Rebels: Culture, Politics, and the Black Working Class* (1994; New York: The Free Press, 1996).

Kennedy, David: *Freedom from Fear: The American People in Depression and War, 1929–1945* (New York: Oxford University Press, 1999).

Kerouac, Jack: *On the Road* (New York: Viking, 1957).

Kerouac, Jack: *Big Sur* (New York: Farrar, Straus and Cudahy, 1962).

Kessell, John L., Rick Hendricks, and Meredith D. Dodge (eds.): *Blood on the Boulders: The Journals of Don Diego de Vargas, New Mexico, 1694–97* (Albuquerque, NM: University of New Mexico Press, 1998).

Kessell, John L., Rick Hendricks, and Meredith D. Dodge (eds.): *That Disturbances Cease: The Journals of Don Diego de Vargas, New Mexico, 1697–1700* (Albuquerque, NM: University of New Mexico Press, 2000).

Kim, Hyung-Chan: *A Legal History of Asian Americans, 1790–1990,* (Westport, CT: Greenwood Press, 1994).

Kimeldorf, Howard: *Reds or Rackets?: The Making of Radical and Conservative Unions on the Waterfront* (Berkeley: University of California Press, 1988).

King, Cameron H. (ed.): *Revised Statutes of Arizona* (Prescott, AZ: State of Arizona, 1887).

King, Joseph E.: *A Mine to Make a Mine: Financing the Colorado Mining Industry, 1859–1902* (College Station: Texas A & M University Press, 1977).

King, Margaret J.: "Disneyland and Walt Disney World: Traditional Values in Futuristic Form." *Journal of Popular Culture* 15 (Summer 1981), 56–62.

Kingston, Hong: *Landscapes of the New West: Gender and Geography in Contemporary Women's Writing* (Chapel Hill: University of North Carolina Press, 1999).

Kinsey, Joni Louise: *Thomas Moran and the Surveying of the American West* (Washington, DC: Smithsonian Institution Press, 1992).

Kittredge, William: *Hole in the Sky: A Memoir* (New York: Knopf, 1992). Kittredge, William: *The Portable Western Reader* (New York: Penguin, 1997).

Klein, Alan M.: "The Political Economy of Gender: A Nineteenth-Century Plains Indian Case Study." In Patricia Albers and Beatrice Medicine (eds.) *The Hidden Half: Studies of Plains Indian Women* (Latham, MD: University Press of America, 1983).

Klein, Kerwin Lee: "Frontier Products: Tourism, Consumerism, and the Southwestern Public Lands, 1890–1990." *Pacific Historical Review* 62 (February 1993), 39–71.

Klein, Kerwin Lee: "Reclaiming the F Word: Or Being and Becoming Postwestern." *Pacific Historical Review* 65 (May 1996), 179–215.

Klein, Kerwin Lee: *Frontiers of Historical Imagination: Narrating the European Conquest of Native America, 1890–1990* (Berkeley: University of California Press, 1997).

Klein, Laura F. and Lillian A. Ackerman (eds.): *Women and Power in Native North America* (Norman: University of Oklahoma Press, 1995).

Kleppner, Paul: "Politics Without Parties: The Western States, 1900–84." In Gerald Nash and Richard Etulain (eds.) *The Twentieth-Century West: Historical Interpretations* (Albuquerque: University of New Mexico Press, 1989).

Kleppner, Paul: "Voters and Parties in Western States, 1876–1900." *Western Historical Quarterly* 14 (January 1983), 49–68.

Kling, Rob, Spencer Olin, and Mark Poster (eds.): *Postsuburban California: The Transformation of Orange County since World War II* (Berkeley: University of California Press, 1991).

Klingle, Matthew: *Urban by Nature: An Environmental History of Seattle, 1880–1970* (PhD dissertation: University of Washington, 2001).

Klyza, Christopher M.: *Who Controls Public Lands? Mining, Forestry, and Grazing Policies, 1870–1990* (Chapel Hill: University of North Carolina Press, 1996).

Knack, Martha C.: *Boundaries Between: The Southern Paiutes, 1775–1995* (Lincoln: University of Nebraska Press, 2001).

Knaut, Andrew L.: *The Pueblo Revolt of 1680: Conquest and Resistance in Seventeenth-Century New Mexico* (Norman, OK: University of Oklahoma Press, 1995).

Knobloch, Frieda: *The Culture of Wilderness: Agriculture as Colonization in the American West* (Chapel Hill: University of North Carolina Press, 1996).

Kohl, Edith Eudora: *Land of the Burnt Thigh* ([1938], rpt. St. Paul: Minnesota Historical Society Press, 1986).

Kolodny, Annette: *The Lay of the Land: Metaphor as Experience and History in American Life and Letters* (Chapel Hill: University of North Carolina Press, 1975).

Kolodny, Annette: *The Land Before Her: Fantasy and Experience of the American Frontiers, 1630–1860* (Chapel Hill: University of North Carolina Press, 1984).

Kolodny, Annette: "Letting Go Our Grand Obsessions: Notes Toward a New Literary History of American Frontiers." *American Literature* 64 (March 1992), 1–18.

Kossoudji, S. A. and S. I. Ranney: "The Labor Market Experience of Female Immigrants: The Case of Temporary Mexican Migration to the United States." *International Migration Review* 18, 3 (1984), 1120–43.

Kowalewski, Michael: *Reading the West: New Essays on the Literature of the American West* (NY: Cambridge University Press, 1996).

Krech, Shepard, III (ed.): *Indians, Animals, and the Fur Trade: A Critique of Keepers of the Game* (Athens: University of Georgia Press, 1981).

Krech, Shepard, III: *The Ecological Indian: Myth and History* (New York: W. W. Norton and Company, 1999).

Kugel, Rebecca: *To Be the Main Leaders of Our People: A History of Minnesota Ojibwe Politics, 1825–1898* (East Lansing: Michigan State University Press, 1998).

Kukla, Jon: *A Wilderness So Immense: The Louisiana Purchase and the Destiny of America* (New York: Knopf, 2003).

Kurashige, Lon: *Japanese American celebration and conflict: A History of Ethnic Identity and Festival, 1934–1990* (Berkeley: University of California Press, 2002).

Kushner, Howard I.: "The Russian–American Diplomatic Contest for the Pacific Basin and the Monroe Doctrine."" *Journal of the West*, 15, 2 (1976), 65–80.

La Forte, Robert S.: *Leaders of Reform: Progressive Republicans in Kansas, 1900–1916* (Lawrence: University Press of Kansas, 1974).

LaFeber, Walter: "A Note on the 'Mercantile Imperialism' of Alfred Thayer Hahan." *The Mississippi Valley Historical Review* 48, 4 (1962), 674–85.

LaFeber, Walter: "The Tensions Between Democracy and Capitalism during the American Century." *Diplomatic History*, 23, 2 (1999), 263–84.

LaGrand, James B.: *Indian Metropolis: Native Americans in Chicago, 1945–75* (Urbana: University of Illinois Press, 2002).

Lamar, Howard R.: *The Far Southwest, 1846–1912: A Territorial History* (New Haven CT: Yale University Press, 1966).

Lamar, Howard R.: "An Overview of Westward Expansion." In William H. Truettner (ed.) *The West as America: Reinterpreting Images of the Frontier, 1820–1920* (Washington, DC: Smithsonian Institution Press, 1991).

Lamar, Howard R. (ed.): *The New Encyclopedia of the American West* (New Haven, CT: Yale University Press, 1998).

Lamar, Howard R. and Leonard Thompson: "Comparative Frontier History." In Howard Lamar and Leonard Thompson (eds.) *The Frontier in History: North America and Southern Africa Compared* (New Haven, 1981).

Lamb, Karl A.: *As Orange Goes: Twelve California Families and the Future of American Politics* (New York: Norton, 1974).

Lamm, Richard D. and Gary Imhoff: *The Immigration Time Bomb: The Fragmenting of America* (New York: Truman Talley Books, 1985).

Lamoreaux, Naomi R. and Daniel M. G. Raff (eds.): *Coordination and Information:*

Historical Perspectives on the Organization of Enterprise (Chicago: University of Chicago Press, 1994).

Lamphere, Louise, Patricia Zavella, Felipe Gonzales, and Peter B. Evans (eds.) *Sunbelt Working Mothers: Reconciling Family and Factory* (Ithaca: Cornell University Press, 1993).

Lane, Roger: *Violent Death in the City: Suicide, Accident, and Murder in Nineteenth-Century Philadelphia* (Cambridge, MA: Harvard University Press, 1979).

Lang, Sabine: *Men as Women, Women as Men: Changing Gender in Native American Cultures* (Austin: University of Texas Press, 1998).

Lange, Dorothea and Paul Taylor: *An American Exodus: A Record of Human Erosion*. (New York: Reynal and Hitchcock, 1939).

Langston, Nancy: *Forest Dreams, Forest Nightmares: The Paradox of Old Growth in the Inland West* (Seattle: University of Washington Press, 1995).

Langum, David J.: *Law and Community on the Mexican California Frontier: Anglo-American Expatriates and the Clash of Legal Traditions, 1821–1846* (Norman, OK: University of Oklahoma Press, 1987).

Langum, David J.: "The Legal System of Spanish California: A Preliminary Study." *Western Legal History* 7 (Winter 1994–Spring 1995), 6–23.

Lapp, Rudolph: *Blacks in Gold Rush California* (New Haven, CT: Yale University Press, 1997).

Larmer, Brook: "Latin U.S.A." *Newsweek* 134, 2 (1999).

Larrain, Jorge: *The Concept of Ideology* (London: Hutchinson and Co., 1979).

Larsen, Laurence: *The Urban West at the End of the Frontier* (Lawrence: University Press of Kansas, 1978).

Larsh, Edward B. and John Nichols: *Leadville, U.S.A.* (Boulder: Pruett Publishing, 1993).

Larson, Robert W.: *Populism in the Mountain West* (Albuquerque: University of New Mexico Press, 1986).

Larson, T. A.: "Petticoats at the Polls: Woman Suffrage in Territorial Wyoming." *Pacific Northwest Quarterly* 44 (April 1953), 74–79.

Larson, T. A.: "Woman Suffrage in Wyoming." *Pacific Northwest Quarterly* 56 (April 1965), 57–66.

Larson, T. A.: "Woman Suffrage in Western America." *Utah Historical Quarterly* 38 (Winter 1970), 7–19.

Larson, T. A.: "Montana Women and the Battle for the Ballot." *Montana: The Magazine of Western History* 21 (1973), 24–41.

Larson, T. A.: "Idaho's Role in America's Woman Suffrage Crusade." *Idaho Yesterdays* 18 (Spring 1974), 2–15.

Larson, T. A.: "The Woman Suffrage Movement in Washington." *Pacific Northwest Quarterly* 67 (April 1976), 49–62.

Lavender, David: *Bent's Fort* (Lincoln, NE: Bison Books, 1954).

Lavender, David: *The Fist in the Wilderness*, (Garden City, NJ: Doubleday, 1964).

Laviera, Tato: *AmeRícan* (Houston: Arte Público Press, 1985).

Lawrence, D. H. *Phoenix: The Posthumous Papers of D. H. Lawrence*, ed. Edward D. McDonald (New York: Viking Press, 1936).

Lawrence, William D.: "Henry Miller and the San Joaquin Valley." (MA thesis: University of California, Berkeley, 1933).

Leclerc, Gustavo, Raúl Villa, and Michael J. Dear (eds.): *La vida latina en L.A.: Urban Latino Cultures* (Thousand Oaks, CA: Sage Publications, 1999).

Lecompte, Janet: *Pueblo, Hardscrabble, and Greenhorn: Society on the High Plains, 1832–1856* (Norman: University of Oklahoma Press, 1978).

Lee, Erika: "Enforcing the Borders: Chinese Exclusion along the U.S. Borders with Canada and Mexico, 1882–1924." *Journal of American History* 89, 1 (June, 2002), 54–86.

Leibhardt, Barbara: "Interpretation and Causal Analysis: Theories in Environmental History." *Environmental Review* 12 (1988), 23–36.

Lemke-Santangelo, Gretchen: *Abiding Courage: African American Migrant Women and the East Bay Community* (Chapel Hill: University of North Carolina Press, 1996).

Leonard, Kevin Allen: "The Impact of World War II on Race Relations in Los Angeles." (PhD dissertation: University of California, Davis, 1992).

Leonard, Kevin Allen: "Migrants, Immigrants, and Refugees: The Cold War and Population Growth in the American West." In Kevin J. Fernlund (ed.) *The Cold War American West, 1945–1989* (Albuquerque: University of New Mexico Press, 1998).

Leonard, Kevin Allen: "'In the Interest of All Races': African Americans and Interracial Cooperation in Los Angeles during and after World War II." In Lawrence B. de Graaf, Kevin Mulroy, and Quintard Taylor (eds.) *Seeking El Dorado: African Americans in California* (Los Angeles: Autry Museum of Western Heritage, in association with the University of Washington Press, 2001).

Leonard, Kevin Allen: *The Battle for Los Angeles: Race, Politics and World War II* (Albuquerque: University of New Mexico Press, forthcoming).

Leopold, Aldo: "Wilderness as a Form of Land Use." In Susan Flader and J. Baird Callicott (eds.) *The River of the Mother of God and Other Essays* (Madison: University of Wisconsin Press, 1991).

Lepore, Jill: *The Name of War: King Philip's War and the Origins of American Identity* (New York: Knopf, 1998).

Lerner, Gerda: "Placing Women in History." In Gerda Lerner *The Majority Finds Its Past* (New York: Oxford University Press, 1979).

Lerner, Gerda: *Teaching Women's History* (Washington, DC: American Historical Association, 1981).

LeSeur, Geta: *Not All Okies are White: The Lives of Black Cotton Pickers in Arizona* (Columbia, MO: University of Missouri Press, 2000).

Lester, William S.: *The Transylvania Colony* (Spencer, IN: S. R. Guard & Co., 1935).

Leuchtenberg, William E.: "The Triumph of Liberal Reform." In David E. Hamilton (ed.) *The New Deal* (Boston: Houghton Mifflin company, 1999).

Levine, Lawrence W.: *Highbrow/Lowbrow: The Emergence of Cultural Hierarchy in America* (Cambridge, MA: Harvard University Press, 1983).

Lewis, Bonnie Sue: *Creating Christian Indians: Native Clergy in the Presbyterian Church* (Norman: University of Oklahoma Press, 2003).

Lewis, David Rich: *Neither Wolf Nor Dog: American Indians, Environment and Agrarian Change* (New York: Oxford University Press, 1994).

Lewis, Meriwether and William Clark: *History of the Expedition Under the Command of Lewis and Clark*, 3 vols. ed. Elliott Coues (New York: Dover, 1965).

Lewis, Merrill and L. L. Lee (eds.): *The Westering Experience in American Literature: Bicentennial Essays* (Bellingham: Bureau for Faculty Research, Western Washington University, 1977).

Libecap, Gary D.: *The Evolution of Private Mineral Rights: Nevada's Comstock Lode* (New York: Arno Press, 1978).

Licht, Walter: *Industrializing America: The Nineteenth Century* (Baltimore: Johns Hopkins University Press, 1995).

Liebman, Ellen: *California Farmland: A History of Large Agricultural Landholdings* (Totowa: Rowman and Allanheld, 1983).

Limerick, Patricia Nelson: *Legacy of Conquest: The Unbroken Past of the American West* (New York: W. W. Norton, 1987).

Limerick, Patricia Nelson: "The Multicultural Islands." *American Historical Review*, 79, 1 (1992), 121–35.

Limerick, Patricia Nelson: "Disorientation and Reorientation: The American Landscape Discovered from the West." *Journal of American History*, 79, 3 (1992), 1021–49.

Limerick, Patricia Nelson: "The Adventures of the Frontier in the Twentieth Century." In James Grossman (ed.) *The Frontier in American Culture* (Berkeley and Los Angeles: California University Press, 1994).

Limerick, Patricia Nelson: "'This Perilous Situation Between Hope and Despair': Meetings Along the Great River of the West." In William L. Lang and Robert C. Carriker (eds.) *Great River of the West: Essays on the Columbia River* (Seattle: University of Washington Press, 1999).

Limerick, Patricia Nelson: "Going West and Ending Up Global." *Western Historical Quarterly*, 32, 1 (2001), 5–23.

Limerick, Patricia Nelson: "Judging Western History: From the Battlefield to the Courtroom." *Western Legal History* 14 (Winter–Spring, 2001), 11–18.

Limerick, Patricia Nelson, Clyde A. Milner, II, and Charles E. Rankin, (eds.): *Trails: Toward a New Western History* (Lawrence, KS.: University Press of Kansas, 1991).

Linderman, Frank B.: *American: The Life Story of A Great Indian, Plenty-Coups, Chief of the Crows* (New York: The John Day Company, 1930).

Linderman, Frank B.: *Red Mother* (New York, 1932); reprinted as *Pretty-shield: Medicine Woman of the Crows* (Lincoln: University of Nebraska Press, 1972).

Lindgren, H. Elaine: *Land in Her Own Name: Single Women as Homesteaders in North Dakota* ([1991], rpt. Norman: University of Oklahoma Press, 1996).

Linford, Orma: "The Mormons and the Law: the Polygamy Cases, Parts I & II." *Utah Law Review* 9 (1965, 1966), 308–70, 543–91.

Lingenfelter, Richard E.: *The Hardrock Miners: A History of the Mining Labor Movement in the American West, 1863–93* (Berkeley: University of California Press, 1974).

Lipsitz, George: "Cruising Around the Historical Bloc: Postmodernism and Popular Music in East Los Angeles." *Cultural Critique* 5 (1986), 157–77.

Lipsitz, George: *Dangerous Crossroads: Popular Music, Postmodernism, and the Poetics of Place* (New York: Verso, 1994).

Lipsitz, George: *The Possessive Investment in Whiteness: How White People Profit From Identity Politics* (Philadelphia: Temple University Press, 1998).

Lipsitz, George: "Their America and Ours: Intercultural Communication in the Context of 'Our America'." In Jeffrey Belnap and Raúl Fernández (eds.) *José Martí's "Our America": From National to Hemispheric Cultural Studies* (Durham: Duke University Press, 1998).

Livingstone, David N. and Charles W. J. Withers (eds.): *Geography and Enlightenment* (Chicago: University of Chicago Press, 1999).

Llewellyn, Karl and E. Adamson Hoebbel: *The Cheyenne Way: Conflict and Case Law in Primitive Jurisprudence* (Norman, OK: University of Oklahoma Press, 1941).

Locke, Mary Lou: "Out of the Shadows and into the Western Sun: Working Women of the Late Nineteenth-Century Urban Far West." *Journal of Urban History* 16, 2 (1990), 175–204.

Loeb, Catherine: "La Chicana: A Bibliographic Survey." *Frontiers* 5, 2 (1980), 59–74.

Lomawaima, K. Tsianina: *They Called It Prairie Light: The Story of Chilocco Indian School* (Lincoln: University of Nebraska Press, 1994).

London, Jack: *Call of the Wild* (New York: Macmillan, 1903).

London, Jack: *Valley of the Moon* (New York: Macmillan, 1913).

Longauex y Vásquez, Enriqueta: "The Mexican-American Woman." In Robin Morgan (ed.) *Sisterhood is Powerful* (New York: Random House, 1970).

Lopez, Barry: *Arctic Dreams: Imagination and Desire in a Northern Landscape* (New York: Charles Scribner's Sons, 1986).

López, David and Yen Espiritu: "Panethnicity in the United States: A Theoretical Framework." *Ethnic and Racial Studies* 13, 2 (1990), 198–224.

López, Elias, Enrique Ramirez, and Refugio I. Rochin: *Latinos and Economic Development in California*, CRB-99-008 (California Research Bureau, 1999).

Lotchin, Roger W. (ed.): *The Martial Metropolis: US Cities in War and Peace* (New York: Praeger, 1984).

Lotchin, Roger W.: *Fortress California, 1910–1961: From Warfare to Welfare* (New York: Oxford University Press, 1992).

Lotchin, Roger W.: "California Cities and the Hurricane of Change: World War II in the San Francisco, Los Angeles, and San Diego Metropolitan Areas." *Pacific Historical Review* 63 (August 1994): 393–420.

Lotchin, Roger: "The Impending Western Urban Past: An Essay on the Twentieth Century West." In Gerald D. Nash and Richard Etulain (eds.) *Researching Western History: Topics in the Twentieth Century* (Albuquerque: University of New Mexico Press, 1997).

Lotchin, Roger W.: *The Way We Really Were: The Golden State in the Second Great War* (Urbana: University of Illinois Press, 2000).

Lotchin, Roger W., Walter Nugent, and Martin Ridge (eds.): *The Bad City in the Good War: San Francisco, Oakland, and San Diego* (Indiana University Press, 2003).

Lowe, Lisa: *Immigrant Acts: On Asian American Cultural Politics* (Durham, NC: Duke University Press, 1996).

Lower, Richard Coke: *A Bloc of One: The Political Career of Hiram W. Johnson* (Stanford: Stanford University Press, 1993).

Lowitt, Richard: *The New Deal and the West* (Bloomington, IN: Indiana University Press, 1984).

Lowitt, Richard: *Bronson M. Cutting: Progressive Politician* (Albuquerque: University of New Mexico Press, 1992).

Lowitt, Richard: *The New Deal in the West* (Bloomington: Indiana University Press, 1984).

Luckingham, Bradford: *The Urban Southwest: A Profile History of Albuquerque, El Paso, Phoenix, Tucson* (El Paso: Texas Western Press, 1982).

Luebke, Frederick C.: *Immigrants and Politics: The Germans of Nebraska, 1880–1900* (Lincoln: University of Nebraska Press, 1969).

Lummis, Charles Fletcher: *A Tramp Across the Continent* ([1892], reprinted Lincoln: University of Nebraska Press, 1982).

Lyon, Thomas J.: "Beyond the Frontier Mind." In Judy Nolte Lensink (ed.) *Old Southwest, New Southwest: Essays on a Region and Its Literature* (Tucson: Tucson Public Library, 1987).

Lyon, Thomas J.: "The Literary West." In Clyde A. Milner, II, Carol A. O'Connor, and Martha Sandweiss (eds.) *The Oxford History of the American West* (New York: Oxford University Press, 1994).

Lyon, Thomas J. (ed.): *The Literary West: An Anthology of Western American Literature* (New York: Oxford University Press, 1999).

Lyon, Thomas J. and J. Golden Taylor (eds.): *Updating the Literary West* (Fort Worth: Texas Christian University Press, 1997).

MacCartney, Leslie: "Hula Dancers Perform at Lip of Berkeley Pit." *The Montana Standard* (July 11, 2000).

Mackay, David: "A Presiding Genius of Exploration: Banks, Cook, and Empire, 1767–1805." In Robin Fisher and Hugh Johnston (eds.) *Captain James Cook and his Times* (Seattle: University of Washington Press, 1979).

McClain, Charles J.: "In re Lee Sing: The First Residential-Segregation Case." *Western Legal History* 3 (1990), 179–96.

McClain, Charles J.: *In Search of Equality: The Chinese Struggle Against Discrimination in Nineteenth-Century America* (Berkeley, CA: University of California Press, 1994).

McClain, Charles J. and Laurene Wu McClain: "The Chinese Contribution to the Development of American Law." In Sucheng Chan (ed.) *Entry Denied: Exclusion and the Chinese Community in America, 1882–1943* (Philadelphia, Temple University Press, 1991).

McConnell, Grant: *Private Power and American Democracy* (New York: Random House, 1966).

McConnell, Michael N.: *A Country Between: The Upper Ohio Valley and Its Peoples, 1724–1774* (Lincoln: University of Nebraska Press, 1992).

McCoy, Drew R.: *The Elusive Republic: Political Economy in Jeffersonian America* (Chapel Hill: University of North Carolina Press, 1980).

McCurdy, Charles W.: "Stephen J. Field and Public Land Law Development in California, 1850–1866: A Case Study of Judicial Resource Allocation in Nineteenth-Century America." *Law and Society Review.* 10 (Fall/Winter, 1976), 235–66.

McDermott, John Francis (ed.): *The Spanish in the Mississippi Valley, 1762–1804* (Urbana: University of Illinois Press, 1974).

McDonald, Terrence: *The Parameters of Urban Fiscal Policy: Socioeconomic Change and Political Culture in San Francisco, 1860–1906* (Berkeley: University of California Press, 1986).

McDowell, Andrea G.: "From Commons to Claims: Property Rights in the California Gold Rush." *Yale Journal of Law and the Humanities* 12. (Winter, 2002), 1–72.

McEvoy, Arthur F.: *The Fisherman's Problem: Ecology and Law in the California Fisheries, 1850–1980* (Cambridge and New York: Cambridge University Press, 1986).

McEvoy, Arthur F.: "Toward an Interactive Theory of Nature and Culture: Ecology, Production, and Cognition in the California Fishing Industry." In Donald Worster (ed.) *The Ends of the Earth: Perspectives on Modern Environmental History* (New York: Cambridge University Press, 1988).

McGerr, Michael: "The Price of the 'New Transnational History.'" *American Historical Review* 96 (1991), 1031–72.

McGinnis, Anthony: *Counting Coup and Cutting Horses: Intertribal Warfare on the Northern Plains, 1738–1889* (Evergreen, CO: Cordillera Press, 1990).

McGirr, Lisa: *Suburban Warriors: The Origins of the New American Right* (Princeton: Princeton University Press, 2001).

McGovern, George and Leonard F. Guttridge: *The Great Coalfield War* (Boston: Houghton Mifflin, 1972).

McGrath, Roger D.: *Gunfighters, Highwaymen, and Vigilantes: Violence on the Frontier* (Berkeley, CA: University of California Press, 1984).

McKanna, Clare V.: *Homicide, Race, and Justice in the American West, 1880–1920* (Tucson, AZ: University of Arizona Press, 1997).

McKanna, Clare V: "Chinese Tongs, Homicide, and Justice in Nineteenth-Century California." *Western Legal History* 13 (Summer–Fall, 2000), 205–38.

McKanna, Clare V.: *Race and Homicide in Nineteenth-Century California* (Reno, NV: University of Nevada Press, 2002).

McKelvey, Susan D.: *Botanical Exploration of the Trans-Mississippi West* (Jamaica Plain, MA: Arnold Arboretum of Harvard University, 1956).

McKenzie, Evan: *Privatopia: Homeowner Associations and the Rise of Residential Private Governments* (New Haven, CT: Yale University Press, 1994).

McKeown, Martha Ferguson: *Them Was the Days: An American Saga of the 70s* (Lincoln: University of Nebraska Press, 1961).

McKinley, Charles: *Uncle Sam in the Pacific Northwest* (Berkeley: University of California Press, 1952).

McLuhan, T. C.: *Dream Tracks: The Railroad and the American Indian, 1890–1930* (New York: Harry N. Abrams, 1985).

McMurtry, Larry: *The Last Picture Show* (New York: Dial Press, 1966).

McMurtry, Larry: *Lonesome Dove* (New York: Simon and Schuster 1985).

McMurtry, Larry: *Texasville* (New York: Simon and Schuster, 1987).

McMurtry, Larry: *Anything for Billy* (New York: Simon and Schuster, 1988).

McMurtry, Larry: *Buffalo Girls* (New York: Simon and Schuster, 1990).

McMurtry, Larry (ed.): *Still Wild: Short Fiction of the American West, 1950 to the Present* (New York: Alfred A. Knopf, 2000).

McNeil, J. R.: *Something New Under the Sun: An Environmental History for the Twentieth-Century World* (New York: W. W. Norton, 2000).

McNickle, D'Arcy: *Native American Tribalism: Indian Survivals and Renewals* (New York: Oxford University Press, 1973).

McPhee, John: *Assembling California* (New York: Farrar, Straus, and Giroux, 1993).

McQuaid, Matilda and Karen Bartlett: "Building an Image of the Southwest: Mary Colter, Fred Harvey Company Architect" In Marta Weigle and Barabar Babcock (eds.) *The Great Southwest of the Fred Harvey Company and the Santa Fe Railway* (Phienix: The Heard Museum, 1996).

McWilliams, Carey: *Factories in the Field: The Story of Migratory Farm Labor in California* (Boston: Little, Brown and Company, 1939).

McWilliams, Carey: *North from Mexico: The Spanish-Speaking People of the United States* ([1949], New York: Greenwood Press, 1968).Madsen, Brigham D: *The Shoshoni Frontier and the Bear River Massacre* (Salt Lake City: University of Utah Press, 1985).

Maffly-Kipp, Laurie F.: *Religion and Society in Frontier California* (New Haven: Yale University Press, 1994).

Maffly-Kipp, Laurie F.: "Eastward Ho! American Religion from the Perspective of the Pacific Rim." In Thomas A. Tweed (ed.) *Retelling U.S. Religious History* (Berkeley: University of California Press, 1997).

Magoc, Chris J.: *Yellowstone: The Creation and Selling of an American Landscape, 1870–1903* (Albuquerque, NM: University of New Mexico Press, 1999).

Magoffin, Susan: *Down the Santa Fe Trail and Into Mexico* (New Haven: Yale University Press, 1926).

Mahoney, Timothy: *River Towns in the Great West: The Structure of Provincial Urbanization in the American Midwest, 1820–1870* (New York: Cambridge University Press, 1990).

Mallery, James: *From a Dangerous to a Dependent and Defective Group of Men: Social Policy, Urban Space, and the Masculinity of Hoboes in San Francisco, 1848–1917* (PhD dissertation: University of California, Los Angeles, 1999).

Malone, Michael P. (ed.): *Historians and the American West* (Lincoln: University of Nebraska Press, 1983).

Malone, Michael P.: "Review of Lowitt *The New Deal and the West.*" *New Mexico Historical Review* 59 (October 1984): 415–18.

Malone, Michael P.: *The Battle for Butte: Mining and Politics on the Northern Frontier, 1864–1906* (Helena: Montana Historical Society Press, 1995).

Malone, Michael P. and Richard W. Etulain: *The American West: A Twentieth-Century History* (Lincoln: University of Nebraska Press, 1989).

Malone, Michael P. and F. Ross Peterson: "Politics and Protests." In Clyde A. Milner, II, Carol A. O'Connor, and Martha Sandweiss (eds.) *The Oxford History of the American West* New York: Oxford University Press, 1994).

Mancall, Peter: *Valley of Opportunity: Economic Culture along the Upper Susquehanna, 1700–1800* (Ithaca: Cornell University Press, 1991).

Mann, Ralph: *After the Gold Rush: Society in Grass Valley and Nevada City, California, 1849–1870* (Stanford: Stanford University Press, 1982).

Marks, Paula Mitchell: *Precious Dust: The American Gold Rush Era, 1848–1900* (New York: W. Morrow, 1994).

Markusen, Ann, Peter Hall, Scott Campbell, and Sabina Deitrick: *The Rise of the Gunbelt: The Military Remapping of Industrial America* (New York: Oxford University Press, 1991).

Marling, Karal Ann (ed.): *Designing Disney's Theme Parks: The Architecture of Reassurance* (Montreal: Canadian Center for Architecture, 1997).

Marling, Karal Ann: *As Seen On TV: The Visual Culture of Everyday Life in the 1950s* (Cambridge: Harvard University Press, 1994).

Marquez, Benjamin: *Power and Politics in a Chicano Barrio: A Study of Mobilization Efforts and Community Power in El Paso* (Lanham, MD: University Press of America, 1985).

Marsh, George Perkins: *The Earth as Modified by Human Action: A New Edition of Man and Nature* ([1864], reprinted New York: Arno Press and the New York Times, 1970).

Marshall, P. J. and Glyndwr Williams: *The Great Map of Mankind: Perceptions of New Worlds in the Age of Enlightenment* (Cambridge, MA: Harvard University Press, 1982).

Martin, Calvin: *Keepers of the Game: Indian–Animal Relationships and the Fur Trade* (Berkeley: University of California Press, 1978).

Martin, Calvin (ed.) The *American Indian and the Problem of History* (New York: Oxford University Press, 1987).

Martin, Joel W.: *The Land Looks After Us: A History of Native American Religion* (New York: Oxford University Press, 2001).

Martin, Russell (ed.): *New Writers of the Purple Sage: An Anthology of Contemporary Western Writing* (New York: Penguin Books, 1992).

Martin, Russell and Marc Barasch: *Writers of the Purple Sage: An Anthology of Recent Western Writing* (New York: Viking Penguin, Inc., 1984).

Martinez, George A.: "The Legal Construction of Race: Mexican Americans and Whiteness." *Harvard Latino Law Review* (1997).

Martinez, John: *Mexican Emigration to the United States* (San Francisco: R&E Research Associates, 1972).

Marx, Karl and Friedrich Engels: *The German Ideology* (New York: International Publishers, 1972).

Massey, D., R. Alarcón, J. Durand, and H. González. *Return to Aztlán: the Social Process of International Migration from Western Mexico* (Berkeley: University of California Press, 1987).

Massey, Douglas S. and Nancy A. Denton: *American Apartheid: Segregation and the Making of the Underclass* (Boston: Harvard University Press, 1993).

Matsumoto, Valerie J. and Blake Allmendinger (eds.): *Over the Edge: Remapping the American West* (Berkeley: University of California Press, 1999).

Matthiessen, Peter: *Wildlife in America*, rev. edn. (New York: Penguin, 1987).

May, Dean L.: *Three Frontiers: Family, Land and Society in the American West, 1850–1900* (Cambridge and New York: Cambridge University Press, 1994).

Mead, Elwood and R. P. Teele: *Report of Irrigation Investigations in Utah,* (Washington, DC: US Government Printing Office, 1903).

Mead, Rebecca: *How the Vote was Won: Woman Suffrage in the Western United States, 1868–1914* (New York: New York University Press, 2004).

Medicine, Beatrice: "Warrior Women – Sex Role Alternatives for Plains Indian Women." In Patricia Albers and Beatrice Medicine (eds.) *The Hidden Half: Studies of Plains Indian Women* (Latham, MD: University Press of America, 1983).

Meier, August and Elliott M. Rudwick *From Plantation to Ghetto: An Interpretive History of American Negroes* (New York: Hill and Wang, 1966).

Meier, Matt S. and Feliciano Rivera: *The Chicanos: A History of Mexican Americans* New York: Hill and Wang, 1972).

Melendez, Edwin: "Understanding Latino Poverty." *Sage Relations Abstracts* 18, 2 (1993).

Meinig, Donald W.: *Southwest: Three Peoples in Geographical Change, 1600–1970* (New York: Oxford University Press, 1971).

Meldrum, Barbara Howard (ed.): *Under the Sun: Myth and Realism in Western American Literature* (Troy, NY: Whitson, 1985).

Merchant, Carolyn: "The Theoretical Structure of Ecological Revolutions." *Environmental Review* 11 (1987), 265–74.

Merchant, Carolyn: "Women of the Progressive Conservation Movement, 1900–1916," *Environmental Review* 8 (Spring 1984), 57–86.

Merk, Frederick: *Manifest Destiny and Mission in American History: A Reinterpretation* (New York: Knopf, 1963).

Merk, Frederick: *Slavery and the Annexation of Texas* (New York: Knopf, 1972).

Merk, Frederick: *The Oregon Question: Essays in Anglo-American Diplomacy and Politics* (Cambridge MA: Harvard University Press, 1967).

Merrell, James H.: *Into the American Woods: Negotiators on the Pennsylvania Frontier* (New York: W. W. Norton, 1999).

Merrill, Karen R.: "In Search of the 'Federal Presence' in the American West." *Western Historical Quarterly* 30 (Winter 1999), 449–73.

Merrill, Karen R.: *Public Lands and Political Meaning: Ranchers, the Government, and the Property Between Them* (Berkeley: University of California Press, 2002).

Merry, Sally Engle: *Colonizing Hawai'i: The Cultural Power of Law* (Princeton: Princeton University Press, 2000).

Messinger Cypess, Sandra: *La Malinche in Mexican Literature: From History to Myth* (Austin: University of Texas Press, 1991).

Metcalf, R. Warren: *Termination's Legacy: The Discarded Indians of Utah* (Lincoln: University of Nebraska Press, 2002).

Meyer, Melissa L.: *The White Earth Tragedy: Ethnicity and Dispossession at a Minnesota Anishinaabe Reservation, 1889–1920* (Lincoln: University of Nebraska Press, 1994).

Mihesuah, Devon A.: *Cultivating the Rosebuds: The Education of Women at the Cherokee Female Seminary* (Urbana: University of Illinois Press, 1993).

Mihesuah, Devon A. (ed.): *Natives and Academics: Research and Writing About American Indians* (Lincoln: University of Nebraska Press, 1998).

Mihesuah, Devon A.: *Indigenous American Women: Decolonization, Empowerment, Activism* (Lincoln: University of Nebraska Press, 2003).

Miller, Beth (ed.): *Women in Hispanic Literature: Icons and Fallen Idols* (Berkeley: University of California Press, 1983).

Miller, Charles: *Jefferson and Nature: An Interpretation* (Baltimore: John Hopkins University Press, 1988).

Miller, Charles W.: *Stake Your Claim! The Tale of America's Enduring Mining Laws* (Tucson, AZ: Westernlore Press, 1991).

Miller, Christopher L.: *Prophetic Worlds: Indians and Whites on the Columbia Plateau* (New Brunswick: Rutgers University Press, 1985).

Miller, Darlis A.: "Cross-Cultural Marriages in the Southwest: The New Mexico Experience, 1846–1900." *New Mexico Historical Review* 57, 4 (October 1962), 355–59.

Miller, Donald E.: *Reinventing American Protestantism: Christianity in the New Millennium* (Berkeley: University of California Press, 1997).

Miller, Henry: "Autobiographical Statement." (Hubert Howe Bancroft Collection: Bancroft Library, University of California, Berkeley).

Miller, Jay, Collin G. Calloway, and Richard A. Sattler (comps.): *Writings in Indian History, 1985–1990* (Norman: University of Oklahoma Press, 1995).

Miller, Loren: *The Petitioners: The Story of the Supreme Court of the United States and the Negro* (New York: Pantheon Books, 1966).

Miller, M. Catherine: *Flooding the Courtrooms: Law and Water in the Far West* (Lincoln: University of Nebraska Press, 1993).

Miller, Perry: *The New England Mind: From Colony to Province.* (Cambridge, Harvard University Press, 1953).

Milner, Clyde A., II: *With Good Intentions: Quaker Work Among the Pawnees, Otos, and Omahas in the 1870s* (Lincoln: University of Nebraska Press, 1982).

Milner, Clyde A., II (ed.): *A New Significance: Re-Envisioning the History of the American West* (New York: Oxford University Press, 1996).

Milner, Clyde A., II, Carol A. O'Connor, and Martha Sandweiss (eds.): *The Oxford History of the American West* New York: Oxford University Press, 1994).

Milner, Clyde A., II, and Floyd A. O'Neil (eds.): *Churchmen and the Western Indians, 1820–1920* (Norman: University of Oklahoma Press, 1985).

Mirandé, Alfredo: *Hombres y Machos: Masculinity and Latino Culture* (Boulder: Westview Press, 1997).

Mirandé, Alfredo and Evangelina Enriquez: *La Chicana: The Mexican-American Woman* (Chicago: University of Chicago Press, 1979).

Mitchell, Gregg: *The Campaign of the Century: Upton Sinclair's Race for Governor of California and the Birth of Media Politics* (New York: Random House, 1992).

Mitchell, Gregg: *Tricky Dick and the Pink Lady: Helen Gahagan Douglas, Sexual Politics, and the Red Scare, 1950* (New York: Random House, 1998).

Mitchell, Rose: *Tall Woman: The Life Story Rose Mitchell, a Navajo Woman*, ed. Charlotte Frisbie (Albuquerque: University of New Mexico Press, 2003).

Mitchell, W. J. T.: *Iconology: Image, Text, Ideology* (Chicago and London: University of Chicago Press, 1986).

Mocho, Jill: *Murder and Justice in Frontier New Mexico, 1821–1846* (Albuquerque, NM: University of New Mexico Press, 1997).

Modell, John: *The Economics and Politics of Racial Accomodation: The Japanese of Los Angeles, 1900–1942* (Urbana: University of Illinois Press, 1977).

Moehring, Eugene P.: *Resort City in the Sunbelt: Las Vegas, 1930–1970* (Reno: University of Nevada Press, 1989).

Mollenkop, John H.: *The Contested City* (Princeton, NJ: Princeton University Press, 1983).

Momaday, N. Scott: *House Made of Dawn* (New York: Harper & Row, 1968).

Momaday, N. Scott: *The Way to Rainy Mountain* (Albuquerque: University of New Mexico Press, 1969).

Monkkonen, Eric H.: *America Becomes Urban: The Development of US Cities and Towns, 1780–1980* (Berkeley: University of California Press, 1988).

Monroy, Douglas: *Thrown Among Strangers: The Making of Mexican Culture in Frontier California* (Berkeley: University of California Press, 1990).

Montejano, David: *Anglos and Mexicans in the Making of Texas, 1836–1986* (Austin: University of Texas Press, 1987).

Montell, William: *Killings: Folk Justice in the Upper South* (Lexington, KY: University Press of Kentucky, 1986).

Mooney, James: *The Ghost-Dance Religion and the Sioux Outbreak of 1890*, Fourteenth Annual Report of the Bureau of Ethnology, 1892–93, pt. 2 (Washington, DC: GPO, 1896).

Mooney, Ralph James: "Matthew Deady and the Federal Judicial Response to Racism in the Early West." In Charles McClain (ed.) *Asian Americans and the Law: Historical and Contemporary Perspectives* (New York: Garland Publishing, 1994).

Moore, Joan W.: "Colonialism: The Case of the Mexican Americans." *Social Problems* 17, 4 (1970): 463–72.

Moore, Joan W. and Harry Pachón: *Hispanics in the United States.* Englewood Cliffs, NJ: Prentice-Hall, 1985.

Moore, Shirley Ann Wilson: *To Place Our Deeds: The African American Community in Richmond, California, 1910–1963* (Berkeley: University of California Press, 2000).

Moran, Rachel F.: *Interracial Intimacy: The Regulation of Race and Romance*. Chicago: University of Chicago Press, 2001.

Morgan, Dale L.: *The Great Salt Lake* (New York: Bobbs-Merrill Company, 1947).

Morgan, David, Mark Busby, and Paul Bryant (eds.): *The Frontier Experience and the American Dream: Essays on American Literature* (College Station: Texas A & M University Press, 1989).

Morgan, Edmund S.: *American Freedom, American Slavery: The Ordeal of Colonial Virginia* (New York: W. W. Norton, 1975).

Morgan, Murray C.: *One Man's Gold Rush: A Klondike Album* (Seattle: University of Washington Press, 1967).

Morlan, Robert L.: *Political Prairie Fire: The Non-Partisan League, 1915–1922* (Minneapolis: University of Minnesota Press, 1955).

Morris, Andrew: "Miners, Vigilantes & Cattlemen: Overcoming Free Rider Problems in the Private Provision of Law." *Land & Water Law Review* 33 (1998), 581–696.

Morris, Gregory L.: *Talking Up a Storm: Voices of the New West* (Lincoln: University of Nebraska Press, 1988).

Morris, John Miller: *El Llano Estacado: Exploration and Imagination on the High Plains of Texas and New Mexico, 1536–1860* (Austin: Texas State Historical Society, 1997).

Morrissey, Katherine G.: *Mental Territories: Mapping the Inland Empire* (Ithaca, NY: Cornell University Press, 1997).

Morrison, Michael A.: *Slavery and the American West: The Eclipse of Manifest Destiny and the Coming of the Civil War* (Chapel Hill: University of North Carolina Press, 1997).

Moses, L. G.: *Wild West Shows and the Images of American Indians, 1883–1933* (Albuquerque: University of New Mexico Press, 1996).

Moulton, Gary E. (ed.): *The Journals of the Lewis and Clark Expedition,* 12 vols. (Lincoln: University of Nebraska Press, 1983–99).

Mourning Dove: *Co-ge-we-a, the Half-Blood: A Depiction of the Great Montana cattle Range* (Boston: The Four Seas Company, 1927).

Mowry, George: *The California Progressives* (Berkeley: University of California Press, 1951).

Moynihan, Ruth Barnes: *Rebel for Rights: Abigail Scott Duniway* (New Haven: Yale University Press, 1983).

Mrozek, Donald J.: "The Image of the West in American Sport." *Journal of the West* 17, 3 (1978), 2–15.

Muir, John: "Wild Parks and Forest Reservations of the West." *Atlantic Monthly* 81 (January 1898), 15.

Mumford, Kevin T.: *Interzones: Black/White Sex Districts in Chicago and New York in the Early Twentieth Century* (New York: Columbia University Press, 1997).

Mumford, Lewis: *The Culture of Cities* (New York: Harcourt, Brace, and Company, 1938).

Muñoz, Carlos: *Youth, Identity, Power: The Chicano Movement.* (New York: Verso, 1989).

Murakami, Naojiro: "Japan's Early Attempts to Establish Commercial Relations with Mexico." In H. Morse Stephens and Herbert E. Bolton (eds.) *The Pacific Ocean in History* (New York: MacMillan, 1917).

Murphy, Mary: "Making Men in the West: The Coming of Age of Miles Cavanaugh and Martin Frank Dunham." In Valerie J. Matsumoto and Blake Allmendinger (eds.) *Over the Edge: Remapping the American West* (Berkeley: University of California Press, 1999).

Myres, Sandra L.: *Westering Women and the Frontier Experience, 1800–1915* (Albuquerque: University of New Mexico Press, 1982).

Nabhan, Gary Paul: *The Desert Smells Like Rain: A Naturalist in Papago Indian Country* (San Francisco: North Point Press, 1982).

Nabhan, Gary Paul: *Enduring Seeds: Native American Agriculture and Wild Plant Conservation* (San Francisco: North Point Press, 1989).

Nabokov, Peter (ed.): *Two Leggings: The Making of a Crow Warrior* (Lincoln: University of Nebraska Press, 1967).

Nabokov, Peter (ed.): *Native American Testimony: A Chronicle of Indian–White Relations from Prophesy to the Present, 1492–2000*, rev. edn (New York: Penguin Putnam, 1999).

Nabokov, Peter and Robert Easton: *Native American Architecture* (New York: Oxford University Press, 1988).

Nasatir, Abraham P. *Before Lewis and Clark: Documents Illustrating the History of the Missouri, 1785–1804* (St. Louis: St. Louis Historical Documents Foundation, 1952).

Nasatir, Abraham P.: *Borderland in Retreat: From Spanish Louisiana to the Far Southwest* (Albuquerque: University of New Mexico Press, 1976).

Nash, Gerald: *The American West in the Twentieth Century: A Short History of an Urban Oasis* (Albuquerque: University of New Mexico Press, 1977).

Nash, Gerald: *The American West Transformed: The Impact of the Second World War* (Bloomington: Indiana University Press, 1985).

Nash, Gerald: *World War II and the West: Reshaping the Economy* (Lincoln: University of Nebraska Press, 1990).

Nash, Gerald: *Creating the West: Historical Interpretations, 1890–1990* (Albuquerque: University of New Mexico Press, 1991).

Nash, Gerald: "A Veritable Revolution: The Global Economic Significance of the California Gold Rush." In James J. Rawls and Richard J. Orsi (eds.) *A Golden State: Mining and Economic Development in Gold Rush California in California History* (Berkeley: University of California Press, 1998/99).

Nash, Gerald: *The Federal Landscape: An Economic History of the Twentieth-Century West* (Tucson: University of Arizona Press, 1999).

Nash, Gerald and Richard Etulain (eds.): *The Twentieth Century West: Historical Interpretations* (Albuquerque: University of New Mexico Press, 1989).

Nash, Roderick: *Wilderness and the American Mind*, 3rd edn. (New Haven: Yale University Press, 1982).

Navin, Thomas R.: "The 500 Largest American Industrials in 1917." *Business History Review* 44 (1970), 360–86.

Neel, Susan Rhoades (ed.): "Tourism and the American West." Special Issue, *Pacific Historical Review* 65 (November 1996).

Nelson, Bruce: *Workers on The Waterfront: Seamen, Longshoremen, and Unionism in the 1930s* (Urbana: University of Illinois Press, 1988).

Nelson, Byron, Jr.: *Our Home Forever: A Hupa Tribal History* (Salt Lake City: University of Utah Printing Service for the Hupa Tribe, 1978).

Nelson, Larry L.: *A Man of Distinction among Them: Alexander McKee and British–Indian Affairs along the Ohio Country Frontier, 1734–1799* (Kent: Kent State University Press, 1999).

Nelson, Paul David: *Anthony Wayne: Soldier of the Early Republic* (Bloomington: Indiana University Press, 1985).

Nelson, Paul David and Andrew R. L. Cayton: *Frontier Indiana* (Bloomington: Indiana University Press, 1996).

Nelson, Paula M.: "No Place for Clinging Vines: Women Homesteaders on the South Dakota Frontier." (MA thesis: University of South Dakota, 1978).

Nelson, Paula M.: *After the West Was Won: Homesteaders and Town-Builders in Western South Dakota, 1900–1917* (Iowa City: University of Iowa Press, 1989).

Nemerov, Alex: "Doing the 'Old America': The Image of the American West, 1880–1920." In William H. Truettner (ed.) *The West as America: Reinterpreting Images of the Frontier, 1820–1920* (Washington, DC: Smithsonian Institution Press, 1991).

Neumann, Mark: *On the Rim: Looking for the Grand Canyon* (Minneapolis: University of Minnesota Press, 1999).

Newman, William H. and Peter L. Halvorson: *Atlas of American Religion: The Denominational Era, 1776–1990* (Walnut Creek, CA: Altamira Press, 2000).

Nichols, Roger L. (ed.): *The Missouri Expedition: The Journal of Surgeon John Gale, with Related Documents* (Norman, University of Oklahoma Press, 1969).

Nichols, Roger L.: *Indians in the United States and Canada: A Comparative History* (Lincoln: University of Nebraska Press, 1998).

Nichols, Roger L. (ed.): *The American Indian: Past and Present*, 5th edn. (New York: McGraw-Hill, 1999).

Nichols, Roger L. and Patrick Halley: *Stephen Long and American Frontier Exploration* ([1980], reprint, Norman: University of Oklahoma Press, 1995).

Nickerson, Michelle: *"Domestic Threats: Women, Gender and Conservatism in Cold War Los Angeles, 1945–1966."* (PhD Dissertation, Yale University, 2003).

Nicolaides, Becky: *My Blue Heaven: Life and Politics in the Working Class Suburbs of Los Angeles, 1920–1965* (Chicago: University of Chicago Press, 2002).

Niemi, Albert, Jr.: *State and Regional Patterns in American Manufacturing* (Westport: Greenwood Press, 1974).

Nobles, Gregory: *American Frontiers: Cultural Encounters and Continental Conquest* (New York: Hill & Wang, 1997).

Nobles, Melissa: *Shades of Citizenship: Race and the Census in Modern Politics* (Stanford: Stanford University Press, 2000).

Nolan, Frederick W.: *The Lincoln County War: A Documentary History* (Norman, OK: University of Oklahoma Press, 1992).

Norris, Frank: *McTeague* ([1899], reprinted New York: Norton, 1977).

Norris, Scott (ed.): *Discovered Country: Tourism and Survival in the American West* (Albuquerque, NM: Stone Ladder Press, 1994).

Norwood, Vera and Janice Monk (eds.): *The Desert is No Lady: Southwestern Landscapes in Women's Writing and Art* (New Haven, CT: Yale University Press, 1987).

Nostrand, Richard L.: *The Hispano Homeland* (Norman: University of Oklahoma Press, 1992).

Nugent, Walter: "Frontiers and Empires in the Late Nineteenth Century." In Patricia Nelson Limerick, Clyde A. Milner, II, and Charles E. Rankin (eds.) *Trails: Toward a New Western History* (Lawrence: University of Kansas Press, 1991).

Nugent, Walter: *Into the West: The Story of Its People* (New York: Alfred A. Knopf, 1999).

Nunis, Doyce B., Jr.: "The 1811 San Diego Trial of the Mission Indian Nazario." *Western Legal History* 4 (Winter 1991–Spring 1992), 47–58.

Oboler, Suzanne: *Ethnic Labels, Latino Lives* (Minneapolis: University of Minnesota Press, 1995).

O'Connor, Alice A.: *Poverty Knowledge: Social Science, Social Policy, and the Poor in the Twentieth Century* (Princeton, NJ: Princeton University Press, 2001).

O'Donnell, James H., III (ed.): "Captain Pipe's Speech: A Commentary on the Delaware Experience, 1775–1781." *Northwest Ohio Quarterly*, 64 (Autumn 1992).

Ogden, Adele: "Trading Vessels on the California Coast, 1786 to 1848." (Ogden Collection: Bancroft Library, University of California, Berkeley).

Oglesby, Richard E.: *Manuel Lisa and the Opening of the Missouri Fur Trade* (Norman: University of Oklahoma Press, 1963).

Okihiro, Gary Y.: *Margins and Mainstream: Asians in American History and Culture* (Seattle: University of Washington Press, 1994).

Olin, Spencer C.: *California's Prodigal Sons: Hiram Johnson and the Progressives, 1911–1917* (Berkeley: University of California Press, 1968).

Olson, James S. and Raymond Wilson: *Native Americans in the Twentieth Century* (Provo: Brigham Young University Press, 1984).

O'Neal, Bill: *Encyclopedia of Western Gunfighters* (Norman, OK: University of Oklahoma Press, 1979).

Onuf, Peter S.: *Statehood and Union: A History of the Northwest Ordinance* (Bloomington: Indiana University Press, 1987).

Onuf, Peter S.: *Jefferson's Empire: The Language of American Nationhood* (Charlottesville: University of Virginia Press, 2000).

Opie, John: *The Law of the Land: Two Hundred Years of American Farmland Policy* (Lincoln: University of Nebraska Press, 1987).

Opie, John: *Ogallala: Water for a Dry Land* (Lincoln: University of Nebraska Press, 1993).

Osborn, John: *Railroads and Clearcuts* (Spokane: Keokee Publishers, 1995).

Osburn, Katherine M. B.: "'To Build Up the Morals of the Tribe': Southern Ute Women's Sexual Behavior and the Office of Indian Affairs, 1895–1932." *Journal of Western History* 9, 3 (Autumn 1997), 10–28.

Osburn, Katherine M. B.: *Southern Ute Women: Autonomy and Assimilation on the Reservation, 1887–1934* (Albuquerque: University of New Mexico Press, 1998).

Ostler, Jeffrey: *Prairie Populism: The Fate of Agrarian Radicalism in Kansas, Nebraska, and Iowa, 1880–1892* (Lawrence: University Press of Kansas, 1993).

Ostrander, Gilbert: *The Prohibition Movement in California, 1848–1933* (Berkeley: University of California Press, 1957).

Outram, Dorinda "On Being Perseus: New Knowledge, Dislocation, and Enlightenment Exploration." In David N. Livingstone and Charles W. J. Withers (eds.) *Geography and Enlightenment* (Chicago: University of Chicago Press, 1999).

Owens, Kenneth N.: "Government and Politics in the Nineteenth-Century West." In Michael P. Malone (ed.) *Historians and the American West* (Lincoln: University of Nebraska Press, 1983).

Padget, Martin: "Claiming, Corrupting, Contesting: Reconsidering "The West" in Western American Literature." *American Literary History* 10 (Summer 1998), 378–92.

Padilla, Felix M.: *Latino Ethnic Consciousness* (Notre Dame: University of Notre Dame Press, 1985).

Paredes, Américo: *"With His Pistol in His Hand": A Border Ballad and Its Hero* (Austin: University of Texas Press, 1958).

Paredes, Américo: "The Problem of Identity in a Changing Culture: Popular Expressions of Culture Conflict Along the Lower Rio Grande Border." In Stanley R. Ross (ed.) *Views across the Border: The United States and Mexico* (Albuquerque: University of New Mexico Press, 1978).

Park, Robert E. and Ernest W. Burgess: *The City: Suggestions for Investigation of Human Behavior in the Urban Environment* (Chicago: University of Chicago Press, 1925).

Parker, Dorothy R.: *Singing an Indian Song: A Biography of D'Arcy McNickle* (Lincoln: University of Nebraska Press, 1992).

Parman, Donald L.: *Indians and the American West in the Twentieth Century* (Bloomington: Indiana University Press, 1994).

Pascoe, Peggy: *Relations of Rescue: The Search for Female Moral Authority in the American West, 1874–1939* (New York: Oxford University Press, 1990).

Pascoe, Peggy: "Introduction: The Challenge of Writing Multicultural Women's History." *Frontiers* XII: 1 (1991), 1–4.

Pascoe, Peggy: "Race, Gender, and Intercultural Relations: The Case of Interracial Marriage." *Frontiers* XII, 1 (1991), 5–18.

Pascoe, Peggy: "Western Women at the Cultural Crossroads." In Patricia Nelson Limerick, Clyde A. Milner II, and Charles E. Rankin (eds.) *Trails: Toward a New Western History* (Lawrence; University Press of Kansas, 1991).

Pastor, Manuel, Jr.: "Economic Inequality, Latino Poverty and the Civil Unrest in Los Angeles." *Economic Development Quarterly* 9, 3 (1995).

Pastor, Manuel, Jr.: "The California Economy: Servant or Master?" In David López (ed.) *Latino Inequality: California's Challenge* (Berkeley: California Policy Seminar, 2000).

Patrick, Kevin: "Mountain Bikes and Baby Boomers." *Journal of American Culture* 11, 2 (1988), 17–24.

Patterson, Richard M.: *Butch Cassidy: A Biography* (Lincoln, NE: University of Nebraska Press, 1988).

Patterson-Black, Sheryll: "Women Homesteaders on the Great Plains Frontier." *Frontiers* 1, 2 (Spring 1976), 67–88.

Paul, Rodman W.: *California Gold. The Beginning of Mining in the Far West* (Cambridge, MA: Harvard University Press, 1947).

Paul, Rodman W.: *Mining Frontiers in the Far West, 1848–1880* (New York: Holt, Rinehart and Winston, 1963).

Paul, Rodman: *The Far West and the Great Plains in Transition, 1859–1900* (New York, Harper & Row, 1988).

Paul, Rodman W.: "Mining Law." In Howard R. Lamar (ed.) *The New Encyclopedia of the American West.* (New Haven, CT: Yale University Press, 1998).

Peavy, Linda and Ursula Smith: *The Gold Rush Widows of Little Falls* (St. Paul: Minnesota Historical Society Press, 1990).

Peavy, Linda and Ursula Smith: *Women in Waiting in the Westward Movement: Life on the Home Frontier* (Norman: University of Oklahoma Press, 1994).

Peck, Gunther: *Reinventing Free Labor: Padrones and Immigrant Workers in the North American West, 1880–1930* (New York: Cambridge University Press, 2000).

Peffer, E. Louise: *The Closing of the Public Domain: Disposal and Reservation Policies, 1900–1950* (Stanford: Stanford University Press, 1951).

Peiss, Kathy: *Cheap Amusements: Working Women and Leisure in Turn-of-the-Century New York* (Philadelphia: Temple University Press, 1986).

Perales, Marian: "Empowering 'The Welder': A Historical Survey of Women of Color in the West." In Elizabeth Jameson and Susan Armitage (eds.) *Writing the Range: Race, Class, and Culture in the Women's West* (Norman: University of Oklahoma Press, 1997).

Perea, Juan F. (ed.): *Immigrants Out: The New Nativism and the Anti-Immigrant Impulse in the United States* (New York: New York University Press, 1997).

Perdue, Theda: *Slavery and the Evolution of Cherokee Society, 1540–1866* (Knoxville: University of Tennessee Press, 1979).

Perdue, Theda: *Nations Remembered: An Oral History of the Cherokees, Chickasaws, Choctaws, Creeks, and Seminoles, 1865–1907* (Norman: University of Oklahoma Press, 1993).

Perdue, Theda: *Cherokee Women: Gender and Culture Change, 1700–1835* (Lincoln: University of Nebraska Press, 1998).

Perdue, Theda and Michael D. Green (eds.): *The Cherokee Removal: A Brief History with Documents* (Boston: St Martin's Press, 1995).

Perkins, Elizabeth A.: *Border Life: Experience and Memory in the Revolutionary Ohio Valley* (Chapel Hill: University of North Carolina Press, 1998).

Perry, David C. and Alfred J. Watkins (eds.): *The Rise of the Sunbelt Cities* (Beverly Hills, CA: Sage, 1977).

Perry, Tony: "Rights and Rites Clash in Mine Plan." *Los Angeles Times* (February 9, 1998).

Peterson, Charles S.: "Hubert Howe Bancroft: First Western Regionalist." In *Writing Western History*, 43–70.

Peterson, Jacqueline, and Jennifer S. H. Brown (eds.): *The New Peoples: Being and Becoming Métis in North America* (Lincoln: University of Nebraska Press, 1985).

Peterson, Merrill D. (ed.): *Thomas Jefferson: Writings* (New York: Viking-Library of America, 1984).

Peterson, Richard: *The Bonanza Kings: The Social Origins and Business Behavior of Western Mining Entrepreneurs, 1870–1900* (Lincoln: University of Nebraska Press, 1977).

Petrik, Paula: *No Step Backward: Women and Family on the Rocky Mountain Mining Frontier* (Helena: Montana Historical Society Press, 1987).

Petrik, Paula: "'Send the Bird and Cage': The Development of Divorce Law in Wyoming, 1868–1900." *Western Legal History* 6 (Summer–Fall 1993), 153–81.

Petrik, Paula and John R. Wunder: "Women, Legal History, and the American West." *Western Legal History* 7 (Summer–Fall 1994), 193–9.

Pfeffer, George Anthony: "Forbidden Families: Emigration Experiences of Chinese Women Under the Page Law, 1875–1882." *Journal of American Ethnic History* 6 (1986), 28–46.

Phelps, Robert: "The Search for a Modern Industrial City: Urban Planning, the Open Shop, and the Founding of Torrance, California." *Pacific Historical Review* 64, 4 (1995): 503–35.

Phillips, Charles and Alan Axelrod (eds.): *Encyclopedia of the American West*, 4 vols. (New York: Simon and Schuster Macmillan, 1996).

Phillips, Paul C.: *The Fur Trade*, vol. 2 (Norman, OK: University of Oklahoma Press, 1961).

Phillips, Rachel: "Marina/Malinche: Masks and Shadows." In Beth Miller (ed.) *Women in Hispanic Literature: Icons and Fallen Idols* (Berkeley: University of California Press, 1983).

Philp, Kenneth R.: *John Collier's Crusade for Indian Reform, 1920–1954* (Tucson: University of Arizona Press, 1977).

Philp, Kenneth R.: *Termination Revisited: American Indians on the Trail to Self-Determination, 1933–1953* (Lincoln: University of Nebraska Press, 1999).

Philpott, William: "Visions of a Changing Vail: Fast-Growth Fallout in a Colorado Resort Town." (Master's thesis: University of Wisconsin, Madison, 1994).

Pierce, Bessie Louise: *A History of Chicago*, vol. 1, *The Beginning of a City* (New York: Knopf, 1937).

Pierson, George Wilson: "American Historians and the Frontier Hypothesis in 1941." In Lawrence O. Burnette, Jr. (comp.) *Wisconsin Witness to Frederick Jackson Turner: A Collection of Essays on the Historian and the Thesis* (Madison: The State Historical Society of Wisconsin, 1961).

Pinkerton, Allan: *Strikers, Communists, Tramps and Detectives* (New York: G. W. Carleton & Co., 1878).

Pisani, Donald: *From the Family Farm to Agribusiness: The Irrigation Crusade in California and the West, 1850–1931* (Berkeley: University of California Press, 1983).

Pisani, Donald J.: *From the Family Farm to Agribusiness: The Irrigation Crusade in California and the West, 1850–1931* (Berkeley: University of California Press, 1984).

Pisani, Donald: "Forests and Conservation, 1865–1890." *Journal of American History* 72 (1985), 340–59.

Pisani, Donald J.: "Irrigation, Water Rights, and the Betrayal of Indian Allotment." *Environmental History Review* (Fall 1986), 157–76.

Pisani, Donald J.: *To Reclaim a Divided West: Water, Law, and Public Policy, 1848–1902* (Albuquerque: University of New Mexico Press, 1992).

Pisani, Donald J.: *Water, Land, and Law in the West: The Limits of Public Policy, 1850–1920* (Lawrence: University Press of Kansas, 1996).

Pitt, Leonard: *The Decline of the Californios: A Social History of the Spanish-Speaking Californians, 1846–1890* (Berkeley: University of California Press, 1966).

Pitti, Stephen: *The Devil in Silicon Valley: Northern California, Race, and Mexican Americans* (Princeton: Princeton University Press, 2003).

Pletcher, David M.: *The Diplomacy of Annexation: Texas, Oregon and the Mexican War* (Columbia: University of Missouri Press, 1973).

Poesch, Jessie: *Titian Ramsay Peale and his Journals of the Wilkes Expedition* (Philadelphia: American Philosophical Society, 1961).

Pomeroy, Earl: "Toward A Reconsideration of American Western History." *Mississippi Valley Historical Review* 41 (March 1955), 579–600.

Pomeroy, Earl: *In Search of the Golden West: The Tourist in Western America* ([1957], reprinted Lincoln: University of Nebraska Press, 1990).

Pomeroy, Earl: *The Pacific Slope: A History of California, Oregon, Washington, Idaho, Utah, and Nevada* ([1965], Lincoln and London: University of Nebraska Press, 1991).

Pommersheim, Frank: *Braid of Feathers: American Indian Law and Contemporary Tribal Life* (Berkeley: University of California Press, 1995).

Porte, Joel (ed.): *Ralph Waldo Emerson: Essays and Lectures* (New York: Viking-Library of America, 1983).

Porter, Charlotte M.: *The Eagle's Nest: Natural History and American Ideas, 1812–1842* (University, AL: University of Alabama Press, 1986).

Porter, Joseph C.: *Paper Medicine Man: John Gregory Bourke and His American West* (Norman: University of Oklahoma Press, 1986).

Portes, Alejandro (ed.): *The New Second Generation* (New York: Russell Sage Foundation, 1996).

Portes, Alejandro and Rubén G. Rumbaut: *Legacies: The Story of the Immigrant Second Generation* (Berkeley: University of California Press, 2001).

Powell, John Wesley, Grove Karl Gilbert, Clarence E. Dutton, A. H. Thompson, and Willis Drummond, Jr.: *Report on the Lands of the Arid Region of the United States* (Washington, DC: Government printing Office, 1878).

Powell, Peter J.: *Sweet Medicine*, 2 vols. (Norman: University of Oklahoma Press, 1969).

Powell, Peter J.: *People of the Sacred Mountain: A History of the Northern Cheyenne Chiefs and Warrior Societies, 1830–1879, with an Epilogue, 1969–1974*, 2 vols. (New York: Harper and Row, 1981).

Prassel, Frank R.: *The Western Peace Officer: A Legacy of Law and Order* (Norman, OK: University of Oklahoma Press, 1972).

Prassel, Frank R.: *The Great American Outlaw: A Legacy of Fact and Fiction* (Norman, OK: University of Oklahoma Press, 1993).

Prendergast, Schoelwer and Howard R. Lamar: *Discovered Lands, Invented Pasts: Transforming Visions of the American West* (New Haven: Yale University Press, 1992).

Preston, William: "Serpent in the Garden: Environmental Change in Colonial California." In Ramón Gutiérrez and Richard J. Orsi (eds.) *Contested Eden: California Before the Gold Rush* (Berkeley: University of California Press, 1998).

Preston, William: *Vanishing Landscapes: Land and Life in the Tulare Lake Basin* (Berkeley: University of California Press, 1981).

Price, Catherine: *The Oglala People, 1841–1879: A Political History* (Lincoln: University of Nebraska Press, 1996).

Price, L. Bradford (ed.): *General Laws of New Mexico* (Albany, NY: W. C. Little & Co., 1880).

Proulx, Annie: *Close Range: Wyoming Stories* (New York: Scribner, 1999).

Prown, Jules David, Nancy K. Anderson, William Cronon, Brian W. Dippie, Martha A. Sandweiss, Susan.

Prucha, Francis Paul: *A Bibliographical Guide to the History of Indian–White Relations in the United States* (Chicago: University of Chicago Press, 1977).

Prucha, Francis Paul: *Indian–White Relations in the United States: A Bibliography of Works Published 1975–1980* (Lincoln: University of Nebraska Press, 1982).

Prucha, Francis Paul. *The Great Father: The United States Government and the American Indians,* 2 vols. (Lincoln: University of Nebraska Press, 1984).

Prucha, Francis Paul: *American Indian Treaties: The History of a Political Anomaly* (Berkeley: University of California Press, 1994).

Przybyszewski, Linda C. A.: "Judge Lorenzo Sawyer and the Chinese: Civil Rights Decisions in the Ninth Circuit." *Western Legal History* 1 (1988), 23–56.

Putnam, Jackson K.: *Old-Age Politics in California from Richardson to Reagan* (Stanford: Stanford University Press, 1970).

Putnam, John: *The Emergence of a New West: The Politics of Class and Gender in Seattle, Washington, 1880–1917* (PhD dissertation: University of California, San Diego, 2000).

Pyne, Stephen J.: *Fire in America: A Cultural History of Wildland and Rural Fire* (Princeton, NJ: Princeton University Press, 1982).

Pyne, Stephen J.: *Vestal Fire: An Evironmental History, Told through Fire, of Europe and Europe's Encounter with the World* (Seattle: University of Washington Press, 1997).

Pyne, Stephen J.: *World Fire: The Culture of Fire on Earth* (Seattle: University of Washington Press, 1997).

Raban, Jonathan: *Bad Land: An American Romance,* (New York: Pantheon Books, 1996).

Rae, John B.: *The American Automobile: A Brief History* (Chicago: University of Chicago Press, 1965).

Rae, John B.: *The Road and the Car in American Life* (Cambridge, MA: MIT Press, 1971).

Ramonofsky, Ann F.: *Vectors of Death: The Archeology of European Contact* (Albuquerque: University of New Mexico Press, 1987).

Rasmussen, Linda, Lorna Rasmussen, Candace Savage, and Anne Wheeler: *A Harvest Yet to Reap: A History of Prairie Women* (Toronto: Women's Press, 1976).

Rawls, James J. and Richard J. Orsi (eds.): *A Golden State: Mining and Economic Development in Gold Rush California in California History,* (Berkeley: University of California Press, 1998/99).

Ray, Arthur J.: *Indians in the Fur Trade: Their Role as Hunters, Trappers, and Middlemen in the Lands Southwest of Hudson Bay, 1660–1870* (Toronto: University of Toronto Press, 1974).

Reddy, Marlita A. (ed.): *Statistical Record of Native North Americans* (Detroit: Gale, 1993).

Redfield, H. V.: *Homicide North and South* (Philadelphia: J. B. Lippincott & Co., 1880).

Reich, Peter L.: "Western Courts and the Privatization of Hispanic Mineral Rights since 1850: An Alchemy of Title." *Columbia Journal of Environmental Law* 23 (1998), 57–87.

Reichard, David A.: "The Politics of Village Water Disputes in Northern New Mexico, 1882–1905" *Western Legal History* 9 (Winter 1996–Spring 1997), 8–33.

Reid, John Philip: *A Law of Blood: The Primitive Law of the Cherokee Nation* (New York: New York University Press, 1970).

Reid, John Philip: *Law for the Elephant: Property and Social Behavior on the Overland Trail,* (San Marino, CA: The Huntington Library, 1980).

Reid, John Philip: "The Layers of Western Legal History." In John McLaren, Hamar Foster and Chet Orloff (eds.) *Law for the Elephant, Law for the Beaver: Essays in the Legal History of the North American West* (Pasadena, CA: Ninth Judicial Circuit Historical Society, 1992).

Reid, John Phillip: *Policing the Elephant: Crime Punishment, and Social Behavior on the Overland Trail* (San Marino, CA: Huntington Library, 1997).

Reid, John Philip: *Patterns of Vengeance: Cross-cultural Homicide in the North American Fur Trade,* (Pasadena, CA: Ninth Judicial Circuit Historical Society, 1999).

Reid, John Philip: *Contested Empire: Peter Skene Ogden and the Snake River Expeditions* (Norman, OK: University of Oklahoma Press, 2002).

Reisler, Marc: *By the Sweat of Their Brow: Mexican Immigrant Labor in the United States* (Westport, CT: Greenwood Press, 1976).

Reisner, Marc and Sarah Bates: *Overtapped Oasis: Reform or Revolution for Western Water* (Washington, DC: Island Press, 1990).

Revised Codes of North Dakota (Bismarck, N.D.: State of North Dakota, 1896).

Rhode, Paul: "The Nash Thesis Revisited: An Economic Historian's View." *Pacific Historical Review* 63 (August 1994) 363–92.

Rice, Ross R.: *Carl Hayden: Builder of the American West* (Lanham, MD: University Press of America, 1994).

Rich, E. E.: *Hudson's Bay Company, 1670–1870* (New York: Macmillan Books, 1961).

Richter, Daniel K.: *The Peoples of the Longhouse: The Iroquois League in the Era of European Colonialism* (Chapel Hill: University of North Carolina Press, 1992).

Richter Daniel K.: *Facing East from Indian Country: A Native History of Early America* (Cambridge, MA: Harvard University Press, 2001).

Richter, Daniel K. and James H. Merrell (eds.): *Beyond the Covenant Chain: The Iroquois and Their Neighbors in Indian North America, 1600–1800* (Syracuse: Syracuse University Press, 1987).

Ridge, Martin: "Disorder, Crime, and Punishment in the California Gold Rush." *Montana, the Magazine of Western History* 49, 3 (Autumn 1999), 12–27.

Ridington, Robin: *"Fox and Chickadee."* In Calvin Martin (ed.) *The American Indian and the Problem of History* (New York: Oxford University Press, 1987).

Rieff, David: *Los Angeles: Capital of the Third World* (New York: Simon and Schuster, 1991).

Righter, Robert: "National Monuments to National Parks: The Use of the Antiquities Act of 1906." *Western Historical Quarterly* 13 (August 1989), 281–301.

Riley, Glenda: *Frontierswomen: The Iowa Experience* (Ames, IA: Iowa State University Press, 1981).

Riley, Glenda: *Women and Nature: Saving the "Wild" West* (Lincoln: University of Nebraska Press, 1999).

Rinehart, Mary Roberts: "My Country Tish of Thee." *Saturday Evening Post* (1 April 1916), 3–6, 54–55, 58–59, 62, 65–66; (8 April 1916), 19–22, 43, 47, 50–51.

Rinehart, Mary Roberts: "On the Trail in Wonderland II." *Wide World* (November 1916), 59–68.

Rinehart, Mary Roberts: "The Family Goes A-Gypsying." *Outlook* (12 June 1918), 263–6.

Rinehart, Mary Roberts: *Tenting Tonight* (Boston: Houghton Mifflin, 1918).

Rinehart, Mary Roberts: *The Out Trail* (New York: George H. Doran, 1923).

Rinehart, Mary Roberts: *Through Glacier National Park in 1915,* reprint (Boulder, CO: Roberts, Rinehart, Inc., 1983).

Riney, Scott: *The Rapid City Indian School, 1898–1933* (Norman: University of Oklahoma Press, 1999).

Robbins, Jim: "Butte Breaks New Ground to Mop Up a World-Class Mess." *The New York Times* (July 21, 1998).

Robbins, William G.: *Hard Times in Paradise: Coos Bay, Oregon, 1850–1986* (Seattle: University of Washington Press, 1988).

Robbins, William G.: *Colony and Empire: The Capitalist Transformation of the American West* (Lawrence: University Press of Kansas, 1994).

Robbins, William G.: *Landscapes of Promise: The Oregon Story, 1800–1940* (Seattle: University of Washington Press, 1997).

Robbins, William G. and James C. Foster (eds.) *Land in the American West: Private Claims and the Common Good* (Seattle: University of Washington Press, 2000).

Roberts, Brian: *American Alchemy: The California Gold Rush and Middle-Class Culture* (Chapel Hill: University of North Carolina Press, 2000).

Roberts, David: *Once They Moved Like the Wind: Cochise, Geronimo, and the Apache Wars* (New York: Simon and Schuster, 1993).

Roberts, David: *A Newer World: Kit Carson, John C. Fremont and the Claiming of the American West* (New York: Simon and Schuster, 2000).

Robertson, Paul: *The Power of the Land: Identity, Ethnicity, and Class among the Oglala Lakota* (New York: Routledge, 2002).

Robertson, R.G.: *Competitive Struggle: America's Western Fur Trading Posts, 1764–1865* (Boise: Tamarack Books, 1999).

Rodarte, Irene: "Machismo vs. Revolution." In Dorinda Moreno (ed.) *La mujer en pie de lucha* (Mexico City: Espina del Norte Publications, 1973).

Rodgers, Daniel T.: *Atlantic Crossings: Social Politics in a Progressive Age* (Cambridge, MA: Harvard University Press, 1998).

Rodríguez, Clara A.: *Changing Race: Latinos, the Census, and the History of Ethnicity in the United States* (New York: New York University Press, 2000).

Rodriguez, Richard: *Hunger of Memory: The Education of Richard Rodriguez* (Boston: D. R. Godine, 1981).

Rodriguez, Richard: *Days of Obligation: An Argument with My Mexican Father* (New York: Viking, 1992)

Rogin, Michael Paul: *Fathers and Children: Andrew Jackson and the Subjugation of the American Indian* (New York: Alfred A. Knopf, 1975).

Rogin, Michael Paul and John L. Shover: *Political Change in California: Critical Elections and Social Movements, 1890–1966* (Westport, CT: Greenwood Press, 1970).

Rohe, Randall E.: "Hydraulicking in the American West: The Development and Diffusion of a Mining Technique." *Montana: The Magazine of Western History* (1985), 18–35.

Rohrbough, Malcolm J.: *The Land Office Business: The Settlement and Administration of American Public Lands, 1789–1837* (New York: Oxford University Press, 1968).

Rohrbough, Malcolm J.: *The Trans-Appalachian Frontier: People, Societies, and Institutions, 1775–1850* (New York: Oxford University Press, 1978).

Rohrbough, Malcolm J.: *Aspen: The History of a Silver Mining Town, 1879–1893* (New York: Oxford University Press, 1986).

Rohrbough, Malcolm J.: *Days of Gold. The California Gold Rush and the American Nation* (Berkeley: University of California Press, 1997)

Rolle, Andrew: *John Charles Fremont: Character as Destiny* (Norman: University of Oklahoma Press, 1991).

Rome, Adam: *Bulldozer in the Countryside: Suburban Sprawl and the Rise of American Environmentalism* (New York: Oxford University Press, 2001).

Romero, Mary: *Maid in the U.S.A* (New York: Routledge, 1992).

Romo, Ricardo: *East Los Angeles, History of a Barrio* (Austin: University of Texas Press, 1983).

Ronda, James P.: *Lewis and Clark among the Indians* (Lincoln: University of Nebraska Press, 1984).

Ronda, James P.: "Before Covered Wagons: The Early History of the Oregon Trail." *Idaho Yesterdays*, 37 (1993), 5–15.

Ronda, James P.: *Astoria and Empire* (Lincoln: University of Nebraska Press, 1990).

Ronda, James P.: *The Exploration of North America* (Washington, DC: American Historical Association, 1992).

Ronda, James P.: "Dreaming the Pass: The Western Imagination and the Landscape of South Pass." In Leonard Engel (ed.): *The Big Empty: Essays on the Land as Narrative* (Albuquerque: University of New Mexico Press, 1994).

Ronda, James P.: *Revealing America: Image and Imagination in the Exploration of North America* (Lexington: D.C. Heath, 1996).

Ronda, James P.: "A Promise of Rivers: Thomas Jefferson and the Exploration of Western Waterways." In Robert C. Ritchie and Paul A. Hutton (eds.) *Frontier and Region: Essays in Honor of Martin Ridge* (Albuquerque: University of New Mexico Press, 1997).

Ronda, James P.: "Exploring the American West in the Age of Jefferson." In John L. Allen (ed.) *The Continent Comprehended* (Lincoln: University of Nebraska Press, 1997).

Ronda, James P. (ed.): *Voyages of discovery: Essays on the Lewis and Clark Expedition* (Helena: Montana Historical Society Press, 1998).

Rony, Dorothy Fujita: *Facing America: Filipina/o Seattle, 1919–1941,* (Berkeley: University of California Press, forthcoming).

Rosa, Joseph G.: *The Gunfighter: Man or Myth?* (Norman, OK: University of Oklahoma Press, 1969).

Rosa, Joseph G.: *Wild Bill Hickok: The Man and his Myth* (Lawrence, KS: University Press of Kansas, 1996).

Rosaldo, Renato: "Imperialist Nostalgia." *Representations* 26 (Spring 1989), 107–22.

Rose, Mark: *Interstate: Express Highway Politics, 1941–1956* (Lawrence: University Press of Kansas, 1979).

Rosenbaum, Robert J.: *Mexicano Resistance in the Southwest: "The Sacred Right of Self-Preservation?"* (Austin: University of Texas Press, 1981).

Ross, Alexander: *Adventures of the First Settlers on the Oregon or Columbia River, 1810–1813* ([London: 1849], Lincoln: University of Nebraska Press, 1989).

Rothman, Hal K.: *Preserving Different Pasts: The American National Monuments* (Urbana: University of Illinois Press, 1989).

Rothman, Hal K.: *The Greening of America? Environmentalism in the United States Since 1945* (New York: Harcourt Brace, 1997).

Rothman, Hal K.: *Devil's Bargains: Tourism in the Twentieth-Century American West* (Lawrence, KS: University Press of Kansas, 1998).

Rothman, Hal K.: *Neon Metropolis: How Las Vegas Started the Twenty-First Century* (New York: Routledge, 2002).

Rothman, Hal K.:(ed.): *The Culture Of Tourism, The Tourism Of Culture* (Albuquerque, NM: University of New Mexico Press, 2003).

Rouse, Roger: "Mexican Migration and the Social Space of Postmodernism." *Diaspora* 1, 1 (1991), 8–23.

Rowley, William D.: "The West as a Laboratory and Mirror of Reform." In Gerald Nash and Richard Etulain (eds.) *The Twentieth-Century West: Historical Interpretations* (Albuquerque: University of New Mexico Press, 1989).

Ruby, Robert H. and John A. Brown: *Indians of the Pacific Northwest: A History* (Norman: University of Oklahoma Press, 1981).

Ruby, Robert H. and John A. Brown: *Indian Slavery in the Pacific Northwest* (Spokane, WA: A. H. Clark & Co., 1993).

Ruiz, Vicki: *Cannery Women, Cannery Lives: Mexican American Women, Unionization, and the California Food Processing Industry* (Albuquerque: University of New Mexico Press, 1987).

Ruiz, Vicki L. and Susan Tiano: *Women on the U.S-.-Mexico Border: Responses to Change* (Boston: Allen and Unwin, 1987).

Runte, Alfred: *National Parks: The American Experience*, 2nd edn. (Lincoln: University of Nebraska Press, 1987).

Runte, Alfred: *Trains of Discovery: Western Railroads and the National Parks* (Niwot, CO: Roberts Rinehart, 1994).

Rush, Richard: "Richard Rush to James Monroe, London, October 1, 1818." (The Papers of James Monroe: Library of Congress, Washington, DC).

Sánchez, George. *Becoming Mexican American: Ethnicity, Culture and Identity in Chicano Los Angeles, 1900–1945* (New York: Oxford University Press, 1993).

Sadler, Richard W. and Richard C. Roberts: *The Weber River Basin: Grass Roots Democracy and Water Development* (Logan: Utah State University Press, 1994).

Sahlins, Marshall: "Cosmologies of Capitalism: The Trans-Pacific Sector of 'The World System'." In Marshall Sahlins (ed.) *Culture in Practice: Selected Essays* (New York: Zone Books, 2000).

Saldívar, José David: *Border Matters: Remapping American Cultural Studies* (Berkeley: University of California Press, 1997).

Salyer, Lucy E.: *Laws Harsh as Tigers: Chinese Immigrants and the Shaping of Modern Immigration Law* (Chapel Hill, NC: University of North Carolina Press, 1995).

Sando, Joe S.: *Nee Hemish: A History of Jemez Pueblo* (Albuquerque: University of New Mexico Press, 1982).

Sankewicz, Robert M.: *Vigilantes in Gold Rush San Francisco* (Stanford, CA: Stanford University Press, 1985).

Sarasohn, David: "The Election of 1916: Realigning the Rockies." *Western Historical Quarterly* 11 (July 1980), 285–306.

Sargent, Aaron A.: "Irrigation and Drainage," *Overland Monthly* 8 (July 1886), 19.

Sarris, Greg: *Mabel McKay: Weaving the Dream* (Berkeley: University of California Press, 1994).

Sassen, Saskia: Globalization and Its Discontents: Essays on the New Mobility of People and Money (New York: New Press, 1998).

Savage, W. Sherman: *Blacks in the West* (Westport, CT: Greenwood Press, 1976).

Saxton, Alexander: *The Indispensable Enemy: Labor and the Anti-Chinese Movement in California* (Berkeley, CA: University of California Press, 1971).

Saxton, Alexander: *The Rise and Fall of the White Republic: Class Politics and Mass Culture in Nineteenth-Century America* (London: Verso, 1990).

Scales, James R. and Danney Goble: *Oklahoma Politics: A History* (Norman: University of Oklahoma Press, 1982).

Schafer, Joseph: "The Western Ocean as a Determinant in Oregon History." In H. Morse Stephens and Herbert E. Bolton (eds.) *The Pacific Ocean in History* (New York: MacMillan, 1917).

Schafer, Joseph: *A History of the Pacific Northwest* (New York: MacMillan Company, 1922).

Scharff, Virginia: "The Case for Domestic Feminism: Woman Suffrage in Wyoming." *Annals of Wyoming* 56, 2 (Fall 1984), 29–37.

Scharff, Virginia: "Mobility, Women, and the West." In Valerie J. Matsumoto and Blake Allmendinger (eds.) *Over the Edge: Remapping the American West* (Berkeley: University of California Press, 1999).

Scharff, Virginia: *Twenty Thousand Roads: Women, Movement, and the West* (Berkeley: University of California Press, 2003).

Scharnhorst, Gary: "In Defense of Western Literary Biography." *Western American Literature*, 33 (Winter 1999), 345–53.

Scheiber, Harry N. and Charles W. McCurdy: "Eminent Domain Law and Western Agriculture, 1849–1900." *Agricultural History* 49 (1975), 112–30.

Schlesinger, Arthur, Jr.: *The Disuniting of America* (New York: W. W. Norton, 1992).

Schlissel, Lillian: *Women's Diaries of the Westward Journey* (New York: Schocken Books, 1982).

Schlissel, Lillian and Catherine Lavender: *The Western Women's Reader* (New York: Harper Perennial, 2000).

Schlissel, Lillian, Vicki Ruiz, and Janice Monk (eds.) *Western Women: Their Land, Their Lives* (Albuquerque: University of New Mexico Press, 1988).

Schmitt, Peter J.: *Back to Nature: The Arcadian Myth in Urban America* (Baltimore: Johns Hopkins University Press, 1990).

Schuele, Donna C.: "Community Property Law and the Politics of Married Women's Rights in Nineteenth-Century California." *Western Legal History* 7 (Summer–Fall, 1994), 244–81.

Schulman, Bruce: *From Cotton Belt to Sunbelt: Federal Policy, Economic Development and the Transformation of the South, 1938–1980* (New York: Oxford University Press, 1990).

Schultz, Duane P.: *Month of the Freezing Moon: The Sand Creek Massacre* (New York: St Martin's Press, 1991).

Schusky, Ernest L.: *Political Organization of Native North Americans* (Washington, DC: University Press of America, 1980).

Schwantes, Carlos A.: "The Concept of the Wageworkers' Frontier: A Framework for Future Research." *Western Historical Quarterly* 18 (January 1987), 39–55.

Schwantes, Carlos A.: *Railroad Signature Across the Pacific Northwest* (Seattle: University of Washington Press, 1993).

Scott, Allen J. and Edward Soja (eds.): *The City: Los Angeles and Urban Theory at the End of the Twentieth Century* (Berkeley: University of California Press, 1996).

Scott, James C.: *Seeing Like a State: How Certain Schemes to Improve the Human Condition Have Failed* (New Haven: Yale University Press, 1998).

Seager, Richard Hughes: *The World's Parliament of Religions: The East/West Encounter, Chicago, 1893* (Bloomington: Indiana University Press, 1995).

Sears, David O. and Jack Citrin: *Tax Revolt: Something for Nothing in California* (Cambridge, MA: Harvard University Press, 1982).

Sears, John F.: *Sacred Places: American Tourist Attractions in the Nineteenth Century* (New York: Oxford University Press, 1989).

Secoy, Frank Raymond: *Changing Military Patterns of the Great Plains Indians* (Lincoln, NE: University of Nebraska Press, 1992).

Self, Robert: *American Babylon: Race and the Struggle for Postwar Oakland* (Princeton, NJ: Princeton University Press, 2003a).

Self, Robert: "California's Industrial Garden: Remaking Postwar Oakland and the Greater Bay Area." In Jefferson Cowie and Joseph Heathcott (eds.) *Beyond the Ruins: Deindustrialization and the Meanings of Modern America* (Ithaca: Cornell University Press, 2003b).

Sellars, Richard West: *Preserving Nature in the National Parks: A History* (New Haven: Yale University Press, 1997).

Sellers, Charles Grier: *James Knox Polk, Jacksonian: 1795–1843*, 2 vols. (Princeton: Princeton University Press, 1957).

Sellers, Charles Grier: *The Market Revolution: Jacksonian America, 1815–1846* (New York: Oxford University Press, 1991).

Shaffer, Marguerite S.: *America First: Tourism and National Identity, 1880–1940* (Washington, DC: Smithsonian Institution Press, 2001).

Shagun, Louis: "As U.S., Canadian Lawyers Wrangle, a Colorado Mine Emits Its Poisons." *Los Angeles Times* (March 3, 1998).

Shah, Nayan: *Contagious Divides: Epidemics and Race in San Francisco's Chinatown* (Berkeley: University of California Press, 2001).

Sharp, Paul F.: "Three Frontiers: Some Comparative Studies of Canadian, American, and Australian Settlement." *Pacific Historical Review* 24, 4 (1955), 369–77.

Sheidley, Nathaniel. "Unruly Men: Indians, Settlers, and the Ethos of Frontier Patriarchy in the Upper Tennessee Watershed, 1763–1815." (PhD dissertation: Princeton University, 1999).

Shelford, Victor: "Preservation of Natural Biotic Communities." *Ecology* 14 (1933), 240–5.

Sherow, James Earl: *Watering the Valley: Development along the High Plains Arkansas River, 1870–1950* (Lawrence: University Press of Kansas, 1990).

Shindo, Charles J.: *Dust Bowl Migrants in the American Imagination* (Lawrence, KS: University Press of Kansas, 1997).

Shinn, Charles H.: *Mining Camps: A Study in American Frontier Government* ed. Rodman W. Paul ([1885]; New York: Harper & Row, 1965).

Shipps, Jan: *Mormonism: The Story of A New Religious Tradition* (Urbana: University of Illinois Press, 1985).

Shipps, Jan: *Sojourner in the Promised Land: Forty Years Among the Mormons* (Urbana: University of Illinois Press, 2000).

Shoemaker, Nancy: "Urban Indians and Ethnic Choices: American Indian Organizations in Minneapolis, 1920–1950." *Western Historical Quarterly* 19 (November 1988), 431–48.

Shoemaker, Nancy (ed.): *Negotiators of Change: Historical Perspectives on Native American Women* (New York: Routledge, 1995).

Shoemaker, Nancy (ed.): *Clearing a Path: Theorizing a Past in Native American Studies* (New York: Routledge, 2002).

Sides, Josh: "Battle on the Home Front: African American Shipyard Workers in World War II Los Angeles." *California History* (Fall 1996), 250–63.

Sides, Josh: "'You understand my condition': The Civil Rights Congress in the Los Angeles African American Community, 1946–1952." *Pacific Historical Review* 67 (May 1998), 233–57.

Sides, Josh: *L.A. City Limits: African American Los Angeles from the Great Depression to the Present* (Berkeley: University of California Press, 2004).

Simonson, Harold P.: *Beyond the Frontier: Writers, Western Regionalism and a Sense of Place* (Fort Worth: Texas Christian University Press, 1989).

Simpson, Lee Michelle: *Selling the City: Women and the California City Growth Games* (PhD dissertation: University of California, Riverside, 1996).

Sitkoff, Harvard (ed.): *Fifty Years Later: The New Deal Evaluated* (New York: Alfred A. Knopf, 1985).

Sitton, Tom: *John Randolph Haynes: California Progressive* (Stanford: Stanford University Press, 1992).

Sklar, Martin J.: *The Corporate Reconstruction of American Capitalism, 1890–1916* (Cambridge: Cambridge University Press, 1988).

Skocpol, Theda and Kenneth Finegold: "State Capacity and Economic Intervention in the Early New Deal." *Political Science Quarterly*, 97, 2 (Summer 1982), 255–78.

Skogen, Larry C.: *Indian Depredation Claims, 1796–1920* (Norman, OK: University of Oklahoma Press, 1996).

Slatta, Richard W: "Comparative Frontier Social Life: Western Saloons and Argentine Pulperias." *Great Plains Quarterly* 7 (1987).

Slotkin, Richard: *Regeneration Through Violence: The Mythology of the American Frontier, 1600–1860* (Middletown, CT: Wesleyan Press, 1973).

Slotkin, Richard: *The Fatal Environment: The Myth of the Frontier in the Age of Industrialization, 1800–1890* (New York: Atheneum, 1985).

Slotkin, Richard: *Gunfighter Nation: The Myth of the Frontier in Twentieth-Century America* (New York: Atheneum, 1992).

Slotkin, Richard: "Buffalo Bill's 'Wild West' and the Mythologization of the American Empire." In Amy Kaplan and Donald E. Pease (eds.) *Cultures of United States Imperialism* (Durham, Duke University Press, 1993).

Smith, Duane: *Rocky Mountain Mining Camps: The Urban Frontier* (Bloomington: Indiana University Press, 1967).

Smith, Duane A.: *Silver Sage: The Story of Caribou, Colorado* (Boulder, CO: Pruett Publishing Co., 1974).

Smith, Duane A.: *Mining America: The Industry and the Environment, 1800–1980* (Lawrence: University Press of Kansas, 1987).

Smith, Gordon: "Dreams of Gold: Mining's Massive Scale." *San Diego Union-Tribune* (January 20, 1998).

Smith, Helena Huntington: *The War on Powder River* (New York: McGraw-Hill, 1966).

Smith, Henry Nash: *Virgin Land: The American West as Symbol and Myth* (Cambridge, MA: Harvard University Press, 1950).

Smith, Justin H.: *The War With Mexico* (New York: Macmillan, 1919).

Smith, Marian W; "The War Complex of the Plains Indians." *Proceedings of the American Philosophical Society* 78 (1937), 425–61.

Smith, Paul Chaat and Robert Warrior: *Like a Hurricane: The Indian Movement From Alcatraz to Wounded Knee* (New York: Basic Books, 1996).

Smith, Sherry L.: "Lost Soldiers: Re-Searching the Army in the American West." *Western Historical Quarterly* 29 (1998), 149–63.

Smith, William: *An Historical Account of the Expedition Against the Ohio Indians in the Year 1764* (Philadelphia: W. Bradford, 1765).

Smythe, William: *The Conquest of Arid America* (New York: The Macmillian Company, 1905).

Sneider, Allison Lee: "Reconstruction, Expansion, and Empire: The United States Woman Suffrage Movement and the Re-Making of National Political Community." (PhD dissertation: University of California at Los Angeles, 1999).

Snodgrass, Mary Ellen: *Encyclopedia of Frontier Literature* (Santa Barbara, CA: ABC-CLIO, 1997).

Sonenshein, Raphael: *Politics in Black and White: Race and Power in Los Angeles* (Princeton: Princeton University Press, 1993).

Sonnichsen, C. L.: *I'll Die Before I'll Run: The Story of the Great Feuds of Texas* (New York: Harper, 1951).

Sorkin, Michael: "See You in Disneyland." In Michael Sorkin (ed.) *Variations on a Theme Park: The New American City and the End of Public Space* (New York: Hill and Wang, 1992).

Spence, Clark C.: *British Investments and the American Mining Frontier, 1860–1901* (Ithaca: Cornell University Press, 1958).

Spence, Clark C.: *Mining Engineers and the American West: The Lace-Boot Brigade* (New Haven: Yale University Press, 1970).

Spence, Mark David: *Dispossessing the Wilderness: Indian Removal and the Making of the National Parks* (New York: Oxford University Press, 1999).

Spicer, Edward H.: *Cycles of Conquest: The Impact of Spain, Mexico, and the United States on the Indians of the Southwest, 1533–1960* (Tucson: University of Arizona Press, 1962).

St Clair, David J.: "The Gold Rush and the Beginnings of California Industry." In James J. Rawls and Richard J. Orsi (eds.) *A Golden State: Mining and Economic Development in Gold Rush California in California History* (Berkeley: University of California Press, 1998/99).

Stannard, David E.: *Before the Horror: The Population of Hawai'i on the Eve of Western Contact* (Honolulu: University of Hawaii Press, 1989).

Starita, Joe: *The Dull Knifes of Pine Ridge: A Lakota Odyssey* (New York: G. P. Putnam's Sons, 1995).

Starr, Kevin. *Material Dreams: Southern California Through the 1920s* (New York: Oxford University Press, 1990).

Starr, Kevin: *Endangered Dreams: The Great Depression in California* (New York: Oxford University Press, 1996).

Starr, Kevin: *The Dream Endures: California Enters the 1940s* (New York: Oxford University Press, 1997).

Stauffer, Helen Winter and Susan Rosowski: *Women and Western American Literature* (Troy, NY: Whitstone, 1982).

Stefanco, Carolyn: "Networking on the Frontier: The Colorado Women's Suffrage Movement, 1876–1893." In Susan Armitage and Elizabeth Jameson (eds.) *The Women's West* (Norman: University of Oklahoma Press, 1987).

Stegner, Wallace: *The Gathering of Zion: The Story of the Mormon Trail* (New York: McGraw Hill, 1964).

Stegner, Wallace: *Angle of Repose* (New York: Doubleday, 1971).

Stegner, Wallace: *Where the Bluebird Sings to the Lemonade Springs: Living and Writing in the American West* (New York: Henry Holt, 1992).

Stegner, Wallace and Richard W. Etulain: *Stegner: Conversations on History and Literature* (Reno: University of Nevada Press, 1996).

Stegner, Wallace: *Marking the Sparrows Fall: The Making of the American West* (New York: Henry Holt, 1998).

Steinbeck, John: *The Grapes of Wrath* (New York: Viking, 1939).

Steinbeck, John: *Cannery Row* (New York: Viking, 1945).

Steinbeck, John: *The Harvest Gypsies: On the Road to The Grapes of Wrath* (Berkeley, CA: Heydey Books, 1996).

Steiner, Michael C.: "Frontierland as Tomorrowland: Walt Disney and the Architectural Packaging of the Mythic West." *Montana* 48 (Spring 1998), 2–17.

Stephanson, Anders: *Manifest Destiny: American Expansionism and the Empire of Right* (New York: Hill and Wang, 1995).

Stephens, H. Morse and Herbert E. Bolton (eds.) *The Pacific Ocean in History* (New York: MacMillan, 1917).

Stern, Alexandra: *Eugenics Beyond Borders: Science and Medicalization in Mexico and the United States West, 1900–1950* (PhD dissertation: University of Chicago, 1999).

Stevens, Todd: "Tender Ties: Husbands' Rights and Racial Exclusion in Chinese Marriage Cases, 1882–1924." *Law and Social Inquiry* 27, 2 (Spring 2002), 271–305.

Stewart, Elinore Pruitt: *Letters of a Woman Homesteader* (Lincoln: University of Nebraska Press, 1961).

Stewart, George R.: *Committee of Vigilance: Revolution in San Francisco, 1851* (Boston: Houghton Mifflin, 1964).

Stilgoe, John R.: *Metropolitan Corridor: Railroads and the American Scene* (New Haven: Yale University Press, 1983).

Stoddard, Ellwyn R. *U.S.–Mexico Borderlands Studies: An Inventory of Scholars, Appraisal of Funding Resources, and Research Prospects* (El Paso: Univerisyt of Texas at El Paso, Center for Inter-American Studies, 1974).

Stoddard, Ellwyn R. and Richard L. Nostrand (eds.): *Borderlands Sourcebook: A Guide to the Literature on Northern Mexico and the American Southwest* (Norman: University of Oklahoma Press, 1983).

Stoeltje, Beverly: "A Helpmate for Man Indeed: The Image of the Frontier Woman." *Journal of American Folklore* 88, 347 (January–March 1975), 27–31.

Stoll, Steven: *The Fruits of Natural Advantage: Making the Industrial Countryside in California* (Berkeley: University of California Press, 1998).

Storper, Michael and Richard Walker: *The Capitalist Imperative: Territory, Technology, and Industrial Growth* (New York: Oxford University Press, 1989).

Storti, Craig: *Incident at Bitter Creek: The Story of the Rock Springs Chinese Massacre* (Ames: Iowa State University Press, 1991).

Strickland, Rennard: *Fire and the Spirits: Cherokee Law from Clan to Court* (Norman, OK: University of Oklahoma Press, 1975).

Strickland, Rennard: *The Indians in Oklahoma* (Norman: University of Oklahoma Press, 1980).

Sturtevant, William C. (gen. ed.): *Handbook of North American Indians*, 20 vols. (Washington DC: Smithsonian Institution, 1978–present).

Svensson, Frances: "The Final Crisis of Tribalism: Comparative Ethnic Policy on the American and Russian Frontiers." *Ethnic and Racial Studies* 1, 1 (1978), 100–23.

Swagerty, William R.: "Marriage and Settlement Patterns of Rocky Mountain Trappers and Traders." *Western Historical Quarterly* 11, 2 (April 1980), 150–80.

Swagerty, William. R. (ed.): *Scholars and the Indian Experience: Critical Reviews of Recent Writing in the Social Sciences* (Bloomington: Indiana University Press, 1984).

Sweeney, Judith: "Chicana History: A Review of the Literature." In Rosaura Sánchez (ed.) *Essays on La Mujer* (Los Angeles: UCLA Chicano Studies Research Center Publications, 1977).

Sweet, William Warren: *Religion on the American Frontier: The Baptists, 1783–1830* (New York: Henry Holt & Co., 1931).

Sweet, William Warren: *Religion on the American Frontier: The Presbyterians, 1783–1840* (New York: Harper Brothers, 1936).

Sweet, William Warren: *Religion on the American Frontier: The Congregationalists, 1783–1850* (Chicago: University of Chicago Press, 1939).

Sweet, William Warren: *Religion on the American Frontier: The Methodists, 1783–1840* (New York: Henry Holt & Co., 1946).

Sweet, William Warren: *The American Churches, An Interpretation* (New York: Abingdon-Cokesbury Press, 1947).

Sword, Wiley: *President Washington's Indian War: The Struggle for the Old Northwest, 1790–1795* (Norman: University of Oklahoma Press, 1985).

Szabo, Joyce: *Howling Wolf and the History of Ledger Art* (Albuquerque: University of New Mexico Press, 1994).

Szasz, Ferenc Morton: *Religion in the Modern American West* (Tucson: The University of Arizona Press, 2000).

Szasz, Margaret Connell: *Between Indian and White Worlds: The Cultural Broker* (Norman: University of Oklahoma Press, 1994).

Takaki, Ronald: *Strangers from a Different Shore* (Boston: Little, Brown and Company, 1989).

Tan, Amy: *The Joy Luck Club* (New York: Putnam's, 1989).

Taussig, Rudolf J.: "The American Inter-Oceanic Land: An Historical Sketch of the Canal Idea." In H. Morse Stephens and Herbert E. Bolton (eds.) *The Pacific Ocean in History* (New York: MacMillan, 1917), 114–36.

Taylor, Alan: *William Cooper's Town: Power and Persuasion on the Frontier of the Early American Republic* (New York: Alfred A. Knopf, 1995).

Taylor, Alan: "'Wasty Ways': Stories of American Settlement." *Environmental History* 3 (1998), 291–310.

Taylor, Alan: *American Colonies* (New York: Viking, 2001).

Taylor, Graham D.: *The New Deal and American Indian Tribalism: The Administration of the Indian Reorganization Act, 1934–45* (Lincoln: University of Nebraska Press, 1980).

Taylor, Joseph E., III: *Making Salmon: An Environmental History of the Northwest Fisheries Crisis* (Seattle: University of Washington Press, 1999).

Taylor, Quintard: "The Emergence of Black Communities in the Pacific Northwest, 1865–1910." *Journal of Negro History* 64, 4 (Fall, 1979), 342–51.

Taylor, Quintard: "the Great Migration: The Afro-American Communities of Seattle and Portland during the 1940s." *Arizona and the West* 23, 2 (Summer 1981), 109–26.

Taylor, Quintard: "Blacks and Asians in a White City: Japanese Americans and African Americans in Seattle, 1890–1940." *Western Historical Quarterly* 22, 4 (November 1991) 401–29.

Taylor, Quintard: "Reflections on Two Decades in Pursuit of African American History in the Pacific Northwest." In Linda Harris, Joseph Franklin, and Stephen McPherson (eds.) *Voices of Kuumba III: An Anthology of the Northwest African American Writers Workshop* (Portland OR: Portland Public Schools, 1991).

Taylor, Quintard: *The Forging of a Black Community: Seattle's Central District, from 1870 through the Civil Rights Era* (Seattle: University of Washington Press, 1994).

Taylor, Quintard: "The Civil Rights Movement in the American West: Black Protest in Seattle, 1960–1970." *The Journal of Negro History* 80, 1 (1995), 1–14.

Taylor, Quintard : *In Search of the Racial Frontier: African Americans in the American West, 1528–1990* (New York: W.W. Norton, 1998).

Taylor, Quintard and Shirley Anne Wilson Moore: *African American Women in the American West* (Norman: University of Oklahoma Press, 1999).

Taylor, Quintard and Shirley Anne Wilson Moore: *African American Women Confront the West, 1600–2000* (Norman: University of Oklahoma Press, 2003).

Taylor, William B.: *Drinking, Homicide, and Rebellion in Colonial Mexican Villages* (Stanford, CA: Stanford University Press, 1979).

Telles, Edward A. and Edward Murguía: "Phenotypic Discrimination and Income Differences Among Mexican Americans." *Social Science Quarterly* 71 (1990), 682–96.

Thomas, Clive S. (ed.): *Politics and Public Policy in the Contemporary American West* (Albuquerque: University of New Mexico Press, 1991).

Thomas, David Hurst (ed.): *Archeological and Historical Perspectives on the Spanish Borderlands East*, vol. 2 of *Columbian Consequences* (Washington, DC: Smithsonian Institution Press, 1990).

Thompson, Sharon Elaine: "Roots of the Turquoise Trade." *Lapidary Journal* (1966).

Thornton, Russell: *We Shall Live Again: The 1870 and 1890 Ghost Dance Movements as Demographic Revitalization* (New York: Cambridge University Press, 1986).

Thornton, Russell: *American Indian Holocaust and Survival: A Population History since 1492* (Norman: University of Oklahoma Press, 1987).

Thornton, Russell (ed.): *Studying Native America: Problems and Prospects* (Madison: University of Wisconsin Press, 1998).

Tijerina, Andres: *Tejano Empire: Life on the South Texas Ranchos* (College Station: Texas A&M University Press, 1998).

Tiller, Veronica Velarde: *The Jicarilla Apache Tribe: A History, 1846–1970* (Lincoln: University of Nebraska Press, 1983).

Tiller, Veronica Velarde: *The Jicarilla Apache Tribe: A History, 1846–1970* (Lincoln: University of Nebraska Press, 1983).

Timberlake, James: *Prohibition and the Progressive Movement, 1900–1920.* (Cambridge, MA: Harvard University Press, 1963).

Tolbert, Emory J.: *The U.N.I.A. and Black Los Angeles: Ideology and Community in the American Garvey Movement* (Los Angeles: UCLA Center for Afro-American Studies, 1980).

Toll, William: *The Making of an Ethnic Middle Class: Portland's Jewry over Four Generations* (Albany: State University of New York Press, 1982).

Tompkins, Jane: *West of Everything: The Inner Life of Westerns* (New York: Oxford University Press, 1992).

Tong, Benson: *Unsubmissive Women: Chinese Prostitutes in Nineteenth-Century San Francisco* (Norman: University of Oklahoma Press, 1994).

Torres, Rodolfo D., Louis F. Mirón, and Jonathan Xavier Inda (eds.) *Race, Identity, and Citizenship: A Reader* (Malden, MA: Blackwell Publishers, 1999).

Trachtenberg, Alan: *The Incorporation of America: Culture and Society in the Gilded Age* (New York: Hill and Wang, 1982).

Trafzer, Clifford: *The Kit Carson Campaign: The Last Great Navajo War* (Norman, OK: University of Oklahoma Press, 1990).

Traub, Stuart H.: "Rewards, Bounty Hunting, and Criminal Justice in the West: 1856–1900." *Western Historical Quarterly* 19 (August, 1988), 287–301.

Treadwell, Edward F.: *The Cattle King: A Dramatized Biography* (New York, Macmillan, 1931).

Trennert, Robert A., Jr.: *The Phoenix Indian School: Forced Assimilation in Arizona, 1891–1935* (Norman: University of Oklahoma Press, 1984).

Trigger, Bruce G.: *Natives and Newcomers: Canada's "Heroic Age" Reconsidered* (Kingston, Ontario: McGill-Queen's University Press, 1986).

Trimble, Stephen: *The People: Indians of the American Southwest* (Santa Fe: School of American Research Press, 1993).

Truett, Samuel: "Neighbors by Nature: Rethinking Region, Nation, and Environmental History in the U.S.–Mexico Borderlands." *Environmental History* 2 (1997), 160–78.

Truettner, William H. (ed.): *The West as America: Reinterpreting Images of the Frontier, 1820–1920* (Washington, DC: Smithsonian Institution Press, 1991).

Truettner, William H.: "Ideology and Image: Justifying Westward Expansion." Introduction to William H. Truettner (ed.) *The West as America: Reinterpreting Images of the Frontier, 1820–1920* (Washington, DC: Smithsonian Institution Press, 1991).

Truettner, William H.: "Prelude to Expansion: Repainting the Past." In William H. Truettner (ed.) *The West as America: Reinterpreting Images of the Frontier, 1820–1920* (Washington, DC: Smithsonian Institution Press, 1991), 55–96.

Tsai, Shih-shan Henry: *China and the Overseas Chinese in the United States 1868–1911* (Fayetteville: University of Arkansas Press, 1983).

Tsai, Shih-shan Henry: "Chinese Immigration, 1848–1882." In Sucheng Chan, Douglas Henry Daniels, Mario T. Garcia, and Terry P. Wilson (eds.) *People of Color in the American West* (Lexington, MA: D.C. Heath and Company, 1994).

Tuan, Yi-fu: *Topophilia: A Study of Environmental Perception, Attitudes, and Values* (Englewood Cliffs, NJ: Prentice Hall, 1974).

Tuan, Yi-Fu: "Humanistic Geography," *Annals of the Association of American Geographers* 66, 2 (June 1976), 266–76.

Tuan, Yi-fu: *Space and Place: The Perspective of Experience* (Minneapolis: University of Minnesota Press, 1977).

Tugwell, Rexford G.: *The Battle for Democracy* (New York: Columbia University Press, 1935).

Turner, Frederick Jackson: "The Significance of the Frontier in American History." American Historical Association *Annual Report* (1893), 199–227.

Turner, Frederick Jackson: *Rediscovering America: John Muir in His Time and Ours* (San Francisco: Sierra Club Books, 1985).

Turner, Frederick Jackson: "The Significance of the Frontier in American History." In John Mack Faragher (ed.) *Rereading Frederick Jackson Turner:"The Significance of the Frontier in American History" and Other Essays* (New York: Henry Holt and Co., 1994).

Turner, Frederick Jackson: "Sections and Nation." In John Mack Faragher (ed.) *Rereading Frederick Jackson Turner:"The Significance of the Frontier in American History" and Other Essays* (New York: Henry Holt and Co., 1994).

Turner, Frederick Jackson: "The Significance of Sections in American History." In John Mack Faragher (ed.) *Rereading Frederick Jackson Turner:"The Significance of the Frontier in American History" and Other Essays* (New York: Henry Holt and Co., 1994).

Tuska, Jon and Vicki Piekarski (eds.): *The Frontier Experience: A Reader's Guide to the Life and Literature of the American West* (Jefferson, NC: McFarland and Co., Inc., 1984).

Twain, Mark. *Roughing It* (New York: Houghton Mifflin Co., 1980).

Tweed, Thomas A.: "Introduction: Narrating U.S. Religious History." In Thomas A. Tweed *Retelling U.S. Religious History* (Berkeley: University of California Press, 1997).

Tyau, Kathleen: "The City I Colored White." In Kathleen Tyau *A Little Too Much is Enough* (New York: Farrar, Straus and Giroux, 1995).

Tyrrell, Ian: "American Exceptionalism in an Age of International History." *American Historical Review* 96 (1991), 1031–72.

Umbeck, John R.: *A Theory of Property Rights: With Application to the California Gold Rush* (Ames, IA: Iowa State University Press, 1981).

Umphrey, Martha Merrill: "The Dialogics of Legal Meaning: Spectacular Trials, the Unwritten Law, and Narratives of Criminal Responsibility." *Law and Society Review* 33 (1999), 393–423.

Unruh, John D. Jr.: *The Plains Across: The Overland Emigrants and the Trans-Mississippi West, 1840–1860* (Urbana, IL: University of Illinois Press, 1979).

Urrea, Luis Alberto: *Nobody's Son: Notes from an American Life* (Tucson: University of Arizona Press, 1998).

Usner, Daniel H., Jr.: *Indians, Settlers, and Slaves in a Frontier Exchange Economy: The Lower Mississippi Valley before 1783* (Chapel Hill: University of North Carolina Press, 1992).

Utley, Robert M.: *The Last Days of the Sioux Nation* (New Haven, CT: Yale University Press, 1963).

Utley, Robert M.: *Frontiersmen in Blue: The United States Army and the Indian, 1848–1865* (New York: Macmillan, 1967).

Utley, Robert M.: *Frontier Regulars: The United States Army and the Indian, 1866–1891* (New York: Macmillan, 1973).

Utley, Robert M.: *A Clash of Cultures: Fort Bowie and the Chiricahua Apaches* (Washington, DC: Department of the Interior, National Park Service, Division of Publications, 1977).

Utley, Robert M.: *The Indian Frontier of the American West, 1846–1890* (Albuquerque: University of New Mexico Press, 1984).

Utley, Robert M.: *Billy the Kid: A Short and Violent Life* (Lincoln, NE: University of Nebraska Press, 1989).

Utley, Robert M.: *A Life Wild and Perilous: Mountain Men and the Path to the Pacific* (New York: Henry Holt and Co., 1997).

Valdes Fallis, Guadalupe: "The Liberated Chicana: A Struggle against Tradition." *Women: A Journal of Liberation* 3, 4 (1974): 20–21.

Valdez, Luis and Stan Steiner (eds.): *Atzlan: An Anthology of Mexican American Literature* (New York: Knopf, 1972).

Van Alstyne, Richard: *The Rising American Empire* (New York: Oxford University Press, 1960).

Vancouver, George: *A Voyage of Discover to the North Pacific Ocean and Round the World, 1791–1795*, 4 vols. ed. W. Kaye Lamb (Cambridge: The Hakluyt Society, 1984).

Vandal, Gilles. *Rethinking Southern Violence: Homicides in Post-Civil War Louisiana, 1866–1884* (Columbus, OH: Ohio State University Press, 2000).

van der Woude, A. M., Akira Hayami, and Jan de Vries (eds.): *Urbanization in History: A Process of Dynamic Interactions* (New York: Oxford University Press, 1990).

Van de Water, Frederic F.: *The Family Flivvers to Frisco* (New York: D. Appleton & Company, 1927).

Van Kirk, Sylvia: *"Many Tender Ties": Women in Fur Trade Society in Western Canada, 1670–1870* (Norman: University of Oklahoma Press, 1980).

Van Orman, Richard: *The Explorers: Nineteenth Century Expeditions in Africa and North America* (Albuquerque: University of New Mexico Press, 1984).

Van Wagenen, Lola: "In Their Own Behalf: The Politicization of Mormon Women and the 1870 Franchise." *Dialogue: A Journal of Mormon Thought* 24, 4 (Winter 1991), 31–43.

Vaughan, Benjamin F., IV: "Property-rights problems and Institutional Solutions: Water Rights and Water Allocation in the Nineteenth-Century American West." (PhD dissertation: University of California, Berkeley, 1997).

Vaughan, Tom: "Bisbee's Transition Years, 1899–1918." *Cochise Quarterly* 14 (1984), 4–7.

Vaught, David: *Cultivating California: Growers, Specialty Crops, and Labor, 1875–1920* (Baltimore: Johns Hopkins University Press, 1999).

Vestal, Stanley: *Warpath and Council Fire: The Plains Indians' Struggle for Survival in War and in Diplomacy, 1851–1891* (New York: Random House, 1948).

Vevier, Charles: "American Continentalism: An Idea of Expansion, 1845–1910." *American Historical Review* 65, 2 (1960), 323–35.

Vicenti-Carpio, Myla Thyrza: "'Let Them Know We Still Exist': Indians in Albuquerque." (PhD dissertation, Arizona State University, 2001).

Vidal, Mirta: *Chicanas Speak Out* (New York: Pathfinder Press, 1971).

Viehe, Fred: "The First Recall: Los Angeles Urban Reform or Machine Politics?" *Southern California Quarterly* 70 (1988), 1–28.

Vigil, James Diego: *From Indians to Chicanos: The Dynamics of Mexican American Culture* (St Louis: C.V. Mosby Co., 1980).

Vila, Pablo Sergio: "Everyday Life, Culture, and Identity on the Mexican-American Border: the Ciudad Juárez-El Paso Case." (PhD Thesis, University of Texas, 1994).

Vivekananda: "Hinduism." In John Henry Barrows (ed.) *The World's Parliament of Religions: An Illustrated and Popular Story of the World's Parliament of Religions, Held in Chicago in Connection with the World's Columbian Exposition,* 2 vols. (Chicago: Parliament Publishing Co., 1893).

Voynick, Stephen: *The Making of a Hardrock Miner: An Account of the Experiences of a Worker in Copper, Molybdenum, and Uranium Mines in the West* (Berkeley, CA: Howell-North Books, 1978).

Wade, Richard: *The Urban Frontier: The Rise of Western Cities, 1790–1830* (Cambridge, MA: Harvard University Press, 1959).

Walker, Rander Jones: "Liberators for Colonial Anahuac: A Rumination on North American Civil Religions." *Religion and American Culture: A Journal of Interpretation* 9, 2 (1999), 183–203.

Walker, Richard: "California's Debt to Nature: Nature Resources and the Golden Road to Capitalist Growth, 1848–1940." *Annals of the American Association of Geographers* (forthcoming).

Wall, Wendy L.: "Gender and the 'Citizen Indian'." In Elizabeth Jameson and Susan Armitage (eds.) *Writing the Range: Race, Class, and Culture in the Women's West* (Norman: University of Oklahoma Press, 1997).

Wallace, Anthony F. C.: *Jefferson and the Indians: The Tragic Fate of the First Americans* (Cambridge, MA: Harvard University Press, 1999).

Wallace, Mike: "Mickey Mouse History: Portraying the Past at Disney World." In Mike Wallace *Mickey Mouse History and Other Essays on American Memory* (Philadelphia: Temple University Press, 1996).

Wallach, Alan: "The Battle over 'The West as America.'" In Alan Wallach *Exhibiting Contradiction: Essays on the Art Museum in the United States* (Amherst: University of Massachusetts Press, 1998).

Warren, Louis: *The Hunter's Game: Poachers and Conservationists in Twentieth-Century America* (New Haven: Yale University Press, 1997).

Washburn, Wilcomb E.: *"The Writing of American Indian History: A Status Report."* Pacific *Historical Review* 40 (August 1971), 261–81.

Watkins, Marilyn P.: *Rural Democracy: Family Farmers and Politics in Western Washington, 1890–1925* (Ithaca: Cornell University Press, 1995).

Watson, J. Wreford: "The Role of Illusion in North America Geography." *Canadian Geographer* 13 (1969), 10–27.

Watts, Steven: *The Magic Kingdom: Walt Disney and the American Way of Life* (Boston: Houghton Mifflin, 1997).

Webb, Walter Prescott: *The Great Plains* (New York: Grosset & Dunlap, 1931).

Webb, Walter Prescott: *Divided We Stand: The Crisis of a Frontierless Democracy* (New York: Farrar and Rinehart, 1937).

Webb, Walter Prescott: *The Great Frontier* ([1931], Boston: Houghton Mifflin, 1952).

Webb, Walter Prescott: "The American West: Perpetual Mirage." *Harper's Magazine* 214 (1957), 25–31.

Weber, David J.: *The Taos Trappers: The Fur Trade in the Far Southwest, 1540–1846* (Norman: University of Oklahoma Press, 1971).

Weber, David J.: *The Mexican Frontier, 1821–1846: The American Southwest under Mexico* (Albuquerque, NM: University of New Mexico Press, 1982).

Weber, David. "Turner, the Boltonians, and the Borderlands," *American Historical Review*, 91 (January 1986), 66–81.

Weber, David J.: *The Spanish Frontier in North America* (New Haven, CT: Yale University Press, 1992).

Weber, Devra: *Dark Sweat, White Gold: California Farm Workers, Cotton, and the New Deal* (Berkeley: University of California Press, 1994).

Weigle, Marta: "From Desert to Disney World: The Santa Fe Railway and the Fred Harvey Company Display the Indian Southwest." *Journal of Anthropological Research* 45 (1989), 115–37.

Weigle, Marta: "Southwest Lures: Innocents Detoured, Incensed, Determined." *Journal of the Southwest* 32 (1990): 499–540.

Weigle, Marta: "Exposition and Mediation: Mary Colter, Erna Fergusson, and the Santa Fe/Harvey Popularization of the Native Southwest, 1902–1940." *Frontiers: A Journal of Women Studies* 12 (Summer 1991), 117–50.

Weigle, Marta and Kathleen L. Howard: "'To *experience* the real Grand Canyon': Santa Fe/Harvey Panopticism, 1910–1935". In Marta Weigle and Barbara Babcock (eds.) *The Great Southwest of the Fred Harvey Company and the Santa Fe Railway* (Phoenix: The Heard Museum, 1996).

Weinberg, Albert K.: *Manifest Destiny: A Study of Nationalist Expansionism in American History* (Baltimore: The Johns Hopkins Press, 1935).

Weiner, Lynn Y.: "There is Great Big Beautiful Tomorrow: Historic Memory and Gender in Walt Disney's Carousel of Progress." *Journal of Popular Culture* 20, 1 (1997): 111–16.

Weinstein, Raymond M.: "Disneyland and Coney Island: Reflections of the Evolution of the Modern Amusement Park." *Journal of Popular Culture* 26, 1 (1992), 131–64.

Weir, Darlene Godat: *Leadville's Ice Palace: A Colossus in the Colorado Rockies* (Lakewood, CO: Ice Castle Editions, 1994).

Weiselberg, Erik Lawrence: "Ascendancy of the Mazamas: Environment, Identity and Mountain Climbing in Oregon, 1870 to 1930." (PhD dissertation: University of Oregon, 1999).

Welch, James: *Fools Crow* (New York: Viking Penguin, 1986).

West, Elliott: *Growing Up With the Country: Childhood on the Far Western Frontier* (Albuquerque: University of New Mexico Press, 1989).

West, Elliott: "Stories." In Elliott West (ed.) *The Way to the West: Essays on the Central Plains* (Albuquerque: University of New Mexico Press, 1995).

West, Elliott: "Selling the Myth: Western Themes in Advertising." *Montana: The Magazine of Western History* (Summer 1996), 36–50.

West, Elliott: *The Contested Plain: Indians, Goldseekers, and the Rush to Colorado* (Lawrence: University of Kansas Press, 1998).

West, Elliott: *The Way to the West: Essays on the Central Plains* (Albuquerque: University of New Mexico Press, 1995).

Wheat, Carl I. (ed.): *Mapping the Trans-Mississippi West*, 5 vols. (San Francisco: Institute of Historical Cartography, 1958–62).

Wheeler, B. Gordon: *Black California: The History of African Americans in the Golden State* (New York: Hippocrene Books, 1993).

Wheeler, Kenneth: *To Wear a City's Crown: The Beginnings of Urban Growth in Texas, 1836–1965* (Cambridge: Harvard University Press, 1968).

White, Evelyn C.: "Black Women and the Wilderness." In Teresa Jordan and James Hepworth (eds.): *The Stories that Shape Us: Contemporary Women Write About the West* (New York: W. W. Norton, 1995).

White, Richard: "The Winning of the West: The Expansion of the Western Sioux in the Eighteenth and Nineteenth Centuries." *Journal of American History* 65 (1978).

White, Richard: *Land Use, Environment, and Social Change: The Shaping of Island County, Washington* (Seattle: University of Washington Press, 1980).

White, Richard: *The Roots of Dependency: Subsistence, Environment, and Social Change Among the Choctaws, Pawnees, and Navajos* (Lincoln: University of Nebraska Press, 1983).

White, Richard: "American Environmental History: The Development of a New Historical Field." *Pacific Historical Review* 54 (1985), 297–335.

White, Richard: *"It's Your Misfortune and None of My Own": A History of the American West* (Norman, OK: University of Oklahoma Press: 1991).

White, Richard: *The Middle Ground: Indians, Empires, and Republics in the Great Lakes Region, 1650–1815* (New York: Cambridge University Press, 1991).

White, Richard: "Discovering Nature in North America." *Journal of American History* 79:3 (December 1992), 877.

White, Richard: "Animals and Enterprise." In Clyde A. Milner, Carol A. O'Connor, and Martha A. Sandweiss (eds.) *The Oxford History of the American West* (New York: Oxford University Press, 1994).

White, Richard: *The Organic Machine: The Remaking of the Columbia River* (New York: Hill and Wang, 1995).

White, Richard: "The Gold Rush: Consequences and Contingencies." *California History* 77 (Spring 1998), 43–54.

White, Richard: "The Nationalization of Nature." *Journal of American History* 86 (Dec. 1999), 976–84.

White, Richard and Patricia Nelson Limerick: "Frederick Jackson Turner and Buffalo Bill." In James R. Grossman (ed.) *The Frontier in American Culture* (Berkeley: University of California Press, 1994).

Whitehead, John S.: "Hawai'i: The First and Last Far West?" *Western Historical Quarterly* 23, 2 (1992): 153–77.

Whitehead, John S.: "The Frontier Legacy in the Pacific Basin." In Arrell Morgan Gibson *Yankees in Paradise: The Pacific Basin Frontier* (Albuquerque: University of New Mexico Press, 1993).

Whitehead, John S.: "Noncontiguous Wests: Alaska and Hawai'i." In David M. Wrobel and Michael C. Steiner (eds.) *Many Wests: Culture and Regional Identity* (Lawrence: University Press of Kansas, 1997).

Wickens, James F.: *Colorado in the Great Depression* (New York: Garland, 1979).

Wiebe, Robert H.: *The Search for Order, 1877–1920* (New York: Hill and Wang, 1967).

Wiley, Peter and Robert Gottlieb: *Empires in the Sun: The Rise of the New American West* (Tucson: University of Arizona Press, 1982).

Wilkins, David E.: *American Indian Sovereignty and the U.S. Supreme Court: The Masking of Justice* (Austin: University of Texas Press, 1997).

Wilkins, David E. and K. Tsianina Lomawaima: *Uneven Ground: American Indian Sovereignty and Federal Law.* Norman: University of Oklahoma Press, 2001).

Wilkinson, Charles F.: *Crossing the Next Meridian: Land, Water, and the Future of the West* (Washington, DC: Island Press, 1992).

Wilkinson, Charles: *Eagle Bird: Mapping a New West* (New York: Pantheon, 1992).

Wilkinson, Charles: *Fire on the Plateau: Conflict and Endurance in the American Southwest* (Washington, DC: Island Press, 1999).

Williams, Michael: *Americans and Their Forests: A Historical Geography* (Cambridge: Cambridge University Press, 1989).

Williams, Peter W.: *America's Religions: Traditions and Cultures* (New York: MacMillan Publishing Company, 1990).

Williams, Peter W.: *Houses of God: Region, Religion and Architecture in the United States* (Urbana, IL: University of Illinois Press, 1997).

Williams, Raymond: *Keywords: A Vocabulary of Culture and Society* (New York: Oxford University Press, 1985).

Williams, Ted: "Killer Weeds." *Audubon* 99 (March–April 1997), 22–8.

Williams, William Appleman: "The Frontier Thesis and Foreign Policy." *Pacific Historical Review* 24, 4 (1955) 379–95.

Williams, Walter L.: "United States Indian Policy and the Debate over Philippine Annexation: Implications for the Origins of American Imperialism." *Journal of American History*, 66, 4 (1980): 810–31.

Williams, William Appelman: *The Roots of Modern American Empire: A Study of the Growth and Shaping of Social Consciousness in a Marketplace Society* (New York: Random House, 1969).

Wills, Morris W.: "Sequential Frontiers: The Californian and Victorian Experience, 1850–1900." *Western Historical Quarterly* 9, 4 (1978): 483–94.

Wilson, Gilbert L.: *Goodbird the Indian: His Story* ([1914], rpt. St. Paul: Minnesota Historical Society Press, 1965).

Wilson, Gilbert L.: *Buffalo Bird Woman's Garden* ([1917], rpt. St. Paul: Minnesota Historical Society Press, 1987).

Wilson, Gilbert L.: *Waheenee: An Indian Girl's Story* ([1921], rpt. Lincoln: University of Nebraska Press, 1981).

Wilson, James: *The Earth Shall Weep: A History of Native America* (New York: Grove Press, 1998).

Wilson, Raymond: *Ohiyesa: Charles Eastman, Santee Sioux* (Urbana: University of Illinois Press, 1983).

Wilson, William: *Hamilton Park: A Planned Black Community in Dallas* (Baltimore: Johns Hopkins University Press, 1998).

Winter, Irene J.: "The Affective Properties of Styles: An Inquiry into Analytic Process and the Inscription of Meaning in Art History." In Caroline A. Jones and Peter Galison (eds.) *Picturing Science, Producing Art* (New York and London: Routledge, 1998).

Winther, Oscar O.: *Express and Stagecoach Days in California, From the Gold Rush to the Civil War* (Stanford: Stanford University Press, 1936).

Winther, Oscar O.: *The Old Oregon Country: A History of Frontier Trade, Transportation and Travel* (Stanford: Stanford University Press, 1950).

Winther, Oscar O.: *The Transportation Frontier: The Trans-Mississippi West, 1865–1890* (New York: Holt, Rinehart and Winston, 1964).

Wirth, John: *Smelter Smoke in North America: The Politics of Transborder Pollution* (Lawrence, Kansas: University Press of Kansas, 2000).

Wise, Winifred E.: *Fray Junípero Serra and the California Conquest* (New York: Scribner, 1967).

Wishart, David J.: *The Fur Trade of the American West, 1807–1840* (Lincoln: University of Nebraska Press, 1979).

Wister, Owen: *The Virginian* (New York: Macmillan,1902).

Woll, Allen J.: *The Latin Image in American Film* (Los Angeles: UCLA Latin American Center Publications, 1997).

Wong, K. Scott and Sucheng Chan (eds.): *Claiming America: Constructing Chinese American Identities During the Exclusion Era* (Philadelphia: Temple University Press, 1998).

Wood, Richard G. *Stephen Harriman Long, 1784–1864: Army Engineer, Explorer, Inventor* (Glendale, CA: A. H. Clark Co., 1966).

Wood, W. Raymond: "Plains Trade in Prehistoric and Protohistoric Intertribal Relations." In W. Raymond Wood and Margot Liberty (eds.) *Anthropology on the Great Plains* (Lincoln: University of Nebraska Press, 1980).

Wood, W. Raymond and Thomas D. Thiessen (eds.): *Early Fur Trade on the Northern Plains: Canadian Traders Among the Mandan and Hidatsa Indians, 1738–1818* (Norman: University of Oklahoma Press, 1985).

Woodcock, Deborah: "Of Posterosional Landscapes, Arrivals, and Extinctions: A Natural History of O'ahu." in D. W. Woodcock (ed.) *Hawai'i: New Geographies* (Honolulu: University of Hawai'i, 1999).

Woolsey, Ronald C.: "Crime and Punishment: Los Angeles County, 1850–1865." *Southern California Quarterly* 61 (1979).

Worcester, Donald E.: *The Apaches: Eagles of the Southwest* (Norman: University of Oklahoma Press, 1979).

Worcester, Donald E.: "Herbert Eugene Bolton: The Making of a Western Historian." In Richard W. Etulain (ed.) *Writing Western History: Essays on Major Western Historians* (Albuquerque: University of New Mexico Press, 1991).

Work, James C. (ed.): *Prose and Poetry of the American West* (Lincoln: University of Nebraska Press, 1990).

Worster, Donald: *Dust Bowl: The Southern Plains in the 1930s* (New York: Oxford University Press, 1979).

Worster, Donald: *Rivers of Empire: Water, Aridity, and the Growth of the American West* (New York: Pantheon, 1985).

Worster, Donald: "World Without Borders: The Internationalizing of Environmental History." In Kendall E. Bailes (ed.) *Environmental History: Critical Issues in Comparative Perspective* (Lanham, MD: University Press of America, 1985).

Worster, Donald: "New West, True West: Interpreting the Region's History." *Western Historical Quarterly* (1987), 141–56.

Worster, Donald: "Beyond the Agrarian Myth." In Patricia Nelson Limerick, Clyde A. Milner, II, and Charles E. Rankin (eds.) *Trails: Toward a New Western History* (Lawrence, KS: University Press of Kansas, 1991).

Worster, Donald: *Under Western Skies: Nature and History in the American West* (New York: Oxford University Press, 1992).

Worster, Donald: *The Wealth of Nature: Environmental History and the Ecological Imagination* (New York: Oxford, 1993).

Worster, Donald: *An Unsettled Country: Changing Landscapes of the American West* (Albuquerque: University of New Mexico Press, 1994).

Worster, Donald: *Nature's Economy: A History of Ecological Ideas*, 2nd ed. (New York: Cambridge University Press, 1994).

Worster, Donald: *A River Running West: The Life of John Wesley Powell* (New York: Oxford University Press, 2001).

Wright, James Edward: *The Politics of Populism: Dissent in Colorado* (New Haven: Yale University Press, 1974).

Wrobel, David M.: *The End of American Exceptionalism: Frontier Anxiety from the Old West to the New Deal* (Lawrence: University Press of Kansas, 1993).

Wrobel, David M.: "Beyond the Frontier-Region Dichotomy." *Pacific Historical Review* 65 (August 1996), 401–29.

Wrobel, David M. and Patrick T. Long (eds.): *Seeing the Being Seen: Tourism in the American West* (Lawrence, KS: University Press of Kansas, 2001).

Wrobel, David M. and Michael C. Steiner (eds.) *Many Wests: Place, Culture, and Regional Identity* (Lawrence: University Press of Kansas, 1997).

Wroth, William (ed.): *Ute Indian Arts & Crafts: From Prehistory to the New Millenium* (Albuquerque: University of New Mexico Press, 2001).

Wunder, John R.: *Inferior Courts, Superior Justice: A History of the Justices of the Peace on the Northwest Frontier, 1853–1889* (Westport, CT: Greenwood Press, 1979).

Wunder, John R.: "The Chinese and the Courts in the Pacific Northwest: Justice Denied?" *Pacific Historical Review* 52, 2 (May 1983), 191–211.

Wunder, John R.: "Territory of New Mexico v Yee Shun: A Turning Point in Chinese Legal Relations in the Trans-Mississippi West." *New Mexico Historical Review* 65 (July 1990), 305–18.

Wunder, John R.: *"Retained By the People": A History of American Indians and the Bill of Rights* (New York: Oxford University Press, 1994).

Wunder, John R.: *Native Americans and the Law: Contemporary and Historical Perspectives on American Indian Rights, Freedoms and Sovereignty* (New York: Garland Publishing, 1996).

Wunder, John R.: "Law. (What's Old about the New Western History?)." *Western Legal History.* 10 (Spring–Fall 1997), 85–116.

Wyatt, Victoria: "Alaska and Hawai'i." In Clyde A. Milner, II, Carol A. O'Connor, and Martha A. Sandweiss (eds.) *The Oxford History of the American West* (New York: Oxford University Press, 1994).

Wyman, Mark: *Hard Rock Epic: Western Miners and the Industrial Revolution, 1860–1910* (Berkeley, University of California Press, 1979).

Yates, Emma Hayden Eames: *Seventy Miles from a Lemon* (London: Hammond, Hammond Co., 1949).

Yoo, David: *Growing Up Nisei: Race, Generation, and Culture Among Japanese Americans of California, 1924–49* (Urbana: University of Illinois Press, 2000).

Young, James A. and B. Abbott Sparks: *Cattle in the Cold Desert* (Logan: Utah State University Press, 1985).

Young, Mary: "The Cherokee Nation: Mirror of the Republic." *American Quarterly* 33 (1981): 3–25.

Young, Otis E. and Robert Lenon: *Western Mining: An Informal Account of Precious Metals Prospecting, Placering, Lode Mining, and Milling, on the American Frontier from Spanish Times to 1893* (Norman: University of Oklahoma Press, 1970).

Yung, Judy: *Unbound Feet: A Social History of Chinese Women in San Francisco* (Berkeley: University of California Press, 1995).

Yung, Judy: *Unbound Voices: A Documentary History of Chinese Women in San Francisco* (Berkeley: University of California Press, 1999).

Zanjani, Sally S.: *Goldfield: The Last Gold Rush on the Western Frontier* (Athens, OH: Swallow Press/Ohio University Press, 1992).

Zavella, Patricia: *Women's Work and Chicano Families: Cannery Workers of the Santa Clara Valley* (Ithaca: Cornell University Press, 1987).

Zerbe, Richard O. and C. Leigh Anderson: "Culture and Fairness in the Development of Institutions in the California Gold Fields." *Journal of Economic History* 61 (2001), 114–43.

Zhu, Liping: *A Chinaman's Chance: The Chinese on the Rocky Mountain Mining Frontier* (Niwot, CO: University Press of Colorado, 1997).

Zimmerman, Tom: "Paradise Promoted: Boosterism and the Los Angeles Chamber of Commerce." *California History* 44 (Winter 1985), 22–33.

Zunz, Olivier: *Making America Corporate, 1870–1920* (Chicago: University of Chicago Press, 1990).

Zweigenhaft, Richard L. and G. William Domhoff: *Diversity in the Power Elite: Have Women and Minorities Reached the Top?* (New Haven: Yale University Press, 1998).

Index

Abbey, Edward 93, 261, 265
Abbott, Carl 418, 431–2
Abbott, John 301
Abert, John J. 68, 70
abolitionists 207
abortion, forced 191
Ackerman, Lillian 152
Acuña, Rodolfo 398, 399
Adam, David 154
Adamic, Louis 243
Adams, Brook 277
Adams, John 365
Adams, John Quincy 65, 363
Adams–Onis treaty 67
Adelman, Jeremy 7
AFL (American Federation of Labor) 247; and CIO 422; cities 248, 421; and IWW 241; Japanese/Filipinos 249; National Industrial Relations Act 243; white supremacy 226
African Americans: alienation 234–5; Cherokees 207, 209; civil rights 330, 433; class 224–5, 231; community 222, 235; Compton 235–6; distribution of 222; employment 246; Exodusters 37, 179, 263; film representations 228–9; gangs 234; Gold Rush 212; history 37, 221; housing 231; landowners 169; living conditions 225; Los Angeles 221–2, 225–6, 474; military service 224; music 222, 228; nationalism 234; politics 222, 227–8, 428, 433; population statistics 224, 236; poverty 173; Progressive Movement 452; religion 291; San Francisco 222, 232; Seattle 222, 223, 225; slavery 72–3, 181, 207, 209; urban history 221–2, 223–4; World War II 229, 230–3; *see also* Black Panthers
Afro-American Council 227
agribusiness 100, 101, 263, 449
Agricultural Adjustment Act 349, 353–4, 356, 357
agriculture: agribusiness 100, 101, 263, 449; capitalism 58; cash crops 85; colonization 34; democracy 83–4; diseases 85; domesticated animals 85–6; environment 87, 355; family 186; Indians 449; irrigation 94; Jefferson 59, 62, 67; labor 100, 244, 358–9; landscape 84; mining 125; New Deal 350, 353–4, 356;

Oregon 30; overgrazing 86; producer ideology 203; railroads 169, 243; technology 353; timber 103; Turner 83–4
Akwesasne Notes 330
Alamo, Battle of 164
Alaska 280; African Americans 222; Arctic National Wildlife Refuge 267; Bering 309; environment 257, 263; gold mining 121; men/women ratios 185; Metlakakans 340; purchase of 97; Russian American Company 63, 257
Alaska Lands Bill (1980) 266, 267
Alaska National Interest Lands Conservation Act 266–7
Alaska Native Claims Settlement Act 340
Albanese, Catherine L. 289
Albers, Patricia 333
Albuquerque 341
Alcatraz Island 330, 341
alcoholism 329
Aldrich, John 98
Alien Land Laws 424, 426
alienation 232, 234–5
Allen, John L. 62
Allen, Michael 33
Allmendinger, Blake 287, 465
allotment policy 135–6, 187, 209–10, 359
Almaguer, Tomás 212–13, 248, 398–9, 425, 426
Alta California 309
Althusser, Louis 366–7
Alvarez, David 294
Amana 315
Ambler, Marjane 340
Ambrose, Stephen 26, 31
AmeRica 403
American Association for the Advancement of Science 260
American Bison Society 261
American Farm Board Federation 356
American Farm Economics Association 356
American Federation of Labor: *see* AFL
American Forestry Association 260
American Historical Association 274
American Indian Movement 330
American Indian Quarterly 156